Lecture Notes in Computer Science   13827

Founding Editors

Gerhard Goos
Juris Hartmanis

The series Lecture Notes in Computer Science (LNCS), including its subseries Lecture Notes in Artificial Intelligence (LNAI) and Lecture Notes in Bioinformatics (LNBI), has established itself as a medium for the publication of new developments in computer science and information technology research, teaching, and education.

LNCS enjoys close cooperation with the computer science R & D community, the series counts many renowned academics among its volume editors and paper authors, and collaborates with prestigious societies. Its mission is to serve this international community by providing an invaluable service, mainly focused on the publication of conference and workshop proceedings and postproceedings. LNCS commenced publication in 1973.

Roman Wyrzykowski · Jack Dongarra ·
Ewa Deelman · Konrad Karczewski
Editors

Parallel Processing and Applied Mathematics

14th International Conference, PPAM 2022
Gdansk, Poland, September 11–14, 2022
Revised Selected Papers, Part II

Springer

Editors
Roman Wyrzykowski
Czestochowa University of Technology
Czestochowa, Poland

Jack Dongarra
University of Tennessee
Knoxville, TN, USA

Ewa Deelman
University of Southern California
Marina del Rey, CA, USA

Konrad Karczewski
Czestochowa University of Technology
Czestochowa, Poland

ISSN 0302-9743   ISSN 1611-3349 (electronic)
Lecture Notes in Computer Science
ISBN 978-3-031-30444-6   ISBN 978-3-031-30445-3 (eBook)
https://doi.org/10.1007/978-3-031-30445-3

This Springer imprint is published by the registered company Springer Nature Switzerland AG
The registered company address is: Gewerbestrasse 11, 6330 Cham, Switzerland

Preface

This volume comprises the proceedings of the 14th International Conference on Parallel Processing and Applied Mathematics – PPAM 2022, which was held in Gdańsk, Poland, September 11–14, 2022. It was organized by the Department of Computer Science of the Częstochowa University of Technology together with the Gdańsk University of Technology, under the patronage of the Committee of Informatics of the Polish Academy of Sciences, in technical cooperation with the Poznań Supercomputing and Networking Center. Scheduled initially for the year 2021, the fourteenth edition of PPAM was postponed to 2022 because of the COVID-19 pandemic. PPAM 2022 was primarily an in-person event. However, the organizers also made provision for authors and delegates to present, attend, and interact online.

PPAM is a biennial conference. Thirteen previous events have been held in different places in Poland since 1994, when the first conference took place in Częstochowa. The proceedings of the last ten conferences have been published by Springer in the Lecture Notes in Computer Science series (Nałęczów, 2001, vol. 2328; Częstochowa, 2003, vol. 3019; Poznań, 2005, vol. 3911; Gdańsk, 2007, vol. 4967; Wrocław, 2009, vols. 6067 and 6068; Toruń, 2011, vols. 7203 and 7204; Warsaw, 2013, vols. 8384 and 8385; Kraków, 2015, vols. 9573 and 9574; Lublin, 2017, vols. 10777 and 10778; Białystok, 2019, vols. 12043 and 12044.

The PPAM conferences have become an international forum for exchanging ideas between researchers involved in parallel and distributed computing, including theory and applications, as well as applied and computational mathematics. The focus of PPAM 2022 was on models, algorithms, and software tools that facilitate efficient and convenient utilization of modern parallel and distributed computing architectures, as well as on large-scale applications, including artificial intelligence and machine learning problems. Special attention was given to the future of computing beyond Moore's Law.

This meeting gathered about 170 participants from 25 countries, including about 130 in-person participants. One hundred thirty-two articles were submitted for review. Each paper secured at least three single-blind reviews from program committee members. A thorough peer-reviewing process that included discussion and agreement among reviewers whenever necessary resulted in the acceptance of 76 contributed papers for publication in the conference proceedings. For regular conference tracks, 33 papers were selected from 62 submissions, giving an acceptance rate of about 53%.

The regular tracks covered such important fields of parallel/distributed/cloud computing and applied mathematics as:

- Numerical algorithms and parallel scientific computing
- GPU computing
- Parallel non-numerical algorithms
- Performance analysis and prediction in HPC (high performance computing) systems
- Scheduling for parallel computing
- Environments and frameworks for parallel/cloud computing

- Applications of parallel and distributed computing
- Soft computing with applications

The keynote talks were presented by:

- Anima Anandkumar from the California Institute of Technology and Nvidia (USA)
- Hartwig Anzt from the Karlsruhe Institute of Technology (Germany) and University of Tennessee (USA)
- Ivona Brandic from the Vienna University of Technology (Austria)
- Ümit V. Çatalyürek from Georgia Institute of Technology (USA)
- Jack Dongarra from the University of Tennessee and ORNL (USA)
- Torsten Hoefler from ETH Zurich (Switzerland)
- Georg Hager from the University of Erlangen-Nuremberg (Germany)
- Simon Knowles from Graphcore (UK)
- Satoshi Matsuoka from the Tokyo Institute of Technology (Japan)
- Michał Mrozek from Intel (Poland)
- Simon McIntosh-Smith from the University of Bristol (UK)
- Manish Parashar from Rutgers University (USA)
- Voica Radescu from IBM (Germany)
- Enrique S. Quintana-Orti from the Universitat Politècnica de València (Spain)
- John Shalf from the Lawrence Berkeley National Laboratory (USA)
- Michela Taufer from the University of Tennessee (USA)
- Christian Terboven from RWTH Aachen (Germany)
- Manuel Ujaldon from the University of Malaga Nvidia

Important and integral parts of the PPAM 2022 conference were the workshops:

- The 9th Workshop on Language-Based Parallel Programming (WLPP 2022) organized by Ami Marowka from the Bar-Ilan University (Israel).
- The 6th Workshop on Models, Algorithms and Methodologies for Hybrid Parallelism in New HPC Systems (MAMHYP 2022) organized by Marco Lapegna, Giulliano Laccetti and Valeria Mele from the University of Naples Federico II (Italy), Raffaele Montella from the University of Naples "Parthenope" (Italy), and Sokol Kosta from Aalborg University Copenhagen (Denmark).
- The First Workshop on Quantum Computing and Communication organized by Krzysztof Kurowski, Cezary Mazurek, and Piotr Rydlichowski from the Poznań Supercomputing and Networking Center (Poland)
- The First Workshop on Applications of Machine Learning and Artificial Intelligence in High Performance Computing organized by Sergio Iserte from the Universitat Jaume I (Spain) and Krzysztof Rojek from the Częstochowa University of Technology (Poland).
- The 9th Workshop on Scheduling for Parallel Computing organized by Maciej Drozdowski from the Poznań University of Technology (Poland).
- The 4th Workshop on Applied High Performance Numerical Algorithms for PDEs organized by Piotr Krzyżanowski and Leszek Marcinkowski from Warsaw University (Poland), Talal Rahman from Bergen University College (Norway), and Jan Valdman from the University of South Bohemia (Czech Republic).

– The 5th Minisymposium on HPC Applications in Physical Sciences organized by Grzegorz Kamieniarz and Michał Antkowiak from Adam Mickiewicz University in Poznan (Poland).
– The 8th Minisymposium on High Performance Computing Interval Methods organized by Bartłomiej J. Kubica from the Warsaw University of Technology (Poland).
– The 7th Workshop on Complex Collective Systems organized by Jarosław Wąs from the AGH University of Science and Technology (Poland), Tomasz Gwizdałła from the University of Łódz (Poland) and Krzysztof Małecki from the West Pomeranian University of Technology (Poland).

The PPAM 2022 meeting began with four tutorials:

– Introduction to Programming Graphcore IPU, by Graphcore (Pawel Gepner team).
– Fundamentals of Deep Learning using the Nvidia Deep Learning Institute infrastructure, by Manuel Ujaldon from the University of Malaga (Spain) and Nvidia.
– Quantum Computing, by IBM, and Poznań Supercomputing and Networking Center (Poland).
– LUMI European Pre-Exascale Supercomputer Hands-on, by Maciej Szpindler and Marek Magryś from the Academic Computer Centre Cyfronet AGH (Poland).

The PPAM Best Paper Award is given upon recommendation of the PPAM Chairs and Program Committee in recognition of the research paper quality, originality, and significance of the work in high performance computing. For the main track, the PPAM 2022 winners were:

– Rafael Ravedutti Lucio Machado, Jan Eitzinger, Harald Köstler and Gerhard Wellein from the University of Erlangen-Nuremberg and Erlangen Regional Computing Center, who submitted the paper "MD-Bench: A generic proxy-app toolbox for state-of-the-art molecular dynamics algorithms".
– Anna Sasak-Okoń from the Maria Curie-Skłodowska University and Marek Tudruj from the Polish Academy of Sciences and Polish-Japanese Academy of Information Technology, who presented the paper "RDBMS speculative support improvement by the use of the query hypergraph representation".

For workshops, the PPAM 2022 winners were Yu-Hsiang Tsai, Natalie Beams, and Hartwig Anzt from the Karlsruhe Institute of Technology and the University of Tennessee, who submitted the paper "Mixed Precision Algebraic Multigrid on GPUs". To stimulate potential authors' interest in submitting high-quality articles to the PPAM conference, one author of each winning paper will receive a significant reduction in the conference fee for the next PPAM.

New Topic at PPAM 2022: First Workshop on Applications of Machine Learning and Artificial Intelligence in High Performance Computing

Machine learning and artificial intelligence methods have become pervasive in recent years due to numerous algorithmic advances and the accessibility of computational power. In high performance computing, these methods have been used to replace, accelerate, or enhance existing solvers.

Research topics of this workshop focused on: (i) disruptive uses of HPC technologies in the field of AI (artificial intelligence), ML (machine learning), and DL (deep learning);

(ii) integration of predictive models to improve the performance of scientific applications in terms of execution time and/or simulation accuracy; (iii) workflow of applying AI/ML/DL to scientific applications in HPC infrastructures; (iv) characterization and study of how to use HPC techniques with AI/ML/DL; (v) HPC tools and infrastructure to improve the usability of AI/ML/DL for scientific applications; (vi) optimized HPC systems design and setup for efficient AI/ML/DL.

These topics were covered at a session that consisted of five presentations:

- adaptation of AI-accelerated CFD simulations to the IPU platform (by P. Rościszewski, A. Krzywaniak, S. Iserte, K. Rojek, and P. Gepner)
- performance analysis of convolution algorithms for deep learning on edge processors (by P. Alonso-Jorda, H. Martinez, E. S. Quintana-Orti, and C. Ramirez)
- machine learning-based online scheduling in distributed computing (by V. Toporkov, D. Yemelyanov, and A. Bulkhak)
- high performance computing queue time prediction using clustering and regression (by S. Hutchison, D. Andresen, M. Neilsen, W. Hsu, and B. Parsons)
- acceptance rates of invertible neural networks on electron spectra from near-critical laser-plasmas: a comparison (by T. Miethlinger, N. Hoffmann, and T. Kluge).

New Topic at PPAM 2022: First Workshop on Quantum Computing and Communication

The dedicated workshop focused on two relevant quantum technology areas: quantum computation and communication. The main goal of this event was to bring together scientists and practitioners experimenting with different software and hardware in the existing Noisy Intermediate-Scale Quantum (NISQ) era. This workshop was also an excellent opportunity to catch up on taking advantage of quantum computing, particularly Adiabatic Quantum Computing, and communication technologies from theoretical and practical angles. There are many exciting research topics today, from the design of quantum algorithms, experiments on early access quantum devices, and performance analysis of classical-quantum approaches to early experiences with quantum communication applications and distributed quantum testbeds.

Therefore, the workshop consisted of nine presentations on various exciting topics delivered during two sessions:

- An analysis of the potential of quantum computing by examining problems involved with determining the worst-case execution time of a restricted set of programs (by Gabriella Bettonte, Stephane Louise, and Renaud Sirdey)
- A study of LDPC decoding using quantum annealing (by Aditya Das Sarma, Utso Majumder, Vishnu Vaidya, M Girish Chandra, Anil Kumar, and Sayantan Pramanik)
- An overview of ongoing Quantum Key Distribution (QKD) communication technology in operational networks within commercial network operators and national research and education networks in Europe (by Piotr Rydlichowski)
- A new QUBO-based algorithm for the scheduling of heterogeneous tasks on unrelated parallel machines problem solved using quantum annealing (by F. Orts, A. M. Puertas, E. M. Garzon, and G. Ortega)
- An approach to studying specific aspects of quantum entanglement contained in the bipartite pure quantum states (by Roman Gielerak and Marek Sawerwain)

- A study of a set of early experiments with a photonic quantum simulator for solving the job shop scheduling problem (by Mateusz Slysz, Krzysztof Kurowski, and Jan Weglarz)
- A proposal for solving the traveling salesman problem with a hybrid quantum-classical feedforward neural network (by Justyna Zawalska, and Katarzyna Rycerz)
- An analysis of the Eisert-Wilkens-Lewenstein scheme of quantum extension for selected games on the example of Prisoners Dilemma (by Piotr Kotara, Tomasz Zawadzki, and Katarzyna Rycerz)
- A new approach to generative quantum machine learning and description of a proof-of-principle experiment (by Karol Bartkiewicz, Patrycja Tulewicz, Jan Roik, and Karel Lemr).

The organizers are indebted to PPAM 2022's sponsors, whose support was vital to the conference's success. The main sponsors were the Intel Corporation and Graphcore; the others were Hewlett Packard Enterprise, Koma Nord, and Inspur. We thank all the International Program Committee members and additional reviewers for their diligent work in refereeing the submitted papers. Finally, we thank all of the local organizers from the Częstochowa University of Technology and the Gdańsk University of Technology, who helped us to run the event very smoothly. We are especially indebted to Łukasz Kuczyński, Marcin Woźniak, Tomasz Chmiel, Piotr Dzierżak, Anna Woźniak, and Ewa Szymczyk from the Częstochowa University of Technology; and to Paweł Czarnul and Mariusz Matuszek from the Gdańsk University of Technology.

We hope that this volume will be useful to you. We would like everyone who reads it to feel invited to the next conference, PPAM 2024, which will be held on September 8–11, 2024.

January 2023

Roman Wyrzykowski
Jack Dongarra
Ewa Deelman
Konrad Karczewski

Organization

Program Committee

Jan Węglarz (Honorary Chair)	Poznań University of Technology, Poland
Roman Wyrzykowski (Chair of Program Committee)	Częstochowa University of Technology, Poland
Ewa Deelman (Vice-chair of Program Committee)	University of Southern California, USA
Konrad Karczewski (Vice-chair for Publication)	Częstochowa University of Technology, Poland
Marco Lapegna (Vice-chair for Tutorials)	University of Naples Federico II, Italy
Robert Adamski	Intel Corporation, Poland
Francisco Almeida	Universidad de La Laguna, Spain
Pedro Alonso	Universidad Politécnica de Valencia, Spain
Alexander Antonov	Moscov State University, Russian Federation
Hartwig Anzt	Karlsruhe Institute of Technology, Germany, and University of Tennessee, USA
Peter Arbenz	ETH Zurich, Switzerland
Cevdet Aykanat	Bilkent University, Turkey
Marc Baboulin	University of Paris-Sud, France
David A. Bader	New Jersey Institute of Technology, USA
Michael Bader	TU Munchen, Germany
Bartosz Baliś	Institute of Computer Science AGH, Poland
Piotr Bała	ICM, Warsaw University, Poland
Krzysztof Banaś	AGH University of Science and Technology, Poland
Jorge G. Barbosa	Universidade de Porto, Portugal
Olivier Beaumont	Inria Bordeaux, France
Włodzimierz Bielecki	West Pomeranian University of Technology, Poland
Paolo Bientinesi	Umea University, Sweden
Jacek Błażewicz	Poznań University of Technology, Poland
Pascal Bouvry	University of Luxembourg, Luxembourg
Jerzy Brzeziński	Poznań University of Technology, Poland
Marian Bubak	AGH Kraków, Poland, and University of Amsterdam, The Netherlands

Sebastiano F. Schifano	University of Ferrara, Italy
Jurij Silc	Jozef Stefan Institute, Slovenia
Renata Słota	Institute of Computer Science, AGH, Poland
Masha Sosonkina	Old Dominion University, USA
Leonel Sousa	Technical University of Lisbon, Portugal
Vladimir Stegailov	Joint Institute for High Temperatures of RAS and MIPT/HSE, Russian Federation
Przemysław Stpiczyński	Maria Curie-Skłodowska University, Poland
Robert Strzodka	University of Heidelberg, Germany
Lukasz Szustak	Częstochowa University of Technology, Poland
Boleslaw Szymanski	Rensselaer Polytechnic Institute, USA
Domenico Talia	University of Calabria, Italy
Andrei Tchernykh	CICESE Research Center, Mexico
Christian Terboven	RWTH Aachen, Germany
Parimala Thulasiraman	University of Manitoba, Canada
Sivan Toledo	Tel-Aviv University, Israel
Victor Toporkov	National Research University "MPEI", Russian Federation
Roman Trobec	Jozef Stefan Institute, Slovenia
Giuseppe Trunfio	University of Sassari, Italy
Denis Trystram	Grenoble Institute of Technology, France
Marek Tudruj	Polish Academy of Sciences and Polish-Japanese Academy of Information Technologies, Poland
Bora Ucar	École Normale Supérieure de Lyon, France
Marian Vajtersic	Salzburg University, Austria
Vladimir Voevodin	Moscow State University, Russian Federation
Bogdan Wiszniewski	Gdańsk University of Technology, Poland
Andrzej Wyszogrodzki	Institute of Meteorology and Water Management, Poland
Ramin Yahyapour	University of Göttingen/GWDG, Germany
Krzysztof Zielinski	Institute of Computer Science, AGH, Poland
Julius Žilinskas	Vilnius University, Lithuania
Jarosław Żola	University of Buffalo, USA

Steering Committee

Jack Dongarra	University of Tennessee and ORNL, USA
Leszek Rutkowski	Częstochowa University of Technology, Poland
Boleslaw Szymanski	Rensselaer Polytechnic Institute, USA

Contents – Part II

9th Workshop on Language-Based Parallel Programming (WLPP 2022)

Kokkos-Based Implementation of MPCD on Heterogeneous Nodes 3
    Rene Halver, Christoph Junghans, and Godehard Sutmann

Comparison of Load Balancing Schemes for Asynchronous Many-Task
Runtimes 14
    Lukas Reitz, Kai Hardenbicker, and Claudia Fohry

New Insights on the Revised Definition of the Performance Portability
Metric 27
    Ami Marowka

Inferential Statistical Analysis of Performance Portability 39
    Ami Marowka

NPDP Benchmark Suite for Loop Tiling Effectiveness Evaluation 51
    Marek Palkowski and Wlodzimierz Bielecki

Parallel Vectorized Implementations of Compensated Summation
Algorithms 63
    Beata Dmitruk and Przemysław Stpiczyński

6th Workshop on Models, Algorithms and Methodologies for Hybrid Parallelism in New HPC Systems (MAMHYP 2022)

Malleability Techniques for HPC Systems 77
    Jesus Carretero, David Exposito, Alberto Cascajo, and Raffaele Montella

Algorithm and Software Overhead: A Theoretical Approach
to Performance Portability 89
    Valeria Mele and Giuliano Laccetti

Benchmarking a High Performance Computing Heterogeneous Cluster 101
    Luisa Carracciuolo, Davide Bottalico, Davide Michelino,
    Gianluca Sabella, and Bernardino Spisso

A Generative Adversarial Network Approach for Noise and Artifacts
Reduction in MRI Head and Neck Imaging 115
  Salvatore Cuomo, Francesco Fato, Lorenzo Ugga, Gaia Spadarella,
  Reanto Cuocolo, Fabio Giampaolo, and Francesco Piccialli

A GPU Accelerated Hyperspectral 3D Convolutional Neural Network
Classification at the Edge with Principal Component Analysis
Preprocessing 127
  Gianluca De Lucia, Marco Lapegna, and Diego Romano

Parallel gEUD Models for Accelerated IMRT Planning on Modern HPC
Platforms 139
  Juan José Moreno, Janusz Miroforidis, Ignacy Kaliszewski,
  and Gracia Ester Martín Garzón

First Workshop on Quantum Computing and Communication

On Quantum-Assisted LDPC Decoding Augmented with Classical
Post-processing 153
  Aditya Das Sarma, Utso Majumder, Vishnu Vaidya, M Girish Chandra,
  A Anil Kumar, and Sayantan Pramanik

Quantum Annealing to Solve the Unrelated Parallel Machine Scheduling
Problem 165
  Francisco Orts, Antonio M. Puertas, Ester M. Garzón, and Gloria Ortega

Early Experiences with a Photonic Quantum Simulator for Solving Job
Shop Scheduling Problem 177
  Mateusz Slysz, Krzysztof Kurowski, and Jan Węglarz

Some Remarks on Super-Gram Operators for General Bipartite Quantum
States 187
  Roman Gielerak and Marek Sawerwain

Solving the Traveling Salesman Problem with a Hybrid Quantum-Classical
Feedforward Neural Network 199
  Justyna Zawalska and Katarzyna Rycerz

Software Aided Analysis of EWL Based Quantum Games 209
  Piotr Kotara, Tomasz Zawadzki, and Katarzyna Rycerz

First Workshop on Applications of Machine Learning and Artificial Intelligence in High Performance Computing (WAML 2022)

Adaptation of AI-Accelerated CFD Simulations to the IPU Platform   223
   Paweł Rościszewski, Adam Krzywaniak, Sergio Iserte, Krzysztof Rojek, and Paweł Gepner

Performance Analysis of Convolution Algorithms for Deep Learning on Edge Processors   236
   Pedro Alonso-Jordá, Héctor Martínez, Enrique S. Quintana-Ortí, and Cristian Ramírez

Machine Learning-Based Online Scheduling in Distributed Computing   248
   Victor Toporkov, Dmitry Yemelyanov, and Artem Bulkhak

High Performance Computing Queue Time Prediction Using Clustering and Regression   260
   Scott Hutchison, Daniel Andresen, Mitchell Neilsen, William Hsu, and Benjamin Parsons

Acceptance Rates of Invertible Neural Networks on Electron Spectra from Near-Critical Laser-Plasmas: A Comparison   273
   Thomas Miethlinger, Nico Hoffmann, and Thomas Kluge

4th Workshop on Applied High Performance Numerical Algorithms for PDEs

MATLAB Implementation of Hp Finite Elements on Rectangles Using Hierarchical Basis Functions   287
   Alexej Moskovka and Jan Valdman

Adaptive Parallel Average Schwarz Preconditioner for Crouzeix-Raviart Finite Volume Method   300
   Leszek Marcinkowski and Talal Rahman

Parareal Method for Anisotropic Diffusion Denoising   313
   Xiujie Shan and Martin B. van Gijzen

Comparison of Block Preconditioners for the Stokes Problem with Discontinuous Viscosity and Friction   323
   Piotr Krzyżanowski

On Minimization of Nonlinear Energies Using FEM in MATLAB   331
   Alexej Moskovka, Jan Valdman, and Marta Vohnoutová

A Model for Crowd Evacuation Dynamics: 2D Numerical Simulations   343
  Maria Gokieli

5th Minisymposium on HPC Applications in Physical Sciences

Parallel Identification of Unique Sequences in Nuclear Structure
Calculations   357
  Daniel Langr and Tomáš Dytrych

Experimental and Computer Study of Molecular Dynamics of a New
Pyridazine Derivative   370
  Sebastian Wołoszczuk, Aneta Woźniak-Braszak, Andrzej Olejniczak,
  and Michał Banaszak

Description of Magnetic Nanomolecules by the Extended Multi-orbital
Hubbard Model: Perturbative vs Numerical Approach   382
  Romuald Lemański and Michał Antkowiak

Structural and Electronic Properties of Small-Diameter Carbon
NanoTubes: A DFT Study   392
  Bartosz Brzostowski, Artur P. Durajski, Konrad M. Gruszka,
  and Jacek Wojtkiewicz

8th Minisymposium on High Performance Computing Interval Methods

Need for Techniques Intermediate Between Interval and Probabilistic Ones   405
  Olga Kosheleva and Vladik Kreinovich

A Cross-Platform Benchmark for Interval Computation Libraries   415
  Xuan Tang, Zachary Ferguson, Teseo Schneider, Denis Zorin,
  Shoaib Kamil, and Daniele Panozzo

Testing Interval Arithmetic Libraries, Including Their IEEE-1788
Compliance   428
  Nathalie Revol, Luis Benet, Luca Ferranti, and Sergei Zhilin

A Survey of Interval Algorithms for Solving Multicriteria Analysis
Problems   441
  Bartłomiej Jacek Kubica

7th Workshop on Complex Collective Systems

Social Fragmentation Transitions in Large-Scale Parameter Sweep
Simulations of Adaptive Social Networks 459
  Hiroki Sayama

Parking Search in Urban Street Networks: Taming Down the Complexity
of the Search-Time Problem via a Coarse-Graining Approach 470
  Léo Bulckaen, Nilankur Dutta, and Alexandre Nicolas

A Multi-agent Cellular Automata Model of Lane Changing Behaviour
Considering the Aggressiveness and the Autonomy 481
  Krzysztof Małecki, Piotr Wróbel, and Patryk Górka

Comparison of the Use of UWB and BLE as Positioning Methods
in Data-Driven Modeling of Pedestrian Dynamics 492
  Dariusz Pałka, Robert Lubaś, Giuseppe Vizzari, and Jarosław Wąs

An Insight into the State-of-the-Art Vehicular Fog Computing
with an Opportunistic Flavour 502
  Krzysztof Ostrowski and Krzysztof Małecki

Author Index 515

Contents – Part I

Numerical Algorithms and Parallel Scientific Computing

How Accurate Does Newton Have to Be? 3
  Carl Christian Kjelgaard Mikkelsen, Lorién López-Villellas,
  and Pablo García-Risueño

General Framework for Deriving Reproducible Krylov Subspace
Algorithms: BiCGStab Case 16
  Roman Iakymchuk, Stef Graillat, and José I. Aliaga

A Generalized Parallel Prefix Sums Algorithm for Arbitrary Size Arrays 30
  Andrzej Sikorski, Izajasz Wrosz, and Michał Lewandowski

Infinite-Precision Inner Product and Sparse Matrix-Vector Multiplication
Using Ozaki Scheme with Dot2 on Manycore Processors 40
  Daichi Mukunoki, Katsuhisa Ozaki, Takeshi Ogita,
  and Toshiyuki Imamura

Advanced Stochastic Approaches for Applied Computing in Environmental
Modeling 55
  Venelin Todorov, Ivan Dimov, Maria Ganzha, and Marcin Paprzycki

Parallel Non-numerical Algorithms

Parallel Suffix Sorting for Large String Analytics 71
  Zhihui Du, Sen Zhang, and David A. Bader

Parallel Extremely Randomized Decision Forests on Graphics Processors
for Text Classification 83
  Julio Cesar Batista Pires and Wellington Santos Martins

RDBMS Speculative Support Improvement by the Use of the Query
Hypergraph Representation 95
  Anna Sasak-Okoń and Marek Tudruj

GPU Computing

Mixed Precision Algebraic Multigrid on GPUs 113
  Yu-Hsiang Mike Tsai, Natalie Beams, and Hartwig Anzt

Compact In-Memory Representation of Decision Trees
in GPU-Accelerated Evolutionary Induction 126
    Krzysztof Jurczuk, Marcin Czajkowski, and Marek Kretowski

Neural Nets with a Newton Conjugate Gradient Method on Multiple GPUs 139
    Severin Reiz, Tobias Neckel, and Hans-Joachim Bungartz

Performance Analysis and Prediction in HPC Systems

Exploring Techniques for the Analysis of Spontaneous Asynchronicity
in MPI-Parallel Applications 155
    Ayesha Afzal, Georg Hager, Gerhard Wellein, and Stefano Markidis

Cost and Performance Analysis of MPI-Based SaaS on the Private Cloud
Infrastructure 171
    Oleg Bystrov, Arnas Kačeniauskas, and Ruslan Pacevič

Building a Fine-Grained Analytical Performance Model for Complex
Scientific Simulations 183
    Jelle van Dijk, Gabor Zavodszky, Ana-Lucia Varbanescu,
    Andy D. Pimentel, and Alfons Hoekstra

Evaluation of Machine Learning Techniques for Predicting Run Times
of Scientific Workflow Jobs 197
    Bartosz Balis and Michal Grabowski

Smart Clustering of HPC Applications Using Similar Job Detection
Methods 209
    Denis Shaikhislamov and Vadim Voevodin

Scheduling for Parallel Computing

Distributed Work Stealing in a Task-Based Dataflow Runtime 225
    Joseph John, Josh Milthorpe, and Peter Strazdins

Task Scheduler for Heterogeneous Data Centres Based on Deep
Reinforcement Learning 237
    Jaime Fomperosa, Mario Ibañez, Esteban Stafford, and Jose Luis Bosque

Shisha: Online Scheduling of CNN Pipelines on Heterogeneous
Architectures 249
    Pirah Noor Soomro, Mustafa Abduljabbar, Jeronimo Castrillon,
    and Miquel Pericàs

Proactive Task Offloading for Load Balancing in Iterative Applications 263
Minh Thanh Chung, Josef Weidendorfer, Karl Fürlinger,
and Dieter Kranzlmüller

Environments and Frameworks for Parallel/Cloud Computing

Language Agnostic Approach for Unification of Implementation Variants
for Different Computing Devices 279
Anshu Dubey and Tom Klosterman

High Performance Dataframes from Parallel Processing Patterns 291
Niranda Perera, Supun Kamburugamuve, Chathura Widanage,
Vibhatha Abeykoon, Ahmet Uyar, Kaiying Shan, Hasara Maithree,
Damitha Lenadora, Thejaka Amila Kanewala, and Geoffrey Fox

Global Access to Legacy Data-Sets in Multi-cloud Applications
with Onedata 305
Michał Orzechowski, Michał Wrzeszcz, Bartosz Kryza, Łukasz Dutka,
Renata G. Słota, and Jacek Kitowski

Applications of Parallel and Distributed Computing

MD-Bench: A Generic Proxy-App Toolbox for State-of-the-Art Molecular
Dynamics Algorithms 321
Rafael Ravedutti Lucio Machado, Jan Eitzinger, Harald Köstler,
and Gerhard Wellein

Breaking Down the Parallel Performance of GROMACS,
a High-Performance Molecular Dynamics Software 333
Måns I. Andersson, Natarajan Arul Murugan, Artur Podobas,
and Stefano Markidis

GPU-Based Molecular Dynamics of Turbulent Liquid Flows with OpenMM ... 346
Daniil Pavlov, Daniil Kolotinskii, and Vladimir Stegailov

A Novel Parallel Approach for Modeling the Dynamics of Aerodynamically
Interacting Particles in Turbulent Flows 359
Ahmad Ababaei, Antoine Michel, and Bogdan Rosa

Reliable Energy Measurement on Heterogeneous Systems–on–Chip
Based Environments 371
Alberto Cabrera, Pavel Nichita, Sergio Afonso, Francisco Almeida,
and Vicente Blanco

Distributed Objective Function Evaluation for Optimization of Radiation
Therapy Treatment Plans 383
   Felix Liu, Måns I. Andersson, Albin Fredriksson, and Stefano Markidis

Soft Computing with Applications

GPU4SNN: GPU-Based Acceleration for Spiking Neural Network
Simulations 399
   Nitin Satpute, Anna Hambitzer, Saeed Aljaberi, and Najwa Aaraj

Ant System Inspired Heuristic Optimization of UAVs Deployment
for *k*-Coverage Problem 414
   Krzysztof Trojanowski, Artur Mikitiuk, and Jakub Grzeszczak

Dataset Related Experimental Investigation of Chess Position Evaluation
Using a Deep Neural Network 429
   Dawid Wieczerzak and Paweł Czarnul

Using AI-based Edge Processing in Monitoring the Pedestrian Crossing 441
   Łukasz Karbowiak and Mariusz Kubanek

**Special Session on Parallel EVD/SVD and its Application in Matrix
Computations**

Automatic Code Selection for the Dense Symmetric Generalized
Eigenvalue Problem Using ATMathCoreLib 453
   Masato Kobayashi, Shuhei Kudo, Takeo Hoshi, and Yusaku Yamamoto

On Relative Accuracy of the One-Sided Block-Jacobi SVD Algorithm 464
   Gabriel Okša and Martin Bečka

Author Index 477

9th Workshop on Language-Based Parallel Programming (WLPP 2022)

Kokkos-Based Implementation of MPCD on Heterogeneous Nodes

Rene Halver[1][iD], Christoph Junghans[2][iD], and Godehard Sutmann[1,3]([✉])[iD]

[1] Jülich Supercomputing Centre, Institute for Advanced Simulation,
Forschungszentrum Jülich, 52425 Jülich, Germany
{r.halver,g.sutmann}@fz-juelich.de
[2] Los Alamos National Laboratory, CCS-7, 87545 Los Alamos, NM, USA
junghans@lanl.gov
[3] ICAMS, Ruhr-University Bochum, 44801 Bochum, Germany

Abstract. The Kokkos based library Cabana, which has been developed in the Co-design Center for Particle Applications (CoPA), is used for the implementation of Multi-Particle Collision Dynamics (MPCD), a particle-based description of hydrodynamic interactions. It allows a performance portable implementation, which has been used to study the interplay between CPU and GPU usage on a multi-node system. As a result, we see most advantages in a homogeneous GPU usage, but we also discuss the extent to heterogeneous applications, using both CPU and GPU concurrently.

Keywords: Kokkos · Multi-particle collision dynamics ·
GPU-computing · particle simulations · performance portability

1 Introduction

The recent development of high-end parallel architectures shows a clear trend to a heterogeneity of compute components, pointing towards a dominance of General Purpose Graphics Processing Units (GPU) as accelerator components, compared to the Central Processing Units (CPU). According to the Top 500 list [4], more than 25% of the machines have GPU support while the overall performance share is more than 40%, i.e., heterogeneous cluster architectures have a large impact for high compute performance. Often these nodes consist of only a few multicore CPUs, while supporting 2–6 GPUs. In many applications one can observe a trend that the most powerful component of the nodes, i.e. the GPUs, is addressed, while the CPUs are used as administrating or data management components. A reason might be the additional overhead in writing/maintaining two different code versions for each architecture, as usually a CPU code cannot simply run on a GPU or vice versa.

With the advent of performance portable programming models, such as Kokkos [6] or Raja [16] it has become possible to use the same code base for different architectures, most prominently including CPUs or GPUs. It might

R. Wyrzykowski et al. (Eds.): PPAM 2022, LNCS 13827, pp. 3–13, 2023.
https://doi.org/10.1007/978-3-031-30445-3_1

be tempting to use the full capacity of a compute-node concurrently, i.e. not wasting compute resources because of the disparate character of the architecture and programming model. In this case one encounters both different performance characteristics of components and possibly a non-negligible data transfer between components. This discrepancy might be targeted by load balancing strategies which would need to take into account hardware and software specific characteristics to achieve an overall performance gain.

In the present paper we consider a stochastic particle based method for the simulation of hydrodynamic phenomena, i.e. the Multi-Particle Collision Dynamics (MPCD) [8] algorithm and its implementation with Cabana [2,14,17], a Kokkos based library. We first introduce the underlying MPCD method and then describe the Cabana library. We then present some benchmark results and finally draw conclusions from our findings and give some outlook for further research.

2   Multi-Particle Collision Dynamics

MPCD is a particle-based description for hydrodynamic interactions in an incompressible fluid. The method is based on a stochastic collision scheme in which particles, that describe the simulated fluid are rotated in velocity space while conserving linear momentum and energy (variants exist which also conserve angular momentum [8]). The method proceeds by sorting particles into a regular mesh with grid cells of size of a characteristic length scale. In order to transport momentum and energy across the system, the mesh is randomly shifted in each time step, changing the local environment of each particle stochastically. For each particle in a cell its relative velocity with respect to the center-of-mass (*com*) velocity of the cell is computed. This velocity is split into a parallel and perpendicular component with respect to a randomly oriented axis in the cell. Consequently, the perpendicular component is rotated around that axis by a fixed angle, which determines together with the particle mass and density, the time step and the cell length the diffusion and viscosity of the fluid under consideration. This procedure can be shown to mimic hydrodynamic behaviour and, in a limiting case, enters into the Navier Stokes equations [8]. Using this procedure the conservation of linear momentum and energy is guaranteed and can also be coupled to embedded particles, simulated by other methods, e.g. molecular dynamics, thereby coupling particle dynamics to a hydrodynamic medium [8,12].

From an algorithmic point of view, three main parts can be identified, i.e. (i) the local identification of particles in the underlying cell structure and the computation of *com* velocities of cells; (ii) the computation of the relative velocities of particles with respect to the *com* velocity of a cell; (iii) rotation of perpendicular velocity component of particles around a random axis. These parts will be discussed separately in Sect. 3 in more detail in the context of the Cabana implementation.

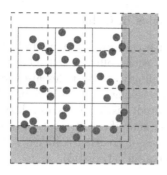

Fig. 1. Illustration of the shifted collision cell grid (black, dashed) in comparison to the static logical cell grid (black, solid). The grey cells mark the periodic images of the shifted grid. (Color figure online)

3 Implementation with Cabana

The aim of the implementation was to write a code, that is performance portable between clusters consisting of CPU and clusters with GPU nodes, which often consist of one or two CPUs and a number of GPUs ranging from two to six. Maintaining two or more codebases for all targeted architectures increases the overhead time of, e.g., design or maintenance time, and calls for solutions which allow a unified approach for various architectures.

For this reason performance portable programming models are attractive for reducing time spent with porting codes to various architectures. One of the more popular programming models in this regard is Kokkos [6], which provides an abstraction layer for data structures, called *Views*, while providing different *ExecutionSpaces* which can either be on the host (usually the CPU) or on devices, i.e. GPUs or other accelerator cards, e.g. Intel KNLs. Kokkos uses different backends to provide this performance portability, e.g. CUDA for the use of NVIDIA GPUs or ROCm for the use of AMD GPUs. Furthermore, OpenMP or PThread backends can be used among others to utilise multicore architectures of CPUs.

Within the Exascale Computing Project (ECP) [5] funded by the Department of Energy (DoE) in the USA, the Co-Design Center for Particle Applications (CoPA) [3] developed a performance portable library, based on Kokkos, with the main focus of supporting the development of particle and grid based codes on HPC systems. Cabana not only provides data structures based on Kokkos *Views* but also provides routines in order to facilitate data transfer between different processes in a distributed-memory environment, based on MPI.

Since the MPCD method is a mixture of a particle and a grid based method (due to the requirement to sort the particles into cells), the implementation of the MPCD code using Cabana was considered reasonable. In the rest of the section the main points of the implementation will be presented.

3.1   Collection of Particles in Cells

Before the *com* velocity for a cell can be calculated, it is necessary to identify the particles that reside in each collision cell. One technique to achieve this is the linked-cell list. Accordingly, all particles are checked and flagged with a cell identifier to which they belong to. In addition, a (linked) list of particles belonging to the cell is created. Listing 1.1 shows how such a list is created in Cabana. The use of Cabana simplifies the creation of such a linked cell list, as Cabana deals with the issues of creating a linked cell list in a multithreaded environment, as described e.g. in [11] or [15].

Listing 1.1. Creation of the linked cell list of the shifted collision cell grid

```
// boundaries of spacial domains
double gridMin[3], gridMax[3];
for (int d = 0; d < 3; ++d)
{
    gridMin[d] = domBorders(2*d) - (double)haloWidth
                 * cellSize(d) + offset(d);
    gridMax[d] = domBorders(2*d+1) + (double)haloWidth
                 * cellSize(d) + offset(d);
}
// creating the linked cell list
// r = list of particle positions
// cellSize = size of linked cells (3d)
Cabana::LinkedCellList<DeviceType>
    linkedList( r, cellSize, gridMin, gridMax );
// permute the particle AoSoA to correspond to the cells
Cabana::permute( linkedList, particles );
```

3.2   Communication of Required Information

As described in Sect. 2, it is necessary to compute the *com* velocity, i.e. the velocity in a zero momentum frame with regard to the local collision cell [7], in order to calculate the collisions within each mesh cell, which requires all velocities and masses of particles that reside within the given collision cell. The underlying parallel algorithm is based on a domain decomposition, where compute resources administrate geometrical spatial regions which are connected. Since the underlying mesh is shifted in each time step cells might be split among several domains. To compute a unique value for the *com* velocity, one can either collect all particles together with their properties on a local domain or one can compute the partial *com* velocities on each local domain and then reduce this value among those processes which share the given cell.

The first of these methods has the advantage that since all particles are collected on a single domain, the computation of the *com* velocity and the following rotation of velocities can be executed without the need of additional communication steps in between. The disadvantage is that it requires the communication of particle data in each time step, since the collision cell mesh needs to be shifted in each time step to avoid artefacts in the computation of the hydrodynamic inter-actions. Listing 1.2 shows the necessary steps to prepare the particle migration between domains. Shown here is a way to try to avoid unnecessary branching while determining the target processes for particles. This is done by masking the target processes with a base-3 number, where each 'bit' indicates either a shift down(0) or up (1) or residing in the domain's boundary concerning that Carte-sian direction. As an example a base-3 number of $(201)_3$ would be assigned to a particle leaving the local domain in positive x-direction and negative y-direction, while stay in the same z-region, as the local domain. This way to determine tar-get processes should improve execution on GPU, with the tertiary operator being removed, in case that true is cast to integer one and false to integer zero.

Listing 1.2. Particle based communication with Cabana

```
Kokkos :: parallel_for (
  Kokkos :: RangePolicy < ExecutionSpace >(0, nParticles),
  KOKKOS_LAMBDA (const size_t i)
  {
    int dims = 1, index = 0;
    // compute the direction of the neighbour the particle
    // needs to be moved to and use dims to compute a
    // base 3 mask:
    // (xyz)_3 with 0 (left), 1 (remains), 2 (right)
    // r = list of particle positions
    for (int d = 2; d >= 0; --d)
    {
        index += dims *
          ( 1 - ((r(i,d) < domBorders(2*d))?1:0) +
          ((r(i,d) >= domBorders(2*d+1))?1:0) );
        dims *= 3;
    }
    // tag the particle with the target neighbour rank
    export_ranks(i) = neigs(index);
  });
Kokkos :: fence ();

// create particles distribution object and
// migrate particles to targets
Cabana :: Distributor < DeviceType > dist ( mpiCart,
                        export_ranks, neighbours );
Cabana :: migrate(dist, particles);
```

In contrast, the second method allows the use of a stable, halo-based commu-nication scheme, where particles are not necessarily communicated in each time step, but only when leaving a halo region around the local domain, allowing the distributed computation of partial *com* velocities, that are reduced with a static communication scheme. The result is then sent back to the domains sharing the same cell. Listing 1.3 shows the required function calls to Cabana to do the halo exchange. This work, related to mesh administration, is implemented in *Cajita*,

which is part of Cabana. In addition, it provides methods for particle-grid interactions, e.g. interpolation of particle properties to a grid, which is, however, not
used in this work. Furthermore, Cajita provides a domain-based load balancing
based on a tensor decomposition scheme, provided by the ALL library [9].

Listing 1.3. Grid based halo communication with Cabana

```
// create the halo communication object based
// on the Cajita grid
auto arrHalo = Cajita::createHalo( *arrNode,
                Cajita::NodeHaloPattern<3>());
// [...] computation of com velocities
// bring the data to the halo cells
arrHalo->gather(ExecutionSpace(), *arrNode);
// collect the data from the halo cells
arrHalo->scatter(ExecutionSpace(),
    Cajita::ScatterReduce::Sum(), *arrNode);
```

For the implementation of the two different communication schemes two different kinds of communication in Cabana were used. For the former method, the
particle-based one, Cabana provides a *Distributor* class, which allows the transfer of particle data between processes. This requires that particles are tagged
with the target process, so that the *Distributor* object can generate a communication topology for this specific transfer. As a consequence this object needs to
be recreated in every time step, since the communication pattern in each time
step changes due the random shift of the collision cell grid and particle movements across domain borders.

For the second communication pattern, reducing the partial results and redis-
tributing them, a halo-based communication on a grid is used. For this purpose,
two different grids are combined, i.e. a logical collision grid which is used for
communication and a linked-cell list, which sorts the particles into the shifted
collision cell grid. Since the number and size of mesh cells in each grid is identical, both grids can be perfectly matched onto each other. The particles are
sorted into the linked-cell list (Sect. 3.1) from where the *com* momentum of each
cell is computed. For collision cells, overlapping with domain borders (Fig. 1),
a halo-based communication reduces the partial results on the process which
administrates the logical cell. This process redistributes the reduced sum back
to each participating neighbour, where the rotations of velocities are computed
for residing particles. Since the number of cells is usually far smaller than the
number of particles, this leads to (i) a static communication scheme (for each
iteration step the same operations on the same amount of data) and (ii) a reduced
and constant amount of data that needs to be communicated.

During the development, it became apparent that the second communication
scheme leads to a better performance due to the reduced amount of transferred
data and the strongly reduced necessity to recreate communication patterns, due
to the stable communication scheme of the halo exchange (this needs to be done

only once in the beginning or after possible load balancing steps, after which
the communication pattern is static). In addition, the transfer of particles can
be reduced to cases, where particles left the halo region surrounding the local
domain, instead of being required in every time step.

3.3 Rotation of Velocities

To simplify the computation of the velocity rotation, the linked cell list mentioned in Sect. 3.1 is used to sort particles into the correct cell of the collision cell
grid. Using the *com* velocity, gathered by one of the two previously described
methods, the linked-cell list provides the particles which belong to the given cell
and their velocity vector rotated.

Listing 1.4. Using the linked cell list from listing 1.1 to compute the com velocity

```
// Kokkos parallel_for iterates over
// all cells on local domain
// vcm = Kokkos::View containg the center
//        of mass velocites for each
//        collision cell
// v   = Cabana::slice containing
//        particle velocities
// m   = Cabana::slice containing
//        particles masses
Kokkos::parallel_for(Kokkos::RangePolicy<ExecutionSpace>
  (0, linkedList.totalBins()),
  KOKKOS_LAMBDA( const size_t i)
  {
     int ix, iy, iz;
     // computing the cartesian coordinates of the cell
     linkedList.ijkBinIndex(i, ix, iy, iz);
     int binOff = linkedList.binOffset(ix, iy, iz);
     // compute com velocity
     for (int d = 0; d < 4; ++d)
       vcm(ix,iy,iz,d) = 0.0;
     // computing com momentum and sum of mass
     for (int n = 0; n < linkedList.binSize(ix,iy,iz); ++n)
     {
       for (int d = 0; d < 3; ++d)
         vcm(ix,iy,iz,d) += v(binOff + n, d) *
                            m(binOff + n);
       vcm(ix,iy,iz,3) += m(binOff + n);
     }
  });
Kokkos::fence();
```

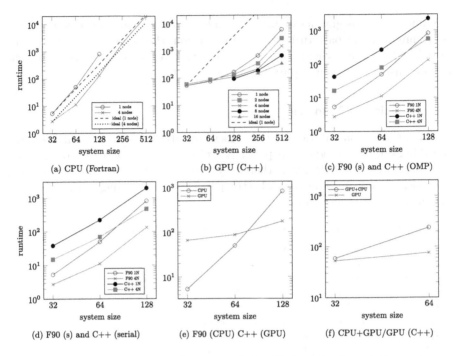

Fig. 2. Performance comparison between existing Fortran implementation and new Cabana implementation using multiple nodes.

4   Benchmarks and Discussion

For the benchmark runs simple fluid systems were used, i.e. a pure MPCD fluid in 3d periodic boundary conditions. Each cubic collision cell has an edge length of one length unit, while containing $\langle N_c \rangle = 10$ particles on average. Each system in the benchmarks is cubic with side length L (the edge length L given as the system size in the following graphs, i.e. Fig. 2), from where the total number of particles in a system is computed as $N = L^3 \langle N_c \rangle$. To check the performance of the newly implemented code, it was compared to an existing Fortran implementation of the MPCD algorithm [12,18].

The benchmarks were performed on the Juwels booster module [13] at Jülich Supercomputing Centre, consisting of GPU nodes with four NVIDIA A100 cards and two AMD EPYC 7402 processors, with 24 cores each. To maintain comparability of the benchmarks the pure CPU runs were also performed on these nodes. Since the GPU nodes are much more powerful in their computing capabilities, we performed the benchmarks for the GPU runs on node numbers from one to 16, doubling the node count each time. For the CPU, expecting longer runtimes we chose to compare single node runs with runs on four nodes, while also restricting the system size to a maximum edge length of 128 while for the GPU runs we performed the benchmarks to a maximum edge length of 512. The edge length directly influences the number of particles in the simulation, since

Table 1. Tables of runtimes for the different implementations. Empty cells indicate combinations of node numbers and system sizes, for which additional measurements did not show additional information. All runtimes presented are given in seconds.

(a) Runtimes for GPU C++ variant, using 4 GPUs on each node.

size	1 node	2 nodes	4 nodes	8 nodes	16 nodes
32	52.96	59.47	53.36		
64	75.55	86.48	78.77		
128	162.88	130.27	107.29	92.11	
256	652.25	335.12	211.51	182.18	144.60
512	5897.44	2774.35	1429.14	648.252	327.49

(b) Runtimes for CPU variants, Fortran (F90) and the C++ based variants, i.e. OpenMP-based (OMP) or serial, i.e. no hybrid parallelization, using one or four nodes (N). OMP uses 8 MPI ranks with 6 threads each on a node, the Fortran and serial version 48 MPI ranks per node. Only system sizes up to edge length 128 are presented due to the longer runtimes.

size	F90 1 N	F90 4 N	OMP 1 N	OMP 4 N	serial 1 N	serial 4 N
32	5.36	2.75	42.62	16.37	38.33	15.06
64	49.59	11.20	284.73	78.79	221.38	69.06
128	819.06	132.06	2268.80	555.42	1967.42	474.67

there are about l^3 collision cells in the system, with l being the edge length of the system, each collision cell containing ten particles on average.

As backends for Kokkos were the AMD and Ampere70 used, since these corresponded best to the available hardware. No further optimization on the basis of compiler flags was attempted yet due to time constraints, but these tests will be performed in the future. Table 1 and Fig. 2 show results for four different benchmarks: (i) C++/Kokkos implementation with GPU variant (Table 1a and Fig. 2b); (ii) C++/Kokkos variant with OpenMP (Table 1b and Fig. 2c); (iii) C++/Kokkos variant with serial backend and (iv) the previous implementation of the MPCD algorithm in Fortran (Table 1b and Fig. 2a) for comparison with the new implementation.

The original Fortran code shows a quite good scaling behaviour for all studied cases (edge lengths $L \in [32, 512]$), as can be seen in Fig. 2a. In comparison to that the scaling behaviour of the GPU variant of the C++ implementation shows for the smaller system sizes a super-linear scaling behaviour, before reaching linear behaviour at system sizes 256 and 512, indicating that smaller sizes not fully utilise the GPU (Fig. 2b).

When comparing the performance of the Fortran implementation (Fig. 2a) and the CPU based variants of the C++ version, i.e. OpenMP based or serial, it can be seen that Fortran achieves much better results (Figs. 2c, 2d). An explanation for this behaviour still needs to be analysed in more depth. But first results point towards a different level of optimization (which is not the main focus of this article). In contrast, the GPU variant is able to outperform the Fortran implementation given sufficiently large system sizes, as can be seen in Fig. 2e, comparing the benchmark results on a single node, respectively. Here only the results for system sizes 32 and 64 are shown, since the measurement strongly hint that for larger system sizes the gap between hybrid execution and pure GPU execution will only widen.

Furthermore, it was tested on a single node if the combination of GPU and CPU could result in a better performance than only GPU computations. Due to the obtained performance of the CPU-based C++ variants, the results indicate at this stage no performance gain for hybrid execution (Fig. 2f). In case of a performance improvement of the CPU-based variants, this result might change for smaller system sizes. Note that for small systems load balancing GPU and CPU ranks can improve the overall performance for hybrid execution significantly, but not sufficiently in order to outperform either pure CPU or GPU. This does not lead to a recommendation of a hybrid execution model at this stage.

5   Conclusion and Outlook

Considering the benchmark results of the new implementation of the MPCD code the following conclusions can be drawn:

(i) It is possible to implement a scalable MPCD algorithm with Cabana, that for large enough systems is faster on GPUs than the existing Fortran implementation. The CPU variant of the Cabana implementation needs to be improved upon to bring the performance closer to the one of the Fortran code.

(ii) Load balancing between CPU and GPU can support hybrid execution, but was not found to increase performance beyond the one of pure CPU or GPU usage.

(iii) The porting effort from a pure CPU variant to a multi-architecture variant was significantly decreased by using Cabana, which offers an architecture independent development and code implementation which provides a unified and transparent view for the programmer. Porting effort is therefore dramatically reduced by maintaining performance (which was not the focus here, but which is demonstrated for other use cases [1,6,10]).

(iv) The implementation of the MPCD algorithm allows further investigation of coupled simulations of MPCD fluids with embedded Molecular Dynamics (MD) systems, e.g. polymer chains. For this, an implementation based on a unified formulation of MD and MPCD, as described, e.g., in [8,12], is required. Since the ratio of MD- to MPCD particles is often small, this could profit from a hybrid implementation and execution model, which invites to further investigations, including execution models for modular supercomputing.

References

1. Artigues, V., Kormann, K., Rampp, M., Reuter, K.: Evaluation of performance portability frameworks for the implementation of a particle-in-cell code. Concurr. Comput. Pract. Exp. **32**(11), e5640 (2020). https://doi.org/10.1002/cpe.5640
2. Cabana. https://github.com/ECP-copa/Cabana
3. Co-Design Center for Particle Applications. https://www.exascaleproject.org/research-project/particle-based-applications/
4. Dongarra, J., Luszczek, P.: TOP500, pp. 2055–2057. Springer, US, Boston, MA (2011). https://doi.org/10.1007/978-0-387-09766-4_157
5. Exascale Computing Project. https://www.exascaleproject.org/
6. Edwards, H.C., Trott, C.R., Sunderland, D.: Kokkos: Enabling manycore performance portability through polymorphic memory access patterns. J. Parallel Distrib. Comput. **74**(12), 3202–3216 (2014). https://doi.org/10.1016/j.jpdc.2014.07.003
7. Goldstein, H., Poole, C., Safko, J.: Classical Mechanics. Addison Wesley, San Francisco (2002)
8. Gompper, G., Ihle, T., Kroll, D.M., Winkler, R.G.: Multi-Particle Collision Dynamics: A Particle-Based Mesoscale Simulation Approach to the Hydrodynamics of Complex Fluids. In: Advanced Computer Simulation Approaches for Soft Matter Sciences III, pp. 1–87. Springer, Berlin Heidelberg (2008). https://doi.org/10.1007/978-3-540-87706-6_1
9. Halver, R., Schulz, S., Sutmann, G.: ALL - A loadbalancing library, C++/Fortran library. https://gitlab.version.fz-juelich.de/SLMS/loadbalancing/-/releases
10. Halver, R., Meinke, J.H., Sutmann, G.: Kokkos implementation of an Ewald coulomb solver and analysis of performance portability. J. Parallel Distrib. Comput. **138**, 48–54 (2020). https://doi.org/10.1016/j.jpdc.2019.12.003
11. Halver, R., Sutmann, G.: Multi-threaded construction of neighbour lists for particle systems in OpenMP. In: Parallel Processing and Applied Mathematics 11th International Conference, PPAM 2015, Krakow, Poland, 6–9 September 2015. Revised Selected Papers, Part II. 11th International Conference on Parallel Processing and Applied Mathematics, Krakow (Poland), 6 Sep 2015–9 Sep 2015 (2015). https://juser.fz-juelich.de/record/279249
12. Huang, C., Winkler, R., Sutmann, G., Gompper, G.: Semidilute polymer solutions at equilibrium and under shear flow. Macromolecules **43**, 10107–10116 (2010)
13. Juwels. https://www.fz-juelich.de/ias/jsc/EN/Expertise/Supercomputers/JUWELS/JUWELS_node.html
14. Mniszewski, S.M., et al.: Enabling particle applications for exascale computing platforms. Int. J. High Perform. Comput. Appl. **35**(6), 572–597 (2021). https://doi.org/10.1177/10943420211022829
15. Ohno, K., Nitta, T., Nakai, H.: SPH-based fluid simulation on GPU using verlet list and subdivided cell-linked list. In: 2017 Fifth International Symposium on Computing and Networking (CANDAR), pp. 132–138 (2017). https://doi.org/10.1109/CANDAR.2017.104
16. RAJA Performance Portability Layer. https://github.com/LLNL/RAJA
17. Slattery, S., et al.: Cabana: a performance portable library for particle-based simulations. J. Open Source Softw. **7**(72), 4115 (2022). https://doi.org/10.21105/joss.04115
18. Sutmann, G.: MP2C (2022). https://fz-juelich.de/en/ias/jsc/about-us/structure/simulation-and-data-labs/sdl-molecular-systems/mp2c

Comparison of Load Balancing Schemes for Asynchronous Many-Task Runtimes

Lukas Reitz[✉], Kai Hardenbicker, and Claudia Fohry

Research Group Programming Languages/Methodologies, University of Kassel,
Kassel, Germany
{lukas.reitz,fohry}@uni-kassel.de

Abstract. A popular approach to program scalable irregular applications is Asynchronous Many-Task (AMT) Programming. Here, programs define tasks according to task models such as dynamic independent tasks (DIT) or nested fork-join (NFJ). We consider cluster AMTs, in which a runtime system maps the tasks to worker threads in multiple processes.

Thereby, dynamic load balancing can be achieved via work-stealing or work-sharing. A well-performing work-stealing variant is the lifeline scheme. While previous implementations are restricted to single-worker processes, a recent hybrid extension combines the scheme with intra-process work-sharing between multiple workers. The hybrid scheme comes at the price of a higher complexity.

This paper investigates whether this complexity is indispensable by contrasting the scheme with a pure work-stealing extension of the lifeline scheme introduced in the paper. In an experimental comparison based on independent DIT and NFJ implementations and three benchmarks, the pure work-stealing scheme is on a par or even outperforms the hybrid one by up to 3.8%.

Keywords: Work Stealing · Work Sharing · Runtime Systems · Asynchronous Many-Tasking · Task-based Parallel Programming

1 Introduction

Asynchronous Many-Task (AMT) programming, as exemplified by Cilk [2], OpenMP tasks [14], and HPX [7], is a popular approach to tackle irregularity in parallel applications. AMT programs partition the computation into units called *tasks*, and a runtime system (briefly called AMT, as well) maps the tasks to lower-level resources called *workers*. We consider cluster AMTs, for which the workers correspond to threads of multiple processes that may run on different nodes.

AMTs can be classified by their model of task cooperation [6]. In particular, *dynamic tasks* are allowed to spawn child tasks to which their parent task may pass parameters. We consider two subclasses:

© The Author(s), under exclusive license to Springer Nature Switzerland AG 2023
R. Wyrzykowski et al. (Eds.): PPAM 2022, LNCS 13827, pp. 14–26, 2023.
https://doi.org/10.1007/978-3-031-30445-3_2

1. *Dynamic Independent Tasks* (DIT) do not communicate, but yield a task result. The final result is calculated from the task results by reduction, e.g., by integer summation. Examples for DIT runtimes include GLB [27] and Blaze-Tasks [15].
2. *Nested Fork-Join* (NFJ) programs begin the computation with one root task. Then each task returns its result to its parent, and the root task yields the final result. Examples for NFJ runtimes include Cilk and Satin [12].

Many AMTs deploy dynamic load balancing, which may be accomplished via *work stealing* or *work sharing*. In work stealing, idle workers (*thieves*) take tasks from other workers (*victims*), whereas in work sharing, busy workers give tasks to others.

A well-performing work stealing variant is Lifeline-based Global Load Balancing, briefly called the *lifeline scheme* [22]. It was first implemented in the Global Load Balancing (GLB) library of the parallel programming language X10 [3] and later ported to Java [17]. Unfortunately, these implementations allow only one worker per process.

A recent *hybrid scheme* overcomes this limitation by combining the lifeline scheme for work stealing between the processes with work sharing among multiple workers within a process. This scheme has been implemented in Java GLB variants for DIT and NFJ, which we denote by $\mathbf{DIT}_{hybrid}$ [5] and $\mathbf{NFJ}_{hybrid}$ [21], respectively.

While the hybrid scheme overcomes the single-worker limitation, its hybrid design has the drawback of a higher complexity. This led us to our research question: Is the complexity of the hybrid scheme indispensable for an efficient extension of the lifeline scheme to multiple workers per process?

To answer the question, we extended the lifeline scheme so that it solely relies on work stealing, but still has multiple workers per process. Our new scheme, which we call *lifeline-pure*, is essentially identical to the lifeline scheme, except that threads instead of processes take over the role of workers. In particular, each worker (thread) within a process maintains its own task queue. When a worker runs empty, it tries to steal tasks from a random worker, which is any thread in the same or in a different process. As will be discussed later, preferring local over global victims may increase the efficiency. Nevertheless, even without such locality optimization in place, we were able to show that the lifeline-pure scheme is on a par or even outperforms the more complicated hybrid scheme by up to 3.8 %.

We conducted our experiments with up to 1280 workers and three benchmarks. Two implementations of the lifeline-pure scheme were used. Both are based on Java GLB, and are called $\mathbf{DIT}_{pure}$ and $\mathbf{NFJ}_{pure}$, respectively. To strengthen our results, the DIT and NFJ implementations were developed independently by the second and first authors of this paper, respectively.

The remainder of the paper is organized as follows. Section 2 provides further details on the load balancing schemes and task models. Then, Sect. 3 discusses the design and implementation of DIT_{pure} and NFJ_{pure}. Experimental results are presented and discussed in Sect. 4. The paper finishes with related work and conclusions in Sects. 5 and 6, respectively.

2   Background

2.1   Lifeline Scheme

The lifeline scheme [22] deploys *cooperative* work stealing, i.e., thieves ask their victims for tasks, and victims respond by sending tasks or a reject message. When a worker runs out of tasks, it first attempts to steal from up to w random victims. If all random steal attempts fail, it informs z so-called *lifeline buddies*, which are neighbored workers in a connected graph, called the *lifeline graph*. The lifeline buddies record all lifeline steal attempts and possibly answer them later.

Each worker maintains an own local task queue. It takes out tasks for processing and inserts child tasks at one end, and extracts loot for thieves at the other. The workers communicate in work stealing by calling a function on the remote worker, where it is executed by an additional thread. For example, to answer a successful random steal request, the victim calls a function on the thief and passes the tasks as a parameter. The function inserts the tasks into the thief's local task queue, which is synchronized for this purpose.

Listing 1.1 depicts pseudocode for the main loop of each worker. Workers process tasks in chunks of k tasks (line 3), after which they respond to recorded steal requests (line 4). When a worker runs out of tasks, it first tries to steal from random victims (line 6). If all random steal attempts fail, the worker notifies its lifeline buddies and enters an idle state (line 8), from which it can be restarted if a lifeline buddy delivers tasks later.

```
1   do {
2     do {
3        processUpToKTasks();
4        answerStealRequests();
5     } while (tasksAvailable());
6     attemptRandomSteals();
7   } while (tasksAvailable());
8   informBuddiesAndBecomeIdle();
```

Listing 1.1. Main loop of Lifeline-based Global Load Balancing

2.2   Hybrid Scheme

As mentioned in Sect. 1, the hybrid scheme [5] couples the lifeline scheme for work stealing between the processes with work sharing among the workers within a process. It uses two shared queues, which are synchronized to allow accesses from multiple threads:

- an *intra queue* for intra-process work sharing, and
- an *inter queue* chiefly for inter-process work stealing.

Listing 1.2 depicts pseudocode for the main loop of each worker. A process begins with a single worker. After its own spawn, each worker repeatedly tries to spawn additional workers and gives them some tasks (line 4), until some desired maximum number of workers is reached. Then, if one of the shared queues is empty, the worker puts any surplus tasks there (lines 6–11). Afterwards, it processes up to k tasks, and repeats the previous steps as long as it has tasks. When a worker runs out of tasks, it first attempts to take all tasks from the intra queue (lines 14–16), or otherwise from the inter queue (lines 17–19). If both shared queues are empty, the worker shuts down (end of code) and has to be spawned again later.

```
1   do {
2      do {
3         if (numWorkers < numMaxWorkers) {
4            attemptToSpawnAdditionalWorker();
5         }
6         if (intraQueueEmpty) {
7            shareTasksToIntraQueue();
8         }
9         if (interQueueEmpty) {
10           shareTasksToInterQueue();
11        }
12        processUpToKTasks();
13     } while (tasksAvailable());
14     if (!intraQueueEmpty) {
15        takeTasksFromIntraQueue();
16     }
17     if (!tasksAvailable() && !interQueueEmpty) {
18        takeTasksFromInterQueue();
19     }
20  } while (tasksAvailable());
```

Listing 1.2. Main loop of Lifeline-based Global Load Balancing

2.3 Nested Fork-Join and Dynamic Independent Tasks

As already noted, the NFJ and DIT task models deploy dynamic tasks. We assume that the tasks are free of side effects.

For **NFJ**, Listing 1.3 depicts pseudocode of a naive recursive Fibonacci program. The code is invoked on worker 0 by calling `fib(n)`. The **spawn** keyword in line 5 generates a child task and passes `n-1`. The child task calculates `fib(n-1)` recursively. Afterwards, the result is assigned to variable `a` of the parent task. The **sync** keyword pauses the execution of the parent task until all child tasks have returned their results. Thus, the structure of the computation can be regarded as a *task tree*, in which the root task returns the final result.

```
1   fib (n) {
2      if (n < 2) {
3         return 1;
4      }
5      a = spawn fib (n−1);
6      b = fib (n−2);
7      sync;
8      return a + b;
9   }
```

Listing 1.3. Nested fork-join: naive recursive Fibonacci

Work stealing in NFJ$_{hybrid}$ is implemented with the *work-first* policy: When a worker spawns a child task, it puts a description of the parent task into the task queue and branches into the child. The description is called a *continuation* and represents the remaining computation of this task. For instance, the continuation that is generated in line 5 of Listing 1.3 denotes the code in lines 6 to 9 enhanced by the value of n and the knowledge that a will be provided by the child task. The continuation may be processed by the worker itself after having finished the child, or be stolen away. In NFJ$_{hybrid}$, a thief always takes a single task (*steal-one*).

Thus, any work stealing scheme for NFJ must keep track of the parent-child relations and incorporate child results into their parent. We denote these activities as the *fork-join protocol*. The fork-join protocol of NFJ$_{hybrid}$ [21] was adapted from [8] and passes the result of a child task directly to the parent task if the parent is still in the local queue when the child returns. Otherwise, the worker saves the child result in a data structure that is shared between all workers of the process. Saved results are eventually collected as follows: When a task has to wait for its child tasks in a `sync`, this task is sent back to its previous victim. Child results may already reside there, if the child has finished. Otherwise, they are eventually inserted. Since the parent task may have been stolen multiple times, child results may exist on further victims, and the result collection continues there. In contrast to [8], where tasks are returned to their last thief after incorporating all child results, we process them at their first victim.

Unlike NFJ tasks, **DIT** tasks only cooperate through parameter passing from parents to children. Task results are accumulated into worker results, by combining them with a commutative and associative binary operator (e.g., integer summation). Later, each process combines its local worker results to a process result, and finally the process results are combined to the final result.

Listing 1.4 depicts pseudocode of a naive recursive Fibonacci program in DIT. The code is invoked on worker 0 by calling `fib(n)`. Like before, the `spawn` keyword in line 5 generates a task. Method `incrementResult()` adds 1 to the worker result, since `fib(0)` = `fib(1)` = 1. After global termination of all tasks, worker 0 initiates the calculation of the process and final results. Afterwards, the final result may be queried from the system.

Work stealing in DIT$_{hybrid}$ is implemented with the *help-first* policy: When a worker encounters a spawn, it puts the child task into the local task queue

```
1    fib (n) {
2       if (n < 2) {
3          incrementResult ();
4       } else {
5          spawn fib (n−1);
6          fib (n−2);
7       }
8    }
```

Listing 1.4. Dynamic independent tasks: naive recursive Fibonacci

and continues to execute the parent task. In DIT_{hybrid}, thieves steal half of the available tasks of a victim (*steal-half*).

3 Design and Implementation of Lifeline-Pure Scheme

The lifeline-pure scheme extends the lifeline scheme with support for multi-worker processes. As noted in Sect. 1, the scheme is essentially identical to the lifeline scheme, except that the workers correspond to threads. Each worker maintains an own local task queue and participates in the work stealing independently of other workers. Also, the lifeline graph and the random victim selection operate at the granularity of workers.

Unlike in NFJ_{hybrid}, we decided to perform all activities of the fork-join protocol separately for each worker within a process in order to reduce contention on the shared data structures. For DIT, as in the hybrid scheme, we first combine the worker results within each process, and then perform a global reduction.

A modification of the lifeline scheme refers to the realization of the communication between a pair of workers. Whereas workers directly communicate with each other in the lifeline scheme, they use a so-called *coordinator* in the lifeline-pure scheme. The coordinator handles all communication, i.e., a worker that is going to send a message to another worker calls a function of its coordinator. The coordinator then sends a message to the remote worker's coordinator. The remote coordinator then forwards the message to the target worker. Global and local worker ids are translated into each other in an obvious way. Figure 1 shows the communication paths, where several workers, denoted as W, communicate with each other through their coordinators, denoted as C@.

Obviously it would be profitable to prefer local over global victims, since process internal stealing has lower communication costs. As of yet, the lifeline-pure scheme does not incorporate such locality optimizations, but the scheme could be easily extended accordingly.

All implementations are based on the "APGAS for Java" library [23], which is a Partitioned Global Address Space (PGAS) platform. We used a modified version of it, which is available in a public git repository [16].

In our implementations, the coordinator is a Java class. Messages between workers of the same process do not get serialized and passed through the network, but are executed in one or more separate threads of Java's fork-join pool.

4   Experimental Evaluation

This section compares the running times of the lifeline-pure and hybrid DIT and NFJ variants, respectively.

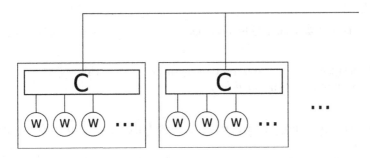

Fig. 1. Communication paths between workers (W) through the coordinator (C) in the lifeline-pure scheme

All experiments were conducted with Java version 17.0.2. We run our programs on the Goethe cluster of the University of Frankfurt [25], where we used a partition of homogeneous Infiniband-connected nodes. Each node is equipped with two 20-core Intel Xeon Skylake Gold 6148 CPUs and 192 GB of main memory. We used up to 32 nodes, with one process per node and one worker per core, resulting in a total of 1280 workers. We report averages over 15 runs.

We used three benchmarks:

- **Fib** (for NFJ): The naive Fibonacci benchmark was presented in Sect. 2. It computes `fib(n)`.
- **UTS**: The Unbalanced Tree Search benchmark dynamically generates a highly-irregular tree and counts its nodes [13]. Users provide a tree depth d, a branching factor b, an initial seed s of a pseudorandom generator, and a probability distribution that determines the tree shape (binomial or geometric).
- **Syn**: The synthetic benchmark counts the nodes of a perfect w-ary tree [19]. Users provide a desired running time T_{calc}, a number m specifies the number of tree nodes per worker, and a task duration variance v as percentage. Each task repeatedly calculates the 5th Fibonacci number recursively until it reaches its task duration. An execution with GLB then takes time $T = T_{\text{calc}} + \epsilon$, where ϵ is the additional time taken by the runtime system, called the runtime system *overhead*. In the case of DIT, ϵ is caused by the load balancing scheme. In the case of NFJ, ϵ is caused by the load balancing scheme and the fork-join protocol.

In all benchmarks, task results are `long` values and the reduction operator is sum.

In preliminary experiments, we found that a so-called *sequential cut-off* reduced the execution times of the NFJ GLB variants significantly: The sequential cut-off c defines a remaining depth (e.g., `fib(n)` calls with $n \leq c$), where the `spawn` statement causes workers to jump into the given function instead of spawning a child task. We implemented a sequential cut-off for Fib and UTS@. Syn did not require one, because the task granularity can be controlled by its benchmark parameters.

Table 1. Benchmark parameters

Benchmark	Parameters
Fib	$n = 67$
	$c = 30$
UTS	$d = 19$
	$b = 4$
	$c = 6$
	geometric tree shape
Syn	$T_{\mathrm{calc}} = 100\,\mathrm{s}$
	$m = 10^6$
	$v = 20\,\%$

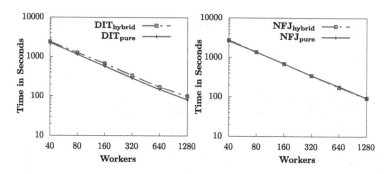

Fig. 2. Strong scaling performance of UTS

For DIT, we used existing implementations of the benchmarks [19]. For NFJ, we slightly improved an existing implementation of Fib [21], and implemented UTS and Syn from scratch.

The used benchmark parameters are shown in Table 1. Recall that both the lifeline-pure and the hybrid scheme process tasks in chunks of k tasks (see Sect. 2). In preliminary experiments, we tried different chunk sizes for each benchmark and found that the following values for k yield the lowest execution times: $k = 511$ (for UTS in DIT), $k = 16$ (for UTS in NFJ), $k = 10$ (for Fib in NFJ), and $k = 1$ (for Syn).

Figures 2 and 3 show execution times for UTS and Fib. They employ strong scaling to convey an impression of the magnitudes. For each run, we doubled the number of nodes, and thus the number of workers. The measured execution times decrease approximately linearly. Speedups over the execution with one worker are between 1103 and 1243 for 1280 workers.

The strong scaling results for DIT show a bigger difference between the hybrid and the lifeline-pure scheme than those for NFJ@. For DIT, the gap between the two schemes is clearly visible. For NFJ, the gap between the schemes is small and barely visible. This is likely due to the fact, that the used load balancing scheme impacts all the communication in DIT (except the final reduction), but only part of the communication in NFJ (not the fork-join protocol).

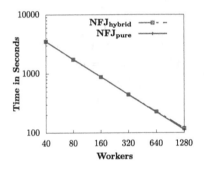

Fig. 3. Strong scaling performance of Fib

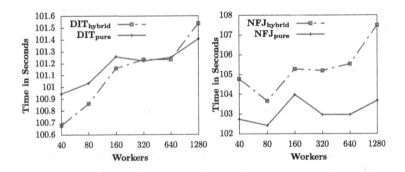

Fig. 4. Weak scaling performance of Syn

Figure 4 shows execution times measured with Syn. We employ weak scaling by keeping T_{calc} constant for all runs. We calculate the overhead as the difference between the measured execution time and T_{calc}. Since $T_{\text{calc}} = 100\,\text{s}$ for all runs, an execution time of $101\,\text{s}$ means, that the runtime system overhead is $1\,\%$. Overheads increase slowly with the number of workers.

For DIT, the overhead is $1.54\,\%$ for 1280 workers and the hybrid scheme, and $1.41\,\%$ for the lifeline-pure scheme. For NFJ, the overhead is higher than in DIT, since it includes the cost of the fork-join protocol. Because the hybrid and the lifeline-pure scheme both use the same fork-join protocol, we can still compare the overhead. The highest overhead difference between both schemes is about $3.8\,\%$ for 1280 workers, where the hybrid scheme has an overhead of about $7.5\,\%$, and the lifeline-pure scheme has an overhead of about $3.7\,\%$.

5 Related Work

AMT, also called task-based parallel programming, goes back until at least the invention of Cilk in the 1990s [2]. Over the years, a variety of AMT programming environments have been proposed, and, especially on shared-memory machines, already found their way into programming practice (e.g., OpenMP tasks [14]).

From a user perspective, major differences between the AMT environments can be seen in their target architectures and task models [6,10,24]. The latter comprise DIT and NFJ, but also several types of dataflow-based, side effect-based, and actor-based coordination. The runtime systems differ in whether they support dynamic load balancing and dynamic task generation, and if they do so, in whether they realize it with work stealing or work sharing.

Work stealing became popular with Cilk [2], but several authors see work sharing on a par or prefer it [4,9]. Both work stealing and work sharing can be implemented in a coordinated way, in which queues are shared between workers, or in a cooperative way, in which they are private. The performance is about the same [1,17]. The work stealing variants also differ in their realization of victim selection and termination detection. Reitz [21] compared different strategies for choosing the number of tasks to be stolen. He used the same NFJ_{hybrid} scheme as we did in this paper.

While the lifeline scheme has traditionally been restricted to single-worker processes, other work stealing variants permit multiple workers. For instance, they combine shared- and distributed-memory work stealing into a two-level algorithm [20], or combine the process-internal load balancing of Java's fork-join pool with the lifeline scheme for inter-process work stealing [18].

These two-level algorithms prefer local over global steals to save communication costs, as do $\textbf{DIT}_{hybrid}$ and $\textbf{NFJ}_{hybrid}$. The idea of incorporating locality optimization into work stealing was also applied to hierachical architectures, e.g., [11]. Its usage may further improve the efficiency of our $\textbf{DIT}_{pure}$ and $\textbf{NFJ}_{pure}$ schemes.

As mentioned in Sect. 2.3, the fork-join protocol of our NFJ GLB variants was adapted from Kestor et al. [8] where tasks are returned to their last thief after incorporating all child results instead of to their first victim. Similar to the coordinators in the lifeline-pure scheme, they deploy a coordinator per process who communicate with each other by calling functions on remote coordinators.

The first GLB variant for X10 that allows multiple workers per process was presented by Yamashita and Kamada [26]. It was later improved by some tuning mechanism and re-implemented as DIT_{hybrid} in Java [5]. We did not employ the tuning mechanism, since it is irrelevant for our benchmarks.

6   Conclusions

This paper has shown that the lifeline scheme can be efficiently extended to multi-worker processes, without introducing the complexity of a hybrid scheme. Our extension, called lifeline-pure, solely relies on work stealing. We implemented it for DIT and NFJ.

Then we performed an experimental comparison between the lifeline-pure and hybrid schemes for DIT and NFJ, respectively. The experiments were run with three benchmarks and up to 1280 workers on a supercomputer. Even though the lifeline-pure scheme does not use any locality optimizations, we observed it to be on a par or even slightly outperform the hybrid scheme. Interestingly, our results were similar for DIT and NFJ, despite significant differences such as help-first vs. work-first, steal-half vs. steal-one, and the fact that the implementations have been developed independently by different people.

This similarity indicates that our findings may be of a more general nature. In particular, it would be interesting to compare other work stealing variants than the lifeline scheme with hybrid counterparts. Future research should also incorporate locality optimization into the lifeline-pure scheme and quantify the additional performance gain. Moreover, the experiments may be extended to larger benchmarks and other task models.

References

1. Acar, U.A., Charguéraud, A., Rainey, M.: Scheduling parallel programs by work stealing with private deques. SIGPLAN Notices **48**(8), 219–228 (2013). https://doi.org/10.1145/2442516.2442538
2. Blumofe, R.D., Leiserson, C.E.: Scheduling multithreaded computations by work stealing. J. ACM **46**(5), 720–748 (1999). https://doi.org/10.1145/324133.324234
3. Charles, P., et al.: X10: An object-oriented approach to non-uniform cluster computing. SIGPLAN Notices **40**(10), 519–538 (2005). https://doi.org/10.1145/1103845.1094852
4. Dinan, J., Olivier, S., Sabin, G., Prins, J., Sadayappan, P., Tseng, C.W.: Dynamic load balancing of unbalanced computations using message passing. In: Proceedings of International Parallel and Distributed Processing Symposium (IPDPS), pp. 1–8. IEEE (2007). https://doi.org/10.1109/IPDPS.2007.370581
5. Finnerty, P., Kamada, T., Ohta, C.: Self-adjusting task granularity for global load balancer library on clusters of many-core processors. In: Proceedings of International Workshop on Programming Models and Applications for Multicores and Manycores (PMAM), ACM (2020). https://doi.org/10.1145/3380536.3380539
6. Fohry, C.: An overview of task-based parallel programming models. In: Tutorial at European Network on High-performance Embedded Architecture and Compilation Conference (HiPEAC) (2019)

7. Kaiser, H., Heller, T., Adelstein-Lelbach, B., Serio, A., Fey, D.: HPX: a task based programming model in a global address space. In: Proceedings of International Conference on Partitioned Global Address Space Programming Models (PGAS), pp. 1–11. ACM (2014). https://doi.org/10.1145/2676870.2676883

8. Kestor, G., Krishnamoorthy, S., Ma, W.: Localized fault recovery for nested fork-join programs. In: Proceedings International Symposium on Parallel and Distributed Processing (IPDPS), pp. 397–408. IEEE (2017). https://doi.org/10.1109/ipdps.2017.75

9. Klinkenberg, J., Samfass, P., Bader, M., Terboven, C., Müller, M.: CHAMELEON: reactive load balancing for hybrid MPI+openMP task-parallel applications. J. Parallel Distri. Comput. **138** (2019). https://doi.org/10.1016/j.jpdc.2019.12.005

10. Kulkarni, A., Lumsdaine, A.: A comparative study of asynchronous many-tasking runtimes: Cilk, Charm++, ParalleX and AM++. CoRR abs/1904.00518 (2019). http://arxiv.org/abs/1904.00518

11. Min, S.J., Iancu, C., Yelick, K.: Hierarchical work stealing on manycore clusters. In: Proceedings of the International Conference on Partitioned Global Address Space Programming Models (PGAS), ACM (2011)

12. Nieuwpoort, R.V.V., Wrzesińska, G., Jacobs, C.J.H., Bal, H.E.: Satin: a high-level and efficient grid programming model. Trans. Program. Lang. Syst. (TOPLAS) **32**(3), 1–40 (2010). https://doi.org/10.1145/1709093.1709096

13. Olivier, S., et al.: UTS: an unbalanced tree search benchmark. In: Almási, G., Caşcaval, C., Wu, P. (eds.) LCPC 2006. LNCS, vol. 4382, pp. 235–250. Springer, Heidelberg (2007). https://doi.org/10.1007/978-3-540-72521-3_18

14. OpenMP Architecture Review Board: OpenMP application programming interface (version 5.2). openmp.org (2021)

15. Pirkelbauer, P., Wilson, A., Peterson, C., Dechev, D.: Blaze-tasks: a framework for computing parallel reductions over tasks. Trans. Architect. Code Optim. (TACO) **15**(4) (2019). https://doi.org/10.1145/3293448

16. Posner, J.: Plm-apgas. https://github.com/posnerj/PLM-APGAS

17. Posner, J., Fohry, C.: Cooperation vs. coordination for lifeline-based global load balancing in APGAS. In: Proceedings of SIGPLAN Workshop on X10, pp. 13–17. ACM (2016). https://doi.org/10.1145/2931028.2931029

18. Posner, J., Fohry, C.: Hybrid work stealing of locality-flexible and cancelable tasks for the APGAS library. J. Supercomput. **74**(4), 1435–1448 (2018). https://doi.org/10.1007/s11227-018-2234-8

19. Posner, J., Reitz, L., Fohry, C.: Task-level resilience: checkpointing vs. supervision. Int. J. Netw. Comput. (IJNC) **12**(1), 47–72 (2022). https://doi.org/10.15803/ijnc.12.1_47

20. Ravichandran, K., Lee, S., Pande, S.: Work stealing for multi-core HPC clusters. In: Jeannot, E., Namyst, R., Roman, J. (eds.) Euro-Par 2011. LNCS, vol. 6852, pp. 205–217. Springer, Heidelberg (2011). https://doi.org/10.1007/978-3-642-23400-2_20

21. Reitz, L.: Load balancing policies for nested fork-join. In: Proceedings of International Conference on Cluster Computing (CLUSTER), Extended Abstract, pp. 817–818. IEEE (2021). https://doi.org/10.1109/Cluster48925.2021.00075

22. Saraswat, V.A., Kambadur, P., Kodali, S., Grove, D., Krishnamoorthy, S.: Lifeline-based global load balancing. In: Proceedings of SIGPLAN Symposium on Principles and Practice of Parallel Programming (PPoPP), pp. 201–212. ACM (2011). https://doi.org/10.1145/1941553.1941582

23. Tardieu, O.: The APGAS library: resilient parallel and distributed programming in java 8. In: Proceedings of SIGPLAN Workshop on X10, pp. 25–26. ACM (2015). https://doi.org/10.1145/2771774.2771780
24. Thoman, P., et al.: A taxonomy of task-based parallel programming technologies for high-performance computing. J. Supercomput. **74**(4), 1422–1434 (2018). https://doi.org/10.1007/s11227-018-2238-4
25. TOP500.org: Goethe-hlr. https://www.top500.org/system/179588
26. Yamashita, K., Kamada, T.: Introducing a multithread and multistage mechanism for the global load balancing library of X10. J. Inf. Process. **24**(2), 416–424 (2016). https://doi.org/10.2197/ipsjjip.24.416
27. Zhang, W., et al.: GLB: lifeline-based global load balancing library in X10. In: Proceedings of Workshop on Parallel Programming for Analytics Applications (PPAA), pp. 31–40. ACM (2014). https://doi.org/10.1145/2567634.2567639

New Insights on the Revised Definition of the Performance Portability Metric

Ami Marowka$^{(\boxtimes)}$ (iD)

Parallel Research Lab, TelAviv-Yafo, Israel
amimar2@yahoo.com

Abstract. The rise in the demand for new performance portability frameworks for heterogeneous computing systems has brought with it a number of proposals of workable metrics for evaluating the performance portability of applications.

This article compares the revised definition and criteria of the Ψ metric and the $\bar{\Psi}$ metric that was derived from it and improves it. The comparison is based on a detailed analysis of nine properties and recent studies of the performance portability of various applications.

Keywords: Performance Portability · Performance Efficiency · Metrics

1 Introduction

Heterogeneous computing is ubiquitous, from supercomputers to core processors in every smartphone. The paradigm shift to heterogeneous computing has brought back to the mainstream of scientific computing R&D the problem of *performance portability.*

One of the major unresolved issues of the performance portability problem is the lack of a definition and a workable metric that the research community will accept as a de facto standard [1]. In 2016, three researchers from Intel, Pennycook, Sewall, and Lee proposed an innovative metric to assess the performance portability of an application among a set of architectures [2,3]. The innovation of the proposed metric stemmed from the clear methodology adopted by the researchers. They defined the criteria that the definition and the metric of performance portability should satisfy and then turned to formulating the metric, which they denoted by the symbol Ψ. The uniqueness of the Ψ metric is that it is based on the performance efficiencies that a given application achieves on top of a given set of architectures.

Since the Ψ metric was proposed, many in the HPC community have studied it and used it in their research. As often happens with innovative ideas, over time, the limitations and shortcomings of the new Ψ metric were discovered [4–10]. Some critics argue that there are significant flaws in its definition, that is difficult to understand the theory behind it, and that it is inconvenient to use. Others have argued that the metric is not intuitive and that its results are

© The Author(s), under exclusive license to Springer Nature Switzerland AG 2023
R. Wyrzykowski et al. (Eds.): PPAM 2022, LNCS 13827, pp. 27–38, 2023.
https://doi.org/10.1007/978-3-031-30445-3_3

not reasonable. Along with the criticism hurled against the metric, various ways were proposed to overcome its stumbling blocks, such as rephrasing it to fit the criteria and proposing alternative metrics. Needless to say, all the criticisms and proposed solutions have one goal, to achieve a better performance portability metric.

Recently, the designers of the Ψ metric responded to the criticism in a detailed article [11]. In an extensive part of the article the authors presented a mathematical analysis of the key principles that guided them in developing the Ψ metric. In the rest of the article, they clarified how, in their opinion, the products of the metric should be interpreted and how to use it correctly and updated the criteria to something that they believe a good performance portability metric should satisfy.

Now that the basic principles that guided the designers of the Ψ metric have been well clarified, the limitations of the metric can be discussed in a better and more informed way. For example, in their early article [2,3] the designers of the Ψ metric referred the readers to Smith's article [12] on which they relied but without elaborating. On the other hand, the article provided a clearer impression of the authors' reliance on Smith's article as their source of inspiration. Therefore, the Ψ metric can now be examined in the light of Smith's article.

This article compares and analyzes in detail the differences between the Ψ metric and the proposed $\overline{\Psi}$ metric [4,5]. The $\overline{\Psi}$ metric was designed to solve the problems and shortcomings that have arisen with regard to the Ψ metric in many studies that used it during the five years since it was first published.

To that end, this article makes the following contributions:

- Examining whether the Ψ and $\overline{\Psi}$ metrics meet the requirements of consistency, linearity and lossless information.
- Presenting the core of Smith's article and examining its relevance to the Ψ metric.
- Showing the weighting relationship that exists between the harmonic mean and the arithmetic mean and proving it mathematically.

2   Definition of the Ψ and $\overline{\Psi}$ Metrics

This section presents the original and revised criteria and definition of the Ψ metric and explains the reasons that motivate a rephrasing of the Ψ metric denoted $\overline{\Psi}$. The criteria and definition of the $\overline{\Psi}$ metric as proposed and presented in [5] are then presented.

The **original** set of criteria for the Ψ metric defines it to be:

1. measured specific to a set of platforms of interest H
2. independent of the absolute performance across H
3. zero if a platform in H is unsupported, and approach zero as the performance of platforms in H approach zero
4. increased if performance increases on any platform in H
5. directly proportional to the sum of scores across H

After it was proved that the $\mathcal{P}$ metric is not directly proportional to the sum of scores across H, Pennycook and Sewall [11] admitted that they made a mistake but chose to exclude only criterion (5) from the definition and to leave the rest of the $\mathcal{P}$ metric definition intact.

The $\mathcal{P}$ metric is defined as the harmonic mean of an application's performance efficiency observed across a set of platforms. If the application fails on any measured platform(s), it defines the performance portability to be 0. Formally, for a given set of platforms H, the performance portability $\mathcal{P}$ of an application a solving problem p is:

$$\mathcal{P}(a, p, H) = \begin{cases} \frac{|H|}{\sum_{i \in H} \frac{1}{e_i(a,p)}} & \text{if } i \text{ is supported } \forall i \in H \\ 0 & \text{otherwise} \end{cases} \tag{1}$$

where $e_i(a, p)$ is the performance efficiency of application a solving problem p on platform i.

The following discussion addresses the three main aspects that appear in the original criteria and the definition of the $\mathcal{P}$ metric and that motivated us to propose the revised metric, $\overline{\mathcal{P}}$:

First, it has been proved that the harmonic mean does not satisfy criterion (5), or in other words, that the $\mathcal{P}$ metric is not directly proportional to the sum of scores across the given set of platforms H. As a result, it is argued that the $\mathcal{P}$ metric is inconsistent and cannot be considered comparable, as we have shown in [5]; Sect. 3 further elaborates on this matter. Therefore, we proposed to replace the harmonic mean by the arithmetic mean because the arithmetic mean is directly proportional to the sum of scores across the set of platforms H, as was proved in [5]. Pennycook and Sewall admitted that they had made a mistake but chose to exclude only criterion (5) from the definition and to leave the rest of the $\mathcal{P}$ metric definition intact. We admit that we do not understand the rationale of this act [11].

Second, we claim that criterion (3) is a constraint imposed on the designers of the $\mathcal{P}$ metric because the harmonic mean is not applicable when one of its components is zero. Reference [5] shows a sample of observations from previous studies on performance portability that demonstrate the practical implications of this constraint for performance portability scores.

For example, it does not make sense to determine that an application's performance portability on H is 0% just because there is, at present, no implementation of the application for one or more platforms in H. Therefore, we have suggested that such cases be defined as *not applicable*, thus avoiding unrealistic and biased results. It is important to emphasize that the arithmetic mean, unlike the harmonic mean, does not suffer from this limitation, i.e., the arithmetic mean is applicable when one of its components is zero.

Although the $\overline{\mathcal{P}}$ metric can include platforms that are not supported by the application, the decision was made here not to include them in the calculations so as not to distort the resulting score. Notwithstanding, and after some thought, we accept the recommendation of Pennycook and Sewall not to include a non-numerical value in the metric definition and therefore the decision was made to refine the definition of the $\overline{\Phi}$ metric to contain only platforms that are supported by the application.

Third, the emergence of heterogeneous computing has rekindled research into performance portability. For this arises the desire to evaluate the performance portability of an application in the heterogeneous environment of platforms like CPUs and GPUs.

The performance portability studies of recent years explicitly show that the performance efficiencies of CPUs are significantly lower, on average, than the performance efficiencies of GPUs. For example, Pennycook, Sewall, and Lee studied the performance portability of GPU-STREAM 2.0 [3] and reported that the performance efficiency of GPUs could be twice that of CPUs. They explicitly stated that "The Φ measurements across CPUs are notably lower than the equivalent measurements across GPUs, and this is reflected in the measurements across the union of both subsets."

Therefore, the $\overline{\Phi}$ metric was redefined to consider only platforms from the *same architecture class*. In the authors' opinion, the performance portability of each class should be calculated individually. In addition, it is highly desirable to present the overall calculation for a heterogeneous system.

The next step is to present the criteria and definition of the $\overline{\Phi}$ metric. Given a set of supported platforms $S \subseteq H$, the set of criteria of the $\overline{\Phi}$ metric defines it to be:

1. measured specific to a set of platforms of interest S
2. independent of the absolute performance across S
3. zero if none of the platforms is supported
4. increasing or decreasing if performance increases or decreases on any platform in S
5. directly proportional to the sum of scores across S

The $\overline{\Phi}$ metric is defined as the arithmetic mean of an application's performance efficiency observed across a set of platforms from the same architecture class. Formally, for a given supported set of platforms $S \subseteq H$ from the same architecture class, the performance portability of a case-study application a solving problem p is:

$$\overline{\Phi}(a, p, S, H) = \begin{cases} \frac{\sum_{i \in S} e_i(a,p)}{|S|} & \text{if } |S| > 0 \\ 0 & \text{otherwise} \end{cases} \tag{2}$$

where $S := \{i \in H | e_i(a,p) > 0\}$ and $e_i(a,p)$ is the performance efficiency of case-study application a solving problem p on platform i.

3   Proportionality

One of the desirable properties of a good single-number performance portability metric, based on summarizing a set of observations, is *direct proportionality*. In

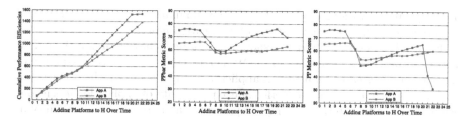

Fig. 1. Comparison of the Performance Portability of two applications according to the Φ (right) and $\overline{\Phi}$ (center) metrics over time. (Left) The cumulative performance efficiencies of the two applications over time.

other words, its score should be directly proportional to the sum of the scores of the observations it represents. Consequently, if the sum of the observation scores change by a certain ratio then the score of the metric should change by the same ratio. This property makes the metric naturally attractive to users.

We believe that this motivated the designers of the Φ metric to include this property in the criteria of the Φ metric definition [3]. Once it had been proved that the Φ metric, which is based on the harmonic mean, does not satisfy this criterion [5] , Pennycook and Sewall admitted that it was a mistake to include it in the definition and decided to exclude it henceforth, but without providing further explanation [11]. In authors' opinion, this approach is wrong. Following is an explanation and a demonstration that support this belief.

First of all, it is important to emphasize that removing the direct proportionality criterion from the definition of the Φ metric in itself does not solve anything because, even after the criterion is removed, the Φ metric remains not directly proportional to the sum of scores of the observations it represents.

Let us clarify that our proposal to reformulate the Φ metric, which is based on the harmonic mean, to the $\overline{\Phi}$ metric, which is based on the arithmetic mean, stemmed primarily from the desire not to remove the direct proportionality criterion because we believe that it is essential to the definition of the metric. Recall that we have proven that the $\overline{\Phi}$ metric is directly proportional [5].

The Φ and $\overline{\Phi}$ metrics are single number-metrics and are therefore lossy metrics by definition. Therefore, it is essential to avoid losing additional information unnecessarily. Removing the direct proportionality criterion from the Φ metric definition means losing additional vital information. In fact, the relationship between the Φ metric and the observations it represents has become looser. Moreover, the Φ metric without this criterion cannot be considered comparable and its consistency is significantly impaired. In [5] we presented a simple example of this claim. We will present it in a more graphic and tangible way.

Figure 1 shows a comparison of the performance portability of two applications based on the Φ and $\overline{\Phi}$ metrics as platforms are added to the set of platforms H over time. The Excel file that generated the graphs in Fig. 1 can be downloaded from [18]. Figure 1(left) shows how the cumulative scores of two applications change over time. The scores shown were taken from real applications reported in various studies [15–17]. The cumulative scores of application a are larger than the cumulative scores of application b over time.

Figures 1(center) and 1(right) show the scoring behavior of the $\overline{\Psi}$ and Ψ metrics respectively. According to the $\overline{\Psi}$ metric, the performance portability of application a is greater than that of application b over time. On the other hand, according to the Ψ metric, the performance portability of application a is inconsistent and is alternately changing compared to the performance portability of application b over time. Sometimes its performance portability is greater than the performance portability of application b, and sometimes the opposite is true. The fact that the cumulative score of application a is always greater than that of application b does not affect the zigzag behavior of the Ψ metric. The direct proportionality property of the $\overline{\Psi}$ metric makes it possible to predict that as long as the cumulative score of application a is greater than that of application b, it is guaranteed that the performance portability of application a will be greater than the performance portability of application b. The induced inconsistency of the Ψ metric makes it difficult to compare and predict the performance portability of different applications over time. It does not reflect the real performance portability relationship of the two applications over time and poorly represents their cumulative performance efficiency behavior over time.

4   Smith's Article

The main source of inspiration for the development of the criteria and definition of the Ψ metric was Smith's article [12]. Hence, it was expected that Pennycook and Sewall would discuss Smith's article at length in their articles [3,11]. In practice, they only referred the readers to Smith's article and noted that, "The harmonic mean has been previously demonstrated by researchers as a superior way to aggregate multiple performance numbers and, unlike the geometric and arithmetic means, satisfies criteria (5) and (5)". This section presents what Smith's article is about, examines the relevance of Smith's article to the criteria and definition of the Ψ metric, and presents the reference of Hennessy and Patterson to Smith's article [13].

Smith studied the ways of reducing benchmark performance results to a single number that maintains the accuracy of the original benchmark. For this purpose, Smith used a hypothetical example of a benchmark that includes two programs running on three computers. The first rows of Table 1 shows the running times of each program on each computer and the total times measured on each computer. From the total time it can be deduced that computer 3 is almost three times as fast as computer 2 and that computer 2 is nine times faster than computer 1.

Next, Smith chose to express the performance in rates (mflop/s). To that end, he assumed that each program operates at 100 mflop. The calculated results are presented in the last rows of Table 1, including the arithmetic, harmonic, and geometric means of the rates for each computer. From these results Smith concluded that only the harmonic mean preserves the relative performance between the computers as calculated in Table 1 - in other words, that computer 3 is three times faster than computer 2 and that computer 2 is nine times faster than computer 1.

Based on these findings Smith formulated two properties:

Property 1. A single-number performance measure for a set of benchmarks expressed in units of time **should be directly proportional** to the total (weighted) time consumed by the benchmarks.

Property 2. A single-number performance measure for benchmarks expressed as a rate **should be inversely proportional** to the total (weighted) time consumed by the benchmarks.

The above discussion constitutes the core of Smith's article.

Now, the reader's attention is directed to three observations related to the properties that Smith formulated and the criteria and definition of the Ψ metric:

1. Smith proved nothing. He used only one hypothetical example and deduced from it two properties that would have been desirable to include in practical and realistic benchmarks.
2. Smith was looking at how to summarize rates (mflop/s). In contrast, the Ψ metric deals with summarizing performance efficiencies that are fractions (or ratios) and are unitless.
3. Smith emphasized in both properties that the single-number performance measure must be directly or inversely proportional to the total time. In other words, Smith required the existence of a criterion (5) that Pennycook and Sewall chose to exclude from the criteria of the Ψ metric.

Due to lack of space, we do not present Hennessy and Patterson's criticism to Smith's paper.

Table 1. Reprint from Smith's Article [12]

Benchmark	mflop	Computer 1	Computer 2	Computer 3
Program 1 (seconds)	100	1	10	20
Program 2 (seconds)	100	1000	100	20
Total Time (seconds)		**1001**	**110**	**40**
Program 1 (mflop/s)		100.0	10.0	5.0
Program 2 (mflop/s)		.1	1.0	5.0
Arithmetic Mean (mflop/s)		50.1	5.5	5.0
Geometric Mean (mflop/s)		3.2	3.2	5.0
Harmonic Mean (mflop/s)		**.2**	**1.8**	**5.0**

5 The Principles

In their responding article [11], Pennycook and Sewall presented the underlying principles from which they derived the criteria and definition of the Ψ metric. Throughout the mathematical development of their ideas, they discovered a weighting relationship between the Ψ and $\overline{\Psi}$ metrics. In other words, they discovered a weighting relationship between the arithmetic and harmonic means.

They showed that the achieved aggregate throughput as normalized against the peak aggregate throughput of a set of platforms is equal to the harmonic mean of the performance efficiencies when work is weighted accordingly to the peak throughput of each platform, and is equal to the arithmetic mean of the performance efficiencies when work is weighted accordingly to the achieved throughput of each platform.

These principles are mathematically correct but are not backed by a clear model as we showed in Sect. 4. Moreover, these principles are only correct for the *architectural efficiency* approach based on throughputs. They are not correct for the popular *application efficiency* approach based on runtimes [2,8,16,17]. We will demonstrate this by an example. After the discussion, an explanation is given of why, after all, use of the $\overline{\Psi}$ metric is preferable.

First, it should come as no surprise that there is a weighting relationship between the arithmetic and harmonic means. After all, *the harmonic mean is the reciprocal of the arithmetic mean of the reciprocals.*

Let $E = (a_1/p_1, a_2/p_2, ..., a_n/p_n)$ be a set of performance efficiencies based on application efficiency of runtimes; $A = (a_1 + ... + a_n)$ the sum of the total achieved runtimes; $P = (p_1 + ... + p_n)$ the sum of the total peak runtimes; $WA = (a_1/A, ..., a_n/A)$ the set of the weights of the achieved runtimes and $WP = (p_1/P, ..., p_n/P)$ the set of the weights of the peak runtimes.

The next step is to prove that the weighted arithmetic mean (WAM) of a set E of performance efficiencies, weighted by peak runtime, is equivalent to the weighted harmonic mean (WHM) of the set E, weighted with achieved runtime:

$$\text{WAM(E, WP)} = \text{WHM (E, WA)} \tag{3}$$

The proof:

$$\text{WAM(E, WP)} = wp_1 \cdot \frac{a_1}{p_1} + ... + wp_n \cdot \frac{a_n}{p_n} = \frac{p_1}{P} \cdot \frac{a_1}{p_1} + ... + \frac{p_n}{P} \cdot \frac{a_n}{p_n}$$

$$= \frac{a_1 + ... + a_n}{P} = \frac{A}{P} = \frac{1}{\frac{p_1}{A} + ... + \frac{p_n}{A}}$$

$$= \frac{1}{\frac{a_1}{a_1} \cdot \frac{p_1}{A} + ... + \frac{a_n}{a_n} \cdot \frac{p_n}{A}} = \frac{1}{\frac{a_1}{A} \div \frac{a_1}{p_1} + ... + \frac{a_n}{A} \div \frac{a_n}{p_n}}$$

$$= \frac{1}{\frac{wa_1}{E_1} + ... + \frac{wa_n}{E_n}} = \text{WHM(E, WA)}$$

Let us demonstrate this relation by an example. Let E be the following performance efficiency set based on achieved and peak runtimes:

$$(20/50, 80/100, 200/300, 40/200, 80/200)$$

Therefore, the total achieved runtime A is:

$$(20 + 80 + 200 + 40 + 80) = 420$$

The total peak runtime P is:

$$(50 + 100 + 300 + 200 + 200) = 850$$

Thus, the overall performance efficiency is: $420/850 = \mathbf{0.49411}$.

The weights of the achieved runtimes WA are:

$$(20/420, 80/420, 200/420, 40/420, 80/420)$$

The weights of the peak runtimes WP are:

$$(50/850, 100/850, 300/850, 200/850, 200/850)$$

Now, WAM and WHM can be calculated:

$$
\begin{aligned}
\text{WAM(E,WP)} &= 20/50 * 50/850 + 80/100 * 100/850 \\
&\quad + 200/300 * 300/850 + 40/200 * 200/850 \\
&\quad + 80/200 * 200/850 \\
&= 42/85 = \mathbf{0.49411}
\end{aligned}
\tag{4}
$$

$$
\begin{aligned}
\text{WHM(E,WA)} &= 1/((20/420)/(20/50) + (80/420)/(80/100) \\
&\quad + (200/420)/(200/300) + (40/420)/(40/200) \\
&\quad + (80/420)/(80/200)) \\
&= 42/85 = \mathbf{0.49411}
\end{aligned}
\tag{5}
$$

From (4) and (5), it is evident that the same result is obtained whether the weighted harmonic mean or the weighted arithmetic mean used. Therefore, either the weighted arithmetic mean or the weighted harmonic mean can be used to find the average of a given set of performance efficiencies if appropriate weights can be properly applied. However, we prefer to use the unweighted arithmetic mean because *neither the weighted arithmetic mean nor the weighted harmonic mean is directly proportional to the sum of the scores of its observations*. The next step is to calculate the scores of the unweighted arithmetic and harmonic means while using the performance efficiencies of the current example:

$$
\begin{aligned}
&\text{AM}(20/50, 80/100, 200/300, 40/200, 80/200) \\
&= 37/75 = \mathbf{0.49333}
\end{aligned}
$$

$$
\begin{aligned}
&\text{HM}(20/50, 80/100, 200/300, 40/200, 80/200) \\
&= 20/51 = 0.39215
\end{aligned}
$$

Without a doubt, the unweighted arithmetic mean obtained a similar result of 0.49333, which is a negligible difference compared to the result obtained by the WAM and the WHM and far better than the unweighted harmonic mean score. It is worth noting that the relationship between the harmonic mean and arithmetic mean, known as HM-AM inequality, states that HM $\leq$ AM.

Table 2. Reprint From [11] and [8], $\mathcal{P}$ vs. $\bar{\mathcal{P}}$.

	$\mathcal{P}$ vs. $\bar{\mathcal{P}}$ (Per Problem)										P_D	$\mathcal{P}$	$\bar{\mathcal{P}}$
	1		2		3		4		5				
	$\mathcal{P}$	$\bar{\mathcal{P}}$	$\mathcal{P}$	$\bar{\mathcal{P}}$	$\mathcal{P}$	$\bar{\mathcal{P}}$	$\mathcal{P}$	$\bar{\mathcal{P}}$	$\mathcal{P}$	$\bar{\mathcal{P}}$			
ep	0.90	0.91	0.84	0.85	0.85	0.86	0.82	0.83	0.83	0.83	19.02	0.85	0.86
cg	0.72	0.80	0.76	0.80	0.91	0.92	0.97	0.97	1.00	1.00	23.70	0.86	0.89
sp	1.00	1.00	1.00	1.00	1.00	1.00	1.00	1.00	0.00	0.00	0	**0.00**	1.00
bt	0.98	0.98	0.91	0.93	1.00	1.00	0.00	0.00	0.00	0.00	5.78	**0.00**	0.97
stencil	0.62	0.78	0.85	0.90	0.94	0.95	1.00	1.00	1.00	1.00	28.69	0.85	0.93
lbm	0.87	0.88	0.99	0.99	0.00	0.00	0.00	0.00	0.00	0.00	11.02	**0.00**	0.94
mri-q	0.95	0.96	1.00	0.99	0.00	0.00	0.00	0.00	0.00	0.00	3.73	**0.00**	0.98

6 Lossy Metrics

Single-number metrics, such as the $\mathcal{P}$ and $\bar{\mathcal{P}}$ metrics, cannot accurately characterize performance portability. On the other hand, practitioners find them attractive, simple to use and intuitive. This section shows, using an example, that the $\mathcal{P}$ metric by definition loses more information than the $\bar{\mathcal{P}}$ metric.

Pennycook and Sewall refer in their article to the work of Daniel and Panetta [8], in which they presented their P_D metric. The P_D metric calculates the variability average of the performance efficiencies of a number of input sizes of a given application on top of a given set of architectures. Pennycook and Sewall claimed that Daniel and Panetta compared the scores of the $\mathcal{P}$ metric with the scores of the P_D metric, but did so separately for each problem size. They argued that the $\mathcal{P}$ metric summarizes the individual $\mathcal{P}$ scores for different problem sizes because calculating the harmonic mean of several harmonic means is equivalent to calculating a harmonic mean using all the data.

Table 2 was taken from the article of Pennycook and Sewall that contained data collected from the article of Daniel and Panetta. It shows the scores of each problem size separately and the total scores. In this study, the scores of the $\bar{\mathcal{P}}$ metric have been added to the original table for comparison. Out of seven total scores, according to the $\mathcal{P}$ metric, four are zero. In contrast, the $\bar{\mathcal{P}}$ metric does not lose any information. How do the Pennycook and Sewall explain this? They claim that "This should not be surprising: both averaging over average values and extending an average to more dimensions of a data set should be expected to **destroy** more information". Does information destruction always occur in such cases? Clearly not, as the $\bar{\mathcal{P}}$ metric shows. Data destruction is inherent to the criteria and definition of the $\mathcal{P}$ metric.

7 Properties of a Good Metric

Throughout the article the $\mathcal{P}$ and $\bar{\mathcal{P}}$ metrics have been compared according the Pennycook and Sewall's articles, our articles and dozens of other studies published in the literature in the last five years.

Table 3. Properties of A Good Performance Portability Metric

	Measurable	Objective	Comparable	Linearity	Consistency	Intuitiveness	Ease-of-use	Lossless	Familiar
	Properties of Good Performance Portability Metric								
$\overline{\Phi}$	Yes	Yes	Yes	Yes	Yes	Yes	Yes	Yes	Yes
Φ	Yes	Yes	Partly	No	No	No	Partly	No	No

Now, it is time for a summary. This paper has presented to the reader the criteria and definition of each metric and the revised versions. The key aspects that motivated us to offer a revised metric have been presented, as well as studies that encountered problems using the Φ metric. The discussions have shown that a measure that is inconsistent is not comparable over time and how important it is that a single-number metric be directly proportional. The core of Smith's article and its relevance to the Φ metric have also been presented, and the weighting relationship between the harmonic and arithmetic means has been demonstrated. It has been explained that single-number metrics lose information by definition and how important it is not to lose additional information. Examples have been given illustrating that the Φ metric loses additional information by definition, whereas the $\overline{\Phi}$ metric preserves information. Beyond all these criteria, a good metric should be objective, easy to use, intuitive, and familiar to users. Table 3 summarizes the comparison using all the properties that make a metric a good one.

8   Conclusions

The top 500 list of the most powerful supercomputers in the world is considered a success story. Despite its criticisms and shortcomings, the HPC community has accepted it as the de facto ranking system for supercomputers in the last three decades. Why? Because it is based on a simple metric that is easy to measure and intuitive.

This paper has shown that the $\overline{\Phi}$ metric is not only intuitive, simple, easy to use and familiar, but also consistent and does not lose information. The authors call upon the HPC community to use the metric, criticize it if necessary, and suggest ways to improve it or to propose a better metric.

References

1. DOE Centers of Excellence Performance Portability Meeting, Glendale, AZ, Post-meeting Report, 19-21 April 2016
2. Pennycook, S.J., Sewall, J.D., Lee, V.W.: A metric for performance portability, arXiv preprint arXiv:1611.07409 (2016)
3. Pennycook, S.J., Sewall, J.D., Lee, V.W.: Implications of a metric for performance portability, Future Generation Computer Systems, Aug 2017. https://doi.org/10.1016/j.future.2017.08.007

4. Marowka, A.: Toward a better performance portability metric. In: Proceeding of 29th Euromicro International Conference on Parallel, Distributed and Network-based Processing (PDP 2021), Valladolid, Spain, 10–12 March 2021
5. Marowka, A.: Reformulation of the performance portability metric. Softw. Pract. Experience **52**(1), 154–171 (2022)
6. Dreuning, H., Heirman, R., Varbanescu, A.L.: A beginner's guide to estimating and improving performance portability. In: Yokota, R., Weiland, M., Shalf, J., Alam, S. (eds.) ISC High Performance 2018. LNCS, vol. 11203, pp. 724–742. Springer, Cham (2018). https://doi.org/10.1007/978-3-030-02465-9_52
7. Siklosi, B., Reguly, I.Z., Mudalige, G.R.: Heterogeneous CPU GPU execution of stencil applications. In: 2018 IEEE/ACM International Workshop on Performance, Portability and Productivity in HPC (P3HPC), pp. 71–80 (2018)
8. Daniel, D.F., Panetta, J.: On applying performance portability metrics. In: 2019 IEEE/ACM International Workshop on Performance, Portability and Productivity in HPC (P3HPC), pp. 50–59 (2019)
9. Sedova, A., Eblen, J.D., Budiardja, R., Tharrington, A., Smith, J.C.: High-performance molecular dynamics simulation for biological and materials sciences: challenges of performance portability. In: 2018 IEEE/ACM International Workshop on Performance, Portability and Productivity in HPC (P3HPC), pp. 1–13 (2018)
10. Bertoni, C., Kwack, J., Applencourt, T., Ghadar, Y., Homerding, B., Knight, C., Videau, B., Zheng, H., Morozov, V., Parker, S.: Performance portability evaluation of Opencl benchmarks across intel and Nvidia platforms. In: IEEE International Parallel and Distributed Processing Symposium Workshops (IPDPSW), vol. 2020, pp. 330–339 (2020)
11. Pennycook, S.J., Sewall, J.D.: Revisiting a metric for performance portability. In: 2021 International Workshop on Performance, Portability and Productivity in HPC (P3HPC), pp. 1–9 (2021)
12. Smith, J.E.: Characterizing computer performance with a single number. Commun. ACM **31**(10), 1202–1206 (1988). https://doi.org/10.1145/63039.63043
13. Hennessy, J.L., Patterson, D.A.: Computer Architecture; A Quantitative Approach. Morgan Kaufmann Publishers Inc., Burlington (1990)
14. Williams, S., Waterman, A., Patterson, D.: Roofline: an insightful visual performance model for multicore architectures. Commun ACM. **52**(4), 65–76 (2009)
15. Deakin, T., Price, J., Martineau, M., McIntosh-Smith, S.: GPU-STREAM v2.0: benchmarking the achievable memory bandwidth of many-core processors across diverse parallel programming models. In: Taufer, M., Mohr, B., Kunkel, J.M. (eds.) ISC High Performance 2016. LNCS, vol. 9945, pp. 489–507. Springer, Cham (2016). https://doi.org/10.1007/978-3-319-46079-6_34
16. Deakin, T., et al.: Performance portability across diverse computer architectures. In: 2019 IEEE/ACM International Workshop on Performance, Portability and Productivity in HPC (P3HPC), Denver, CO, USA, pp. 1–13 (2019)
17. Deakin, T.J., Poenaru, A., Lin, T., Mcintosh-Smith, S.N.: Tracking performance portability on the yellow brick road to exascale. In: Proceedings of the Performance Portability and Productivity Workshop P3HPC: Supercomputing 2020 Institute of Electrical and Electronics Engineers (IEEE) (2020). (Accepted/In press)
18. Zigzag graph. https://www.dropbox.com/scl/fi/xfsvlf7pbbrx3f6isrybq/zigzag-graph.xlsx?dl=0&rlkey=u9vah2sjduvr3ckb9o8wt2et4

Inferential Statistical Analysis
of Performance Portability

Ami Marowka⁽⊠⁾ 🆔

Parallel Research Lab, Haifa, Israel
amimar2@yahoo.com

Abstract. The assessment of the performance portability of hybrid programming models is based on many unverifiable observations. Drawing from the assessment by knowledgeable analysts, subjective conclusions from unverifiable data are incomplete without descriptive and inferential statistical analysis.

In this article, a knowledgeable analyst's assessment of the performance portability of OpenACC, OpenMP, Kokkos and Raja, on CPU and GPU architectures is confronted with inferential statistical analysis of two types of hypothesis tests while carefully examining the effect of outliers.

Keywords: Performance Portability · Performance Efficiency · Metrics

1 Introduction

One of the challenging problems of contemporary high-performance programming is to allow advanced scientific applications to be performance portable. To enable porting high-performance applications between diverse and heterogeneous computing architectures while sustaining their performance efficiency and without the need to rewrite the code.

New performance portability frameworks such as Kokkos [1] and Raja [2] alongside mature hybrid programming models such as OpenMP [3] and OpenACC [4] are the leading software development tools available to the high-performance community today for the development of performance portable scientific applications.

Recently, a formal definition and associated metric have been proposed to quantitatively assess the degree of the performance portability of these performance portability frameworks [7]. Dozens of case studies of various applications, mini-applications, kernels, and scientific benchmarks of different characteristics are required to assess the performance portability of such development environments. In addition, these case studies should be examined on many types of platform architectures and backend compilers. This task cannot be accomplished by one research group. Therefore, the only way to complete such complex research is to use the professional scientific literature and collect publications of studies that reported on performance portability experiments.

The present innovative metrics for evaluating performance portability are based on calculating the performance efficiencies average of the case studies chosen in the research [5–7]. The score obtained from this calculation is the performance portability of the application or the performance portability framework under assessment. The following question arises: how can one determine and classify the range of score values that provide acceptable performance portability and those that do not?

Moreover, when it comes to a research experiment based on hundreds of case studies, it is expected that some of the observations obtained will present extreme values, outliers, that are not typical of the vast majority of the data collected in the experiment. These observations require re-examination to ascertain whether the results can be reproduced or whether they are measurement errors and accordingly decide whether to remove these observations from the experiment. Here, a second question arises: how should one proceed if the observations are based on studies that have been published in the scientific literature? In such cases, it is impossible to ascertain whether the results originate from measurement errors or not. The scientific publications do not contain the information needed to reproduce the experiment in most cases. Even when this information exists, setting up the same testbed is almost unattainable.

It turns out that there are no objective criteria to determine whether an application or performance portability framework has sufficient performance portability or not. Such assessment is subjective and is determined in practice by an analyst with the subject-area knowledge needed to establish a sound and plausible assessment that determines how to handle outliers. However, a knowledgeable analyst's assessment may not be sufficient. It needs to be confronted with the help of objective statistical analysis that will examine the assessment with and without outliers [21]. Such statistical analysis can discover additional insights that may strengthen the assessment or allow the analysts to consider refining their initial assessment in accordance with the statistical findings. Identifying outliers cannot be done using statistical rules because it depends on subject area knowledge and how observations are collected. However, there are techniques, plots, and statistical tests that can help to identify potential outliers [15–18].

In this article, we confront an analyst's assessment of a recently published paper with a statistical analysis of the case study results provided in the research [7]. The research studied the performance portability of OpenACC, OpenMP, Kokkos, and Raja using various applications, mini-applications, and kernels that were tested on different CPU and GPU architectures. Specifically, this article makes the following contributions.

- First, we present a detailed descriptive statistical analysis of OpenACC observations, including Shapiro-Wilk normality tests and Q-Q plots.
- We confront the analyst's performance portability assessment of OpenACC against two nonparametric hypothesis tests, while carefully examining the effect of outliers.

- We present an inferential statistical analysis of OpenACC using two statistical hypothesis tests: Wilcoxon signed-rank test and the bootstrapping method.
- We apply the above inferential statistical analysis to OpenMP, Kokkos, and Raja and discuss the obtained findings.

For convenience, throughout the article, we will call the group of 141 OpenACC observations that include outliers and the subgroup of 109 observations without outliers groups A and B, respectively.

To perform the descriptive and inferential statistical tests mentioned in this study, we used several statistical tools. Some are proprietary software packages, and others are online statistic calculators available for free: Minitab [8], Stat 101 [9], Statistic Kingdom [10], Real Statistics [11], GraphPad [12], R language [13] and Microsoft Excel [14].

The raw data of the statistical tests presented in this article can be viewed and downloaded at the following link [20].

2   OpenACC Performance Portability

Recently, a new metric for assessing the performance portability of high-level parallel programming models was proposed [7]. In this research, we used the new metric for evaluating the performance portability of OpenACC, OpenMP, Kokkos, and RAJA based on 324 case studies in various application domains, CPU and GPU architectures, and high-performance compilers.

In this section, we present the definition of the proposed metric and the results of the performance portability of OpenACC obtained using this metric. We also explain how we treated the outliers and the assumptions that guided us to determine which observations would be marked as outliers. Later in this article, we use OpenACC's observations collected in this research for our in-depth statistical analysis.

The new metric definition was formulated as follows.

Definition: Performance Portability of a Model
The arithmetic mean of the performance efficiencies, which are the achieved performance values of a given portable model as a fraction of the performance values of a non-portable architecture-specific model, obtained from collections of case studies carried out on platforms of the same class of pairs (application, problem).

Formally, the performance portability metric $\overline{\mathbf{\Phi}}_M$ of a high-level portable parallel programming model M executing a set of case studies T, where each $t \in T$ corresponds to application a solving problem b on platform c is:

$$\overline{\mathbf{\Phi}}_M = \frac{\sum_{i \in T} e_i(a, b, c)}{|T|} \tag{1}$$

where $e_i(a, b, c)$ is the performance efficiency of application a solving problem b on platform c.

The performance efficiency used in this evaluation is the achieved performance of a given portable model M as a fraction of the performance of a non-portable architecture-specific parallel programing model. For example, OpenACC is a portable programming model, whereas CUDA is a non-portable architecture specific programming model. Therefore, assuming that performance values are given in gigaflop/s, the performance efficiency of each case study i in this evaluation is:

$$e_i(a, b, c) = \frac{OpenACC\ Performance}{CUDA\ Performance} \tag{2}$$

Table 1. Performance Portability of OpenACC on GPUs.

Performance Portability												
	Exc. outliers					Inc. outliers					# of outliers		
Model	Case Studies	$\overline{\Phi}_M$	std. dev.	max	min	Case Studies	$\overline{\Phi}_M$	std. dev.	max	min	< 50%	50% - 100%	> 100%
GPU													
OpenACC	109	**81%**	13%	100%	51%	141	**77%**	28%	200%	3%	23	109	9

Table 1 shows the calculated performance portability scores of OpenACC as obtained by the proposed new metric $\overline{\Phi}_M$ on the GPUs, without outliers less than 50% and greater than 100%, alongside the calculated performance portability scores that include outliers. In addition, the table presents statistics such as the minimum and maximum values of the calculated performance efficiencies, the standard deviation, and the number of outliers less than 50%, greater than 100%, and in the range 50%-100%. It can be observed that the total number of case studies used in this evaluation is 141, while 32 of them were marked as outliers (23%). Moreover, the calculated performance portability without outliers is 81% and with outliers is 77%.

The following question arises: what is the rationale behind our decision that observations whose scores are less than 50% and greater than 100% will be classified as outliers? To answer this question, let us use the previous example where OpenACC is the performance portability framework being tested, and CUDA is the reference non-portable programming model. If the performance efficiency of a given case study shows a score greater than 100%, it means that the performance of the implementation developed by OpenACC is better than the implementation developed by CUDA. This is in contrast to what is expected from the implementation that was developed using non-portable and architecture-specific programming models such as CUDA. Therefore, this almost certainly indicates that the optimization of the implementation developed by CUDA requires improvement.

This is what motivated us to classify case studies showing scores greater than 100% as outliers. On the other hand, if a given case study shows a score of less than 50%, it means that the performance of the implementation developed using OpenACC is less than half the performance of the implementation developed using CUDA. In the subjective opinion of the authors, it should be classified as an outlier. Other analysts could determine threshold values less or greater than 50%. In the following sections, we will confront and analyze this decision using statistical tools.

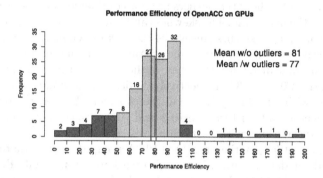

Fig. 1. Histogram of Performance Efficiencies of OpenACC on GPUs. The dark bars represent potential outliers.

Table 2. Statistics Summary of the Case Study Observations.

Groups	Descriptive Statistics									
	Mean	Std. Error	Median	Std. Dev.	Kurtosis	Skewness	Range	Min.	Max.	Count
A	77	2.41	78	28	3.5	0.6	197	3	200	141
B	81	1.25	81	13	-0.9	-0.2	49	51	100	109

3 OpenACC's Observation Statistics

In this section, we present the summary statistics of OpenACC's observations that we are analyzing. Figure 1 shows the histogram of 141 observations representing the performance efficiencies of 141 OpenACC case studies of various applications on different GPU platforms as studied and reported in [7]. Table 2 presents the descriptive statistics of the distribution of observations.

The bars in the histogram that are highlighted in a dark color represent potential outliers marked by the analysts of the study. Recall, these outliers are the performance efficiencies that yield scores greater than 100% and less than 50%. It can also be discerned by examining the histogram, that calculating the mean without outliers yields a score of 81% (for 109 observations) compared to a score of 77% (for 141 observations) including the outliers.

Table 2 shows additional descriptive statistics of groups A and B. The most notable statistic is the standard deviation, which is double in the case where the outliers are considered. This indicates a wider dispersion of observations compared to the case where the outliers are not considered. This is seen visually from looking at the histogram. The skewness and kurtosis characteristics describe the distribution shape. Skewness measures the lack of symmetry, while kurtosis measures whether the distribution is heavy-tailed (has outliers) or light-tailed relative to a normal distribution. When outliers are considered, the skewness and the kurtosis of 0.6 and 3.5, respectively, indicate an asymmetrical and right-positive shape with long heavy tails. On the other hand, when the outliers are removed, skewness and kurtosis are -0.2 and -0.9, respectively, indicating an almost symmetrical shape with short thin tails.

Usually, a quantile-quantile plot (Q-Q Plot) alongside a statistic test of normality is used for determining whether observations are normally distributed. Figure 2 presents the Q-Q plots with and without outliers, respectively, while the Shapiro-Wilk test was chosen as the normality test [19]. The Shapiro-Wilk test rejects the H_0 hypothesis for the two groups, and hence the observations are not normally distributed.

The p-values that were calculated by the Shapiro-Wilk test are 1.297e-7 and 0.00095 for groups A and B, respectively. Since the p-values are less than the significance level (α) of 0.05 it can be concluded that the difference between the distribution of the observations and the normal distribution is big enough to be statistically significant. In the next section we elaborate further about the concept of hypothesis tests, P-values and the significance level (α).

The Shapiro-Wilk test uses the Kolmogorov-Smirnov effect size to measure the deviation from the normal. The observed effect sizes of groups A and B were 0.1552 and 0.09838, respectively, indicating that the magnitude of the difference between the distribution of the observations and the normal distribution is large for group A and small for group B.

Now, let's look at the Q-Q plots shown in Fig. 2. To visually assess whether the points representing the observations follow a normal distribution, we check that the points follow a straight line.

By looking at the Q-Q plot in Fig. 2 (left), it can be observed that the straight distribution fit line covers only some of the points, while the points at the ends move away from the line. These points are suspected to be outliers. On the other hand, it can be observed from the Q-Q plot in Fig. 2 (right) that the straight distribution fit line covers most of the points. These findings are consistent with the results obtained using the Shapiro-Wilk test.

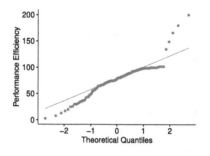 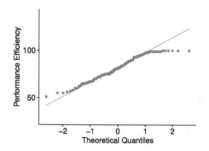

Fig. 2. Q-Q Plots of the 141 tested observations including outliers (left) and 109 tested observations without outliers (right).

Figure 3 shows beeswarm-boxplots. A beeswarm-boxplot, is a graph that is a combination of a beeswarm plot on top of a boxplot. A boxplot, also known as a box and whisker diagram, is a graph that shows how the observations are spread out in a different perspective compared with histograms and Q-Q plots. A boxplot displays the distribution of observations based on a five number summary ("minimum", first quartile (Q1), median, third quartile (Q3), and "maximum"). It also shows potential outliers and their values.

Figure 3 (left) shows the beeswarm-boxplot of the 141 observations including the outliers. The numbers 65 and 94 represent the first and third quartiles, respectively. The line that crosses the box represents the median (78). The box represents the interquartile range (IQR), the range from the 25th to 75th percentile (IQR = Q3-Q1 = 29). The "maximum" and "minimum" values (135 and 25, respectively), also known as Tukey fences, are 1.5 times the interquartile range from the quartiles. The observations below and above the Tukey fences are outliers (3, 8, 13,17, 20, 149, 166, 180, and 200).

Hence, according to the statistical analysis there are nine outliers compared to the thirty-two outliers acknowledged by the analyst. Figure 3 (right) shows the beeswarm-boxplot of 109 observations, of which the analysts determined none were outliers. It can be noted that according to our statistical analysis, none of the observations are below or above the Tukey fences, 51 and 100, respectively, and therefore none of them are outliers.

Beeswarm plots are designed to show the underlying distribution of the observations in a way that avoids overlapping. They provide a better visualization of the distribution of the observations and thus allows new conclusions and insights to be drawn.

For example, statistical analysis of the beeswarm-boxplot in Fig. 3 (left) shows that there are a few extreme outliers above the 100% upper threshold as determined by the analysts. That is, there are a very small number of case studies whose implementations in OpenACC yield a better performance than their implementations in CUDA. This finding is consistent with the analysts' determination that the observations showing performance efficiency scores of greater than 100% are outliers.

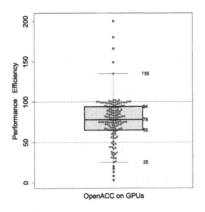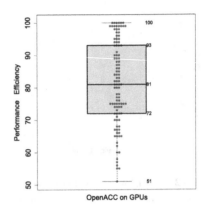

Fig. 3. Beeswarm boxplots of the 141 observations including the outliers (left) and 109 observations without outliers(right).

On the other hand, most outliers marked by the analysts are in the range between the "minimum" Tukey fence (25%) and the lower threshold value set by the analysts (50%). This finding allows analysts to re-examine whether their early determination that set the lower threshold to 50% is appropriate and to consider changing it to a lower threshold value.

4 Hypothesis Testing

Hypothesis testing is a statistical analysis that uses a sample of observations to assess two conflicting hypotheses about the properties of a population: the null hypothesis (H_0) and the alternative hypothesis (H_1). When the null hypothesis is rejected, the results are statistically significant, meaning that there is a difference between the population value and the null hypothesis value.

Statistical hypothesis tests use several parameters to determine whether to reject the null hypothesis and give an estimated range of values that is likely to include an unknown population moment. The parameters used in this article are p-value, significance level, and 95% confidence interval. The significance level (α) is the probability threshold value of rejecting a true null hypothesis. The p-value represents the probability of the observation distribution and to what extent it contradicts the null hypothesis. When the p-value is less than or equal to the significance level, the null hypothesis is rejected. A confidence interval represents a range of values that an estimation is expected to fall within a certain percentage of the time. For example, a 95% confidence interval of [50 60] indicates 95% confidence that the population mean falls within this range.

In this section, we test our case studies using two nonparametric tests (1-sample Wilcoxon and nonparametric bootstrap).

4.1 One-sample Wilcoxon Signed-Rank Test

The one-sample Wilcoxon signed-rank test is a powerful nonparametric test since the ranking of the observations is considered as well as the signs, thus giving more accurate results. The assumptions for the one-sample Wilcoxon test are similar to those of the paired test, but it adds an assumption that the distribution of the observations is symmetric around the median, or at least not very skewed. The Wilcoxon test can be applied on our case studies because the skewness of the distribution of the observations is approximately symmetric (0.58).

The one-sample Wilcoxon signed-rank test has the following hypotheses (two-sided test):

- $H_0 : \eta = \eta_0$
- $H_1 : \eta \neq \eta_0$

where η is the population median and η_0 is the hypothesized value of the median in the population. In our test $\eta_0 = 80$.

We analyze the outcome of the one-sample Wilcoxon signed-rank test we performed for groups A and B.

Wilcoxon signed-rank test - Group A
V = 4290.5, p-value = 0.2835
H_1: true median is not equal to 80
95 percent confidence interval: 73 82
sample estimates: median 78

Wilcoxon signed rank test - Group B
V = 3206.5, p-value = 0.2427
H_1: true median is not equal to 80
95 percent confidence interval: 79 84
sample estimates: median 82

For group A, the null hypothesis states that the median equals 80. As the p-value is approximately 0.28, greater than the significance level of 0.05, we cannot reject the null hypothesis. We do not have enough evidence to conclude that the median is different from 80. The 95% confidence interval estimates that the actual population median is likely to be between 73 and 82. The 95% confidence interval includes the hypothesized value of 80, which is why we can be 95% confident that the population median is between 73 and 82. Therefore, we cannot conclude that the population mean is different from 80.

The one-sample Wilcoxon signed-rank test for group B yields a similar outcome except that the 95% confidence interval is narrower [79 84]. The hypothetical value of 80 falls within this range and indicates that our hypothesis is closer to the population median.

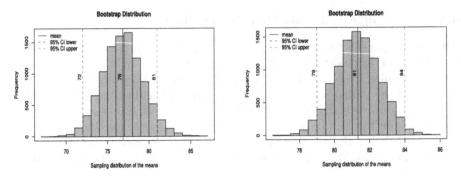

Fig. 4. Bootstrap histograms of Group A (left) and Group B (right).

Table 3. Statistical Analysis of OpenACC, OpenMP, Kokkos and RAJA.

Performance Portability												
			Knowledgeable Analyst (without outliers)					Statistics Analysis (with outliers)				
Model	Case Studies	Num. Outliers	$\bar{\Phi}_M$	Normal Distribution	95% CI	Skewness	Kurtosis	$\bar{\Phi}_M$	Normal Distribution	95% CI	Skewness	Kurtosis
CPU												
OpenACC	8	5	71	Yes	[60..80]	S	Nt	105	Yes	[84..123]	S	Nt
OpenMP	25	4	88	No	[81..93]	As	Lht	97	No	[86..119]	As	Nt
Kokkos	27	12	85	No	[76..90]	As	Lht	92	No	[77..113]	As	Lht
Raja	9	4	82	Yes	[75..92]	S	Nt	109	Yes	[73..162]	S	Nt
GPU												
OpenACC	141	32	81	No	[78..83]	S	Stt	76	No	[72..81]	As	Lht
OpenMP	83	21	83	No	[79..86]	S	Nt	77	No	[71..82]	S	Nt
Kokkos	20	6	86	Yes	[78..91]	S	Nt	85	Yes	[74..95]	S	Nt
Raja	11	5	85	Yes	[72..94]	S	Nt	80	No	[61..93]	S	Nt

S: Symmetrical; **As**: Asymmetrical; **Stt**: Short thin tails; **Lht**: Long Heavy tails; **Nt**: Normal tails; **95% CI**: 95% Confidence Interval

4.2 Nonparametric Bootstrap

Bootstrapping is a technique that resamples a sample of observations with replacement, to create many simulated samples without making assumptions about the sample distribution. Each of the simulated samples has its own statistics, such as the mean. The histogram of the distribution of these means is called the *sampling distribution of the means*. By using this technique, it is possible to calculate a variety of sample statistics, such as the median, mean, and standard deviation. This article focuses on calculating the mean and the 95% confidence interval.

Figure 4 (left) shows the bootstrap distribution of the means and the 95% confidence interval for the 141 observations. The bootstrap distribution was generated by re-sampling the observations from Fig. 1 10,000 times and then calculating each sample's mean. The sampling distribution of the means is the histogram shown in Fig. 4 (left). It can be observed that the calculated mean of the bootstrap distribution yields a score of 76, similar to the mean of the observations in Fig. 1. The confidence interval of the bootstrap distribution is

[72 81], which means that we can be 95% confident that the population mean falls within this range. It can also be noticed that the sampling distribution of the histogram in Fig. 4 (left) approximates a normal distribution even though the underlying distribution of the observations is skewed. This is a direct outcome of the Central Limit Theorem. Figure 4 (right) shows the sampling distribution of the means and the 95% confidence interval for the 109 observations. It approximates a normal distribution around the mean (81) while the confidence interval of the bootstrap distribution is narrower [79 84]. This means that we can be 95% confident that the population mean falls within this range, and we know that our hypothesis is closer to the population mean.

5   OpenMP, Kokkos, and Raja

The statistical analysis described in detail for the case of OpenACC on GPUs was also applied to OpenMP, Kokkos, and Raja on GPUs and CPUs, based on the case studies of the research in [7]. Table 3 shows the results obtained. Each row in the table refers to one of the performance portability frameworks and indicates the number of case studies considered, the performance portability score obtained, the number of outliers detected, whether the distribution of the observations is normal or not as obtained by the Shapiro-Wilk test, the 95% confidence interval, and a literary assessment of the skewness and kurtosis values obtained.

An analysis of the data in Table 3 reveals the following. As the number of observations increases, the number of outliers increases. The distribution of the observations tends to be non-normal, and the 95% confidence intervals tend to be narrower, thus the statistical reliability is better. In contrast, the smaller the number of observations, the wider the 95% confidence interval, and the ability to draw a reliable statistical assessment decreases. The conclusion is that the accuracy of the calculation of the performance portability score of a given performance portability framework increases as the number of observations increases. This finding makes sense and is not surprising, but now it also has the support of statistical tests.

6   Conclusions

Descriptive and inferential statistical analysis using powerful statistical hypothesis tests constitute complementary tools for the performance portability evaluation of an analyst. They are used to conduct an overall reliable assessment of the capability of a given performance portability framework to generate performance portable applications. Confrontation of an analyst's assessment with statistical analysis is necessary when performance portability assessment is based on unverifiable and unreproducible case studies.

In this article, we presented the method for performing a comprehensive statistical analysis for OpenACC on GPUs when many case studies are available. On one hand, we showed how statistical analysis strengthens the evaluation of an analyst, and on the other hand, we showed how statistical analysis allows an analyst to refine his initial conclusions. Finally, we presented statistical analysis for OpenMP, Kokkos and Raja on CPUs and GPUs, and for samples of a small number of case studies.

References

1. Carter Edwards, H., Trott, C.R., Sundrland, D.: Kokkos: enabling manycore performance portability through polymorphic memory access patterns. J. Parallel Distrib. Comput. (2014)
2. Hornung, R.D., Keasler, J.A.: The RAJA Portability Layer: Overview and Status. LLNL-TR-661403 (2014)
3. OpenMP. OpenMP 4.5 Specifications. http://www.openmp.org/specifications/. Accessed 11 Feb 2017
4. OpenACC: Directive-Based Parallel Programming Model for Accelerators (2018). http://www.openacc.org
5. Marowka, A.: Toward a better performance portability metric. In: Proceeding of 29th Euromicro International Conference on Parallel, Distributed and Network-based Processing (PDP 2021), Valladolid, Spain, 10–12 March 2021
6. Marowka, A.: Reformulation of the performance portability metric. Softw. Pract. Exp. **52**(1), 154–171 (2022)
7. Marowka, A.: On the Performance Portability of OpenACC, OpenMP, Kokkos and RAJA. In: ACM Proceeding of HPCAsia 2022, pp. 103–114, January 2022
8. Minitab. https://www.minitab.com/en-us/
9. Stat101. http://www.statistics101.net/statistics101web_000003.htm
10. Statistic Kingdom. https://www.statskingdom.com/
11. Real Statistic. https://www.real-statistics.com/
12. GraphPAD. https://www.graphpad.com/
13. R language. https://www.r-project.org/
14. Excel. https://www.microsoft.com/en-us/microsoft-365/excel
15. Cumming, J., Finch, S.: Inference by eye: confidence intervals and how to read pictures of data. Am. Psychol. 170–180 (2005)
16. DeWinter, J., Dodou, D.: Five-Point Likert Items: t test versus Mann-Whitney-Wilcoxon, pp. 1–16. Practical Assessment, Research and Evaluation (2010)
17. Freedman, D., Pisani, R., Purves, R.: Statistics, 3rd edn. W.W. Norton and Company, New York (1998)
18. Goldstein, H., Healy, M.J.: The graphical presentation of means. J. R. Statist. Soc. 170–180 (1995)
19. Shapiro-Wilk test. https://en.wikipedia.org/wiki/Shapiro%E2%80%93Wilk_test
20. Raw Statistic. https://www.dropbox.com/s/q84gh1jdg3xz8ip/0-statistics-merged.pdf?dl=0
21. Torsten, H., Roberto, B.: Scientific benchmarking of parallel computing systems: Twelve ways to tell the masses when reporting performance results. In: Proceedings of the International Conference for High Performance Computing, Networking, Storage and Analysis (SC 2015) (Austin, Texas). ACM, New York, Article 73, 12 p. (2015)

NPDP Benchmark Suite for Loop Tiling Effectiveness Evaluation

Marek Palkowski[✉] and Wlodzimierz Bielecki

West Pomeranian University of Technology in Szczecin Faculty of Computer Science
and Information Systems, Zolnierska 49, 71210 Szczecin, Poland
{mpalkowski,wbielecki}@wi.zut.edu.pl
http://www.wi.zut.edu.pl

Abstract. The paper introduces ten non-serial polyadic dynamic programming (NPDP) kernels as a benchmark suite dedicated to effectiveness evaluation of tiled code generated by means of polyhedral optimization compilers. Most of the applications implement bioinformatics algorithms which are challenging and ongoing tasks for automatic loop nest tiling transformations. The paper describes mathematically examined kernels and uniformizes them in the form of loop nests presented in the C language. In an experimental study, we applied the two automatic source-to-source compilers, TRACO and PluTo, to generate cache-efficient codes and analysed their performance on three multi-core machines. We discuss the limitations of well-known tiling approaches and outline future tiling strategies for the introduced NPDP Benchmark suite.

Keywords: RNA folding · high-performance computing ·
computational biology · loop tiling · benchmarks

1 Introduction

A collection of non-serial polyadic dynamic programming (NPDP) benchmarks is introduced to evaluate the performance of tiled code automatically generated by means of state-of-the-art optimizing compilers. Tiling is a very important loop nest transformation allowing for increasing code locality and task grain size as well as task parallelism. The suite consists of 10 kernels belonging to NPDP algorithms that in general are difficult for automatic generation of effective parallel tiled code. Eight of them present dynamic programming recurrences, which are ones of the commonly-known approaches in computational biology, to nucleic acid structure prediction (the folding of an RNA molecule), and sequence alignment (determining similar regions between two strings of nucleic acid sequences or protein sequences). Two kernels implement classic algorithms of computer science.

The contribution of the paper is i) to expose disadvantages of existing benchmarks for evaluation of dynamic programming code generated by means of optimizing compilers ii) collect a new benchmark suite to evaluate the effectiveness

© The Author(s), under exclusive license to Springer Nature Switzerland AG 2023
R. Wyrzykowski et al. (Eds.): PPAM 2022, LNCS 13827, pp. 51–62, 2023.
https://doi.org/10.1007/978-3-031-30445-3_5

of compilers optimizing dynamic programming code; iii) optimization of presented benchmarks by means of the PLUTO and TRACO compilers and the presentation of evaluation results for those optimized codes.

Each benchmark is specified as a C code with a short description of what the code is supposed to do. This is sufficient in the context of automated loop transformations implemented within source-to-source compilers. Presented kernels involve mathematical computations, which are easily implemented as affine control loop nests [7,8], thus, the iteration space can be represented by the polyhedral model for optimizing their locality and parallelism. It provides a powerful theoretical framework that can analyze regular loop programs with static dependences [14].

Dynamic programming kernels involve opportunities for polyhedral loop transformations such as tiling for improving code locality via allowing reuse when the tile fits in local memory. However, NPDP irregular loop dependence patterns prevent generation of effective tiled code by means of polyhedral optimization techniques [14].

In the suite, we included only such NPDP kernels that expose non-uniform dependences (the non-uniform dependence is represented with a dependence vector whose elements are affine expressions, i.e., they are not constants) and are challenging for state-of-the-art tiling strategies based on affine transformation framework (ATF) [14,23] and the transitive closure of dependence graphs [9].

In the next section, we describe introduced NPDP kernels. In the experimental study section, we demonstrate applying of two well-known polyhedral compilers to parallelize and optimize benchmarks. In the relation work section, we discuss related polyhedral benchmarks. In conclusion, we define future tasks to optimize the introduced NPDP Benchmark Suite in order to outperform code generated by means of state-of-the-art compilers.

2   NPDP Kernels

The *nussinov* kernel implements Nussinov's algorithm [17] and solves the problem of RNA folding through computing the maximum number of base pairs for subsequences, starting with subsequences of length 1 and building upwards, storing the result of each subsequence in a dynamic programming array.

Let N be an $n \times n$ Nussinov matrix and $\sigma(i,j)$ be a pairing function. Then the following recursion $N(i,j)$ is defined over the region $1 \leq i \leq j \leq n$ as

$$N(i,j) = max(N(i+1,j-1) + \sigma(i,j), \max_{1 \leq j \leq n}(N(i,k) + N(k+1,j))) \quad (1)$$

and zero elsewhere.

The *zuker* kernel implements Zuker's algorithm [25] for RNA folding and calculates the minimal free energy of the input RNA sequence on recurrence relations. It defines two energy matrices, $W(i,j)$ and $V(i,j)$, as the total free energy of a sub-sequence defined with values of i and j, and of a sub-sequence starting with i and ending with j, respectively, if i and j pairs (otherwise $V(i,j) = \infty$).

The main recursion of Zuker's algorithm for all i, j with $1 \leq i < j \leq N$, where N is the length of a sequence, is the following.

$$W(i,j)) = min \begin{cases} W(i+1,j) \\ W(i,j-1) \\ V(i,j) \\ \min_{i<k<j} \{W(i,k) + W(k+1,j)\} \end{cases} \qquad (2)$$

Below, we present the computation of matrix V.

$$V(i,j)) = min \begin{cases} eH(i,j) \\ V(i+1,j-1) + eS(i,j) \\ \min_{\substack{i \leq i' \leq j' \leq j \\ 2 < i'-i+j-j' < d}} \{V(i',j') + eL(i,j,i',j')\} \\ \min_{i<k<j-1} \{W(i+1,k) + W(k+1,j-1)\} \end{cases} \qquad (3)$$

where eH (hairpin loop), eS (stacking) and eL (internal loop) are the structure elements of energy contributions in Zuker's algorithm.

The Smith-Waterman algorithm (sw kernel) explores all the possible alignments between two sequences and as a result it returns the optimal local alignment guarantying the maximal sensitivity [21].

It constructs a scoring matrix H, which is used to keep track of the degree of similarity between the cells a_i and b_j of two sequences to be aligned, where $1 \leq i \leq N, 1 \leq j \leq M$. The size of the scoring matrix is $(N+1)*(M+1)$. Matrix H is first initialized with $H_{0,0} = H_{0,j} = H_{i,0} = 0$ for all i and j.

Each element $H_{i,j}$ of matrix H is calculated as follows.

$$H_{i,j} = max \begin{cases} H_{i-1,j-1} + s(a_i, b_j) \\ \max_{1 \leq k < i} (H_{i-k,j} - W_k) \\ \max_{1 \leq k < j} (H_{i,j-k} - W_k) \\ 0 \end{cases} \qquad (4)$$

where $s(a_i, b_j)$ is a similarity score of elements a_i, b_j that constitute the two sequences, and W_k is a penalty of a gap that has length k.

The benchmark $sw3d$ finds local alignment for three sequences [21]. Multiple sequence alignments are computationally difficult to produce (much harder than that of pairwise alignment) and most formulations of the problem lead to NP-complete combinatorial optimization problems.

Scoring matrix H is similarly constructed to align cells a_i, b_j, and c_l of three sequences, where $1 \leq i \leq N, 1 \leq j \leq M, 1 \leq l \leq P$. The size of the scoring matrix is $(N+1)*(M+1)*(P+1)$. Matrix H is first initialized with $H_{0,0,0} = H_{i,0,0} = H_{0,j,0} = H_{0,0,l} = 0$ for all i, j, and l. Each element $H_{i,j,l}$ is calculated as follows.

$$H_{i,j,l} = \max \begin{cases} H_{i-1,j-1,l-1} + s(a_i, b_j) + s(b_j, c_l) + s(a_i, c_l) \\ \max_{1 \le k < min(j,l)} (H_{i,j-k,l-k} + s(b_j, c_l) - W_k) \\ \max_{1 \le k < min(i,j)} (H_{i-k,j-k,l} + s(a_i, b_j) - W_k) \\ \max_{1 \le k < min(i,l)} (H_{i-k,j,l-k} + s(a_i, c_l) - W_k) \\ \max_{1 \le k < i} (H_{i-k,j,l} - 2 * W_k) \\ \max_{1 \le k < j} (H_{i,j-k,l} - 2 * W_k) \\ \max_{1 \le k < l} (H_{i,j,l-k} - 2 * W_k) \\ 0. \end{cases}$$

Multiple entries of matrix H are much more complicated by data dependences, whereby each cell entry depends on the values of seven entries. The filling stage requires one more loop for l. The number of loop nest statements for q sequences is equal to 2^q-1. For two and three sequences with the same length n, computation of one element growths from $3*n^2$ to $7*n^3$ iterations.

The Needleman-Wunsch (nw) algorithm finds global sequence alignment according to the scheme below [16].

$$F(i, j) = \max \begin{cases} F(i - 1, j - 1) + \sigma(a_i, b_j), \\ \max_{1 \le k < i} (F(i - k, j) - \gamma(k)), \\ \max_{1 \le k < j} (F(i, j - k) - \gamma(k)). \end{cases} \tag{5}$$

where $\sigma(a_i, b_j)$ is a score of a_i, b_j (match or mutation), $\gamma(k)$ is a gap penalty score with the length k.

The *counting* algorithm computes the exact number of nested structures for a given RNA sequence. It was introduced by Michael S. Waterman and Temple F. Smith [22]. It populates the matrix C by means of the following recursion.

$$C_{i,j} = C_{i,j-1} + \sum_{\substack{i \le k < (j-l) \\ S_k, S_j \text{ pair}}} C_{i,k-1} \cdot C_{k+1,j-1}, \tag{6}$$

where l is the minimal number of enclosed positions, and the entry $C_{i,j}$ provides the exact number of admissible structures for the sub-sequence from position i to j. The upper right corner $C_{1,n}$ presents the overall number of admissible structures for the sequences.

The John S. McCaskill kernel (*mccaskill*) computes the partition function $Z = \sum_P exp(-E(P)/RT)$ over all possible nested structures P that can be formed by a given RNA sequence S with $E(P)$ as energy of structure P, gas constant R, and temperature T [12].

Each base pair of a structure contributes a fixed energy term E_{bp} independent of its context in a Nussinov-like energy scoring scheme. Given this, two dynamic programming tables Q and Q_{bp} are populated. Q_{ij} provides the partition function for a subsequence from position i to j, while the array Q_{bp} stores the partition function of the subsequences which form a base pair or 0 if base pairing is not possible. Q and Q^{bp} are populated as follows.

$$Q_{i,j} = Q_{i,j-1} + \sum_{i \le k < (j-l)} Q_{i,k-1} \cdot Q^{bp}_{k,j}, \tag{7}$$

$$Q^{bp}_{i,j} = \begin{cases} Q_{i+1,j-1} \cdot \exp(-E_{bp}/RT) & \text{if } S_i, S_j \text{ can form} \\ & \text{base pair} \\ 0 & \text{otherwise} \end{cases} \tag{8}$$

The *mea* kernel predicts the structure with the maximum expected accuracy for a given RNA sequence using the algorithm introduced by Zhi J. Lu et al., 2009 [11] applying the sequence's base pair and unpaired probabilities. The kernel consists of six NPDP program loops (Q, QBP, PB, PU, PUU, M) and follows a Nussinov-like recursion using the probabilities derived from John S. McCaskill's algorithm.

The computation of PB is the sum of the Boltzmann probabilities of all the structures that contain the base pair [6]. PB covers both the case when (i, j) is an external base pair and that when (i, j) is directly enclosed by an outer base pair (p, q). The PB recursions are used to compute the probabilities of individual base pairs P^{bp} according to the formula below.

$$P^{bp}_{i,j} = \frac{Q_{1,i-1} \cdot Q^{bp}_{i,j} \cdot Q_{j+1,n}}{Q_{1,n}} + \sum_{p<i,j<q} P^{bp}_{p,q} \cdot \frac{\exp(-E_{bp}/RT) \cdot Q_{p+1,i-1} \cdot Q^{bp}_{i,j} \cdot Q_{j+1,q-1}}{Q^{bp}_{p,q}} \tag{9}$$

Analogously to base pair probabilities, we can also compute the probability when a given subsequence $Si...Sj$ of an RNA sequence is not involved in any intramolecular base pair. We call this kernel as PU and use the scheme below.

$$P^u_{i,j} = \frac{Q_{1,i-1} \cdot 1 \cdot Q_{j+1,n}}{Q_{1,n}} + \sum_{p<i,j<q} P^{bp}_{p,q} \cdot \frac{\exp(-E_{bp}/RT) \cdot Q_{p+1,i-1} \cdot 1 \cdot Q_{j+1,q-1}}{Q^{bp}_{p,q}} \tag{10}$$

The following formula is used to populate the probability P^u_i when a given sequence position S_i is not paired. We call it PUU and apply the formula below.

$$P^u_i = 1 - \sum_{k<i} P^{bp}_{k,i} - \sum_{i<j} P^{bp}_{i,j} \tag{11}$$

Finally, the MEA structure prediction uses the following recursion to fill a dynamic programming table M. The overall score of $M_{i,j}$ and the subsequence $S_i..S_j$ is hold in $M_{1,n}$ for a sequence of length n. γ is a constant base pair weighting. We call this kernel MEA.

$$M_{i,j} = \max \begin{cases} M_{i,j-1} + P_j^u & S_j \text{ unpaired} \\ \max_{i \leq k < (j-l)} \left(M_{i,k-1} + M_{k+1,j-1} + \gamma \cdot P_{k,j}^{bp} \right) & S_k \text{ paired with } S_j \end{cases}$$
(12)

In the optimal (polygon) triangulation problem (the *triang* kernel), we are given a convex polygon and a weight function defined on triangles formed by sides and chords [5]. The problem is to find a triangulation that minimizes the sum of the weights of the triangles in the triangulation.

Let cost $w(i, j, k)$ denotes the length of the perimeter of $\triangle v_i v_j v_k = |v_i v_j| + |v_j v_k| + |v_k v_i|$. Then minimal cost polygon triangulation is calculated as follows.

$$c[i][j] = \begin{cases} 0 & j < i + 2, \\ \max_{i < k < j} (c[i][k] + c[k][j] + w(i, j, k)) & \text{otherwise.} \end{cases}$$
(13)

The *knuth* kernel is the optimal binary search tree (OBST) [10], the case when the tree cannot be modified after it has been constructed. Knuth's OBST algorithm populates matrix C and is represented with the following recurrence

$$C_{i,j} = \min \begin{cases} C_{i,j} \\ \min_{1 \leq i < k < j \leq n} (C_{i,k} + C_{k,j} + W_{i,j}) \end{cases},$$
(14)

where $W(i, j)$ is the sum of the probabilities that each of the items i through j will be accessed.

The source codes of all considered benchmarks are available in the sub-directory *input* on the website https://github.com/markpal/NPDP_Bench.

Table 1 presents characteristics of the presented NPDP C kernels. For each kernel, it describes the number of nested loops, the number of arrays, the number of relations representing loop dependences, and memory capacity. The data presented in the last two columns are discussed in the experimental study section.

3   Related Work

The commonly known benchmark suite for polyhedral optimizers is PolyBench introduced by Louis-Noel Pouchet in 2011 [19]. PolyBench is a collection of 30 numerical computations containing static control parts. The kernels are extracted from problems in various application domains (linear algebra computations, image processing, physics simulation, dynamic programming, statistics, etc.). PolyBench is dedicated to evaluate code performance generated by means of techniques based on affine transformations. In previous versions, Polybench includes the dynamic programming kernel *dynprog*. However, this implementation uses a temporary three-dimensional array to avoid non-uniform dependences. In current version 4.2, the kernel is removed. Instead of it, the Nussinov kernel is added.

Table 1. Characteristics of the NPDP kernels.

Kernel	No. of nested loops	No. of arrays	No. of dep. relations	Memory	TRACO exact R+	PluTo limits
counting	3	1	14	N^2	yes	***
knuth	3	2	10	$2*N^2$	yes	*
mcc	3	3	26	$2*N^2+N$	yes	****
mea	4	6	104	$4*N^2+N$	no	
nussinov	3	2	24	N^2+N	yes	*
nw	3	6	22	$3*N^2+3*N$	yes	*
sw	3	6	22	$3*N^2+3*N$	yes	*
sw3d	4	6	98	$3*N^23+3*N$	no	
triang	3	1	22	N^2	yes	*
zuker	4	4	104	$4*N^2$	no	**

* - unitled innermost loop nest, ** - unitiled one before innermost loop nest
*** - untiled outermost loop nest, **** - serial tiled code

The Livermoore loops [13] measure numerical computation to benchmark supercomputers. It was proposed by Francis H. McMahon from scientific source code run on computers at the Lawrence Livermore National Laboratory. The suite consist of 24 loops representing different mathematical kernels, and some of them can be presented within the polyhedral model.

The polyhedral compilers are practiced to generate optimized codes for the NAS benchmark suite (NPB) [15] derived from computational fluid dynamics. It is a branch of fluid mechanics that uses numerical analysis and algorithms to solve and analyse problems that involve fluid flows. The NAS parallel benchmarks suite in version 3.3 consists of eleven kernels targeting performance evaluation of highly parallel supercomputers.

The UTDSP Benchmark Suite [26] was created in 1992 at the University of Toronto to evaluate the quality of code generated by a high-level language (such as C) compiler targeting a programmable digital signal processor (DSP). This evaluation was used to drive the development of specific compiler optimizations to improve the quality of generated code and to modify the architecture of the target processor to simplify compiler's task. The code is provided in multiple styles, versions with arrays are represented as polyhedral loop nests.

The LORE loop repository for the evaluation of compilers maintains a large amount of loop nests in the C language (about 2500 loops) extracted from popular benchmarks, libraries, and real applications [3]. Those loops cover a variety of properties that can be tested by optimization compilers to expose their strengths and weaknesses. The kernels help to evaluate auto-vectorization, tiling, interchange, unrolling, and other possible transformations implemented within optimizers. It is worth noting that LORE contains only necessary codes to execute the kernel loops (not all source programs) to investigate speedup and efficiency of optimization techniques. The authors tested the Intel C++ Compiler

(ICC), GNU C Compiler (GCC), and Clang (frontend of LLVM). Using those compilers, authors provided the time execution results on an Intel Haswell generation Xeon E5-1630 v3 with -O3 flag and enabled more aggressive optimization settings depending on the compiler. However, LORE does not contain NPDP kernels presented in our benchmark suite. Furthermore, not all LORE loops can be directly represented within the polyhedral model because they contain, for example, pointers, typecasting, and arrow operators.

The disadvantage of the benchmark suites discussed above is the absence of multiple dynamic programming kernels that is hard to be tiled to obtain the maximal tile dimension, which has crucial impact on target code locality. This makes it difficult to evaluate the effectiveness of loop tiling approaches implementing in optimizing compilers for essential real-life applications.

4   Experimental Study

In this section, we present the results of an experimental study with the discussed benchmark codes generated applying PLuTo and TRACO. All parallel tiled codes were compiled using the Intel C++ Compiler (icc) and GNU C++ Compiler (g++) with the -O3 flag of optimization.

To carry out experiments, we used three multi-processor machines: an Intel Xeon Platinum 9242 CPU (2.30 GHz, 96 thrads, 71.5/48/3 MB Cache, compiler icc 21.3.0), an Intel i7-8700 (3.2 GHz, 4.6 GHz in turbo, 6 cores, 12 threads, 12 MB/1.5 MB/6*32 kB (D and I) Cache, compiler icc 19.0.1), and an AMD Epyc 7542 (2.35 GHz, 32 cores, 64 threads, 128/16/2 MB Cache, compiler g++ 9.3.0).

For all examined codes, the tile size along each axis was chosen as 16. Experimentally we discovered that such a tile size is optimal or near to optimal regarding to target tiled code performance.

Source codes of the benchmarks with generated codes are available at the open repository github with the following link https://github.com/markpal/NPDP_Bench. Original (sequential and without any modification) input codes are placed in sub-folder *input*. Arrays are filled with random data.

For experimental study, we chose two polyhedral compilers PluTo and TRACO, which are maintained projects with source code repositories, source-to-source parallelizers and cache efficiency optimizers dedicated to optimize C/C++ program loops.

The state-of-the-art source-to-source PluTo compiler [2] is able to tile all examined loop nests automatically. For this purpose, it extracts and applies affine transformations to generate tiled code within the polyhedral model.

TRACO does not find and use any affine function to transform the loop nest. It is based on the iteration space slicing framework [20], which envisages applying the transitive closure of a dependence graph to carry out corrections of original rectangular tiles so that all dependences available in the original loop nest are preserved under the lexicographic order of target tiles. As a result, the inter-tile dependence graph does not contain any tile cycle and any technique of

Table 2. Times of the original and parallel tiled code execution in seconds.

Kernel	counting	knuth	mcc	mea	nussinov	nw	sw	sw3d	triang	zuker
Size	10000	10000	10000	2500	10000	10000	10000	500	10000	2000
XEON Platinum 9242, 96 threads, 2019										
Original	409,91	730,09	3043,21	6240,48	1667,69	2221,84	2357,07	291,32	2562,11	436,76
PluTo	15,34	21,075	1299,29	185,6	80,44	112,43	114,15	29,63	82,11	21,59
TRACO	17,5	12,55	1096,88	175,6	51,91	69,43	62,15	34,01	62,9	45,99
AMD Epyc 7542, 64 threads, 2019										
Original	354,51	853,09	3676,3	8296,33	4008,76	4 567,33	4 433,91	309,87	3574,98	415,55
PluTo	45,77	37,63	1005,44	356,8	217,69	188,32	173,37	24,28	180,67	30,99
TRACO	38,12	74,06	135,01	483,16	113,17	65,22	61,88	27,17	314,63	63,7
Intel i7-8700, 12 threads, 2017										
Original	339,81	744,68	2066,33	3826,6	1507,17	3452,11	3389,89	240,19	2134,83	317,8
PluTo	82,43	145,45	854,9	747,76	618,66	687,22	700,76	91,29	470,26	63,8
TRACO	48,54	77,35	399,16	729,73	134,15	205,22	218,25	99,24	297,42	45,2

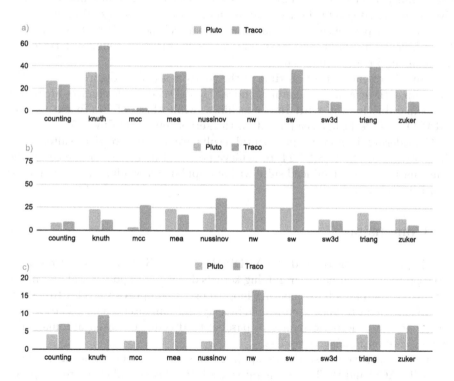

Fig. 1. Speedups of parallel tiled codes generated by applying TRACO and PluTo for a) Intel Xeon Platinum 9242, b) AMD Epyc 7542, and c) Intel i7-8700.

loop parallelization can be used [1]. TRACO parallelizes tiled cods by means of the commonly known wave-fronting technique.

For *mea, sw3d,* and *zuker,* the following lengths of randomized sequences were studied, 2500, 500 and 2000, respectively. The rest of benchmarks were considered with 10000 size of a problem.

Both compilers accelerate the NPDP benchmarks on all machines. PluTo is not able to tile the innermost loop nest for *nussinov, sw, nw, knuth,* and *triang.* It is not able also to tile the outermost loop for *counting,* and the one before the inner loop nest for *zuker,* and it does not parallelize the *mccaskill* kernel. PluTo fails to generate tiles of the maximal dimension for NPDP codes because the tile dimensionality is limited to the number of linearly independent solutions to the space/time partition constraints. The above observations are presented in the last column of Table 1.

TRACO codes demonstrate lower or comparable speed-up for *sw3d* and *zuker* because for those source codes, it uses not an accurate but approximated transitive closure of dependence graphs. For calculation of transitive closure, TRACO uses a corresponding function of the ISL library, which it is not able to return exact transitive closure for those kernels. Calculation of an approximated transitive closure envisages introducing addition dependences (not existing in sourced code) in the dependence graph that worsens parallel tiled code performance. For those kernels, TRACO generates complex code due to a complex form of an approximated transitive closure.

Table 2 presents execution time of the codes in seconds. Figure 1 depicts the speed-up of the examined generated codes. TRACO code performances are better or comparable for the both Intel machines, while those of PluTo outperform TRACO code performances for half of the kernels on AMD Epyc 7542.

Considering the above experimental results, we plan to investigate alternative tiling strategies [4, 14, 18, 23, 24] to achieve potential higher performance for the benchmarks of the introduced suite without applying any affine function and/or transitive closure.

5   Conclusion

In this paper, we introduced the NPDP Benchmark Suite as a set of ten non-serial polyadic dynamic programming kernels dedicated to polyhedral automatic optimizing compilers implementing loop tiling. It comprises C codes to resolve real-life problems from computational biology and computer science. Those codes are to evaluate the performance of parallel tiled code generated automatically by means of optimizing compilers.

In the experimental study, we applied two source-to-source optimizing compilers, TRACO and PluTo, to generate parallel tiled code and evaluate its speed-up on three multi-core machines. Obtained results demonstrate some limitations of techniques implemented in those compilers. PluTo does not expose tiling or parallelism for each kernel, while TRACO does not produce efficient code for each complex non-uniform dependence patterns. We may conclude that approaches implemented in those compilers do not allow us to get the maximal possible cache efficiency for examined kernels.

In the future, we plan to extend the suite with new NPDP kernels. Using that suite, we are going to study alternative tiling strategies to outperform code generated by means of well-known automatic compilers.

References

1. Bielecki, W., Palkowski, M.: Tiling of arbitrarily nested loops by means of the transitive closure of dependence graphs. Int. J. Appl. Math. Comput. Sci. (AMCS) **26**(4), 919–939 (2016)
2. Bondhugula, U., et al.: A practical automatic polyhedral parallelizer and locality optimizer. SIGPLAN Not. **43**(6), 101–113 (2008). https://doi.org/10.1145/1379022.1375595
3. Chen, Z., et. al.: Lore: a loop repository for the evaluation of compilers. In: 2017 IEEE International Symposium on Workload Characterization (IISWC), pp. 219–228. IEEE (2017)
4. Chowdhury, R., et. al.: Autogen. ACM Trans. Parallel Comput. **4**(1), 1–30 (2017). https://doi.org/10.1145/3125632
5. Cormen, T.H., et al.: Introduction to Algorithms, 3rd edn. The MIT Press, Cambridge (2009)
6. Freiburg bioinformatics group: freiburg RNA Tools, Teaching RNA algorithms. https://rna.informatik.uni-freiburg.de/teaching (2022)
7. Griebl, M.: Automatic parallelization of loop programs for distributed memory architectures (2004)
8. Irigoin, F., Triolet, R.: Supernode partitioning. In: Proceedings of the 15th ACM SIGPLAN-SIGACT Symposium on Principles of Programming Languages, pp. 319–329. POPL 1988, ACM, New York (1988)
9. Kelly, W., et al.: Transitive closure of infinite graphs and its applications. Int. J. Parallel Program. **24**(6), 579–598 (1996)
10. Knuth, D.E.: Optimum binary search trees. Acta Informatica **1**(1), 14–25 (1971)
11. Lu, Z.J., Gloor, J.W., Mathews, D.H.: Improved RNA secondary structure prediction by maximizing expected pair accuracy. RNA **15**(10), 1805–1813 (2009). https://doi.org/10.1261/rna.1643609
12. McCaskill, J.S.: The equilibrium partition function and base pair binding probabilities for RNA secondary structure. Biopolymers **29**(6–7), 1105–1119 (1990)
13. McMahon, F.H.: The livermore fortran kernels: A computer test of the numerical performance range. Technical Report, UCRL-53745, Lawrence Livermore National Laboratory, Livermore, California (1986)
14. Mullapudi, R.T., Bondhugula, U.: Tiling for dynamic scheduling. In: Rajopadhye, S., Verdoolaege, S. (eds.) Proceedings of the 4th International Workshop on Polyhedral Compilation Techniques, Vienna, Austria (2014)
15. NAS benchmarks suite. http://www.nas.nasa.gov (2013)
16. Needleman, S.B., Wunsch, C.D.: A general method applicable to the search for similarities in the amino acid sequence of two proteins. In: Molecular Biology, pp. 453–463. Elsevier (1989). https://doi.org/10.1016/b978-0-12-131200-8.50031-9
17. Nussinov, R., et al.: Algorithms for loop matchings. SIAM J. Appl. Math. **35**(1), 68–82 (1978)
18. Palkowski, M., Bielecki, W.: Tiling nussinov's RNA folding loop nest with a space-time approach. BMC Bioinf. **20**(1) (2019). https://doi.org/10.1186/s12859-019-2785-6

19. The Polyhedral Benchmark suite (2012). http://www.cse.ohio-state.edu/pouchet/software/polybench/

20. Pugh, W., Wonnacott, D.: An exact method for analysis of value-based array data dependences. In: Banerjee, U., Gelernter, D., Nicolau, A., Padua, D. (eds.) LCPC 1993. LNCS, vol. 768, pp. 546–566. Springer, Heidelberg (1994). https://doi.org/10.1007/3-540-57659-2_31

21. Smith, T., Waterman, M.: Identification of common molecular subsequences. J. Mol. Biol. **147**(1), 195–197 (1981)

22. Waterman, M., Smith, T.: RNA secondary structure: a complete mathematical analysis. Math. Biosci. **42**(3–4), 257–266 (1978)

23. Wonnacott, D., Jin, T., Lake, A.: Automatic tiling of "mostly-tileable" loop nests. In: IMPACT 2015: 5th International Workshop on Polyhedral Compilation Techniques, At Amsterdam, The Netherlands (2015)

24. Zhao, C., Sahni, S.: Cache and energy efficient algorithms for Nussinov's RNA folding. BMC Bioinf. **18**(15), 518 (2017)

25. Zuker, M., Stiegler, P.: Optimal computer folding of large RNA sequences using thermodynamics and auxiliary information. Nucleic Acids Res. **9**(1), 133–148 (1981)

26. UTDSP benchmark suite. http://www.eecg.toronto.edu/corinna/DSP/infrastructure/UTDSP.html (2012)

Parallel Vectorized Implementations
of Compensated Summation Algorithms

Beata Dmitruk and Przemysław Stpiczyński

Maria Curie-Skłodowska University, Institute of Computer Science,
ul. Akademicka 9, 20-031 Lublin, Poland
{beata.dmitruk,przemyslaw.stpiczynski}@umcs.pl

Abstract. The aim of this paper is to show that Kahan's and Gill-Møller compensated summation algorithms that allow to achieve high accuracy of summing long sequences of floating-point numbers can be efficiently vectorized and parallelized. The new implementation uses Intel AVX-512 intrinsics together with OpenMP constructs in order to utilize SIMD extension of modern multicore processors. We describe in detail the vectorization technique and show how to define custom reduction operators in OpenMP. Numerical experiments performed on a server with *Intel Xeon Gold 6342* processors show that the new implementations of the compensated summation algorithms achieve much better accuracy than ordinary summation and their performance is comparable with the performance of the ordinary summation algorithm optimized automatically. Moreover, the experiments show that the vectorized implementation of the Gill-Møller algorithm is faster than the vectorized implementation of Kahan's algorithm.

Keywords: Summation · Accuracy · Kahan and Gill-Møller algorithms · Vectorization · SIMD intrinsics · OpenMP

1 Introduction

Summation of floating point numbers is one of the most common and basic numerical algorithms. The accuracy and stability of many more complex numerical algorithms depend on the quality of the summation method used. It is clear that the ordinary summation defined recursively is one of the basic of various possible methods. Chapter 4 of the book [7] and [6] provide an overview of several simple and more complicated methods that achieve better accuracy than the ordinary method. Further, more sophisticated methods can be found in [1,3,5,15–17,24]. They can be used if the highest accuracy is desired and the performance is not so important.

Compensated summation methods rely on ordinary recursive summation supplemented with correction terms calculated in order to diminish rounding errors. It should be noticed that compensated summation can be profitable when computations are performed at the highest precision supported by underlying hardware [7]. There are two basic methods that apply this approach, namely Kahan's

R. Wyrzykowski et al. (Eds.): PPAM 2022, LNCS 13827, pp. 63–74, 2023.
https://doi.org/10.1007/978-3-031-30445-3_6

compensated summation [13] and the Gill-Møller method [18]. Although these summation methods are relatively simple and can be described with single loops, their optimization by compilers is not possible due to data dependencies in successive steps. On the other hand, vectorization and parallelization is crucial to utilize potential power of modern multicore processors [2,21–23,25].

The paper [19] shows how to vectorize Kahan's compensated summation in order to utilize AVX2 and AVX-512 SIMD extension of Intel processors, while the papers [8,9] discuss how to apply low-level cache optimization techniques together with the assembly language to improve the performance of the Kahan's algorithm applied for computing the dot product. The aim of this paper is to compare the accuracy and performance of serial, vectorized and parallel implementations of both Kahan's and Gill-Møller compensated summation algorithms. We show how to use Intel AVX-512 intrinsics [12] together with OpenMP [20] constructs in order to utilize SIMD extension of modern multicore processors. We describe in detail the high-level vectorization technique and explain how to define custom reduction operators in order to obtain simple high performance implementations of the compensated summation methods that achieve the performance comparable with the ordinary summation algorithm optimized automatically by the compiler.

2   Compensated Summation Algorithms

Let us consider the summation of n floating point numbers $a_1, a_2, \ldots, a_n$ using an arithmetic with t mantissa bits using the ordinary algorithm based on the recursive formula

$$s_i = \begin{cases} 0 & \text{for } i = 0 \\ s_{i-1} + a_i & \text{for } i = 1, \ldots, n. \end{cases} \tag{1}$$

The relative error of the computed value of s_n satisfies [10,26]

$$e_n = \frac{|s_n - \sum_{i=1}^n a_i|}{\sum_{i=1}^n |a_i|} \leq (1 + 2^{-t})^{n-1} - 1. \tag{2}$$

Moreover, if $n \cdot 2^{-t} \leq 0.1$, then $e_n \leq 1.06(n-1)2^{-t}$. It means that for large n such a possible relative error may be unacceptable. Therefore in order to improve the accuracy of the summation one can consider the use of so-called *compensated summation* algorithms that use correction terms that estimate $(x+y) - fl(x+y)$ to reduce rounding errors of add operations [7, Section 4.3].

Algorithm 1 shows Kahan's compensated summation [4,7,13]. It uses the correction term e on every step of summation. As soon as each partial sum is evaluated, the correction is added to the next term before that term is added to the partial sum. In case of the Gill-Møller algorithm (see [14,18] and Algorithm 2) correction terms are accumulated separately by ordinary summation and finally the global correction is added to the computed sum.

Algorithm 1: Kahan	Algorithm 2: Gill-Møller
1 $s \leftarrow 0$	1 $s \leftarrow 0$
2 $e \leftarrow 0$	2 $p \leftarrow 0$
3 **for** $i = 1, \ldots, n$ **do**	3 $sold \leftarrow 0$
4 $\quad temp \leftarrow s$	4 **for** $i = 1, \ldots, n$ **do**
5 $\quad y \leftarrow a_i + e$	5 $\quad s \leftarrow sold + a_i$
6 $\quad s \leftarrow temp + y$	6 $\quad p \leftarrow p + (a_i - (s - sold))$
7 $\quad e \leftarrow (temp - s) + y$	7 $\quad sold \leftarrow s$
8 **end**	8 **end**
9 **return** s	9 **return** $s + p$

It can be proven [4, 6, 7, 10, 14] respectively, that in case of both compensated summation algorithms, the computed sums satisfy

$$\hat{s}'_n = \sum_{i=1}^{n} a_i(1 + \varepsilon'_i), |\varepsilon'_i| \le 2u + O(nu^2) \text{ (Kahan)} \tag{3}$$

and

$$\hat{s}''_n = \sum_{i=1}^{n} a_i(1 + \varepsilon''_i), |\varepsilon''_i| \le 2u + n^2 u^2 \text{ (Gill-Møller)}, \tag{4}$$

where the *unit roundoff* u is equal to 2^{-24} or 2^{-53} for IEEE single and double precision arithmetic, respectively. As long as $nu \le 1$, the constant in (3) is independent of n. In case of Gill-Møller (see [7, 11, 14]) if we assume that $n^2 u \le 0.1$, then the relative error satisfies $|\varepsilon''_i| \le 2.1u$. It means that if n is not too large, then s_n computed by Algorithm 1 or 2 is the exact sum of slightly perturbed input data. Moreover, if all $a_i > 0$, then the relative error of both algorithms is of the same order as u.

3   Implementation of Parallel Vectorized Algorithms

It is clear that the ordinary summation algorithm (Fig. 1, SumOrd) can be automatically optimized by the compiler to utilize SIMD extensions of modern processors. Moreover, it can be easily parallelized using the OpenMP `parallel for` construct [20] with the `reduction` clause (Fig. 1, PSumOrd). However, the optimization of the Kahan and Gill-Møller algorithms (Fig. 1, SumK and SumGM, respectively) is not so straightforward because of their main loops with obvious data dependencies. It should be noticed that in case of the Intel OneAPI compiler, one should remember to compile the functions SumK and SumGM using the option `-fprotect-parens` which tells the optimizer to honor parentheses when floating-point expressions are evaluated. Otherwise, the optimizer may reorder expressions without regard for parentheses if it produces faster executing code and then the benefits (i.e. the accuracy) of the compensated summation algorithms can be lost.

```
//ordinary summation(SumOrd)
double s = 0;
for (int i=0; i<n; i++)
    s += a[i];
return s;
```

```
//Gill-Møller (SumGM)
double s=0, p=0, sold=0;
for(int i=0;i<n;i++){
    s=sold+a[i];
    p=p+((a[i]-(s-sold)));
    sold = s;
}
return s+p;
```

```
//vectorized Gill-Møller
//summation(VSumGM)
__m512d vx,vs,vp,vsold,vt;
vp = _mm512_setzero_pd();
vs = _mm512_setzero_pd();
vsold = _mm512_setzero_pd();
for (int k = 0; k<n; k=k+8){
    vx=_mm512_load_pd(&a[k]);
    vs=_mm512_add_pd(vsold,vx);
    vt=_mm512_sub_pd(vs,vsold);
    vt=_mm512_sub_pd(vx,vt);
    vp=_mm512_add_pd(vp,vt);
    vsold=vs;
}
vs=_mm512_add_pd(vs,vp);
// then apply SumGM to vs
...
```

```
//parallel summmation
//(PSumOrd)
double s = 0;
#pragma omp parallel for
    ↪ reduction(+:s)
    ↪ schedule (static)
for (int i = 0; i<n; i++)
    s += a[i];
return s;
```

```
//Kahan summation (SumK)
double s=0, e=0;
for(int i=0;i<n;i++){
    double temp=s;
    double y=a[i]+e;
    s=temp+y;
    e=(temp-s)+y;
}
return s;
```

```
//vectorized Kahan (VSumK)
__m512d vx,vs,ve,vy,vt;
vs=ve=_mm512_setzero_pd();
for (int k=0;k<n;k=k+8){
    vt=vs;
    vx=_mm512_load_pd(&a[k]);
    vy=_mm512_add_pd(vx,ve);
    vs=_mm512_add_pd(vt,vy);
    vt=_mm512_sub_pd(vt,vs);
    ve=_mm512_add_pd(vt,vy);
}
// then apply SumK to vs
```

Fig. 1. Ordinary summation (SumOrd), parallelized ordinary summation (PSumOrd), Kahan summation (SumK), Gill-Møller summation (SumGM), vectorized Kahan summation (VSumK) and vectorized Gill-Møller summation (VSumGM)

The general idea that can be applied to develop vectorized versions of summation is the *divide-and-conquer* approach. The main loop of the functions SumK and SumGM can be divided into v separate loops, where v is the length of vectors used in particular SIMD extension. For the sake of simplicity let us assume that n is a multiple of v. In case of 512-bit Intel Advanced Vector Extensions (AVX-512) for double precision $v = 8$ and $v = 16$ for single precision, respectively. Then the loop number k, $k = 0, \ldots, v-1$, will perform summation of the numbers a_{k+iv}, where $i = 1, \ldots, n/v$. Note that such partial summations can

```
//parallelized and vectorized Kahan summation(PVSumK)
void avkadd(__m512d *vnew,__m512d *vold){
    __m512d vs,ve,vy,vt;
    vt = *vold;
    vy = *vnew;
    vs = _mm512_add_pd(vt,vy);
    vt = _mm512_sub_pd(vt,vs);
    ve = _mm512_add_pd(vt,vy);
    *vnew = _mm512_add_pd(vs,ve);
}
#pragma omp declare reduction(vkadd:__m512d:avkadd      (&
    ↪ omp_out,&omp_in) initializer( omp_priv =
    ↪ _mm512_setzero_pd())
double PVSumK(int n, double *a){
    __m512d vsold,vx,vs,ve,vy,vt;
    ve = _mm512_setzero_pd();
    vs = _mm512_setzero_pd();
#pragma omp parallel for firstprivate(vx,vt,vy,ve)
    ↪ reduction(vkadd:vs) schedule(static)
    for (int k = 0; k < n; k=k+8){
    ...
    }
    // the rest of the code as in VSumK
    ...
}
```

Fig. 2. Parallel vectorized Kahan summation (PVSumK)

be performed using both Kahan's and Gill-Møller algorithms. Finally, v partial sums are added using the appropriate algorithm (again, Kahan's or Gill-Møller).

In order to take advantages of AVX-512 and develop vectorizable implementations of the considered algorithms we will use intrinsics for SIMD instructions which allow to write constructs that look like C/C++ function calls corresponding to actual AVX-512 instructions [12]. Such calls are automatically replaced with assembly code inlined directly into programs. The algorithms VSumK and VSumGM presented in Fig. 1 use two variables of the type _m512d allocated in processor's registers: vx is used to store a sequence of $v = 8$ consecutive numbers loaded by the intrinsic _mm512_load_pd(), while vs works as the accumulator. The intrinsic _mm512_add_pd() is used to perform vectorized summation. VSumK and VSumGM also need a few auxiliary variables of the type _m512d to compute corrections using the intrinsic _mm512_sub_pd() which performs a subtraction of two vectors. The vectorized version of the Gill-Møller algorithm uses _mm512_add_pd() to add the vector of v corrections to previously evaluated partial sums.

```
//parallelized and vectorized Gill-Møller summation
//(PVSumGM)
typedef struct GMSum{
  __m512d vs,vp;
} GMSum;
void avzero(GMSum *vnew){
  vnew->vp = _mm512_setzero_pd();
  vnew->vs = _mm512_setzero_pd();
}
void avgmadd(GMSum *vnew,GMSum *vold){
    __m512d tvs,tvp;
    tvs = _mm512_add_pd(vold->vs,vnew->vs);
    tvp = _mm512_sub_pd(tvs,vold->vs);
    tvp = _mm512_sub_pd(vnew->vs,tvp);
    tvp = _mm512_sub_pd(vnew->vp,tvp);
    vnew->vp = _mm512_add_pd(vold->vp,tvp);
    vnew->vs = tvs;
}
#pragma omp declare reduction (vgmadd:GMSum:avgmadd (&
  ↪ omp_out, &omp_in)initializer(avzero(&omp_priv))

double PVSumGM(int n, double *a){
  __m512d vx,vs,vt,vp,old;
  GMSum vsold;   avzero(&vsold);
#pragma omp parallel for private (vx,vt,vs) reduction(
  ↪ vgmadd:vsold) schedule (static)
  for (int k = 0; k < n; k=k+8){
    vx = _mm512_load_pd(&a[k]);
    vs = _mm512_add_pd(vsold.vs,vx);
    vt = _mm512_sub_pd(vs,vsold.vs);
    vt = _mm512_sub_pd(vx,vt);
    vsold.vp = _mm512_add_pd(vsold.vp,vt);
    vsold.vs = vs;
  }
  vs = _mm512_add_pd(vsold.vs,vsold.vp);
  // the rest of the code as in VSumGM
    ...
}
```

Fig. 3. Parallel vectorized Gill-Møller summation (PVSumGM)

The parallelization of the vectorized algorithms VSumK and VSumGM using the
OpenMP parallel for construct with the reduction clause requires a custom reduction operator to be defined. For that one should use the declare
reduction directive. Figure 2 shows how to define the new vkadd operator providing its *initializer* and *combiner*. The first one is responsible for the production
of the neutral element, while the second one shows how to combine two partial
results. We use the intrinsic _mm512_setzero_pd() as the *initializer* and the

user-defined function avkadd() as the *combiner*. It is responsible for a single compensated addition of two vectors that hold partial sums computed by two separate OpenMP threads. Note that both *initializer* and *combiner* operate on the predefined variables omp_priv, omp_in, and omp_out.

Figure 3 shows parallel vectorized Gill-Møller summation (PVSumGM). Parallelization of the main loop is more sophisticated because one should define two helper functions avzero() and avgmadd() that work as the *initializer* and *combiner* of another reduction operator vgmadd. Note that we also have to define the type GMSum that stores two vectors that holds partial sums and their corrections. Finally, these two vectors are added using the intrinsic _mm512_add_pd() in the main OpenMP thread (i.e. outside the parallel region).

4   Results of Experiments

All considered methods have been tested on a server with two *Intel Xeon Gold 6342* processors (totally 48 cores with hyperthreading, 2.8 GHz, 36 MB of cache memory), 256 GB RAM, running under Linux with Intel OneAPI version 2022. This compiler suite consists of C/C++ and Fortran compilers and high performance numerical libraries like MKL. As our test problem we have chosen

$$S_n = \sum_{k=1}^{n} a_k = \sum_{k=0}^{n-1} \frac{1}{(k \bmod m + 1)(k \bmod m + 2)}, \tag{5}$$

where for simplicity we assume that n and m are powers of two. It is well known that $s_m = \sum_{k=0}^{m-1} \frac{1}{(k+1)(k+2)} = \frac{m}{m+1}$, thus $S_n = \frac{n}{m} s_m = \frac{n}{m+1}$. The generated numbers have been shuffled using $2n$ random swaps of two elements. The methods have been tested for $n = 2^c$, $c = 15, \ldots, 30$, and $m = 2^j$, $j = 2, \ldots, 6$. We have measured the execution time, selected speedups and accuracy. The results have been presented in Tables 1 and 2, and Figs. 4 and 5. Note that we have two implementations of the ordinary summation algorithm, SumOrd – vectorized by the compiler (column V) and PSumOrd – additionally parallelized using OpenMP (column P+V). In case of the compensated summation algorithm, we have their three implementations, namely scalar (columns S, functions SumK and SumGM), vectorized using intrinsics (columns V, functions VSumK and VSumGM), and the implementations additionally parallelized using OpenMP (column P+V, functions PVSumK and PVSumGM). It should be noticed that all functions have been compiled using the compiler option O3, i.e. the highest optimization level. It enables vectorization, inlining of intrinsics, and it is recommended for applications that have loops using floating-point calculations.

Table 1 presents the relative error for all considered methods but for each value of n it contains only the results for one value of m, namely the value for which the ordinary algorithm has achieved the worst accuracy in order to show how the use of compensated summation improves the accuracy. However, for fixed value of n, the accuracy of SumOrd for various m is always of the same order. We can observe that the accuracy of SumOrd and PSumOrd decreases when the problem size n increases. PSumOrd achieves slightly better accuracy because the *parallel reduction* implements a kind of the *pairwise summation* approach, which gives more accurate results [6]. Both compensated summation algorithms mostly give accurate results. For a few cases, the relative error is of the same order as the unit roundoff, what corresponds to the theoretical properties presented in Sect. 2. Indeed, for all problem sizes $nu < 1$, the relative error of Kahan's algorithm should not exceed $O(u)$. In case of the Gill-Møller algorithm the inequality $n^2u \leq 0.1$ is not satisfied for $n \geq 2^{25}$ but even for such values of n, the relative error is still of order u. Our parallel and vectorized versions of the algorithms preserve these properties with a reduced number of cases for which exact results are obtained. It was to be expected because *divide and conquer* implementations of compensated summation preserve $|\varepsilon_i| \leq cu$ but at cost of a slight increase in the size of the constant c [6,10].

Table 1. Relative error for all considered methods

n	m	Ordinary		Kahan			Gill-Møller		
		V	P+V	S	V	P+V	S	V	P+V
2^{15}	2^3	3.7e−14	1.0e−15	0.0e−00	0.0e−00	0.0e−00	0.0e−00	0.0e−00	1.2e−16
2^{16}	2^2	3.6e−14	1.7e−15	0.0e−00	1.4e−16	0.0e−00	0.0e−00	1.4e−16	1.4e−16
2^{17}	2^2	6.1e−14	1.5e−15	0.0e−00	0.0e−00	1.4e−16	0.0e−00	1.4e−16	0.0e−00
2^{18}	2^2	1.4e−13	6.1e−15	0.0e−00	0.0e−00	1.4e−16	0.0e−00	0.0e−00	1.4e−16
2^{19}	2^2	2.4e−13	5.8e−15	0.0e−00	0.0e−00	0.0e−00	0.0e−00	0.0e−00	1.4e−16
2^{20}	2^3	1.0e−12	2.1e−14	0.0e−00	0.0e−00	1.3e−16	0.0e−00	0.0e−00	0.0e−00
2^{21}	2^4	1.3e−12	2.5e−14	0.0e−00	0.0e−00	0.0e−00	0.0e−00	0.0e−00	1.2e−16
2^{22}	2^2	2.3e−12	1.0e−13	0.0e−00	0.0e−00	0.0e−00	1.4e−16	0.0e−00	1.4e−16
2^{23}	2^3	8.6e−12	8.4e−14	0.0e−00	0.0e−00	0.0e−00	0.0e−00	0.0e−00	1.2e−16
2^{24}	2^4	1.6e−11	5.5e−15	0.0e−00	0.0e−00	0.0e−00	0.0e−00	0.0e−00	0.0e−00
2^{25}	2^3	3.6e−11	6.9e−13	0.0e−00	0.0e−00	0.0e−00	0.0e−00	0.0e−00	0.0e−00
2^{26}	2^2	3.7e−11	1.6e−12	0.0e−00	0.0e−00	1.4e−16	0.0e−00	1.4e−16	0.0e−00
2^{27}	2^3	1.5e−10	3.7e−12	0.0e−00	0.0e−00	0.0e−00	0.0e−00	0.0e−00	1.2e−16
2^{28}	2^2	1.5e−10	6.5e−12	0.0e−00	0.0e−00	1.4e−16	0.0e−00	0.0e−00	1.4e−16
2^{29}	2^5	3.3e−10	1.2e−11	0.0e−00	0.0e−00	0.0e−00	0.0e−00	0.0e−00	0.0e−00
2^{30}	2^4	4.2e−10	3.5e−11	0.0e−00	0.0e−00	0.0e−00	0.0e−00	0.0e−00	0.0e−00

The performance of SumK and SumGM is up to 8× slower than the performance of SumOrd because the source code of these functions cannot be vectorized automatically. Unexpectedly, SumGM is really faster than SumK (up to 2×). The same is true for VSumK and VSumGM. Both algorithms have the same number of flops, but probably in case of SumGM, the optimizer can make better use of the scalar units of the processor. Both vectorized implementations of compensated summation algorithms are up to 8× faster than their scalar counterparts (Fig. 4). It can also be observed that for bigger problem sizes, the performance of VSumGM is comparable with the performance of SumOrd.

The timing results presented in Table 2, and Figs. 4 and 5 have been obtained for KMP_HW_SUBSET=1s,24c,1t and KMP_AFFINITY=scatter. These environment variables allow to control how the OpenMP runtime uses the hardware threads on the processors. We can recommend to use only one thread per core and to distribute the threads sequentially among the cores of a processor. The use of parallel implementations of considered algorithms, namely the functions PSumOrd, PVSumGM, and PVSumK, is profitable for really big problem sizes, i.e. $n > 2^{24}$ (Fig. 4). Then the execution time of the algorithms is almost the same. However, the efficiency of using parallel processing is not very high, because the parallel loops are not computationally intensive. The speedup of PVSumGM over SumGM (up to 38×) is worse than speedup of PVSumK over SumK (up to 81×) because its implementation of parallel reduction is more complicated. Note that the speedup of PVSumK over SumOrd, and the speedup of PVSumGM over SumOrd, are almost the same as speedup of PSumOrd over SumOrd, namely up to 8.5× for sufficiently large problems.

Table 2. Execution time [s] for all considered methods

n	m	Ordinary		Kahan			Gill-Møller		
		V	P+V	S	V	P+V	S	V	P+V
2^{15}	2^3	6.2e–6	0.0022	0.0002	2.5e–5	0.0023	0.0001	1.7e–5	0.0023
2^{16}	2^2	1.1e–5	0.0038	0.0003	4.6e–5	0.0038	0.0001	3.1e–5	0.0033
2^{17}	2^2	2.1e–5	0.0041	0.0006	0.0001	0.0041	0.0003	0.0001	0.0040
2^{18}	2^2	5.5e–5	0.0043	0.0012	0.0002	0.0041	0.0006	0.0001	0.0041
2^{19}	2^2	0.0001	0.0045	0.0024	0.0003	0.0044	0.0011	0.0001	0.0043
2^{20}	2^3	0.0002	0.0061	0.0049	0.0006	0.0061	0.0022	0.0003	0.0060
2^{21}	2^4	0.0005	0.0065	0.0097	0.0012	0.0064	0.0040	0.0005	0.0063
2^{22}	2^2	0.0017	0.0068	0.0194	0.0025	0.0070	0.0082	0.0013	0.0069
2^{23}	2^3	0.0040	0.0071	0.0389	0.0056	0.0072	0.0182	0.0040	0.0071
2^{24}	2^4	0.0080	0.0075	0.0779	0.0111	0.0079	0.0364	0.0080	0.0104
2^{25}	2^3	0.0162	0.0129	0.1558	0.0222	0.0117	0.0730	0.0165	0.0098
2^{26}	2^2	0.0322	0.0142	0.3116	0.0445	0.0137	0.1461	0.0328	0.0129
2^{27}	2^3	0.0647	0.0190	0.6234	0.0889	0.0206	0.2917	0.0652	0.0202
2^{28}	2^2	0.1290	0.0273	1.2468	0.1775	0.0268	0.5833	0.1299	0.0235
2^{29}	2^5	0.2577	0.0397	2.4950	0.3552	0.0420	1.1664	0.2582	0.0405
2^{30}	2^4	0.5138	0.0604	4.9954	0.7125	0.0613	2.3437	0.5165	0.0609

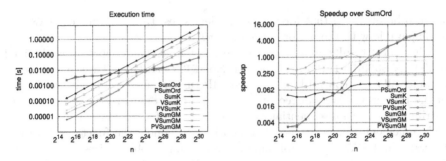

Fig. 4. Execution time (left) and speedup over SumOrd (right) for all considered methods and their implementations

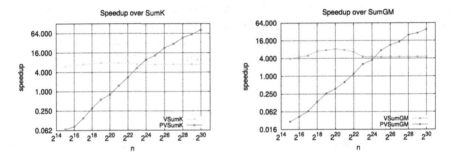

Fig. 5. Speedup over based methods: SumK (left) and SumGM (right)

5 Conclusions and Future Work

We have shown that Kahan's and Gill-Møller compensated summation algorithms that allow to achieve high accuracy of summation of floating-point numbers can be efficiently vectorized using Intel AVX-512 intrinsics and parallelized with OpenMP constructs in order to utilize SIMD extension of modern multicore processors. Numerical experiments show that for sufficiently large problem sizes the vectorized Gill-Møller summation algorithm is as fast as the ordinary summation algorithm optimized automatically by the compiler. Kahan's algorithm is slower, however, both compensated summation algorithms achieve the same accuracy, much better than accuracy achieved by the ordinary summation algorithm. Both vectorized implementations of the summation algorithms can also be parallelized using rather easy-to-use and flexible the "declare reduction" construct in order to speedup their execution, but it can be profitable for really big problem sizes. However, if summation is only a part of implemented problem, for example when summed numerical values are computed during summation using a more complicated procedure, then the use of multiple processors can be profitable even for smaller problem sizes. In the future, we plan to implement several algorithms for solving such problems (numerical integration, solving ordinary differential equations) in order to examine how the use of the parallel vectorized compensated summation algorithms affects accuracy and performance.

References

1. Ahrens, P., Demmel, J., Nguyen, H.D.: Algorithms for efficient reproducible floating point summation. ACM Trans. Math. Softw. **46**, 22:1–22:49 (2020). https://doi.org/10.1145/3389360
2. Amiri, H., Shahbahrami, A.: SIMD programming using intel vector extensions. J. Parallel Distrib. Comput. **135**, 83–100 (2020). https://doi.org/10.1016/j.jpdc.2019.09.012
3. Collange, S., Defour, D., Graillat, S., Iakymchuk, R.: Numerical reproducibility for the parallel reduction on multi- and many-core architectures. Parallel Comput. **49**, 83–97 (2015). https://doi.org/10.1016/j.parco.2015.09.001
4. Goldberg, D.: What every computer scientist should know about floating-point arithmetic. ACM Comput. Surv. **23**, 5–48 (1991). https://doi.org/10.1145/103162.103163
5. He, Y., Ding, C.H.Q.: Using accurate arithmetics to improve numerical reproducibility and stability in parallel applications. J. Supercomput. **18**, 259–277 (2001). https://doi.org/10.1023/A:1008153532043
6. Higham, N.J.: The accuracy of floating point summation. SIAM J. Sci. Comput. **14**, 783–799 (1993). https://doi.org/10.1137/0914050
7. Higham, N.: Accuracy and Stability of Numerical Algorithms. SIAM, Philadelphia (1996)
8. Hofmann, J., Fey, D., Riedmann, M., Eitzinger, J., Hager, G., Wellein, G.: Performance analysis of the Kahan-enhanced scalar product on current multicore processors. In: Wyrzykowski, R., Deelman, E., Dongarra, J., Karczewski, K., Kitowski, J., Wiatr, K. (eds.) PPAM 2015. LNCS, vol. 9573, pp. 63–73. Springer, Cham (2016). https://doi.org/10.1007/978-3-319-32149-3_7
9. Hofmann, J., Fey, D., Riedmann, M., Eitzinger, J., Hager, G., Wellein, G.: Performance analysis of the Kahan-enhanced scalar product on current multi-core and many-core processors. Concurr. Comput. Pract. Exp. **29**(9) (2017). https://doi.org/10.1002/cpe.3921
10. Jankowski, M., Smoktunowicz, A., Woźniakowski, H.: A note on floating-point summation of very many terms. Elektronische Informationsverarbeitung und Kybernetik **19**, 435–440 (1983)
11. Jankowski, M., Woźniakowski, H.: The accurate solution of certain continuous problems using only single precision arithmetic. BIT Num.l Math. (1985). https://doi.org/10.1007/BF01936142
12. Jeffers, J., Reinders, J., Sodani, A.: Intel Xeon Phi Processor High-Performance Programming. Knights Landing Edition. Morgan Kaufman, Cambridge (2016)
13. Kahan, W.: Pracniques: further remarks on reducing truncation errors. Commun. ACM **8**, 40 (1965). https://doi.org/10.1145/363707.363723
14. Kiełbasiński, A.: The summation algorithm with correction and their applications. Math. Appl. (Matematyka Stosowana) (1973). 10.14708/ma.v1i1.295
15. Lefèvre, V.: Correctly rounded arbitrary-precision floating-point summation. IEEE Trans. Comput. **66**, 2111–2124 (2017). https://doi.org/10.1109/TC.2017.2690632

16. Lei, X., Gu, T., Graillat, S., Jiang, H., Qi, J.: A fast parallel high-precision summation algorithm based on AccSumK. J. Computut. Appl. Math. **406**, 113827 (2022). https://doi.org/10.1016/j.cam.2021.113827
17. Lutz, D.R., Hinds, C.N.: High-precision anchored accumulators for reproducible floating-point summation. In: Burgess, N., Bruguera, J.D., de Dinechin, F. (eds.) 24th IEEE Symposium on Computer Arithmetic, ARITH 2017, London, UK, 24–26 July 2017, pp. 98–105. IEEE Computer Society (2017). https://doi.org/10.1109/ARITH.2017.20
18. Møller, O.: Quasi double-precision in floating point addition. BIT Num.l Math. **5**, 37–50 (1965). https://doi.org/10.1007/BF01975722
19. Neuman, B., Dubois, A., Monroe, L., Robey, R.W.: Fast, good, and repeatable: Summations, vectorization, and reproducibility. Int. J. High Perform. Comput. Appl. **34** (2020). https://doi.org/10.1177/1094342020938425
20. van der Pas, R., Stotzer, E., Terboven, C.: Using OpenMP - The Next Step. Affinity, Accelerators, Tasking, and SIMD. MIT Press, Cambridge (2017)
21. Stojanov, A., Toskov, I., Rompf, T., Püschel, M.: SIMD intrinsics on managed language runtimes. In: Proceedings of the 2018 International Symposium on Code Generation and Optimization, pp. 2–15. ACM, New York, NY (2018). https://doi.org/10.1145/3168810
22. Stpiczyński, P.: Language-based vectorization and parallelization using intrinsics, OpenMP, TBB and Cilk Plus. J. Supercomput. **74**(4), 1461–1472 (2018). https://doi.org/10.1007/s11227-017-2231-3
23. Stpiczyński, P.: Algorithmic and language-based optimization of Marsa-LFIB4 pseudorandom number generator using OpenMP, OpenACC and CUDA. J. Parallel Distrib. Comput. **137**, 238–245 (2020). https://doi.org/10.1016/j.jpdc.2019.12.004
24. Uguen, Y., de Dinechin, F., Derrien, S.: Bridging high-level synthesis and application-specific arithmetic: the case study of floating-point summations. In: Santambrogio, M.D., Göhringer, D., Stroobandt, D., Mentens, N., Nurmi, J. (eds.) 27th International Conference on Field Programmable Logic and Applications, FPL 2017, Ghent, Belgium, 4–8 September 2017, pp. 1–8. IEEE (2017). https://doi.org/10.23919/FPL.2017.8056792
25. Wang, H., Wu, P., Tanase, I.G., Serrano, M.J., Moreira, J.E.: Simple, portable and fast SIMD intrinsic programming: generic SIMD library. In: Proceedings of the 2014 Workshop on Programming Models for SIMD/Vector Processing, pp. 9–16. ACM, New York, NY (2014). https://doi.org/10.1145/2568058.2568059
26. Wilkinson, J.: Rounding Errors in Algebraic Processes. Prentice-Hall, Englewood Cliffs (1963)

6th Workshop on Models, Algorithms and Methodologies for Hybrid Parallelism in New HPC Systems (MAMHYP 2022)

Malleability Techniques for HPC Systems

Jesus Carretero[1]([✉]) [iD], David Exposito[1] [iD], Alberto Cascajo[1] [iD],
and Raffaele Montella[2] [iD]

[1] Universidad Carlos III de Madrid. Departamento de Informática,
Leganes, Madrid, Spain
{jcarrete,dexposit,acascajo}@inf.uc3m.es
[2] Computer Science at the Department of Science and Technologies (DiST),
University of Naples "Parthenope" (UNP), Naples, Italy
raffaele.montella@uniparthenope.it

Abstract. Abstract The current static usage model of HPC systems is
becoming increasingly inefficient due to the continuously growing complexity of system architectures, combined with the increased usage of
coupled applications, the need for strong scaling with extreme scale parallelism, and the increasing reliance on complex and dynamic workflows.
Malleability techniques adjust resource usage dynamically for HPC systems and applications to extract maximum efficiency. In this paper, we
present FlexMPI, a tool being developed in the ADMIRE project that
provides an intelligent global coordination of resource usage at the application level. FlexMPI considers runtime scheduling of computation, network usage, and I/O across all system architecture components. It can
optimize the exploitation of HPC and I/O resources while minimizing the
makespan of applications in many cases. Furthermore, FlexMPI provides
facilities such as application world recomposition to generate a new consistent state when processes are added or removed to the applications,
data redistribution to the new application world, and I/O interference
detection to migrate congesting processes. We also present an environmental use case co-designed using FlexMPI. The evaluation shows its
adaptability and scalability.

Keywords: Malleability · Scheduling · High-Performance
Computing · Environmental applications

1 Introduction

One major challenge for efficiently exploiting HPC infrastructures is finding a
balance between the computational and storage I/O resources. This goal is even

This work has been partially funded by the European Union's Horizon 2020 under the
ADMIRE project "Adaptive multi-tier intelligent data manager for Exascale", grant
Agreement number 956748-ADMIRE-H2020-JTI-EuroHPC-2019-1, and by the Spanish
Ministry of Science and Innovation.

R. Wyrzykowski et al. (Eds.): PPAM 2022, LNCS 13827, pp. 77–88, 2023.
https://doi.org/10.1007/978-3-031-30445-3_7

more complex when we consider the structure of the I/O stack that includes multiple storage levels (burst buffers, *ad-hoc* and back-end storage systems, etc.) and their interaction with the executing applications. In this context, the use of malleability provides a new dimension to this problem by allowing it to expand or shrink both the number of application processes and the number of storage nodes.

When considering a platform where both the applications and the I/O subsystem are malleable, it is difficult to determine a proper balance between these components: HPC applications exhibit significant disparities in I/O requirements, which may change when the application is reconfigured by malleability. In this context, new libraries and components of the platform I/O stack are needed to enhance the existing components with malleable capabilities. In addition, novel control mechanisms are also required to execute malleable applications efficiently and to adapt the I/O stack to the characteristics of each application. In this context, ADMIRE project, depicted in the next section, provides a solution to this challenge. This work is mainly focused on depicting the application malleability provided by the FlexMPI library, developed in the context of ADMIRE project. This work describes the main features of FlexMPI and how it is integrated with the WaComM++ application to improve its performance -by means of malleability- under different execution scenarios.

The rest of this paper is organized as follows: Sect. 2 contextualizes this work in the framework of the ADMIRE project; a detailed description of the malleability features implemented by the Flex-MPI library is in Sect. 3; Sect. 4 is about the ADMIRE environmental application focusing on the WaComM++ component; finally, Sect. 5 is about the conclusions and the future research directions.

2   ADMIRE Project

The ADMIRE project pursues the creation of an active I/O stack that dynamically adjusts, computes, and storage requirements through intelligent global coordination, the elasticity of computation and I/O, and the scheduling of storage resources at all levels of the storage hierarchy. We are developing a software-defined framework based on scalable monitoring and control principles, separating control and data paths and orchestrating key system components and applications through embedded control points.

The framework consists of the following new active main components:

- an *ad-hoc* parallel storage system, such as GekkoFS [18] and Hercules [14] reducing the pressure on the back-end parallel file system and improve checkpointing performance;
- malleability management will cost-effectively balance I/O and compute performance via dynamic scaling of application resources;
- an I/O scheduler [8] will offer end-to-end quality-of-service guarantees for the whole storage stack and reduce data movement. The orchestration of

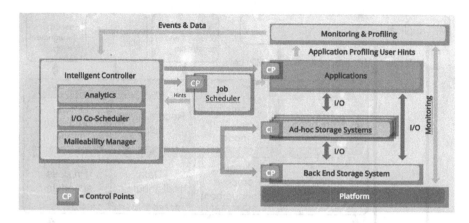

Fig. 1. ADMIRE architecture.

the entire system, the global monitoring, and performance profiling feed the intelligent controllers coordinating storage allocation and access through control points installed in these three new active components, the job scheduler, and the applications. Our software-only solution will offer quality-of-service (QoS), energy efficiency, and resilience. The approach proposed in the ADMIRE project enables I/O interference mitigation. This feature is enforced by a globally coordinated minimization of data transfers between storage tiers. Furthermore, the minimization is performed while conveying and enforcing end-to-end QoS needs.

– an Intelligent Controller that holistically coordinates with each other based on global monitoring information and application profiles through control points embedded in each of them.

Figure 1 shows the architectural blocks of the ADMIRE framework.

However, to efficiently balance the computational and storage I/O resources of the platform by combining malleability and I/O control mechanisms to enhance the execution of multiple applications is a challenging goal in HPC systems [13]. Therefore, in ADMIRE project, new strategies for improving the system performance are based on closer cooperation between the I/O software stack, the scheduler, and the running applications. To achieve those goals, we enhance the FlexMPI environment developed by UC3M [7] to cope with these challenges.

3   FlexMPI

FlexMPI is a library based on MPI whose primary goal is to provide malleability facilities for MPI-based applications. FlexMPI is implemented on top of the MPICH implementation. It makes it fully compatible with the MPI features and

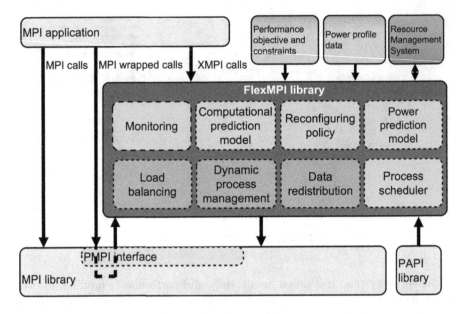

Fig. 2. FlexMPI architecture.

allows it to integrate with any existing MPI-based application easily. Currently, FlexMPI can be implemented with C/C++ and FORTRAN applications. The structure of FlexMPI includes several blocks (See Fig. 2) that provide four main functionalities: monitoring, load balancing (LB), dynamic process management, and data redistribution. FlexMPI also provides prediction features for computational needs, I/O behavior, and power prediction models. This work describes the four basic blocks that provide essential support for malleability.

The purpose of the *monitoring* block is to collect performance metrics for each parallel application process during its execution. The applications we target are iterative and alternate computation and communication phases. The computation phases are monitored using hardware counters (via PAPI [2]), and the communication routines are tracked by using the MPI profiling interface (PMPI), which allows profiling the communications without modifying the source code of the application. The implementation uses low-level PAPI interfaces to track the number of floating point operations, $FLOPs$, the real-time, $Treal$ (i.e. the wall-clock time), and the CPU time, $Tcpu$ (i.e. the time during which the processor is running in user mode).

The *dynamic process management* is responsible for assigning the unused computational resources (compute cores) to the newly executed process or to the ones already being executed when the number of processes has been changed through malleability. The dynamic process management determines how many processes have to be created or destroyed, and the Resource Manager is responsible for deciding, for each reconfiguration, which specific cores must be allocated or released.

The *load balancing* functionality receives as input the per-process values for the performance metrics measured via monitoring. When load imbalance is detected, the algorithm determines the new distribution of workload based on the per-process performance metrics. Although monitoring can be performed at every iteration, load balancing is only triggered every sampling interval-consisting of a fixed number of iterations-to reach a trade-off between the overhead of this operation and the performance gain related to it.

$$MFLOPS_i = \frac{FLOP_i}{Treal} \qquad (1)$$

The load balancing algorithm first computes the $MFLOPS$ that each process i has executed during the previous sampling interval. $MFLOPS_i$ is defined in Eq. 1 as the ratio between the number of floating point operations $FLOP_i$ and the actual execution time $Treal_i$ during a given sampling interval.

$$RCP_i = \frac{MFLOPS_i}{\sum_{I=0}^{p} MFLOPS_i} \qquad (2)$$

The fraction of the workload assigned to process i is computed in Eq. 2. It depends on the relative computing power (RCP_i) of a process i, which is computed as the $MFLOPS_i$ divided by the total MFLOPS for all of the processes. RCP estimates workload distribution on parallel applications since it provides a normalized value of a process's computational power relative to the whole system's computational power.

Figure 3 shows the integration of FlexMPI with the Intelligent Controller in ADMIRE framework. FlexMPI is linked with applications for exploiting computing and storage malleable features. As a result, the application's source code modifications are reduced. Four operations are introduced in the code: initialize FlexMPI, declare the redistributed data structures, define the malleable code section, and start or stop the application monitoring.

When FlexMPI is active, the application workload is redistributed when: (1) the application is executed in exclusive compute nodes but is unbalanced or (2) the application is executed in non-exclusive compute nodes, and long-term external load is detected. Note that short and isolated external workloads do not affect the application's overall performance and do not trigger the load balance feature.

In HPC applications, the data is usually distributed -rather than replicated-between processes, which requires redistribution to move the data between processes each time a load balance operation is carried out. FlexMPI includes a *data redistribution* functionality which handles both one-dimensional (e.g. vectors) and two-dimensional (e.g. matrices) data structures, which may be either dense or sparse. The developer must register each data structure, which will need to be redistributed due to load balance operations. The registering function (XMPI Register) receives as input the pointer to the data structure and the size of the data structure.

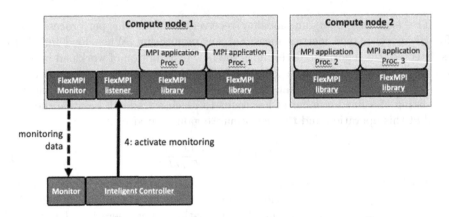

Fig. 3. FlexMPI integration with the Intelligent Controller.

Depending on domain decomposition, a Flex-MPI-enabled application leverages the provided data structure footprint, the number of elements, and the dimensions of rows and columns.

FlexMPI can manage several data structures when registered using the same type of domain decomposition.

Once the load balancing functionality has computed the RCP of each PE and the new workload distribution has been mapped to a data partition, the data redistribution functionality: (i) computes the range of data associated with the new workload partition of every process, and (ii) moves the data from the previous to the new processes.

`XMPI-Monitor-end` returns -on behalf of the data redistribution functionality- the new count and displacement for the new data mapping used by each process. MPI standard messages are used to move data between MPI processes efficiently.

4   A Malleability Use Case: WaComM++

The *Environment Application* workflow produces operational weather and marine forecasts and/or on-demand ad-hoc environmental simulations for scenarios and what-if analysis [9].

The *Environment Application* workflow can be seen in Fig. 4.

The computation starts when the initial and boundary conditions from NCEP Global Forecast System (GFS) are available for download. Once the GFS data has been downloaded, the computation workflow engine *DagOn-Star*[1] [10,16,17] performs data pre-processing, operation that is required by the Weather Research and Forecasting (WRF) numerical model engine. Finally, the results from WRF, both raw and a more processed and refined output, are

---

[1] https://github.com/dagonstar.

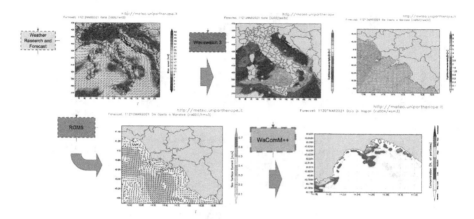

Fig. 4. Environmental application workflow.

moved into a high-performance accessible and available storage. The refined output is converted to be represented in the spatial domain (regular latitude and longitude), and diagnostic variables enrich it. Note that the results provided by WRF are also used for other models to predict marine and air quality in the evaluated regions.

WaComM++ (Water Community Model) is a pollutant transport and diffusion model that operates over the model outputs. In this case, the WRF model outputs feed the WaComM++ model alongside the Campania Region coastal pollution emission sources database.

WaComM++ is a Lagrangian model that simulates marine pollutants' transport and diffusion processes. WaComM++ is a model component of the operational model chain at the Center for Monitoring and Modelling Marine and Atmosphere applications (CMMMA)[2] of the University of Naples "Parthenope". The WaComM++ system can be used in different ways: (i) as an ex-ante decision-support tool, for example, to aid in selecting the best suitable areas for farming activity deployment; (ii) as an ex-post simulation tool for improving the management of offshore activities. WaComM++ supports three levels of hierarchical parallelization: (i) the distributed memory enforced by the use of the Message Passing Interface (MPI) library; (ii) the shared memory paradigm to leverage on the modern multicore architectures thanks to the OpenMP library; (iii) the multi-GPU computing implemented with the NVIDIA CUDA toolkit.

WaConM++ is characterized by a parallelization schema based on hierarchical and heterogeneous computation.

WaComM++ has been designed with hierarchical parallelism in mind. Nevertheless, some requirements have been strongly driven by the transport and diffusion Lagrangian model, for example, the need for data exchange using standard and well-known formats. For each time interval to simulate (i.e., one hour),

---

[2] https://meteo.uniparthenope.it.

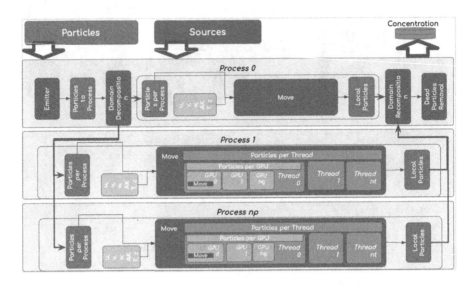

Fig. 5. The WaComM++ data-flow and parallelization schema.

the total number of particles is distributed between the available processors in an MPI distributed memory fashion. Each processor distributes its duty between the available threads leveraging OpenMP. If one or more CUDA-enabled GPUs are available, each thread partitions its particles' computational burden between the GPUs. The application has been designed to exploit a three level heterogeneous parallelization model supporting multiple CPUs, multi core CPUs and NVIDA CUDA general purpose GPUs (Fig. 5).

WaComM++ [11] algorithm is an evolution on the Lagrangian Assessment for Marine Pollution 3D (LAMP3D) algorithm [1]. This algorithm computes the pollutants and evaluates the water quality near the mussel farms. To increase the potential of LAMP3D, WaComM++ has optimized its internal algorithms, and some features, such as parallel-computing techniques in shared memory environments or checkpointing and restarting, have been included.

WaComM++ aims to predict the concentration of pollutants surrounding the mussels' farming areas, giving the expert a tool to estimate the potential risks to human health.

In the ADMIRE project, WaComM++ has been selected as a use case for testing the malleability features by integrating FlexMPI. This decision is motivated by means of WaComM++ because it supports distributed memory parallelization (MPI), and the main algorithm is iterative (note that FlexMPI is designed for iterative applications).

Figure 6 shows the integration of FlexMPI and WaComM++. In order to include malleability features in the source code, FlexMPI provides a set of function calls that have to be included by the developers. These functions wrap specific MPI function calls to configure the FlexMPI environment and expand or shrink the application processes. Algorithm 1 describes the WaComM++ ker-

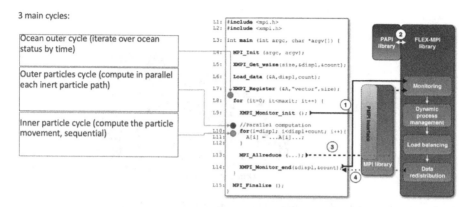

Fig. 6. Application co-design using FlexMPI.

nel iteration schema, including the code sections where the FlexMPI function calls should be placed -at the beginning and end of the main function and the beginning and end of the parallel loop-.

Algorithm 1 *WaComM++* kernel simplified algorithm.

1: $MPI\_Init()$
2: **while** $sim\_time < total\_time$ **do**
3:      $EMPI\_Monitor\_init()$
4:      **if** $rank == 0$ **then**
5:          $Generate\_new\_particles()$
6:          $Calculate\_displacements\_vcounts()$
7:      **end if**
8:      $MPI\_Broadcast(displacements, vcounts)$
9:      $MPI\_Scatter(particles)$
10:     **for all** $HCAs$ *in the Subnet* **do**
11:         $Compute\_particles()$
12:     **end for**
13:     $MPI\_Gather(particles)$
14:     **if** $rank == 0$ **then**
15:         $Remove\_died\_particles()$
16:         $Do\_checkpoint()$
17:     **end if**
18:     $sim\_time + +$
19:     $EMPI\_Monitor\_end()$
20: **end while**
21: $MPI\_Finalize()$

Figure 7 shows the behavior and the performance of a malleable execution of WaComM++ when the particles increase every iteration. Note that the computation will become a bottleneck if the number of processes keeps constant.

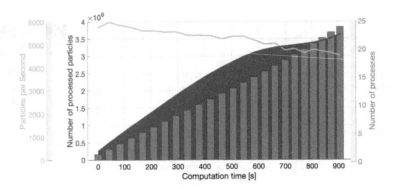

Fig. 7. Scenario with constant increasing load.

However, this problem can be avoided by expanding the number of processes in runtime when the load achieves a certain threshold. In this case, the computation becomes a bottleneck when the application has allocated the maximum number of resources the scheduler provides.

Figure 8 shows the behavior and the performance of another malleable execution of WaComM++. However, in this case, the algorithm focuses on those particles in a concrete region of the spatial domain. As the particles are constantly moving, the algorithm will compute only those within a range of longitudes and latitudes. So, in this case, the particles can increase and decrease every iteration. The most exciting characteristic of Fig. 8 is given by the line that shows the particles per second (in yellow) and the bars that show the number of processes (in orange). As can be seen, if the number of particles increases, FlexMPI expands the application processes to provide extra computation resources. However, if the number of particles decreases, FlexMPI shrinks the processes. FlexMPI includes load-balancing algorithms to expand and shrink the application processes trying to maintain the same computation load between the processes, achieving a good trade-off in terms of computation power *versus* resource utilization.

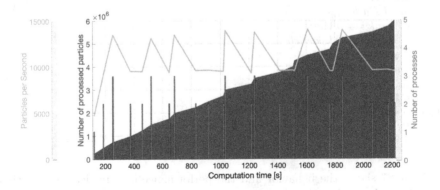

Fig. 8. Scenario with variable load.

5 Conclusions

This paper describes FlexMPI, an MPI extension that provides malleable capabilities to iterative SPMD MPI applications and is developed in the scope of the ADMIRE project. FlexMPI enables MPI applications to expand or shrink the application processes at runtime to adapt the application performance to the existing execution conditions. The results described in this paper demonstrate the computational malleability as a promising paradigm in HPC that could be fully exploited in GPU, cloud, and edge computing scenarios [4,15]. In this paper, the evaluation has been done using WaComM++ as a use case, a three-dimensional Lagrangian model that implements an evolution of the LAMP3D algorithm.

The experimental section shows two evaluation scenarios of WaComM++. The first is a scenario in which the particles (as well as the computational load) increase every iteration. In the second, the particles increase or decrease in every iteration, depending on their position in the spatial domain. Both use cases leverage FlexMPI to adapt the number of processes to the current workload depending on the number of existing particles. As a future work, in the scope of the ADMIRE project, we propose extending FlexMPI to provide compatibility with other programming languages, such as Python, and including MPI Sessions for managing the existing and newly created group processes. Furthermore, WaComM++ will be extended to support other ADMIRE components as the intelligent controller and the *ad-hoc* file system [3,6]. Finally, from the computational malleability perspective, WaComM++ will be tested in virtualized/remoted GPU environments [12] and real-world applications [5].

References

1. De Gaetano, P., Doglioli, A.M., Magaldi, M.G., Vassallo, P., Fabiano, M.: FOAM, a new simple benthic degradative module for the LAMP3D model: an application to a Mediterranean fish farm. Aquac. Res. **39**(11), 1229–1242 (2008)
2. Dongarra, J., London, K., Moore, S., Mucci, P., Terpstra, D.: Using PAPI for hardware performance monitoring on Linux systems. In: Conference on Linux Clusters: The HPC Revolution, vol. 5. Linux Clusters Institute (2001)
3. Duro, F.R., Blas, J.G., Carretero, J.: A hierarchical parallel storage system based on distributed memory for large scale systems. In: Proceedings of the 20th European MPI Users' Group Meeting, pp. 139–140 (2013)
4. Lapegna, M., Balzano, W., Meyer, N., Romano, D.: Clustering algorithms on low-power and high-performance devices for edge computing environments. Sensors **21**(16), 5395 (2021)
5. Marcellino, L., et al.: Using GPGPU accelerated interpolation algorithms for marine bathymetry processing with on-premises and cloud based computational resources. In: Wyrzykowski, R., Dongarra, J., Deelman, E., Karczewski, K. (eds.) PPAM 2017, Part II. LNCS, vol. 10778, pp. 14–24. Springer, Cham (2018). https://doi.org/10.1007/978-3-319-78054-2_2
6. Marozzo, F., Rodrigo Duro, F., Garcia Blas, J., Carretero, J., Talia, D., Trunfio, P.: A data-aware scheduling strategy for workflow execution in clouds. Concurrency Comput.: Pract. Experience **29**(24), e4229 (2017)

7. Martín, G., Marinescu, M.-C., Singh, D.E., Carretero, J.: FLEX-MPI: an MPI extension for supporting dynamic load balancing on heterogeneous non-dedicated systems. In: Wolf, F., Mohr, B., an Mey, D. (eds.) Euro-Par 2013. LNCS, vol. 8097, pp. 138–149. Springer, Heidelberg (2013). https://doi.org/10.1007/978-3-642-40047-6_16

8. Miranda, A., Jackson, A., Tocci, T., Panourgias, I., Nou, R.: NORNS: extending Slurm to support data-driven workflows through asynchronous data staging. In: 2019 IEEE International Conference on Cluster Computing (CLUSTER), pp. 1–12. IEEE (2019)

9. Montella, R., et al.: Using the face-it portal and workflow engine for operational food quality prediction and assessment: An application to mussel farms monitoring in the bay of Napoli, Italy. Futur. Gener. Comput. Syst. **110**, 453–467 (2020)

10. Montella, R., Di Luccio, D., Kosta, S.: DagOn*: executing direct acyclic graphs as parallel jobs on anything. In: 2018 IEEE/ACM Workflows in Support of Large-Scale Science (WORKS), pp. 64–73. IEEE (2018)

11. Montella, R., Di Luccio, D., Troiano, P., Riccio, A., Brizius, A., Foster, I.: WaComM: a parallel water quality community model for pollutant transport and dispersion operational predictions. In: 2016 12th International Conference on Signal-Image Technology & Internet-Based Systems (SITIS), pp. 717–724. IEEE (2016)

12. Montella, R., Giunta, G., Laccetti, G.: Virtualizing high-end GPGPUs on arm clusters for the next generation of high performance cloud computing. Clust. Comput. **17**(1), 139–152 (2014)

13. Panziera, J.P., et al.: Strategic research agenda 2017. Technical Report (2017)

14. Rodrigo Duro, F., Marozzo, F., Garcia Blas, J., Talia, D., Trunfio, P.: Exploiting in-memory storage for improving workflow executions in cloud platforms. J. Super-comput. **72**(11), 4069–4088 (2016). https://doi.org/10.1007/s11227-016-1678-y

15. Romano, D., Lapegna, M.: A GPU-parallel image coregistration algorithm for InSar processing at the edge. Sensors **21**(17), 5916 (2021)

16. Sánchez-Gallegos, D.D., Di Luccio, D., Gonzalez-Compean, J.L., Montella, R.: Internet of things orchestration using DaGon* workflow engine. In: 2019 IEEE 5th World Forum on Internet of Things (WF-IoT), pp. 95–100. IEEE (2019)

17. Sánchez-Gallegos, D.D., Di Luccio, D., Kosta, S., Gonzalez-Compean, J., Montella, R.: An efficient pattern-based approach for workflow supporting large-scale science: the DagOnStar experience. Futur. Gener. Comput. Syst. **122**, 187–203 (2021)

18. Vef, M.A., et al.: Gekkofs-a temporary distributed file system for HPC applications. In: 2018 IEEE International Conference on Cluster Computing (CLUSTER), pp. 319–324. IEEE (2018)

Algorithm and Software Overhead: A Theoretical Approach to Performance Portability

Valeria Mele[(✉)] [ID] and Giuliano Laccetti[ID]

University of Naples "Federico II", Naples, Italy
valeria.mele@unina.it

Abstract. In the last years, the *portability* term has enriched itself with new meanings: research communities are talking about how to measure the degree to which an application (or library, programming model, algorithm implementation, etc.) has become *"performance portable"*. The term *"performance portability"* has been informally used in computing communities to substantially refer to: (1) the ability to run one application across multiple hardware platforms; and (2) achieving some decent level of performance on these platforms [1,2]. Among the efforts related to the *"performance portability"* issue, we note the annual performance portability workshops organized by the US Department of Energy [3]. This article intends to add a new point of view to the performance portability issue, starting from a more theoretical point of view, that shows the convenience of splitting the proper algorithm from the emphoverhead, and exploring the different factors that introduce different kind of overhead. The paper explores the theoretical framework to get a definition of the execution time of a software but that definition is not the point. The aim is to show and understand the link between that execution time and the beginning of the design, to exploit what part of any program is really environment-sensitive and exclude from performance portability formulas everything is not going to change, as theoretically shown.

Keywords: parallel computing · performance portability · overhead · algorithms · software

1 Introduction

In the last years, the *portability* term has enriched itself with new meanings: research communities are talking about how to measure the degree to which an application (or library, programming model, algorithm implementation, etc.) has become *"performance portable"* [4]. The terms *"performance portability"* has been informally used in computing communities to substantially refer to: (1) the ability to run one application across multiple hardware platforms; and

(2) achieving some notional level of performance on these platforms [1]. Among the efforts related to the *"performance portability"* issue, we note the annual performance portability workshops organized by the US Department of Energy [3].

Notes from a meeting on the subject held in 2016 highlight the lack of a "universally accepted definition of performance portability", observing that "several attempts were made by various speakers to take a crack at it" [5]. How could so many researchers be said to be working towards a common goal, if they could not agree upon what it was? The attendees all ascribed importance to the term performance portability even if no precise meaning was agreed upon. Increasing microarchitectural diversity and specialization had created challenges to address in software, impacting the performance and portability of applications and the productivity of the programmers creating them. An ecosystem was beginning to develop around frameworks promising to improve performance portability and maintainability [6]. In the absence of precise definitions, subjectivity prevailed, community has made significant progress towards shared terminology, and we are closer to a universally adopted methodology for assessing performance portability and programmer productivity than ever before [7], but in our opinion they are still very vague concepts, too difficult to define first that to measure.

This article intends to add a new contribute to the performance portability issue, starting from a more theoretical point of view, that shows the convenience of splitting the proper algorithm characteristics from the *overhead*, and exploring the different factors that introduce different kinds of overhead. The aim is to show and understand the link between that execution time and the beginning of the design, to exploit what part of any program is really environment-sensitive, suggesting to exclude from performance portability formulas - that generally involves the execution time of the software on a given hardware - everything that is not going to change, as theoretically shown.

The performance evaluation framework we start from is the one described in [8–12] and here briefly described in the first section to get the definition we need. In [9] authors also show examples of application of the framework to get parameters for a matrix-matrix multiply problem.

The framework is modular and can be as complicated as we want to match hybrid and/or heterogeneous parallel architectures. The increasing need for parallel and scalable software, ready to exploit the new exascale architectures, leads to the development of many performance models, mainly based on architecture features [13–17] or especially made for choosen algorithm classes [18–20]. The model we present here is mainly focused on the dependencies among the computational tasks of the algorithm and is meant to be as general as possible.

2   The Performance Evaluation Framework

Starting from some preliminary concepts about a new performance evaluation framework described in a conference paper [8], we summarize a performance model useful to estimate the execution time of an algorithm on a specific piece of hardware, when an actual measurement is not an option (e.g. unavailability of hardware). That framework allows to choose a level of abstraction for problem decomposition and algorithm description which determines the level of granularity in the performance analysis. A set of parameters are used both to describe the problem and to compute cost and overhead of the algorithm, starting from the problem decomposition.

In that paper, the authors address basic structural features of algorithms which are dictated by data and operator dependencies [8–10,21]: by giving the key definition of *dependency relation* on a set, they consider the set of all computational problems Γ and any element $B_N \in \Gamma$ where N is the input data size, called the *problem size*.

2.1 Decomposition of a Problem

Any B_N can always be decomposed in at least one finite set of other computational problems, called *decomposition of B_N*. Given a decomposition in k sub-problems B_{N_i}, called D_k, and taking into account the dependencies among such sub-problems, they build a *dependency matrix* or *decomposition matrix*[1] $\mathcal{M}_{D_k}$ where in each row we put sub-problems independent of one another, but dependent on those in the previous rows.

Given D_k, the number of column of $\mathcal{M}_{D_k}$, say c_{D_k}, is the *concurrency degree* of B_N, and its number of rows, say r_{D_k}, is the *dependency degree* of B_N, according to the actual decomposition, so that the dependency degree measures the amount of dependencies induced by the chosen decomposition. Hence, number and size of sub-problems determine the granularity of such decomposition. By choosing a proper granularity, we can modulate the level of detail for the performance analysis of an algorithm with this approach. Therefore, the decomposition matrix allows us to identify some properties of the algorithm design, such as the concurrency available in a problem when we choose a decomposition rather than another.

2.2 Algorithm

The next step is to assign the identified sub-problems to the computing machine. Let $\mathcal{M}_P$ be a computing machine equipped with $P \geq 1$ processing elements with specific logical-operational capabilities[2] called computing operators of $\mathcal{M}_P$, and collected in the set without repetitions $Cop_{\mathcal{M}_P} = \{I^j\}_{j \in [0,q-1]}$, where $q \in \mathbb{N}$, characterizes logical-operational capabilities of the machine $\mathcal{M}_P$.

In [8] the definition of *algorithm* is given as the partially ordered set of k operators $A_{k,P}$, with not necessarily distinct elements, where each operator solves a sub-problem in the decomposition D_k. Operators of $A_{k,P}$ inherit the

---

[1] *Decomposition matrix* is the name we preferred in this work, but in [8] it is referred as *dependency matrix*.

[2] These can be basic operations (arithmetic,...), special functions evaluations (sin, cos, ...), solvers (integrals, equations system, non-linear equations...).

dependencies existing between sub-problems in D_k, but not the independences, e.g. two operators may depend on the availability of computing units in $\mathcal{M}_P$ during their executions [21]. Therefore, each algorithm is related to a problem decomposition, and each problem decomposition can be related to more than one algorithm, inducing an equivalence relationship among algorithms used to the same problem. As a consequence, all the algorithms are split in *equivalence classes* based on the problem decomposition they come from. They are also characterized by a unique complexity value, where the definition for *complexity* is the cardinality of the decomposition:

Definition 1 (Complexity). *The cardinality of $A_{k,P}$ is called complexity of $A_{k,P}$. It is denoted as $C(A_{k,P})$. That is $C(A_{k,P}) := card(A_{k,P}) = k$.*

Defining a second *dependency relation* between operators in an algorithm, the so-called *execution matrix* $\mathcal{E}_{k,P}$ of order $r_\mathcal{E} \times P$ can be defined, where in each row we put operators independent of one another and dependent on those in the previous rows. These dependencies refer to relations among computations which need to be satisfied in order to compute the problem solution correctly. Inside an equivalence class, the algorithm which solves a problem according to a decomposition and which is executed on a machine with just one processor is a *sequential algorithm* and its execution matrix has just one column, since $P = 1$.

In [8] other definitions and results are given, under the strong hypothesis that all the operators in considered algorithms have the same execution time t_{calc}, but there is the general cases, taking into account algorithms that consist of different steps, each with specific computing characteristics.

In both the cases the number of rows $r_\mathcal{E}$ of $\mathcal{E}_{k,P}$ is directly related to the execution time of the algorithm executed with P processing units. We will see that the execution matrix size is related to the algorithm *cost*, and, in case of zero elements in the matrix, to the algorithm *overhead*.

Let's associate execution time t_i (measured, for instance, in seconds) to each $I^i \in Cop_{\mathcal{M}_P}$. If $I^i \equiv \varnothing$, we set $t_\varnothing = 0$.

Let t_{calc} be the execution time for one floating-point operation that here is considered the time unit. We assume that[3] all the operators have the same execution time t_{calc}[4] in order to define:

Definition 2 (Execution time). *Given the algorithms $A_{k,P}$ executed with P computing units, the quantity*

$$T(A_{k,P}) := r_{\mathcal{E}_{k,P}} \cdot t \qquad (1)$$

is called execution time of $A_{k,P}$.

Given the well known general definition of Speed Up [22] as the ratio between the execution times of a sequential algorithm and a parallel one, authors in [8] specify the Speed Up for algorithms in the same equivalence class,

---

[3] For the general case, look at [12].
[4] This assumption is necessary to compare two algorithms.

Definition 3 (Speed Up). *Given the algorithms $A_{k,P}$ executed with P computing units, the ratio*

$$S(A_{k,P}) := \frac{k}{r_{\mathcal{E}_{k,P}}} \tag{2}$$

is called Speed Up of $A_{k,P}$ in its equivalence class.

Notice that, according to Definition 1, k is the unique complexity value characterizing the algorithms class, proportional to the execution time of the sequential algorithm in the class.

Given two different decompositions D_{k_i} and D_{k_j}, with $k_j \neq k_i$, given two different machines with two different number of processors $P_1 = 1$ and $P > 1$, for the two corresponding algorithms, $A_{k_j,P}$ and $A_{k_i,1}$ we define the *General Speed Up* of the parallel one respect to the sequential one, as the product of the *Scale Up* between the two decompositions[5] and the classical speed up of the parallel one.

Definition 4 (General Speed Up). *The ratio*

$$GS(A_{k_j,P}, A_{k_i,1}) := SC(D_{k_i}, D_{k_j}) \cdot S(A_{k_j,P}) = \frac{k_i}{k_j} \cdot \frac{k_j}{r_{\mathcal{E}_{A_{k_j,P}}}} = \frac{r_{\mathcal{E}_{A_{k_i,1}}}}{r_{\mathcal{E}_{A_{k_j,P}}}} \tag{3}$$

is called General Speed Up of $A_{k_j,P}$ respect to $A_{k_i,1}$.

Note that the ideal value of the General Speed Up is not limited by the number of processing units P.

2.3   Algorithm Overhead

Let Q denote the cost of $A_{k,P}$. The cost is defined as the product of the execution time and the number of processors utilized [22]. In this mathematical settings it holds that

Proposition 1. *The cost Q can be written as*

$$Q(A_{k,P}) = c_{\mathcal{E}_{k,P}} \cdot r_{\mathcal{E}_{k,P}} \cdot t. \tag{4}$$

Notice that, if $c_{\mathcal{E}_{k,P}} = 1$, the cost is the same of the execution time.

The definition of *overhead* of $A_{k,P}$ that we found in [8] is the first one we deal with in this article: it is intended as the total time spent by all the processing elements waiting for other processing elements to complete their tasks. Notice that is doesn't depend on the hardware/software environment, but for the number of computing unit of the machine.

---

[5] Scale Up is defined in [8] as the ratio $SC(D_{k_i}, D_{k_j}) := \frac{k_i}{k_j}$ and it measures the difference between the two algorithm respect to the number of operations they perform to solve the same problem.

Definition 5 *(Algorithm Overhead). Given the algorithms $A_{k,P}$ executed with P computing units, the quantity*

$$Oh(A_{k,P}) := (Q(A_{k,P}) - k) \cdot t = \left(c_{\mathcal{E}_{k,P}} \cdot r_{\mathcal{E}_{k,P}} - C(A_{k,P})\right) \cdot t \qquad (5)$$

is called overhead of $A_{k,P}$.

Since the cost of an algorithm is related to the size of the execution matrix, they also show that

Theorem 1. *It holds*

$$Oh(A_{k,P}) \geq 0. \qquad (6)$$

It follows that the overhead is minimum when the matrix has zero empty elements.

In [12] authors remarks that the so-defined overhead depends directly on the operators "time weight". Since, they are here seen as black boxes with their own execution time, we don't need to know the way they work, and the weight could be different on different machines. However, given an operator and a particular execution machine, the weight is to be considered as fixed. Notice that the operator itself may contain other kind of "overhead" (for example memory access overhead), that should be treated separately, in a modular fashion, in order to understand which one introduces it more and which one can be substituted with a more efficient one. This can also suggest to change the problem decomposition, if needed.

Let $Ef(A_{k,P}) := \frac{S(A_{k,P})}{P}$ be the efficiency of $A_{k,P}$ where $P \geq 1$. It is also proved that it is inversely proportional to the size of the execution matrix $\mathcal{E}_{k,P}$.

Theorem 2. *It holds that*

$$Ef(A_{k,P}) = \frac{k}{c_{\mathcal{E}_{k,P}} \cdot r_{\mathcal{E}_{k,P}}}. \qquad (7)$$

It is easy to verify that it's always $Ef(A_{k,P}) \leq 1$ and we get the maximum value of efficiency when the overhead is minimum.

2.4   Memory and Communication

From now on, we consider memory accesses performed by an algorithm and we assume, for simplicity, that to each access corresponds one read/write of a single data. Moreover, we assume that computations and memory accesses are not performed simultaneously, instead they depend each other[6].

Given the set of elementary operators of $\mathcal{M}_P$ we introduce memory access operators corresponding to the memory access (read $r(\cdot)$/write $w(\cdot)$) of processing elements of $\mathcal{M}_P$ and the set

$$OA_{\mathcal{M}_P} = \{r(\cdot), w(\cdot)\}$$

Now we can define

---

[6] This is an initial, not realistic, assumption.

Definition 6 *(**Memory Accesses set**). The ordered set (whose elements should not be different) of accesses operators of $\mathcal{M}_P$*

$$AC_{k,P} = \{oa_0(\cdot), oa_1(\cdot), \ldots oa_k(\cdot)\}$$

where

$$oa_i(\cdot) \in OA_{\mathcal{M}_P}$$

is called memory accesses set *of the algorithm $A_{k,P}$. Moreover we consider the surjective correspondence*

$$\bar{\gamma} : oa_i(\cdot) \in OA_{\mathcal{M}_P} \longleftrightarrow I_i^{j_i} \in A_{k,P}. \tag{8}$$

Note that $card(AC_{k,P}) \geq card(A_{k,P}) = k$.

Let us remind that $\beta_{i_j,\mathcal{E}_{k,P}}$ is the "time weight" of each considered operator (seen as a working black box), according to the chosen decomposition and respect to the execution time unit t_{calc}, but let us assume from now on, that they are all equal to 1, that is all the computing operators have the same execution time t_{calc}[7].

Suppose that[8]

- memory hierarchy has $L \geq 2$ levels[9],
- the data type is fixed
- we can access no more than nd data of the fixed type in the (mean) memory access time unit at level l t_{mem}^l (*bandwidth*)
- $t_{mem}^l = t_{calc} \cdot \delta^l$, with $\delta \geq 1$ and $0 \leq l < L$ is a level of the memory hierarchy

We will say that an operator needs *meanly* time t_{mem} to get a data of the fixed type from the memory hierarchy on the given machine.

Then we say that two operators $oa_i \in AC_{k,P}$ and $oa_j \in AC_{k,P}$ are *independent* from each other if they correspond (according to $\bar{\gamma}$) to independent operators in $A_{k,P}$ or they correspond to the same operator in $I_i^{j_i} \in A_{k,P}$ but are related to different data and they must be executed both before or after $I_i^{j_i}$. In this case we write $oa_i \nleftarrow oa_j$ and $oa_j \nleftarrow oa_i$, or $oa_i \nleftrightarrow oa_j$.

Definition 7 *(**Memory Matrix**). Given the algorithm $A_{k,P}$, its execution matrices $\mathcal{E}_{k,P}$ and its memory accesses set $AC_{k,P}$, we define the* memory matrix *of $A_{k,P}$ as $AM_{k,P,nd}$ defined in $AC_{k,P}$ of order $r_{AM} \times c_{AM}$, with $c_{AM} = nd$[10], such that $\forall i \in [0, r_{AM} - 1], j \in [0, c_{AM} - 1]$:*

- *its elements $ac_{i,j} \equiv oa_k \in AC_{k,P}$ or $ac_{i,j} = \varnothing$;*

---

[7] There is no loss of generality because any operator can be rewritten as a number of elementary operators with execution time t_{calc}.

[8] This is a semplified and very general logical description of a memory hierarchy behavior useful to the aim of the framework. Of course it could be adapted to an actual architecture, but the following definitions hold the same.

[9] Level 0 is the fastest one.

[10] In general $c_{AM} \leq nd$, but we can assume $c_{AM} = nd$ without loss of generality.

- $\forall j \in [0, c_{AM} - 1],\quad \forall k \in [0, c_{AM} - 1],\quad \forall i \in [0, r_{AM} - 1]$ it is $ac_{0,j} \nleftrightarrow ac_{i,k}$
- $\exists q \in [0, c_{AM} - 1]$ such that $ac_{i,j} \leftarrow ac_{i-1,q} \forall j \in [0, c_{AM} - 1]$
- $\forall i \in [1, r_{AM} - 1], j \in [0, c_{AM} - 1], k \in [0, c_{AM} - 1]\quad ac_{i,j} \leftrightarrow ac_{i,k}$

Basically the *memory matrix* is built in the same way of the decomposition and execution matrices, possibly much greater of the execution matrix if the access operator we consider moves a single data and the algorithm is data-driven.

Definition 8 (Memory Time). *Algorithm* $A_{k,P}$, *with memory matrix* $AM_{k,P,nd}$, *has memory access time:*

$$T_M(A_{k,P}, nd) = r_{AM} \cdot t_{mem} \tag{9}$$

where t_{mem} *is the (mean) memory access time unit in the memory hierarchy.*

Let now consider the *communication matrix* $CM_{k,P}$ of order $r_{CM} \times c_{CM}$ where $c_{CM} \leq P$, defined in $AC_{k,P}$ considering a communication like the $(L + 1)-th$ level of the memory hierarchy (the lowest), with an unitary communication time $t_{mem}^L = t_{comm}$ [23], and built analogously to the *memory matrix*. Then we can define

Definition 9 (Communication Time). *Be the algorithm* $A_{k,P}$ *and* $T_M(A_{k,P}, nd)$ *its memory access time, we define the* communication time *as*

$$T_{COMM}(A_{k,P}, nd) = r_{CM} \cdot t_{comm} \tag{10}$$

2.5   Software Execution Time

Consider that memory access, communication and computation can be performed partially in parallel. This means that we need to build a new matrix

Definition 10 (Global Matrix). *The* global matrix *of the software related to the* $A_{k,P}$ *algorithm, of order* $r_{global} \times c_{global}$ *with* $c_{global} \leq c_E + nd + c_{CM}$ *columns, is such that* $\forall i \in [0, r_{global} - 1], j \in [0, c_{global} - 1]$:

- *its elements* $el_{i,j} \equiv oa_k \in AC_{k,P}$ *or* $el_{i,j} \equiv I^j \in Cop_{\mathcal{M}_P}$ *or* $el_{i,j} = \varnothing$;
- $\forall j \in [0, c_{global} - 1],\quad \forall k \in [0, c_{global} - 1],\quad \forall i \in [0, r_{global} - 1]$ it is $el_{0,j} \nleftrightarrow el_{i,k}$
- $\exists q \in [0, c_{global}^j - 1]$ such that $el_{i,j} \leftarrow el_{i-1,q} \forall j \in [0, c_{global} - 1]$
- $\forall i \in [1, r_{global} - 1], j \in [0, c_{global} - 1], k \in [0, c_{global} - 1]\quad el_{i,j} \leftrightarrow el_{i,k}$

The shape of the *global matrix* does not depend only on the number of rows and columns of the three matrices, because we know that their rows have different "weights": each row has a different weight according to the maximum weight of its elements. Several rows of $\mathcal{E}_{k,P}$ can correspond to one row of $AM_{k,P,nd}$ or $CM_{k,P}$ and several rows of $AM_{k,P,nd}$ can correspond to one row of $CM_{k,P}$.

Definition 11 *(Global i-th row Execution Time).* *The* global i-th row execution time *is defined as*

$$
Tg_{SW}^i(A_{k,P}, nd) = \begin{cases} t_{comm} & \textit{if the i-th row includes a comm. op.} \\ t_{mem} & \textit{if the i-th row includes a mem. op. and no (new) comm.} \\ t_{calc} & \textit{if there isn't any mem. or comm. op.} \end{cases}
$$

$$(11)$$

Then we can define at the end

Definition 12 *(Global Software Execution Time).* *The* global software execution time *is defined as*

$$
Tg_{SW}(A_{k,P}, nd) = \sum_{i=0}^{r_{global}-1} Tg_{SW}^i(A_{k,P}, nd).
$$

$$(12)$$

3   Performance Portability

It is clear from this theoretical description that the most of a good design is portable everywhere. What a programmer have to deal with is

- Avoiding communications [4, 25–27] to keep the communication matrix as short as possible
- Avoiding to access the memory to keep the memory matrix as short as possible
- Work with the principle of locality in mind to keep t_{mem} as lower as possible [28]
- Decompose the problem keeping the concurrency degree as higher as possible
- Coding minimizing the algorithm overhead

    Parameters that can help are

- *Computational Intensity* of the software (see [11, 24]): the number of operations per memory accesses. It measures how intensely $A_{k,P}$ computes with data, once it has been received, and is defined as the ratio

$$
C_I(SW) = \frac{r_E}{\sum_{l\,=\,0}^{L-1} r_{AM}^l} \geq 1.
$$

- *Communication Intensity* of the software (see [11]): the number of communication per operations. It measures how intensely $A_{k,P}$ needs to communicate to compute the solution, and is defined as the ratio

$$
Com_I(SW) = \frac{r_{CM}}{r_E}
$$

Now, we want to distinguish two kind of *software overhead*:

- *Memory Overhead*: the ratio $Oh_{MEM} = \frac{t_{mem}}{t_{calc}}$ describing how much slower[11] than computing the access to a level of memory is, and

---

[11] Meanly.

– *Communication Overhead*: the ratio $Oh_{COMM} = \frac{t_{comm}}{t_{calc}}$ describing how much slower[12] than computing the communication of a single data is.

Oh^l_{MEM} and Oh_{COMM} are the characteristic of the hardware/software environment that we need to know once we have build the *global software execution matrix*, and they are the only two parameters we really need to compare each time we move the algorithm from an environment to another one, in order to estimate the actual performance.

They do not depend on the algorithm or the application we developed, and this estimation are not portable.

4   Conclusions

The paper explores the theoretical framework to get a definition of the execution time of a software but that definition is not the point, of course: moreover, it is easy to show that the definition is a rewriting of other well known formulas [21,22], so we don't discuss the "execution time prediction" and keep the hypothesis about the machine very general, even if the framework is modular and can be as complicated as we want to match hybrid and/or heterogeneous parallel architectures[13]. The aim of the description we make in the previous sections is to show and understand the link between that execution time and the beginning of the design, or the decomposition of the problem. The parameters we exploit are useful to understand the characteristics of an algorithm and the software we build from it. Basically, our point is that the key for a *good* performance portability is in the decomposition. We notice that today the discussions about performance portability go so far as to suggest to loose performance as long as it is portable: is this something that can have sense in HPC field? This is the question. Of course, a good algorithm and software design means a lack of productivity in many cases, because it needs many hours of coding and lots of trials, so the answer can be that the community looks for a portability solution, but we believe that a strong theoretical background about decomposition, performance parameters, and modular parallel design can be the most helpful tool for programmers to improve the performance portability of their application, or at least what is possible to port of their performance.

References

1. Pennycook, S.J., Sewall, J.D., Lee, V.W.: Implications of a metric for performance portability. Future Gener. Comput. Syst. **92**, 947–958 (2017). https://doi.org/10.1016/j.future.2017.08.007

---

[12] Meanly.
[13] For example: in case of an algorithm like the one in [13], where the architecture is a heterogeneous GPU and Multicore based system, we can build different matrices for different parts of the algorithm.

2. Kwack, J., et al.: Evaluating performance portability of HPC applications and benchmarks across diverse HPC architectures. Exascale Computing Project (ECP) Webinar. https://www.exascaleproject.org/event/performance-portability-evaluation/. Accessed 20 May 2020
3. DOE centres of excellence performance portability meeting: post-meeting report technical report LLNL-TR-700962. Lawrence Livermore National Laboratory, Livermore (2016). https://asc.llnl.gov/sites/asc/files/2020-09/COE-PP-Meeting-2016-FinalReport_0.pdf
4. Carracciuolo, L., Mele, V., Szustak, L.: About the granularity portability of block-based Krylov methods in heterogeneous computing environments. Concurr. Comput. Pract. Exp. **33**(4), e6008 (2021). https://doi.org/10.1002/cpe.6008
5. Neely, J.R.: DOE centers of excellence performance portability meeting. Technical report LLNL-TR-700962, 4. Lawrence Livermore National Laboratory (2016). https://doi.org/10.2172/1332474
6. Edwards, H.C., Trott, C.R., Sunderland, D.: Kokkos: enabling manycore performance portability through polymorphic memory access patterns. J. Parallel Distrib. Comput. **74**(12), 3202–3216 (2014). https://doi.org/10.1016/j.jpdc.2014.07.003
7. Pennycook, J., Sewall, J., Jacobsen, D.W., Deakin, T., McIntosh-Smith, S.N.: Navigating performance, portability and productivity. Comput. Sci. Eng. **23**(5), 28–38 (2021). https://doi.org/10.1109/MCSE.2021.3097276
8. Mele, V., Romano, D., Constantinescu, E.M., Carracciuolo, L., D'Amore, L.: Performance evaluation for a PETSc parallel-in-time solver based on the MGRIT algorithm. In: Mencagli, G., et al. (eds.) Euro-Par 2018. LNCS, vol. 11339, pp. 716–728. Springer, Cham (2019). https://doi.org/10.1007/978-3-030-10549-5_56
9. D'Amore, L., Mele, V., Laccetti, G., Murli, A.: Mathematical approach to the performance evaluation of matrix multiply algorithm. In: Wyrzykowski, R., Deelman, E., Dongarra, J., Karczewski, K., Kitowski, J., Wiatr, K. (eds.) PPAM 2015. LNCS, vol. 9574, pp. 25–34. Springer, Cham (2016). https://doi.org/10.1007/978-3-319-32152-3_3
10. Mele, V., Constantinescu, E.M., Carracciuolo, L., D'amore, L.: A PETSc parallel-in-time solver based on MGRIT algorithm. Concurr. Comput. Pract. Exp. **30**(24), e4928 (2018). https://doi.org/10.1002/cpe.4928
11. D'Amore, L., Mel, V., Romano, D., Laccetti, G.: Multilevel algebraic approach for performance analysis of parallel algorithms. Comput. Inform. **38**(4), 817–850 (2019). https://doi.org/10.31577/cai_2019_4_817
12. Romano, D., Lapegna, M., Mele, V., Laccetti, G.: Designing a GPU-parallel algorithm for raw SAR data compression: a focus on parallel performance estimation. Future Gener. Comput. Syst. **112**(6), 695–708 (2020). https://doi.org/10.1016/j.future.2020.06.027
13. Laccetti, G., Lapegna, M., Mele, V., Romano, D.: A study on adaptive algorithms for numerical quadrature on heterogeneous GPU and multicore based systems. In: Wyrzykowski, R., Dongarra, J., Karczewski, K., Waśniewski, J. (eds.) PPAM 2013. LNCS, vol. 8384, pp. 704–713. Springer, Heidelberg (2014). https://doi.org/10.1007/978-3-642-55224-3_66
14. Laccetti, G., Lapegna, M., Mele, V.: A loosely coordinated model for heap-based priority queues in multicore environments. Int. J. Parallel Prog. **44**(4), 901–921 (2015). https://doi.org/10.1007/s10766-015-0398-x
15. Laccetti, G., Lapegna, M., Mele, V., Montella, R.: An adaptive algorithm for high-dimensional integrals on heterogeneous CPU-GPU systems. Concurr. Comput. Pract. Exp. **31**(19), e4945 (2019). https://doi.org/10.1002/cpe.4945

16. Montella, R., Giunta, G., Laccetti, G.: Virtualizing high-end GPGPUs on ARM clusters for the next generation of high performance cloud computing. Cluster Comput. **17**(1), 139–152 (2014). https://doi.org/10.1007/s10586-013-0341-0

17. Marcellino, L., et al.: Using GPGPU accelerated interpolation algorithms for marine bathymetry processing with on-premises and cloud based computational resources. In: Wyrzykowski, R., Dongarra, J., Deelman, E., Karczewski, K. (eds.) PPAM 2017. LNCS, vol. 10778, pp. 14–24. Springer, Cham (2018). https://doi.org/10.1007/978-3-319-78054-2_2

18. D'Amore, L., Campagna, R., Mele, V., Murli, A., Rizzardi, M.: ReLaTIve. An Ansi C90 software package for the Real Laplace Transform Inversion. Numerical Algorithms **63**(1), 187–211 (2013). https://doi.org/10.1007/s11075-012-9636-0

19. D'Amore, L., Campagna, R., Mele, V., Murli, A.: Algorithm 946. ReLIADiff. An C++ software package for real Laplace transform inversion based on automatic differentiation. ACM Trans. Math. Softw. **40**(4), 31:1–31:20 (2014). Article 31. https://doi.org/10.1145/2616971

20. D'Amore, L., Mele, V., Campagna, R.: Quality assurance of Gaver's formula for multi-precision Laplace transform inversion in real case. Inverse Probl. Sci. Eng. **26**(4), 553–580 (2018). https://doi.org/10.1080/17415977.2017.1322963

21. Tjaden. G.S., Flynn. M.J.: Detection and parallel execution of independent instructions. IEEE Trans. Comput. **C-19**(10), 889–895 (1970). https://doi.org/10.1109/T-C.1970.222795

22. Flatt, H.P., Kennedy, K.: Performance of parallel processors. Parallel Comput. **12**(1), 1–20 (1989). https://doi.org/10.1016/0167-8191(89)90003-3

23. Maddalena, L., Petrosino, A., Laccetti, G.: A fusion-based approach to digital movie restoration. Pattern Recogn. **42**(7), 1485–1495 (2009). https://doi.org/10.1016/j.patcog.2008.10.026

24. Hockney, R.W.: The Science of Computer Benchmarking. SIAM (1996)

25. Ballard, G., Demmel, J., Knight, N.: Avoiding communication in successive band reduction. ACM Trans. Parallel Comput. **1**(2), 37 (2015). Article 11. https://doi.org/10.1145/2686877

26. Koanantakool, P., et al.: Communication-avoiding parallel sparse-dense matrix-matrix multiplication. In: IEEE International Parallel and Distributed Processing Symposium (IPDPS), pp. 842–853 (2016). https://doi.org/10.1109/IPDPS.2016.117

27. Sao, P., Kannan, R., Li, X.S., Vuduc, R.: A communication-avoiding 3D sparse triangular solver. In: Proceedings of the ACM International Conference on Supercomputing (ICS 2019), pp. 127–137. Association for Computing Machinery, New York (2019). https://doi.org/10.1145/3330345.3330357

28. Kennedy, K., McKinley, K.S.: Optimizing for parallelism and data locality. In: Proceedings of the 6th International Conference on Supercomputing (ICS 1992), pp. 323–334. Association for Computing Machinery, New York (1992). https://doi.org/10.1145/143369.143427

Benchmarking a High Performance Computing Heterogeneous Cluster

Luisa Carracciuolo[1]([✉]) [ID], Davide Bottalico[2,3] [ID], Davide Michelino[2,3] [ID], Gianluca Sabella[2] [ID], and Bernardino Spisso[3] [ID]

[1] CNR - National Research Council, Rome, Italy
luisa.carracciuolo@cnr.it
[2] University of Naples Federico II, Naples, Italy
[3] INFN - National Institute for Nuclear Physics, Rome, Italy

Abstract. The paper describes the results of some benchmarking tests aimed to verify and validate all the solutions implemented during the deployment of a HPC heterogeneous resource acquired by the data center of the University of Naples "Federico II" thanks to the funds of the IBiSCo (Infrastructure for Big data and Scientific COmputing) Italian National Project. The first set of benchmarks evaluates how the network interconnection technologies affect the inter- and intra-node communications of GP-GPU workloads. The second set evaluates the performance of the Lustre parallel file system to ensure an efficient environment for data-intensive applications. The tests, especially those that analyze the lower level of the middleware (micro-benchmarks), seem to confirm the ability of the resource to guarantee the expected performance.

Keywords: Benchmarking · High Performance Computing · Heterogeneous Computing · GP-GPU · InfiniBand · NVLink · Lustre · CUDA · RDMA · UCX · MPI

1 Introduction

In the first half of the 1990s, Thomas Sterling and Donald Becker built a cluster of networked computers, called *Beowulf* [35], as an alternative to large supercomputers. At the time, their idea of providing *"Commodity Off The Shelf (COTS)"* based systems has been a great success. This idea is still valid and can inspire the realization of HPC computing systems, whose computational power is far from that of the most powerful computers in the world, but whose architecture is already compliant to incoming exascale era systems (e.g., see The Exascale Computing Project (ECP) of U.S. Department of Energy [32]). Most likely, these systems will respond to the following description: multi-node systems, connected by high performance networks, where each node will have a high level of internal parallelism which will be also made available by technologies such as NVIDIA®and Intel®Xe GPUs.

R. Wyrzykowski et al. (Eds.): PPAM 2022, LNCS 13827, pp. 101–114, 2023.
https://doi.org/10.1007/978-3-031-30445-3_9

In such context, the data center of the University of Naples "Federico II" acquired, thanks to the IBiSCo (Infrastructure for Big data and Scientific COmputing) project funds [28], a heterogeneous computational resource [2]. The use of heterogeneous features aims to ensure the best use of resources for different scenarios applications, such as distributed memory computing, GP-GPU (General-Purpose computing on Graphics Processing Units) accelerated workloads and their combinations (e.g., see [3,4,6,7,10]).

In the context of High Performance Computing, it is a common practice to evaluate performance (in terms of speedup, throughput, I/O speed, etc.) as a response to the HPC workload [17]. For this purpose, there are different suites of benchmarks, among the main ones:

- The Standard Performance Evaluation Corporation (SPEC) [31] is a consortium whose goals are to provide the industry with performance measurement tools since 1994. The development of the benchmark suites includes tools to analyze all the components of computing systems: from processors to compilers, from interconnects to run-time libraries. In the context of HPC systems can be considered: the SPECmpi for evaluating MPI-parallel performance across a wide range of cluster and SMP hardware emphasizing the performance of the type of computer processor, the number of computer processors, the communication interconnect, and the shared file system. The SPEChpc provides a set of application benchmark suites using a comprehensive measure of real-world performance offering well-selected science and engineering codes that are representative of HPC workloads.
- The HPC Challenge (HPCC) benchmark suite [15] was developed to provide a set of standardized hardware probes based on commonly occurring computational software kernels such as some parallel BLAS operations [1] as well as tools to analyze communications performance, attempting to span from high to low-level components of an HPC system.
- The CORAL Benchmarks: CORAL is a U.S. Department of Energy (DOE) project that will culminate in three ultra-high performance supercomputers at Lawrence Livermore, Oak Ridge, and Argonne national laboratories. In such context, a suite of benchmarks was developed to evaluate performances on supercomputers deployed during the project [8]. CORAL Benchmark categories represent DOE Workloads and among them should be considered: the Throughput Benchmarks representing full applications; The Skeleton Benchmarks investigating various platform characteristics including network performance, threading overheads, I/O, memory, system software, and programming models.

The benchmarks described above use one of three possible strategies: high-level, low-level, and hybrid. In the first case, the benchmarks evaluate performance by testing the application-level components; in the second case, they test

---

[1] The BLAS (Basic Linear Algebra Subprograms) are routines that provide optimized standard building blocks for performing basic vector and matrix operations. Some vendors supply its optimized implementation of the BLAS.

low-level system functions. The strategy we use is *"hybrid"* also according to the approach described in [21,23]: the tests evaluate the performance of the highest level components (macro benchmark tests), which can be considered tests from "the applications point of view"; down to the evaluation of the lowest level components (micro benchmark test).

Our work tests and analyzes all the IBiSCo cluster components. The first set of benchmarks evaluates how the network interconnection technologies affect the inter- and intra-node communications of GP-GPU workloads. The second set evaluates the performance of the Lustre parallel file system to ensure efficient access to data storage which is a critical issue for data-intensive applications. In Sect. 2 we describe the cluster architecture and its middleware layer which implements all the necessary software tools for communication and data storage services. Section 3 shows tests carried out to validate what is described in the previous section. In Sect. 4 we discuss positive aspects, observed deficiencies, and suggestions on how to improve the obtained results. The conclusion (Sect. 5) will summarize the contents of the work.

2   The Architecture of the Hybrid High Performance Computing Cluster

The architecture of this cluster is depicted as a set of multiple layers (Fig. 1). The highest layer of the architecture consists of the application layer. The lowest one consists of the hardware resources, which comprises 32 computing nodes and 4 storage nodes. In particular, it provides 1) 128 NVIDIA Volta GPUs and about 1600 physical cores (from Intel Gen 2 Xeon Gold CPUs) distributed on 32 nodes whose connections are based on InfiniBand [18] and NVLink2 [12] technologies; 2) 320 TB distributed on 4 storage nodes connected to the computing nodes by an InfiniBand network. The top one is the application layer which is exposed to users. The efficient use of cluster technologies is made possible by a software layer interposed between the lowest and the highest levels, namely the middleware, which is based on a combination of the following technologies:

1. OpenFabrics Enterprise Distribution (OFED) [26] for drivers and libraries needed by the Mellanox InfiniBand network cards.
2. CUDA Toolkit [25] for drivers, libraries and, development environments, enables NVIDA GP-GPU.
3. *"MPI-CUDA aware"* [22] implementation of OpenMPI [27] through the UCX open-source framework [29].
4. Lustre [33] - a distributed, parallel and open source file system - provides high performance access to storage resources.

Bandwidth and latency in message exchange among processes is one of the issues preventing the full exploitation of GP-GPU potential. In this regard, NVIDIA introduced CUDA Inter-Process Copy (IPC) [19] and GPUDirect Remote Direct Memory Access (RDMA) [14] technologies for intra- and inter-node GPU process communications to make this solution available for

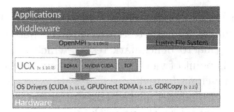

Fig. 1. The Layered Cluster Architecture

InfiniBand-based clusters. To optimize inter-node GPU-to-GPU communications for small messages, NVIDIA offers NVIDIA gdrcopy [30]. To combine these technologies with communication libraries (i.e., OpenMPI), we used the UCX open-source framework. UCX is a communication framework optimized for modern, high-bandwidth, low-latency networks. It exposes a set of abstract communication primitives that automatically choose the best available hardware resources. Supported technologies include RDMA (both InfiniBand and RoCE), TCP, GPU, shared memory, and atomic network operations.

As previously stated, a key aspect of high-performance computing is the efficient delivery of data to and from the computing nodes. The implementation adopted in the IBiSCo cluster is based on Lustre, a high-performance, parallel, and distributed file system. High-performance is guaranteed by Lustre flexibility in supporting multiple storage technologies, from the common ones based on Ethernet and TCP/IP to those with high-speed and low latency such as Infini-Band, RDMA and RoCE. Storage nodes host the OSTs^2 for the two Lustre exposed file systems, one for user home directories and one for jobs scratch area. In particular, the home file system is characterized by large disk space needs and fault tolerance, therefore it is made up of RAID-5 SAS HDD array. On the other hand, the scratch area needs fast disk access times and no redundancy requirement, hence it is hosted on SATA SSD disks.

3   Cluster Benchmarking

We have created a set of micro- and macro-benchmarks to study communication and access to resources. As for the communication tests: the micro-benchmarks have highlighted some limitations, mainly because they work with either very small or very large problems. For both intra- and inter-node communication, although peak performance is achieved (50 and 10 GB/s respectively), the tests show sudden increases. Growth should be "softened" by decreasing intermediate peaks. The discontinuity is due to several factors: first of all to the technologies used, such as the GDRCopy, which works with small message sizes. The growth of the message size leads to an automatic deactivation of the technology. This

---

^{2} The Lustre Object Storage Targets (OST) are the block devices on which data is distributed.

feature is essential. Depending on the type of application that uses the resources, it may be more appropriate to use one configuration of the benchmarking algorithm than another. For this reason, the choice of a benchmark that keeps pace with current technologies is indispensable for the evaluation of the cluster. As for the macro-benchmarks, the real limitation is given by Linpack: all communications to and from GPU devices are obtained using the PCI Channel and not NVLink (since the implementation of these benchmarks does not provide for GPU-to-GPU), this implies that the cluster resources are not fully exploited. Summing up, benchmark results are provided which should be useful for:

1. filling the lack of deep understanding on how modern GP-GPU can be connected and the actual impact of "state-of-the-art" hardware/software technologies on multi-GPU application performance;
2. evaluating the usage of parallel file systems in applications with intensive parallel data access.

3.1   Communication and Computation

Micro-benchmark Tests. We evaluate the basic characteristics of the four GPU interconnections focusing on both MPI Peer-to-Peer (P2P) and MPI Collective (CL) GPU-TO-GPU communication patterns. Both for intra- and inter-node P2P, we pay special attention to assessing the communication technologies in terms of latency and bandwidth on message size. Eventually, we evaluate the latency of the collective communication patterns on both intra- and inter-node scenarios. The tool used for measuring latency and bandwidth is the CUDA-aware version of MPI OSU Micro-Benchmarks [5] which evaluates latency and bandwidth of P2P tests as follows:

Latency Test: the latency tests are performed in a ping-pong fashion, by using blocking versions of the MPI functions (`MPI_Send` and `MPI_Recv`). The sender sends a message with certain data size and waits for a reply. The recipient receives the message and returns a response with the same data size. Many iterations of this test are performed and average one-way latency numbers are obtained[3].

Bandwidth Test: Non-blocking versions of the MPI functions (`MPI_Isend` and `MPI_Irecv`) are used in this case. The sender sends a fixed number of consecutive messages to the recipient and waits for its reply. The recipient sends the reply only after all these messages are received. This process is repeated for several iterations and the bandwidth is calculated based on elapsed time (until the sender receives the reply from the recipient) and the number of bytes sent by the sender. The goal of this bandwidth test is to determine the maximum sustained data rate which can be achieved at thethe network level.

Conversely, the latency of collective communications is measured via the following procedure: fixing a message size, many calls of `MPI_BCast`, `MPI_Gather`,

---

[3] We used the default number of iterations that the benchmark provides: 1000 iterations for small messages and 100 iterations for large messages.

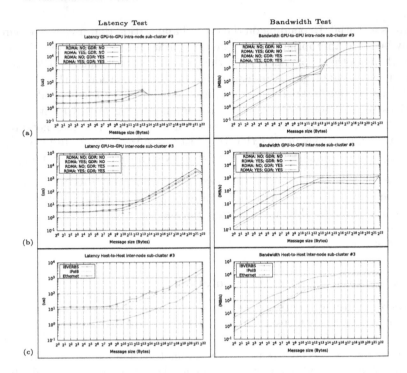

Fig. 2. Communication and computation micro-benchmarks results. Latency and bandwidth of P2P GPU-TO-GPU intra-node (a) and inter-node (b) communication and of Host-to-Host (c) communication on the considered sub-clusters (Color figure online)

`MPI_Reduce` (with `MPI_SUM` operation type) functions are carried out to compute time spent in a single call. All those time values are averaged to compute the latency number of the **Broadcast**, **Gather**, and **Reduce** tests respectively for each considered message size.

All the tests described above are carried out to evaluate the performance of both intra- and inter-node communications of the cluster where different combinations of RDMA, IPC, and gdrcopy are used as summarized in the description of Fig. 2. Plots of trends (as a function of message size) for P2P intra- and inter-node communications are respectively reported in Fig. 2-(a) and 2-(b). As a term of comparison, Fig. 2-(c) shows the behavior of P2P Host-to-Host communications. In all latency plots, we show, as an error bar, the value of σ where σ^2 is the *Sample Variance* [4] of the measured latency times used for each mean computation: just in very few cases the variance appears significant).

---

[4] The following formula is used to compute the *Sample Variance* σ^2 of a set of n values $\{x_i\}_{i=1,...,n}$ whose mean value is $\bar{x}$: $\sigma^2 = \frac{\sum_{i=1}^{n-1}(x_i-\bar{x})^2}{n-1}$.

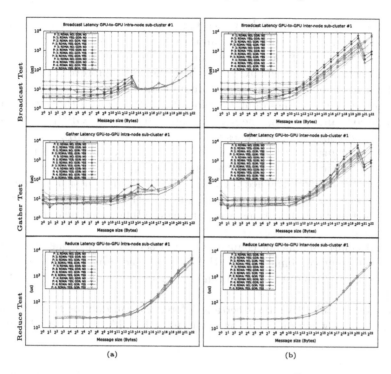

(a)   (b)

Fig. 3. Communication and computation micro-benchmarks results. Latency of GPU-to-GPU collective communications on the cluster: intra-node (a) and inter-node (b) communications

In Fig. 3-(a) and 3-(b) are respectively reported plots (as a function of message size) for collective intra- and inter-node communications where different combinations of RDMA, IPC, and gdrcopy are used. During the tests, in the case of intra-node collective communications, all the tasks are spawned on a single node. Conversely, when inter-node collective communication is considered one task is spawned on a single node. Tests are performed with different task numbers P. Lines in the plots representing tests executed on $P = 2, 3, 4$ are marked respectively with ■, ◆ and ▼ symbols.

All plots use a logarithmic scale with base 2 and 10 respectively for the x and y coordinate axis. From Figs. 2 and 3, we can state the following:

- Significant differences can be found between the performance of intra- and inter-node P2P communications. The intra-node communication seems to reach the maximum bandwidth performance of 50 GB/s, guaranteed by the NVLink technology, already with medium-sized messages. The same behavior cannot be witnessed during inter-node communication since the performance (about 10 GB/s) is comparable to the peak performance of the InfiniBand technology achieved only transmitting large-sized messages.

- The use of gdrcopy technology (see blue and green lines of all the plots in Fig. 2-(a) and 2-(b)) significantly improves the performance of P2P communications with small messages. A combination of gdrcopy and GPUDirect RDMA technologies seems to be the best choice to improve performance in all the tested configurations: it is more noticeable in P2P inter-node communications (see green lines of all the plots in Fig. 2-(a) and 2-(b)) although the best performance for large messages is obtained using the GPUDirect RDMA without gdrcopy (see green lines of all the plots in Fig. 2-(b)).
- All the configurations tested show equivalent performance when P2P intra-node communication uses large messages (see Fig. 2-(a)).
- The sustainable performance values for GPU-TO-GPU inter-node communications seem to be, in most cases, about a tenth of the value measured for Host-to-Host communications, which reach the InfiniBand peak performance (see Fig. 2-(c)).
- No particularly significant changes can be observed in the Collective Reduce test if different combinations of RDMA, IPC, and gdrcopy are used. These differences seem more noticeable in inter-node communications (see Fig. 3-(b))
- In the other Collective Tests certain differences, can only be found for small message sizes when different combinations of RDMA, IPC, and gdrcopy are used.

Macro-benchmark Tests. To evaluate how the implemented multi-GPU heterogeneous computational resource responds to a typical parallel workload from Scientific Computing, the CUDA-Aware version of the High Performance Linpack (HPL) Benchmark is used. The HPL benchmark [1] is a software package that solves a (random) dense linear system in double precision arithmetic on distributed-memory architectures. The HPL package provides a timing program to quantify the time it took to compute it. The best performance evaluation, in terms of thethe number of floating operations per second, is currently used to compile the list of the most powerful computers in the world [34]. The CUDA-Aware HPL benchmark [11] uses CUDA libraries to accelerate the HPL benchmark on heterogeneous clusters, where both CPUs and GPUs are used with minor or no modifications to the source code of HPL. A host library intercepts the calls to BLAS $DGEMM$ and $DTRSM$ procedures and executes them simultaneously on both GPUs and CPU cores. However, the benchmark has a limit: all communications to and from GPU devices are performed using the PCI channel.

In Fig. 4 we show the results of the CUDA-Aware HPL benchmark executed on some nodes of the IBiSCo cluster: the number of total MPI tasks is $4P$ where P is the number of involved nodes. The tests are performed using different values for the problem dimension N. The graphs show:

$T(P, N)$: The execution time of the benchmark as a function of the number P of nodes for some values of N;

$S(P, N)$: The Speed-Up of the execution as a function of the number P of nodes for some values of N. So, $S(P, N) = \frac{T(1,N)}{T(P,N)}$;

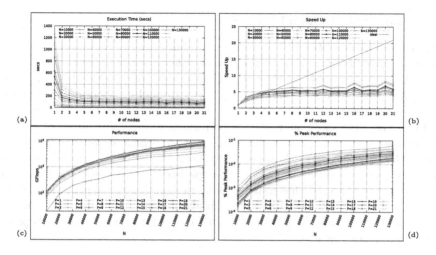

Fig. 4. Communication and computation macro-benchmarks results: The CUDA-Aware HPL benchmark Execution Time $T(P)$ (a), Speed-Up $S(P)$ (b), the Sustained Performance $SP(P, N)$ (c) and the fraction of Peak Performance $SPF(P, N)$ (d).

$SP(P, N)$: The Sustained Performance (expressed in GigaFLOPS) is obtained during the execution as a function of the problem dimension N for some values of P. It represents the number of Floating Point operations executable by an algorithm in a time range;

$SPF(P, N)$: The fraction of Peak Performance is obtained during the execution as a function of the problem dimension N for some values of P. So, $SPF(P, N) = \frac{SP(P,N)}{PP(P)}$ where $PP(P)$ is the Peak Performance of P nodes when for each node all four GPU devices are considered[5].

From the plots in Fig. 4 we can observe:

- the super linear speedup which is most remarkable for large problems. We think this is due to the increased time spent on CPU-GPU communications mainly as a consequence of a saturated PCI channel (indeed that all the four GPUs of a node are involved in computations);
- the very low scalability of the benchmark as the number of parallel tasks increase;
- the very small fraction of the Peak Performance scored during executions: if we consider very large problems we get just under 10% of max computational power which can be guaranteed by the computational resources.

---

[5] Let $PP(P) = (4NCores_{GPU}Clock_{GPU} + NCores_{CPU}Clock_{CPU})P$.

3.2   Communication and Data Storage

Micro-benchmark Tests. We evaluate the basic characteristics of the implemented Lustre file systems using the IOzone File system Benchmark [20], which generates and measures the time to complete a set of file operations as read, write, re-read, re-write. In Fig. 5 we show the throughput performance for the same above-mentioned operations both with and without the SYNC IOZone option[6]. The plots show single stream performance as a *"Heat Map"* of file size and request size for two Lustre-based file systems which are an aggregation of SAS HDDs and SATA SSDs respectively both available on storage nodes. In the same plots, we show, as a term of comparison, the results of the same test performed using two XFS file systems configured on different types of local disks (SATA SSD and PCIe NVMe SSD) available on computing nodes. All plots use a logarithmic scale with base 2 for the x and y coordinate axes. From such plots, the following statements can be argued:

- on read operations, all the tested file systems show comparable performance and suffer from large file size;
- the Lustre file system seems to be especially performing on write operations when file size increases. This is more noticeable if the option SYNC is activated;
- on write operations, the performance of Lustre file systems seems to be comparable (in terms of order of magnitude) with results obtained on slow local disks (especially if the option SYNC is disabled);

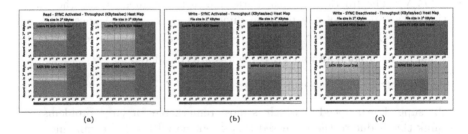

Fig. 5. Communication and storage micro-benchmarks results: IOZone throughput performance (in KB/s) for read (a) and write operations with (b) and without (c) the SYNC options. For better readability, we preferred to use a different color map in each plot.

Macro-benchmark Tests. We use a benchmark based on the Block-Tridiagonal (BT) problem of the NAS Parallel Benchmarks (NPB) [24], which is employed to test the I/O capabilities of high-performance computing systems, especially parallel systems. As improvements were made to parallel systems, the

---

[6] When this option is activated, IOZone will open the files with the O_SYNC flag. This forces all writes to the file to go completely to disk before returning to the benchmark.

speed with which computed results are being written to and read from files still represents a bottleneck in practical applications. The benchmark, named BT-IO, is based on the MPI I/O Application Programmer Interface [9] which is part of the MPI. In Fig. 6 we report the results of th BT-IO benchmark in its *"simple"* configuration where data, scattered in memory across the processors, are written to the same file. What is considered here is the class *"E"* problem dimension. During execution, one MPI task is allocated to each node, and both the Lustre file systems described above are considered. From such plots we can argue:

- time spent during the IO stages might account for a significant portion (>50%) of total execution time when the number of parallel tasks is large;
- the write pattern used by the tests, where each processor writes the data elements it is responsible for directly into an output file, confirms the weak performance due to a very high degree of fragmentation [36]. The Lustre file system based on SSD disks better manages the such type of pattern also when the number of processors becomes large;
- IO throughput seems far from the values measured by micro-benchmarks which appear to be about a bigger order of magnitude.

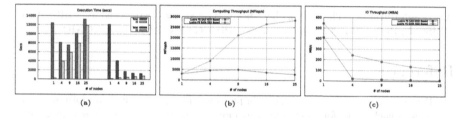

Fig. 6. Communication and storage macro-benchmarks results. BT-IO results: the total time of execution versus the time spent during IO phases (a), the throughput of computing (b) and IO (c) stages expressed in MFlops/sec and MB/s respectively

4 Discussion on the Results

The tests that analyze the lower level of the middleware (micro-benchmarks), seem to confirm the ability of the resource to guarantee the expected performance.

All the macro-benchmarks confirm that the goal of achieving the maximum performance of IT systems is extremely demanding. Although useful for evaluating the cluster created and highlighting the strengths of its resources, the benchmarks are also intended to bring out any issues. In this case, the problems in some of the results shown depend largely on the chosen benchmarks. In fact, for the most part, they cannot fully keep up with new technologies.

Our future work will be to find (or create) a version of macro benchmarks that can to make the most of the heterogeneity of the systems with solutions that: 1) use both the CPU and GPU present on the individual nodes, 2) exploit all the most performing communications channels available, 3) by CUDA-Aware messages passing library and innovative tools such as the Software for Linear Algebra Targeting Exascale (SLATE) library [13] or innovative approach as the HPL-AI Mixed-Precision Benchmark [16].

5   Conclusion

The paper describes the results of some benchmarking tests aimed to verify and validate all the solutions implemented during the deployment of a computing cluster within the Italian National Project IBiSCo able to satisfy the different computing needs of the project partners. All the strategies implemented have been verified and evaluated by the appropriate tools used to estimate some significant performance indexes of all the components of the system from a micro and macro point of view. From the communication between nodes with multiple GP-GPU in a distributed memory environment to the efficiency of the application during the IO phases.

Acknowledgment. This work has been funded by project code PIR01_00011 "IBISCo", PON 2014–2020, for all three entities (INFN, UNINA, and CNR).

References

1. Petitet, A., et al.: A portable implementation of the high-performance linpack benchmark for distributed-memory computers. https://www.netlib.org/benchmark/hpl/index.html
2. Barone, G.B., et al.: Designing and implementing a high-performance computing heterogeneous cluster. In: 2022 International Conference on Electrical, Computer and Energy Technologies (ICECET), pp. 1–6 (2022). https://doi.org/10.1109/ICECET55527.2022.9872709
3. Bertero, M., et al.: MedIGrid: a medical imaging application for computational grids. In: Proceedings International Parallel and Distributed Processing Symposium, p. 8 (2003). https://doi.org/10.1109/IPDPS.2003.1213457
4. Boccia, V., Carracciuolo, L., Laccetti, G., Lapegna, M., Mele, V.: HADAB: enabling fault tolerance in parallel applications running in distributed environments. In: Wyrzykowski, R., Dongarra, J., Karczewski, K., Waśniewski, J. (eds.) PPAM 2011, Part I. LNCS, vol. 7203, pp. 700–709. Springer, Heidelberg (2012). https://doi.org/10.1007/978-3-642-31464-3_71
5. Bureddy, D., Wang, H., Venkatesh, A., Potluri, S., Panda, D.K.: OMB-GPU: a micro-benchmark suite for evaluating MPI libraries on GPU clusters. In: Träff, J.L., Benkner, S., Dongarra, J.J. (eds.) EuroMPI 2012. LNCS, vol. 7490, pp. 110–120. Springer, Heidelberg (2012). https://doi.org/10.1007/978-3-642-33518-1_16
6. Carracciuolo, L., et. al: Implementation of a non-linear solver on heterogeneous architectures. Concurr. Comput. Pract. Exp. **30**(24), e4903 (2018). https://doi.org/10.1002/cpe.4903

7. Carracciuolo, L., et al.: About the granularity portability of block-based Krylov methods in heterogeneous computing environments. Concurr. Comput. Pract. Exp. **33**(4), e6008 (2021). https://doi.org/10.1002/cpe.6008
8. CORAL procurement benchmarks. https://asc.llnl.gov/sites/asc/files/2020-06/CORALBenchmarksProcedure-v26.pdf
9. Corbett, P., et al.: Overview of the MPI-IO parallel I/O interface. In: Jain, R., Werth, J., Browne, J.C. (eds.) Input/Output in Parallel and Distributed Computer Systems. SECS, vol. 362, pp. 127–146. Springer, Boston (1996). https://doi.org/10.1007/978-1-4613-1401-1_5
10. D'Amore, L., et al.: a scalable space-time domain decomposition approach for solving large scale nonlinear regularized inverse ill posed problems in 4D variational data assimilation. J. Sci. Comput. **91**(2), 59 (2022). https://doi.org/10.1007/s10915-022-01826-7
11. Fatica, M.: Accelerating Linpack with CUDA on heterogenous clusters. In: 2nd Workshop on General Purpose Processing on Graphics Processing Units. GPGPU-2, pp. 46–51. Association for Computing Machinery, New York (2009). https://doi.org/10.1145/1513895.1513901
12. Foley, D., et al.: Ultra-performance pascal GPU and NVLink interconnect. IEEE Micro **37**(2), 7–17 (2017). https://doi.org/10.1109/MM.2017.37
13. Gates, M., et al.: SLATE: design of a modern distributed and accelerated linear algebra library. In: International Conference for High Performance Computing, Networking, Storage and Analysis (2019). https://doi.org/10.1145/3295500.3356223
14. GPUDirect RDMA - CUDA Toolkit DOC. https://docs.nvidia.com/cuda/gpudirect-rdma/index.html
15. HPC Challenge Benchmark. https://hpcchallenge.org/hpcc/
16. HPL-AI Mixed-Precision Benchmark. https://hpl-mxp.org/
17. Ihde, N., et al.: A survey of big data, high performance computing, and machine learning benchmarks. In: Nambiar, R., Poess, M. (eds.) TPCTC 2021. LNCS, vol. 13169, pp. 98–118. Springer, Cham (2022). https://doi.org/10.1007/978-3-030-94437-7_7
18. InfiniBand network standard. https://en.wikipedia.org/wiki/InfiniBand
19. Interprocess Communication - Programming Guide : CUDA Toolkit DOC. https://docs.nvidia.com/cuda/cuda-c-programming-guide/index.html#interprocess-communication
20. IOzone Filesystem Benchmark. https://www.iozone.org/
21. Khorassani, K.S., Chu, C.-H., Subramoni, H., Panda, D.K.: Performance evaluation of MPI libraries on GPU-enabled OpenPOWER architectures: early experiences. In: Weiland, M., Juckeland, G., Alam, S., Jagode, H. (eds.) ISC High Performance 2019. LNCS, vol. 11887, pp. 361–378. Springer, Cham (2019). https://doi.org/10.1007/978-3-030-34356-9_28
22. Kraus, J.: An introduction to CUDA-aware MPI. https://developer.nvidia.com/blog/introduction-cuda-aware-mpi/
23. Li, A., et al.: Tartan: evaluating modern GPU interconnect via a multi-GPU benchmark suite. In: 2018 IEEE International Symposium on Workload Characterization (IISWC), pp. 191–202 (2018). https://doi.org/10.1109/IISWC.2018.8573483
24. NAS Parallel Benchmarks. https://www.nas.nasa.gov/software/npb.html
25. Nickolls, J., et al.: Scalable parallel programming with CUDA. Queue **6**(2), 40–53 (2008). https://doi.org/10.1145/1365490.1365500
26. NVIDIA Mellanox OFED DOC. https://docs.mellanox.com/display/MLNXOFEDv531001/NVIDIA+MLNX_OFED+Documentation+Rev+5.3-1.0.0.1

27. Open MPI: Open Source High Performance Computing. https://www.open-mpi.org/
28. Programma Operativo Nazionale Ricerca e Innovazione 2014–2020: Progetto IBiSCo. https://www.na.infn.it/fondi-esterni/pon
29. Shamis, P., et al.: UCX: an open source framework for HPC network APIs and beyond. In: IEEE 23rd Annual Symposium on High-Performance Interconnects, pp. 40–43 (2015). https://doi.org/10.1109/HOTI.2015.13
30. Shi, R., et al.: Designing efficient small message transfer mechanism for inter-node MPI communication on InfiniBand GPU clusters. In: 21st International Conference on High Performance Computing (HiPC), pp. 1–10 (2014). https://doi.org/10.1109/HiPC.2014.7116873
31. Standard Performance Evaluation Corporation. https://www.spec.org/
32. The Exascale Computing Project Website. https://www.exascaleproject.org/
33. The Lustre file system. https://www.lustre.org/
34. The Top 500 list Website. https://www.top500.org/
35. Sterling, T., et al.: BEOWULF: a parallel workstation for scientific computation. In: 24th International Conference on Parallel Processing, pp. 11–14. CRC Press (1995)
36. Wong, P., et al.: NAS parallel benchmarks I/O version 2.4. NAS Technical report NAS-03-002 (2003)

A Generative Adversarial Network Approach for Noise and Artifacts Reduction in MRI Head and Neck Imaging

Salvatore Cuomo[1], Francesco Fato[1], Lorenzo Ugga[2], Gaia Spadarella[2], Reanto Cuocolo[3], Fabio Giampaolo[1], and Francesco Piccialli[1](✉)

[1] Department of Mathematics and Applications "R. Caccioppoli", University of Naples Federico II, Naples, Italy
`{salvatore.cuomo,fabio.giampaolo,francesco.piccialli}@unina.it`
[2] Department of Advanced Biomedical Sciences, University of Naples Federico II, Naples, Italy
[3] Department of Medicine, Surgery and Dentistry, University of Salerno, Baronissi, Italy

Abstract. As the volume of data available to healthcare and life sciences specialists proliferates, so do the opportunities for life-saving breakthroughs. But time is a key factor. High-Performance Computing (HPC) can help practitioners accurately analyze data and improve patient outcomes, from drug discovery to finding the best-tailored therapy options. In this paper, we present and discuss an Artificial Intelligent methodology based on a Generative Adversarial Network to improve the perceived visual quality of MRI images related to the head and neck region. The experimental results demonstrate that once trained and validated, our model performs better with respect to the state of art methods and testing it on unseen real corrupted data improved the quality of the images in most cases.

Keywords: Deep Learning · Generative Adversarial Networks · MRI · Imaging

1 Introduction

The region of the head and neck (HN), while representing a relatively small area of the whole body, is of great interest in clinical practice. Indeed, there are numerous pathological processes that involve the HN with significant potential to reduce patients' quality of life as well as being life threatening in the case of malignancies. In this setting, medical imaging represents a crucial step in the diagnostic workflow for lesion characterization, staging and follow up. While the main modality for first level assessment is represented by ultrasound, magnetic resonance imaging (MRI) is the exam of choice for final evaluation of HN lesions [1]. MRI presents several advantages making it particularly suitable for HN studies [2,3]. Noise and artifacts reduction of 2D magnetic resonance of HN images is an interesting research topic in medical image analysis. Many algorithms have been proposed to this topic, but in recent years, there has been a growing interest in deep learning methodologies [4,5,14]. An emerging and challenging approach to dealing with this problem is based on generative adversarial networks (GANs) [4]. GANs are a class of methods in which two neural networks, the Generator and the Discriminator, are competitively and separately trained to classify or predict information. In other words, the main idea is to design a coupled neural network where a Generator learns to generate plausible data, and a Discriminator can distinguish the generator's fake data from real ones. The Discriminator penalizes the Generator for producing implausible results. Unfortunately, the learning process, in practical GAN usage, may have many difficulties and several open issues have to be addressed. How to train the Discriminator and Generator separately, by updating the architecture parameters, and how to find hyperparameters for the Generator such that the Discriminator is fooled completely are two crucial aspects in the study of the GANs. Goodfellow et. al. in [4] identified the difficulty of these networks to convergence as an issue that may cause the underfitting of the data. However, radiomics and machine learning models based on this type of data have not yet transitioned from academic research to real world clinical practice. This has been due to several reasons, in large part related to issues of reproducibility across different institutions and scanners [8,9,12,13]. In other anatomical regions, GANs have already been proven to attenuate this limitation of radiomics analysis [10]. Therefore, the potential impact of image quality improvement techniques, such as those presented in our study, on quantitative image analysis are another avenue for future research. To overcome some practical problems in the GAN implementation, we propose a method based on the residual encoder-decoder of the Wasserstein generative adversarial network class. The aim of this work is to design a stable GAN learning scheme able to improve the perceived visual quality of HN images and at the same time to reduce the artifacts that can often affect imaging with extra features, not present in the acquired MRI, that can be confused with some disease. The paper is organized as follows: Sect. 2 reports materials and methods; in Sect. 3 experimental results are presented. Finally, Sect. 4 is devoted to some discussions.

2   Materials and Methods

In this section, we show some aspects of designing a GAN for noise and artifacts removal in MRI neck images. We first describe the MRI acquired data and some information on the dataset information to train the network. Moreover, some considerations about data augmentation are reported in the preprocessing discussion. The designed GAN architecture, named M-GAN, is described in depth to highlight the main computational tasks of the network. Finally, evaluation metrics to show how M-GAN works are reported in the last paragraph.

2.1   The GAN Methodology

GANs [4,5] are a class of AI methods, in which two neural networks, the Generator and the Discriminator, are competitively and separately trained within a minimax game framework that involves the following objective function:

where Z is the latent space with a priori distribution p_z as input of the Generator, X is the space of the real data distributed as pdata, the Discriminator $D(x, \theta_D)$ acting as a classifier, outputs the probabilities that x comes from the distribution of real data p_{data} or from the distribution of generated data p_G and finally the Generator $G(z, \theta_G)$ outputs the new generated data in order to fool the Discriminator. A crucial step is the training of a GAN and some issues have to be addressed. More in detail, the main three steps of training a GAN are resumed as follows: i) train separately Discriminator and Generator updating the parameters; ii) find parameters θ_G and θ_D such that the Discriminator is completely fooled; iii) once the Discriminator is fooled, it is discarded and the output is then the Generator. In the applications, however, the general form is modified by obtaining two losses, which are in a kind of mutual relationship, one for the Generator and one for the Discriminator.

2.2   MRI Dataset Description and Splitting

This observational retrospective study was approved by the local Institutional Review Board, and the need for written informed consent was waived. All acquisitions were performed on a 1.5-Tesla (Gyroscan Intera, Philips, Eindhoven, The Netherlands) or 3T MRI scanner (Magnetom Trio, Siemens Medical Solutions, Erlangen, Germany). Both protocols included an axial T2-weighted TSE sequence, which was used for the analysis. The geometrical parameters varied but minimum in plane image resolution was $0.8 \times 0.8\,\mathrm{mm}$, and maximum slice thickness was $4\,\mathrm{mm}$. The available dataset includes 3170 slices of the neck area from 90 patients, selected from the zone just up the clavicle to the cheekbones with 35 slices for patients on average. The data were classified by doctors according to the noise level on a Likert scale, from 1 (more noise) to 4 (less noise), and on a dichotomous scale for the presence of artifacts (indicated with 1) and the absence (indicated with zero). About the dataset splitting the entire dataset has been divided into:

- Training set. 625 target slices collected from 18 patients with 0 artifacts and level noise of 3 and 4 used as target;
- Validation set. 155 slices collected from 4 patients with 0 artifacts and level noise of 3 and 4 used as target;
- Test set. 128 slices randomly selected among 64 patients(two per patient) in which there are some with presence of artifacts at different levels of noise(from 1 to 3) and some with absence of artifacts but with high level of noise (1 and 2).

In addition 4 patients, for a total of 150 slices with low noise level (3 or 4) and no artifacts were used for a comparison with the state of the art.

2.3   Data Pre-processing

Most of the images are 384×384 pixels in size, those that were larger have been resized to 384×384 with a center crop rather than compression to add no more noise and those of smaller size have been readapted by immersion in a black background. After the dimensions standardization, a normalization was carried out which led the tensor containing the whole set of images to assume values between 0 and 1. In order to simulate degradation and noise that can occur in MRI diagnosis we combined *Gaussian blur* and *Rician noise*. For the Training data, given y_i, a target image, we obtain:

$$j_{j,i} = y_i + G_{\sigma_j} + (y_i + noise_j)$$

with $j = 1, 2, 3, 4$, $i = 1, \cdots, 625$ where with $*$ we denote the convolutional product between Gaussian distribution and our target image. So for each target image y_i, we obtained four corrupted versions of itself, so starting from the initial 625 slices used as target, we have 2500 corrupted slices. The value chosen for the parameters is shown in Table 1.

Table 1. Selected parameters used for training data simulation.

Gaussian Blur (G_{σ_j})	Racian Noise ($noise_j$)
1	(80, 80)
0.9	(87, 87)
0.8	(90, 90)
0.7	(100, 100)

About the Validation data, 155 slices obtained by corrupting the 155 target slices with unseen parameters for Gaussian blur and Rician noise used as input of Generator have been considered. Finally for the comparisons with state-of-the-art (S.O.T.A.) denoising algorithms we consider 150 slices obtained by corrupting the 150 target slices with unseen parameters for Gaussian blur and Rician noise used as input of Generator.

2.4   The M-GAN Architecture

We propose a GAN-based model for noise and artifacts reduction. Our model comprises a generator and discriminator (see Fig. 1).

In Fig. 1 we report the M-GAN architecture. More in detail, the Generator is composed of four convolutional 2D layers and four deconvolutional 2D layers. The number of filters is respectively (4, 8, 16, 32, 16, 8, 4, 1). Each kernel used in convolutional and deconvolutional layers is 3×3 dimensions with stride and padding equals to 1. In the encoding phase each convolution operation is followed by batch normalization and a LeakyReLU activation function. During the

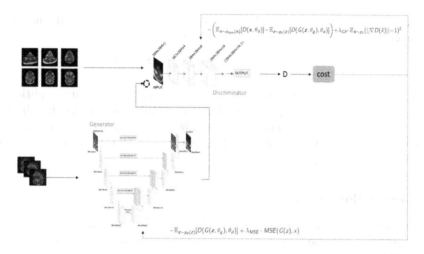

Fig. 1. The M-GAN architecture.

decoding phase, the first layer is composed of deconvolution followed by batch normalization and a LeakyReLU activation function. In the second and third layers, each deconvolution operation is preceded by a features concatenation with the correspondent encoding part and a features pooling (2D convolution between encoding and decoding features), then deconvolution followed by batch normalization and a LeakyReLU. The last deconvolutional layer is preceded by concatenation with the correspondent encoding part and a features pooling and is followed by the output layer composed respectively by concatenation with input, a features pooling, and a ReLU activation function. Discriminator architecture: it is composed of four layers, three convolutional layers with a number of filters respectively 4,8,16, each convolution followed only by LeakyReLU without batch normalization, and the last layer is a dense layer which outputs the result of classification. Each kernel used in the convolutional layers is 3×3 dimensions with stride and padding equal to 1. About the Loss functions, during the training phase the Generator and the Discriminator are competitively and separately trained both with the aim of minimizing in turn their loss functions. Loss functions, written as follows, are of Wasserstein type [6]:

$$Loss_D = -(\mathbb{E}_{x \sim p_{data(x)}}[D(x)] - \mathbb{E}_{z \sim p_z}) \cdot$$

$$\cdot [D(G(z)) - \lambda_{gp} \mathbb{E}_{x \sim p(x)}[||D(x)|| - 1)^2]$$

and,

$$Loss_G = -\mathbb{E}_{z \sim p_{(z)}}[D(G(z))] + \lambda_{MSE} MSE(G(z), x)$$

here z and x are respectively the corrupted image and the ground truth, $D(x)$ is the Discriminator output on the ground truth, $D(G(z))$ is the Discriminator output on generated data, w and h are respectively the width and the height of the images, λ_{gp} and λ_{MSE} are two hyperparameters.

$$\mathbb{E}_{x \sim p_{(x)}} = (||D(x)|| - 1)^2$$

is the gradient penalty term and it is used to enforce the Lipschitz condition of the Discriminator improving the stability of the model, $p(x)$ is the distribution obtained by uniformly sampling along a straight line between the real and generated distributions. The MSE term helps Generator to better reconstruct the details.

2.5   Evaluation Metrics

To evaluate the performance of our model we used four measures. The first one is the peak signal-to-noise ratio (PSNR), which considers the root mean square error (RMSE) between the ground truth and reconstructed or corrupted images. The second is the structural similarity index measure (SSIM) [11] reconstruction, which measures the similarity between ground truth and reconstructed or corrupted images. The third is the L1 distance that measures the pixel-wise average distance between the ground truth and reconstructed or corrupted images, and the last is the Artifacts Power which consider the L2 squared difference between the ground truth and reconstructed or corrupted images divided by the L2 squared norm of the ground truth image. Higher is the AP, higher is the corruption level in the images.

3   Experimental Results

In this section we discuss overall results in terms of accuracy in MRI image reconstruction. Several accuracy metrics on the training, the validation and the test sets are analyzed. Finally, some results on S.O.T.A. denoising methods are considered.

3.1   Results on the Training Set

After training the model, it was tested on all 2500 input slices, recording an improvement in quality in terms of measurements on all of them (Fig. 2).

Table 2 shows performances on four selected slice levels (the area just under the lower jaw, the mouth area, the area between the superior jaw and just under the nose, and the nose area) for each patient in the training set, an improvement of at least one order of magnitude in terms of L1 and Artifacts power and an improvement of at least 0.3 in terms of SSIM can be noted after M-GAN correction. The M-GAN reaches the 98% of the SSIM value with improvements in edge detection. The reconstructed image is close to the ground truth.

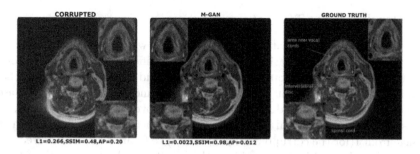

Fig. 2. Results on a randomly selected image from the dataset.

Table 2. Performance metrics of M-GAN generator.

SLICE	M-GAN			CORRUPTED		
LEVEL	L1 Distance	Artifacts power	SSIM	L1 Distance	Artifacts power	SSIM
0th	0.0061 ± 0.0104	0.029 ± 0.007	0.98 ± 0.016	0.0273 ± 0.053	0.31 ± 0.33	0.64 ± 0.056
1st	0.0052 ± 0.0079	0.015 ± 0.003	0.98 ± 0.003	0.0276 ± 0.0152	0.21 ± 0.11	0.66 ± 0.056
2nd	0.0060 ± 0.0069	0.012 ± 0.002	0.97 ± 0.007	0.0291 ± 0.0162	0.16 ± 0.06	0.64 ± 0.048
3rd	0.0066 ± 0.0073	0.011 ± 0.003	0.97 ± 0.007	0.0299 ± 0.0167	0.14 ± 0.05	0.70 ± 0.051

3.2   Results on the Validation Set

Validation set was used to set the hyperparameters, the model with final setting hyperparameters registered an improvement in terms of measures on all slices. For the validation slices quality assessment, we selected the same slices level chosen in the training set.

Table 3. Performance metrics of M-GAN generator on four selected slice levels for each patient in the validation set.

SLICE	M-GAN			CORRUPTED		
LEVEL	L1 Distance	Artifacts power	SSIM	L1 Distance	Artifacts power	SSIM
0th	0.027 ± 0.026	0.076 ± 0.03	0.68 ± 0.019	0.057 ± 0.032	0.311 ± 0.24	0.32 ± 0.039
1st	0.027 ± 0.025	0.064 ± 0.01	0.70 ± 0.012	0.059 ± 0.031	0.227 ± 0.11	0.35 ± 0.027
2nd	0.029 ± 0.027	0.067 ± 0.01	0.71 ± 0.007	0.060 ± 0.033	0.213 ± 0.09	0.37 ± 0.020
3rd	0.030 ± 0.028	0.063 ± 0.02	0.71 ± 0.006	0.059 ± 0.030	0.191 ± 0.07	0.36 ± 0.019

Table 3 presents the M-GAN results in terms of perceived visual quality and main metrics. An improvement of at least one order of magnitude in terms of Artifacts power and an improvement of at least 0.3 in terms of SSIM can be observed like in the training set, referring to the L1 Loss, we have an improvement for all four selected slice levels, but less than those obtained in the training set.

3.3   Results on the Test Set

After the training and validation phases, the model was tested on 128 slices randomly selected among 64 patients, obtaining a significant improvement through
the quality control of doctors in terms of noise and artifacts on 80% of them
(103/128). An improvement regarding noise was measured with an increased
score on a Likert scale by doctors, while an improvement about artifacts, not
necessarily the total removal but also only the reduction, was denoted with the
passage from 1(for the corrupted original image) to 0 (after M-GAN correction).
In Fig. 3, Fig. 4 and Fig. 5 were shown the results on three randomly selected
slices in the test set before and after M-GAN correction.

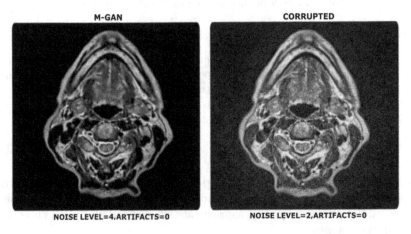

Fig. 3. Ability of M-GAN to reduce the noise. It appears in the real corrupted acquisition as a grainy effect on the scanned object.

Figure 3 shows the improvement in terms of noise measured by doctors on
a Likert scale. After M-GAN correction, an increase in contrast that allows
better recognition of the elements in the image can be noted resulting in a
smoother image with a notable reduction of grainy effect.   In Fig. 4 we report
the performance of the M-GAN in terms of noise measured by doctors on a
Likert scale and in terms of artifacts on a dichotomous scale. After correction the
artifact due to motion is reduced with better-defined edges, resulting in an image
that makes the diagnosis less complicated for doctors than the corrupted one.
Finally, Fig. 5 shows better results of M-GAN for reducing artifacts registered
from the passage from 1 to 0 on a dichotomous scale. After correction the intra-
pixel variation due to noise is alleviated and the "ghost effect" due to motion
artifacts is reduced with the restoration of details.

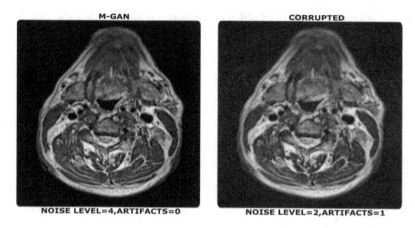

Fig. 4. Ability of M-GAN to reduce artifacts and noise. The corrupted image is affected by a lack of sharpeness.

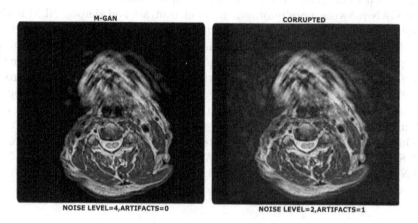

Fig. 5. Ability of M-GAN to reduce motion artifacts and noise. Due to motion, the edges of the corrupted version repeat outside the object appearing on the image black background and inside it overlapping the real structure by altering the morphology.

3.4   Comparison with the S.O.T.A

After training, validating and testing of our model, we compared it with some of state of art denoising filters like Anisotropic, Non-local-means and Bilateral [7], selecting and corrupting 150 slices from 4 new patients with unseen values of Gaussian blur and Rician noise. Reconstruction results are reported in Table 4.

In Table 4, we show that M-GAN performs better than typically denoising filters, recovering more information about contrast and shapes. NLM shows good performances, especially in terms of SSIM, where the increase compared to the corrupted image and the other two filters are considerable. Anisotropic filter doesn't perform better like NLM and M-GAN but it is able to get an improve-

Table 4. Performance metrics of different methods on four selected slice levels (the same levels of validation and training stages) for each patient in the test set

SLICE	CORRUPTED			ANISOTROPIC			BILATERAL		
LEVEL	PSNR	AP	SSIM	PSNR	AP	SSIM	PSNR	AP	SSIM
0th	26.9 ± 0.5	0.17 ± 0.01	0.57 ± 0.03	27.7 ± 0.7	0.14 ± 0.001	0.69 ± 0.01	26.9 ± 0.5	0.17 ± 0.01	0.57 ± 0.03
1st	26.2 ± 0.7	0.16 ± 0.02	0.58 ± 0.01	26.9 ± 0.8	0.14 ± 0.01	0.70 ± 0.01	26.2 ± 0.7	0.16 ± 0.02	0.58 ± 0.01
2nd	25.7 ± 0.5	0.15 ± 0.01	0.60 ± 0.01	26.2 ± 0.6	0.13 ± 0.004	0.72 ± 0.01	25.7 ± 0.5	0.15 ± 0.01	0.60 ± 0.01
3rd	25.3 ± 0.5	0.15 ± 0.01	0.61 ± 0.01	25.8 ± 0.6	0.13 ± 0.01	0.72 ± 0.01	25.3 ± 0.5	0.15 ± 0.01	0.61 ± 0.01

NLM			M-GAN		
PSNR	AP	SSIM	PSNR	AP	SSIM
28.2 ± 0.7	0.13 ± 0.01	0.96 ± 0.01	32.9 ± 1.01	0.04 ± 0.001	0.99 ± 0.003
27.3 ± 0.8	0.12 ± 0.01	0.96 ± 0.004	31.9 ± 1.1	0.04 ± 0.001	0.99 ± 0.001
26.5 ± 0.6	0.13 ± 0.004	0.96 ± 0.002	31.1 ± 0.8	0.04 ± 0.001	0.98 ± 0.001
26.1 ± 0.6	0.12 ± 0.001	0.95 ± 0.003	30.5 ± 0.7	0.05 ± 0.001	0.98 ± 0.001

ment in terms of measures. Bilateral filters get an improvement in terms of measurements only after at least the fifth decimal digit.

M-GAN recovers more information about contrast and shapes. NLM is able to restore the morphology of the image with an improvement in terms of contrast; the edges are preserved but slightly blurred, as reported in Fig. 6. Anisotropic filter partially restores contrast reducing noise. Bilateral filters seem to leave the image unchanged. Finally, we observe that if we require that the Anisotropic and Bilateral filters reduce more noise by changing their parameters, it happens that large structures are preserved while small ones are considered as noise and so blurred.

Our experiments have been conducted on a server with the Intel Core i9-9900 K 8-core CPU with 128 GB of RAM, and two GPUs: Nvidia RTX 3090 and Nvidia RTX 3070. The programming language used is Python 3.9 with the framework Pytorch 1.9.1 for the Deep Learning model (Table 5).

Table 5. Comparing computational time on four selected patients of our approach with the current state-of-art technique for all 150 slices.

Method	Total execution time
Anisotropic	1 s
Bilateral	0.2 s
NLM	21.6 s
M-GAN	8.7 s

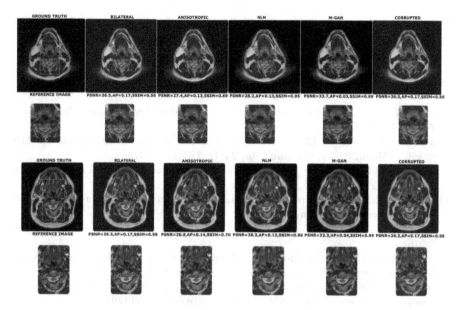

Fig. 6. Quality assessment dealing with two slices selected from one patient.

4   Discussion and Conclusions

In this work, we propose a method based on the Wasserstein generative adversarial network to reduce noise and artifacts in MRI images while effectively preserving the structural details. This network aims to process 2D data using 2D convolutional layers. The Generator has an auto-encoder structure, while the discriminator acting as a classifier, through 3 convolutional layers and 1 dense layer, takes an image as input and provides a value as output. Training stage performed on a GPU, takes approximately 40 min and it is the costliest step. The experimental results demonstrate that once trained and validated our model, it performs better with respect to the state of art methods and testing it on unseen real corrupted data improved the quality of the images in most cases. The reduction of imaging artifacts and improvement of SNR will hopefully lead to improvements in diagnostic accuracy of MRI HN examinations as well as potentially reducing exam duration. Nonetheless, the clinical impact of our results has to be investigated in future studies designed for this task. A further consideration has to be made on the potential impact of GANs and denoising techniques in general on quantitative analysis of medical images. Our work has some limitations that should be acknowledged. First of all, it has a retrospective design which limits the possibility for clinical validation. However, from a technical point of view a prospective design would not have impacted significantly the network architecture. All the data was collected from a single center and MRI scanner, therefore the generalizability of our results has to be proven in a different setting. In conclusion, the results obtained are encouraging and efficiently demonstrate the potential of deep learning-based methods for MRI denoising and artifacts reduction.

References

1. Dai, Y.L., King, A.D.: State of the art MRI in head and neck cancer. Clin. Radiol. **73**(1), 45–59 (2018)
2. Jansen, J.F.A., et al.: Evaluation of head and neck tumors with functional MR imaging. Magn. Reson. Imaging Clin. **24**(1), 123–133 (2016)
3. Zhuo, J., Gullapalli, R.P.: MR artifacts, safety, and quality control. Radiographics **26**(1), 275–297 (2006)
4. Goodfellow, I., et al.: Generative adversarial nets. In: Advances in Neural Information Processing Systems **27** (2014)
5. Goodfellow, Y., Bengio, Y., Courville, A.: Deep Learning. MIT press, Cambridge (2016)
6. Arjovsky, M., Chintala, S., Bottou, L.: Wasserstein generative adversarial networks. In: International Conference on Machine Learning, PMLR (2017)
7. Mohan, J., Krishnaveni, V., Guo, Y.: A survey on the magnetic resonance image denoising methods. Biomed. Signal Proc. Control **9**, 56–69 (2014)
8. Spadarella, G., et al.: MRI based radiomics in nasopharyngeal cancer: systematic review and perspectives using radiomic quality score (RQS) assessment. Eur. J. Radiol. **140**, 109744 (2021)
9. Lohmann, P., et al.: Radiomics in neuro-oncology: basics, workflow, and applications. Methods **188**, 112–121 (2021)
10. Marcadent, S., et al.: Generative adversarial networks improve the reproducibility and discriminative power of radiomic features. Radiol.: Artif. Intell. **2**(3), e190035 (2020)
11. Wang, Z., Bovik, A.C., Sheikh, H.R., Simoncelli, E.P.: Image quality assessment: from error visibility to structural similarity. IEEE Trans. Image Process. **13**(4), 600–612 (2004)
12. Piccialli, F., Cuomo, S., De Michele, P.: A regularized MRI image reconstruction based on hessian penalty term on CPU/GPU systems. Procedia Comput. Sci. **18**, 2643–2646 (2013)
13. Palma, G., et al.: 3D Non-local means denoising via multi-GPU. In: 2013 Federated Conference on Computer Science and Information Systems, vol. 13884786 (2013)
14. Chianese, A., Marulli, F., Piccialli, F., Valente, I.: A novel challenge into multimedia cultural heritage: an integrated approach to support cultural information enrichment. In: International Conference on Signal-Image Technology & Internet-Based Systems, pp. 217–224 (2013)

A GPU Accelerated Hyperspectral 3D Convolutional Neural Network Classification at the Edge with Principal Component Analysis Preprocessing

Gianluca De Lucia[1]([✉]) [iD], Marco Lapegna[2] [iD], and Diego Romano[1] [iD]

[1] Institute for High Performance Computing and Networking (ICAR), CNR,
80131 Naples, Italy
{gianluca.delucia,diego.romano}@icar.cnr.it
[2] Department of Mathematics and Applications, University of Naples Federico II,
80126 Naples, Italy
marco.lapegna@unina.it

Abstract. The Edge Computing paradigm promises to transfer decision-making processes based on artificial intelligence algorithms to the edge of the network without the need to query servers far from the data collection point. Hyperspectral image classification is one of the application fields that can benefit most from the close relationship between Edge Computing and Artificial Intelligence. It consists of a framework of techniques and methodologies for collecting and processing images related to objects or scenes on the Earth's surface, employing cameras or other sensors mounted on Unmanned Aerial Vehicles. However, the computing performance of the edge devices is not comparable with those of high-end servers, so specific approaches are required to consider the influence of the computing environment on the algorithm development methodology. In the present work, we propose a hybrid technique to make the Hyperspectral Image classification through Convolutional Neural Network affordable on low-power and high-performance sensor devices. We first use the Principal Component Analysis to filter insignificant wavelengths to reduce the dataset dimension; then, we use a process acceleration strategy to improve the performance by introducing a GPU-based form of parallelism.

Keywords: Hyperspectral classification · Edge Computing · Principal Component Analysis · GPU computing

1 Introduction

Edge computing refers to the enabling technologies to process data at the network's edge near the data source before being sent to the cloud data center. For some authors, edge computing is interchangeable with fog computing [1], although it focuses more on the devices at the edge, whereas fog computing focuses more on the whole network infrastructure. This type of computing paradigm has several advantages over traditional cloud computing, e.g., as the results of [15] show, energy savings can reach up to 40%. There are various metrics to consider in Edge computing, including energy and transmission rate, especially for big data [3,13]. In addition to the network signal strength [11], data size and available bandwidth will also influence the transmission energy overhead [27]. For this reason, as shown in [17], new High-Performance Edge devices mount GPUs capable of performing complex calculations by finding a trade-off between performance and power consumption.

One stimulating application field for Edge computing is Remote Sensing (RS). RS is the science of acquiring, processing, and interpreting images and related data from aircraft and satellites that record the interaction between matter and electromagnetic energy [30]. In recent years, deep learning techniques have revolutionized how RS images are processed and classified. In particular, standard optical, RGB, and IR (infrared) images have benefited from deep convolutional neural networks (CNNs) for classification, object detection, or semantic segmentation tasks [6,25,33].

A promising RS technology focuses on hyperspectral images (HSIs), allowing simultaneous radiance capture at different wavelengths, and generating various spectral bands. HSI data have an exceptionally high range and resolution in the spectral dimension. In particular, the branch of Hyperspectral Imaging deals with collecting and processing information on the nature of materials by analyzing their reflectance in a part of the electromagnetic spectrum [12]. Hyperspectral imaging aims to obtain a spectral vector for each pixel of an image to find objects, detect processes, or identify and classify materials [8,10].

Some classifiers preprocess the HSI to reduce the image depth to three spectral bands (RGB) through Principal Component Analysis (PCA) or other strategies [23,31] and only use a 2D CNN architecture to perform the classification. However, this approach may result in the loss of some hyperspectral properties. For this reason, we propose to use PCA to reduce the length of the HSI spectral dimension while maintaining the multidimensional nature of the data. This strategy allows adoption of more accurate and faster classification tools than the above methods.

In this paper, we will present an HSI classifier[1] that exploits the computational power of the GPU on High-Performance Edge Devices. For the development, we used a PyTorch-based deep learning toolbox for classifying hyperspectral data called DeepHyperX [4]. We focused on three-dimensional convolutional networks (3D CNNs). Indeed, since we can interpret HSIs as volumes, we can classify them with the aid of 3D CNNs using three-dimensional convolutions [20]. Instead of producing 2D feature maps, these 3D CNNs create 3D feature maps suitable for spectral pattern recognition and seem theoretically more relevant for HSI classification. This approach slightly improves classification performance compared to 2D+1D models [19]. In [9], the author showed that 3D CNNs for the classification of hyperspectral images performed better than their 2D counterparts. Indeed, compared to spectral CNNs or 2D+1D counterparts, 3D CNNs combine spatial and spectral pattern recognition strategies in one filter, requiring fewer parameters and layers.

---

[1] Source code: https://github.com/gigernau/PCAHyperspectralClassifier.

Many architectures in the literature handle 3D convolutional neural networks for hyperspectral data [7,9,16,18,21,22]. The authors of [5] compare several variants, pointing out their ability to recognize more complex 3D reflectance patterns, such as spectral signatures and absorption differences between bands.

With this work, we want to show how High-Performance Edge Computing can enable onboard classification with a limited energetic impact, eventually improving the transmission stage towards the ground station. The idea is to preprocess raw data using a GPU-parallel PCA to reduce the spectral dimension of the HSI while retaining the information content. Then, a properly chosen GPU-accelerated 3D CNN classifier [20] can process the hyperspectral-reduced data in a shorter time while maintaining high accuracy.

2   HSI Pipeline

HSIs have a data structure similar to RGB images, consisting of the superposition of three wavelengths, one for each primary color: red, green, and blue. Even if the visible spectrum has a broader range of wavelengths, RGB images appear to the human eye in almost any color, thanks to the tristimulus mechanism. In hyperspectral cameras, images have higher information content. HSI cameras allow the simultaneous capture of radiance at different wavelength bands of the electromagnetic spectrum, providing informative spectral details for each material. An HSI has spatial pixels corresponding to geographical locations, each with a spectral depth of several wavelength bands depending on the specific sensor. Thus, an HSI is a volume graphically representable with a so-called cube of hyperspectral data (Fig. 1).

If we cut the cube perpendicularly to the spectral bands, we obtain a plane appearing as an image whose pixels represent the reflectance at a specific wavelength λ. Therefore, the pixel's intensity, with a value usually normalized between 0 and 1, measures the surface efficiency of the sampled material in radiative reflection at λ.

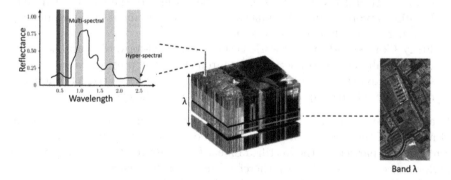

Fig. 1. Graphical representation of a hyperspectral data cube.

Two main methods of reducing datasets are PCA and Multidimensional Scaling (MDS). We preferred to focus on using PCA, which operates on the spectral dimension, rather than MDS. The output of the HSI classification produces labels for each pixel, so we have to preserve the spatial details, while MDS focuses mainly on reducing the spatial dimensions.

Thanks to PCA, we can reduce the spectral dimension by projecting the vector corresponding to each spatial point onto the first principal components only, where the variance of the data and the information content are most relevant. We can define the first principal component as the direction that maximizes the variance of the projected data. The i-th principal component is the direction orthogonal to the first $i - 1$ principal components that maximize the variance of the projected data [28]. The main steps of PCA are [32]:

- Dataset normalization.
- Calculating covariance matrix for the features in the dataset.
- Calculating eigenvalues and eigenvectors for the covariance matrix.
- Ordering eigenvalues and corresponding eigenvectors.
- Selection of k eigenvalues and creation of the eigenvectors matrix.

The eigenvector associated with the largest eigenvalue indicates the direction in which the data have the greatest variance.

In general, dimensionality reduction inevitably results in a loss of information, leading to less accurate data classification. However, PCA minimizes this information loss. Moreover, available parallel implementations on SIMD architectures can exploit GPU acceleration using a SIMT execution model [29]. Indeed, optimized versions of GPU-parallel cuBLAS-based PCA are up to 12 times faster than the CPU-optimised BLAS versions [2]. Our high-performance PCA cuBLAS implementation uses the Gram-Schmidt orthogonalization, as described in [2]. Therefore, we will perform PCA on the dataset before the classification phase to speed up the process without sacrificing prediction accuracy.

For HSI classification through Deep Learning, many authors use CNNs [5]. In general, classifiers built with CNNs usually have the following layers:

- **Convolutional layers:** filters extract the features of the images analyzed.
- **Pooling layers:** reduce the dimension of the feature maps by downsampling, and increase the level of *abstraction.*
- **Fully Connected layers:** work as traditional feed-forward neural networks, in which all neurons connect to all neurons from the previous layer.
- **Output layer:** a fully connected layer using *softmax* as a trigger function to obtain the selected input's probabilities for a specific class.

In a fully connected layer, an **activation function** computes the weighted sum of neurons of the previous layer and consequently activates neurons on the current layer. In particular, the Rectified Linear Units (ReLU) function has excellent performance on deep networks; therefore, many authors currently prefer it.

We will use a 3D-CNN, where the filters used in the convolutional layers are three-dimensional and move along the three directions to calculate feature representations (Fig. 2).

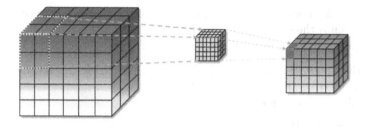

Fig. 2. Example of three-dimensional convolution.

Hence, the pipeline of our classifier (Fig. 3) takes hyperspectral data as input, then performs a GPU-parallel PCA by executing the code in CUDA. Next, the reduced dataset becomes the input for the inference via the appropriately trained 3D-CNN network model. The output is an RGB image in which each pixel has a color representing the class of the corresponding material.

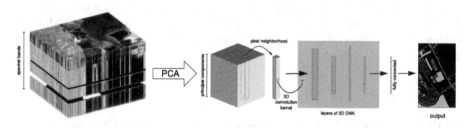

Fig. 3. Pipeline of the HSI classifier with PCA preprocessing.

3   Experiments

We developed a hyperspectral image classifier trained on two datasets to test our approach. There are few public datasets [14] acquired using hyperspectral sensors. In particular, for this work, we used:

- **Indian Pines (IP):** collected by the AVIRIS sensor on a NASA flight over northwestern Indiana in 1992, with a ground pixel resolution of 17 m. The acquired data consist of 145×145 pixels with 220 spectral bands, but after removing the water absorption bands $(104 - -108, 150 - -163,$ and $220)$, they result in 200 bands. The ground truth has 16 classes, not all of which are mutually exclusive.
- **Pavia University (PU):** detected by the ROSIS sensor on a DLR flight in 2002 over Pavia, Italy, with a ground pixel resolution of 1.3 m. After removing samples without information, the dataset consists of 610×340 pixels, with 103 spectral bands. The ground truth differentiates 9 classes.

We used double precision for both datasets to present coherent results during our tests, even if the original formats differed.

We experimented on two different platforms:

- PC with a 2.60 GHz Intel Core i7-9750H CPU, 16 GB RAM, Nvidia GeForce RTX 2060 GPU, and running Ubuntu Linux;
- Nvidia Jetson Nano developer kit.

We exploited the GPUs on both platforms to accelerate each step of the classification pipeline. To test our code in the High-Performance Edge Computing environment, we used the Jetson Nano activating both 5W and 10W modalities and reporting their impact on the inference time and the energy absorption.

Firstly, we selected the best 3D-CNN model in inference time and prediction accuracy for both datasets on the Jetson Nano. This step is essential to identifying the most promising model for the Edge computing environment. Then, we tested the overall classification performance in prediction accuracy and inference time by changing the selected number of components in the PCA preprocessing. We used a customized parallel version of the PCA developed in CUDA using the cuBLAS library for this task. We also compared the execution time of the PCA preprocessing using our CUDA version and the scikit-learn module of Python. Finally, we evaluated the energy consumption using both Jetson Nano modalities.

4   Results

Firstly, we present in Table 1 the execution times of a few 3D-CNN models from the literature (He et al. [16], Li et al. [21], Hamida et al. [7]), implemented in DeepHyperX and executed on Jetson Nano. We did not include Lee et al. [18], Luo et al., [22] and Chen et al. [9] because they are not competitive in inference execution times (more than 5 min in 10 W modality).

Table 1. Execution times on Jetson Nano and classification accuracy of some models from DeepHyperX on IP and PU datasets

| | Indian Pines | | | Pavia University | | |
| | Inference Time | | | Inference Time | | |
Model	10 W	5 W	Accuracy	10 W	5 W	Accuracy
He et al.	01:05	01:24	95.35%	04:19	06:10	96.14%
Li et al.	00:23	00:27	97.08%	00:56	01:20	97.72%
Hamida et al.	00:24	00:29	85.72%	01:07	01:40	97.59%

The best results in terms of accuracy and execution time for both datasets and power modalities are those of Li et al. All the subsequent reasonings and tests will suppose the adoption of this promising model, considering our context of on-board processing of remote sensing data.

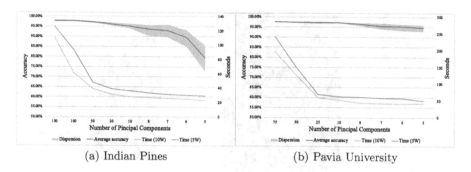

(a) Indian Pines   (b) Pavia University

Fig. 4. Accuracy and execution time of inference using our pipeline with several numbers K of Principal Components.

By applying the PCA, if we decrease the number of Principal Components K used for the 3D-CNN, classification accuracy and execution time decrease simultaneously (Fig. 4). The curve steepness of the execution time is greater than that of the accuracy. Hence, we do not need to sacrifice significant accuracy to reduce the execution time.

Moreover, the dispersion area of multiple testing increases when using fewer Principal Components. This result means that excessive reduction of the input components during the CNN training implies a less reliable prediction. Indeed, prediction accuracy strictly depends on the model and the training set. We used a random approach to sample the training set when repeating the tests, so we trained with different random samples each time. Consequently, an increasing accuracy dispersion means that the training samples' choice becomes highly relevant. Hence, the excessive reduction in the number of principal components directly impacts the training quality of the neural network.

Following these observations, we think a good trade-off between accuracy and execution time is $K = 50$ for IP (Fig. 4a), thus reducing the dimension of the initial dataset by 75%. However, if we need to reduce the execution time further, we could choose $K = 10$ while keeping a 95% prediction accuracy and a 95% dimensional reduction. The numbers change for PU (Fig. 4b) since the hyperspectral bands are fewer. To maintain at least a 97% accuracy, we can choose an optimal $K = 10$, obtaining an approximate 90% reduction in the dataset dimension. On the other hand, we can choose $K = 5$ for an approximate 95% dimensional reduction and a 95% accuracy. We will use the K values mentioned above to control the prediction accuracy in the following testing.

Visual comparisons between ground truth and prediction for PU (Fig. 5) and IP (Fig. 6) datasets show that the results of our pipeline represent reliable classifications, as confirmed by the diagonal of the confusion matrices in Fig. 5c and Fig. 6c.

Regarding power consumption, we tested our pipeline on the Jetson Nano using both energy modalities: 10 W (Table 2) and 5 W (Table 3). We can notice that the advantage of using our pipeline with PCA preprocessing for the PU

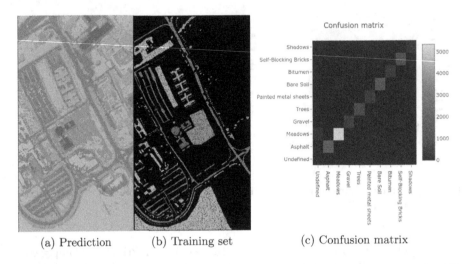

(a) Prediction   (b) Training set   (c) Confusion matrix

Fig. 5. Pavia University prediction with 95% accuracy (a), the training set with 70% samples from ground truth (class Undefined in black) (b), and relative confusion matrix (c).

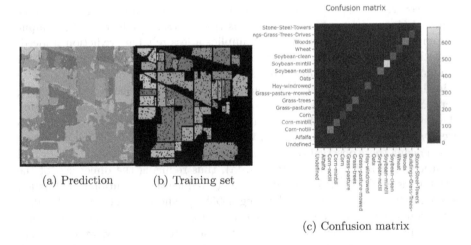

(a) Prediction   (b) Training set

(c) Confusion matrix

Fig. 6. Indian Pines prediction with 95% accuracy (a), the training set with 70% samples from ground truth (class Undefined in black) (b), and relative confusion matrix (c).

dataset is evident, as it halves energy consumption and markedly reduces the execution time. There is a slight improvement for the IP dataset when using the $10\,W$ modality. Instead, with $5\,W$, we only see an improvement in energy consumption when reducing the accuracy to 95%. This limitation is due to the HSI shape, which is spatially small but spectrally big in IP, and therefore the GPU-parallel PCA weights more on total time and energy consumption. To bet-

Table 2. Comparison of energy consumption and execution times on Jetson Nano (10 W modality) for Li et al. model without and with PCA preprocessing

	Without PCA		With PCA accuracy 95%		With PCA accuracy 97%	
	Secs	Joules	Secs	Joules	Secs	Joules
Pavia University	80	320.3	42	152.41	52	199.7
IndianPines	39	175.78	28	90.80	39	173.25

Table 3. Comparison of energy consumption and execution times on Jetson Nano (5 W modality) for Li et al. model without and with PCA preprocessing

	Without PCA		With PCA accuracy 95%		With PCA accuracy 97%	
	Secs	Joules	Secs	Joules	Secs	Joules
Pavia University	107	354.97	48	166.21	62	204.07
IndianPines	50	148.58	36	102.3	48	186.24

ter understand the energetic performance of our proposed pipeline, we compare in Table 4 several items. We calculated energy consumption on the RTX 2060 in joules, multiplying the GPU's Thermal Design Point (160 W) by the execution time.

It appears evident that for the overall measuring, the execution on the RTX is less time-consuming at the cost of more energy absorption. On the other hand, using both Jetson's modalities for the PCA implemented with cuBLAS, we measured a saving of about 95% of energy compared to RTX, but with an increment of only 55 − 61% in the execution time. This result is fascinating when considering possible future data processing implementations at the Edge. Regarding the performance of the PCA from scikit-learn, it does not exploit the GPU and therefore is non-competitive.

Looking at overall measuring, including 3D-CNN, we report an increase of about 90% in execution time, saving 70 − 80% in terms of power consumption. That proportion is not promising as the PCA case, probably due to PyTorch inefficiencies. However, it is still an interesting option when connection bandwidth is critical. If we think of a situation with a poor transfer connection, processing at the Edge can reduce bandwidth requests. For example, in our case of HSI classification, the PU dataset consists of 33.2 MB, while the classification output is an image of 610x340 bytes.

Table 4. Comparison of energy consumption and execution times on both platforms, isolating PCA preprocessing contributions. In italic, measures for PCA using scikit-learn as reference. The totals refer to PCA with cuBLAS plus inference, setting the accuracy to 95%.

			RTX (160 W)	Jetson (10 W)	Jetson (5 W)
PaviaUniversity	**PCA Cublas**	Joules	28.8	1.34	1.21
		Secs	0.18	0.4	0.42
	PCA scikit-learn	*Joules*		*18.02*	*23.11*
		Secs	*3.09*	*5.38*	*7.64*
	Total	Joules	481.6	152.41	138.59
		Secs	3.01	42	48
IndianPines	**PCA Cublas**	Joules	43.2	2.49	2.10
		Secs	0.27	0.7	0.7
	PCA scikit-learn	*Joules*		*12.12*	*17.10*
		Secs	1.48	*3.41*	*5.7*
	Total	Joules	432.0	90.80	102.3
		Secs	0.27	28	36

5   Conclusions

This work shows an innovative perspective on the HSI classification problem contextualized in High-Performance Edge Computing. By adopting the Nvidia Jetson Nano system-on-chip, which can be attached to remote sensors of various types, we developed an HSI classifier optimized for the Edge to enable onboard processing. In such a context, the processing time is focal; therefore, we chose the most promising 3D-CNN model in prediction accuracy and inference time using a GPU.

Then, to further speed up the processing, we applied a Principal Component Analysis to the original dataset to obtain up to a 90% reduction in size without significantly depleting accuracy.

To exploit the acceleration available on the Jetson Nano and achieve high performance, we implemented a GPU-parallel version of the PCA in CUDA. Furthermore, we analyzed the energy absorption on the Jetson Nano to identify the best energy configuration for our problem. The 10W modality resulted in the shortest execution time, even if it did not correspond to greater energy consumption for both considered datasets.

Results are encouraging to further investigate the problem by analyzing datasets from more recent sensors that are not yet publicly available. Moreover, additional analysis of the two energy modalities in the Jetson Nano on other applications can result in possibly interesting evidence about Edge energy consumption. Another improvement could be considering a scenario where the GPU is remoted and the actual computation executed on low-power devices or single-board computers, as in [24,26].

References

1. Ai, Y., Peng, M., Zhang, K.: Edge cloud computing technologies for internet of things: a primer. Digit. Commun. Netw. **4**, 77–86 (2017)
2. Andrecut, M.: Parallel GPU implementation of iterative PCA algorithms. J. Comput. Biol. **16**(11), 1593–1599 (2009)
3. Armbrust, M., et al.: A view of cloud computing. Commun. ACM **53**(4), 50–58 (2010)
4. Audebert, N.: Deephyperx. https://github.com/nshaud/DeepHyperX
5. Audebert, N., Le Saux, B., Lefèvre, S.: Deep learning for classification of hyperspectral data: a comparative review. IEEE Geosci. Remote Sens. Mag. **7**(2), 159–173 (2019)
6. Audebert, N., Le Saux, B., Lefèvre, S.: Semantic segmentation of earth observation data using multimodal and multi-scale deep networks. In: Lai, S.-H., Lepetit, V., Nishino, K., Sato, Y. (eds.) ACCV 2016. LNCS, vol. 10111, pp. 180–196. Springer, Cham (2017). https://doi.org/10.1007/978-3-319-54181-5_12
7. Ben Hamida, A., Benoit, A., Lambert, P., Ben Amar, C.: 3-D deep learning approach for remote sensing image classification. IEEE Trans. Geosci. Remote Sens. **56**(8), 4420–4434 (2018)
8. Chang, C.I.: Hyperspectral Imaging: Techniques for Spectral Detection and Classification, vol. 1. Springer, Cham (2003)
9. Chen, Y., Jiang, H., Li, C., Jia, X., Ghamisi, P.: Deep feature extraction and classification of hyperspectral images based on convolutional neural networks. IEEE Trans. Geosci. Remote Sens. **54**(10), 6232–6251 (2016)
10. De Lucia, G., Lapegna, M., Romano, D.: Towards explainable AI for hyperspectral image classification in edge computing environments. Comput. Electr. Eng. **103**, 108381 (2022)
11. Ding, N., Wagner, D., Chen, X., Pathak, A., Hu, Y.C., Rice, A.: Characterizing and modeling the impact of wireless signal strength on smartphone battery drain. ACM SIGMETRICS Perform. Eval. Rev. **41**(1), 29–40 (2013)
12. Grahn, H., Geladi, P.: Techniques and Applications of Hyperspectral Image Analysis. John Wiley, Hoboken (2007)
13. Greenberg, A., Hamilton, J., Maltz, D.A., Patel, P.: The cost of a cloud: research problems in data center networks. SIGCOMM Comput. Commun. Rev. **39**(1), 68–73 (2009)
14. Grupo de Inteligencia Computacional (GIC): Hyperspectral dataset. http://www.ehu.eus/ccwintco/index.php/Hyperspectral_Remote_Sensing_Scenes
15. Ha, K., Chen, Z., Hu, W., Richter, W., Pillai, P., Satyanarayanan, M.: Towards wearable cognitive assistance. In: Proceedings of the 12th Annual International Conference on Mobile Systems, Applications, and Services, MobiSys 2014, pp. 68–81. Association for Computing Machinery, New York (2014)
16. He, M., Li, B., Chen, H.: Multi-scale 3D deep convolutional neural network for hyperspectral image classification. In: 2017 IEEE International Conference on Image Processing (ICIP), pp. 3904–3908 (2017)
17. Lapegna, M., Balzano, W., Meyer, N., Romano, D.: Clustering algorithms on low-power and high-performance devices for edge computing environments. Sensors **21**(16), 5395 (2021)
18. Lee, H., Kwon, H.: Going deeper with contextual CNN for hyperspectral image classification. IEEE Trans. Image Process. **26**(10), 4843–4855 (2017)

19. Li, J., Cui, R., Li, B., Li, Y., Mei, S., Du, Q.: Dual 1d–2d spatial-spectral CNN for hyperspectral image super-resolution. In: IGARSS 2019–2019 IEEE International Geoscience and Remote Sensing Symposium, pp. 3113–3116 (2019)
20. Li, Y., Zhang, H., Shen, Q.: Spectral-spatial classification of hyperspectral imagery with 3D convolutional neural network. Remote Sens. 9(1), 67 (2017)
21. Li, Y., Zhang, H., Shen, Q.: Spectral-spatial classification of hyperspectral imagery with 3D convolutional neural network. Remote Sens. 9(1) (2017)
22. Luo, Y., Zou, J., Yao, C., Zhao, X., Li, T., Bai, G.: HSI-CNN: a novel convolution neural network for hyperspectral image. In: 2018 International Conference on Audio, Language and Image Processing (ICALIP), pp. 464–469 (2018)
23. Makantasis, K., Karantzalos, K., Doulamis, A., Doulamis, N.: Deep supervised learning for hyperspectral data classification through convolutional neural networks. In: 2015 IEEE International Geoscience and Remote Sensing Symposium (IGARSS), pp. 4959–4962. IEEE (2015)
24. Marcellino, L., et al.: Using GPGPU accelerated interpolation algorithms for marine bathymetry processing with on-premises and cloud based computational resources. In: Wyrzykowski, R., Dongarra, J., Deelman, E., Karczewski, K. (eds.) PPAM 2017. LNCS, vol. 10778, pp. 14–24. Springer, Cham (2018). https://doi.org/10.1007/978-3-319-78054-2_2
25. Marmanis, D., Wegner, J.D., Galliani, S., Schindler, K., Datcu, M., Stilla, U.: Semantic segmentation of aerial images with an ensemble of CNSS. ISPRS Ann. Photogrammetry Remote Sens. Spat. Inf. Sci. 2016(3), 473–480 (2016)
26. Montella, R., Giunta, G., Laccetti, G.: Virtualizing high-end GPGPUS on arm clusters for the next generation of high performance cloud computing. Cluster Comput. 17(1), 139–152 (2014)
27. Raychaudhuri, D., Nagaraja, K., Venkataramani, A.: Mobilityfirst: a robust and trustworthy mobility-centric architecture for the future internet. ACM SIGMOBILE Mob. Comput. Commun. Rev. 16(3), 2–13 (2012)
28. Rodarmel, C., Shan, J.: Principal component analysis for hyperspectral image classification. Surv. Land Inf. Syst. 62(2), 115–123 (2002)
29. Romano, D., Lapegna, M.: A GPU-parallel image coregistration algorithm for InSar processing at the edge. Sensors 21(17), 5916 (2021)
30. Sabins, F.F.: Remote sensing for mineral exploration. Ore Geol. Rev. 14(3–4), 157–183 (1999)
31. Slavkovikj, V., Verstockt, S., De Neve, W., Van Hoecke, S., Van de Walle, R.: Hyperspectral image classification with convolutional neural networks. In: Proceedings of the 23rd ACM International Conference on Multimedia, pp. 1159–1162 (2015)
32. Tharwat, A.: Principal component analysis-a tutorial. Int. J. Appl. Pattern Recognit. 3(3), 197–240 (2016)
33. Volpi, M., Tuia, D.: Dense semantic labeling of subdecimeter resolution images with convolutional neural networks. IEEE Trans. Geosci. Remote Sens. 55(2), 881–893 (2016)

Parallel gEUD Models for Accelerated IMRT Planning on Modern HPC Platforms

Juan José Moreno[1][✉], Janusz Miroforidis[2], Ignacy Kaliszewski[2], and Gracia Ester Martín Garzón[1]

[1] Informatics Department, ceiA3, University of Almería, Almería, Spain
{juanjomoreno,gmartin}@ual.es
[2] Systems Research Institute, Polish Academy of Sciences, Warsaw, Poland

Abstract. Radiotherapy treatments apply high doses of radiation to tumorous cells to break the structure of cancer DNA, trying at the same time to minimize radiation doses absorbed by healthy cells. The personalized design of radiotherapy plans has been a relevant challenge since the beginning of these therapies. A wide set of models have been defined to translate complex clinical prescriptions into optimization problems. The model based on the generalized equivalent uniform dose, gEUD, is very relevant for IMRT radiotherapy planning in clinical practice. This way, the expert physicists can tune plans near the prescriptions, solving the optimization problem based on gEUD in a trial-and-error process. The gradient descent methods can be applied for solving these models personalized for every patient. However, their computational requirements are huge. So, to facilitate their use in clinical practice it is necessary to apply HPC techniques to implement such models. In this work, we have developed two parallel implementations of an gEUD model for IMRT planning on multi-core and GPU architectures, as they are increasingly available in clinical settings. Both implementations are evaluated with two Head&Neck clinical tumor cases on modern GPU and multi-core CPU platforms. Our implementations are very useful since they help expert physicists obtain fast plans that can satisfy all the prescriptions.

Keywords: Radiotherapy Planning · Intensity Modulated Radiation Therapy (IMRT) · gEUD models · Gradient Descent · GPU computing · multi-core CPU

1 Introduction

External beam radiation therapies kill the diseased tissue cells with radiation emitted by a source from outside the body. To achieve this goal, it is necessary to design personalized RadioTherapy Plans (RTPs) to get specific 3D distribution

This work has been supported by the projects: RTI2018-095993-B-I00 and PID2021-123278OB-I00 (funded by MCIN/AEI/10.13039/501 100011033/FEDER "A way to make Europe"); UAL18-TIC-A020-B (funded by Junta de Andalucía and the European Regional Development Fund, ERDF).

R. Wyrzykowski et al. (Eds.): PPAM 2022, LNCS 13827, pp. 139–150, 2023.
https://doi.org/10.1007/978-3-031-30445-3_12

radiation doses which effectively destroy diseased cells with minimal side effects on the healthy ones.

IMRT devices deliver beams of radiation to radiated patients from different angles with varied intensities within a beam. The angles are fixed by the IMRT equipment. To control the radiation dose deposition each beam is decomposed in a regular grid of (thousands of) beamlets, whose radiation intensity can be individually controlled. Every RTP is defined by the specific intensities of all the beamlets, referred to as a fluence map. This way, the goal is to determine the fluence maps that deliver doses near the prescriptions on tumors and healthy tissues. The prescribed doses are defined by the segmentation of the patients' tomography images composed of millions of voxels. Therefore, the definition of effective RTPs has been a challenge from the very beginning of the development of this type of therapy, due to the contradictory aims and the high dimensions of the involved data [1]. So, intensive efforts have been developed to obtain software tools which help medical physicists to find the most effective RTPs. Such tools are based on the definition of optimization models, whose solutions are developed using high-performance computing (HPC) techniques.

The model based on generalized equivalent uniform dose (gEUD) is very relevant in clinical practice and it is the focus of this work [7,13]. Such model allows to compute RTPs near to a subset of prescriptions by solving the optimization problem based on gEUD. It can be solved by gradient methods, as it is proposed in [2]. These RTPs are used by the medical physicist as an important tool in the trial-and-error process to design clinical feasible RTPs according to the whole set of oncologist's criteria for every patient. The workflow for the personalized RTP design is complex and the use of fast and accurate tools in such process is essential.

In contrast, all the main processes related with the design of IMRT planning have huge computational demands. Consequently, in addition to the design of efficient algorithms, it is necessary to apply HPC techniques to accelerate and extend the application of such algorithms. There are many works focused on the exploitation of the parallelism involved in the RTP design on several platforms, for example, on multicore and vector units on CPU [14], or on reconfigurable hardware architectures (FPGAs) [15].

Graphics Processing Units (GPUs) deserve special mention as HPC platforms which can accelerate the computationally intensive tasks in the design of RTPs, such as tomography reconstruction, high spatial/temporal resolution image processing, Monte Carlo radiation dose simulations and radiotherapy planning [3,6,12]. Such computations exhibit massive parallelism which can squeeze the architecture of GPU platforms. Moreover, currently, GPUs are consolidated resources which can be integrated into the cloud platforms or servers applied in clinical practices. The design of RTPs can be strongly accelerated on GPU platforms. However, it is necessary to reprogram the algorithms or even to propose new methods to better exploit the parallelism of the GPU platforms.

This work aims to develop fast planners based on the main biological criteria, gEUD, accelerated on GPUs and multicore platforms. The convexity proprieties of the corresponding objective functions allow us to apply gradient methods to find near-optimal RTPs, as suggested from the definition of gEUD [13]. Therefore, we have selected the Gradient Descent (GD) method since it is a well-known optimization method [4,10] which has been already used for solving a penalty-based quadratic optimization model for IMRT planning on GPU [5].

The main goal of this work is to express the GD for the RTP design based on gEUD in terms of efficient matrix operations on GPUs and multi-core CPUs and to develop the corresponding parallel planner, reducing the communications overload and tuning the memory access performance. As far as we know, such fast planners are not referred to in the literature, despite the great interest as it has been motivated above.

The outline of the paper is as follows. Section 2 presents the formulation of IMRT planning based on gEUD criteria as an optimization problem solved by the GD method. The main issues related to the efficient GPU and multi-core CPU implementations are described. In Sect. 3 both implementations of the planner based on gEUD and GD are evaluated with two clinical cases in terms of computational performance and accuracy of the planning in relation to the prescriptions. Section 4 presents directions for further research and conclusions.

2   Formulation of Radiotherapy Planning

Oncological radiotherapy planning is needed when a number (from one to several) tumorous cell locations (Planning Target Volumes – PTVs) have to be radiated to kill the malignant tissue and several healthy organs (Organs at Risk – OARs) have to be spared as much as possible. Neutral (or normal) tissue (NT) is also to be spared. PTVs, OARs and NT form a predefined set of Regions of Interest (ROIs). In the general case, this calls for a multiobjective optimization setting, but the optimization model based on gEUD translates all goals to one function to maximize. To facilitate the reading, we introduce Table 1 to define the notation used.

In the Intensity Modulated Radiotherapy (IMRT) technique the process is controlled by the intensities of radiating rays (beamlets) to which the field radiated from the head is discretized. There are several (usually more than six) positions of the radiating head (beams) from which the radiation is delivered to a patient in one session.

An effective optimization model for IMRT planning is based on the generalized equivalent uniform dose (gEUD) using a linear-quadratic cell survival model [7]. It is possible to define an objective function that not only defines a penalty factor for every planning constraint but also it expresses the dose uniformity by the integration of generalized equivalent uniform dose (gEUD) in such a model. This approach was introduced by [13] where the optimal fluence map is defined by the argument that maximizes $F(x)$:

$$\max F(x) \tag{1}$$

Table 1. Notation for the formulation of optimization model based on gEUD

Notation	Meaning
M	Number of voxels
N	Number of beamlets
x	Array related to fluence map
D	Sparse dose deposition matrix
$d(x) = Dx$	Array of doses for each voxel as function of fluence map x
S_s	Array of voxel indices for region s
$gEUD_s^0$	Prescribed/constraining dose for region s
T	Set of all PTVs
$t \in T$	Index of a specific PTV
R	Set of all OARs and virtual PTVs
$r \in R$	Index of a specific OAR
S	Set of all ROIs
$s \in S$	Index of a specific ROI structure

with

$$F(x) = \prod_{r \in R} f_r(x) \prod_{t \in T} f_t(x) \qquad (2)$$

and

$$f_r(x) \equiv \frac{1}{1 + \left(\frac{gEUD_r(x)}{gEUD_r^0} \right)^{n_r}} \qquad (3)$$

$$f_t(x) \equiv \frac{1}{1 + \left(\frac{gEUD_t^0}{gEUD_t(x)} \right)^{n_t}} \qquad (4)$$

where $gEUD_t^0$ is the min desired doses at the PTV with index t and $gEUD_r^0$ is the max dose at the region of index r with constrains doses according to the prescriptions; the parameters n_r, n_t indicate the importance of the structure-specific in the optimization model and its role is similar to a weight or penalty of such structure. The $gEUD_r(x)$ and $gEUD_t(x)$ functions are related to a biological metric which defines the generalized equivalent uniform dose which gets the same effect than the actual nonuniform dose distribution on the regions of interest. Such functions are defined by the same relations independently of the kind of structure with index s:

$$gEUD_s(x) = \left(\frac{1}{|S_s|} \sum_{j \in S_s} d_j(x)^{a_s} \right)^{\frac{1}{a_s}} \qquad (5)$$

where $|S_s|$ is the number of voxels of the region s, $d_j(x)$ is the element j of the dose vector related to voxel j in s region for the fluence map, x and it is computed as the product of deposition matrix and the vector x, $d(x) = Dx$; and a_s is a parameter related to the radiation effect on the specific region s, it can be empirically adjusted by calibration processes. In practice such parameters are fixed by the values available in the literature for a wide set of organs. In general, we can say that a_t (a_r) gets large negative (or positive) values.

As described, the proposed model clearly distinguishes between Organs at Risk (OARs) and Planning Target Volumes (PTVs), defining different objective functions for each one. Equation 3 controls the maximum (or average maximum, depending on the value of a_r) dose irradiated to a given OAR does not exceed the respective constraint, while Eq. 4 controls the minimum dose irradiated to a given PTV.

However, for PTVs, avoiding overdosage inside the volume is also important. Therefore, is it common to define a new structure for each PTV (commonly called "Virtual PTV") which is treated as an OAR. On this work, we have defined virtual PTVs for each PTV and, to lighten the optimization costs, linked their parameters. Therefore, for each PTV t, there is a virtual PTV r with $gEUD_0^r = gEUD_0^t + 1$, $a_r = -a_t$ and $n_r = n_t$. These virtual PTVs are treated as OARs and included into the R set, so no special treatment or changes to the algorithm are required.

2.1 Gradient Descent

The objective function $F(x)$ is non-linear and differentiable, so a gradient descent method can be used to explore possible plans that maximize $F(x)$. To facilitate the computation of the derivatives, we can transform optimization model bearing in mind that functions $F(x)$ and $\ln F(x)$ share their optimal arguments because $0 < F(x) \leq 1$, $\forall x$. So, the gradient function to look for the arguments x that maximize $F(x)$ can be decomposed by the gradients of $\ln f_r(x)$ and $\ln f_t(x)$ which are computed as

$$\nabla \ln f_r(x) = \frac{-n_r f_r(x)}{\sum_{j \in S_r} d_j(x)^{a_r}} \left(\frac{gEUD_r(x)}{gEUD_r^0} \right)^{n_r} D^T \begin{pmatrix} A_1^r(x) \\ \cdots \\ A_M^r(x) \end{pmatrix} \quad (6)$$

$$\nabla \ln f_t(x) = \frac{n_t f_t(x)}{\sum_{j \in S_t} d_j(x)^{a_t}} \left(\frac{gEUD_t^0}{gEUD_t(x)} \right)^{n_t} D^T \begin{pmatrix} A_1^t(x) \\ \cdots \\ A_M^t(x) \end{pmatrix} \quad (7)$$

where $A_j^s(x) = d_j(x)^{a_s - 1}$ if $j \in S_s$ and $A_j^s(x) = 0$ in other case. This way, Eqs. 6 and 7 are the keys to compute the gradient vector at every x.

Algorithm 1 describes the sequential implementation of the proposed model. This model does not require a feasible starting fluence map, so it can be initialized to zero. After the initialization, we start the iterative gradient descent process, which begins by computing the dose deposition in the patient body. This sparse matrix – dense vector multiplication is the most computationally intensive part of the algorithm. Subsequently, for each region, we calculate the gEUD (lines 4–6) and the region-specific components of Eq. 9 and 12 (lines 7–12). Afterwards, we calculate the voxel-specific components (lines 13–19). The resulting partial gradients (one for each ROI) are summed together to obtain a

Algorithm 1. Simplified gEUD-based Gradient Descent implementation

1: $x \leftarrow \mathbf{0}$ ▷ Initialize fluence vector to zero
2: **while** *running* **do**
3:    $\mathbf{d} \leftarrow \mathbf{D} \cdot \mathbf{x}$ ▷ Compute dose deposition from fluence
4:    **for** $s \in S$ **do**   ▷ For all ROIs
5:      $SUM_s \leftarrow \sum_{j \in S_s} d_j^{a_s}$
6:      $gEUD_s \leftarrow \left(\frac{1}{|S_s|} \cdot \sum_{j \in S_s} d_j^{a_s} \right)^{\frac{1}{a_s}}$ ▷ Calculate current gEUD value
7:    **for** $r \in R$ **do**   ▷ For each OAR
8:      $f_r \leftarrow \frac{1}{1+\left(\frac{gEUD_r}{gEUD_r^0}\right)^{n_r}}$ ▷ OAR objective function (Eq. 3)
9:      $\frac{\partial lnF}{\partial gEUD_r} \leftarrow \frac{-n_r f_r}{gEUD_r} \cdot \left(\frac{gEUD_r}{gEUD_r^0}\right)^{n_r}$ ▷ Common part of Eq. 6
10:    **for** $t \in T$ **do**   ▷ For each PTV
11:      $f_t \leftarrow \frac{1}{1+\left(\frac{gEUD_t^0}{gEUD_t}\right)^{n_t}}$ ▷ PTV objective function (Eq. 4)
12:      $\frac{\partial lnF}{\partial gEUD_t} \leftarrow \frac{n_t f_t}{gEUD_t} \cdot \left(\frac{gEUD_t^0}{gEUD_t}\right)^{n_t}$ ▷ Common part of Eq. 7
13:    **for** $s \in S$ **do**   ▷ For each ROI
14:      **for** $i \in M$ **do**   ▷ For each voxel
15:        **if** $i \in S_s$ **then**   ▷ If the voxel belongs to the ROI
16:          $\frac{\partial gEUD_s}{\partial d_i} \leftarrow gEUD_s \cdot \frac{d_i^{a_s-1}}{SUM_s}$ ▷ Voxel-specific part of Eq. 6 and 7
17:          $V_i^s \leftarrow \frac{\partial gEUD_s}{\partial d_i} \cdot \frac{\partial lnF}{\partial gEUD_s}$ ▷ From line 16 & 9 (12) for OARs (PTVs)
18:        **else**
19:          $V_i^s \leftarrow 0$
20:    **for** $i \in M$ **do**   ▷ For each voxel
21:      $V_i \leftarrow \sum_{s \in S} V_i^s$ ▷ Reduce the partial gradients for each ROI
22:    $\nabla \mathbf{x} \leftarrow \mathbf{D^T} \cdot \mathbf{V}$ ▷ Find the delta of the fluence for the gradient
23:    $x \leftarrow x + \nabla x \cdot step$ ▷ Move the fluence in the direction of the gradient
24:    $x \leftarrow \mathbf{smooth}(x)$ ▷ Smooth the fluence using a simple convolution kernel

vector of size M, which is multiplied by the transposed Dose Deposition Matrix D to obtain the delta, which is finally added to the current fluence to move it in the direction of the gradient.

During the final planning stage, the optimized fluence map is converted into multileaf collimator movements by leaf-sequencing algorithms. As leaf-sequencing can drastically change a fluency map, especially in zones with high inhomogeneity, some precautions must be taken to produce fluences that can be sequenced with minimal changes. With this objective, we smooth the fluence using the beams' geometry and a simple 3×3 convolution kernel. Our experimentation shows that giving 99% of the weight to the center does not substantially modify the beam shape, while providing enough smoothing so the adjustment done by leaf-sequencing algorithms is minimal.

In this listing, we do not describe the stopping criteria used by our iterative algorithm, as it depends on the clinical needs, available planning time and computational power. For this work, our implementations stop when all the constraints are fulfilled and at least 20000 descent steps have been processed.

The main results of this work are two implementations of the algorithm previously described: A GPU implementation for high-end systems containing CUDA-capable devices and multi-core CPU implementation able to run in most modern computers.

2.2 GPU Implementation

As described in the previous section, the most computationally intensive parts of this program are the sparse matrix – dense vector multiplications (lines 3 and 22, Algorithm 1) and the calculation of the gradient contributions from regions at every voxel (lines 13–19, Algorithm 1). All three of these procedures efficiently conform to the SIMD execution model used by modern Graphics Processing Units (GPU).

Therefore, the first implementation provided alongside this work has been built with the CUDA programming interface [8] to target modern NVIDIA GPUs. We use the cuSPARSE library (part of the CUDA SDK) for the sparse matrix multiplications [9] and we have developed several custom kernels to solve the different parts of the Gradient Descent, always trying to achieve the best data-level parallelism and performance. Furthermore, in terms of CPU–GPU memory transfers, this algorithm performs efficiently, as it only requires transferring the patient data before the iterative process and the final computed fluence at the end of the program.

2.3 Multi-core Implementation

For situations where CUDA-capable GPUs are not available or heterogeneous computing platforms are employed (such as modern HPC clusters) we have developed a second implementation to target Multi-core CPUs. This program uses the Intel Math Kernel Libraries (MKL) for the sparse matrix operations and custom OpenMP-accelerated code for the calculation of the gradient of each ROI. Additionally, we have carried some optimizations to take advantage of the (usually) bigger memory pools available and to make this implementation more competitive compared to the GPU one. As an example, both the Dose Deposition Matrix D and its transpose D^T are precalculated and stored in optimized forms to reduce SpMV computing time.

3 Experimental Results

For the experimentation of this study, we have solved two Head and Neck (H&N) IMRT cases. Both cases aim to fulfill physician dose prescriptions on PTVs while keeping the dose in OAR below the physician prescribed maximum (for serial organs) or average maximum (for parallel organs). Furthermore, to be able to generate the dose deposition, our optimizer uses a dose deposition model developed by researchers at the Warsaw University of Technology [11]. Table 2 shows the parameters of the two cases. Case 1 has three delineated PTV, while Case 2 only has two. Although both are treated by the same number of beam angles, the beam geometry makes Case 2 bigger than Case 1, which is reflected in the number of nonzero values of the sparse Dose Deposition Matrix.

Table 3 shows the gEUD parameters used by the optimization model. Six OARs are delineated, including the special "Normal tissue", defined as a region of the patient body outside all other OARs and PTVs. Showcasing the ease of use of the provided implementation, both cases share the same values of a_s and n_s parameters for the same kind of region (serial OARs, parallel OARs or PTVs). For each organ, the value of $gEUD_r^0$ corresponds to the maximum (or average maximum) dose allowed by the physician. For PTVs, $gEUD_t^0$ is the prescribed dose in the target volume. PTVs are usually named using their prescribed dose, defined in Table 3 as x.

Table 2. Plan specifications for each test case.

Parameter	Case 1	Case 2
Beam angles	9	9
Beamlets (N)	30265	33911
Voxels (M)	94647	160786
Regions	12	11
D nonzero	64,991,188	106,792,251
PTVs	3	2
PTV$_0$ pr. dose (Gy)	54.0	59.4
PTV$_1$ pr. dose (Gy)	60.0	66.0
PTV$_2$ pr. dose (Gy)	66.0	–

Table 3. gEUD optimization model parameters for both cases.

Region of Interest	gEUD Parameters		
	$gEUD_s^0$	a_s	n_s
Normal Tissue	74.25	10	5
Mandible	70.00	10	5
Salivary Gland R	26.00	1	5
Salivary Gland L	26.00	1	5
Spinal C. +3mm	50.00	10	5
Brainstem +3mm	60.00	10	5
PTV x	x	-50	50

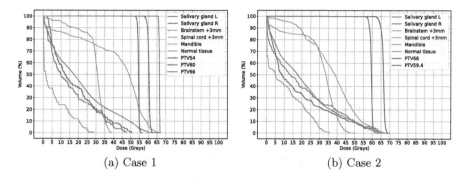

Fig. 1. Dose-volume histograms (DVH) of the resulting plans.

Using the model defined in Sect. 2 and the parameters defined above, we ran the GPU implementation for 30 s (approximately 9000 iterations for Case 1 and 5700 iterations for Case 2), obtaining the plans whose DVHs are exhibited in Fig. 1. These DVHs prove that both plans achieve good PTV coverage, while keeping the dose in OARs below the prescribed maximums.

Table 4 displays, in increased detail, statistics and metrics for the different ROIs. For the PTVs, the minimum or nearly minimum ($d98\%$) dose is expected to be higher than 95% of the prescribed dose. The maximum or nearly maximum ($d2\%$) dose is expected to be lower than 107% of the prescribed dose. $d98\% > 95\%$ means that at least 98% of the PTV's volume should be covered by 95% of prescribed doses. $d2\% < 107\%$ means that only at most 2% of PTV's volume can receive a dose higher than 107% of the prescribed dose.

From this table we can swiftly understand the characteristics of the plans. Firstly, we confirm that, in both plans, all OARs are below the physician prescribed doses. Secondly, for both cases, all PTVs are inside the upper and lower dose-volume constraints. These results show that simple parameter selection can achieve good results with the proposed gEUD model. However, per-case fine tuning is still necessary for clinical-grade results.

Furthermore, Fig. 2 displays two sample Beam's Eye Views from the fluence maps of the resulting plans. Thanks to the smoothing procedure carried out after each descend step of the gradient algorithm, these fluence maps can be easily converted to MLC motions using common leaf-sequencing algorithms.

Finally, the evaluation of both implementations has been carried out using two compute nodes from the HPC cluster of the "Supercomputación–Algoritmos" research group at the University of Almería. The first platform (alias Zen2) contains two AMD EPYC 7642 (for a total of 96 cores) and 512 GB of DDR4 3200 MHz MHz RAM. The second platform (alias Volta) contains two AMD EPYC 7302 (for a total of 32 cores), 512 GB of DDR4 3200 MHz MHz RAM and one NVIDIA Tesla V100 GPU with 32 GB or VRAM. Both platforms run CentOS 8.2 (OpenHPC 2), MKL 2020.1.217 and CUDA 11.7. As seen

Table 4. Statistics and metrics of the two proposed plans. $\bar{d}$ is the average dose, d^{max} is the maximum dose and $dx\%$ is a dose-volume metric, where x is a percentage of the volume.

ROI	Parameter (Gy)	Constraint	Case 1	Case 2
Salivary Gland L.	$\bar{d}$	26.00	15.10	19.55
Salivary Gland R.	$\bar{d}$	26.00	17.31	17.26
Spinal C. +3mm	d^{max}	50.00	38.74	49.30
Brainstem +3mm	d^{max}	60.00	28.68	35.73
Mandible	d^{max}	70.00	66.26	67.60
PTV 54	$\bar{d}$	54.00	54.45	–
	$d98\%$	51.30	53.30	–
	$d2\%$	57.78	55.50	–
PTV 60	$\bar{d}$	60.00	60.39	–
	$d98\%$	57.00	58.60	–
	$d2\%$	64.20	62.00	–
PTV 66	$\bar{d}$	66.00	66.37	–
	$d98\%$	62.70	65.80	–
	$d2\%$	70.62	66.80	–
PTV 59.4	$\bar{d}$	60.00	–	59.46
	$d98\%$	56.43	–	57.50
	$d2\%$	63.56	–	61.10
PTV 66	$\bar{d}$	66.00	–	66.22
	$d98\%$	62.70	–	63.30
	$d2\%$	70.62	–	68.20

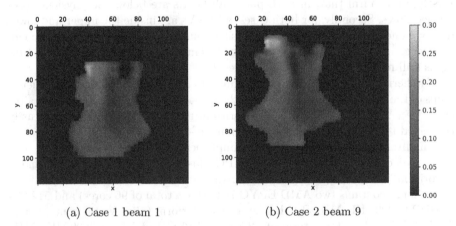

(a) Case 1 beam 1   (b) Case 2 beam 9

Fig. 2. Representation of two Beam's Eye Views (BEV).

Table 5. Time per iteration (in milliseconds) and acceleration of the sequential, multi-core and GPU implementations for the two platforms. For the multi-core implementations, 32 threads have been deployed in both platforms.

Platform	Implementation	Case 1		Case 2	
		T (ms)	Accel.	T (ms)	Accel.
Zen2	MKL Sequential	98.8	1.0 ×	144.1	1.0 ×
	MKL OpenMP	14.0	7.1 ×	20.2	7.1 ×
Volta	MKL Sequential	105.8	1.0 ×	153.8	1.0 ×
	MKL OpenMP	14.8	7.1 ×	21.1	7.3 ×
	CUDA cuSPARSE	3.4	31.1 ×	5.3	29.0 ×

in Table 5, both parallel implementations perform well compared to sequential execution.

4 Conclusions and Future Works

In this work, we have developed two fast implementations of the gEUD model for IMRT planning, applying specific HPC techniques on two implementations to efficiently exploit modern multicore CPUs and GPUs. The performance of these new implementations has been tested with real clinical data of two patients with Head and Neck tumors on two multi-core CPU platforms and a GPU. On multi-core CPUs an acceleration factor of 7 × in relation to the sequential version has been achieved, while on GPU we have achieved accelerations of up to 31 ×.

To conclude, modern HPC platforms can enable experts to generate feasible IMRT plans in a matter of seconds. As planning time is one of the most important clinical constraints, it is very relevant to improve the performance of the optimizers. Moreover, these HPC implementations allow us to address, as future work, the combination of this model with additional physical criteria to improve the quality of the automatically computed RTPs.

Acknowledgements. The authors wish to express their deep gratitude to following persons: Paweł Kukołowicz and Anna Zawadzka form Department of Medicine Physics, Memorial Skłodowska-Curie Cancer Center and Institute of Oncology, Warsaw, Poland, for data acquisition and methodological guidance; Jacek Starzyński, Robert Szmurło, Faculty of Electrical Engineering, Warsaw University of Technology, Warsaw, Poland, for access to their stand-alone dose deposition calculation software.

References

1. Breedveld, S., Craft, D., van Haveren, R., Heijmen, B.: Multi-criteria optimization and decision-making in radiotherapy. Eur. J. Oper. Res. **277**(1), 1–19 (2019). https://doi.org/10.1016/j.ejor.2018.08.019. http://www.sciencedirect.com/science/article/pii/S0377221718307148
2. Choi, B., Deasy, J.O.: The generalized equivalent uniform dose function as a basis for intensity-modulated treatment planning. Phys. Med. Biol. **47**(20), 3579–3589 (2002). https://doi.org/10.1088/0031-9155/47/20/302
3. Jia, X., Ziegenhein, P., Jiang, S.B.: GPU-based high-performance computing for radiation therapy. Phys. Med. Biol. **59**(4), R151–R182 (2014). https://doi.org/10.1088/0031-9155/59/4/r151
4. Lemaréchal, C.: Cauchy and the gradient method. Doc. Math. Extra **251**(254), 10 (2012)
5. Men, C., et al.: GPU-based ultrafast IMRT plan optimization. Phys. Med. Biol. **54**(21), 6565–6573 (2009). https://doi.org/10.1088/0031-9155/54/21/008
6. Neph, R., Ouyang, C., Neylon, J., Yang, Y., Sheng, K.: Parallel beamlet dose calculation via beamlet contexts in a distributed multi-GPU framework. Med. Phys. **46**(8), 3719–3733 (2019)
7. Niemierko, A.: Reporting and analyzing dose distributions: a concept of equivalent uniform dose. Med. Phys. **24**(1), 103–110 (1996)
8. NVIDIA: Cuda toolkit documentation v11.2.1 (2021). https://docs.nvidia.com/cuda/index.html. Accessed 9 Mar 2021
9. NVIDIA: cuSPARSE library (2022). https://docs.nvidia.com/cuda/cusparse/index.html. Accessed 18 May 2022
10. Snyman, J., Wilke, D.: Practical Mathematical Optimization - Basic Optimization Theory and Gradient-Based Algorithms. Springer, Cham (2018)
11. Starzyński, J., Szmurło, R., Chaber, B., Krawczyk, Z.: Open access system for radiotherapy planning. In: 2015 16th International Conference on Computational Problems of Electrical Engineering (CPEE), pp. 204–206 (2015). https://doi.org/10.1109/CPEE.2015.7333376
12. Tian, Z., et al.: Multi-GPU implementation of a VMAT treatment plan optimization algorithm. Med. Phys. **42**(6), 2841–2852 (2015)
13. Wu, Q., Mohan, R., Niemierko, A., Schmidt-Ullrich, R.: Optimization of intensity-modulated radiotherapy plans based on the equivalent uniform dose. Int. J. Radiat. Oncol. Biol. Phys. **52**(1), 224–235 (2002)
14. Ziegenhein, P., Kamerling, C., Fast, M.F., Oelfke, U.: Real-time energy/mass transfer mapping for online 4D dose reconstruction. Sci. Rep. **8**(1), 1–10 (2018)
15. Ziegenhein, P., et al.: Towards real time radiotherapy simulation. J. Signal Process. Syst. **92**(9), 949–963 (2020)

First Workshop on Quantum Computing and Communication

On Quantum-Assisted LDPC Decoding Augmented with Classical Post-processing

Aditya Das Sarma[1], Utso Majumder[1], Vishnu Vaidya[2], M Girish Chandra[3(✉)], A Anil Kumar[3], and Sayantan Pramanik[2]

[1] Jadavpur University, Kolkata, India
[2] TCS Incubation, Bengaluru, India
{vaidya.vishnu,sayantan.pramanik}@tcs.com
[3] TCS Research, Bengaluru, India
{m.gchandra,achannaanil.kumar}@tcs.com

Abstract. Utilizing present and futuristic Quantum Computers to solve difficult problems in different domains has become one of the main endeavors at this moment. Of course, in arriving at the requisite solution both quantum and classical computers work in conjunction. With the continued popularity of Low Density Parity Check (LDPC) codes and hence their decoding, this paper looks into the latter as a Quadratic Unconstrained Binary Optimization (QUBO) and utilized D-Wave 2000Q Quantum Annealer to solve it. The outputs from the Annealer are classically post-processed using simple minimum distance decoding to further improve the performance. We evaluated and compared this implementation against the decoding performance obtained using Simulated Annealing (SA) and belief propagation (BP) decoding with classical computers. The results show that implementations of annealing (both simulated and quantum) are superior to BP decoding and suggest that the advantage becomes more prominent as block lengths increase. Reduced Bit Error Rate (BER) and Frame Error Rate (FER) are observed for simulated annealing and quantum annealing, at useful SNR range - a trend that persists for various codeword lengths.

Keywords: LDPC code · Quantum annealing · Simulated annealing · Minimum distance decoding · QUBO

1 Introduction

Low Density Parity Check (LDPC) codes are linear block codes originally proposed in the 1960s by Gallager in his seminal doctoral work. The name reflects the fact that the parity check matrix used in LDPC coding is sparse with low density of 1s in the matrix. The performance of the LDPC codes approach theoretically described capacity limits, and therefore are very powerful. LDPC codes have established themselves as appropriate candidates for wireless systems based on multi-antenna multi-carrier transmission. Suitably designed LDPC codes are also proven to be excellent candidates for Hybrid Automatic Repeat Request

R. Wyrzykowski et al. (Eds.): PPAM 2022, LNCS 13827, pp. 153–164, 2023.
https://doi.org/10.1007/978-3-031-30445-3_13

(HARQ) schemes. The success and the consequent popularity of the LDPC codes over the years has resulted in support and proposals for its utilization in various applications and standards. Some examples are DVB-S2 (2nd Generation Digital Video Broadcasting via Satellite), 5G New Radio (NR) access technology standards, recent revisions of the 802.11Wi-Fi protocol family and various storage applications. Practically utilizable codes should constitute certain favourable properties, especially low encoding and decoding complexities, good waterfall regions, low error floors and flexibility in the context of getting different rates and frame lengths. There are various code designs available, starting from the pseudo-random constructions to sophisticated algebraic and graph-based techniques. See [10,11] and [3] and some of the original references therein for more details.

Good performance of LDPC codes can be achieved with a proper choice of code and decoding algorithm. Belief Propagation algorithms, like the Sum-Product algorithm are widely used in classical LDPC decoding. The Sum-Product algorithm can be viewed as a message passing algorithm operating on the Tanner graph, which is a bipartite graph representing the parity check matrix, and consisting of variable nodes and check (or constraint) nodes. Each iteration of the algorithm can be divided into two halves. In the first half, message is passed from each check node to all adjacent variable nodes and in the second, from each variable node to its adjacent check nodes. The decoding performance is achieved through multiple iterations of the message passing along the edges of the graph, until some stopping criterion is reached. In the direction of reducing the complexity of the (regular) Sum-Product algorithm, many variants of it have been proposed in the literature, one example being, min-sum algorithm (see [5,11] and the references there in for details).

Currently, we are in an exciting period in Quantum Technologies. With the intermediate-scale commercial quantum computers becoming increasingly available, Quantum Information Processing is witnessing spectacular developments (see [17,19,20] and the relevant references there in). Before quantum processors become scalable, capable of error correction and universality [17], the current and near-term devices, referred to as the Noisy Intermediate-Scale Quantum (NISQ) [20] devices are getting explored for solving certain hard problems to achieve significant speedups over the best known classical algorithms. Promising results are already reported for solutions in the areas like, optimization, machine learning and chemistry. Apart from speedup considerations, quantum mechanical properties of superposition, entanglement and interference are being explored for solving problems differently with possible performance improvements. In the NISQ era, the hybrid quantum-classical processing has established itself as an essential combination, and this "cooperation" will continue for a long time.

Considering the hardness and complexity of the some of the important problems in the current and emerging Communication Systems, research efforts have been under way to explore Quantum Computing paradigms to solve them. Some references in this direction are [6,13,15–17] and [2], among many others. Needless to say, due to the present requirements of Quantum Computers (QCs), like dilution refrigerators to maintain superconducting cooling, the usage of QCs are targeted to the Centralized Data Centers (Radio Access Networks), see for example, [17] and [15]. In this paper, similar to some of the references mentioned in this paragraph, we would be considering the baseband processing, in particular the LDPC decoding (in fact, we use [13] as the starting point). The relevance of LDPC codes in modern wireless networks can be seen in the search for computationally efficient decoders and their ASIC/FPGA implementations in [13]. As a futuristic notion, it is also useful to see how Quantum Processing Unit (QPU) enhanced (or accelerated) processing together with the classical computation can be worked out to carry out some of the complex and computationally heavy processing at the data center.

It has been well established for the last few years that QCs can "naturally" solve the discrete combinatorial optimization problems. Many of these problems fall under the unifying model of Quadratic Unconstrained Binary Optimization (QUBO) (see [18]). One of the approaches to finding the solution to a QUBO formulation is to construct a physical system, typically a set of interacting spin particles (two-state particles) whose lowest energy state encodes the solution to the problem, so that solving the problem is equivalent to finding the ground state of the system. Two main approaches have been identified to find the ground state of interacting spin systems (quantum optimization) on NISQ processors [17,19]: Quantum Annealing (QA) and Quantum Approximate Optimization Algorithms (QAOA) [7]. QA is an approximate or non-ideal implementation of Adiabatic Quantum Computing, which is an analog quantum computation. QA has been developed theoretically in the early nineties but realized experimentally in a programmable device by D-Wave Systems, nearly two decades later. A digitized version of Quantum Adiabatic Computing leads to QAOA, a gate-circuit based quantum computing.

In this paper, we have taken up the study of LDPC Decoding using Quantum Annealers similar to [13]. But, the following novelties are brought in. Keeping in mind the tandem working of Quantum and Classical computers, we have attempted to exploit the inherent randomness of the QCs and the outputs or the results of the runs/shots are subjected to classical postprocessing to arrive at better inference (in particular, better decoding) performance. In this direction, instead of just picking up the minimum-energy solution as prevalent in the Quantum Computing literature, the different outputs are post-processed using simple minimum distance computation to the received codeword vector to arrive at the final decoding. This approach sets the direction to consider appropriate and more sophisticated post processing for Quantum-Enhanced baseband processing. We have taken this route to bring out a notion of diversity emerging from the runs/shots. In fact, different outputs emerging from the runs/shots are seen as a kind of "diversity", which to the best of our knowledge are not interpreted this way in the existing literature. Preliminary results with length 32 and 96 rate half LDPC codes [1] demonstrate the improved performance of the quantum-enhanced decoders, even with these short lengths, over conventional Sum-Product Algorithm. The paper also spell out certain new

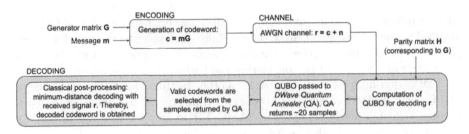

Fig. 1. Schematic of the approach

remarks/observations about different formulations considered and is organized as follows: In Sect. 2, we capture aspects related to classical Sum-Product and Min-Sum algorithms, QUBO and Annealing (both Simulated and Quantum). Section 3 provides the details about the Proposed augmented method; results and the discussions are covered in Sect. 4.

2   Brief Elaboration on Quantum Annealer and QUBO

2.1   D-Wave Quantum Annealer

Quantum Annealing (QA) is a metaheuristic for solving QUBO problems [9]. The adiabatic theorem of quantum mechanics states that Quantum Annealing, in a closed system, will find the final ground state encoding the solution, provided the annealing time is appropriately large compared to the inverse of the energy gap in quantum ground state. However, this does not guarantee that QA will always perform better than classical optimization algorithms, as the relative success of QA depends on the suitability of the optimization landscape to obtain an quantum advantage. D-Wave provides access to their devices which implement Quantum Annealing on Quantum hardware, through its cloud access provision Leap. Here, we are not capturing information on D-Wave Annealers, since nice documentation/information is available in their website. Also see [8,12].

2.2   QUBO

The concept of a QUBO formulation is fundamental to utilizing a Quantum Annealer to solve a given optimization problem.

Let $f : B^n \to R$ be a quadratic polynomial with $q_i \in B = \{0, 1\}$ for $1 \leq i \leq n$:

$$f_{\bar{\alpha}}(x) = \sum_{i=1}^{n} \sum_{j=1}^{i} \alpha_{ij} q_i q_j \tag{1}$$

The QUBO problem then consists of finding q^* such that:

$$q^* = \underset{q \in B^n}{\mathrm{argmin}} f_{\bar{\alpha}}(q) \tag{2}$$

The QUBO form of (1) can be written, separating the linear and quadratic terms, and noting that $q_i^2 = q_i$, and setting $\alpha_i = \alpha_{ii}$, as:

$$f_{\bar{\alpha}}(q) = \sum_{i=1}^{n} \alpha_i q_i + \sum_{i=1}^{n} \sum_{j=1}^{i} \alpha_{ij} q_i q_j \tag{3}$$

α_i is called the bias of the variable q_i, and α_{ij} is called the bias/coupling of the quadratic term $q_i q_j$.

Any optimization problem that we wish to solve with the QA, must first be formulated as a QUBO problem. We discuss the QUBO formulation of LDPC decoding in the next section.

3 Proposed Approach

The flowchart given in Fig. 1 summarizes the proposed solution approach. In the following sub-sections requisite details are elaborated.

3.1 Encoding

- To implement the LDPC encoding, we consider a valid parity matrix $\mathbf{H}$ and the corresponding generator matrix $\mathbf{G}$.
- For a randomly generated message $\mathbf{m}$, codeword $\mathbf{c}$ corresponding to $\mathbf{m}$ is obtained by multiplying $\mathbf{c}$ with the generator matrix $\mathbf{G}$.

$$\mathbf{mG} = \mathbf{c} \tag{4}$$

  where the multiplication is mod-2.
- To simulate the effect of the channel on the transmission of the codeword, we add Additive White Gaussian Noise (AWGN) to the transmitted codeword, to obtain the received signal $\mathbf{r}$:

$$\mathbf{r} = \mathbf{c} + \mathbf{n} \tag{5}$$

  where $\mathbf{n} \sim \mathcal{N}_N(\mathbf{0}, \sigma \mathbf{I})$. We can adjust SNR by adjusting the variance σ.

3.2 Decoding

- To decode the received signal $\mathbf{r}$, we first put in place the corresponding QUBO formulation. The QUBO for $\mathbf{r}$ is composed of two parts:

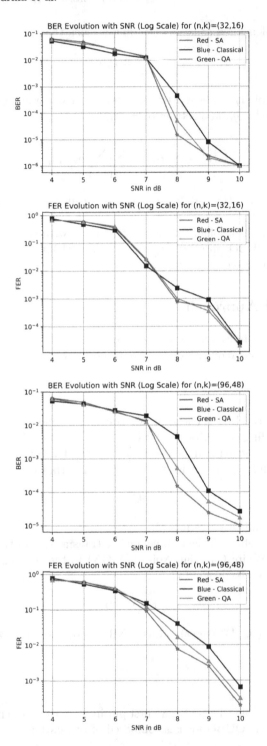

Fig. 2. BER, FER vs SNR for different problems

1. Distance Metric: Let binary variable q_i represent the ith bit of the decoded codeword. We compute the expectation of q_i given the received symbol r_i, as $P(q_i = 1|r_i)$. For an AWGN Channel with Binary Phase Shift Keying (BPSK) Modulation, this quantity, as given in [13], is:

$$Pr(q_i = 1|r_i) = \frac{1}{1 + \exp \frac{2r_i}{\sigma^2}} \tag{6}$$

We expect that the transmitted codeword is "proximal" to the received signal. Therefore, to find the transmitted codeword, we seek to minimize the following Distance Metric δ that computes the proximity of a codeword to the received information:

$$\delta = \sum_{i=1}^{n} (q_i - Pr(q_i = 1|r_i))^2 \tag{7}$$

A minimum of (7) is an estimate of the transmitted codeword, computed with the quantities $Pr(q_i = 1|r_i)$ alone.

2. Constraint Satisfaction Metric: The LDPC constraints ensure that the modulo-2 sum at each check node c_n is 0. These equality constraints need to be incorporated into an objective function that can be minimized. We implement this with the following function. For each check node c_i one can define LDPC satisfier function (see also [7]):

$$L_{sat}(c_i) = ((\Sigma_{\forall j:h_{ij}=1} q_j) - 2L_e(c_i))^2 \tag{8}$$

Through minimization of the above function, we can force the sum at that check node to be even: that is, force the modulo-2 sum at that node to zero. $L_e(c_i)$ is implemented with additional ancillary qubits. Next enters the Constraint Satisfaction Metric L:

$$L = \sum_{i} L_{sat}(c_i) \tag{9}$$

Minimizing L would result in the satisfaction of the LDPC constraints at the check nodes.

Finally, we combine the two components with Langrange weights W_1 and W_2, to compose the final QUBO. Minimizing the QUBO in general tends to minimize both the composite components. We can prioritize the minimization of one component over the other with a high choice for the Langrange weight for that component relative to the other. We have experimented with variations on W_1, keeping W_2 fixed at 1.0. The resulting QUBO is:

$$F = W_1\delta + W_2L \tag{10}$$

– The QUBO is then passed to the D-Wave annealer. Several samples are collected by running the annealer multiple times.

- Valid codewords (codewords that satisfy LDPC constraints) are filtered out from the samples and then minimum distance decoding is performed with the received signal to obtain the final decoded codeword.

As can be seen from the above description this QA-based framework doesn't require message passing iterations typically used to perform LDPC decoding with classical BP algorithms. Instead, a Quantum Annealer implemented on real Quantum hardware "naturally settles" to the optimal state for the QUBO, thereby performing the LDPC decoding.

4   Results and Discussion

Decoding was performed on LDPC parity matrices of dimensions (32, 16) and (96, 48), using quantum and simulated annealing, and classical Belief Propagation algorithms (see [1]). Quantum methods provide an inherent mode of diversity, due to its stochastic nature, giving different outputs for the same r, for different runs of the experiment. This advantage is not available for classical BP algorithms, which are deterministic in nature. In other words, for successive runs of the experiment, using the same r results in different outputs due to the inherent randomness in quantum information processing. On the other hand, it is trivial to observe that the same output, and not the "different copies" of information related to the transmitted codeword. Of course, this benefit is coming because of the use of Quantum Computers.

4.1   Results for Fixed SNR Channel

For this scenario, different SNRs are considered for experimentation. For each SNR, the BER and FER estimate is obtained with 10^6 Monte Carlo iterations. The term "fixed" refers to the fact that the SNR remains the same for all these 10^6 "transmissions". Elaborating little more, the number of times the quantum annealer used for a given SNR was the same as that of the number of received codewords used for assessing the performance, that is 10^6. Further, the number of reads per anneal used was 20. Coming to the results, based on the four plots in Fig. 2, the following observations are evident:

- In the moderate SNR regime, Quantum Annealing (QA) and Simulated Annealing (SA) perform better than the classical BP.
- At lower SNRs, performance of QA and SA is close to the performance of classical BP.
- However, a sharp drop is seen in BER, as well as in FER, around 7.5 to 8 dB range for both simulated and quantum annealing. When SNR reaches 10 dB, the noise becomes small enough such that all the methods achieves the similar BER and FER.

In the limited amount of studies we carried out using two short codewords, Simulated Annealing performs slightly better than Quantum Annealing. It is to be noted that the QA results are obtained from the actual D-Wave Annealer, and these realistic machines do have imperfections ("noisy behavior") at present. Of course, as remarked earlier, both SA and QA performed better than classical BP.

4.2   Results for Time-Varying SNR

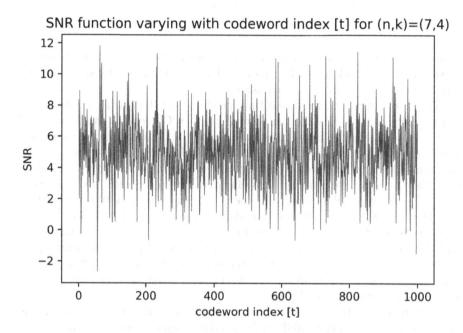

Fig. 3. Variation of SNR with respect to time

In order to simulate a time-varying SNR function and observe how the proposed approach performs in this case, the following procedure was undertaken and observations were recorded.

- For each of the 1000 codewords transmitted, the SNR is varied. In our experimentation, the samples have been drawn from the normal distribution with $\mu = 5$, $\sigma = 2$. A realization of the SNR is depicted in Fig. 3
- It is again observed that simulated annealing has the highest fraction of correct codewords decoded, followed by quantum annealing and classical belief propagation, as given in Table 1.

In this paper, we have just considered a time-varying SNR to assess the performance of the proposed methodology. In the direction of considering the more

Table 1. Fraction of correct codewords for time-varying SNR (for 10^6 Monte Carlo instances)

Methods	Fraction of correct codewords
Classical Belief Propagation	0.848
Simulated Annealing	0.946
Quantum Annealing	0.902

realistic scenarios, we are in the process of implementing complex-baseband processing with the Rayleigh fading channel. The possible modifications to QUBO formulation for this case is also envisaged.

The results for both fixed and time-varying SNR demonstrated the correct functionality of the QUBO formulation of the LDPC decoding augmented with post-processing which exploits the special diversity mentioned. Experimentations with longer codewords may bring out the beneficial aspects of the proposed approach compared to classical counterparts. Elaborating further, it is expected that the Quantum Computers, including the Annealers will only improve in terms of number of qubits, quality of the qubits, the connectivity between them, etc. They can then not only accommodate larger-sized problems (for instance, longer code lengths of practical importance, etc.), but also naturally solve them with better performance and speed compared to the fully classical counterparts (both Simulated Annealing and the variants of Sum-Product). Additionally, the right integration of classical and quantum computing systems may result in useful energy savings as well [14].

Keeping in mind the number of available qubits with D-Wave Annealers and hence the corresponding capability of supporting larger number of variables in an optimization problem, we focused our study in this paper using QA. QUBO problems can also be solved through Gate Model based Quantum Computing through different algorithms like QAOA, Variational Quantum Eigensolvers (VQE, see [4] and the references therein), etc. When futuristic gate-based hardware capable of running the "good-sized" problems are available, the Decoding problem can be systematically examined using the Quantum-Classical combination. The notion of "diversity" suggested in this paper also consider the fact that in Quantum Computing the probability amplitudes can interfere unlike in classical probabilistic computing. Together with other quantum effects, in principle, one can see a different potential of Quantum compared to classical; this thread can be further scrutinized through both theoretical and empirical angles for decoding as well as other communication signal processing.

5   Conclusion

Classical post-processing assisted quantum annealing is proposed for LDPC decoding which exploits the stochastic nature of quantum computers to arrive at improved solutions at SNRs of practical relevance, when compared with classical BP decoding. Unlike classical BP decoding, iterations are not required for this QA-based approach. The candidate solutions obtained through runs were post-processed based on minimum distance decoding and this can be extended to more refined methods. There is plenty of scope for expanding this work which uses both quantum and classical computations in co-operative manner for different baseband processing techniques.

References

1. https://www.uni-kl.de/channel-codes/channel-codes-database
2. Ahmed, F., Mähönen, P.: Quantum computing for artificial intelligence based mobile network optimization. In: 2021 IEEE 32nd Annual International Symposium on Personal, Indoor and Mobile Radio Communications (PIMRC), pp. 1128–1133 (2021). https://doi.org/10.1109/PIMRC50174.2021.9569339
3. Bae, J.H., Abotabl, A., Lin, H.P., Song, K.B., Lee, J.: An overview of channel coding for 5G NR cellular communications. APSIPA Trans. Sig. Inf. Process. **8**, e17 (2019). https://doi.org/10.1017/ATSIP.2019.10
4. Bharti, K., et al.: Noisy intermediate-scale quantum algorithms. Rev. Mod. Phys. **94**(1), 015004 (2022). https://doi.org/10.1103/revmodphys.94.015004
5. Chandra, M., Harihara, S., Adiga, B., Balamuralidhar, P., Subramanian, P.: Effect of check node processing on the performance of message passing algorithm in the context of LDPC decoding for DVB-S2. In: 2005 5th International Conference on Information Communications Signal Processing, pp. 1369–1373 (2005). https://doi.org/10.1109/ICICS.2005.1689281
6. Choi, J., Oh, S., Kim, J.: Quantum approximation for wireless scheduling. Appl. Sci. **10**(20), 7116 (2020). https://doi.org/10.3390/app10207116. https://www.mdpi.com/2076-3417/10/20/7116
7. Farhi, E., Goldstone, J., Gutmann, S.: A quantum approximate optimization algorithm applied to a bounded occurrence constraint problem (2015)
8. Finnila, A.B., Gomez, M., Sebenik, C., Stenson, C., Doll, J.D.: Quantum annealing: a new method for minimizing multidimensional functions. Chem. Phys. Lett. **219**(5–6), 343–348 (1994)
9. Hen, I., Spedalieri, F.M.: Quantum annealing for constrained optimization. Phys. Rev. Appl. **5**(3), 034007 (2016)
10. Janakiram, B., Chandra, M.G., Harihara, S., Adiga, B., Balamuralidhar, P.: On the usage of projective geometry based LDPC codes for wireless applications. In: 2009 7th International Conference on Information, Communications and Signal Processing (ICICS), pp. 1–5 (2009). https://doi.org/10.1109/ICICS.2009.5397612
11. Johnson, S.J.: Iterative Error Correction: Turbo, Low-Density Parity-Check and Repeat-Accumulate Codes. Cambridge University Press, Cambridge (2009). https://doi.org/10.1017/CBO9780511809354
12. Kadowaki, T., Nishimori, H.: Quantum annealing in the transverse Ising model. Phys. Rev. E **58**, 5355–5363 (1998). https://doi.org/10.1103/PhysRevE.58.5355
13. Kasi, S., Jamieson, K.: Towards quantum belief propagation for LDPC decoding in wireless networks. Association for Computing Machinery, New York (2020). https://doi.org/10.1145/3372224.3419207

14. Kasi, S., Warburton, P.A., Kaewell, J., Jamieson, K.: A cost and power feasibility analysis of quantum annealing for NextG cellular wireless networks (2021). https://doi.org/10.48550/ARXIV.2109.01465. https://arxiv.org/abs/2109.01465
15. Kim, M., Kasi, S., Lott, P.A., Venturelli, D., Kaewell, J., Jamieson, K.: Heuristic quantum optimization for 6G wireless communications. IEEE Netw. **35**(4), 8–15 (2021). https://doi.org/10.1109/MNET.012.2000770
16. Kim, M., Mandrà, S., Venturelli, D., Jamieson, K.: Physics-inspired heuristics for soft MIMO detection in 5G new radio and beyond, pp. 42–55. Association for Computing Machinery, New York (2021). https://doi.org/10.1145/3447993.3448619
17. Kim, M., Venturelli, D., Jamieson, K.: Leveraging quantum annealing for large MIMO processing in centralized radio access networks. In: Proceedings of the ACM Special Interest Group on Data Communication, SIGCOMM 2019, pp. 241–255. Association for Computing Machinery, New York (2019). https://doi.org/10.1145/3341302.3342072
18. Kochenberger, G.A., Glover, F.W.: A unified framework for modeling and solving combinatorial optimization problems: a tutorial. In: Hager, W.W., Huang, S.J., Pardalos, P.M., Prokopyev, O.A. (eds.) Multiscale Optimization Methods and Applications. NOIA, vol. 82, pp. 101–124. Springer, Boston (2006). https://doi.org/10.1007/0-387-29550-X_4
19. Pramanik, S., Chandra, M.G.: Quantum-assisted graph clustering and quadratic unconstrained D-ary optimisation (2021)
20. Preskill, J.: Quantum computing in the NISQ era and beyond. Quantum **2**(79), 10 (2018). https://doi.org/10.22331/q-2018-08-06-79

Quantum Annealing to Solve the Unrelated Parallel Machine Scheduling Problem

Francisco Orts[1]([✉]), Antonio M. Puertas[2], Ester M. Garzón[1], and Gloria Ortega[1]

[1] Informatics Department, University of Almería, ceiA3, Almería, Spain
{francisco.orts,gmartin,gloriaortega}@ual.es
[2] Department of Chemistry and Physics, University of Almería, ceiA3, Almería, Spain
apuertas@ual.es

Abstract. Quantum computing has emerged in recent years as an alternative to classical computing, which could improve the latter in solving some types of problems. One of the quantum programming models, Adiabatic Quantum Computing, has been successfully used to solve problems such as graph partitioning, traffic routing and task scheduling. Specifically, in this paper we focus on the scheduling on unrelated parallel machines problem. It is a workload-balancing problem where the processing time of any procedure executed on any of the available processing elements is known. Here, the problem is expressed as Quadratic Unconstrained Binary Optimisation, which can be subsequently solved using quantum annealers. The quantum nonlinear programming framework discussed in this work consists of three steps: quadratic approximation of cost function, binary representation of parameter space, and solving the resulting Quadratic Unconstrained Binary Optimisation. One of the novelties in tackling this problem has been to compact the model bearing in mind the repetitions of each task, to make it possible to solve larger scheduling problems.

Keywords: Adiabatic Quantum Computing · Quadratic Unconstrained Binary Optimisation · Scheduling on unrelated parallel machines problem

1 Introduction

Quantum computing takes advantage of the quantum mechanical effects to process information. The quantum hardware implements such principles to solve general computational problems. There are two ways of performing computational operations on a quantum computer. The most well-known is the approach based on a quantum circuit model of computation. This approach provides both a framework for formulating quantum algorithms and an architecture for the physical construction of quantum computers. This model of computation might provide a complete design of quantum computing in the long run, but nowadays is severely limited by the small number of qubits that make up real quantum platforms and by the errors introduced by each quantum gate. The other model relies on the adiabatic theorem.

Adiabatic Quantum Computing (AQC) is focused on the solution of combinatorial optimization problems. Although the goal of AQC is particular, it is of great interest since many of these problems are NP-complete and they are a challenge for conventional computation when the input problem grows. Moreover, these problems are involved in a wide set of applications as illustrated in [8]. AQC can solve such problems efficiently because their solution can be expressed as the ground state of an Ising Hamiltonian, which evolves in polynomial time [12]. The Ising Hamiltonian is used to model quadratic unconstrained binary optimization (QUBO). So, the QUBO problem is formulated to find the minimum of a quadratic polynomial with unitary variables. The physical realization of AQC are unreachable since the non-ideals conditions avoid the adiabatic evolution of the quantum hardware. Quantum Annealing (QA) is based on the AQC principles but in a flexible sense. Currently the Ising solvers are realized with quantum annealer, such as the D-Wave platform [7]. Thus, the translation of combinatorial optimization problems in QUBO models is the key for their QA solution.

Scheduling is one of the active areas of discrete optimization that plays a crucial role in manufacturing and service industries. The scheduling theory has been a focus of interest by researchers in management science, industrial engineering, and operations research. Many classical approaches to solve the different types of scheduling problems can be found in the literature, just to name a few [5,16,17]. In recent years, quantum computing has been postulated as an alternative and several authors have studied the behavior of these problems on quantum platforms. In [11] authors formulate the uncapacitated task allocation problem as a QUBO model. The work by Carugno et al. [3] studies the application of quantum annealing to solve the job shop scheduling problem and compares the solution quality with various classical solvers. In the present work, we focused our attention on the unrelated parallel machine problem.

The unrelated parallel machines problem consists of balancing the computational load among the available (heterogeneous) processing elements, when the processing time of any procedure executed on any of the available processing elements is 'a priori' known. In this work, the scheduling problem is transformed into a QUBO formulation, thereby allowing the use of Ising solvers such as D-Wave's quantum annealer. This transformation to QUBO is done by the quadratic approximation of cost function, binary encoding of the integer variables, and solving the problem using a quantum annealer.

The main contributions of this work are the following: (1) QUBO model has been designed and implemented in a real quantum annealer supplied by D-Wave to solve the unrelated parallel machine scheduling problem; (2) thanks to a technique based on the use of binary variables for setting the number of repetitions of every tasks, the number of required qubits has been considerably decreased and case studies with about 5000 variables have been solved on quantum annealers;

and (3) the proposed methodology can be extended to solve other combinatorial optimization problems.

The paper has been organized as follows. Section 2 is devoted to describing the quantum annealing computational model. Section 3 introduces the load balancing problem addressed in this work. Section 4 shows the QUBO formulation for the unrelated parallel machine scheduling problem and how it is solved on the D-wave annealer. In Sect. 5 the obtained results are shown and discussed. Finally, in Sect. 6 the main conclusions are drawn.

2   Quantum Annealing Computing

The adiabatic theorem assures that if we start at a state of minimum energy of a simple Hamiltonian and it evolves slowly, it will always remain in the state of lowest energy, ground state. So, the idea of quantum adiabatic computing is to select a ground state of a simple Hamiltonian, H_0, and make the system evolve during a time T to the state of minimum energy of the Hamiltonian of the problem H_p. So, we can define a Hamiltonian as a function of time to model its temporal evolution:

$$H(t) = (1 - \frac{t}{T})H_0 + \frac{t}{T}H_p \qquad (1)$$

In practice it is difficult to guarantee the adiabatic conditions, and quantum annealing s used as a heuristic approach which combines the adiabatic theorem and the Ising model [13] to build solvers of combinatorial optimization problems. It consists of:

1. $H_0 = -\sum_{i=1}^{n} Y_i$ is defined as initial Hamiltonian where n is the number of qubits,
2. H_p is defined as the target Ising Hamiltonian,
3. The system evolves from H_0 to H_p without adiabatic conditions being guaranteed,
4. The final state is measured to compute a possible minimum,
5. The process is repeated several times to compute various approximations of minima.

We recall that the Ising Hamiltonian defines a model of ferromagnetism in statistical mechanics with unitary discrete variables, since they represent magnetic spins that can be in one of two states. Therefore, QA is useful to solve combinatorial optimization problems with unitary variables. Moreover the Ising model can be translated to the QUBO model, which unifies a rich variety of combinatorial optimization problems [6].

Currently, D-Wave Systems Inc. has developed quantum hardware based on QA with a large number of qubits. This technology still suffers from limitations such as resource scarcity and control errors, among others. However, a wide set of practical optimization applications are being currently adapted to this technology since potentially it offers a huge computational power for solving large combinatorial optimization problems which are NP-complete.

The next sections are focused on the application of the QA methodology for solving Unrelated parallel machine scheduling. Therefore, we develop the steps related to the described methodology: (1) quadratic approximation of cost function of a compact model, (2) binary representation of the discrete variables, and (3) solving and testing the resulting QUBO model on the D-wave annealer.

3   Unrelated Parallel Machine Scheduling Problem Using Quantum Annealing

3.1   Definition of the Unrelated Parallel Machine Scheduling Problem

The problem of distributing N tasks, of J different types, in M processing units has been already described in the literature [14]; thus here we only give a short account. Briefly, the optimal distribution that minimizes the total time to execute all tasks is sought, namely:

$$
\begin{array}{lll}
\text{Find:} & n_{j,\alpha} & \\
\text{to minimize} & max \left\{ T_\alpha \right\} & \\
\text{with} & T_\alpha = \sum_j n_{j,\alpha} t_{j,\alpha} & \alpha = 1, \ldots, M \\
\text{subject to} & \sum_\alpha n_{j,\alpha} = x_j & j = 1, \ldots, J
\end{array}
$$

Here $\{n_{j,\alpha}\}$ is the number of tasks of type j assigned to Processing Unit (PU) named α, T_α is time needed by PU α to complete all of its tasks, and $\{t_{j,\alpha}\}$ is the runtime matrix of all tasks j in all PUs α. The J restrictions (last line) indicate that all jobs of type j, x_j, must be assigned.

The inputs to the problem are the number of PUs, M, the number of tasks of every type that must be assigned, $\{x_j\}$, and the runtime matrix, $t_{j,\alpha}$. Different strategies have been proposed to solve this problem, and commercial software is available, such as AMPL [4] and CPLEX [2].

3.2   From Binary Integer Programming (BIP) to QUBO

In order to solve this problem with quantum annealing, it has been reformulated as a quadratic unconstrained binary optimization (QUBO) problem following [6]. Let us define the function:

$$
O_0 = \sum_\alpha T_\alpha^2 \tag{2}
$$

The summation in O_0 is dominated by the largest term, i.e. by $max \{T_\alpha\}$, and therefore, minimizing $max \{T_\alpha\}$ is equivalent to minimizing O_0.

The first, brute force, approach to the problem is to consider that all tasks are different: $n_{j,\alpha}$ becomes then a binary variable, $n_{j,\alpha} = 1$ if task j is run in PU α and 0 otherwise, and the restriction now reads $\sum_\alpha n_{j,\alpha} = 1$ for all j, ensuring

that all tasks are run once. This restriction must be incorporated in the function
to be minimized:

$$O = \sum_\alpha T_\alpha^2 + \sum_j P_j \left(1 - \sum_\alpha n_{j,\alpha}\right)^2$$

$$= \sum_\alpha \left[\sum_j n_{j,\alpha}^2 t_{j,\alpha}^2 + 2 \sum_{k,l;k\neq l} n_{k,\alpha} n_{l,\alpha} t_{k,\alpha} t_{l,\alpha}\right] + \sum_j P_j \left(1 - \sum_\alpha n_{j,\alpha}\right)^2 \quad (3)$$

where P_j are "large" constants [6], and the expression of T_α has been substituted
in the second line to get an explicit expression. This formulation corresponds to
a QUBO problem, as expected.

This approach, however, requires as many unitary variables as elements in
the matrix $n_{j,\alpha}$, i.e. tasks to be assigned times the number of PUs, what restricts
importantly the size of the problem that can be studied. To overcome this issue,
we make use of the repetition of jobs for the same task. In this case, $n_{j,\alpha}$ is subject
to the last condition in the problem definition, $\sum_\alpha n_{j,\alpha} = x_j$, and therefore it is
no longer an unitary variable. To continue within the QUBO formulation, it can
be, nevertheless, expressed using unitary variables for the digits in the binary
representation [12]:

$$n_{j,\alpha} = \sum_{k=0}^{B} n_{j,\alpha,k} 2^k \quad (4)$$

where $B = int\left[log_2(R+1)+1\right]$, with $R = max\{x_j\}$; variables $n_{j,\alpha,k}$ are unitary.
Introducing this representation of $n_{j,\alpha}$ in the expression of O_0 and the restriction
yields finally:

$$O = \sum_\alpha T_\alpha^2 + \sum_j P_j \left(1 - \sum_\alpha n_{j,\alpha}\right)^2$$

$$= \sum_\alpha \left[\sum_j t_{j,\alpha} \sum_{k=0}^{B} n_{j,\alpha,k} 2^k\right]^2 + \sum_j P_j \left(x_j - \sum_\alpha \sum_{k=0}^{B} n_{j,\alpha,k} 2^k\right)^2 \quad (5)$$

It can be easily confirmed that this expression corresponds to a QUBO problem, and allows finding the distribution of $J \times R$ tasks in M processing units
using $J \times B \times M$ unitary variables. Since $B \sim log_2 R$, this implies an important
reduction in computing resources with respect to the initial formulation, given
by Eq. 3.

4   D-Wave Implementation

This section shows how to formulate the problem to be solved using D-Wave [9,
15, 18]. The code has been written in Python.

The implementation is oriented to receive, as inputs, the number of PUs, the number of different tasks, and the number of repetitions for each type of task. It must also be indicated the maximum possible value of completion time, and how long each type of task takes on each type of PU. The latter times can be specified in the form of a matrix, with each row being a type of task, each column a PU, and thus each element of the matrix represents the necessary time taken for each possible combination of type of task and PU. An example of how this can be easily represented is shown in Fig. 1. Based on Sect. 3, it is assumed that there are no dependencies between tasks and that each PU can only execute a single task at a time.

```
#Num of different jobs: 3
#Num of repetitions: 5
#Num of machines: 2


type id    machine 0      machine 1
---------  ---------      ---------

   0            1              2
   1            2              3
   2            3              1
```

Fig. 1. Example of an input file for a problem with 2 PUs, 3 different type of tasks, and 5 repetitions. Since tasks of the same type share execution times, the time is only shown once for each type of task.

Following the nomenclature used in the previous section, the following parameters have been considered to represent the problem in the code:

- **J**: is the number of different tasks.
- **R**: is the number of repetitions.
- **M**: is the number of PUs.
- **j**: is the set of different tasks $(1, 2, ..., J)$.
- **α**: is the set of PUs $(1, 2, ..., M)$.
- **$t_{j,\alpha}$**: is the processing duration that PU α needs for tasks of type j.
- **V**: maximum possible completion time (make-span).

To simplify the problem, all tasks are considered to have the same number of repetitions R. However, it is easy to modify the code so that each type of task can be assigned its own number of repetitions. This decision does not limit the conclusions of our work. These variables have also been used to work with the model:

- **O**: is a positive integer variable that defines the completion time (make-span).
- **B**: is the number of necessary binary digits to represent the number of repetitions (Eq. 4).
- $\{n_{j,\alpha,k}\}$: is the matrix of the distribution of tasks, where $n_{j,\alpha,k}$ represents the k-th digit in the binary representation of $n : j, \alpha$, which stands for the number of tasks of type j that are assigned to PU α.

We recall that the aim is to minimize the make-span (O, as it is defined in Eq. 3 and Eq. 5). It is important to clarify that V and O are different variables. V is a value entered by the user and indicates the maximum value allowed for the make-span (assuming it is possible to solve the problem in that time). O will contain the make-span found by the software.

According to the model described in the previous section, only one constraint needs to be established. This constraint is focused on ensuring that each task is executed only R times:

$$\sum_{\alpha} n_{j,\alpha} = R \tag{6}$$

where R will be 1 if we use the model set out in Eq. 3, or any other natural number if we work with the model in Eq. 5.

```
#Number of jobs: 15
#Number of machines: 2
#Completion time: 11.0
```

		machine 0			machine 1	
job id	type	start	dur	type	start	dur
0	0	0	1	0	0	0
1	0	1	1	0	0	0
2	0	2	1	0	0	0
3	0	3	1	0	0	0
4	0	4	1	0	0	0
5	1	5	2	0	0	0
6	1	7	2	0	0	0
7	1	9	2	0	0	0
8	0	0	0	1	0	3
9	0	0	0	1	3	3
10	0	0	0	2	6	1
11	0	0	0	2	7	1
12	0	0	0	2	8	1
13	0	0	0	2	9	1
14	0	0	0	2	10	1

Fig. 2. Example of an output file for the problem shown in Fig. 1. Each row corresponds to an executed task. The first column assigns a unique id to each task for the sake of clarity. The following columns, in groups of three, correspond to each PU. For each task/PU, the type of task, the start time, and its duration are indicated. If the duration is 0, it is understood that the task has not been executed on that PU.

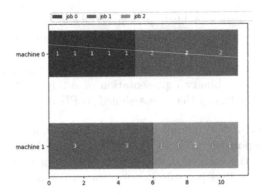

Fig. 3. Example of an output file for the problem shown in Fig. 1. Each row corresponds to an executed task. This results is the same as the one shown in Fig. 2, but represented graphically.

D-Wave returns the results using the representation specified in Eq. 4 through variable n. This matrix is not suitable for quick human interpretation. Therefore, once the results have been obtained, a further process is carried out to represent the data in a more readable and tractable format. To this end, the procedure carried out in Ku et al. [10] has been followed. For each task, the PU on which it is going to be executed, the start time, and the duration are represented. This representation is shown in text form (producing an output file with the indicated information), and also in graphical form. The work of Ku et al. [10] is focused on the problem called "Job Shop Scheduling", similar to the one discussed in this paper but with its own characteristics (tasks composed of subtasks, dependencies between tasks, etc.). Several implementations based on this problem are available on the D-Wave website [1]. These implementations include useful routines to transform the output of the problem into a more user-friendly format. The adaptation of these data processing routines to the unrelated parallel machine scheduling problem is simply a matter of Python programming skills. Examples of the output in text and graphical format can be seen in Figs. 2 and 3, respectively.

5   Evaluation

The evaluation of the software has been split up in two parts. First, the possible problem sizes to be addressed are studied using first the model described by Eq. 3 and second by Eq. 5. The size of each problem depends on the number of tasks and the number of PUs for the case of Eq. 3, and on the number of different tasks, the maximum number of repetitions, and the number of PUs for the case of Eq. 5. Second, the accuracy of the results has been validated.

5.1 Resource Assessment

The D-Wave device on which the software has been tested has 5000 qubits. According to the CQM model, an integer variable will be dedicated to the make-span, and $J \times M$ binary variables for the case where all tasks are different (model described by in Eq. 3). Ideally, the variable-qubit correspondence is direct. This approach allows us to solve any problem with J different tasks and M PUs as long as $J \times M < 5000$. That is, if we set a number of PUs M, the number of possible tasks will be a maximum of $4999/M$, and if we set a number of tasks of J, the maximum number of PUs we can include in the planning will be $4999/J$. However, in practice, some extra qubits are needed for topology reasons, so it is not possible to use the 5000 qubits in the way described. Table 1 shows the maximum possible values of each variable as a function of the value of the other.

Table 1. Maximum number of tasks and PUs using 5000 qubits and the model defined in Eq. 3.

Number of tasks	Number of PUs
4	1249
8	624
16	312
32	156
64	78
128	39
256	19
512	9
1024	4
2048	2

For the case where tasks can be grouped by type, an integer variable is still dedicated for the makespan, but in this case the problem needs $J \times R \times M$ binary variables. However, according to Eq. 5, the number of repetitions is being represented as $B = int[log2(R + 1) + 1]$, so the actual number of variables will be $J \times B \times M$ (again, a certain number of qubits must be dedicated to allow correct transpilation to the topology of the quantum computer). Again, $J \times B \times M < 5000$ must be satisfied, so any combination of J, R and M values that satisfies this expression is feasible to be solved by the proposed software. In this case, the introduction of B allows the number of executed tasks to be greatly increased if they can be grouped into types. Since the representation of the number of tasks is the one that allows to express larger numbers occupying fewer qubits, R (B) is the variable that can grow the most, so that if the problem contains few PUs and types of tasks, it can be solved involving millions of tasks. This is in contrast to the data shown in Table 1. Table 2 shows an example with

16 PUs ($M = 16$) and 7 types of tasks ($J = 7$). It can be seen how more than $4.8E + 12$ repetitions can be allowed for in each task type. That is, more than $3.3E + 13$ tasks can be executed in total). This is much higher than the 300 or so tasks we could solve with 7 PUs using the former formulation.

Table 2. Number of variables (qubits) used varying R for an example with $M = 16$ and $J = 7$. In the quantum device, R is expressed as $B = int[log_2(R + 1) + 1]$ so, for clarity of display, B is also shown. Furthermore, column 'Executed' identifies the total number of executed tasks, calculated by multiplying the number of task types by the number of repetitions ($J \times R$).

R	B	Variables	Executed
4	3	336	28
8	4	448	56
16	5	560	112
32	6	672	224
64	7	784	448
128	8	896	896
256	9	1008	1792
512	10	1120	3584
5.72E+5	20	2240	4.00E+6
5.86E+8	30	3360	4.10E+9
6.00E+11	40	4480	4.20E+12
1.20E+12	41	4592	8.40E+12
2.40E+12	42	4704	1.68E+13
4.80E+12	43	4816	3.36E+13

5.2   Validation of Results

To test the accuracy of the software, it has been used to solve more than 50 scheduling random problems by varying J, M, and R and keeping the number of executed tasks as small as possible. To perform this, a Python script was developed to generate input files with the corresponding configurations quickly and easily. This script accepts as input per command J, M, R, the maximum time that a task can last (we will denote t), and optionally the name of the output file. The name of the output file is, by default, instance_J_R_M.txt. The file will be in the format specified by Fig. 1, but naturally adapted to the specific parameters. The time for each type of task on each PU will be a random value between 1 and t, both values included.

Once the test files have been obtained, the optimal time for the planning of the problems they represent has been calculated using AMPL [4] and CPLEX [2].

The optimal value of each problem has been established as the maximum make-span for the execution of that problem with the proposed software with the aim of verifying whether it is capable of finding a schedule in that time. A maximum execution time in D-Wave of 10 seconds has been set. In all tested cases, the software was able to find a valid schedule in the optimal time. As a simple test, times shorter than the optimal time have also been tested. In such cases, the software has correctly indicated that it is not possible to find a task/PU configuration that solves the problem in the given time.

6   Conclusions

In this work, the scheduling of heterogeneous tasks on unrelated parallel machines has been solved using quantum annealing. The problem has been formulated using modularity mathematically and transform it to QUBO. The results obtained have been compared with classical methods such as CPLEX and AMPL to demonstrate that the quantum solution is of the same quality as the based on classical computing. D-Wave platform has been considered to perform the quantum annealing version of the scheduling of heterogeneous tasks. The obtained results are very promising since, thanks to the trick of using the binary representation to indicate the number of repetitions of each task, the number of qubits needed to represent them is reduced, thus being able to solve larger problems. Finally, it should be noted that the methodology used in this work can be applied to other combinatorial optimization problems.

Acknowledgements. This work has been supported by the projects: RTI2018-095993-B-I00 and PID2021-123278OB-I00 (funded by MCIN/AEI/10.13039/501 100011033/FEDER "A way to make Europe"); P20_00748, UAL2020-TIC-A2101, UAL18-FQM-B038-A and UAL18-TIC-A020-B (funded by Junta de Andalucía and the European Regional Development Fund, ERDF).

Authors would also like to thank Professor Dr. Elías F. Combarro, from the Informatics Department, University of Oviedo, Spain, because this work has been possible thanks to the contents of his interesting lectures about Quantum Computing at Almería University.

References

1. Ocean SDK demos. https://github.com/dwavesystems/demos
2. Bliek, C., Bonami, P., Lodi, A.: Solving mixed-integer quadratic programming problems with IBM-CPLEX: a progress report. In: Proceedings of the Twenty-Sixth RAMP Symposium, pp. 16–17 (2014)
3. Carugno, C., Ferrari Dacrema, M., Cremonesi, P.: Evaluating the job shop scheduling problem on a D-Wave quantum annealer. Sci. Rep. **12**(1), 1–11 (2022)
4. Fourer, R., Gay, D.M., Kernighan, B.W.: AMPL. A Modeling Language for Mathematical Programming. Thomson (2003)
5. Gehrke, J.C., Jansen, K., Kraft, S.E.J., Schikowski, J.: A PTAS for scheduling unrelated machines of few different types. In: Freivalds, R.M., Engels, G., Catania, B. (eds.) SOFSEM 2016. LNCS, vol. 9587, pp. 290–301. Springer, Heidelberg (2016). https://doi.org/10.1007/978-3-662-49192-8_24

6. Glover, F., Kochenberger, G., Hennig, R., Du, Y.: Quantum bridge analytics I: a tutorial on formulating and using QUBO models. Ann. Oper. Res. **314**, 141–183 (2022). https://doi.org/10.1007/s10479-022-04634-2
7. Grant, E.K., Humble, T.S.: Adiabatic quantum computing and quantum annealing. Oxford Research Encyclopedia of Physics, July 2020
8. Kochenberger, G., et al.: The unconstrained binary quadratic programming problem: a survey. J. Comb. Optim. **28**(1), 58–81 (2014). https://doi.org/10.1007/s10878-014-9734-0
9. Koshikawa, A.S., Ohzeki, M., Kadowaki, T., Tanaka, K.: Benchmark test of blackbox optimization using D-Wave quantum annealer. J. Phys. Soc. Jpn. **90**(6), 064001 (2021)
10. Ku, W.Y., Beck, J.C.: Mixed integer programming models for job shop scheduling: a computational analysis. Comput. Oper. Res. **73**, 165–173 (2016)
11. Lewis, M., Alidaee, B., Kochenberger, G.: Using xQx to model and solve the uncapacitated task allocation problem. Oper. Res. Lett. **33**(2), 176–182 (2005)
12. Lucas, A.: Ising formulations of many NP problems. Front. Phys. **2**, 5 (2014)
13. Mohseni, N., McMahon, P.L., Byrnes, T.: Ising machines as hardware solvers of combinatorial optimization problems. Nat. Rev. Phys. **4**(6), 363–379 (2022). https://doi.org/10.1038/s42254-022-00440-8
14. Orts, F., Ortega, G., Puertas, A.M., García, I., Garzón, E.M.: On solving the unrelated parallel machine scheduling problem: active microrheology as a case study. J. Supercomput. **76**(11), 8494–8509 (2020). https://doi.org/10.1007/s11227-019-03121-z
15. Phillipson, F., Bhatia, H.S.: Portfolio optimisation using the D-Wave quantum annealer. In: Paszynski, M., Kranzlmüller, D., Krzhizhanovskaya, V.V., Dongarra, J.J., Sloot, P.M.A. (eds.) ICCS 2021. LNCS, vol. 12747, pp. 45–59. Springer, Cham (2021). https://doi.org/10.1007/978-3-030-77980-1_4
16. Sels, V., Coelho, J., Dias, A., Vanhoucke, M.: Hybrid tabu search and a truncated branch-and-bound for the unrelated parallel machine scheduling problem. Comput. Oper. Res. **53**, 107–117 (2015)
17. Wang, T., Liu, Z., Chen, Y., Xu, Y., Dai, X.: Load balancing task scheduling based on genetic algorithm in cloud computing. In: Proceedings of the 2014 IEEE 12th International Conference on Dependable, Autonomic and Secure Computing, DASC 2014, pp. 146–152. IEEE Computer Society (2014)
18. Willsch, D., et al.: Benchmarking advantage and D-Wave 2000Q quantum annealers with exact cover problems. Quantum Inf. Process. **21**(4), 1–22 (2022). https://doi.org/10.1007/s11128-022-03476-y

Early Experiences with a Photonic Quantum Simulator for Solving Job Shop Scheduling Problem

Mateusz Slysz[1]($\boxtimes$)(iD), Krzysztof Kurowski[1](iD), and Jan Węglarz[2](iD)

[1] Poznań Supercomputing and Networking Center, IBCH PAS, Poznań, Poland
{mslysz,krzysztof.kurowski}@man.poznan.pl
[2] Institute of Computing Science Poznań, Poznań University of Technology,
Poznań, Poland
jan.weglarz@put.poznan.pl

Abstract. Quantum computing is a rapidly developing technology that, in theory, can solve complex computational problems practically intractable for classical computers. Although the technology offers promising breakthroughs, it is only in the early stages of development, and various quantum computer architectures are emerging. One such new development is the photonic quantum computer. Since the work on discrete optimization using different quantum computer architectures is well studied, in this paper, we experiment with solving a toy instance of the Job-Shop Scheduling problem using a hybrid learning algorithm on a photonic quantum computer simulator. The promising results, combined with some highly desirable properties of photonic quantum computers, show that this new architecture is worth considering for further development and investment in the quantum technology landscape.

Keywords: Job Shop Scheduling Problem · Quantum Computing · Photonic Quantum Computer

1 Introduction

With the dynamic and rapid development of programmable and scalable photonic circuits, there is a natural question about potential algorithms and application areas for optical quantum computers as near-term quantum devices. This paper presents our early experiences with a new quantum simulation framework supporting bosonic sampler capabilities. We use the recent advent of the simulation tool to model and solve a well-known Job Shop Scheduling Problem. The Job Shop Scheduling Problem (JSSP) is an NP-hard optimization problem in computer science and operations research. A complete set of solutions for larger instances of this problem is practically intractable, so typically, solving it requires using heuristics or local search algorithms. However, even dedicated algorithms using classical machines have many constraints due to the limited scalability of computer architectures and their other parameters, such as processor sizes and

R. Wyrzykowski et al. (Eds.): PPAM 2022, LNCS 13827, pp. 177–186, 2023.
https://doi.org/10.1007/978-3-031-30445-3_15

energy consumption. Encouraged by our recent work on using quantum computers to solve the JSSP problem - in the quantum annealing (QA) model [9], as well as in the gate-based model using the QAOA algorithm [5], we propose in this paper yet another approach to verify if and how we can solve it by using upcoming photonic-based quantum computers.

2   Problem Formulation

2.1   Photonic Quantum Computer

Quantum computers based on photonic technologies bring a number of highly desirable features, such as scalability, due to parallel developments in classical photonics - a well-established industrial sector, the ability to perform room-temperature computing, as well as the possibility of combining into hybrid architectures, due to the growing field of photonic-based quantum communications.

In this research, we are going to use a photonic quantum computer simulator provided by ORCA Computing [2]. The photonic quantum computer is an implementation of a computation technique called Boson Sampling [7]. In a few words, it is based on passing a number of singular photons through a linear optical system, which consist of parameterized gates. It includes beam-splitters that create optical path intersections with parameters ϑ determining the transition probabilities of photons moving along the respective paths, as well as parameterized phase-shifters, which change the phase of the photon based on the value of the parameter ψ. Each time a particle passes through such an intersection, it generates a quantum superposition. Furthermore, each meeting point of the paths of two or more photons produces an entangled state. The large number of potential paths and branches that the particles can travel through gives the potential to obtain very large entangled states, even for a small number of photons, which determines the quantum advantage of such a device over classical simulation. A readout of the result involves sampling the probability distribution by measuring the number of photons in each of the single photon detectors at the output of the system.

$$|\xi(\boldsymbol{\vartheta}, \boldsymbol{\psi})\rangle = \sum_n \alpha_n |n_1, \ldots, n_M\rangle \tag{1}$$

This measurement of the so-called Foch state can be further mapped by a parity function to a binary tuple $\boldsymbol{x}$ with a corresponding energy function E for an observable H.

$$E(\boldsymbol{\vartheta}, \boldsymbol{\psi}) = \langle \boldsymbol{x}|H|\boldsymbol{x}\rangle \tag{2}$$

The quantum circuit composed of the parametrized phase-shifters and beam-splitters acting on the input quantum state can be denoted as a unitary operator $U(\boldsymbol{\vartheta}, \boldsymbol{\psi})$ and the readout from the circuit can be denoted as (Fig. 1):

$$\langle \boldsymbol{x}|U^\dagger(\boldsymbol{\vartheta}, \boldsymbol{\psi})\, O U(\boldsymbol{\vartheta}, \boldsymbol{\psi})|\boldsymbol{x}\rangle. \tag{3}$$

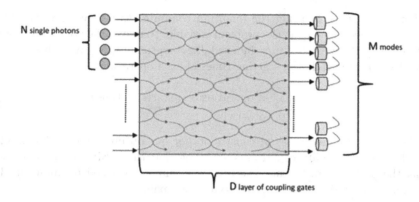

Fig. 1. Boson Sampling based photonic quantum computer architecture [6].

One can derive that this holds true for any observable O in the form of:

$$O = \sum_{i=1}^{M} o_{ii} a_i^\dagger a_i + \sum_{i,j=1}^{M} o_{ij} a_i^\dagger a_j \tag{4}$$

This notation can be easily mapped into a class of quadratic unconstrained binary optimization (QUBO) problems, which are already well described as a basic case to solve on other quantum architectures, such as quantum annealers [4] and gate-based quantum computers [5].

$$E(\boldsymbol{x}) = \sum_i Q_{ii} x_i + \sum_{i<j} Q_{ij} x_i x_j, \tag{5}$$

Finding an optimal solution to a QUBO problem is equivalent to minimizing a classical Ising Hamiltonian, where the minimal energy eigenstate encodes the solution to the binary optimization problem:

$$\min_{\boldsymbol{x}} \boldsymbol{x}^T Q \boldsymbol{x}, \tag{6}$$

where the diagonal terms Q_{ii} are the linear coefficients and the nonzero off-diagonal terms Q_{ij} are the quadratic coefficients.

2.2 JSSP Formulation

The JSSP formulation we are considering is defined as follows. There are J jobs $\mathcal{J} = \{j_1, \ldots, j_J\}$, each consisting of O_j operations $\mathcal{O}_j = \{O_{j1}, \ldots, O_{jO_j}\}$, which are supposed to be processed in a predefined order. Each operation $O_{j,k}$ has a duration time $l_{j,k}$ and must be processed on a specified machine from a set of M machines $\mathcal{M} = \{m_1, \ldots, m_M\}$. A set of operations $O_{j,k}$ that have to be executed on the machine m_m can be denoted as I_m. Each machine can process at most one operation at a given time.

For the purpose of using the quantum computer as a solver for the JSSP problem, we need to encode the problem variables to match the QUBO notation. Inspired by [11] we use the time-indexed JSSP representation. We define binary variables, which encode the starting times of each operation:

$$
x_{j,k,t} = \begin{cases} 1 & \text{if operation } O_{j,k} \text{ starts at time } t \\ 0 & \text{otherwise} \end{cases} \tag{7}
$$

We can now define a set of constraints for our optimization problem. The first three are feasibility constraints, ensuring that the JSSP solution does not break the problem statement. The last constraint is designed to minimize the total duration of all tasks - referred to as makespan.

- **Single-start constraint:** Each job should start once and only once.

$$
h_1(x) = \sum_j^J \sum_k^{O_j} \left(\sum_t^T x_{j,k,t} - 1 \right)^2 \tag{8}
$$

This constraint ensures, that each operation from each job has exactly 1 starting time.
- **Machine sharing constraint:** At a given time no 2 jobs should be running on the same machine.

$$
h_2(x) = \sum_m^M \left(\sum_{j,k,t,j',k',t' \in A_m \cup B_m} x_{j,k,t} x_{j',k',t'} \right) \tag{9}
$$

where

$$
A_m = (j,k,t,j',k',t') : (O_{j,k}, O_{j',k'}) \in I_m \times I_m,
$$
$$
(j,k) \neq (j',k'), \quad 0 < t, t' < T, \quad 0 < t - t' < l_{jk}
$$

$$
B_m = (j,k,t,j',k',t') : (O_{j,k}, O_{j',k'}) \in I_m \times I_m,
$$
$$
(j,k) \neq (j',k'), \quad t = t', \quad l_{jk} > 0, \quad l_{j'k'} > 0
$$

The set A_m is defined so that the constraint forbids operation $O_{j,k}$ from starting at t if there is another operation $O_{j',k'}$ still running, and B_m constrains two operations from starting at the same time.
- **Precedence constraint:** The precedence of operations within jobs should be maintained.

$$
h_3(x) = \sum_j^J \sum_k^{O_j} \sum_{t+l_{jk}<t'} x_{j,k,t} x_{j,k+1,t'} \tag{10}
$$

This ensures that no operation with a lower index within the same job starts, before the previous one has finished.

– **Minimal makespan constraint:** Promotes low-makespan schedules by putting a penalty on any non-optimal schedule (schedule with finish time further away from the maximum time $T_{\max}$).

$$h_4(x) = (J+1)^{\left(T_{\max} - \max_j\{t_{j,O_j} + l_{j,O_j}\}\right)} \tag{11}$$

Encoding the Q matrix coefficients takes the form of a weighted sum of those four constraints between certain pairs of x variables.

$$Q = w_1 h_1(x) + w_2 h_2(x) + w_3 h_3(x) + w_4 h_4(x) \tag{12}$$

2.3 Hybrid Optimization Algorithm

In a nutshell, to find the optimal solution, represented by the binary vector x_{opt}, we need to find the optimal set of parameters (ϑ, ψ) of the quantum circuit. To do so, we use a gradient-based method in a hybrid (classical-quantum) loop. Parameters of the quantum circuit are initialized randomly. Then, we run the quantum circuit on a photonic quantum computer (or simulator) and readout the results. After processing it through a parity function, we can calculate the corresponding energy value using the Q matrix. Then we can use a gradient-based model to calculate a new set of parameters. An example loop passing with sample data for a problem of size seven is schematically shown in Fig. 2.

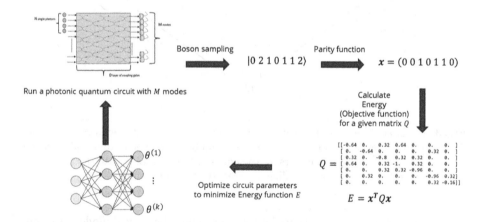

Fig. 2. Hybrid optimization algorithm loop, consisting of quantum computations and classical processing and parameter optimization.

3   Experiments

3.1   Problem Instance

For the first part of the experiments, a photonic quantum computer's simulator was used to perform an optimization of a toy problem consisting of 3 jobs $\mathcal{J}$ = { "cupcakes", "smoothie", "lasagna" } and 2 machines $\mathcal{M}$ = { "mixer", "oven" }. The complete problem notation also shows execution times of each operation on a given machine, along with the order of operations within jobs is given in a dictionary-like format:

$$\{\text{"cupcakes"} : [(\text{"mixer"}, 2), (\text{"oven"}, 1)],$$
$$\text{"smoothie"} : [(\text{"mixer"}, 1)],$$
$$\text{"lasagna"} : [(\text{"oven"}, 2)]\},$$

or in a form of a dependency graph as shown in Fig. 3.

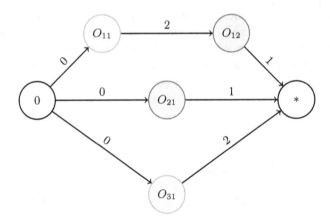

Fig. 3. Example JSSP instance with 3 jobs, 4 operations and 2 machines. O_{jk} nodes denotes k-th operation of job j and colors green and blue correspond to machines *mixer* and *oven* respectively. The numbers on the edges of the graph indicate the processing times of operations labelling preceding vertices. (Color figure online)

The total number of binary variables (represented by optical modes) is calculated as the total number of all operations in all jobs ($|O|$) times the maximum time constant $T_{\max}$, which has been chosen arbitrarily as the problem size. The only limitation is that $T_{\max}$ should not be smaller than the optimal time of a given instance, because if it was, finding a feasible solution would be impossible. In most cases the optimal time is not known, however, one can estimate it based on various factors while preprocessing the instance.

3.2   Variable Prunning

To reduce the number of variables, we can perform basic pruning by eliminating variables that, if selected, would generate infeasible solutions. The exclusion of illegal start times is performed, by removing variables that would cause the job to finish after the maximum time or start the operation before the earliest possible time (due to precedence constraints).

For $T_{max} = 4$ the original number of binary values was 16, however, it can be reduced to 11 after this preliminary preprocessing step as shown in Table 1.

Table 1. Pruning the variables for simple instance with $T_{max} = 4$. Out of initial 16 variables ($|O| \times T_{\text{max}}$), 5 variables marked in red can be pruned.

Cupcakes - mixer	Cupcakes - oven	Smoothie - mixer	Lasagna - oven
$x_{1,1,0}$	$x_{1,2,0}$	$x_{2,1,0}$	$x_{3,1,0}$
$x_{1,1,1}$	$x_{1,2,1}$	$x_{2,1,1}$	$x_{3,1,1}$
$x_{1,1,2}$	$x_{1,2,2}$	$x_{2,1,2}$	$x_{3,1,2}$
$x_{1,1,3}$	$x_{1,2,3}$	$x_{2,1,3}$	$x_{3,1,3}$

3.3   Experiments

During performed experiments, we chose Adam Optimization Algorithm for classical first-order gradient-based optimization [8]. To calculate the gradient, the parameter-shift rule was used, so that it was sufficient to estimate the function value 2 times in each iteration. For each parameter update, the quantum circuit has been executed 1000 times and the results were averaged.

The first batch of experiments was started with equal Q matrix weights: $w_1 = 1$, $w_2 = 1$, $w_3 = 1$ and $w_4 = 1$. The results were promising, as in most cases the returned binary vectors with corresponding low energy values. However, they were not ideal, because many solutions remained infeasible. In order to obtain the desired results, we proposed and implemented two solutions.

First, we tuned the weights using the grid-search method on the parameters w_1, w_2, w_3, setting the value of the optimization factor $w_4 = 1$ as a reference value. The best weights for this problem were found for $w_1 = 1$, $w_2 = 5$, $w_3 = 2$.

Secondly, we added a regularization factor to the objective function. Since the constraint on the number of variables was often broken, it was natural to direct the optimizer to the correct solutions using the $L2$ regularization in which the number of binary variables equal to 1 should equal the total number of operations in all jobs.

$$\min_{\boldsymbol{x}} \boldsymbol{x}^T Q \boldsymbol{x} + \gamma \left(\sum_i^N x_i - |O| \right)^2 \tag{13}$$

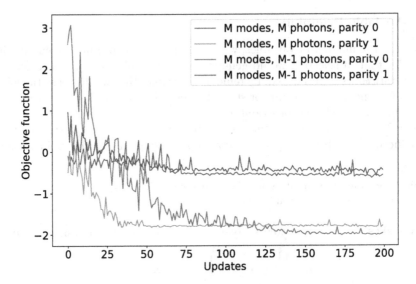

Fig. 4. Learning curve for the energy function, while optimizing the parameters with Adam algorithm.

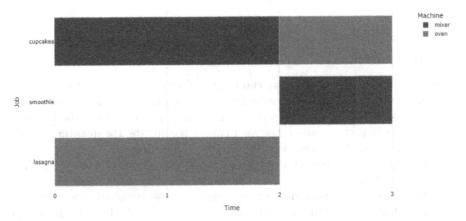

Fig. 5. Gantt chart showing the optimal solution of the given instance with makespan $T = 3$.

The regularization factor was added with an additional weight γ, but for this experiment it was set to $\gamma = 1$ and required no more fine-tuning.

After all these adjustments, the simulator was able to return the binary vector corresponding to the optimal solution with the makespan $T_{opt} = 3$. The learning process is shown in Fig. 4 as a plot of the energy objective function value changing in subsequent iterations. The different learning curves represent different approaches to mapping parameters of the quantum simulator into the binary vector x. We used two different parity functions and two different entanglement strategies, hence four possible combinations are possible. Each time, out of the 4 results, the one with the lowest final energy value is chosen as the best result. The optimal solution for the given instance is shown on the Gantt chart in Fig. 5.

4   Conclusions

This paper discussed another approach to solving the Job-Shop Scheduling Problem on a relatively new class of photonic quantum devices. Our approach used a photonic quantum computer architecture based on the Boson Sampling technique. Similarly to previous methods using the Quantum Annealing model and QAOA algorithm on gate-based quantum computers to solve the JSSP problem, we applied the time-indexed notation, defined a set of constraints, and then formulated a QUBO problem accordingly. Thanks to the QUBO representation, we successfully performed experiments on a toy JSSP instance with only three tasks and four operations, finding the optimal solution. We solved the problem using a photonic quantum computer with classical machine learning techniques in a hybrid (classical-quantum) loop. Some additional techniques, such as grid-searching weights and adding regularization factor, were also introduced and briefly discussed in this paper. Those improvements will be used and applied in our future research and experiments to solve larger JSSP problem instances.

References

1. Aaronson, S., Arkhipov, A.: The computational complexity of linear optics. In: Proceedings of the Forty-Third Annual ACM Symposium on Theory of Computing, pp. 333–342 (2011)
2. Bradler, K., Wallner, H.: Certain properties and applications of shallow bosonic circuits (2021). https://doi.org/10.48550/ARXIV.2112.09766. https://arxiv.org/abs/2112.09766
3. Clifford, P., Clifford, R.: The classical complexity of boson sampling. In: Proceedings of the Twenty-Ninth Annual ACM-SIAM Symposium on Discrete Algorithms, pp. 146–155. SIAM (2018)
4. D-Wave: Solving problems with quantum samplers. D-Wave System Documentation. https://docs.dwavesys.com/docs/latest/c_gs_3.html
5. Farhi, E., Goldstone, J., Gutmann, S.: A quantum approximate optimization algorithm (2014). https://doi.org/10.48550/ARXIV.1411.4028. https://arxiv.org/abs/1411.4028
6. García-Patrón, R., Renema, J.J., Shchesnovich, V.: Simulating boson sampling in lossy architectures. Quantum **3**, 169 (2019)
7. Hamilton, C.S., Kruse, R., Sansoni, L., Barkhofen, S., Silberhorn, C., Jex, I.: Gaussian boson sampling. Phys. Rev. Lett. **119**, 170501 (2017). https://doi.org/10.1103/PhysRevLett.119.170501, https://link.aps.org/doi/10.1103/PhysRevLett.119.170501
8. Kingma, D.P., Ba, J.: Adam: a method for stochastic optimization (2014). https://arxiv.org/abs/1412.6980

9. Kurowski, K., Węglarz, J., Subocz, M., Różycki, R., Waligóra, G.: Hybrid Quantum Annealing Heuristic Method for Solving Job Shop Scheduling Problem. In: Krzhizhanovskaya, V.V., et al. (eds.) ICCS 2020. LNCS, vol. 12142, pp. 502–515. Springer, Cham (2020). https://doi.org/10.1007/978-3-030-50433-5_39

10. Pelucchi, E., et al.: The potential and global outlook of integrated photonics for quantum technologies. Nat. Rev. Phys. **4**(3), 194–208 (2022)

11. Venturelli, D., Marchand, D.J.J., Rojo, G.: Quantum annealing implementation of job-shop scheduling (2015). https://doi.org/10.48550/ARXIV.1506.08479. https://arxiv.org/abs/1506.08479

12. Zhong, H.S., et al.: Quantum computational advantage using photons. Science **370**(6523), 1460–1463 (2020)

Some Remarks on Super-Gram Operators for General Bipartite Quantum States

Roman Gielerak[ID] and Marek Sawerwain[(✉)][ID]

Institute of Control and Computation Engineering, University of Zielona Góra,
Licealna 9, 65-417 Zielona Góra, Poland
{R.Gielerak,M.Sawerwain}@issi.uz.zgora.pl

Abstract. The Gramian matrices approach to study certain aspects of quantum entanglement contained in the bipartite pure quantum states is being extended to the level of a general quantum bipartite states. The corresponding Gram matrices, called here super-gram matrices are being constructed over the Hilbert-Schmidt structure build on the Hilbert space of pure states. The main result is the extension of the widely known realignment criterion to the level of super-operators.

Keywords: gramians · super-matrices · quantum states · numerical computations

1 Introduction

Quantum computing (QC) is an area where the model of computation is expressed by the laws of quantum physics [16]. A recent development of quantum computing (QC) methods allows us to give many application of a new algorithms and solutions. The set of quantum algorithms, especially widely known Shor's prime factorization algorithm [25], and Grover's algorithm [6] are supplied with a new application of QC to machine learning [21,22], methods of classification [23,26] and neural networks [24]. It is also possible to indicate other area of applications as security and cryptography especially in block chains theory [3], where we can found proposal of the usage of quantum methods [5,18]. And also in the area of clustering methods [13] where quantum solutions are also discussed [2].

Many applications in general also entail the development of analytical techniques. In work [8] we use the notion of gramians [12] to study certain aspects of the quantum entanglement in the case of two-partite pure quantum states. Phenomenon of quantum entanglement is of crucial importance in recent research connected to teleportation protocols [15], routing problem [4], and also in the future construction of genuine quantum networks [17].

In the present contribution we extend certain results of [8] to the case of a general bipartite quantum states. From the paper [14] it follows the importance of the gramian technique for general multipartite entanglement problem.

R. Wyrzykowski et al. (Eds.): PPAM 2022, LNCS 13827, pp. 187–198, 2023.
https://doi.org/10.1007/978-3-031-30445-3_16

In particular in the quantum marginal problem which is close to the one of the basic problem known as the AME-states existence and construction. For an extensions to the infinite dimensional setting, see [10].

Below we show how to calculate the so-called super-gram matrices (super-gramians) of a given quantum state for two partite quantum systems. In particular we discuss how to use super-gramians to formulate some sufficient criterion for non-separability of a general quantum states. Also we propose some Python routines (and briefly discuss efficiency of its performance) which can be used in numerical computations with the use of introduced here super-gramians. For a more extended exposition of this topic see our recent paper [11].

The material of this chapter is organised as follows. To finish present section we give introductory material, and outline some basic notation (as Table 1) which is used in the rest of chapter. Section 2 includes precise definition of super-gramians connected to bipartite quantum systems. Section 3 is devoted to show some computational examples related to super-gram matrices notion. A summary of this chapter is provided in Sect. 4. Acknowledgements and bibliography sections are final parts of chapter.

Before we start presentation of super-gramians notion for general quantum states we summarise used notation, symbols, abbreviations and acronyms at Table 1.

Table 1. Some symbols, notations, sets and functions used in the chapter

Notation	Description
d	Integer value representing dimensions of vector/matrix
$d_1 \times d_2$	Dimensions of matrix,
$\mathbb{R}$	Set of real numbers
$\mathbb{C}$	Set of complex numbers
$\mathbb{H}$	Hilbert space
$\mathbb{I}, \mathbb{I}_N$	Identity matrix/operator, identity operator defined in system with N qudits
$\mathbb{I}_A$	Identity operator defined in subsystem A
$A^\star, A^\dagger$	Conjugation of matrix, hermitian adjoint of matrix
$\langle-|-\rangle$	Inner product
$\mathbb{E}(\mathbf{C}^d)$	Set of density matrices on $\mathbf{C}^d$, i.e. $\rho \geq 0$ and $\mathrm{tr}\,(\rho) = 1$
$\mathrm{Sep}(\mathbf{C}^{d_A} \otimes \mathbf{C}^{d_B})$	Set of separable states on $\mathbf{C}^{d_A} \otimes \mathbf{C}^{d_B}$
$\partial\mathbb{E}(\mathbf{C}^d)$	Set of pure states on $\mathbf{C}^d$
$\mathrm{HS}(\mathbf{C}^d)$	The Hilbert-Schmidt structure on the space of all $d \times d$ matrices $\mathcal{M}_d$
$||\rho||_{\mathrm{HS}}^2$	The Frobenius norm of $\rho \in \mathcal{M}_d$, i.e. $||\rho||_{\mathrm{HS}}^2 = \mathrm{tr}\,(\rho^\dagger \rho)$
$\langle-|-\rangle_{\mathrm{HS}}$	The canonical Hilbert-Schmidt scalar product in $\mathrm{HS}(\mathbf{C}^d)$
$\Delta^A(Q), \Delta^B(Q)$	Left and right super-gramians for given Q
$1\!:\!n$	Means the sequence of $1, 2, 3, \ldots, n$
$\mathcal{U}(d)$	Group of unitary matrices acting in $\mathbf{C}^d$

2   Two-Partite System Gramians

In this part of chapter we introduce main definitions and some results related to super-gram matrices.

Let $(e^A_{\alpha\beta})_{\alpha\beta}$, resp. $(e^B_{\gamma\eta})_{\gamma\eta}$ be some HS-orthonormal and complete system in $\mathrm{HS}(\mathbb{C}^{d_A})$, resp. in $\mathrm{HS}(\mathbb{C}^{d_B})$. Then, the system $(e^A_{\alpha\beta} \otimes e^B_{\gamma\eta})_{\alpha\beta \atop \gamma\eta}$ forms HS-orthonormal base in $\mathrm{HS}(\mathbb{C}^{d_A}) \otimes \mathrm{HS}(\mathbb{C}^{d_B})$.

For any $Q \in \mathrm{HS}(\mathbb{C}^{d_A} \otimes \mathbb{C}^{d_B})$ there is decomposition:

$$Q = \sum_{\alpha\beta,\gamma\eta} q_{\alpha\beta|\gamma\eta} e^A_{\alpha\beta} \otimes e^B_{\gamma\eta}, \tag{1}$$

where

$$q_{\alpha\beta|\gamma\eta} = \langle Q|e^A_{\alpha\beta} \otimes e^B_{\gamma\eta}\rangle_{\mathrm{HS}} \quad \text{and} \quad \sum_{\alpha\beta,\gamma\eta} |q_{\alpha\beta|\gamma\eta}|^2 = \|Q\|^2_{\mathrm{HS}}. \tag{2}$$

Let us define the following isometries:

$$J^A(Q): \quad e^A_{\alpha\beta} \longrightarrow \mathcal{F}^A_{\alpha\beta} \in \mathrm{HS}(\mathbb{C}^{d_B}), \tag{3}$$

where

$$\mathcal{F}^A_{\alpha\beta} = \sum_{\gamma\eta} q_{\alpha\beta|\gamma\eta} e^B_{\gamma\eta}, \tag{4}$$

and extended by linearity to the whole space of $\mathrm{HS}(\mathbb{C}^{d_A})$.

Similarly, we define:

$$J^B(Q): \quad e^B_{\gamma\eta} \longrightarrow \mathcal{F}^B_{\gamma\eta} \in \mathrm{HS}(\mathbb{C}^{d_A}), \tag{5}$$

where

$$\mathcal{F}^B_{\gamma\eta} = \sum_{\alpha\beta} q_{\alpha\beta|\gamma\eta} e^A_{\alpha\beta}, \tag{6}$$

and extended then by linearity on the whole space of $\mathrm{HS}(\mathbb{C}^{d_B})$.

Both maps:

$$J^A(Q) : \mathrm{HS}(\mathbb{C}^{d_A}) \longrightarrow \mathrm{HS}(\mathbb{C}^{d_B}) \quad \text{and} \quad J^B(Q) : \mathrm{HS}(\mathbb{C}^{d_B}) \longrightarrow \mathrm{HS}(\mathbb{C}^{d_A}), \tag{7}$$

are isometric maps.

For further use we define the following Gram super-matrices:

$$\Delta^A(Q) := J^A(Q)^\dagger \circ J^A(Q), \quad \mathrm{HS}(\mathbb{C}^{d_A}) \longrightarrow \mathrm{HS}(\mathbb{C}^{d_A}), \tag{8}$$

and

$$\Delta^B(Q) := J^B(Q)^\dagger \circ J^B(Q), \quad \mathrm{HS}(\mathbb{C}^{d_B}) \longrightarrow \mathrm{HS}(\mathbb{C}^{d_B}). \tag{9}$$

Proposition 1. *The Gram super-matrices $\Delta^A(Q)$ and $\Delta^B(Q)$ have the following properties:*

(i) $\Delta^A(Q) \geq 0$ and $\Delta^B(Q) \geq 0$ i.e. are positive super-matrices and therefore hermitian.

(ii) Let $\mathcal{U}(\mathrm{HS}(\mathbf{C}^{d_A}))$, resp. $\mathcal{U}(\mathrm{HS}(\mathbf{C}^{d_B}))$ stands for the groups of unitary super-transformations on the corresponding HS-spaces of matrices. Then:

(1) $\forall_{\Omega \in \mathcal{U}(\mathrm{HS}(\mathbf{C}^{d_B}))} \Delta^A(Q) = \Delta^A((\mathbb{1}_A \otimes \Omega)(Q))$,

(2) $\forall_{\Omega \in \mathcal{U}(\mathrm{HS}(\mathbf{C}^{d_A}))} \Delta^B(Q) = \Delta^B((\Omega \otimes \mathbb{1}_B)(Q))$.

(iii) $\forall_{\substack{\Omega^A \in \mathcal{U}(\mathrm{HS}(\mathbf{C}^{d_A})) \\ \Omega^B \in \mathcal{U}(\mathrm{HS}(\mathbf{C}^{d_B}))}} \Delta(Q) = \Delta^A(Q) \otimes \Delta^B(Q)$ is invariant:

$$(\Omega^A \otimes \Omega^B)\Delta(Q) = \Delta(Q). \tag{10}$$

Proof. Everything follows from the observation that

$$\Delta^A(Q)_{\alpha\beta|\alpha'\beta'} = \langle \mathcal{F}^A_{\alpha'\beta'} | \mathcal{F}^A_{\alpha\beta} \rangle_{\mathrm{HS}(\mathbf{C}^{d_B})}, \tag{11}$$

and

$$\Delta^B(Q)_{\gamma\eta|\gamma'\eta'} = \langle \mathcal{F}^B_{\gamma'\eta'} | \mathcal{F}^B_{\gamma\eta} \rangle_{\mathrm{HS}(\mathbf{C}^{d_A})}, \tag{12}$$

where $\mathcal{F}^A_{\alpha\beta}$, resp. $\mathcal{F}^B_{\gamma\eta}$ are given by Eq. (4) and Eq. (6).

Remark 1. The formulas Eq. (8) and Eq. (9) fully justify the name introduced: "Gram super-matrices" as from these formulas it follows that matrices Δ^A and respectively Δ^B are Gram matrices constructed over the space $\mathrm{HS}(\mathbf{C}^{d_A})$ and $\mathrm{HS}(\mathbf{C}^{d_B})$ respectively.

Example 1. Let $|\Psi\rangle \in \mathbf{C}^{d_A} \otimes \mathbf{C}^{d_B}$ and such that $|||\Psi|| = 1$. Then $|\Psi\rangle\langle\Psi| \equiv Q(\Psi) \in \mathrm{HS}(\mathbf{C}^{d_A} \otimes \mathbf{C}^{d_B})$. Let us consider the canonical Schmidt decomposition of $|\Psi\rangle$:

$$|\Psi\rangle = \sum_{k=1}^{\min(d_A, d_B)} \tau_k |\psi_k^A\rangle \otimes |\theta_k^B\rangle, \tag{13}$$

where $\tau_k \geq 0$, $\sum_k \tau_k^2 = 1$ and the systems $\{|\psi_k^A\rangle, k = 1 : d_A\}$, resp. $\{|\theta_k^B\rangle, k = 1 : d_B\}$ forms complete orthonormal systems in $\mathbf{C}^{d_A}$, resp. in $\mathbf{C}^{d_B}$.

Let us form the following system of linear operators:

$$E^A_{\alpha\beta} = |\psi_\alpha\rangle\langle\psi_\beta| \in \mathrm{HS}(\mathbf{C}^{d_A}), \quad \alpha, \beta = 1 : d_A, \tag{14}$$

and

$$E^B_{\gamma\eta} = |\theta_\gamma\rangle\langle\theta_\eta| \in \mathrm{HS}(\mathbf{C}^{d_B}), \quad \gamma, \eta = 1 : d_B. \tag{15}$$

It is not hard to observe that:

(i) $(E^A_{\alpha\beta})^\dagger = E^A_{\beta\alpha}$, $(E^B_{\gamma\eta})^\dagger = E^B_{\eta\gamma}$,

(ii) $\sum_{\alpha=1}^{d_A} E^A_{\alpha\alpha} = \mathbb{I}_A$, $\sum_{\gamma=1}^{d_B} E^B_{\gamma\gamma} = \mathbb{I}_B$,

(iii) $\langle E^A_{\alpha\beta} | E^A_{\alpha'\beta'} \rangle_{\mathrm{HS}(\mathbf{C}^{d_A})} = \delta_{\alpha\alpha'}\delta_{\gamma\gamma'}$, $\langle E^B_{\gamma\eta} | E^B_{\gamma'\eta'} \rangle_{\mathrm{HS}(\mathbf{C}^{d_B})} = \delta_{\gamma\gamma'}\delta_{\eta\eta'}$,

(iv) the system

$$\{E_{\alpha\beta|\gamma\eta} = E^A_{\alpha\beta} \otimes E^B_{\gamma\eta}\}, \quad \alpha, \beta = 1 : d_A, \quad \gamma, \eta = 1 : d_B, \tag{16}$$

forms a complete, HS-orthonormal system in $\mathrm{HS}(\mathbf{C}^{d_A} \otimes \mathbf{C}^{d_B})$.

From Eq. (13) it follows

$$|\Psi\rangle\langle\Psi| = \sum_{\alpha,\alpha'}^{\min(d_A,d_B)} \tau_\alpha \tau_{\alpha'} E_{\alpha,\alpha'}^A \otimes E_{\alpha,\alpha'}^B. \tag{17}$$

Therefore, the A-frame of $|\Psi\rangle\langle\Psi|$ consist of operators

$$\{\mathcal{F}_{\alpha\alpha'}^A = \tau_\alpha \tau_{\alpha'} E_{\alpha\alpha'}^B\}, \tag{18}$$

and B-frame of

$$\{\mathcal{F}_{\gamma\gamma'}^B = \tau_\gamma \tau_{\gamma'} E_{\gamma\gamma'}^A\}. \tag{19}$$

From Eq. (18) and Eq. (19) the following results follows.

Proposition 2. *Let $|\Psi\rangle \in \partial\mathbb{E}(\mathbf{C}^{d_A} \otimes \mathbf{C}^{d_B})$, then the corresponding super-gramians Δ^A resp. Δ^B of $|\Psi\rangle\langle\Psi|$ are given by the formula (up to the unitary, local transformations in the local HS-spaces $\mathrm{HS}(\mathbf{C}^{d_A})$), and resp. in $\mathrm{HS}(\mathbf{C}^{d_B})$:*

$$\Delta^A \left(|\Psi\rangle\langle\Psi|\right)_{\alpha\alpha'|\beta\beta'} = \tau_\alpha \tau_{\alpha'} \tau_\beta \tau_{\beta'} \delta_{\alpha\beta}\delta_{\alpha'\beta'}, \tag{20}$$

and

$$\Delta^B \left(|\Psi\rangle\langle\Psi|\right)_{\gamma\eta|\gamma'\eta'} = \tau_\gamma \tau_\eta \tau_{\gamma'} \tau_{\eta'} \delta_{\gamma\gamma'}\delta_{\eta\eta'}. \tag{21}$$

Remark 2. The standard reduced density matrices of the density matrix $Q(\Psi) = |\Psi\rangle\langle\Psi|$ defined as

$$Q^A(\Psi) = \mathrm{tr}_B\left(Q(\Psi)\right), \tag{22}$$

and respectively

$$Q^B(\Psi) = \mathrm{tr}_A\left(Q(\Psi)\right), \tag{23}$$

are given by

$$Q^A(\Psi) = \sum_k \tau_k^2 |\psi_k^A\rangle\langle\psi_k^A| \quad \text{and} \quad Q^B(\Psi) = \sum_k \tau_k^2 |\theta_k^B\rangle\langle\theta_k^B|. \tag{24}$$

The formulae Eq. (20) and Eq. (21) yields the following formulae for corresponding partial traces of the operator $QQ = |Q(\Psi)\rangle\langle Q(\Psi)|$ acting in the space $\mathrm{HS}(\mathrm{HS}(\mathbf{C}^{d_A}) \otimes \mathrm{HS}(\mathbf{C}^{d_B})) \simeq \mathrm{HS}(\mathrm{HS}(\mathbf{C}^{d_A})) \otimes \mathrm{HS}(\mathrm{HS}(\mathbf{C}^{d_B}))$:

$$\mathrm{tr}_{\mathrm{HS}(\mathbf{C}^{d_B})}\left(QQ\right) = \Delta^A(|\Psi\rangle\langle\Psi|) \quad \text{and} \quad \mathrm{tr}_{\mathrm{HS}(\mathbf{C}^{d_A})}\left(QQ\right) = \Delta^B(|\Psi\rangle\langle\Psi|). \tag{25}$$

In the case of a general two-qudit state $Q \in \mathbb{E}(\mathbf{C}^{d_A} \otimes \mathbf{C}^{d_B})$ the corresponding super-gram operators are computable with the use of operator Schmidt decomposition of Q.

For this goals let $Q \in \mathrm{HS}(\mathbf{C}^{d_A} \otimes \mathbf{C}^{d_B})$, then there exists a sequence λ_α^0, $\alpha = 1 : d_A \cdot d_B$ of non-negative numbers, called in the following the operator Schmidt coefficients, and such that

$$\sum_\alpha (\lambda_\alpha^0)^2 = \|Q\|^2_{\mathrm{HS}(\mathbf{C}^{d_A} \otimes \mathbf{C}^{d_B})} \quad \text{and} \quad Q = \sum_\alpha \lambda_\alpha^0 S_\alpha^A \otimes S_\alpha^B, \tag{26}$$

where $\{S_\alpha^A\}$, and resp. $\{S_\beta^B\}$ forms HS-orthonormal and complete system in $\mathrm{HS}(\mathbf{C}^{d_A})$, and resp. in $\mathrm{HS}(\mathbf{C}^{d_B})$.

Defining, for any $Q \in \mathrm{HS}(\mathbf{C}^{d_A} \otimes \mathbf{C}^{d_B})$ the following super-projector $\mathfrak{Q} = |Q\rangle\langle Q| \in \mathrm{HS}(\mathrm{HS}(\mathbf{C}^{d_A} \otimes \mathbf{C}^{d_B}))$ and using also Eq. (26) we obtain

$$\mathfrak{Q} = \sum_{\alpha,\beta} \lambda_\alpha^0 \lambda_\beta^0 \mathfrak{S}_{\alpha\beta}^A \otimes \mathfrak{S}_{\alpha\beta}^B, \tag{27}$$

where

$$\mathfrak{S}_{\alpha\beta}^A = |S_\alpha^A\rangle\langle S_\beta^A| \quad \text{and} \quad \mathfrak{S}_{\alpha\beta}^B = |S_\alpha^B\rangle\langle S_\beta^B|. \tag{28}$$

From Eq. (27) it follows, that the corresponding to Q super-gramians, defined as

$$\mathfrak{Q}^A = \mathrm{tr}_{\mathrm{HS}(\mathbf{C}^{d_B})} (\mathfrak{Q}) \quad \text{and} \quad \mathfrak{Q}^B = \mathrm{tr}_{\mathrm{HS}(\mathbf{C}^{d_A})} (\mathfrak{Q}), \tag{29}$$

are given by the following formulas

$$\mathfrak{Q}^A = \sum_\alpha (\lambda_\alpha^0)^2 \mathfrak{S}_{\alpha\alpha}^A \quad \text{and} \quad \mathfrak{Q}^B = \sum_\alpha (\lambda_\alpha^0)^2 \mathfrak{S}_{\alpha\alpha}^B. \tag{30}$$

Thus, we have obtained:

Theorem 1. *Let $Q \in \mathrm{Sep}(\mathbf{C}^{d_A} \otimes \mathbf{C}^{d_B})$ and let $(\lambda_\alpha^{\mathrm{Op}})$ be the sequence of Schmidt coefficients connected to the Schmidt decomposition of the super operator $\mathfrak{Q} \in \mathrm{HS}(\mathrm{HS}(\mathbf{C}^{d_A} \otimes \mathbf{C}^{d_B}))$. Then*

$$\sum_\alpha \lambda_\alpha^{\mathrm{Op}} \leq 1. \tag{31}$$

Remark 3. Note that values of $\lambda_\alpha^{\mathrm{Op}}$ are in general different then those of λ_α^0.

Proof. In follows by an elementary argument that:

$$\mathrm{HS}(\mathrm{HS}(\mathbf{C}^{d_A} \otimes \mathbf{C}^{d_B})) = \mathrm{HS}(\mathrm{HS}(\mathbf{C}^{d_A})) \otimes \mathrm{HS}(\mathrm{HS}(\mathbf{C}^{d_B})). \tag{32}$$

Therefore, the Hilbert-Schmidt Hilbert space structure on the space of super-operators i.e. the linear endomorphism of the space $\mathrm{HS}(\mathbf{C}^{d_A} \otimes \mathbf{C}^{d_B})$ is of tensor product metric structure type.

Let $Q \in \mathrm{HS}(\mathbf{C}^{d_A} \otimes \mathbf{C}^{d_B})$ be a quantum separable state on $\mathbf{C}^{d_A} \otimes \mathbf{C}^{d_B}$. Then, as it is well known [7] (see also [19]) that $\sum_\alpha \lambda_\alpha^0 \leq 1$, where λ_α^0 are the Schmidt numbers of the corresponding operator Schmidt decomposition as given in Eq. (26).

Taking into account formula Eq. (27) it follows the Schmidt numbers of the corresponding super-operator $\mathfrak{Q}$ are given by the products $\lambda_\alpha^0 \lambda_\beta^0$. But,

$$\sum_\gamma \lambda_\gamma^{\mathrm{Op}} = \sum_{\alpha\beta} \lambda_\alpha^0 \lambda_\beta^0 = \left(\sum_\alpha \lambda_\alpha^0\right)^2 \leq 1. \tag{33}$$

and this concludes the proof.

3 Computational Examples

In this section we will briefly discuss a selected functions supporting the concept of gram and super-gram matrices (and also gram matrices which already have been presented in [8]). Newly added functions are part of the EntDetector (ED) package [9]. We also presents its performance in multithread (with several computational nodes) computational environment. Apart of (super-)gram related functions, the ED package provides also a set of functions devoted to the entanglement detection problem, for pure and mixed quantum states (source code of ED package is available at [20]).

The Python programming language is a primary tool which is used to implementation a new set functions to implementation of gramians and super-gramians. The use of Python allows us to give a simple and uncomplicated API which can be used directly in Python scripts. Additionally, the use of the NumPy package enables to utilise available multi-core processors.

To show basic calculations which are necessary to compute left, right gramians we create following state of two qutrits A and B:

$$|\psi\rangle = |0\rangle_A \otimes |+\rangle_B, \tag{34}$$

where $|+\rangle_B = \frac{1}{\sqrt{3}}(|0\rangle + |1\rangle + |2\rangle)$. Using ED package and Python language we need only a few lines of code (in example state $|\psi\rangle$ is represented as variable q) to create necessary state:

```
import entdetector as ed
import numpy as np

q0=ed.create_base_state(3, 1, 0)
q1=ed.create_qutrit_plus_state();
q=np.kron(q0, q1)
```

Calculation of left, right gramian and full gramian can be performed as follows:

```
dRPrime, dLPrime, dFullGramPrime =
                   ed.gram_matrices_of_vector_state(q, 3, 3)
```

The values 3, 3 given in the function argument are the dimensions of the matrix representing the left and the right gramian. We do not present the form of these matrices here, but in [20] there are other examples of source codes presenting the application of the ED package.

To calculate the super-gram matrices we also need to use only one line of Python code:

```
dRSPrime, dLSPrime, dFullSGramPrime =
    ed.super_gram_matrices_of_vector_state(q, 3, 3, base='std')
```

The super-gramians calculations function also allows to give a base form. In the example a standard zero-one base is used. The parameter base can be omitted, so the standard form of the base will be automatically assumed.

Table 2. Computation times (denoted as Time, values given as seconds) for the super-gramians for a bipartite system for different values of the d parameter. We use different NumPy threads number (denoted as Threads). In experiment the Python distribution from Intel One API 2022.0.22 package is used. The numerical experiments were performed in virtual environment WSL2 for Windows 11 (version 10.0.22000.613), Linux kernel 5.10.102.1. The calculations are performed on a workstation machine equipped with Intel Xeon W-2245 3.9 GHZ (base clock) processor and 128 GB of RAM.

d	Threads	Time	d	Threads	Time	d	Threads	Time
3	1	15.31 s	4	1	141.12 s	5	1	501.19 s
3	2	7.23 s	4	2	62.33 s	5	2	230.67 s
3	4	3.31 s	4	4	29.23 s	5	4	64.21 s
3	8	1.61 s	4	8	7.42 s	5	8	13.83 s

The super-gram matrix dimensionality is bigger than the system for which it calculated e.g. a system of two qutrits, the vector dimension for the example state $|\psi\rangle$ described by Eq. (34) is 3^2. The dimension of density matrix is $3^2 \times 3^2$, but the super-gramian dimension is described as $(3^4) \times (3^4)$. With such an increasing dimensionality, it is reasonable to check whether the multithreaded processing offered by the NumPy package allows to shorten the computation time of given super-gramians. Theorem 1 of the present chapter decrease significantly the computational complexity of computations with super-gramians use. Further remarks about computational complexity will be given later at end of this section.

Based on the state Eq. (34), bipartite registers for qudits and computation times for their super-gramians were determined. The time results are shown in Table 2. It is easy to observe that the NumPy package and the given implementation allow for effective use of available computing cores and shortening the entire computing process.

In the second numerical experiment we generate bipartite quantum state with randomly selected values of probability amplitudes and we randomly point one vector from base of given system:

$$|\psi\rangle = \sum_i \alpha_i |e_k\rangle, \tag{35}$$

where $\sum_i |\alpha_i|^2 = 1$ and e_k represents randomly selected vector from given system $(e^A_{\alpha\beta} \otimes e^B_{\gamma\eta})^{\alpha\beta}_{\gamma\eta}$ which forms HS-orthonormal base in $HS(\mathbb{C}^{d_A}) \otimes HS(\mathbb{C}^{d_B})$.

By the use of Theorem 1 the non-separability in a finite given set of quantum states can be detected. This type of computational task can also be computed with parallel programming techniques. Computations can be performed using NumPy threads, but it is necessary to underline that the set of quantum states can be easily distributed to the other nodes. For this purpose, we use mpi4py v3.1.3 package [1] (based on MPI protocol) for communication between computational nodes.

The distribution of cases of separability tests into individual nodes reduces the computation time. The results as an speedup values related to the number of nodes are presented in Fig. 1. Numerical experiment for separability tests shows that increasing the number of nodes shortens the computation time and the scalability of the computation process is correct.

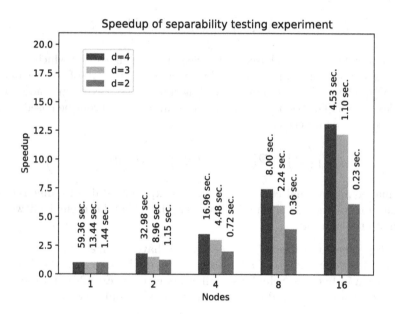

Fig. 1. The speedup values obtained for a separability criterion for various sizes of the quantum system described by the Eq. (35), d means the qudit dimension. The computing system which is used to perform experiment contains sixteen nodes and each one is built of two quad-core Intel Xeon E5420 2.50 GHZ (base clock) processors and 16 GB of RAM. Each node performs eight computational tasks. The MPI protocol is used to communicate available computations nodes. The numerical experiments were conducted in the operating system Debian 8.3.0-6, Linux kernel 4.19.235-1. The numerical values over the bins denotes duration of the experiment in seconds. In the experiment we generate a set of 1024 state examples for different values of d.

Since communication is limited only to passing the parameters, e.g. seeds values to generate pseudo-random numbers to create the state in the form Eq. (35), therefore the influence of communication on the whole computational process is not essential.

It should be added that "brute force" approach (i.e. we perform Schmidt decomposition directly on the super operator $\mathfrak{Q}$) to the applications of the separability test formulated as Theorem 1 depends heavily on the dimensionality of super operator $\mathfrak{Q}$ of examined state Q. Let e.g. $Q \in \mathbb{E}(\mathbb{C}^{d_A} \otimes \mathbb{C}^{d_B})$ be examined pure state, then dimensionality of Q is expressed as following product:

$$\dim Q = d_A \cdot d_B, \tag{36}$$

where d_A, d_B are dimension of space for quantum subsystem A and B, e.g. for two qutrits dimension of the state Q is equal to $3 \times 3 = 9$. For super operator $\mathfrak{Q} = |Q\rangle\langle Q| \in \mathrm{HS}(\mathrm{HS}(\mathbb{C}^{d_A} \otimes \mathbb{C}^{d_B}))$ dimensionality is calculated as:

$$\dim \mathfrak{Q} = \left((d_A)^2 \cdot (d_A)^2 \right)^2 \cdot \left((d_B)^2 \cdot (d_B)^2 \right)^2 = (d_A)^8 \cdot (d_B)^8. \tag{37}$$

The proof of Theorem 1 is based on the Schmidt decomposition which a singular value decomposition (SVD) is used. The general complexity of SVD is denoted as $O(N^3)$, where N represents the leading dimension. Taking into account the complexity of SVD, then the complexity of computational routine based on Theorem 1 should be described as:

$$T_{\text{Thm. }1}\left(\mathfrak{Q} \right) = O\left((d_A)^8 \cdot (d_B)^8 \right)^3 = O\left((d_A)^{24}(d_B)^{24} \right). \tag{38}$$

The final computational complexity remains exponential due to dimensionality of quantum subsystems A and B. However, the use of Theorem 1 allows us to formulate the remark:

Remark 4. The "brute force" complexity (we have assumed $d_A = d_B = d$ for simplicity) is described as $O(d^{24})$. However, taking into account the Theorem 1 and relation in between Schmidt's coefficients given in Eq. (26) and those given in Eq. (27) allows us to reduce the computational complexity as:

– for pure state to $O(d^6)$,
– for a general quantum states to $O(d^{12})$.

4   Conclusions

In the article, we have presented a notion of super-gram matrices as an analytic tool to work with bipartite qubit and qudit systems. We also give some remarks about implementation of computational functions in Python programming language that perform the necessary calculations related to super-gramians.

We introduce also the super-gram matrices notion which are being constructed over the Hilbert-Schmidt structure build on the Hilbert space of pure states. The main results presented in chapter is the extension of the widely known sufficient criterion for the presence of entanglement known under the name realignment criterion on the level of super-operators. Several extensions of results presented in this note are being now under preparations [10]. In particular extensions the genuine infinite-dimensional systems are included there.

We also show that implementation of the set of function to easier processing of super-gramians also possesses scalability property which is important when we process a significant amount of set of quantum states where multicore and many nodes computational environment can be fully utilised.

Acknowledgments. We would like to thank for useful discussions with the *Q-INFO* group at the Institute of Control and Computation Engineering (ISSI) of the University of Zielona Góra, Poland. We would like also to thank to anonymous referees for useful comments on the preliminary version of the chapter. The numerical results were done using the hardware and software available at the "GPU μ-Lab" located at the Institute of Control and Computation Engineering of the University of Zielona Góra, Poland.

References

1. Dalcin, L., Fang, Y.-L.L.: mpi4py: status update after 12 years of development. Comput. Sci. Eng. **23**(4), 47–54 (2021). https://doi.org/10.1109/MCSE. 2021.3083216
2. Decheng, F., Jon, S., Pang, C., Dong, W., Won, C.: Improved quantum clustering analysis based on the weighted distance and its application. Heliyon **4**(11), e00984 (2018). https://doi.org/10.1016/j.heliyon.2018.e00984
3. Devidas, S., Subba Rao, Y.V., Rukma Rekha, N.: A decentralized group signature scheme for privacy protection in a blockchain. Int. J. Appl. Math. Comput. Sci. **31**(2), 353–364 (2021). https://doi.org/10.34768/amcs-2021-0024
4. Farahbakhsh, A., Feng, C.: Opportunistic routing in quantum networks. arXiv preprint (2022). https://doi.org/10.48550/arXiv.2205.08479
5. Faridi, A.R., Masood, F., Shamsan, A.H.T., Luqman, M., Salmony, M.Y.: Blockchain in the quantum world. Int. J. Adv. Comput. Sci. Appl. **13**(1), 542–552 (2022). https://doi.org/10.14569/IJACSA.2022.0130167
6. Grover, L.K.: A fast quantum mechanical algorithm for database search. In: Proceedings of the 28th Annual ACM Symposium on the Theory of Computing (STOC), pp. 212–219 (1996). https://doi.org/10.1145/237814.237866
7. Horodecki, R., Horodecki, P., Horodecki, M., Horodecki, K.: Quantum entanglement. Rev. Mod. Phys. **81**, 865 (2009). https://doi.org/10.1103/RevModPhys.81. 865
8. Gielerak, R., Sawerwain, M.: A Gramian approach to entanglement in bipartite finite dimensional systems: the case of pure states. Quantum Inf. Comput. **20**(13&14), 1081–1108 (2020). https://doi.org/10.26421/QIC20.13-1
9. Gielerak, R., Sawerwain, M., Wiśniewska, J., Wróblewski, M.: EntDetector: entanglement detecting toolbox for bipartite quantum states. In: Paszynski, M., Kranzlmüller, D., Krzhizhanovskaya, V.V., Dongarra, J.J., Sloot, P.M.A. (eds.) ICCS 2021. LNCS, vol. 12747, pp. 113–126. Springer, Cham (2021). https://doi.org/10. 1007/978-3-030-77980-1_9
10. Gielerak, R., Sawerwain, M.: Gramian and super-gramian approach to infinite-dimensional quantum states. In preparation (2022)

11. Gielerak, R., Wiśniewska, J., Sawerwain, M., Wróblewski, M., Korbicz, J.: Classical computer assisted analysis of small multiqudit systems. IEEE Access **10**, 82636–82655 (2022). https://doi.org/10.1109/ACCESS.2022.3196656

12. Kuptsov, L.P. : Gram matrix entry. In: Hazewinkel, M. (ed.) Encyclopaedia of Mathematics: Coproduct - Hausdorff - Young Inequalities, p. 861. Springer, New York (1995). https://doi.org/10.1007/978-1-4899-3795-7

13. Kaliszewska, A., Syga, M.: A comprehensive study of clustering a class of 2D shapes. Int. J. Appl. Math. Comput. Sci. **32**(1), 95–109 (2022). https://doi.org/10.34768/amcs-2022-0008

14. Klyachko, A.: Quantum marginal problem and representations of the symmetric group. arXiv preprint (2004). https://doi.org/10.48550/arXiv.quant-ph/0409113

15. Kopszak, P., Mozrzymas, M., Studziński, M., Horodecki, M.: Multiport based teleportation - transmission of a large amount of quantum information. Quantum **5**, 576 (2021). https://doi.org/10.22331/q-2021-11-11-576

16. Nielsen, M.A., Chuang, I.L.: Quantum Computation and Quantum Information: 10th Anniversary Edition, 10th edn. Cambridge University Press, Cambridge (2011)

17. van Meter, R.: Quantum Networking. Wiley, Hoboken (2014). https://doi.org/10.1002/9781118648919

18. Rajan, D., Visser, M.: Quantum blockchain using entanglement in time. Quantum Rep. **1**(1), 3–11 (2019). https://doi.org/10.3390/quantum1010002

19. Rudolph, O.: Further results on the cross norm criterion for separability. Quantum Inf. Process. **4**, 219–239 (2005). https://doi.org/10.1007/s11128-005-5664-1

20. Sawerwain, M., Wiśniewska, J., Wróblewski, M., Gielerak, R.: GitHub repository for EntDectector package (2022). https://github.com/qMSUZ/EntDetector

21. Schuld, M., Petruccione, F.: Prospects for near-term quantum machine learning. In: Supervised Learning with Quantum Computers. QST, pp. 273–279. Springer, Cham (2018). https://doi.org/10.1007/978-3-319-96424-9_9

22. Schuld, M., Sinayskiy, I., Petruccione, F.: An introduction to quantum machine learning. Contemp. Phys. **56**(2), 172–185 (2014)

23. Schuld, M., Sinayskiy, I., Petruccione, F.: Quantum computing for pattern classification. In: Pham, D.-N., Park, S.-B. (eds.) PRICAI 2014. LNCS (LNAI), vol. 8862, pp. 208–220. Springer, Cham (2014). https://doi.org/10.1007/978-3-319-13560-1_17

24. da Silva, A.J., Ludermir, T.B., de Oliveira, W.R.: Quantum perceptron over a field and neural network architecture selection in a quantum computer. Neural Netw. **76**, 55–64 (2016). https://doi.org/10.1016/j.neunet.2016.01.002

25. Shor, P.W.: Polynomial-time algorithms for prime factorization and discrete logarithms on a quantum computer. SIAM J. Comput. **26**(5), 1484–1509 (1997). https://doi.org/10.1137/S0097539795293172

26. Wiebe, N., Kapoor, A., Svore, K.M.: Quantum algorithms for nearest-neighbor methods for supervised and unsupervised learning. Quantum Inf. Comput. **15**(3&4), 318–358 (2015). https://doi.org/10.26421/QIC15.3-4-7

Solving the Traveling Salesman Problem with a Hybrid Quantum-Classical Feedforward Neural Network

Justyna Zawalska[1,2]([⊠]) and Katarzyna Rycerz[1,2]

[1] Academic Computer Centre Cyfronet AGH, ul. Nawojki 11, 30-950 Krakow, Poland
justyna.zawalska@cyfronet.pl, kzajac@agh.edu.pl
[2] Institute of Computer Science, AGH, al. Mickiewicza 30, 30-059 Krakow, Poland

Abstract. Solving combinatorial optimization problems with the Quantum Approximate Optimization Algorithm (QAOA) is becoming more and more popular. The performance of the QAOA strongly depends on the initial parameters and the optimization procedure. This work presents a benchmark for solving the Traveling Salesman Problem (TSP) that introduces a hybrid feedforward neural network as the QAOA's optimization routine. The strength of this method lies in training the optimization procedure on many instances of the problem and using minibatch updates of the parameters. Although the learning process is costly, the advantage of this method is that after the neural network is trained, it immediately returns optimized parameters for new problem instances. We present the advantage of our method by evaluating it on two sets of initial parameters. The experiments demonstrated that the proposed hybrid quantum-classical feedforward neural network can be successfully used to solve the TSP.

Keywords: Hybrid quantum-classical feedforward neural network ·
Quantum Approximate Optimization Algorithm · Combinatorial
optimization · The Traveling Salesman Problem

1 Introduction

Current quantum computers are Noisy Intermediate-Scale Quantum (NISQ) devices [9] therefore their practical use is limited. An answer to this issue is using hybrid quantum-classical algorithms where a problem is solved using both quantum and classical computational resources. One of the hybrid quantum-classical algorithms is the Quantum Approximate Optimization Algorithm (QAOA). The QAOA is mainly used to find approximate solutions for combinatorial optimization problems [3]. However, the performance of this algorithm is highly dependent on the classical optimization routine [14].

This work describes an approach of utilizing a hybrid quantum-classical feedforward neural network as a QAOA optimizer and presents a benchmark for optimization that introduces the use of fixed QAOA parameters for all problem

R. Wyrzykowski et al. (Eds.): PPAM 2022, LNCS 13827, pp. 199–208, 2023.
https://doi.org/10.1007/978-3-031-30445-3_17

instances. In this study, we focus on solving the Traveling Salesman Problem (TSP).

The article is organized as follows. Section 2 discusses the related work, Sect. 3 introduces the necessary theoretical background, and Sect. 4 describes the method. The experimental setup is outlined in Sect. 5. This is followed by Sect. 6, which examines the obtained results. Finally, Sect. 7 provides a summary and future work.

2   Related Work

The exploration of different approaches to the process of updating the QAOA parameters has started to attract some attention. Several studies have found that the use of machine learning-inspired techniques [12] or hybrid quantum-classical machine learning algorithms such as reinforcement learning [5] or recurrent neural networks [11,13] is beneficial. The QAOA combined with machine learning methods has been used for solving i.e. MAX-2-SAT [12,13], Graph Bisection [13], and Max-Cut [5,11] problems.

In [12] the authors employed a greedy search for the QAOA parameters. The parameter update procedure was learned on the basis of the average response from a training set of problem instances. The optimization procedure generalized well to unseen problem instances.

To find an optimization heuristic, the authors of [13] used a gradient-based technique. They suggested the use of a hybrid quantum-classical Long Short Term Memory (LSTM) recurrent neural network. The LSTM was proven to be a successful meta-learner that was able to approach the global optima. Similarly, the authors of [11] also proposed using an LSTM, however, not as a standalone optimizer, but as a heuristic for finding good initial QAOA parameters.

In our work, we wanted to verify whether a hybrid feedforward neural network could find some fixed parameter values that for different problem instances would yield good result (the phenomenon of parameter concentration has been observed in the MaxCut problem [1]). Similarly to the work presented in [12], we used a method that updated the parameters based on the average responses from the subsets of the training set and returned the parameter values that should generalize well to new problem instances. In contrast to the work presented in [11,13] we tested whether a simple neural network that has no feedback loops could also be useful for the task of finding the correct updates of the parameters.

3   Background

3.1   Traveling Salesman Problem

The TSP is an NP-hard combinatorial optimization problem aimed at determining the shortest possible route that involves visiting each city exactly once and returning to the starting city. Let us assume that N is the number of cities,

$\mathbf{X} = [x_{i,t}]_{N \times N}$ is a Boolean matrix, where $x_{i,t} = 1$ only if the salesperson visits the city i at the timestamp t, and $\mathbf{D} = [d_{i,j}]_{N \times N}$ is a symmetric matrix of distances between cities. The cost function can be expressed in the form of a Quadratic Unconstrained Binary Optimization (QUBO) problem

$$C(\mathbf{X}) = b \cdot \sum_{\substack{i,j=0 \\ i \neq j}}^{N-1} d_{i,j} \sum_{t=0}^{N-1} x_{i,t} x_{j,t+1}$$

$$+ a \cdot \sum_{i=0}^{N-1} \left(1 - \sum_{t=0}^{N-1} x_{i,t}\right)^2 + a \cdot \sum_{t=0}^{N-1} \left(1 - \sum_{i=0}^{N-1} x_{i,t}\right)^2, \tag{1}$$

where $0 < b \cdot \max_{i \neq j}(d_{i,j}) < a$ [7]. The first component of the sum represents the cost of visiting the cities in a given order, and the last two components are the constraints that ensure the correctness of the solution. This discrete optimization problem can be translated into a continuous optimization problem encoded in a quantum subroutine using the QAOA.

3.2 QAOA

The classical cost function $C(\mathbf{X})$ is translated into the cost Hamiltonian H_C. In addition to the cost Hamiltonian, a mixing Hamiltonian is required. The simplest mixing Hamiltonian is $H_M = \sum_{i=1}^{N} X_i$, where X_i is the Pauli-X gate. The goal is to find $2p$ parameters $(\gamma, \beta) \in [0, 2\pi]^p \times [0, \pi]^p$ that minimize the expectation value

$$F_p(\gamma, \beta) = \langle \gamma, \beta | H_C | \gamma, \beta \rangle, \tag{2}$$

where

$$|\gamma, \beta\rangle = e^{-i\beta_p H_M} e^{-i\gamma_p H_C} \cdots e^{-i\beta_1 H_M} e^{-i\gamma_1 H_C} |+\rangle^{\otimes n} \tag{3}$$

$(|+\rangle^{\otimes n}$ is a uniform superposition of n qubits). A quantum device is used to prepare the quantum state, while a classical device is responsible for evaluating the expectation value and updating the values of the parameters (γ, β).

4 Method

We wanted to investigate whether it is possible to obtain a hybrid quantum-classical neural network that, after training on many instances of the TSP, would yield proper parameters (γ, β) for unseen instances of the TSP. To achieve this task, we proposed the use of a hybrid feedforward neural network that consisted of two classical layers: an input layer with a single neuron, a hidden layer with $2p$ neurons, and a quantum layer with a parameterized quantum circuit, cf. Fig. 1. The design of this network was based on the fact that the parameterized quantum circuit had to receive $2p$ parameters, so the layer preceding the quantum layer needed to consist of $2p$ neurons. When it comes to the classical part of this neural network, we tested different configurations of the numbers of neurons and layers;

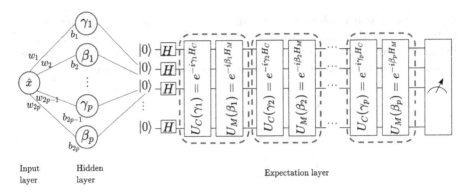

Fig. 1. The quantum layer (in this case the expectation layer) in the hybrid neural network receives classical values as input. These values are applied to the parameterized quantum circuit. The measurement result is the outcome of this layer. Both the input and the output of the quantum layer are classical values.

however, we did not notice any significant improvements compared to this simple setting.

The training begins with the classical part of the hybrid feedforward network sending the set of candidate parameters to the parameterized quantum circuit. The candidate (γ, β) are calculated based on the values of the weights w and biases b connecting the input layer to the hidden layer

$$\gamma_i = \hat{x} \cdot w_{2 \cdot i - 1} + b_{2 \cdot i - 1} \text{ and } \beta_i = \hat{x} \cdot w_{2 \cdot i} + b_{2 \cdot i} \text{ for } i \in \{1, \dots, p\}, \qquad (4)$$

$\hat{x}$ is a hyperparameter provided as input, and it indicates the importance of the weights w. After that, quantum hardware (or a simulator) executes the parameterized circuit. The estimated expectation value is the loss function. The task is to minimize the loss function, so the estimated expectation value is fed back to the classical part, where the neural network uses a gradient-based optimizer to update its weights and biases and to suggest a new set of parameters for the next iteration.

What is interesting in this approach is the method of parameter updates during the optimization procedure. Instead of updating the parameters after every training example, we use a mini-batch approach where the parameters are updated after seeing a subset of training data. As a result, updates based on the average responses of a subset of problem instances are expected to be a good fit for other problem instances.

5   Experimental Setup

All experiments were implemented using TensorFlow Quantum [2] and performed on a quantum computer simulator[1].

---

[1] The implementation is available on GitHub https://github.com/jzawalska/qnn4qaoa.

5.1   Data Preparation and Encoding

The first step was to create a data set consisting of 220 TSP instances by randomly choosing pairs of city coordinates from the range $(0, 10000]$. Since the algorithm was executed on a quantum simulator, a feasible example to solve consisted of four cities ($N = 4$). The matrix D of distances between cities was determined as the Euclidean distance between the city coordinates. From the perspective of optimizing the expectation value, to prevent having very small and very large distances, we normalized the distances between the cities. Normalization consisted in dividing all the distances by the maximum distance. To select the weights for the elements of the QUBO cost function (1) we used a grid search method, which resulted in the following choice of the values: $a = 4, b = 1$. Using this equation, we obtained the cost function and then translated it into the corresponding cost Hamiltonian H_C. As a mixing Hamiltonian, we used the standard version that consists of Pauli-X gates applied on each qubit. Having the cost and mixing Hamiltonians, we were able to generate the parameterized quantum circuits that encoded the problem instances.

5.2   Training Phase

As input, the classical part of the network received the initial values of (γ, β) and the value $\hat{x}$ corresponding to the importance of the weights of the network. The quantum part of the network received 200 parameterized quantum circuits representing the training data set of TSP instances. Training consisted of 20 epochs. The training data has been divided into mini-batches of size 10, so the parameters (γ, β) were updated 400 times. As a classical optimizer, we used Adam [6] (learning rate $= 0.01$, $\beta_1 = 0.9$, $\beta_2 = 0.999$, $\epsilon = 10^{-7}$).

Using the trial-and-error method, it has been observed that if the value of $\hat{x}$ is not equal to 0, then it is very hard to find the parameters (γ, β) that would correctly approximate the cost function. As a result, the neural network's weights were ignored and the parameter values corresponded to the values of the biases $(\gamma_1 = b_1, \beta_1 = b_2, \ldots, \gamma_p = b_{2p-1}, \beta_p = b_{2p})$. The quantum part of this network was differentiated using the Adjoint method [8] which is very efficient for simulations. We did not observe overfitting.

Since the network output depended only on the bias values, after training, we received fixed (universal) parameters (γ, β) that do not rely on the problem instance. To check the influence of the number of QAOA's layers, we trained this hybrid network separately for $p \in \{1, \ldots, 10\}$.

5.3   Testing Phase and Reference Method

We used the test set that contained 20 TSP instances. For $p \in \{1, \ldots, 10\}$ we evaluated each test example by substituting the trained values of the parameters (γ, β) into the parameterized quantum circuit of the problem. For each test example, we measured the expectation value and sampled the circuit 2^{16} times to calculate the number of feasible solutions. The feasible solutions are those that do not violate the TSP constraints; although, they do not need to be optimal.

As a reference method, we used the same hybrid neural network model. However, each test example was optimized separately and the mean and standard deviation were calculated after evaluating the test set with 20 examples. The initial parameters (γ, β) were updated 400 times for each test case anew. This choice of the reference method enabled us to discover if using universal parameters obtained after the training on a larger number of problems with the use of mini-batch updates can yield equally good or better parameter values than optimizing the parameters for each problem instance separately.

6   Results

The QAOA not only is highly dependent on the optimization procedure, but also on the values of the initial parameters. After performing the experiments with different versions of the initial parameters, we present a solution with a high number of correct results and a solution that is trapped in a local minimum but presents the advantage of the introduced method.

6.1   Solution with High Number of Correct Results

For the initial values $\gamma = (0, 0, \dots)$, $\beta = (0, 0, \dots)$ the optimized values of the parameters for $p = 10$ are presented in Fig. 2. This set of parameters returned around 92% feasible solutions for a test 4-city TSP instance.

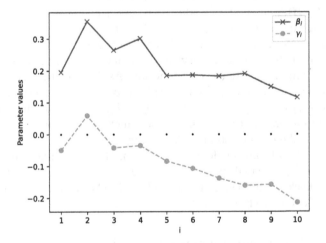

Fig. 2. Optimized values of γ_i and β_i for the circuit with depth $p = 10$.

Although we did not observe the pattern of the parameter values resembling the adiabatic quantum computation process [4] (increasing γ and decreasing β), the obtained results are promising.

The results indicate that the larger the depth p of the circuit, the lower the expectation value of the cost function (cf. Table 1) and the greater the number of correct solutions (cf. Table 2), which is consistent with the theoretical assumptions.

Table 1. Expectation values for the optimization with initial parameters $(\gamma, \beta) = (0, \ldots 0, 0, \ldots, 0)$.

p	Using universal parameters	Reference method
1	17.03 ± 0.19	17.03 ± 0.19
2	13.99 ± 0.24	13.99 ± 0.24
3	10.42 ± 0.25	10.42 ± 0.25
4	9.07 ± 0.25	9.06 ± 0.25
5	7.59 ± 0.28	7.58 ± 0.28
6	5.55 ± 0.27	5.55 ± 0.29
7	4.78 ± 0.27	4.79 ± 0.52
8	4.30 ± 0.27	4.29 ± 0.26
9	3.61 ± 0.25	3.61 ± 0.26
10	3.43 ± 0.25	3.43 ± 0.25

The percentage of feasible solutions is based on the measurement of the output repeated 2^{16} times.

Table 2. Percent of solutions in the feasible space for the optimization with initial parameters $(\gamma, \beta) = (0, \ldots 0, 0, \ldots, 0)$.

p	Using universal parameters	Reference method
1	2.34 ± 0.06	2.34 ± 0.06
2	5.80 ± 0.24	5.85 ± 0.37
3	16.76 ± 0.53	16.78 ± 0.50
4	27.00 ± 0.36	27.05 ± 0.58
5	48.88 ± 0.24	48.88 ± 0.51
6	74.10 ± 0.38	74.17 ± 0.55
7	82.06 ± 0.39	81.90 ± 2.80
8	86.69 ± 0.49	86.75 ± 0.59
9	91.95 ± 0.56	92.00 ± 0.48
10	92.84 ± 0.52	92.95 ± 0.46

There is no significant difference between the results of using the fixed parameters and the results returned by the reference method. It indicates that for a good guess of initial parameter values the proposed method performs as well as optimizing TSP instances separately. However, the proposed method is faster.

The parameter values received as a result of the training are fixed and can be used to solve any 4-city TSP. Obtaining results for a new problem instance requires only a single evaluation.

6.2   Solution Trapped in a Local Minimum

For the initial values $\gamma = (0.05, 0.15, \dots)$, $\beta = (1, 1, \dots)$, the results are worse compared to starting with all the parameters set to 0. We did not observe a decrease in the expectation value with increasing circuit depth. Nevertheless, the use of these initial parameters emphasized the strength of the proposed method. The parameters obtained after the optimization procedure provided results with high precision, e.g., for $p = 10$ using the universal parameters for a test TSP instance yielded the expectation value 7.28 ± 0.7 and $63.60 \pm 3.04\%$ solutions in feasible space. In contrast, the reference method returned the expectation value 11.67 ± 3.43 and $31.64 \pm 15.30\%$ of solutions in feasible space. Figure 3 and Fig. 4 present the comparison of the results obtained after the evaluation of the fixed parameters with the reference method for 20 test instances. In the reference method both the expectation value and the number of solutions in feasible space have large fluctuations. Using universal parameters returned more accurate responses on average.

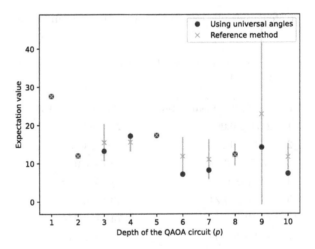

Fig. 3. Estimated expectation value with respect to the QAOA circuit's depth.

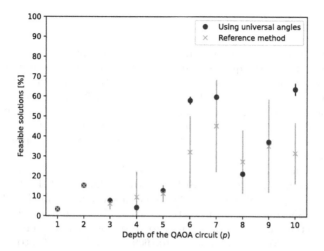

Fig. 4. Percent of correct solutions with respect to the QAOA circuit's depth.

7   Conclusion and Future Work

To sum up, this work has presented a novel way to update the parameters in the QAOA with the use of training data and mini-batch updates. The experiments demonstrated that the proposed hybrid quantum-classical feedforward neural network can be successfully used to solve the TSP. We have obtained encouraging results demonstrating that the introduced method is at least equally good as a simpler optimization method and is faster. Although the learning process is costly, the advantage of this method is that after the neural network is trained, it immediately returns optimized parameters for new problem instances.

However, some shortcomings should be considered. First, the results were not validated on a real quantum device. The effect of noise and decoherence might significantly affect the results. Also, using this method does not prevent being trapped in local optima—if initial parameters are far from almost optimal values, then the optimization process will be unsuccessful.

Future research should consider checking how this method generalizes for larger TSP instances. Also, applying this method to the TSP with time windows [10] or other combinatorial optimization problems, such as MaxCut, Max-2-Sat might provide new insights about the correlations between the nearly optimal parameters for different problems. It might be beneficial to investigate other types of hybrid neural networks that could act as an optimizer and be able to find optimal parameters starting from initial values that are not close to the optimal values.

Acknowledgement. We would like to thank Dr. Adam Glos for valuable discussion. This research was supported in part by PLGrid Infrastructure.

References

1. Brandao, F.G.S.L., Broughton, M., Farhi, E., Gutmann, S., Neven, H.: For fixed control parameters the quantum approximate optimization algorithm's objective function value concentrates for typical instances. https://arxiv.org/abs/1812.04170
2. Broughton, M., et al.: TensorFlow quantum: a software framework for quantum machine learning. https://doi.org/10.48550/ARXIV.2003.02989. https://arxiv.org/abs/2003.02989. Publisher: arXiv Version Number: 2
3. Farhi, E., Goldstone, J., Gutmann, S.: A quantum approximate optimization algorithm. https://arxiv.org/abs/1411.4028
4. Farhi, E., Goldstone, J., Gutmann, S., Sipser, M.: Quantum computation by adiabatic evolution. https://doi.org/10.48550/ARXIV.QUANT-PH/0001106. https://arxiv.org/abs/quant-ph/0001106. Publisher: arXiv Version Number: 1
5. Khairy, S., Shaydulin, R., Cincio, L., Alexeev, Y., Balaprakash, P.: Learning to optimize variational quantum circuits to solve combinatorial problems, vol. 34, no. 3, pp. 2367–2375. https://doi.org/10.1609/aaai.v34i03.5616. https://arxiv.org/abs/1911.11071
6. Kingma, D.P., Ba, J.: Adam: a method for stochastic optimization. https://doi.org/10.48550/ARXIV.1412.6980. https://arxiv.org/abs/1412.6980. Publisher: arXiv Version Number: 9
7. Lucas, A.: Ising formulations of many NP problems 2. https://doi.org/10.3389/fphy.2014.00005. https://journal.frontiersin.org/article/10.3389/fphy.2014.00005/abstract
8. Luo, X.Z., Liu, J.G., Zhang, P., Wang, L.: Yao.jl: extensible, efficient framework for quantum algorithm design. https://doi.org/10.48550/ARXIV.1912.10877. https://arxiv.org/abs/1912.10877. Publisher: arXiv Version Number: 3
9. Preskill, J.: Quantum computing in the NISQ era and beyond. https://doi.org/10.48550/ARXIV.1801.00862. https://arxiv.org/abs/1801.00862. Publisher: arXiv Version Number: 3
10. Salehi, O., Glos, A., Miszczak, J.A.: Unconstrained binary models of the travelling salesman problem variants for quantum optimization. Quantum Inf. Process. **21**(2), 67 (2022). https://doi.org/10.1007/s11128-021-03405-5. https://link.springer.com/10.1007/s11128-021-03405-5
11. Verdon, G., et al.: Learning to learn with quantum neural networks via classical neural networks. https://arxiv.org/abs/1907.05415
12. Wecker, D., Hastings, M.B., Troyer, M.: Training a quantum optimizer. Phys. Rev. A **94**(2), 022309 (2016). https://doi.org/10.1103/PhysRevA.94.022309. https://arxiv.org/abs/1605.05370
13. Wilson, M., Stromswold, R., Wudarski, F., Hadfield, S., Tubman, N.M., Riefel, E.G.: Optimizing quantum heuristics with meta-learning. Quantum Mach. Intell. **3**(1), 13 (2021). https://doi.org/10.1007/s42484-020-00022-w. https://link.springer.com/10.1007/s42484-020-00022-w
14. Zhou, L., Wang, S.T., Choi, S., Pichler, H., Lukin, M.D.: Quantum approximate optimization algorithm: performance, mechanism, and implementation on near-term devices. Phys. Rev. X **10**(2), 021067 (2020). https://doi.org/10.1103/PhysRevX.10.021067. https://arxiv.org/abs/1812.01041

Software Aided Analysis of EWL Based Quantum Games

Piotr Kotara[1,2], Tomasz Zawadzki[2], and Katarzyna Rycerz[2,3]($\boxtimes$) (iD)

[1] IBM Software Laboratory, Kraków, Poland
piotr.kotara@ibm.com
[2] AGH, Institute of Computer Science, al. Mickiewicza 30, 30-059 Krakow, Poland
kzajac@agh.edu.pl
[3] Academic Computer Centre Cyfronet AGH, ul. Nawojki 11, 30-950 Krakow, Poland

Abstract. In this paper, we present the library supporting analysis of Eisert–Wilkens–Lewenstein (EWL) scheme [3] proposed as a quantum extension for 2×2 bimatrix games on the example of Prisoner's Dilemma. Such schemes are often used as a basis for quantization in game theory field [8]. The proposed solution is based on modern approach combining symbolic and numerical calculations with the actual access to quantum simulators and real devices provided by IBM-Q. In particular, the library provides high-level functions for searching Nash equilibria in pure strategies as well as finding the best response cycles which can lead to the existence of Nash equilibria in mixed states [16].

Keywords: quantum games · EWL · Qiskit

1 Introduction and Motivation

Quantum game research combines classical game theory with quantum mechanics and focuses primarily on design, classification and analysis of quantum games, which are an extension of their classical counterparts to the quantum domain [9]. A well-known example of such extension is the formal approach to a general 2×2 game on the case of Prisoner's Dilemma introduced by Eisert, Wilkens and Lewenstain [3], where the use of two-parameter unitary operators as player strategies allows to achieve the Pareto-optimal Nash equilibrium. The scheme is widely used in various research that often requires manual analysis of payoff functions mostly obtained by dedicated tools for symbolical calculations [2,5,16]. In this work, we present and evaluate semi-automatic, software-aided approach towards such analysis. The proposed tool, integrated with actual quantum devices, provides both symbolic and numerical support for quantum games researchers. The results show to which extend the presented approach may be successfully applied for the purpose of theoretical analysis of various properties of quantum games in the EWL protocol, including finding best responses for arbitrary strategies of the opponent, finding Nash equilibria in pure strategies, or proving the lack of existence of such strategy profiles.

R. Wyrzykowski et al. (Eds.): PPAM 2022, LNCS 13827, pp. 209–220, 2023.
https://doi.org/10.1007/978-3-031-30445-3_18

2 Related Work

The general overview of quantum games topic can be found in [9]. One of most common approaches in this area is EWL game scheme [3], that became a basis for further research in this field [12]. The original proposition initiated long discussion as the same approach using fully parameterised operators does not lead to Nash equilibrium and original limitation to two degrees of freedom was accused of being artificial [1]. However, the scheme is widely analysed and used [7], including generalization to arbitrary number of players [4,6], extension to the repeated version of the game [14] or inspiration for different quantisation schemes [8,11]. In [15], instead of using original angle-based parametrizations and trigonometric functions, the authors introduce algebra of quaternions, which cleverly facilitates calculation of probabilities of possible game outcomes.

On the other hand, there exists various software tools related to game theory such as Nashpy [10] or Gambit[1], implementing a wide variety of efficient algorithms for numerical analysis of classical games in terms of the existence of Nash equilibria, Pareto efficiency and other various properties, however with no support for quantum games. The aim of the work presented in this paper is to fill this gap in the context of EWL–based games.

3 Generalized Eisert-Wilkens-Lewenstein Scheme

A 2×2 bimatrix game is a two-players game described by set of payoff matrices:

$$(P_A, P_B) = \begin{pmatrix} (a_{00}, b_{00}) & (a_{01}, b_{01}) \\ (a_{10}, b_{10}) & (a_{11}, b_{11}) \end{pmatrix}. \tag{1}$$

The strategies are identified by the number of the row (for player A) or column (for player B). In particular, if player A chooses row k and player B chooses column l, their payoffs are described by matrix elements a_{kl} and b_{kl}, respectively.

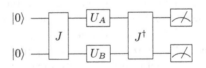

Fig. 1. Quantum circuit for EWL protocol

Generalized form of the Eisert-Wilkens-Lewenstein (EWL) scheme [12] for 2×2 bimatrix games is presented in the Fig. 1. The game depends on the choice of the initial state produced by application of J gate to $|00\rangle$ state.

$$J|00\rangle = |\Psi(\gamma)\rangle = (\cos{(\gamma/2)}|00\rangle + i\sin{(\gamma/2)}|11\rangle, \tag{2}$$

---

[1] http://www.gambit-project.org/.

where $\gamma \in [0, \pi/2]$ is a real parameter which is a measure of the initial state entanglement. If we introduce $W_0 = \begin{pmatrix} 1 & 0 \\ 0 & 1 \end{pmatrix}$ as representation of choosing row (or column) number 0 in (1) and $W_1 = \begin{pmatrix} 0 & i \\ i & 0 \end{pmatrix}$ as representation the of choosing row (or column) number 1 in (1), we can define vectors

$$|\Psi_{kl}(\gamma)\rangle = W_k \otimes W_l |\Psi(\gamma)\rangle \text{ for } k, l \in \{0, 1\} \tag{3}$$

that form a basis of $C^2 \otimes C^2$ for any $\gamma \in [0, \pi/2]$ and therefore are used to define columns of gate J.

In the quantum version of the game, each player (represented by one qubit) applies his strategy as an arbitrary unitary matrix U_A or U_B. The payoff function is calculated as an expectation value of the measurement output after applying $J^\dagger$ gate as follows:

$$p_A(U_A, U_B, \gamma) = \sum_{k,l=0}^{1} a_{kl} |\langle \Psi_{kl}(\gamma)|U_A \otimes U_B|\Psi(\gamma)\rangle|^2 \tag{4}$$

$$p_B(U_A, U_B, \gamma) = \sum_{k,l=0}^{1} b_{kl} |\langle \Psi_{kl}(\gamma)|U_A \otimes U_B|\Psi(\gamma)\rangle|^2, \tag{5}$$

where a_{kl} and b_{kl} for $k, l \in \{0, 1\}$ are the payoffs of (1).

4   EWL Library

4.1   EWL Abstraction

The `ewl` library[2] provides a layer of abstraction for generalized EWL circuits for arbitrary number of players with customizable base strategies representing the possible moves from the classical counterpart of the game. The library comes with several built-in parametrizations for unitary player strategies U_A and U_B commonly used in research [2,3,6], also allowing for the use of custom ones.

The sample usage of the `ewl` library is shown in the Listing 1.1. To construct the EWL circuit, user must define the initial quantum state that can be passed in Dirac notation, W_0 and W_1 operators representing classical strategies and set of quantum strategies U_A and U_B actually used by players. Based on this information, thanks to the integration with Qiskit `operators` package[3], the library automatically derives the corresponding entanglement operator J and its Hermitian conjugate, $J^\dagger$, amplitudes of the final state, game outcome probabilities and payoff functions.

---

[2] https://github.com/tomekzaw/ewl/blob/master/examples/example.ipynb.
[3] https://qiskit.org/documentation/tutorials/circuits_advanced/
02_operators_overview.html.

```
 1 import sympy as sp  # Python library for symbolic calculations
 2 from sympy.physics.quantum.qubit import Qubit
 3
 4 psi = (Qubit('00') + i * Qubit('11')) / sp.sqrt(2)  # initial state
 5
 6 # parametrization for player A
 7 theta1, alpha1, beta1 = sp.symbols('theta1 alpha1 beta1', real=True)
 8 UA = U_theta_alpha_beta(theta=theta1, alpha=alpha1, beta=beta1)
 9
10 # parametrization for player B
11 theta2, alpha2, beta2 = sp.symbols('theta2 alpha2 beta2', real=True)
12 UB = U_theta_alpha_beta(theta=theta2, alpha=alpha2, beta=beta2)
13
14 # construct EWL circuit
15 ewl = EWL(psi, W0, W1, players=[UA, UB], payoff_matrix)
16
17 ewl.J  # J gate of EWL circuit
18 ewl.J_H  # Hermitian conjugate of J
19
20 ewl.amplitudes()  # symbolic amplitudes of the final state of the circuit
21 ewl.probs()  # symbolic probabilities of the final state of the circuit
22
23 ewl.payoff_function(player=n)  # payoff function for player n
24 ewl.payoff_function(player=None)  # payoff function for all players
```

Listing 1.1. Creation of EWL game based on initial state $|\psi\rangle$

The library allows for direct usage of symbolic expressions as an interface. The result can be further processed by symbolic expressions engine integrated with SymPy package[4] which applies well-known mathematical identities to simplify the expression taking advantage of the fact that the parameters are real-valued. The library design allows for easy switching from symbolic to numerical approach if necessary.

4.2 Algorithms

Nash Equilibria. The core functionality of the library allowing EWL-based game analysis is the possibility to calculate the payoff function of each player in a symbolic form as a function of parameters involved in the initial quantum state as well as the quantum operators representing the strategies of the players. Unfortunately, even for two players game symbolic calculations to obtain a general symbolic formula of the best response for arbitrary parameters of the opponent's strategy turned out to be too time-consuming. Therefore we focus on finding best responses for particular strategies using well-known numerical optimization algorithms. This method was also extended to find Nash equilibria.

In a two-player game, Nash equilibrium is a pair of strategies (U_A, U_B) such that U_A is the best response for U_B and simultaneously U_B is the best response for U_A.

---

[4] https://www.sympy.org/.

A pair of strategies $(U(\mathbf{x_A}), U(\mathbf{x_B}))$ is a Nash equilibrium if

$$\mathbf{x_B} \in \text{best response}_B(\mathbf{x_A}) \text{ and } \mathbf{x_A} \in \text{best response}_A(\mathbf{x_B}). \tag{6}$$

Assuming that only a single best response exists, the following pair of statements can be merged into

$$\mathbf{x_A} = \text{best response}_A(\text{best response}_B(\mathbf{x_A})), \tag{7}$$

which can be expressed as a fixed point equation

$$\mathbf{x_A} = f(\mathbf{x_A}) \tag{8}$$

where $f = (\text{best response}_A \circ \text{best response}_B)$ is a composition of best response functions, $\mathbf{x_A}$ is a fixed point of f, and $\mathbf{x_B} = \text{best response}_B(\mathbf{x_A})$.

In case of a symmetric 2×2 game, $\text{best response}_A = \text{best response}_B$, so effectively $f = \text{best response}^2$, or alternatively $\mathbf{x_A}$ is a 2-periodic point of best response function.

If the analytic form of the best response function is unknown, numerous numerical methods of fixed-point search can be employed in order to find Nash equilibria. However, due to discrete nature of numerical computing, this requires searching the entire grid of valid parameter values constrained by appropriate boundaries or running the algorithm multiple number of times with randomizing the initial strategy, as proposed in Algorithm 1.

Algorithm 1: Finding Nash equilibria numerically

Input: $U(\mathbf{x})$ – parametrization of players' strategies
$\quad\quad X$ – space of valid parameter values
$\quad\quad \$_A(\mathbf{x_A}, \mathbf{x_B})$ – Alice's expected payoff function
$\quad\quad \$_B(\mathbf{x_A}, \mathbf{x_B})$ – Bob's expected payoff function
$\quad\quad N$ – number of iterations of the algorithm
Output: E – list of found Nash equilibria in pure strategies
$E \leftarrow []$
$i \leftarrow 0$
while $i < N$ **do**
$\quad$ $\mathbf{x_A} \leftarrow \text{RandomStrategy}(X)$
$\quad$ $\mathbf{x_B} \leftarrow \text{NumericBestResponse}(U, X, \mathbf{x_A}, \$_B)$
$\quad$ $\mathbf{x_A'} \leftarrow \text{NumericBestResponse}(U, X, \mathbf{x_B}, \$_A)$
$\quad$ **if** $U(x_A') \approx U(x_A)$ **then**
$\quad\quad$ $E.\textbf{insert}((\mathbf{x_A}, \mathbf{x_B}))$
$\quad$ **end**
$\quad$ $i \leftarrow i + 1$
end
return E

Best Response Cycles. Assuming that $U_A \to U_B \to U_A$, a pure Nash equilibrium can be seen as a special case of best response cycle. However, in some quantum games there are no such cycles of length 2 and thus no Nash equilibria in pure strategies. The concept of two mutual best responses in two-player games may be easily generalized to cycles of length $2n$ such that

$$U_A^{(1)} \xrightarrow{B} U_B^{(1)} \xrightarrow{A} U_A^{(2)} \xrightarrow{B} U_B^{(2)} \xrightarrow{A} \dots \xrightarrow{A} U_A^{(n)} \xrightarrow{B} U_B^{(n)} \xrightarrow{A} U_A^{(1)} \qquad (9)$$

where $X \xrightarrow{A} Y$ denotes that $Y \in$ best response$_A(X)$ and analogously for $\xrightarrow{B}$.

A proposed numerical approach towards finding best response cycles symbolically is shown in Algorithm 2.

Algorithm 2: Finding best response cycle numerically

Input: $U(\mathbf{x})$ – parametrization of players' strategies
      X – space of valid parameter values
      $\$_A(\mathbf{x}_A, \mathbf{x}_B)$ – Alice's expected payoff function
      $\$_B(\mathbf{x}_A, \mathbf{x}_B)$ – Bob's expected payoff function
Output: C – best response cycle found
$i \leftarrow 0$
$\mathbf{x}_A \leftarrow \text{RandomStrategy}(X)$
$prev \leftarrow [\mathbf{x}_A]$
while *True* **do**
    $\mathbf{x}_B \leftarrow \text{NumericBestResponse}(U, X, \mathbf{x}_A, \$_B)$
    $prev.\text{insert}(\mathbf{x}_B)$
    $\mathbf{x}_A \leftarrow \text{NumericBestResponse}(U, X, \mathbf{x}_B, \$_A)$
    $prev.\text{insert}(\mathbf{x}_A)$
    $i \leftarrow i + 1$
    $j \leftarrow 0$
    while $j \leq i$ **do**
        if $U(\boldsymbol{x}_A) \approx U(prev[2*j])$ **then**
            | **return** $prev[2*j : 2*i]$
        end
        $j \leftarrow j + 1$
    end
end

4.3   Qiskit Integration

Apart from symbolic and numerical software aided EWL games analysis, the library allows to execute games on real quantum devices. Qiskit[5] integration allows for verification of theoretical results on numerous available real IBM-Q quantum devices or simulators including noise models. The library also greatly

---

[5] http://qiskit.org.

simplifies visualizing quantum circuit of the game after transpiling and optimization for a selected quantum device. A sample usage is shown in the Listing 1.2, where a user fixes parameters for particular instance of the game, creates the circuit, transpiles it to the actual device and compares results from IBM QASM simulator and a real device.

```
1
2  # fix actual parameters of parametrization strategies UA and UB
3  ewl_fixed = ewl.fix(theta1=pi / 2, alpha1=pi / 2, beta1=0,
4                      theta2=0, alpha2=0, beta2=0)
5
6  # create and draw IBM-Q circuit
7  ewl_ibmq = EWL_IBMQ(ewl_fixed)
8  ewl_ibmq.draw()
9
10 # draw transpiled circuit
11 ewl_ibmq.draw_transpiled(backend_name='ibmq_quito', optimization_level=3)
12
13 # simulate game using QASM simulator
14 counts_qasm_simulator = ewl_ibmq.simulate_counts()
15
16 # run game on actual device
17 counts_quantum_device = ewl_ibmq.run()
18
19 # plot results
20 plot_histogram(data=[counts_qasm_simulator, counts_quantum_device],
21                legend=['qasm simulator', 'quantum device'])
```

Listing 1.2. Running example of EWL game on a real quantum device

5 Prisoner's Dilemma Use Case

Prisoner's Dilemma is a symmetric bimatrix game example (see Sect. 3) with the following payoff matrix

$$(P_A, P_B) = \begin{pmatrix} (r,r) & (s,t) \\ (t,s) & (p,p) \end{pmatrix}. \tag{10}$$

where r is the reward payoff if both players decide to cooperate, p is the punishment payoff when both players defect, t is temptation payoff and s is sucker's payoff in case the first player defects while the second cooperates, respectively. The values need to satisfy the conditions $s < p < r < t$ and $2r > s + t$ (commonly used values are: $r = 3$, $p = 1$, $t = 5$ and $s = 0$) This condition implies that mutual defection is the unique Nash equilibrium for this game [13] leading to the dilemma, i.e. player payoffs are lower in comparison to the situation when they cooperate with each other.

6   Experiment Results

6.1   Symbolic Calculations of Probability Functions

The execution time of symbolically calculating the probability functions for EWL circuit was measured in relation to the number of qubits and degree of entanglement of initial quantum state. Tests were performed on three classes of quantum states: one maximally entangled, second one with entanglement degree equal to 0.5 and third without entanglement. Tests were performed on the MacBook Pro 16 with 8-core 2.4 GHz with TurboBoost up to 5 GHz Intel Core i9 equipped with 16 MB L3 cache (Table 1).

Table 1. Execution times for calculating EWL schema probabilities

Number of qubits	Execution time [s] (maximally entangled)	Execution time [s] (half-entangled)	Execution time [s] (non-entangled)
2	2.3 ($\sigma = 0.2$)	36 ($\sigma = 1$)	1.28 ($\sigma = 0.12$)
3	443.3 ($\sigma = 5.5$)	10940 ($\sigma = 702$)	10.7 ($\sigma = 0.2$)
4	>18000	>18000	122 ($\sigma = 3$)
5	>18000	>18000	2712 ($\sigma = 27$)

Due to the exponential nature of problem based on qubits number, the results are suggesting, that calculations for the quantum EWL circuits based on large amount of qubits will be impossible to perform in a reasonable amount of time. Nonetheless, for untangled states, the calculation of probabilities is by far the fastest. We are able to obtain formulas in a reasonable time for four-qubit systems.

6.2   Numerical Best Response and Nash Equilibrium Search

The example comparison of numerical search methods for the best response for EWL-based Prisoner's Dilemma is shown in Table 2. Success rate was calculated with 0.01% tolerance. The highest success rate of 99.94% was achieved using Powell method with bounds disabled and zero vector as starting point.

As can be seen, applying the best response function repeatedly (see Algorithm 1) for Quantum Prisoner's Dilemma with original two-parameters EWL parametrisation [3] yields a best response cycle of length 2 which represents a Nash equilibrium as shown in Table 3, which can be generalized to $((0, x), (0, \pi - x))$ where $x \in [0, \pi]$ after running the experiment starting from different initial strategy parameters.

When using Prisoner's Dilemma variant with full parametrization [2] there are no Nash equilibria, but for arbitrary initial startegy there exist best response cycles of length 4 (i.e. 2 moves per each player).

Table 2. Comparison of numerical search for best response

Optimization method	Start point	Bounds	Success rate
Powell	Zero	True	86.94%
Powell	Zero	False	99.94%
Powell	Random	True	76.34%
Powell	Random	False	99.23%
Powell	Alice	True	79.14%
Powell	Alice	False	99.35%
Nelder-Mead	Zero	True	45.89%
Nelder-Mead	Zero	False	96.60%
Nelder-Mead	Random	True	41.47%
Nelder-Mead	Random	False	99.52%
Nelder-Mead	Alice	True	43.55%
Nelder-Mead	Alice	False	99.01%

Table 3. A sequence of best responses leading to Nash equilibrium found numerically in Quantum Prisoner's Dilemma starting from a random strategy

Player	θ	ϕ	Expected payoff
Alice	2.030715	2.818488	n/a
Bob	1.044621	1.510837	4.933883
Alice	6.208956	1.609381	3.499695
Bob	6.278414	1.532301	3.002761
Alice	0.000299	1.609292	3.000011
Bob	0.000019	1.532301	3.0
Alice	6.283184	1.609292	3.0
Bob	6.283185	1.532301	3.0
Alice	6.283185	1.609292	3.0
Bob	6.283185	1.532301	3.0

As shown in Table 4, after only a few iterations, the numerical method was able to find one of the best response cycles $U_{A1} \rightarrow U_{B1} \rightarrow U_{A2} \rightarrow U_{B2} \rightarrow U_{A1}$ composed of the strategies (11)

$$
\begin{aligned}
U_{A1} &= U(-2.267319, 1.453127, 1.484048) \\
U_{B1} &= U(5.408823, -1.484063, 0.117665) \\
U_{A2} &= U(2.267279, -0.117653, -0.086732) \\
U_{B2} &= U(-0.874319, 0.086739, -1.452943).
\end{aligned}
\tag{11}
$$

To sum up, the main advantage of using numerical methods for Finding Nash equilibria as well as best response cycles is the fact that it does not require know-

Table 4. A sequence of best responses found numerically in Quantum Prisoner's Dilemma with $U(\theta, \phi, \alpha)$ parametrization starting from random strategy

Player	θ	ϕ	α	Expected payoff
Alice	2.271152	−0.118018	−0.081848	n/a
Bob	−0.870404	0.081856	−1.452776	5.000000
Alice	−2.270383	1.453049	1.487888	4.999995
Bob	0.871299	1.653691	0.117743	5.000000
Alice	2.270338	−0.117733	−0.082893	5.000000
Bob	−0.871261	0.082902	−1.452838	5.000000
Alice	−2.269523	1.453107	1.486841	4.999995
Bob	0.872155	1.654738	0.117685	5.000000
Alice	2.269483	−0.117675	−0.083941	5.000000
Bob	−0.872115	0.083949	−1.452903	5.000000
Alice	−2.268748	1.453130	1.485877	4.999996
Bob	0.872926	1.655703	0.117663	5.000000
Alice	2.268713	−0.117652	−0.084905	5.000000
Bob	−0.872885	0.084913	−1.452932	5.000000
Alice	−2.268020	1.453131	1.484945	4.999996
Bob	0.873651	1.656635	0.117661	5.000000
Alice	2.267989	−0.117650	−0.085838	5.000000
Bob	−0.873609	0.085846	−1.452939	5.000000
Alice	−2.267319	1.453127	1.484048	4.999996
Bob	5.408823	−1.484063	0.117665	5.000000
Alice	2.267279	−0.117653	−0.086732	5.000000
Bob	−0.874319	0.086739	−1.452943	5.000000

ing the best response functions in analytic form. However, this kind of analysis is strictly dependent on the choice of the initial strategy and it is necessary to run the experiment a number of times and manually generalize the results afterwards in order to draw reasonable conclusions. Moreover, the current solution only finds a single global maximum, while in general there may exist more than one best response.

7   Summary and Future Work

In this paper we showed that existing software for scientific computing may be successfully utilized for the purpose of theoretical analysis of various properties of quantum games in the EWL protocol. In particular, `ewl` library is a useful tool for deriving complex formulas describing generalized variants of such quantum games.

Finding best responses and Nash equilibria using numerical methods is far more efficient than using symbolic algorithms, however involves numerical errors and requires many iterations. Due to performance reasons the symbolic approach can be used only for particular game examples, when the best response function in analytic form is known.

When implementing quantum games for IBM Q, `Operators` library can be used to construct arbitrary quantum gates instead of manual decomposition of entanglement operator.

Despite numerous attempts involving simplification of the input as well as reduction to other kinds of problems, we were not able to obtain a generic formula for the best reply to arbitrary strategy of the opponent using Mathematica or SymPy. If we knew the best response function in analytic form, we could find whole families of Nash equilibria in symbolic form for arbitrary quantum game in the EWL scheme, which is ineffective and challenging with the numerical approach.

The `ewl` library, which was developed as part of the work, greatly facilitates the analysis more general variants of quantum games in the EWL protocol, for instance involving symbolic parameters or simply with more players, and thus provides new opportunities for quantum game theory researchers. A particularly interesting topic seems to be the study of influence of the underlying quantum computer architecture, especially connections between qubits, on the noise levels in quantum games with three or more players.

Acknowledgements. This work is partly supported by IBM Software Laboratory in Kraków. We would like to thank Piotr Frackiewicz and Marek Szopa for fruitful discussions.

References

1. Benjamin, S.C., Hayden, P.M.: Comment on "quantum games and quantum strategies". Phys. Rev. Lett. **87**(6), 069801 (2001). https://doi.org/10.1103/PhysRevLett.87.069801. https://link.aps.org/doi/10.1103/PhysRevLett.87.069801
2. Chen, K.Y., Hogg, T.: How well do people play a quantum prisoner's dilemma? Quantum Inf. Process. **5**(1), 43–67 (2006). https://doi.org/10.1007/s11128-006-0012-7. http://link.springer.com/10.1007/s11128-006-0012-7
3. Eisert, J., Wilkens, M., Lewenstein, M.: Quantum games and quantum strategies. Phys. Rev. Lett. **83**(15), 3077–3080 (1999). https://doi.org/10.1103/PhysRevLett.83.3077. https://link.aps.org/doi/10.1103/PhysRevLett.83.3077. Number: 15. Publisher: American Physical Society
4. Frąckiewicz, P., Rycerz, K., Szopa, M.: Quantum absentminded driver problem revisited. Quantum Inf. Process. **21**(1), 34 (2022). https://doi.org/10.1007/s11128-021-03377-6. https://link.springer.com/10.1007/s11128-021-03377-6
5. Frąckiewicz, P.: Quantum approach to Cournot-type competition. Int. J. Theor. Phys. **57**(2), 353–362 (2017). https://doi.org/10.1007/s10773-017-3567-4
6. Frackiewicz, P., Pykacz, J.: Quantum games with strategies induced by basis change rules. Int. J. Theor. Phys. **56**(12), 4017–4028 (2017). https://doi.org/10.1007/s10773-017-3423-6. https://link.springer.com/10.1007/s10773-017-3423-6

7. Ikeda, K., Aoki, S.: Theory of quantum games and quantum economic behavior. Quantum Inf. Process. **21**(1), 27 (2022). https://doi.org/10.1007/s11128-021-03378-5. https://link.springer.com/10.1007/s11128-021-03378-5

8. Iqbal, A., Abbott, D.: Two-player quantum games: when player strategies are via directional choices. Quantum Inf. Process. **21**(6), 212 (2022). https://doi.org/10.1007/s11128-022-03526-5. https://link.springer.com/10.1007/s11128-022-03526-5

9. Khan, F.S., Solmeyer, N., Balu, R., Humble, T.S.: Quantum games: a review of the history, current state, and interpretation. Quantum Inf. Process. **17**(11), 309 (2018). https://doi.org/10.1007/s11128-018-2082-8. http://link.springer.com/10.1007/s11128-018-2082-8

10. Knight, V., et al.: drvinceknight/Nashpy: v0.0.34, June 2022. https://doi.org/10.5281/ZENODO.6620830. https://zenodo.org/record/6620830

11. Marinatto, L., Weber, T.: A quantum approach to static games of complete information. Phys. Lett. A **272**(5–6), 291–303 (2000). https://doi.org/10.1016/S0375-9601(00)00441-2. http://arxiv.org/abs/quant-ph/0004081. Number: 5–6

12. Nawaz, A., Toor, A.H.: Generalized quantization scheme for two-person non-zero sum games. J. Phys. A: Math. Gen. **37**(47), 11457–11463 (2004). https://doi.org/10.1088/0305-4470/37/47/014. https://iopscience.iop.org/article/10.1088/0305-4470/37/47/014

13. Roth, A.E., Murnighan, J.: Equilibrium behavior and repeated play of the prisoner's dilemma. J. Math. Psychol. **17**(2), 189–198 (1978). https://doi.org/10.1016/0022-2496(78)90030-5. https://linkinghub.elsevier.com/retrieve/pii/0022249678900305

14. Rycerz, K., Frackiewicz, P.: A quantum approach to twice-repeated 2×2 game. Quantum Inf. Process. **19**(8), 269 (2020). https://doi.org/10.1007/s11128-020-02743-0. https://link.springer.com/10.1007/s11128-020-02743-0

15. Shaik, A., Ahmed, A.: Best response analysis in two person quantum games. Adv. Pure Math. **04**(07), 341–356 (2014). https://doi.org/10.4236/apm.2014.47045. http://www.scirp.org/journal/doi.aspx?DOI=10.4236/apm.2014.47045

16. Szopa, M.: Efficiency of classical and quantum games equilibria. Entropy **23**(5), 506 (2021). https://doi.org/10.3390/e23050506. https://www.mdpi.com/1099-4300/23/5/506

First Workshop on Applications of Machine Learning and Artificial Intelligence in High Performance Computing (WAML 2022)

Adaptation of AI-Accelerated CFD Simulations to the IPU Platform

Paweł Rościszewski[1(✉)], Adam Krzywaniak[1,6], Sergio Iserte[2,3], Krzysztof Rojek[4], and Paweł Gepner[1,5]

[1] Graphcore, Gdańsk, Poland
{royr,adamk,pawelg}@graphcore.ai, pawel.gepner@pw.edu.pl
[2] Department of Construction and Mechanical Engineering, Universitat Jaume I, Castellón de la Plana, Spain
siserte@uji.es
[3] Barcelona Supercomputing Center, Barcelona, Spain
sergio.iserte@bsc.es
[4] Institute of Computer and Information Sciences, Częstochowa University of Technology, Częstochowa, Poland
krojek@icis.pcz.pl
[5] Faculty of Mechanical and Industrial Engineering, Warsaw University of Technology, Warszawa, Poland
[6] Department of Computer Architecture Faculty of Electronics, Telecommunications and Informatics, Gdańsk University of Technology, Narutowicza 11/12, 80-233 Gdańsk, Poland

Abstract. Intelligence Processing Units (IPU) have proven useful for many AI applications. In this paper, we evaluate them within the emerging field of *AI for simulation*, where traditional numerical simulations are supported by artificial intelligence approaches. We focus specifically on a program for training machine learning models supporting a *computational fluid dynamics* application. We use custom TensorFlow provided by the Poplar SDK to adapt the program for the IPU-POD16 platform and investigate its ease of use and performance scalability. Training a model on data from OpenFOAM simulations allows us to get accurate simulation state predictions in test time. We show how to utilize the *popdist* library to overcome a performance bottleneck in feeding training data to the IPU on the host side, achieving up to 34% speedup. Due to communication overheads, using data parallelism to utilize two IPUs instead of one does not improve the throughput. However, once the intra-IPU costs have been paid, the hardware capabilities for inter-IPU communication allow for good scalability. Increasing the number of IPUs from 2 to 16 improves the throughput from 560.8 to 2805.8 samples/s.

Keywords: Intelligence processing unit · Computational fluid dynamics · Machine learning

1 Introduction

One of the emerging trends in high performance computing (HPC) is supporting traditional numerical simulations with artificial intelligence (AI) approaches.

R. Wyrzykowski et al. (Eds.): PPAM 2022, LNCS 13827, pp. 223–235, 2023.
https://doi.org/10.1007/978-3-031-30445-3_19

While various names have been proposed for this field of research, such as *simulation intelligence* [7] or *cognitive simulation* [19], we refer to it as simply as *AI for simulation* [11,12]. Another significant trend is designing hardware architectures specifically for the type of workloads that are the backbone of AI [8,13,15]. In this paper, we look into an *AI for simulation* approach, where a machine learning (ML) model supports a computational fluid dynamics (CFD) application, and investigate how it can benefit from a AI-specific hardware architecture: the intelligence processing unit (IPU) processor.

The IPU is a computing accelerator specifically designed for machine learning computation. Each IPU has 1472 cores, with its own on-chip 624KiB SRAM memory per core. The combination of the core and the associated on-chip memory is named a tile. The tile Instruction Set Architecture (ISA) [2] includes focused hardware elements such as Accumulating Matrix Product (AMP) and Slim Convolution (SLIC) units which allow to complete up to 64 multiply-add instructions per clock cycle. There are also hardware support instructions for random number generation and selected transcendental operations generally used in machine learning. Every tile runs 6 hardware execution threads in a time-sliced round-robin schedule, allowing instruction and memory latency to be hidden. With this mechanism, most instructions, including memory access and vectorised floating-point operations, complete within one thread cycle (6 clock cycles). Every thread represents a truly independent program. There is no restriction that threads run in groups executing the same program in lockstep, and no requirement that memory accesses are coalesced to achieve high SRAM bandwidth [2].

IPU accelerators have proven useful for many AI applications, but employing them in *AI for simulation* is a new area of research. In this paper we adapt a training program for AI-accelerated CFD simulations to the IPU-based POD16 platform. This allows us to evaluate the models trained on the IPU-POD16 platform for the selected problem and investigate performance scalability of the training workload. The remainder of the paper is organized as follows: references to related work are given in Sect. 2, implementation details are described in Sect. 3, experimental results are reported and discussed in Sect. 4, while a summary is provided along with proposed future work directions in Sect. 5.

2   Related Work

Kochkov et al. in [6] summarized the applications of ML to accelerating numerical simulations and proposed the following classification:

- supporting simulations with ML for better accuracy but no performance improvement;
- pure ML replacing the entire simulation, allowing for significant performance gains but weak on generalization (when new physical constraints are applied to previously trained model);
- hybrid approach replacing/accelerating iterative solvers inside the simulation without accuracy reduction.

We reviewed several papers which support such a classification of AI-accelerated simulations.

Maulik et. al in their work [9] presented the results of two-dimensional Kraichan turbulence subgrid modeling with a novel data-driven neural network support for predicting the turbulence source. Their work aimed to improve the accuracy of modeling without focusing on increasing its performance.

Kim et al. in their paper [5] proposed a generative model called DeepFluids to synthesize fluid simulations from a set of reduced parameters. They train a convolutional neural network (CNN) for predicting the fluid velocity fields. In their work they propose a fluid-specific loss function to improve the convergence of the trained model. The aim of their work is to replace the simulation in order to use the trained ML model in inference mode and improve the performance of velocity fields reconstruction up to 700x.

Wiewel et al. in their work [18] proposed an approach based on the long short-term memory (LSTM) network for fluid flow modeling, i.e. to predict the changes of pressure fields over time. They achieved practical speed-ups with neural network-based simulation of 3D+time functions of a physics system.

Ribeiro et al. in their paper [10] presented a CNN-based model called Deep-CFD, that efficiently approximates solutions for the problem of non-uniform steady laminar flows. Their proposed model is able to learn complete solutions of the Navier-Stokes equations, for both velocity and pressure fields, directly from ground-truth data generated using a state-of-the-art CFD code. The predictions of the proposed model allow for achieving up to 1000x speedup in obtaining the resulting velocity and pressure fields, when comparing classical simulation on CPU with CNN model running on GPU.

Thuerey et. al in their work [16] investigated the accuracy of deep learning models for the inference of Reynolds-Averaged Navier-Stokes solutions. Their best results allowed them to obtain mean relative pressure and velocity error of less than 3% across a range of previously unseen airfoil shapes.

Um et al. in their paper [17] present a hybrid approach called Solver-in-the-loop. By integrating the learned function into a differentiable physics pipeline, the corrections can interact with the physical system, alter the states, and receive gradients about the future performance of these modifications. This provided the model with realistic input distributions that take previous corrections into account, yielding improvements in accuracy with stable rollouts of several hundred recurrent evaluation steps and surpassing even tailored supervised variants.

In this paper we evaluate the LSTM-based approach for predicting the fluid flow in a homogenization tank which aims to replace the simulation with an OpenFOAM numerical solver. We evaluate the LSTM model on IPU, a new AI-dedicated massively parallel hardware accelerator.

3   Implementation

In this section we describe the details behind the proposed implementation. First, in Sect. 3.1 we describe the original implementation of the model selected for adaptation. Section 3.2 contains a detailed description of the hardware configuration used for the experiments. The basic process of porting the training application to the IPU platform is described in Sect. 3.3. Additionally, Sect. 3.4, describes the improvements that we introduced using the popdist library to alleviate data loader limitations.

3.1   The Original Model for Accelerating CFD Simulations

The case study selected for this paper trains a ML model for accelerating CFD simulations of an industrial homogenization tank. The tank is composed of two interconnected subtanks of 10 m length, 5 m width, and 5 m depth each. Figure 1 depicts the geometry of the tank. The figure highlights the location of the areas of interest. They do not correspond to regular walls and can be parametrized. The flow enters the tank through *Inflow*. The flow is driven to *Outflow* through *Bulkhead wall*. Part of the flow is fed back from the second subtank to the first one using *Recirculator*. Finally, stirrers inside the tank (*Stirrer #1 and #2*) are responsible for impelling the flow.

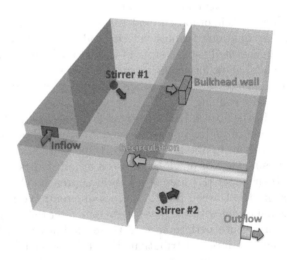

Fig. 1. Geometry of the reactor under study [3]. Arrows represent the flow direction on the highlighted areas.

We have simulated 131 different configurations of the case under study with OpenFOAM[1]. In these simulations, the values of in *Inlet* and *Recirculation* are varied within a minimum and a maximum limit. The OpenFOAM solver models a transient incompressible flow using the Unsteady Reynolds-averaged Navier-Stokes (URANS) equations. The state of the simulation is adjusted to a write

---

[1] http://www.openfoam.com.

interval of 10 s of simulated time. The flow is evolved until the second 4,201, which is translated into 420 stored states per executed simulation. In this regard, taking it all into account, the number of simulated cases, states per case, the cells in the domain, and the velocity dimensions, generate an eventual dataset with a shape $131 \times 420 \times 125,565 \times 3$.

Before feeding the trainable model, each velocity dimension is normalized to have a distribution of mean zero and a standard deviation of one. Moreover, the dataset is split into train and test subsets. For this purpose, cases are shuffled and 80% of them (104 cases) are assigned to the training dataset, while the remaining (27 cases) are assigned to the testing dataset. Notice that 20% of training cases (20 cases) are used for cross-validating the learning.

In order to capture the temporal dependencies in the data, a sequence to sequence model is trained, where features representing 3 consecutive simulation states are used as the input sequence, while output represents 1 succeeding simulation state. The training program is implemented in Python using TensorFlow and the model is constructed sequentially using the Keras API, as shown in Listing 1.1. The main building blocks of the model are the encoder and decoder LSTM layers with 10 hidden units each. Repeated copies of the encoder output are used as the input for the decoder. Finally, temporal slices of the decoder output are used by two dense layers. The rectified linear unit (ReLU) function is used for activation and Adam optimizer is used for training.

It should be noted that considering the input sequence length, the number of cells in the domain and the velocity dimensions, the input sequence dimensionality is $3 \times 125,565 \times 3$ giving $1,130,085$ features per sample. This, in combination with relatively small hidden state numbers in the model layers, makes the training workload highly I/O-bound.

Listing 1.1. Implementation of the model layers

```
from tensorflow.keras.layers import LSTM, RepeatVector,
                                    Dense, TimeDistributed
...
model = Sequential()
model.add(LSTM(10, activation='relu',
               input_shape=(n_timesteps, n_features),
               return_sequences=False))

model.add(RepeatVector(n_outputs))
model.add(LSTM(10, activation='relu', return_sequences=True))

model.add(TimeDistributed(Dense(10, activation='relu')))
model.add(TimeDistributed(Dense(n_features)))

opt = tf.keras.optimizers.Adam(learning_rate=0.00025)

model.compile(loss='mae', optimizer=opt)

model.fit(train, epochs=n_epochs, verbose=1, shuffle=True,
          steps_per_epoch=steps_per_epoch, callbacks=callbacks)
```

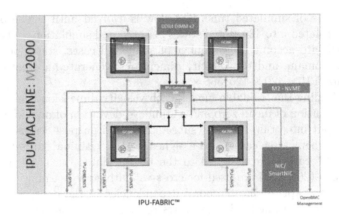

Fig. 2. Schematic and building block of IPU-M2000 Machine [2]

3.2 The IPU Processor, IPU-M2000 System and IPU-POD16 Configuration

From the hardware definition IPUs are distributed memory, massively parallel, multiple-instruction multiple-data (MIMD) devices. With 1472 tiles, the IPU has just under 900 MB of memory in total. This local memory is the only memory directly accessible by tile instructions. It is used for both the code and the data used by that tile. There is no shared memory access between tiles. Tiles cannot directly access each others' memory but can communicate via message passing using an all-to-all high bandwidth exchange (theoretical 8 TB/s). The memory has very low-latency (6 cycles) and ultra-high bandwidth (theoretical 47.5 TB/s). The whole chip is built on the budget of 59.4 billion transistors using the TSMC 7nm manufacturing process [2].

The Graphcore IPU-M2000 system is essentially a 1U server utilizing 4 IPUs. It includes also a gateway chip which connects IPUs into the compute domain and provides access to the DRAM, two 100Gbps IPU-Fabric Links, a PCIe slot for standard Smart NICs, two 1GbE Open BMC management interfaces, and access to an M.2 slot. Figure 2 shows the block diagram of the IPU-M2000 system. The host system accesses the IPU-M2000 platform over 100Gb Ethernet with ROCE (RDMA over Converged Ethernet) with very low-latency access. Such an implementation based on Ethernet avoids the bottlenecks and costs of PCIe connectors and PCIe switches. This enables a flexible host CPU to accelerators combination and provides scaling from a single IPU-M2000 system to massive supercomputer scale including 64,000 IPUs, all networked over standard networking at a lower cost and providing much more flexibility than using e.g., InfiniBand [1].

IPU-Fabric is a totally new scale-out fabric designed from the ground up to support the needs of machine intelligence communication. IPU-Fabric is natively integrated into the IPU processors and IPU-M2000 system. A key difference between IPU-Fabric and other proprietary fabrics is the usage of Compiled

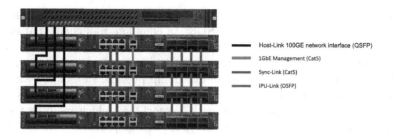

Fig. 3. IPU-POD16 direct attach configuration [2]

Communication and Bulk Synchronous Parallel protocol; both these elements provide deterministic communication behaviour. Every IPU has dedicated IPU-Links providing 64 GB/s of bidirectional bandwidth and an aggregate bandwidth per chip of 320 GB/s. Each IPU-M2000 has 8 external IPU-Links for intra-rack scale out using OSFP copper cables. The intra-rack configuration called IPU-POD16 contains 4 IPU-M2000s connected into a single instance with a daisy chain topology utilizing IPU-Links. Host-Link connectivity is provided from the Gateway through a PCIe NIC or SmartNIC card. Figure 3 shows the IPU-POD16 configuration [1].

The memory model for the IPU-Machine is also quite unique. In addition to in-IPU Memory, each IPU-M2000 system has DDR memory available to the four IPUs. This DDR memory is used differently from memory found in CPUs or GPUs. Instead of a memory hierarchy that requires swapping data and code from the host memory store to the accelerator's memory, the Poplar Graph Compiler creates deterministic code-memory relationships in both the memory on the IPU tile and the DDR memory. In fact, the IPU-M2000 system can use this additional memory in stand-alone mode for inference processing without any attachment to a host server. And thanks to the bulk synchronous parallel (BSP) model compiling both computation and communication, the network communication overhead is kept to a minimum compared to traditional messaging or shared memory constructs commonly used for parallel processing.

Built-in fabrics are becoming a necessity for AI accelerators since model sizes are increasing dramatically, some containing billions of parameters. These large models must be distributed across hundreds or thousands of processors to solve problems in a reasonable time. Graphcore's hybrid model uses a proprietary IPU-Link fabric to communicate across the tiles in an IPU and adjacent rack IPUs, while tunnelling the IPU-Link protocol across standard 100GbE for rack-to-rack scale-out supporting larger configurations [1].

3.3   Porting the Training Program to the IPU Platform

The IPU is based on a sophisticated architecture which offers, to our knowledge, the first ever BSP model implementation in hardware. Fortunately, users do not have to be parallel processing experts to benefit from the performance opportunities offered by the IPU accelerator. The hardware comes with a comprehensive software ecosystem[2] with the Poplar SDK[3], a complete tool chain that enables the user to exploit IPU features. The SDK includes a graph compiler responsible for handling the scheduling and work partitioning of large parallel programs including memory control. To provide maximum possible ease of use, the SDK is integrated with a number of industry-standard ML frameworks. In this paper, we benefit from such an integration with TensorFlow, which requires the user to employ *pip* to install a separate *tensorflow* package provided with the Poplar SDK. Using this approach, porting the original code to the IPU platform requires only a few changes, as outlined in Listing 1.2.

Listing 1.2. Code changes required to port the program to the IPU

```
from tensorflow.python import ipu

config = ipu.config.IPUConfig()
config.auto_select_ipus = FLAGS.num_replicas
config.configure_ipu_system()

strategy = ipu.ipu_strategy.IPUStrategy()

with strategy.scope():
    <code from Listing 1.1>
```

Running the code on the IPU requires the user to import the corresponding module *tensorflow.python.ipu* and use it to configure the IPU system as well as place the adequate variables on the IPU. Running the training on multiple IPUs using data parallelism is as simple as setting the *auto_select_ipus* configuration parameter to the desired value. Tensor and operation placement is performed by wrapping the original code in the scope of a custom implementation of a TensorFlow distribution strategy. Additionally, to avoid frequent host-IPU synchronization, it is worth setting the *steps_per_execution* parameter of the *model.compile()* function to a large value. We use the number of steps per epoch as a rule of thumb in order to run the whole epoch on the IPU before returning to the host. This straightforward approach to porting the code to IPU benefits from the ease of use of the Poplar SDK's TensorFlow integration.

3.4   Using the Popdist Library to Remove the I/O Bottleneck

In many cases a simple porting procedure described in Sect. 3.3 would be sufficient for optimal utilization of the IPU platform. However, as shown in Sect. 4, in the case of the investigated IO-bound CFD application, using a single Python process for feeding multiple IPUs with input data results in a I/O bottleneck.

To remove this bottleneck, we used the *poprun* tool associated with the Poplar distributed configuration library (*popdist*)[4] to execute a separate system process per each IPU. The crucial code changes required are shown in Listing 1.3.

---

[2] https://www.graphcore.ai/developer.

[3] https://docs.graphcore.ai/projects/sdk-overview/en/latest/index.html.

[4] https://docs.graphcore.ai/projects/poprun-user-guide/en/latest/configuration.html.

Listing 1.3. Code changes required to run the training in a distributed setup

```
import popdist
from tensorflow.python.ipu import horovod as hvd
from tensorflow.python.ipu.horovod import popdist_strategy
...
popdist.tensorflow.set_ipu_config(config, ipus_per_replica=1)
hvd.init()
...
train = train.shard(num_shards=popdist.getNumInstances(),
                    index=popdist.getInstanceIndex())
...
strategy = popdist_strategy.PopDistStrategy()
```

Popdist allows the user to automatically configure the desired number of IPUs per model replica. It is used along with an implementation of the Horovod communication scheme [14]. Shards of the training dataset are selected accordingly to the number of instances executed by the *poprun* tool and the corresponding process instance numbers. Finally, instead of the standard IPUStrategy, the PopDistStrategy class ensures the proper variable placement in the context of distributed execution.

4   Experimental Results

In order to evaluate the usefulness of the IPU-POD16 platform for the application we are focusing on in this paper, first we utilized it to train a model and investigated its accuracy. The findings are described in Sect. 4.1. Then, to assess its performance capabilities, we measured training throughput depending on the number of used IPUs and chosen implementation. The performance results are provided in Sect. 4.2. The experiments were run on an IPU-POD16 with 16 IPU-M2000 IPU chips using Graphcore TensorFlow-2.6.3 and Keras 2.6.0 on top of Poplar SDK r2.6.0.

4.1   Model Verification

To develop a model for verification, we executed ten training sessions with a random selection of learning rate between 1e-7 and 1e-5. The runs were stopped when the validation loss has not improved more than 0.0001 for 10 epochs. Out of the ten trained models we selected the one that performed best on the validation set. The accuracy results for this model are presented in Table 1.

To estimate the accuracy, we used statistical metrics such as RMSE (root-mean-square-error) and correlation coefficients that measure the extent to which two variables tend to change together. These coefficients describe both the strength and the direction of the relationship. Here, we use two coefficients, including the Pearson correlation which estimates the linear relationship between two continuous variables, as well as the Spearman correlation which assesses the monotonic relationship between two continuous or ordinal variables. The correlation coefficients can return values from -1 to 1. The RMSE statistic shows that the error is below 0.08 for all the results. Since the range of data is from 0 to 1.1 we conclude that the differences are below 8% of the maximum value for the

10th-time step and below 1% for the steady-state. The correlation coefficients show a strong dependency between trends of the predicted and real values (>0.9 for all the time steps).

Table 1. Accuracy of the trained model for the selected steps of simulation.

Step	Pearson's correlation	Spearman's correlation	Root mean squared error
10	0.949	0.917	0.078
20	0.989	0.982	0.038
100	1.000	0.999	0.008

4.2 Performance and Scalability

Table 2 shows training throughput depending on the number of utilized IPUs and implementation variant averaged from the aforementioned five runs, additionally providing standard deviation. The number of IPUs corresponds to the number of model replicas in the "data parallel" scheme used for training parallelization. The "single process" variant is described in Sect. 3.3 while the "popdist" variant is described in Sect. 3.4. We performed five runs for each parameter combination. In each run, we executed four training epochs and measured the throughput for the three last epochs as the total number of used samples divided by execution time. We treated the first epoch as a warm-up.

While IPUs do not have a particularly high memory capacity, they do not require large batch sizes to achieve good performance, so for all experiments we used mini-batches containing one training sample. As training data, we used random samples generated on the host side, so that the benchmark measures the capability of the host + IPU system as a whole, without considering potential limitations of storage I/O overheads. To overcome the limitations of FP16 data handling on the CPU side, in two cases of single process implementation (8 and 16 IPUs) we used non-standard, increased buffer sizes in the internal TensorFlow data queue.

The results allow us to draw the following conclusions. Firstly, most of the results are statistically significant, with exceptions in the cases where 4, 8 and 16 IPUs are used by the single process implementation. The configuration that results in the most variable results (16 IPUs, single process) is also the one which benefits the most from switching to *popdist* (34% speedup). We performed detailed profiling of the program to determine that there is a bottleneck on the host side: multi-threading limitations of Python result in slow data pre-processing and populating the input data queue by the CPU. As a result, the more IPUs that are used, the more likely that they are starved.

Another interesting observation is related to scalability: increasing the number of used IPUs from 1 to 2 doesn't significantly improve the throughput, and even makes it slightly worse. At the same time, increasing the number of IPUs 8-fold from 2 to 16 improves the throughput around 5-fold, which is relatively good scalability, considering the characteristics of data-parallel deep neural network training. Again, the reason for the lack of scalability between 1–2 IPUs has been determined through detailed profiling. In this case, the bottleneck is on the IPU side: for this particular model, the overhead of introducing additional buffers and exchange operations makes the data-parallel implementation significantly slower on a single IPU.

Table 2. Throughput (samples/s) depending on implementation variant and number of utilized IPUs

No. of IPUs utilized	Average throughput	
	Single process	Popdist
1	571.8 ± 4.31	574.4 ± 3.20
2	558.8 ± 3.92	560.8 ± 1.94
4	862.8 ± 7.14	871.4 ± 1.36
8	1344.2 ± 8.35	1566.4 ± 1.02
16	2099.8 ± 193.19	**2805.8 ± 1.17**

5 Summary and Future Work

In this paper, we adopt a deep neural network training application from the *AI for simulation* field for the IPU platform, demonstrating the ease of use provided by the Poplar SDK software ecosystem. Training a model on data from traditional CFD simulations allows us to get accurate simulation state predictions in test time. Investigating the performance of the training on the IPU-POD16 platform reveals that the main bottleneck of this particular application is feeding training data to the IPU on the host side. We show how to utilize the *popdist* library to overcome the limitations of host-side data loading. Scaling of the program is limited in a small scale of 1–2 IPUs by communication overheads. However, once the intra-IPU costs have been paid, the hardware capabilities for inter-IPU communication allow for good scalability.

In the future, we would like to investigate the scalability of the IPU platform further, utilizing a larger platform such as the IPU-POD64. It could be also beneficial to use the FP8 data type to increase training performance. The predictive model introduced in this work can be leveraged in hybrid CFD-DL solvers such as that presented in [4]. This solver alternates stages of CFD simulation with predictions made by a DL engine in order to reduce the time-to-solution. In their paper, the authors are able to accelerate the simulation interleaving predictions during the CFD simulation. That module could be easily substituted by the IPU-trained model for inference.

Acknowledgements. The authors would like to thank Grzegorz Andrejczuk for his ideas and help with investigating data loading overheads. Big thanks to Charis Fisher for her support and valuable comments. Researcher Sergio Iserte was supported by the postdoctoral fellowship APOSTD/2020/026 from Valencian Region Government (GVA) and European Social Funds (ESF). CFD Simulations were executed on Tirant III cluster of the *Servei d'Informàtica* of the University of Valencia (UV).

References

1. Freund, K., Moorhead, P.: The graphcore second-generation IPU (2020). https://moorinsightsstrategy.com/research-paper-the-graphcore-second-generation-ipu/
2. Gepner, P.: Machine learning and high-performance computing hybrid systems, a new way of performance acceleration in engineering and scientific applications. In: 2021 16th Conference on Computer Science and Intelligence Systems (FedCSIS), pp. 27–36 (2021). https://doi.org/10.15439/2021F004
3. Iserte, S., et al.: Modeling of Wastewater Treatment Processes with HydroSludge. In: Water Environment Research, pp. 1–38 (2021)
4. Iserte, S., Macías, A., Martínez-Cuenca, R., Chiva, S., Paredes, R., Quintana-Ortí, E.S.: Accelerating urban scale simulations leveraging local spatial 3D structure. J. Comput. Sci. **62**, 101741 (2022). https://doi.org/10.1016/j.jocs.2022.101741
5. Kim, B., Azevedo, V.C., Thuerey, N., Kim, T., Gross, M., Solenthaler, B.: Deep fluids: a generative network for parameterized fluid simulations. Comput. Graph. Forum **38**(2), 59–70 (2019)
6. Kochkov, D., Smith, J.A., Alieva, A., Wang, Q., Brenner, M.P., Hoyer, S.: Machine learning-accelerated computational fluid dynamics. In: Proceedings of the National Academy of Sciences, vol. 118, no. 21, p. e2101784118 (2021). https://doi.org/10.1073/pnas.2101784118, https://www.pnas.org/doi/abs/10.1073/pnas.2101784118
7. Lavin, A., et al.: Simulation intelligence: towards a new generation of scientific methods, December 2021. https://arxiv.org/abs/2112.03235
8. Li, Z., Wang, Y., Zhi, T., Chen, T.: A survey of neural network accelerators. Front. Comput. Sci. **11**(5), 746–761 (2017)
9. Maulik, R., San, O., Rasheed, A., Vedula, P.: Subgrid modelling for two-dimensional turbulence using neural networks. J. Fluid Mech. **858**, 122–144 (2019). https://doi.org/10.1017/jfm.2018.770
10. Ribeiro, M.D., Rehman, A., Ahmed, S., Dengel, A.: DeepCFD: efficient steady-state laminar flow approximation with deep convolutional neural networks, November 2021. https://arxiv.org/abs/2004.08826, arXiv:2004.08826 [physics]
11. Rojek, K., Wyrzykowski, R.: Performance and scalability analysis of AI-accelerated CFD simulations across various computing platforms. In: HeteroPar 2022, Springer International Publishing (in press 2022)
12. Rojek, K., Wyrzykowski, R., Gepner, P.: AI-accelerated CFD simulation based on OpenFOAM and CPU/GPU computing. In: Paszynski, M., Kranzlmüller, D., Krzhizhanovskaya, V.V., Dongarra, J.J., Sloot, P.M.A. (eds.) ICCS 2021. LNCS, vol. 12743, pp. 373–385. Springer, Cham (2021). https://doi.org/10.1007/978-3-030-77964-1_29
13. Rościszewski, P., Iwański, M., Czarnul, P.: The impact of the AC922 architecture on performance of deep neural network training. In: 2019 International Conference on High Performance Computing Simulation (HPCS), pp. 666–673, July 2019. https://doi.org/10.1109/HPCS48598.2019.9188164
14. Sergeev, A., Del Balso, M.: Horovod: fast and easy distributed deep learning in TensorFlow. arXiv:1802.05799 [cs, stat], February 2018, https://arxiv.org/abs/1802.05799, arXiv: 1802.05799

15. Sze, V., Chen, Y.H., Emer, J., Suleiman, A., Zhang, Z.: Hardware for machine learning: challenges and opportunities, pp. 1–8, April 2018. https://doi.org/10.1109/CICC.2018.8357072

16. Thuerey, N., Weißenow, K., Prantl, L., Hu, X.: Deep learning methods for reynolds-averaged navier-stokes simulations of airfoil flows. AIAA J. **58**, 1–12 (2019). https://doi.org/10.2514/1.J058291

17. Um, K., Brand, R., Fei, Y.R., Holl, P., Thuerey, N.: Solver-in-the-loop: learning from differentiable physics to interact with iterative PDE-solvers. In: Proceedings of the 34th International Conference on Neural Information Processing Systems, NIPS 2020, Curran Associates Inc., Red Hook, NY, USA (2020)

18. Wiewel, S., Becher, M., Thuerey, N.: Latent space physics: towards learning the temporal evolution of fluid flow. Comput. Graph. Forum **38**(2), 71–82 (2019)

19. Wyatt II, M.R., Yamamoto, V., Tosi, Z., Karlin, I., Van Essen, B.: Is disaggregation possible for HPC cognitive simulation? arXiv:2112.05216 [cs], December 2021, https://arxiv.org/abs/2112.05216

Performance Analysis of Convolution Algorithms for Deep Learning on Edge Processors

Pedro Alonso-Jordá[1]([✉])(ⓘ), Héctor Martínez[2](ⓘ),
Enrique S. Quintana-Ortí[1]([✉])(ⓘ), and Cristian Ramírez[1](ⓘ)

[1] Universitat Politécnica de Valéncia, Valencia, Spain
{palonso,crirabe}@upv.es, quintana@disca.upv.es
[2] Universidad de Córdoba, Córdoba, Spain
el2mapeh@uco.es

Abstract. We provide a complete performance comparison of two realizations of the convolution, based on the lowering approach and a blocked variant of the direct convolution algorithm. The theoretical analysis focuses on the conventional, high performance implementation of the general matrix multiplication (GEMM), which is the key computational kernel underneath these two algorithms. The study leverages a simulator calibrated for the GAP8 edge processor and exploits the determinism of the memory system in this type of architectures to deliver accurate predictions of the arithmetic and data transfer costs.

Keywords: Convolution · deep learning · edge processors · performance analysis

1 Introduction

The deployment of deep learning (DL) at the edge, on IoT (Internet-of-Things) appliances, is crucial to improve safety and privacy, reduce the latency for the end-user, and/or decrease energy consumption [4,9]. The large diversity of IoT applications, with many of them exploiting DL-based technologies, and the strict constraints on power supply and time-to-response have resulted in a large heterogeneity of edge processor architectures, and the utmost need to carefully select the algorithms and then optimize the software running on this type of devices.

In this work we focus on the optimization of convolutional deep neural networks (DNNs) on edge processors by conducting a complete analysis of the theoretical performance for two popular realizations of the convolution operator, based on the lowering approach [2] and a blocked variant of the direct algorithm for this operation [1,10]. Our analysis exploits that 1) both algorithms are built on top of the general matrix multiplication (GEMM); and 2) the determinism of the memory system in edge processors, derived from the integration of user-controlled scratchpads instead of hardware-assisted memory caches. These features provide the means to deliver a valuable performance comparison of the two GEMM-based algorithms prior to their potential implementation. This evaluation is conducted using a simulator enhanced with a few experimental data collected via simple calibration experiments on the RISC-V fabric controller comprised in the GAP8 parallel-ultra-low power platform (PULP) for IoT.

2   Brief Review of the Convolution

The convolution operator

$$O = \text{CONV}(F, I), \tag{1}$$

combines a 4D input tensor I, of size $B \times H_i \times W_i \times C_i$, with a 4D filter tensor F, of size $C_i \times H_f \times W_f \times C_o$, in order to produce a 4D output tensor O, of dimension $B \times H_o \times W_o \times C_o$. Here, B denotes the number of (input and output) images that are to be processed simultaneously in a batch; each input/output image is of size $H_i \times W_i / H_o \times W_o$ (height $\times$ width), and consist of C_i input/C_o output channels; and there are $C_i C_o$ filters, each of size $H_f \times W_f$ (height $\times$ width). For simplicity, we assume that the filter is applied with unit vertical/horizontal strides; and the output is not padded so that $H_o = H_i - H_f + 1, W_o = W_i - W_f + 1$.

While there exist several approaches to realize the convolution operator, the general view of the corresponding optimized implementations of these methods is that the best option from the viewpoints of performance and accuracy is largely dependent on the parameters that define the convolution. In this paper we focus on the lowering approach and the direct algorithm which, compared with the FFT or Winograd-based realizations, offer superior flexibility and numerical stability at the cost of an increased arithmetic count.

3   Convolution via Lowering

The lowering approach leverages the IM2ROW transform [2] in order to cast the convolution operator in terms of a large GEMM. The advantage of this method is that there exist highly optimized implementations of GEMM for virtually any processor architecture. On the negative side, this solution requires a large workspace and a considerable number of data copies.

The Lowering Approach. As argued earlier, this technique transforms the convolution shown in (1), via the IM2ROW transform, into the GEMM:

$$C = A \cdot B, \tag{2}$$

where $C \equiv O$ is the output tensor, viewed as an $M \times N = (BH_oW_o) \times C_o$ matrix; and $B \equiv F$ is the filter tensor, viewed as a $K \times N = (C_iH_fW_f) \times C_o$ matrix. Furthermore, the augmented matrix A, of size $M \times K = (BH_oW_o) \times (C_iH_fW_f)$, results from applying IM2ROW to the input tensor I; see [2].

High Performance Implementation of GEMM. Consider next the GEMM in (2) resulting from the application of IM2ROW. The high performance implementations of this kernel in BLIS, OpenBLAS, AMD AOML and, presumably,

```
 1 void Gemm( C[M][N], A[M][K], B[K][N] ){
 2   for ( jc = 0; jc < N; jc += Nc )              // Loop L1
 3     for ( pc = 0; pc < K; pc += Kc ) {          // Loop L2
 4       Bc := B[pc : pc + Kc - 1][jc : jc + Nc - 1]; //      Pack Bc
 5       for ( ic = 0; ic < M; ic += Mc ) {        // Loop L3
 6         Ac := A[ic : ic + Mc - 1][pc : pc + Kc - 1]; //   Pack Ac
 7         for ( jr = 0; jr < Nc; jr += Nr )       // Loop L4
 8           for ( ir = 0; ir < Mc; ir += Mr )     // Loop L5
 9             // Micro-kernel
10             for ( pr = 0; pr < Kc; pr++ )       // Loop L6
11               Cc[ir : ir + Mr - 1][jr : jr + Nr - 1]
12                   += Ar[ir : ir + Mr - 1][pr] · Bc[pr][jr : jr + Nr - 1];
13 }    } }
```

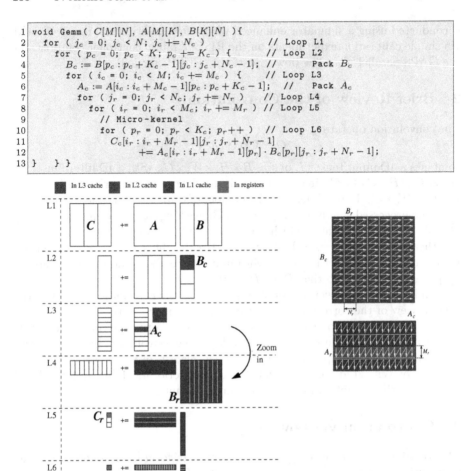

Fig. 1. High performance implementation of GEMM. C_c is a notation artifact, introduced to ease the presentation of the algorithm, while A_c and B_c are actual buffers that maintain copies of certain blocks of A and B.

Intel MKL follow the ideas in GotoBLAS [3] to formulate it as a collection of five nested loops around a *micro-kernel* that performs a small GEMM; see Fig. 1 (top). In some detail, tiling (blocking) is applied to the operands so that a $K_c \times N_c$ block of B is packed into a buffer B_c, and an $M_c \times K_c$ block of A is packed into a buffer A_c. Here, the cache blocking parameters M_c, N_c, K_c are set so that, during the execution of the micro-kernel, B_c "remains" into the L3 cache, A_c into the L2 cache, and a specific $K_c \times N_r$ micro-panel of B_c, say B_r, into the L1 cache [5,8]. Finally, the micro-kernel performs all the arithmetic, retrieving the data of (an $M_r \times K_c$ micro-panel A_r of) A_c from the L2 cache, B_r from the L1 cache, and C directly from memory; see Fig. 1 (bottom-left).

The micro-kernel is usually encoded in assembly (or in C with vector intrinsics). The innermost loop, inside the micro-kernel, updates an $M_r \times N_r$ micro-tile of C, say C_r, by performing an outer product one row of A_r and one column of B_r. The packing of A_c and B_c shown in Fig. 1 (bottom-right) ensures that the entries of A_r, B_r are retrieved with unit stride. Together with a selection of $M_r, N_r \ll K_c$, this amortizes the cost of accessing C_r.

4   GEMM-Like Direct Convolution

The basic algorithm for the convolution consists of 7 nested loops traversing the $(B, H_i/H_o, W_i/W_o, C_i, C_o, H_f, W_f)$ dimensions of the problem; see, e.g. [10]. The ordering of the loops together with the layout of the tensors in memory dictate the memory access pattern. Also, the loops in the algorithm are independent from each other as well as from the memory layout of the tensors. In consequence, the algorithm loops can be reorganized in any other order.

In [1], we combined the blocking ideas in [10] with the packing strategies in the high performance formulation of GEMM, obtaining the blocked variant of the direct convolution in Fig. 2, with the following properties:

- All arithmetic occurs inside a micro-kernel that computes a small GEMM via a sequence of outer products, each updating an $M_r \times N_r$ micro-tile of O.
- The dimensions of the micro-tile are decoupled from the cache blocking parameters $W_{o,b}, C_{o,b}, C_{i,b}$ (respectively analogous to M_c, N_c, K_c for GEMM).
- During the algorithm, (part of) the contents of the input tensor are packed into an $M_c \times N_c$ buffer A_c so that its entries are accessed with stride 1 from the micro-kernel. For clarity, the algorithm in Fig. 2 only indicates the loop inside which this packing is placed but still shows the arithmetic as if operating directly with the input tensor I.
- The filter tensor is re-packed into a 5D tensor, of dimension $H_f \times W_f \times C_o/C_{o,b} \times C_i \times C_{o,b}$. As the filters do not vary during inference, this only needs to be done once for the DNN model and the cost is negligible. The advantage of this type of packing is that it allows accessing the entries of B with unit stride during the execution of the micro-kernel.

As in the case of [10] and in the high performance realization of GEMM, one of the keys to high performance is the re-formulation of the direct convolution in terms of a GEMM, with a blocking mechanism and the utilization of an architecture-specific micro-kernel. The decoupling of the micro-tile dimensions and the cache blocking parameters, combined with the packing of the input tensor, allows that, unlike the proposal in [10], the entries of A_c are accessed from the micro-kernel with stride 1, paving the road to the utilization of micro-kernels specifically tuned for different architectures from the BLIS framework [1].

5   Architecture Model for an Edge Processor

In order to analyze the GEMM-based convolution algorithms described earlier, we make the following considerations for the target edge processor:

```
 1  void ConvDirect_Blocked( I[B][Hᵢ][Wᵢ][Cᵢ],, F[Cᵢ][H_f][W_f][C_o], O[B][H_o][W_o][C_o] )
 2  {
 3    for ( b = 0; b < B; b++ )
 4      for ( i' = 0; i' < Cᵢ/Cᵢ,ᵦ; i'++ )          // Loop L2 in GEMM
 5      for ( l = 0; l < H_o; l++ )
 6        for ( k' = 0; k' < W_o/W_o,ᵦ; k'++ )  // Loop L3 in GEMM
 7        for ( n = 0; n < H_f; n++ )
 8          for ( m = 0; m < W_f; m++ ) {
 9            // Here packing for A_c
10            // Ommitted for simplicity
11            for ( j' = 0; j' < C_o/C_o,ᵦ; j'++ )        // Loop L1 in GEMM
12              for ( jj = 0; jj < C_o,ᵦ; jj += N_r )      // Loop L4 in GEMM
13                for ( kk = 0; kk < W_o,ᵦ; kk += M_r ) { // Loop L5 in GEMM
14                // Micro-kernel
15                for ( ii = 0; ii < Cᵢ,ᵦ; ii++ )          // Loop L6 in GEMM
16                  for ( jᵣ = kk; jᵣ < kk + M_r; jᵣ++ )
17                    for ( iᵣ = C_o,ᵦ; iᵣ < C_o,ᵦ + N_r; iᵣ++ )
18                      O[l][k' · W_o,ᵦ + jᵣ][j' · C_o,ᵦ + iᵣ]
19                        += I[l + n][k' · W_o,ᵦ + jᵣ + m][i' · Cᵢ,ᵦ + ii]
20                        · F[j' · C_o,ᵦ + iᵣ][n][m][i' · Cᵢ,ᵦ + ii];
21  }         }
```

Fig. 2. Blocked variant of the direct convolution. The loops are annotated to specify their counterpart in the GEMM algorithm in Fig. 1. Here loop L1 is re-scheduled to amortize the cost of packing A_c.

- The processor is equipped with a single core, enhanced with a SIMD (single instruction multiple data) arithmetic unit capable of working with 32 vector registers of width 32 bits (4 INT8 numbers). The peak arithmetic rate is R_A MINT8S (millions of INT8 operations per second).
- The memory comprises four levels, from fastest/smallest to slowest/largest, referred to as R (for processor registers), S1, S2, and M (for main memory), and with capacities C_R, C_{S1}, C_{S2}, and C_M, respectively. The transfer rates between two levels will be referred to as $R_{O,D}$, with the subindices O/D specifying the origin/destination memory levels.
- There is a strict control of the data transfers between memory levels. The S1 and S2 levels are "scratchpad" memories instead of conventional caches. The system relies on programmable DMA (direct memory access) units and explicit user-control to manually orchestrate data transfers to/from the main memory and in between S1 and S2 (instead of cache memories and a hardware-assisted coherence mechanism). A relevant consequence of this is the determinism of the memory system behavior.

For reference, Table 1 reports the transfer rates between different levels of the memory hierarchy on the GAP8 edge platform. This system comprises a fabric controller (FC) core for control, communications, and security functions; a cluster of 8 cores for the execution of parallel algorithms; and a specialized accelerator. The experimental data was collected using the RISC-V core in the FC, which has access to its own private 16-KB S1 (data/instructions) and a shared 512-KB S2. The arithmetic of the FC rate, when running at 250 MHz, was experimentally determined to be $R_A = 84$ MINT8OPS.

Table 1. Experimental transfers rates in the GAP8. Note that, since we consider INT8 as the basic datatype, the Bytes/s rates directly translate into INT8/s.

	Bytes/s	GEMM		Bytes/s	GEMM
$R_{\text{M,M}}$	1.44E+05	Packing B to B_c	$R_{\text{M,R}}$	4.39E+05	Stream C to reg.
$R_{\text{M,S2}}$	1.36E+05	Packing A to A_c	$R_{\text{R,M}}$	4.39E+05	Stream C to mem.
$R_{\text{M,S1}}$	1.76E+07	B_c to B_r	$R_{\text{S2,R}}$	6.92E+06	Stream A_r to reg.
			$R_{\text{S1,R}}$	1.82E+07	Stream B_r to reg.

When accessing data that is stored in "chunks" of r consecutive in main memory, the transfer rates in the table for $R_{\text{M,M}}$, $R_{\text{M,S2}}$ (first two rows in the left side, corresponding to the packings of B_c, A_c) have to be multiplied by a factor of r. For all other cases, the memory accesses involve consecutive elements in the corresponding memory level, as is the case of data transfers from the GEMM micro-kernel and the copy of B_c and B_r (right side of the table).

6   Performance Analysis

The goal of our analysis is to experiment with different algorithmic alternatives for this operation, prior to going through the effort of implementing them on a specific edge processor. As a starting point, we remind that we target the FC in the GAP8 operating with INT8 arithmetic (i.e., 4 INT8 numbers per SIMD register); $(M, N, K) = (BH_oW_o, C_o, C_iH_fW_f)$ for the lowering approach (LOW), and $(M_c, N_c, K_c) = (W_{o,b}, C_{o,b}, C_{i,b})$ for the blocked variant of the direct convolution (BDC). Furthermore, the actual values for M_r, N_r are constrained by the number of SIMD registers, and those of M_c, K_c by the capacities of the scratchpad. Finally, in the notation used for the cost in this section, the subindices for the summations specify the bounds defined by the corresponding loop in Fig. 1. Thus, for example, the summation $\sum_{\text{L1}}$ refers to loop L1 there, which iterates from $j_c = 0$ to $N - 1$ in steps of N_c elements.

Micro-kernel. Both GEMM-based realizations of the convolution are based on the same type of micro-kernel, which performs a sequence of K_c outer products, each updating an $M_r \times N_r$ micro-tile C_r using a column of A_r and a row of B_r (with M_r and N_r elements, resp.). Let us first turn our attention to the total cost of executing the micro-kernels when computing the GEMM of dimension (M, N, K) in LOW. Moreover, for simplicity assume these values are respectively integer multiples of M_c, N_c, K_c; and that M_c, N_c are respectively integer multiples of M_r, N_r. We can then easily derive that the total costs due to the streaming of A_r, B_r and C_r from the micro-kernel are respectively given by:

$$T_{\text{streamAr}} = \sum_{\text{L1}} \sum_{\text{L2}} \cdots \sum_{\text{L5}} M_r K_c / R_{\text{S2,R}} = M N K / (R_{\text{S2,R}} N_r) \ s,$$

$$T_{\text{streamBr}} = \sum_{\text{L1}} \sum_{\text{L2}} \cdots \sum_{\text{L5}} K_c N_r / R_{\text{S1,R}} = M N K / (R_{\text{S1,R}} M_r) \ s, \quad (3)$$

$$T_{\text{streamCr}} = \sum_{\text{L1}} \sum_{\text{L2}} \cdots \sum_{\text{L5}} 2 M_r N_r / R_{\text{M,R}} = 2 M N K / (R_{\text{M,R}} K_c) \ s,$$

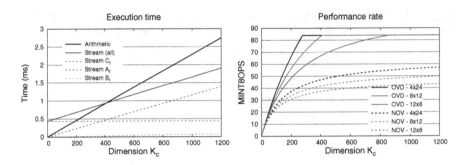

Fig. 3. Performance analysis of the micro-kernels in the GAP8 FC.

which take into account the number of times the micro-kernel is executed, the dimensions of the micro-panels of A, B and the micro-tile of C being transferred, the origin/destination of the data (S2 for A_r, S1 for B_r, and the main memory for C_r), and the fact that C_r is both read from and written to memory (factor 2 in the numerator of the last cost). These expressions bring to light the relationship between M_r, N_r, K_c and the streaming costs for the global GEMM execution in LOW, showing how increasing these parameters reduce the corresponding streaming overheads. The analysis of the micro-kernel in BDC is basically analogous.

In order to gain some quantitative insights from this analysis of the transfer overheads incurred by the micro-kernel, let us consider the arithmetic and memory costs for a single execution of three types of micro-kernels, which differ in that $M_r \times N_r = 4 \times 24$, 8×12, or 12×8. (These three cases were selected because they result in a high utilization of the 32 SIMD registers available in the GAP8 FC. For example, the 8×12 micro-kernel utilizes $8/4 \times 12 = 24$ SIMD registers for C_r, $8/4 = 2$ for the column of A_r, and $12/4 = 3$ for the row of B_r, for a total of 29 SIMD registers.) This study also considers two scenarios (to be achieved using the spare SIMD registers to *prefetch* the data): overlapped vs. non-overlapped data transfers and arithmetic, which result in the execution time for *a single execution of the micro-kernel* respectively being

$$T_{\text{MK}}^{\text{OVD}} = \max(T_{\text{arith}}, T_{\text{streamCr}} + T_{\text{streamAr}} + T_{\text{streamBr}}) \ s \quad \text{or}$$

$$T_{\text{MK}}^{\text{NOV}} = T_{\text{arith}} + T_{\text{streamCr}} + T_{\text{streamAr}} + T_{\text{streamBr}} \ s,$$

where the costs of the individual components are obtained by setting $M, N, K = M_r, N_r, K_c$ in (3).

The left plot in Fig. 3 illustrates the contribution of the arithmetic and memory costs to the time of a single execution of the 8×12 micro-kernel as K_c varies. (The other two micro-kernels offered qualitatively similar results.) This plot shows that the arithmetic becomes the dominant factor from a threshold point $K_c > 410$. Also, the largest contribution to the memory access overhead comes from the load/store of C_r for small values of K_c, up to 380, and the streaming of A_r from then on. In contrast, the contribution of streaming B_r remains almost negligible. In the right plot in the same figure, the higher costs of accessing the data in S2 with respect to S1 explain the faster ramp up of the MINT8OPS rates of the 4×24 micro-kernel compared with those of the other two types of micro-kernels. Concretely, for the same value of K_c, a larger value of M_r implies that the micro-kernel retrieves a larger volume of data for A_r from the slower S2 (compared with B_r in S1). In the same figure we can also observe that, for the overlapped model (label "OVD"), as K_c grows, all micro-kernels eventually saturate the full peak arithmetic rate (84 MINT8OPS), nicely illustrating the effect of the "roofline model" effect. In contrast, none of their non-overlapped (label "NOV") counterparts reaches that value.

Data Transfers Outside the Micro-kernel. Let us continue with the GEMM of dimension (M, N, K) *appearing in* LOW, and consider that the assumptions on the integer multiplicity between M, N, K and M_c, N_c, K_c, and the former two and M_r, N_r, still hold. In LOW, B_c is packed within the first two loops of the GEMM algorithm (see Fig. 1), and per call copies a block of $K_c \times N_c$ elements of B, residing in the main memory, into the buffer B_c, to be stored back in main memory. Thus, the cost for these packing operations is

$$T_{\text{packBc}} = \sum_{\text{L1}} \sum_{\text{L2}} 2 K_c N_c / (R_{\text{M,M}} N_r) = 2 N K / (R_{\text{M,M}} N_r) \ s,$$

which takes into account that 1) the data is read from and written back to the main memory; and that 2) these copies are done in "chunks" of N_r consecutive elements in memory (see Fig. 1, right), and therefore the transfer rate needs to be multiplied by this factor. Similarly, all the copies of A from main memory into the buffer A_c in S2 consume

$$T_{\text{packAc}} = \sum_{\text{L1}} \sum_{\text{L2}} \sum_{\text{L3}} M_c K_c / (R_{\text{M,S2}} M_r) = M N K / (R_{\text{M,S2}} M_r N_c) \ s.$$

Finally, although not included explicitly in the algorithm in Fig. 1, the preparation of the data for the micro-kernel requires copying the micro-panels B_r from the main memory into the S1 scratchpad. This occurs inside loop L4, involves a block of $K_c \times N_r$ elements (per call), and contributes with the cost

$$T_{\text{copyBr}} = \sum_{\text{L1}} \sum_{\text{L2}} \sum_{\text{L3}} \sum_{\text{L4}} K_c N_r / R_{\text{M,S1}} = M N K / (R_{\text{M,S1}} M_c) \ s.$$

In addition, for LOW, the cost of IM2ROW amounts for

$$T_{\text{IM2ROW}} = 2 B C_i W_o H_o W_f H_f / (R_{\text{M,M}} W_f) \ s,$$

as this involves reading entries of I from the main memory, in order to build the augmented matrix B in memory, and can proceed in chunks of W_f elements.

The previous expressions for the data transfer costs of LOW (outside the micro-kernel) expose that increasing M_r, N_r reduces the corresponding overheads, because it provides faster transfer rates between the main memory and the S2 scratchpad. In addition, increasing M_c, N_c diminishes the costs by saving data transfers. *A similar analysis holds for BDC*, taking into account that there is no packing of B_c nor IM2ROW in that case.

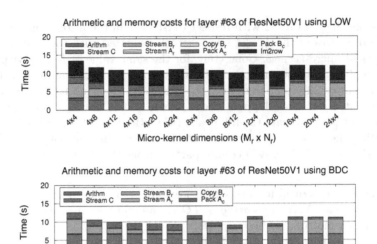

Fig. 4. Arithmetic and memory costs of the GEMM-based convolution algorithms.

The Simulator. The cost expressions derived earlier in this section provide a qualitative tool to explore the effect of modifying the configuration parameters on the performance of the convolution via LOW or BDC. However, when dealing with real convolutional DNNs, the dimensions of the GEMM kernels to be executed are rarely integer multiples of the cache configuration sizes. In such case, the use of the previous formulas may introduce non-negligible approximation errors in the cost calculations. To tackle this, we developed a simulator that takes into account the actual size of the subproblems encountered during the execution of the GEMM-based convolution algorithms[1]. Our simulator accepts the parameters defining the convolution as a tuple $(B, H_i, W_i, C_i, C_o, H_f, W_f)$ and the values for M_r, N_r to be explored. In order to reduce the search space, the simulator automatically selects the values for M_c, N_c, K_c depending on the memory capacity of the architecture, as discussed next.

The S1 scratchpad stores both instructions and data in the GAP8 FC. Therefore, for safety, we leave half of its capacity for the instructions and use the remaining half for storing B_r, of size $K_c \times N_r$. As N_r is "hard-wired" in the implementation of the micro-kernel, the simulator sets $K_c = \min(C_{S1}/(2 N_r), K)$. Along the same line, once K_c is fixed, the "free" dimension of the $M_c \times K_c$ buffer A_c, which has to reside in the (data) S2, is chosen as $M_c = \min(C_{S2}/K_c, M)$. Finally, $N_c = N$ (or the largest value which fits in the available space in the main memory of the GAP8, which plays the role of the L3 cache in this platform).

---

[1] The simulator is based on a performance model for GEMM that was validated in [7], showing a relative error for the estimations below 2% against an actual implementation of that kernel on the GAP8 platform.

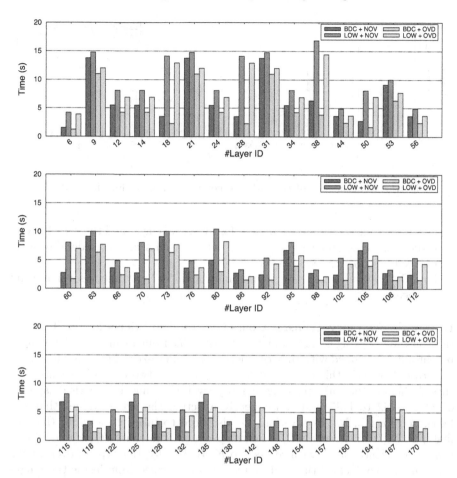

Fig. 5. Execution time of GEMM-based convolution algorithms for ResNet50.

Detailed Cost Analysis of a Single Case. Fig. 4 reports the arithmetic cost and memory access overheads for a layer with $(B, H_i, W_i, C_i, C_o, H_f, W_f) = (1, 28, 28, 128, 128, 3, 3)$, computed using LOW (top) and BDC (bottom), and various types of micro-kernels. There are some aspects to highlight in that figure:

- In both algorithms, the contribution of the arithmetic is constant and independent of the type of micro-kernel. The same holds for the cost of the IM2ROW transform in LOW.
- For both GEMM-based algorithms, the best micro-kernel is $M_r \times N_r = 8 \times 12$.
- The overheads of packing A_c, B_c and copying B_r are negligible compared with the streaming costs incurred by the micro-kernel.
- BDC exhibits a high overhead due to the streaming of C_r, independently of the type of micro-kernel. The reason is that the simulator selects $K_c = C_i = 128$

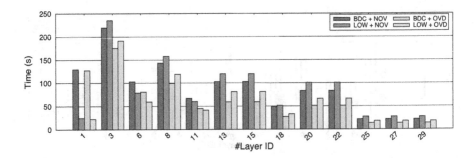

Fig. 6. Execution time of GEMM-based convolution algorithms for VGG16.

for all micro-kernels. In comparison, for LOW, this layer and the 8×12 micro-kernel, the simulator sets $K_c = 341$, which results in a considerably more reduced cost for this component.

– For LOW, assembling the augmented matrix via IM2ROW imposes a significant overhead.

Hiding the Memory Transfer Costs Outside the Micro-kernel. The data transfers for packing A_c, B_c and transferring B_r from memory to S1 can be potentially overlapped with the arithmetic of the micro-kernel by applying *double buffering*. However, this requires space for (at least) two copies of each one of these buffers in the corresponding memory level, reducing the practical capacity of S1 and S2 to half, and consequently affecting the actual values that can be chosen for K_c, M_c. In addition, we also need to take into account that the first packing/transfer cannot be overlapped and, therefore, K_c, M_c should be chosen sufficiently small with respect to K, M. Finally, this type of overlapping can generate conflicts with the data transfers performed from inside the micro-kernel. For those reasons, we do discard the potential overlapping outside the micro-kernel.

Putting it All Together: Global Analysis. For the final evaluation, we target the convolutional layers in VGG16 and ResNet50 (v1.5), combined with the ImageNet dataset with $B = 1$ (single stream case in the MLPerf benchmark [6]).

Figures 5 and 6 report the global execution time of the GEMM-based convolution algorithms for two scenarios: 1) without any type of overlapping; and 2) overlapping only the data transfers occurring within the micro-kernel (streaming A_r, B_r, C_r). We evaluate the same types of micro-kernels consigned in Fig. 4 and select the best one, for each layer and scenario. Therefore, we can have different types of micro-kernels in operation in the same DNN.

Focusing, for example, in the results for VGG16 (Fig. 6) we can make the following observations:

– The benefit of overlapping arithmetic and data transfers in the micro-kernel is visible for both GEMM-based convolution algorithms, showing that this operation is far from being compute-bound in the GAP8 FC.

- In general, BDC outperforms LOW, both with and without overlapping, though the differences between the two are narrower in the second case.
- In a few cases, the execution of BDC takes considerably longer. For example, looking in more detail into layer #1, the reason is that $C_i = 3$ for that layer, which results in the inner loop of the micro-kernel being executed with $k_c = C_i$, and explains the low performance.

7   Concluding Remarks

We have conducted a complete analysis of the memory access overheads for the convolution operator realized via two methods: the lowering approach and a blocked variant of the direct algorithm, both heavily based on the GEMM kernel. Our study for a RISC-V edge processor equipped with two scratchpad memories illustrates the high performance benefits of carefully selecting the micro-kernel prior to its implementation, and the relevance of a proper selection of the scratchpad configuration parameters and, of course, the convolution method.

Acknowledgments. This work was supported by project PID2020-113656RB-C22 of MCIN/AEI/10. 13039/501100011033 C. Ramírez is a "Santiago Grisolía" fellow supported by *Generalitat Valenciana*. H. Martínez is a POSTDOC_21_00025 postdoctoral fellow supported by *Junta de Andalucía*.

References

1. Barrachina, S., et al.: Reformulating the direct convolution for high-performance deep learning inference on ARM processors. Cluster Computing (2022). In review
2. Chellapilla, K., Puri, S., Simard, P.: High performance convolutional neural networks for document processing. In: 10th International Workshop Frontiers in Handwriting Recognition. Université de Rennes, France (2006)
3. Goto, K., van de Geijn, R.A.: Anatomy of a high-performance matrix multiplication. ACM Trans. Math. Softw. **34**(3), 12:1-12:25 (2008)
4. Hazelwood, K., et al.: Applied machine learning at Facebook: a datacenter infrastructure perspective. In: IEEE International Symposium on HPC Architecture, pp. 620–629 (2018)
5. Low, T.M., et al.: Analytical modeling is enough for high-performance BLIS. ACM Trans. Math. Softw. **43**(2), 12:1–12:18 (2016)
6. Mattson, P., et al.: MLPerf training benchmark. CoRR abs/1910.01500 (2019). http://arxiv.org/abs/1910.01500
7. Ramírez, C., Castelló, A., Quintana-Ortí, E.S.: A BLIS-like matrix multiplication for machine learning in the RISC-V ISA-based GAP8 processor. J. Supercomput. **78**(16), 18051–18060 (2022). To appear
8. - Van Zee, F.G., van de Geijn, R.A.: BLIS: a framework for rapidly instantiating BLAS functionality. ACM Trans. Math. Softw. **41**(3), 14:1-14:33 (2015)
9. Wu, C., et al.: Machine learning at Facebook: understanding inference at the edge. In: IEEE International Symposium on HPC Architecture, pp. 331–344 (2019)
10. Zhang, J., et al.: High performance zero-memory overhead direct convolutions. In: Proceedings 35th International Conference on Machine Learning - ICML, vol. 80, pp. 5776–5785 (2018)

Machine Learning-Based Online Scheduling in Distributed Computing

Victor Toporkov[✉][iD], Dmitry Yemelyanov[iD], and Artem Bulkhak

Department of Computing Technologies, National Research University "MPEI",
Moscow, Russia
{ToporkovVV,YemelyanovDM,BulkhakAN}@mpei.ru

Abstract. In this work, we propose and evaluate an online scheduler prototype based on machine learning algorithms. Online job-flow scheduler should make scheduling and resource allocation decisions for individual jobs without any prior knowledge of the subsequent job queue (i.e., online). We simulate and generalize this task to a more formal 0–1 Knapsack problem with unknown utility functions of the knapsack items. In this way we evaluate the implemented machine learning-based solution to classical combinatorial optimization algorithms. A hybrid machine learning and dynamic programming - based approach is proposed to consider and strictly satisfy the knapsack constraint on the total weight. As a main result the proposed hybrid solution showed efficiency comparable to the greedy knapsack approximation.

Keywords: Knapsack · Machine learning · Neural network · Dynamic programming · Resources · Scheduling · Job · Parallel computing

1 Introduction

Today's high-performance parallel and distributed computing systems (HPCS), including network, cloud, and hybrid infrastructures, provide access to vast amounts of resources [1,2]. These resources include compute nodes, network links, software tools, and data stores required to run parallel jobs submitted by HPCS users.

Most HPCS and cloud solutions require some quality of service (QoS) for scheduling, executing, and monitoring user applications. Therefore, QoS constraints typically include a set of requirements for coordinating resources' participation and sharing [3–5], as well as several time and cost criteria and constraints, such as deadlines, response time, total execution cost, etc. [2–7].

One of the most important indicators of the efficiency of a distributed computing environment is both the level of use of system resources and the criteria for the time and cost of performing tasks by users [2–4,8].

Organization and support of the HPCs are associated with certain economic costs: the acquisition and installation of machinery, power supplies, user support, repair work, security, etc. Under such conditions, resource management and job flow scheduling based on economic models is seen as an effective way to reconcile conflicting preferences of participants of the computing system and stakeholders [3–7].

The easiest way to schedule jobs is to use the First Come First Served (FCFS) method. FCFS executes jobs sequentially in the order in which they arrive. The backfill process [4,9] uses advanced resource reservation to prevent starvation of jobs with relatively large resource demands. Micro-scheduling methods [4,5,10] can be added to the backfill to influence the global scheduling efficiency by choosing appropriate secondary optimization criteria.

On the other hand, online scheduling requires the HPCS scheduler to make resource allocation and optimization decisions when submitting jobs. One of the obvious strategies for online scheduling is to select locally available resources for each job. However, in this case, the efficiency of global scheduling is reduced. The CoP micro-scheduling strategy [4] implements a set of heuristic rules to optimize the execution time of job streams according to resource characteristics: performance, cost, utilization, etc. Many scheduling algorithms and methods implement exact or approximate knapsack solutions for the resource selection step [4,11–14]. For example, in [13,14], we study the problem of jointly allocating n windows of simultaneously available computing resources (the fixed-number problem). The topic of performing combinatorial optimization tasks using machine learning methods, including the knapsack problem [15–20], is currently relevant. For example, [16] studied neural network and deep learning based heuristic knapsack solvers in detail. Neural solvers have been successfully tested on instances of up to 200 items and provide near-optimal solutions (usually better than greedy algorithms) in scenarios where there is a correlation between the utility and weight of the items.

A method to solve the traveling salesman problem using reinforcement machine learning and neural networks is proposed in [17]. The flexibility of Neural Combinatorial Optimization is proved by the results of its application on another NP-hard problem of filling a knapsack up to 200 elements. Although the performance of this method is far from the strongest solvers, it provides fair approximations.

Another application [18] combines dynamic programming with machine learning, introducing a neural network instead of the conventional memorization table to solve NP-hard combinatorial optimization problems, in particular the traveling salesman problem. This solution can significantly reduce space complexity and it is flexible in balancing space, runtime, and accuracy. Experimental results show that the method can solve larger-scale problems.

Paper [19] provides a review of well-known combinatorial optimization problems and the most recent approaches to solve them using machine learning. Models with supervised, unsupervised and reinforcement learning are considered. The authors propose ideas for possible overcoming the problem of finding a balance between low accuracy, limited scalability, poor generalization, etc.

The authors of the article [20] consider the integration of machine learning and optimization algorithms to be a more advantageous approach in solving combinatorial problems, in contrast to the vaguely defined and too expensive to calculate handcrafted heuristics.

The main contribution of this paper is a machine learning-based approach that can be trained on efficient scheduling results to perform 0–1 knapsack allocation based on unknown utility functions. With this problem statement we formalize and simulate first step of the online job flow scheduling process.

The structure of the paper is as follows. Section 2 presents the general problem statement and the corresponding machine learning model. Section 3 describes the proposed neural network algorithm and training details. Section 4 contains simulation details, results, and analysis. Conclusion Sect. 5 summarizes the results of the paper.

2   Problem Statement

2.1   Online Resources Selection and Knapsack Problem

It is typically impossible to explain or solve an optimization problem for simultaneous co-allocation of resources of various sorts (computational nodes, data storages, software packets, network connections, etc.). The minimum and maximum required amount of resources, their proportional utility value, and other requirements vary depending on the type of resource being allocated. However, there is always a single common constraint on the price of using all of the resources, i.e., a budget set aside for the job's execution, when many resource types are needed for a single user job.

Co-allocating a variety of heterogeneous resources of various sorts according to user criterion z_i and a single constraint on the total usage cost appears like an unrealistic and erroneous issue formulation. Unbalanced resource combinations may result from the z_i criterion (or preliminary user utility estimations for each accessible resource i calculation features. For instance, a set of solely network resources (without a computational capacity) or a set of only computational nodes (without access to the network or data storages) may be assigned for such a request.

Thus, the resources allocation model in heterogeneous environments with resources of diverse types requires formulation and simultaneous solution of several co-allocation sub-problems specific for each type of resource. For example: allocate n_1 computational nodes, the corresponding number n_2 of software packets, $[n_3; n_4]$ storage drives and at least one network connection for a total allocation budget C. Such a problem formulation guarantees selection of a minimum set of resources of each type required to execute a job, including those having relatively small user utility values z_i.

Therefore, the formulation and simultaneous solution of a number of co-allocation sub-problems unique to each type of resource are required by the resources allocation model in heterogeneous environments with resources of diverse types. For a total allocation budget C, for instance, assign n_1 computational nodes, n_2 software packets, $[n_3; n_4]$ storage drives, and n_1 network connections. The choice of a minimal set of resources of each type, including those with relatively low user utility values z_i, is ensured by this issue formulation.

The 0–1 knapsack issue is crucial for the allocation and selection of resources. There are numerous approaches that can be used to get individual solutions for each resource co-allocation sub-problem with a specific budget constraint C and a single resource type. Each of the m available computing resources has the properties cost c_1 and performance $p_i = z_i$. The maximizing of overall window performance under the total cost restriction C_j is represented by the optimization problem below:

$$Z = \sum_{i=1}^{m} z_i x_i \rightarrow \max, \tag{1}$$

with the following restrictions:

$$\sum_{i=1}^{m} c_i x_i \leq C_j$$

$$\sum_{i=1}^{m} x_i = n$$

$$x_i \in \{0, 1\}, i = 1, .., m,$$

where z_i is a target characteristic value provided by resource i, c_i is its usage price, x_i is a decision variable determining whether to allocate resource i ($x_i = 1$) or not ($x_i = 0$) for the solution. This problem formulation (1) is compatible with the economic scheduling model when computing resources are made available and have cost (c_i) and performance (p_i) attributes.

In practice, specifying the exact number n of the simultaneously required resources usually is not possible or sensible. In a more general case, the suitable number n of resources required to execute a parallel job depends not only on the job structure, but also on the composition and characteristics of the cloud system. Thus, a more flexible resources co-allocation approach should accept an interval $[n_{min}; n_{max}]$ of permissible values for the allocated resources number. In this case, the resource request may be formulated as follows: allocate for a period T a set of $n \in [n_{min}; n_{max}]$ simultaneously available resources satisfying constraints for individual characteristics (OS, minimal performance, RAM, etc.) and an integral constraint for a total allocation cost C.

For instance, a backfilling scheduling technique can reduce the total queue completion time by defining extra restrictions for the task queue execution order. The work queue composition must be known in advance, which is a crucial condition for the backfilling time optimization's effectiveness. The fundamental concept of backfilling is that relatively small jobs at the end of the queue are executed on idle and waiting resources right now.

However, in a more typical case, each user parallel job is submitted separately, and in the online mode, resources should be chosen and assigned right away.

Therefore, our primary objective is to independently plan user jobs in order to maximize overall scheduling criteria, such as the average jobs' finish time or a makespan.

The so-called microsheduling methodologies, such as CoP and PeST [4,10], are based on comparable concepts. On the basis of the resources' meta-parameters and attributes, such as utilization level, performance, local schedules, etc., they put into practice heuristic guidelines for how the resources should be chosen for user jobs.

2.2   Artificial Neural Network Model

We consider a more structured method based on a machine learning model in the current study. It is possible to train an artificial neural network to plan each job separately with equivalent total overall efficiency using the outcomes of efficient job queue scheduling (obtained, for example, through backfilling).

The more variables and characteristics of a suitable reference solution that are considered, the more precise the online solution may be. Online scheduling also places limitations on prior knowledge of the condition of the computer environment. It is possible that the precise values of resource characteristics and utility functions are uncertain or inaccurate.

The main purpose then is to create a model that will solve the 0–1 knapsack problem with utility z_i values that are a priori unknown and using just a set of secondary resource's features.

Accordingly, to sum up this problem we will utilize more complicated scheduling model interpretation with elements having four numeric attributes a_i, b_i, d_i, g_i in an expansion to the weight w_i. Utilities z_i will be determined for every knapsack element as a capability function F_{val} of attributes a_i, b_i, d_i, g_i. This function is used to find out the exact reference knapsack allocation (by using a brute force or dynamic programming calculation). In view of this allocation the AI model will be prepared to choose elements dependent just upon the info attributes a_i, b_i, d_i, g_i, consequently, reproducing the online scheduling features.

For current study we will use five specific functions as different examples of hidden relationships between the elements: attributes and their utility towards the common criteria for the knapsack allocation:

$$F_{val} = a + b + d - g, \tag{2}$$

$$F_{val} = a * b + d * g^2, \tag{3}$$

$$F_{val} = sin(a + b) + cos(d) + g^2, \tag{4}$$

$$F_{val} = a + lg(b + d) * g, \tag{5}$$

$$F_{val} = a + lg(b) + d * e^{g/10}, \tag{6}$$

where a, b, d, g are knapsack elements' attributes notwithstanding the weight. The given functional relationships contain practically the whole numerical complexity range to research at the testing stage how these relationships affect the AI calculation precision and effectiveness.

3 Algorithms Implementation

3.1 Training and Design of the Artificial Neural Network

An artificial neural network (ANN can be addressed as a grouping of layers that can transform input values to return an outcome. Several design and implementation iterations for knapsack problems of smaller sizes were made to choose the ANN configuration and hyperparameters.

The ANN training set was gotten as an exact 0–1 knapsack allocations obtained with dynamic programming algorithm based on randomized problems set.

In the current ANN model we consider a knapsack of twenty elements. Each knapsack item has four parameters a_i, b_i, d_i, g_i (in addition to the weight parameter w_i), the values of which are terms of the (hidden for ANN) utility functions (2)–(6).

Thus, the training sample will contain the following set of vectors: the vector of 20 knapsack elements weights, the vectors of the items' parameters a_i, b_i, d_i, g_i and the vector of the results (obtained using dynamic programming algorithm), characterizing the allocated knapsack (1 - the item is selected for the knapsack, 0 - not). Thus, total number of inputs for 20-elements knapsack is then 100, and the number of outputs is 20.

In case we need to model knapsack problem with $m < 20$, we can provide decidedly large weights $w_i > 1$ for the spare elements $i = m + 1, .., 20$. In this case such extra elements should not be selected into the knapsack.

Eventually, after forming the sample (parameters vectors, weights, and solutions) of the desired size, it is divided into training and test samples. We need that to avoid sample data coincidence, so that the training and testing of ANN takes place correctly on various disjoint datasets.

The sample generation goes according to the following scenario. All the parameters of the knapsack elements are randomly generated. For an array of weights, 20 values are generated from the interval [1; 180], arrays of the rest four parameters (a_i, b_i, d_i, g_i) are generated in a similar way.

The generation is set up in such a way that in the results of the generated knapsack problem, we achieve a uniform distribution of the item's selections (between 0 s and 1 s). That is, there was no obvious bias in any direction. Otherwise, it is difficult to evaluate the accuracy and quality of training.

The interval for generating the limit on the total weight of the knapsack was found experimentally: the lower bound of the interval corresponds to the minimum value in the vector of weights, the upper bound is equal to the number of elements in the knapsack multiplied by an experimentally selected multiplier.

Additionally, the vector of weights was sorted to simplify the training of ANN. That is, an item with the largest weight (and its parameters) is always set at the beginning of the ANN inputs (and outputs), while an item with the smallest weight - in the end. We believe that such an input regularity simplifies the training of the ANN hidden layers of the ANN.

To improve the *perception* of ANN, the input values should be additionally normalized. In order to put the input data in the same conditions for all training samples, it is crucial to carry out the alignment process and provide input values in a certain interval. This helps to avoid possible training errors of ANN, since inappropriate values can be given to it, which in turn won't affect the neurons properly, which will lead to incorrect generalizations. Thus, as an input normalization step, we divide weights vector by the limit C on the total weight of the knapsack (Fig. 1). Weights normalization allows us to generalize the weight constraint in (1) to $C = 1$ for any input sample. Additionally, in this case we don't need to provide the weight constraint as an input to the ANN.

Total Weight: 664

Weight: [15, 27, 31, 48, 49, 56, 73, 78, 87, 92, 105, 117, 134, 138, 143, 152, 153, 157, 166, 177]

Normalized Weight: [0.02259036, 0.04066265, 0.04668675, 0.07228916, 0.07379518, 0.08433735, 0.10993976, 0.11746988, 0.1310241, 0.13855422, 0.15813253, 0.17620482,0.20180723, 0.20783133, 0.21536145, 0.22891566, 0.23042169, 0.23644578, 0.25, 0.26656627]

True Result: [1, 1, 1, 1, 1, 1, 0, 1, 1, 0, 0, 1, 1, 0, 0, 0, 0, 0, 0, 0]

Fig. 1. Input weight normalization example.

Normalization of the input layer of ANN is usually performed by scaling the data supplied to the activation function. However, data normalization can also be performed in hidden layers. Therefore, in addition to standard dense layers, layers with batch normalization are used in the implemented neural network architecture. Batch normalization provides a regularization mechanism, since it introduces a certain noise to the outputs of hidden layers. Thus, we increase performance and stabilize the ANN.

3.2 MLAK Algorithm

While preparing an ANN, it is difficult to work with formal numerical equations and hard constraints, specifically those characterized for the 0–1 knapsack problem (1)).

The primary issue with the ANN knapsack implementation is that even with a high accuracy we cannot rest assured that the weight condition for the knapsack is satisfied.

To consider the restriction on the knapsack weight, we propose to utilize the ANN allocation result as an anticipated utility values u_i which can be used in another algorithmic knapsack solution.

That is, the input data for the task (1)) will contain weight w_i and utility $z_i = u_i$ vectors, where u_i values are calculated for each element based on the item's properties a_i, b_i, d_i, g_i. In this way, the ANN will operate as a conversion module to identify mutual relationships between the knapsack items' properties and map them to the common utility values. Thus, the ANN will work as a transformation layer to distinguish shared relationships and connections between the attributes of knapsack items and predict their utilities.

4 Simulation Study

4.1 Simulation Environment

We assess MLAK performance in comparison with traditional combinatorial optimization knapsack algorithms (i.e., dynamic programming and greedy execution), as well as with pure neural network implementation. Neural network results were fixed to follow the weight limitation: the items with the smallest prediction certainty were eliminated individually until the total weight limitation is fulfilled.

Thus, MLAK and ANN received a_i, b_i, d_i, g_i properties as an input, while Dynamic programming (DP) and *Greedy* implementations used $z_i = F_{val}(a_i, b_i, d_i, g_i)$ calculated utility functions to solve the knapsack problem.

Furthermore, we consider a Random choice calculation to assess MLAK and ANN performance in between the optimal solution received with dynamic programming and a totally random outcome.

Every one of the considered algorithms were given the same set of 1000 randomized knapsack problems as input. We then calculate two performance criteria for each algorithm:

- the resulting knapsack total utility $Z = \sum_{i=1}^{m} z_i x_i$ and its relation to the DP result (average utility);
- the resulting accuracy as element-wise comparison with the DP result for all the experiments.

Both performance criteria depend on DP result as it gives an optimal knapsack allocation based on the known element utilities.

In addition, we measure and compare average calculation times. All considered algorithms were implemented in Python. Run times were observed on a desktop PC with a Core i5 and 8 Gb RAM. The running time of MLAK includes execution of both internal ANN algorithms and DP algorithms.

4.2 Simulation Results and Analysis

For the algorithms comparison and evaluation, we performed over 1000 simulations of 20-items knapsack problem. The results are collected in Tables 1, 2, 3, 4 and 5 for each hidden function (2)–(6).

Table 1. Function (2) Optimization Results.

Algorithm	Average Utility, %	Accuracy, %	Average working time, s
DP	100,0	100	0.0063
Greedy	98,7	48,0	0.00004
MLAK	98,2	39,9	0.0421
ANN	96,1	25,9	0.0237
Random	57,6	0,6	0.00005

Table 2. Function (3) Optimization Results.

Algorithm	Average Utility, %	Accuracy, %	Average working time, s
DP	100	100	0.0061
Greedy	99,2	59,2	0.00004
MLAK	97,7	36,6	0.0415
ANN	94,9	21,6	0.0239
Random	53,5	1,4	0.00005

Table 3. Function (4) Optimization Results.

Algorithm	Average Utility, %	Accuracy, %	Average working time, s
DP	100,0	100	0.00743
Greedy	99,4	64,1	0.00004
MLAK	98,4	42,5	0.04531
ANN	96,6	22,6	0.02380
Random	51,7	1,2	0.00005

Table 4. Function (5) Optimization Results.

Algorithm	Average Utility, %	Accuracy, %	Average working time, s
DP	100	100	0.00734
Greedy	99,0	49,6	0.00004
MLAK	98,7	40,8	0.04556
ANN	96,3	22,6	0.02400
Random	60,0	1,4	0.00005

Table 5. Function (6) Optimization Results.

Algorithm	Average Utility, %	Accuracy, %	Average working time, s
MLAK	96,7	41,2	0.04784
ANN	96,9	24,1	0.02391
DP	100,0	100	0.00823
Greedy	99,8	85,9	0.00004
Random	39,8	1,0	0.00005

The obtained outcomes mainly show that Greedy calculation proved nearly optimal average utility: close to 99% when compared to DP. Such an outcome is expected for 20 items with randomized and uniformly distributed utility attributes. 50–85% accuracy demonstrates that nearly optimal solutions are quite achievable with different allocation configurations.

MLAK and ANN optimization efficiency is generally comparable to the Greedy implementation. Relative difference by the average utility between Greedy and MLAK is less than 1% for functions (2), (4), and (5). ANN provides similar results with less than 1% lower utility compared to MLAK.

For functions (3) and (6) the relative difference is as high as 3%, which can be explained by the much larger absolute values of the utility functions obtained from the same set of randomly generated input properties (see the Average Utility column in Tables 1, 2, 3, 4and 5). ANN prediction works less efficiently when the relationships between properties include multiplication and exponentiation.

And even this under 3% performance loss for MLAK (in the most pessimistic scenario observed) is somewhat reasonable or even negligible when compared to the Random allocation with over 40% loss from DP solution. Remember that in the considered scenarios DP and Greedy performed knapsack calculations using the known utility functions, while Random selection shows average outcomes with no optimization.

Actual running time od MLAK is inferior to all other algorithms. For the 20-element knapsack problem under consideration, MLAK prediction time of 0.05 s may seem ridiculously small, but larger problems will require an increase in ANN structure, training sample size, training time and computational effort.

5 Conclusion

In this paper we considered a machine learning-based approach for resources allocation in online scheduling mode based on global criteria. For a proper comparison we formalized and simulated the problem and compared the results to the classical combinatorial optimization algorithms.

Based on the presented results, the proposed Machine Learning-based Algorithm for the Knapsack problem (MLAK) showed efficiency comparable to the greedy approximation. However, unlike the classical greedy solution, MLAK did not know the knapsack items' utility values, but firstly predicted them based on a set of secondary characteristics. This feature distinguishes this work from other machine learning applications for combinatorial optimization problems.

The obtained results substantiate the possibility of using the same approach for the actual job-flow scheduling data. And thus, we expect the efficiency of the scheduling results to be on par with the classic greedy approximation.

Future work is aimed to gather job-flow execution data from real systems to prepare the training data for the machine learning - based online scheduler.

Acknowledgements. This work was supported by the Russian Science Foundation project no. 22-21-00372.

References

1. Bharathi, S., Chervenak, A.L., Deelman, E., Mehta, G., Su, M., Vahi, K.: Characterization of scientific workflows. In: 2008 Third Workshop on Workflows in Support of Large-Scale Science, pp. 1–10 (2008)
2. Rodriguez, M.A., Buyya, R.: Scheduling dynamic workloads in multi-tenant scientific workflow as a service platforms. Future Gener. Comput. Syst. **79**(P2), 739–750 (2018)
3. Kurowski, K., Nabrzyski, J., Oleksiak, A., Weglarz, J.: multicriteria aspects of grid resource management. In: Nabrzyski, J., Schopf, J.M., Weglarz J. (eds.) Grid Resource Management. State of the Art and Future Trends, pp. 271–293. Kluwer Academic Publishers. (2003)
4. Toporkov, V., Yemelyanov, D.: Coordinated and hindsight resources allocation in distributed computing. In: Proceedings - 2019 20th International Conference on Parallel and Distributed Computing, Applications and Technologies, PDCAT (2019)
5. Toporkov, V., Yemelyanov, D., Toporkova, A.: Coordinated global and private job-flow scheduling in grid virtual organizations. J. Simul. Model. Pract. Theor. **107**, 102228 (2021)
6. Sukhoroslov, O., Nazarenko, A., Aleksandrov, R.: An experimental study of scheduling algorithms for many-task applications. J. Supercomput. **75**, 7857–7871 (2019)
7. Samimi, P., Teimouri, Y., Mukhtar M.: A combinatorial double auction resource allocation model in cloud computing. J. Inf. Sci. **357**(C), 201–216 (2016)
8. Rodero, I., Villegas, D., Bobroff, N., Liu, Y., Fong, L., Sadjadi, S.: Enabling interoperability among grid meta-schedulers. J. Grid Comput. **11**(2), 311–336 (2013)

9. Shmueli, E., Feitelson, D.G.: Backfilling with lookahead to optimize the packing of parallel jobs. J. Parallel Distrib. Comput. **65**(9), 1090–1107 (2005)
10. Khemka, B., et al.: Resource management in heterogeneous parallel computing environments with soft and hard deadlines. In: Proceedings of 11th Metaheuristics International Conference (MIC 2015) (2015)
11. Netto, M.A.S., Buyya, R.: A flexible resource co-allocation model based on advance reservations with rescheduling support. In: Technical Report, GRIDSTR-2007-17, Grid Computing and Distributed Systems Laboratory, The University of Melbourne, Australia (2007)
12. Toporkov, V., Toporkova, A., Yemelyanov, D.: Slot co-allocation optimization in distributed computing with heterogeneous resources. In: Del Ser, J., Osaba, E., Bilbao, M.N., Sanchez-Medina, J.J., Vecchio, M., Yang, X.-S. (eds.) IDC 2018. SCI, vol. 798, pp. 40–49. Springer, Cham (2018). https://doi.org/10.1007/978-3-319-99626-4_4
13. Toporkov, V., Yemelyanov, D.: Optimization of resources selection for jobs scheduling in heterogeneous distributed computing environments. In: Shi, Y., et al. (eds.) ICCS 2018. LNCS, vol. 10861, pp. 574–583. Springer, Cham (2018). https://doi.org/10.1007/978-3-319-93701-4_45
14. Toporkov, V., Yemelyanov, D.: Scheduling optimization in heterogeneous computing environments with resources of different types. In: Zamojski, W., Mazurkiewicz, J., Sugier, J., Walkowiak, T., Kacprzyk, J. (eds.) DepCoS-RELCOMEX 2021. AISC, vol. 1389, pp. 447–456. Springer, Cham (2021). https://doi.org/10.1007/978-3-030-76773-0_43
15. Xu, S., Panwar, S.S., Kodialam, M.S., Lakshman, T.V.: Deep neural network approximated dynamic programming for combinatorial optimization. In: AAAI Conference on Artificial Intelligence, pp. 1684–1691 (2020)
16. Nomer, H.A.A., Alnowibet, K.A., Elsayed, A., Mohamed, A.W.: Neural knapsack: a neural network based solver for the knapsack problem. In: IEEE Access, vol. 8, pp. 224200–224210 (2020)
17. Bello, I., Pham, H., Le, Q.V., Norouzi, M., Bengio, S.: Neural Combinatorial Optimization with Reinforcement Learning. In: International Conference on Learning Representations (2017)
18. Yang, F., Jin, T., Liu, T., Sun, X., Zhang, J.: Boosting dynamic programming with neural networks for solving NP-hard problems. In: Proceedings of The 10th Asian Conference on Machine Learning, PMLR, vol. 95, pp. 726–739 (2018)
19. Yang, X., et al.: A review: machine learning for combinatorial optimization problems in energy areas. Algorithms **15**, 205 (2022)
20. Bengio, Y., Lodi, A., Prouvost, A.: Machine learning for combinatorial optimization: a methodological tour d'horizon. Eur. J. Oper. Res. **290**(2), 405–421 (2021)

High Performance Computing Queue Time Prediction Using Clustering and Regression

Scott Hutchison[1]([✉])(iD), Daniel Andresen[1], Mitchell Neilsen[1], William Hsu[1], and Benjamin Parsons[2]

[1] Kansas State University, Manhattan, KS 66506, USA
{scotthutch,dan,neilsen,bhsu}@ksu.edu
[2] Engineering Research and Development Center, Vicksburg, MS 39180, USA
ben.s.parsons@erdc.dren.mil

Abstract. High Performance Computing (HPC) users are often provided little or no information at job submission time regarding how long their job will be queued until it begins execution. Foreknowledge of a long queue time can inform HPC user's decision to migrate their jobs to commercial cloud infrastructure to receive their results sooner. Various researchers have used different machine learning techniques to build queue time estimators. This research applies the proven technique of K-Means clustering followed by Gradient Boosted Tree regression on over 700,000 jobs actually submitted to an HPC system to predict a submitted job's queue time from HPC system characteristics and user provided job requirements. This method applied to HPC queue time prediction achieves better than 96% accuracy at classifying whether a job will start prior to an assigned deadline. Additionally, this research shows that historic HPC CPU allocation data can be used to predict future increases or decreases in job queue time with accuracy exceeding 96%.

Keywords: HPC · SLURM · Scheduling · K-Means Clustering · Gradient Boosted Tree Regression

1 Introduction

When a job is submitted to a High Performance Computing (HPC) cluster, a scheduling application, like SLURM, PBS, LoadLeveler, etc., handles the allocation of HPC resources in the future to the job's requirements as specified by the submitter. If adequate HPC resources are currently unavailable, the job enters a queue for execution in the future, and future resources are scheduled for that job's use. While a job is queued and awaiting execution, the job is making no forward progress toward its eventual completion. Worse still, it is often unclear to the user how long it will take until the job begins execution. The user knows the job is waiting to start, but there is often no way for the user to know if the job execution will begin in three hours, three days, or three weeks. Users with a time-critical application facing long queue delays may be willing to migrate jobs to commercial cloud infrastructure, like Amazon's AWS, Microsoft's Azure, Google's Cloud Computing, etc. Various techniques for predicting job queue times have been implemented in the past with different trade offs and accuracy. A machine learning pipeline which uses unsupervised K-Means clustering followed by Gradient Boosted Tree Regression has been used to lower error rates when used in other applications. This research investigates if this machine learning technique can also be used to a predict queue times for HPC jobs.

The goal of this research is to answer the following questions: For an HPC system with a given current utilization, can we provide an accurate queue time prediction for a job which factors in the future state of the HPC cluster? Can we predict the execution of a job prior to an assigned deadline?

2   Background

Improving HPC utilization, decreasing job queue time, and decreasing job turnaround time are all active areas of research at Kansas State University (KSU). These areas would typically apply and are of interest to any HPC cluster manager. Developing an accurate queue time predictor can not only help inform job scheduling, but it can also provide additional information to users about their expected job start times, and perhaps more importantly, about the length of time they can expect to wait for their results.

Kumar and Vadhiyar [7] performed a similar job queue time prediction by using k-nearest neighbors followed by support vector machines to classify jobs into time bins of various sizes with their probabilities. Though this technique showed promise, using regression allows for a concrete prediction value for queue time, as opposed to the most likely time bin this job would fall into.

Jancauskas, et al. [6] conducted similar research on queue time prediction using Naive Bayes to return a list of probability estimates (t_i, p_i), where p_i was the probability that a job will start before t_i. They used similar features and achieved excellent accuracy, precision, and recall. An advantage of using clustering and regression over Naive Bayes is that a concrete start time prediction can be generated for the current load on the HPC system for an individual job with certain requirements. This research not only uses different machine learning techniques for prediction, but also factors in changes of the future state of the HPC system and the impact those changes have on job queue times, which Jancauskas, et al. considered outside the scope of their research.

Brown, et al. [2] used a very similar technique as this research, using k-nearest neighbors followed by gradient boosted tree regression, however they also did not factor in the future state of the HPC system.

Unsupervised K-Means [8] clustering followed by Gradient Boosted Tree Regression [3] (GBTR) has been used by various researchers to improve the accuracy of regression models. For instance, Zheng and Wu [4] used this technique to improve on short-term wind forecasting, and Liu et al. [9] used this technique to improve short-term power load forecasting. As this technique has shown promise in improving prediction accuracy in other areas of research, using clustering followed by regression could also improve the accuracy of predicting how long a job will be queued for execution on an HPC system.

3   Methodology

3.1   Data Set

The HPC cluster at KSU is a Beowulf [1] HPC cluster called "Beocat". Beocat currently consists of 362 compute nodes with a total of 10980 compute cores and 5.57 Terabytes of memory, and it uses SLURM [16] as the job scheduler. SLURM logs data from all jobs submitted to Beocat and retains 105 different features about each job. These features include job submission time, start time, end time, the number of CPUs requested by the user, the amount of memory and time requested by the user, etc. The data set used for this research consisted of all jobs submitted in 2018, which totaled approximately 730,000 jobs. Figure 1 shows the CPU and memory allocation over time for Beocat for 2018. The calculated CPU utilization for 2018 was roughly 60%. Jobs can remain queued due to lack of available CPUs or lack of available memory. This data set was thought to be a good representative data set with enough data to produce meaningful results.

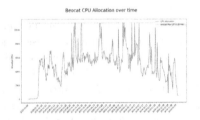 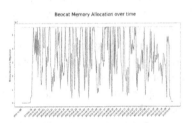

Fig. 1. CPU and memory allocation over time for KSU HPC system for 2018

3.2   Feature Selection and Calculation

The queue time of a job depends primarily on two factors: the amount of resources available in the HPC and the amount of resources a job is requesting. Table 1 summarizes and describes the features used for this research.

To calculate `BeocatCPUsInUse`, the 2018 jobs from the log data were sorted chronologically by their start and end times. Each time a new job began, the number of CPUs in use by the cluster was increased by the number of cores allocated to that job. Each time a job ended, the number of CPUs in use by the cluster was decreased by the number of cores allocated the that job. The same strategy was employed to calculate `BeocatMemoryInUse`.

Table 1. Features used

Category	Feature	Description
HPC features	BeocatCPUsInUse	Current allocated CPUs
	BeocatMemoryInUse	Current allocated memory
	QueueDepth	The queue depth when job was submitted
Job features	ReqCPUs	Number of requested cores for a job
	ReqMem	Amount of memory requested for a job
	ReqMinutes	Amount of minutes requested for a job
	OwnsResources	True if user has priority access to compute nodes; False otherwise
Dependent variable	QueueTimeInSec	Number of seconds from submit until start

To calculate QueueDepth, jobs were sorted by their submit times and their start times. Each time a job is submitted, the queue depth is increased by one. Each time a job starts, the queue depth is decreased by one.

The requested CPUs, requested memory, and requested time for each job were directly pulled from the log data to populate the ReqCPUs, ReqMem, and ReqMinutes features.

There are a number of compute nodes which are available for all Beocat users to use. Certain resources are owned by departments whose members have priority access and who can preempt running jobs. The OwnsResources feature was set to true if there were dedicated resources available which could run that job. If the job was submitted to only the queues common to all, the OwnsResources feature was set to false.

To calculate QueueTimeInSec, the submit time for each job was subtracted from its start time. This time delta object was converted into an integer that represented the number of seconds each job sat in the queue awaiting job execution.

3.3 Feature Normalization and Model Development

Min-Max scaling was used on Beocat CPU and memory allocation to return a value between 0 and 100 which represents the percentage of Beocat currently allocated.

A vector consisting of ScaledBeocatCPUsInUse, ScaledBeocatMemoryInUse, QueueDepth, ReqCPUs, ReqMem, and OwnsResources was constructed, and used to predict QueueTimeInSec. The log data containing roughly 730,000 jobs were randomly split into an 80% training batch and a 20% testing batch. The training batch contained roughly 583,000 jobs, and the test batch contained roughly 146,000 jobs.

A base GBTR model was trained using 5-fold cross validation on the training data, which was then evaluated using the test data. This base model was used later to predict clusters that contained fewer than 100 elements. This model will be referred to as the GBT_{base} in various figures throughout the remainder of this report.

Since the optimal number of clusters required to group the training data was initially unclear, iterative K-Means was used to cluster the data using an increasing number of clusters from 2 to 150. The training data was fed into K-Means and n clusters were returned, where $n = 2, 3, 4, \ldots, 150$. After clustering, a GBTR model was developed using 5-fold cross validation for each cluster containing more than 100 elements. A small cluster containing fewer than 100 elements would use the GBT_{base} model to make queue time predictions. These models were developed using the training data, and then evaluated using the test data. An unseen-before test input would first be classified by the K-means model, and then the appropriate GBTR model was used to develop a prediction of the job's queue time. The machine learning pipeline's error rate overall on the test data was used to determine an ideal number of clusters that minimized the error. The number of clusters producing a local minimum error rate was identified, and then that pipeline was selected for further evaluation. This machine learning pipeline is outlined in Fig. 2.

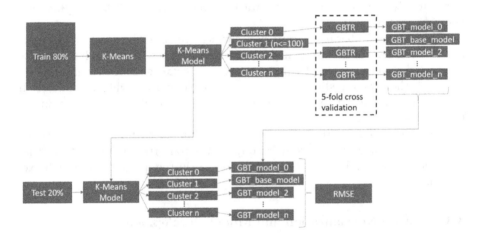

Fig. 2. The machine learning pipeline used for this research.

During actual use, users may have individual and specific deadlines. This information is not currently solicited or collected on Beocat, so it was unavailable in the log data. An arbitrary deadline for each job was set to be the average queue time for all jobs in 2018, or 13423 s (HH:MM:SS = 03:43:43). A queue time prediction was made for each job, and it was assessed whether this prediction was met or exceeded the assigned deadline. Since the actual queue time was known, a confusion matrix was generated to determine the overall accuracy, precision, recall, and F1 scores for the machine learning pipeline.

The above mentioned queue time prediction represents a snapshot in time given the overall HPC system resources allocated for a job with specific requirements. The future state of the HPC may also impact job queue time. For instance, if cluster allocation increases following a job submission when a large number of higher priority jobs are started, this queue time estimate may underestimate when a job would actually begin. Alternatively, an HPC allocation decrease following a job submission due to jobs finishing earlier than expected may cause a job to begin sooner.

Since the average queue time for Beocat in 2018 was roughly 3 h and 45 min, a sliding time window of 4 h was used to assess what impact a change in HPC CPU allocation would have on the change in queue times for HPC jobs. Figure 3 depicts how average Δ_{CPUs} was calculated. Average Δ_{queue_time} was calculated in the same manner. In 2018, there were 1,520 four-hour time windows containing submitted jobs. The time windows were randomly split into an 80% training batch and 20% testing batch. A linear regression model was trained using the average Δ_{CPUs} from the training data and used to predict the average Δ_{queue_time} of the test data. Again, the actual change in queue time was known from the log data, which enabled the calculation of RMSE, accuracy, precision, recall and the F1 Score for this linear regression model.

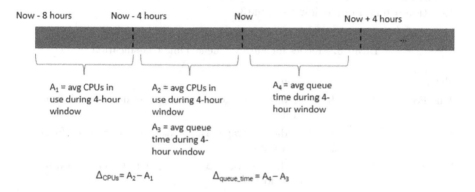

Fig. 3. Depiction of Δ_{CPUs} calculation

3.4 Evaluation

Feature correlation was measured using the Pearson Correlation Coefficient [12]. This statistical measure produces a value between -1 and 1, where correlation coefficient values closer -1 or 1 indicate a stronger correlation between two features and a value closer to 0 indicates no or very little correlation.

Each regression model contained some N elements. The machine learning pipeline and each regression model was evaluated using the Root Mean Squared Error (RMSE) metric, which is calculated according to the following equation:

$$RMSE = \sqrt{\frac{\Sigma_{i=0}^{N}(\text{actual queue time}_i - \text{predicted queue time}_i)^2}{N}}$$

Additionally, the machine learning pipeline was used to compare whether or not the predicted queue time for each job exceeded the assigned deadline. A confusion matrix, along with the metrics of accuracy, precision, recall, and the F1 Score were utilized. The metrics and their descriptions are laid out in Table 2:

Table 2. Metrics for Deadline Classification

Metric	Description
True Positive (TP)	Model predicts job will start before deadline, and it does
True Negative (TN)	Model predicts job will start after deadline and it does
False Positive (FP)	Model predicts job will start before deadline, but job does not
False Negative (FN)	Model predicts job will start after deadline, but job does not

The metrics used to assess the change in queue time given the change in CPU allocation are laid out below in Table 3:

Table 3. Metrics for Future Queue Time Classification

Metric	Description
True Positive (TP)	Model predicts average Δ_{queue_time} will decrease 4 h from now, and it does
True Negative (TN)	Model predicts average Δ_{queue_time} will increase 4 h from now, and it does
False Positive (FP)	Model predicts average Δ_{queue_time} will decrease 4 h from now, and it does not
False Negative (FN)	Model predicts average Δ_{queue_time} will increase 4 h from now, and it does not

These metrics were calculated in the following way:

$$\text{Accuracy} = \frac{TP+TN}{TP+TN+FP+FN} \quad \text{Precision} = \frac{TP}{TP+FP}$$
$$\text{Recall} = \frac{TN}{TP+FN} \quad \text{F1 Score} = \frac{2*TP}{2*TP+FP+FN}$$

4   Results

PySpark is an interface for Apache Spark [17] for the Python [15] programming language. PySpark was utilized for data wrangling and analysis. PySpark's machine learning library, MLlib [10], was utilized for statistical analysis, clustering, and regression tasks. Matplotlib [5] was used to generate plots and charts.

4.1   Correlation of Features

Table 4 lays out the Pearson Correlation Coefficients for the features used. "Slightly correlated" values in Table 4 are displayed using orange text and the stronger "somewhat correlated" features are displayed using red text. Perhaps unsurprisingly, there is a slight correlation between the HPC CPUs in use and the HPC memory in use at any given time, as well as a slight correlation between the amount of CPUs requested by a user and the amount of memory requested by a user. The queue depth and queue time are somewhat correlated, and the queue depth and the amount of memory allocated on the HPC are somewhat correlated. This makes sense given the relatively large amount of time Beocat spends with its allocated memory near or at its maximum (See Fig. 1).

Table 4. Correlation of Features

Feature	BeocatCPUsInUse	BeocatMemoryInUse	QueueDepth	ReqCPUs	ReqMem	ReqMinutes	QueueTimeInSec
BeocatCPUsInUse	1	0.195	0.008	0.008	−0.010	−0.067	−0.009
BeocatMemoryInUse	0.195	1	0.392	−0.047	−0.020	−0.036	0.131
QueueDepth	0.008	0.392	1	−0.061	−0.028	−0.091	0.326
ReqCPUs	0.007	−0.047	−0.047	1	0.119	0.057	−0.002
ReqMem	−0.010	−0.020	−0.027	0.119	1	0.036	0.003
ReqMinutes	−0.067	−0.036	−0.091	0.057	0.036	1	0.074
QueueTimeInSec	−0.009	0.131	0.326	−0.002	0.003	0.074	1

4.2   K-Means Clustering and GBT Regression

The GBT_{base} model had a RMSE of 23229.92. This was compared to two naive guessing strategies of guessing zero queue time for all jobs and guessing the average queue time from 2018 for all jobs. Naively guessing zero seconds produced a RMSE of 42818.2, and naively guessing the average queue time (13423.21 s) produced a RMSE of 40659.8. It is clear that the base model has a lower RMSE than these two naive guessing strategies.

It was identified by iterating through the number of generated k-means clusters that 57 clusters produced a local minimum RMSE of 18119.23. As the number of clusters increased, there was not a significant improvement in accuracy, and it is thought that as the number of clusters continues to increase, the GBT_{base} model will be used for more and more clusters as the number of data points in each cluster decreases. Locating this "elbow" in the data [14] attempts to prevent overfitting and clustering beyond the point of diminishing returns. The RMSE of the machine learning pipeline as the number of clusters was varied is depicted in Fig. 4.

Using 57 clusters produces 42 GBTR models for clusters containing more than 100 elements, and the machine learning pipeline uses the base GBTR model for the remaining 15 clusters. Each test data point was clustered, and then the appropriate GBTR model was used to predict the queue time for a job. Each job's queue time prediction was compared to its actual queue time, and it was evaluated if the predicted and actual queue time exceeded the assigned deadline. The confusion matrix and evaluation metrics can be found in Table 5. Overall, the machine learning pipeline was excellent at predicting future queue times, and its accuracy, precision, recall, and F1 Score were all greater than 96%.

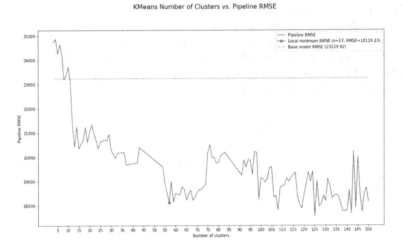

Fig. 4. RMSE of machine learning pipeline as the number of K-Means clusters was varied.

Table 5. Confusion Matrix for Machine Learning Pipeline with Metrics

Total Jobs 145,658		Actual	
		Job runs before Avg Queue Time	Job runs after Avg Queue Time
Predicted	Job runs before Avg Queue Time	TP = 107,208	FP = 1,490
	Job runs after Avg Queue Time	FN = 3,366	TN = 33,594

Metric	Value
Accuracy	96.66%
Precision	98.63%
Recall	96.95%
F1 Score	97.79%

4.3   Future HPC Queue Time Prediction

The $(\Delta_{CPUs}, \Delta_{queue\_time})$ points and the line-of-best-fit provided by the linear regression model are depicted in Fig. 5. The model achieved a RMSE of 14691.17 s. The confusion matrix and evaluation metrics are found in Table 6. Overall, the linear regression model was excellent at predicting future queue times, and its accuracy, precision, recall, and F1 Score were all greater than 96%.

Change in CPU Allocation vs. Change in Queue Time

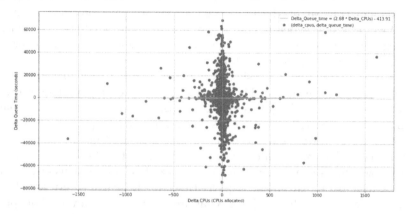

Fig. 5. Change in average CPU allocation vs. change in average queue time

Table 6. Confusion Matrix for Queue Time Increase with Metrics

Total Time Windows 1,520		Actual	
		Future average Δ_{queue_time} decreases	Future average Δ_{queue_time} increases
Predicted	Future average Δ_{queue_time} decreases	TP = 702	FP = 26
	Future average Δ_{queue_time} increases	FN = 24	TN = 768

Metric	Value
Accuracy	96.71%
Precision	96.43%
Recall	96.69%
F1 Score	96.56%

5 Discussion

The correlation between queue depth and the HPC memory in use for Beocat is supported by the memory in use over time depicted in Fig. 1. This confirms the observations made by Beocat's system administrators who have determined that more often than not, Beocat is constrained by its available memory rather than its available CPUs. This alone has informed the equipment requirements for purchases of new servers for the HPC system here at KSU. We now procure servers with larger memory to try to better accommodate our user's requirements. Doing a similar analysis might allow managers of other HPC systems to better identify hardware that can support the types of jobs their users often run.

As depicted in Table 5, the accuracy, precision, recall, and F1 Score were all greater than 96%. Although a somewhat arbitrary deadline was used for each user's deadline, this data could be provided by the users at submission time. This would give more meaningful information to the users of Beocat depending on how time sensitive their jobs are. Various other values for deadlines were used (1 h, 8 h, and 12 h), all of which produced similar accuracy, precision, recall, and F1 scores exceeding at least 90%. It can only be concluded that the machine learning pipeline does a good job at predicting a reasonable start time for most jobs regardless of the pipeline RMSE.

Using clustering and regression as opposed to other techniques provides a concrete queue time estimate. The pipeline RMSE was roughly 5 h of error, and the average queue time for jobs submitted to Beocat in 2018 was approximately 3 h and 45 min. The HPC at KSU has comparatively low queue times for jobs, and other HPC clusters may have queue time measured in the range of days, or even weeks. An overall 5 h error rate for the prediction for Beocat somewhat overshadows the average queue time in our case, but in other clusters, it might be more meaningful. In practice, queue times for Beocat are very left-skewed, and most of the jobs submitted to Beocat are executed after a very short period of time. Only very large jobs spend any significant amount of time in the queue waiting for resources.

It was shown that the average allocation of HPC CPUs over a 4 h window was an effective predictor for an increase or decrease of future queue time for jobs. This information could further inform machine learning models attempting to predict queue time for jobs. For instance, the linear regression model could be run before the queue time deadline assessment to determine if this contributes to an increase in the accuracy of the queue time prediction from the machine learning pipeline.

Finally, this queue time estimation tool could inform a decision to migrate a job to cloud resources instead of facing a long queue delay. Okanlawon, et al. [11] conducted research to better inform a user's decision to either resubmit a job with different resources or migrate that job to commercial cloud infrastructure. An accurate queue time estimation tool could offer another data point informing a user's decision.

6   Conclusion and Future Work

This research demonstrated that clustering and regression can also be applied to the task of queue time estimation for HPC systems. The machine learning pipeline described in this paper was more than 96% accurate at classifying whether a job would start before an assigned deadline. A simple linear regression model also achieved greater than 96% when attempting to predict if future queue times will increase or decrease. These pieces of information could prove vital to a researcher with a time critical application. It is also a meaningful metric for all HPC users, so they will be better informed about the start times of their jobs.

Additional analysis is needed to determine why certain jobs were grouped together into the clusters provided by K-Means. This research fed the cluster and job feature vector into the K-Means algorithm in search of the number of cluster producing a local minimum error rate. It is thought that additional analysis of clusters might shed light onto what is causing certain kinds of jobs to queue for longer times. Are there certain characteristics of jobs that cause them to sit in the queue longer? Are there certain characteristics or limitations of the HPC cluster itself which is contributing to longer queue times? Could additional HPC user education or better documentation mitigate queue time in some way? These remain open questions.

Our experience has been that users tend to drastically overestimate their job requirements at submission times. There is very little downside for a user who overestimates their resources at submission time. However, there is a very large downside if a job is killed before completion due to a user requesting insufficient resources at submit time. In the aggregate, however, mass overestimation of required resources leads to longer queue times for all users, which can negatively impact user experience overall. Tanash, et al. [13] have looked to machine learning to determine how actual allocated resources compared to what users have requested at submit time. Since this queue time predictor relied upon user submitted requirements for each job, adding a more accurate estimate of actual resources used would presumably improve the accuracy of a model predicting queue time.

Finally, informing the machine learning pipeline with the future queue time prediction may further improve the accuracy of the prediction made by the machine learning pipeline. It remains to be seen if first applying the future state of the HPC queue time prediction has measurable impacts on the accuracy of the clustering and regression pipeline.

References

1. Becker, D.J., Sterling, T., Savarese, D., Dorband, J.E., Ranawak, U.A., Packer, C.V.: Beowulf: a parallel workstation for scientific computation. In: Proceedings, International Conference on Parallel Processing, vol. 95, pp. 11–14 (1995)
2. Brown, N., Gibb, G., Belikov, E., Nash, R.: Predicting batch queue job wait times for informed scheduling of urgent hpc workloads. arXiv preprint arXiv:2204.13543 (2022)
3. Friedman, J.H.: Greedy function approximation: a gradient boosting machine. Ann. Stat. **29**, 1189–1232 (2001)
4. Henriques, J., Caldeira, F., Cruz, T., Simões, P.: Combining k-means and xgboost models for anomaly detection using log datasets. Electronics **9**(7), 1164 (2020)
5. Hunter, J.D.: Matplotlib: a 2d graphics environment. Comput. Sci. Eng. **9**(3), 90–95 (2007). https://doi.org/10.1109/MCSE.2007.55
6. Jancauskas, V., Piontek, T., Kopta, P., Bosak, B.: Predicting queue wait time probabilities for multi-scale computing. Philos. Trans. Roy. Soc. A **377**(2142), 20180151 (2019)
7. Kumar, R., Vadhiyar, S.: Prediction of queue waiting times for metascheduling on parallel batch systems. In: Cirne, W., Desai, N. (eds.) JSSPP 2014. LNCS, vol. 8828, pp. 108–128. Springer, Cham (2015). https://doi.org/10.1007/978-3-319-15789-4_7
8. Likas, A., Vlassis, N., Verbeek, J.J.: The global k-means clustering algorithm. Pattern Recogn. **36**(2), 451–461 (2003)

9. Liu, Y., Luo, H., Zhao, B., Zhao, X., Han, Z.: Short-term power load forecasting based on clustering and xgboost method. In: 2018 IEEE 9th International Conference on Software Engineering and Service Science (ICSESS), pp. 536–539. IEEE (2018)

10. Meng, X., et al.: Mllib: machine learning in apache spark. J. Mach. Learn. Res. **17**(1), 1235–1241 (2016)

11. Okanlawon, A., Yang, H., Bose, A., Hsu, W., Andresen, D., Tanash, M.: Feature selection for learning to predict outcomes of compute cluster jobs with application to decision support. In: 2020 International Conference on Computational Science and Computational Intelligence (CSCI), pp. 1231–1236. IEEE (2020)

12. Pearson, K.: Vii. note on regression and inheritance in the case of two parents. In: Proceedings of the Royal Society of London, vol. 58, pp. 347–352, 240–242 (1895)

13. Tanash, M., Dunn, B., Andresen, D., Hsu, W., Yang, H., Okanlawon, A.: Improving hpc system performance by predicting job resources via supervised machine learning. In: Proceedings of the Practice and Experience in Advanced Research Computing on Rise of the Machines (learning), pp. 1–8 (2019)

14. Thorndike, R.L.: Who belongs in the family. Psychometrika, pp. 267–276 (1953)

15. Van Rossum, G., Drake, F.L.: Python 3 Reference Manual. CreateSpace, Scotts Valley (2009)

16. Yoo, A.B., Jette, M.A., Grondona, M.: SLURM: simple linux utility for resource management. In: Feitelson, D., Rudolph, L., Schwiegelshohn, U. (eds.) JSSPP 2003. LNCS, vol. 2862, pp. 44–60. Springer, Heidelberg (2003). https://doi.org/10.1007/10968987_3

17. Zaharia, M., et al.: Apache spark: a unified engine for big data processing. Commun. ACM **59**(11), 56–65 (2016)

Acceptance Rates of Invertible Neural Networks on Electron Spectra from Near-Critical Laser-Plasmas: A Comparison

Thomas Miethlinger[1,2(✉)], Nico Hoffmann[1], and Thomas Kluge[1]

[1] Helmholtz -Zentrum Dresden -Rossendorf, 01328 Dresden, Germany
{t.miethlinger,n.hoffmann,t.kluge}@hzdr.de
[2] Technische Universität Dresden, 01069 Dresden, Germany

Abstract. While the interaction of ultra-intense ultra-short laser pulses with near- and overcritical plasmas cannot be directly observed, experimentally accessible quantities (observables) often only indirectly give information about the underlying plasma dynamics. Furthermore, the information provided by observables is incomplete, making the inverse problem highly ambiguous. Therefore, in order to infer plasma dynamics as well as experimental parameter, the full distribution over parameters given an observation needs to considered, requiring that models are flexible and account for the information lost in the forward process. Invertible Neural Networks (INNs) have been designed to efficiently model both the forward and inverse process, providing the full conditional posterior given a specific measurement. In this work, we benchmark INNs and standard statistical methods on synthetic electron spectra. First, we provide experimental results with respect to the acceptance rate, where our results show increases in acceptance rates up to a factor of 10. Additionally, we show that this increased acceptance rate also results in an increased speed-up for INNs to the same extent. Lastly, we propose a composite algorithm that utilizes INNs and promises low runtimes while preserving high accuracy.

Keywords: Invertible Neural Networks · Inverse Problems · Machine Learning · Particle-in-Cell · Laser-Plasma Physics

1 Introduction

Relativistic plasmas driven by ultra-intense ultra-short laser pulses are currently increasingly investigated due to various prospective applications in e.g. medicine, materials science and laboratory astrophysics. While the dynamics of *underdense* plasmas, i.e. plasmas with electron density n_e smaller than the critical plasma density n_c, can in principle be studied with optical methods as incoming light there is mostly transmitted, the situation is much more difficult for *near-critical* (mostly absorption, $n_e \approx n_c$) and *overdense* (mostly reflection, $n_e > n_c$) plasmas. Indeed, inferring experimental parameter values and consequently determining

© The Author(s), under exclusive license to Springer Nature Switzerland AG 2023
R. Wyrzykowski et al. (Eds.): PPAM 2022, LNCS 13827, pp. 273–284, 2023.
https://doi.org/10.1007/978-3-031-30445-3_23

the relevant underlying plasma dynamics is highly elaborate, heavily depending on comparisons with observables computed from plasma simulations where typically the Particle-in-Cell (PIC) method is employed [3,11]. Furthermore, the information provided by observables is incomplete in the sense that multiple experimental parameter and plasma dynamics can cause the same values for observables, but also retrieving information is regarded non-trivial since this process usually depends on fitting (scalar) quantities to analytical expressions which have been derived under strong assumptions.

This is, depending on the context, also the case for the *electron spectrum*, which counts the number of electrons dN_e in an energy interval dE:

$$f_e(E) := \frac{dN_e}{dE}. \tag{1}$$

In this work, we study *laser-driven ion acceleration* [9,15]. In this research field, where objectives concern ion-related properties, the electron spectrum is a secondary quantity that is sometimes measured in conjunction with the ion spectrum. Being a high-dimensional vector, however, the electron spectrum is difficult to interpret, infer parameters and draw conclusions from. Typically, one resorts to computing the *mean (kinetic) energy* of the laser-driven electrons[1]:

$$T_e := \frac{\int_{E_e^{\text{laser}}}^{\infty} E f_e(E) dE}{\int_{E_e^{\text{laser}}}^{\infty} f_e(E) dE}, \tag{2}$$

where the lower integration boundary E_e^{laser} is introduced to distinguish between electrons in thermal equilibrium and laser-driven electrons exhibiting an exponential distribution for high energies. One can then show, using analytical considerations, that the *ion cutoff energy*[2] scales linearly with the mean kinetic energy of the electrons, $E_i^{\max} \propto T_e$, and that the mean kinetic energy of the electrons itself mostly depends on the laser intensity I: $T_e = T_e(I)$ [14,16].

However, retrieving information from the electron spectrum beyond T_e in general requires an automatized, data-driven approach. This is all the more the case because PIC simulations are computationally (potentially very) expensive, which motivates researchers to this day to improve PIC simulation codes, for example, algorithmically or by improved hardware utilization [4,5]. Therefore, employing machine learning (ML) algorithms and ML-based surrogate models is essential to decrease the overall computational effort which would otherwise be needed due to the necessity of performing an excessive amount of simulations. For example, Djordjević et al. used deep learning to predict the time evolution of ion cutoff energies and electron mean kinetic energies in overdense laser-ion acceleration [8].

2   PIC Simulation Setup and Data Generation

In this work, we employ the PIC-code *Smilei* [5] to generate data for our ML models. Since the predominant acceleration mechanism in laser-ion acceleration is target-normal sheath-acceleration (TNSA), which is a one-dimensional

---

[1] Sometimes (unfortunately) also called *electron temperature*.

[2] Or, equivalently, the maximum ion energy in a laser-driven ion spectrum.

physical effect, and in order to significantly reduce the computational effort for this study, we use a narrow simulation box with $240\,\mu$m $\times$ $0.2\,\mu$m and impose periodic boundary conditions in the y-direction [19]. The cell size is $\Delta x = \Delta y = \frac{\lambda_0}{\text{resolution}} = \frac{800\text{ nm}}{64} = 12.5\,$nm, and the time step is $\Delta t = 0.995\frac{1}{\sqrt{2}}\frac{\Delta x}{c}$ corresponding to a Courant-Friedrichs-Lewy (CFL) value of 0.995. We initialize our plasma with 50 particles per cell. The target is a pre-expanded hydrogen foil with thickness D. Pre-plasma with exponential scale length ℓ is included at the front side of the target such that the density reaches a maximum n_0 at $x_{\text{f}} = 100\,\mu$m. Moreover, the pre-plasma is cut-off where the density is less than $0.01n_{\text{c}}$, i.e. $\forall x : n(x) < 0.01n_{\text{c}} \implies n(x) = 0$. The back side is not pre-expanded, i.e. the density is step-function-like shaped. The laser pulse is a Gaussian with full width at half maximum (FWHM) τ and normalized vector potential $a_0 = E/E_0 = E/(e^{-1}m_e c\omega_0)$, where E is the corresponding electric field, e is the elementary charge, m_e the electron mass, c the speed of light and $\omega_0 = 2\pi\frac{c}{\lambda_0}$ the angular frequency corresponding to the laser's central wavelength $\lambda_0 = 800\,$nm.

In this work, we performed 5000 simulations in total, varying the five parameters a_0, τ, n_0, D and ℓ. An overview of the parameter space that we studied in this work is given in Table 1. Thus, the laser intensity is in the range between $10^{20} \leq I(a_0)/\text{Wcm}^{-2} \leq 10^{21}$.

Table 1. Parameter space for PIC simulations.

Quantity	Symbol	Unit	Min	Max	Scaling
Normalized vector potential	a_0	1	6.8	21.5	Linear
Full width at half maximum	τ	fs	25	50	Linear
Number density (bulk)	n_0	n_{c}	15	60	Linear
Target thickness	D	μm	0.25	5	Linear
Pre-plasma scale length	ℓ	μm	0.01	1	Square

Since ML usually strongly benefits from using normalized and/or standardized values, we designed our experiments as follows:

- In an effort to have our simulations as space-filling as possible in parameter space, we obtained our parameter vectors $\mathbf{x} = [x_1, ..., x_5]^{\mathsf{T}}$ from a low-discrepency sequence. In particular, we used the *Halton sequence*, which is a common low-discrepancy sequence used in Monte Carlo integration and design of experiment, with dimension $n_{\mathbf{x}} = 5$ and support $\hat{x}_k \in [0,1] \forall k \in \{1, ..., 5\}$ [17].
- Since ℓ spans two orders of magnitude, we account for that by using a nonlinear transformation to obtain the parameter values x_k as used in our simulations. This can be expressed as follows:

$$x_k = \hat{x}_k^{\text{s}}(x_k^{\text{max}} - x_k^{\text{min}}) + x_k^{\text{min}}, \tag{3}$$

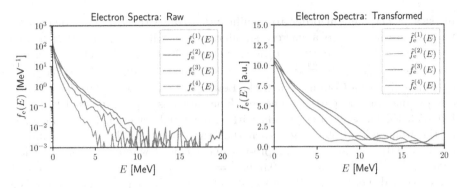

Fig. 1. Examples of electron spectra. Left: Raw spectra $f_e(E)$ as measured in the PIC simulations (note the logarithmic scale). Right: Nonlinearly transformed spectra $\tilde{f}_e(E)$.

where $x_k^{\min}$ and $x_k^{\max}$ refer to the parameter range of the kth parameter x_k, as defined in Table 1, and where the scaling exponent s refers to s $= 1$ for $k \leq 4$ (linear), and s $= 2$ for $k = 5$ (squared scaling for ℓ).

In each simulation, we measured the electron spectra 500 fs after the laser maximum reaches the target. The electron spectra were computed by binning the weights of electron macroparticles onto 200 bins with energies between 0 and 40 MeV. Furthermore, aiming to bridge the more than five orders of magnitude present in the raw electron spectra, we made a nonlinear transformation $\tilde{f}_e(E) = \left(\log\left(f_e/10^{-3} + 1\right) * g\right)(E)$, which ensures that $\min_E \tilde{f}_e(E) \geq 0$. Here, $*$ relates to the convolution operation, i.e. we smoothed our spectra with a Gaussian filter $g(E) = \frac{1}{\sqrt{2\pi}}e^{-E^2/2}$ to make the data more robust. A comparison of the raw electron spectra to the transformed spectra is provided in Fig. 1.

Given the limited data size, especially in relation to the relatively high number of bins, we experienced in our initial attempts of training a ML model from parameter vectors[3] $\mathbf{x}$ to electron spectra $\tilde{f}_e(E)$ that the training process is rather difficult and sensitive to hyperparameter. Therefore, in order to further simplify the training process, we expressed our transformed spectra in terms of a linear regression model. In particular, we performed principle component regression (PCR) using $n_\mathbf{y} = 6$ principle components $b_k(E)$:

$$\tilde{f}_e(E) \approx \sum_{k=1}^{6} c_k b_k(E) + \bar{\tilde{f}}_e, \tag{4}$$

where the c_k's are the coefficients corresponding to the basis functions $b_k(E)$, and $\bar{\tilde{f}}_e$ is the mean transformed spectrum. Thus, altogether we train our ML models to learn mappings between $\mathbf{x}$ and $\mathbf{y} := [c_1, ..., c_6]^{\mathsf{T}}$. Further information about

---

[3] Note that we use, for the sake of better of readability, henceforth the symbol $\mathbf{x}$ both for our simulation parameter $\mathbf{x}$ as well as normalized ML parameter $\hat{\mathbf{x}}$.

the ML models used and studied in this work and their training is provided in Sects. 3 and 4, respectively.

3   Invertible Neural Networks

In this work, we employ invertible neural networks (INNs) as described by Ardizzone et al. in [1]. They have been designed having in mind a common problem in natural sciences, namely that there exists a forward process (experiment, simulation, ...) f that maps a parameter vector $\mathbf{x} \in \mathbb{R}^{n_{\mathbf{x}}}$ onto experimentally accessible quantities which we call *observables* $\mathbf{y} = f(\mathbf{x}) \in \mathbb{R}^{n_{\mathbf{y}}}$. Typically, this forward process, at least formally, is well understood in the sense that there exists a (often highly sophisticated) theory that supports this mapping. However, one is most often interested in the *inverse process*, i.e. to gain information about experimentally inaccessible parameter given an experimental result. Furthermore, since the forward process intrinsically has in general accompanying information loss, the inverse direction can only be expressed probabilistically as this loss of information renders the inverse process ambiguous. In other words, multiple parameter vectors may correspond to the same observable. Therefore, we are interested in the complete set of solutions $\{\mathbf{x} \in \mathbb{R}^{n_{\mathbf{x}}} \mid f(\mathbf{x}) = \mathbf{y}\}$, i.e. the full *conditional posterior distribution* $p(\mathbf{x}|\mathbf{y})$ has to be determined.

In order to account for the information loss, INNs introduce a *latent space* of dimension $n_{\mathbf{z}}$ and elements $\mathbf{z} \sim \mathcal{N}(\mathbf{z}; \mathbf{0}, \mathbf{I})$. Then, the latent vectors are concatenated with the observables as $[\mathbf{y}, \mathbf{z}]$. Note that invertibility requires that $n_{\mathbf{x}} = n_{\mathbf{y}} + n_{\mathbf{z}}$, which can be realized by including zero-padding as required. In our case, since already $n_{\mathbf{x}} = 5 < n_{\mathbf{y}} = 6$, we fulfilled the aforementioned condition by padding our parameter vectors as $[\mathbf{x}, \mathbf{0}]$, where $\mathbf{0}$ stands for a $(n_{\mathbf{y}} + n_{\mathbf{z}} - n_{\mathbf{x}})$-dimensional zero vector. Then, INNs attain invertibility by composition of *affine coupling blocks* (ACBs), which are invertible themselves. While various different architectures for ACBs have been developed, in this work we use the Glow architecture[4], that is very similar on the RealNVP design [7,13]. In each ACB, the input is split into two parts $\mathbf{u} = [\mathbf{u}_1, \mathbf{u}_2]$ of equal size which are then transformed by an affine function using element-wise multiplication ($\odot$) and vector addition to an output $\mathbf{v} = [\mathbf{v}_1, \mathbf{v}_2]$:

$$
\begin{aligned}
\mathbf{v}_1 &= \mathbf{u}_1 \odot \exp(s_2(\mathbf{u}_2)) + t_2(\mathbf{u}_2), \\
\mathbf{v}_2 &= \mathbf{u}_2 \odot \exp(s_1(\mathbf{u}_1)) + t_1(\mathbf{u}_1).
\end{aligned}
\tag{5}
$$

Then, given the output $\mathbf{v} = [\mathbf{v}_1, \mathbf{v}_2]$, we can easily retrieve $\mathbf{u} = [\mathbf{u}_1, \mathbf{u}_2]$ as follows:

$$
\begin{aligned}
\mathbf{u}_2 &= (\mathbf{v}_2 - t_1(\mathbf{v}_1)) \odot \exp(-s_1(\mathbf{v}_1)), \\
\mathbf{u}_1 &= (\mathbf{v}_1 - t_2(\mathbf{u}_2)) \odot \exp(-s_2(\mathbf{u}_2)).
\end{aligned}
\tag{6}
$$

The functions $[s_i(\cdot), t_i(\cdot)]$, which are typically implemented as feedforward neural networks and hence called *subnetworks*, can be arbitrarily complicated functions

---

[4] Not including ActNorm, invertible 1×1 convolutions, etc. relevant for their specific application, but only the coupling part itself.

that need not be invertible themselves. We further elaborate on the design of the subnetworks in Sect. 4.

INNs are bi-directionally trained with losses $\mathcal{L}_{\mathbf{x}}, \mathcal{L}_{\mathbf{y}}$ and $\mathcal{L}_{\mathbf{z}}$ defined for $\mathbf{x}, \mathbf{y}$ and $\mathbf{z}$, respectively. While $\mathcal{L}_{\mathbf{y}}$ in general can be any supervised loss, we use the mean-squared loss (MSE) loss, $\mathcal{L}_{\mathbf{y}} = \mathbb{E}[(\mathbf{y} - f_{\mathbf{y}}(\mathbf{x}))^2]$. For $\mathcal{L}_{\mathbf{x}}$ and $\mathcal{L}_{\mathbf{z}}$ we use *maximum mean discrepancy* (MMD), which is a kernel-based, unsupervised loss on the space of probability distributions and which is based on reproducing kernel Hilbert spaces [10]. For our study, we used a multiscale inverse multiquadratic kernels as follows $k(\mathbf{x}, \mathbf{x}') = \sum_h 1/(1 + \|(\mathbf{x} - \mathbf{x}')/h\|_2^2)$, where the *bandwidth parameter* $h \in \{0.04, 0.16, 0.64\}$ are similar to the ones employed by Ardizzone et al. [1].

4   Results

We ran our experiments on the Taurus cluster at ZIH/TU Dresden. We used nodes of type Haswell, each node having two Intel Xeon E5-2680v3 @ 2.50 GHz processors with 30 MB L3 cache and 12 cores each, amounting to 24 cores per node. Each observation (1000 altogether), i.e. electron spectrum, was analyzed with one core. Each core has $2 \cdot 32$ KB L1 cache and 256 KB L2 cache. Each program is written in Python 3.9.12 and imports NumPy 1.21.5 and PyTorch 1.10.2.

We performed two different experiments: **(1)** we made a comparison of acceptance rates between different methods for solving the inverse problem and **(2)** then measured the actual time needed to find one accepted solution. These experiments were performed on hyperparameter optimized models as follows:

ML Models and Training. In this study, we both employ a multilayer perceptron (MLP) that we use as our reference model for the forward process $f(\cdot)$ only, and an INN for solving the inverse problem. For the training of the MLP, we again use MSE loss, corresponding to the $\mathcal{L}_{\mathbf{y}}$ loss of the INN. For both models we splitted our data into 80% train and 20% test set[5], and we used in both cases the *Adam* optimizer with learning rate $\alpha = 0.001$ and betas $\beta_1 = 0.9, \beta_2 = 0.999$ for training [12]. Furthermore, we performed a hyperparameter optimization for the MLP with regards to:

1. the activation function $\sigma(\cdot)$: ReLU$(\cdot)$, Tanh$(\cdot)$,
2. widths of hidden layers: 12, 16, 20, 24, 30,
3. number of layers: 3, 4, 5,

where we found that the setting MLP: $\{\text{Tanh}(\cdot), 16, 4\}$ shows the lowest loss for the test set. For the INN, we extend the hyperparameter optimization with regards to the dimension of the latent space $n_{\mathbf{z}}$, and the number of affine coupling blocks (ACBs):

---

[5] I.e. 4000 and 1000 data points for the train and test set, respectively.

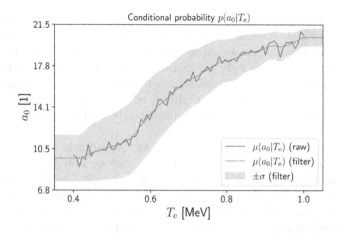

Fig. 2. Conditional probability $p(a_0|T_e)$ used as prior in the modified ABC routine.

1. the activation function $\sigma(\cdot)$: ReLU$(\cdot)$, Tanh$(\cdot)$,
2. widths of layers in subnetworks: 12, 16, 20, 24, 30,
3. number of layers in subnetworks: 2, 3, 4,
4. dimension $n_{\mathbf{z}}$: 2, 3, 4, 5, 6,
5. number of ACBs: 2, 3, 4, 5, 6,

where the best results, in terms of $\mathcal{L}_{\mathbf{x}} + \mathcal{L}_{\mathbf{y}}$, were obtained with the setting INN: {Tanh$(\cdot)$, 20, 3, 6, 5}. Note that the optimal number of ACBs in our case is larger than proposed by Dinh who generally suggests to use four ACBs [6].

4.1   Acceptance Rate

In the first experiment we compared, in terms of their acceptance rates, different methods suitable for (approximately) solving the inverse problem, i.e. to find a set of samples $\{\mathbf{x}\}$ that is representative for the conditional posterior $p(\mathbf{x}|\mathbf{y}^\star)$ conditioned on a specific measurement $\mathbf{y}^\star$. We call a parameter vector $\mathbf{x}$ to be accepted if the acceptance condition:

$$d(\mathbf{y}^\star, f(\mathbf{x})) \leq \epsilon, \tag{7}$$

is fulfilled, where $f(\cdot)$ is, in this study, the hyperparameter optimized MLP, $d(\cdot, \cdot)$ is a suitable distance function and ϵ is a non-negative threshold.

Approximate Bayesian Computation. If a surrogate model for the forward process is available, then one standard method to find an approximate solution for the inverse problem is *approximate Bayesian computation* (ABC) [2]. In ABC, the forward process f is embedded in a rejection-sampling scheme, i.e. the forward model is employed by randomly sampling $\mathbf{x}$ from the parameter space and subsequently checking for the acceptance condition.

In practice, depending on the problem's complexity as well as $\mathbf{y}^\star$ and ϵ, finding an appropriately sized set of solutions might require the evaluation of f for millions of times. Furthermore, since the algorithm is, per construction, subject to randomness, one can simply get "unlucky", consequently spending excessive amounts of compute time. Therefore, in order to speed up the expected convergence, we also performed an experiment where we again used quasi-random numbers produced from the Halton sequence instead of purely randomly generated numbers.

Moreover, since in naive ABC we don't include prior knowledge as we draw samples (quasi)randomly from the parameter space and therefore implicitly assume a multivariate uniform distribution as our prior, we don't sample optimally and thus increase the computational effort. Consequently, in order to study the effect of a non-uniform prior, we also conducted an experiment in which we draw a_0 based on a probability density function $p(a_0|T_e)$, since $T_e = T_e(I(a_0))$. The corresponding probability distribution is illustrated in Fig. 2 and was numerically computed by applying Bayes' rule on the train set data.

Hill-Climbing. On the other hand, instead of randomly trying different parameter vectors $\mathbf{x}$ as in ABC, local search algorithms such as hill-climbing (HC) and related methods try to find solutions by incrementally improving the current state [18]. While typically gradient-based approaches are preferred, hill-climbing can be used also if only a black-box model is available. Arguably it's simplest form, and also as implemented in this work, is first-choice hill-climbing, where the current solution is updated directly as soon as a better candidate solution has been found. Considering that ABC produces a set of uncorrelated samples, however, it is necessary in HC, once having found the first solution, to restart the search for the next solution at a randomly chosen location in order also obtain a statistically uncorrelated sample. A pseudocode of our implementation of first-choice hill-climbing is provided in the procedure FirstChoiceHillClimbing in Algorithm 1. For our experiments, we used a learning rate of $\alpha = 10^{-3}$, as commonly used in ML, and a learning rate of $\alpha = 10^{-2}$ for comparison.

Comparison. A comparison of the three different methods (ABC, HC and INN) and their specific settings is provided in Fig. 3. First, we chose our test set of 1000 electron spectra $f_e(E)$ and computed their PCR coefficients as described in Sect. 2. Second, with the intention of obtaining a *relative* measure of similarity, we define our distance function $d(\cdot, \cdot)$ based on the L^2 distance as follows:

$$d[f(E), g(E)] = \frac{\sqrt{\int (f(E) - g(E))^2 \mathrm{d}E}}{\sqrt{\int g^2(E) \mathrm{d}E}}, \tag{8}$$

where $f(E)$ represents an electron spectrum containing errors, e.g. as proposed by one of our inverse solver, and $g(E)$ is the reference ground truth spectrum function. In this work, $g(E)$ corresponds to the transformed electron spectrum

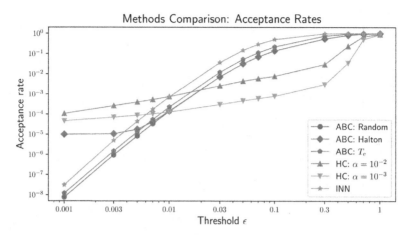

Fig. 3. Acceptance rates of different approaches for obtaining $p(\mathbf{x}|\mathbf{y}^\star)$ in dependence of acceptance threshold ϵ, averaged over 1000 different electron spectra.

of the reference model, i.e. after the PCR procedure, and the lower and upper limits of integration are again $0\,\mathrm{MeV}$ and $40\,\mathrm{MeV}$, respectively. At last, using 10 iterations with $m_{\mathrm{trial}} = 10^5$, we compute the acceptance rate as the ratio of accepted solutions to all$(= 10 \cdot m_{\mathrm{trial}} = 10^6)$ tested solutions.

From Fig. 3 can see that the efficiency of a method heavily depends on the acceptance threshold ϵ. Not surprisingly, naive ABC using random numbers shows a rather low acceptance rate regardless of ϵ. Furthermore, ABC using quasi-random numbers behaves the same as naive ABC for larger ϵ, since then the law of large numbers becomes relevant, and shows significantly better performance for smaller thresholds where $\epsilon \leq 5 \cdot 10^{-3}$. A further improvement can be achieved by using an informed prior for a_0: On average, the acceptance rate increases approximately by a factor of 2 when compared to uninformed ABC. However, interestingly, it can be seen that the acceptance rate is more than two orders of magnitude smaller than simply using ABC with the Halton sequence for $\epsilon = 10^{-3}$. This can be understood by noting that in this case parameters are again sampled randomly, and thus don't exhibit the enhanced space-filling property as in the Halton case. The largest acceptance rates for small ϵ were obtained by the hill-climbing methods, which are higher by around one order of magnitude. We can deduce, from the big drop in the acceptance rate of HC for large ϵ, that HC first needs many steps to approach a region of reasonably small distance after which, however, it apparently only takes minimal effort to further optimize the solution. While HC with learning rate $\alpha = 10^{-2}$ always beats HC with learning rate of $\alpha = 10^{-3}$, we can also see that the difference significantly decreases for decreasing ϵ. On the other hand, the largest acceptance rates for $\epsilon \geq 10^{-2}$ were obtained by the INN. For $\epsilon \leq 5 \cdot 10^{-3}$, the INN shows worse performance than both configurations of HC. Then, around $\epsilon \approx 3 \cdot 10^{-3}$, the INN also exhibits lower acceptance rates than Halton-based ABC. Again, the reason is that latent vectors $\mathbf{z}$ are sampled randomly from the multivariate

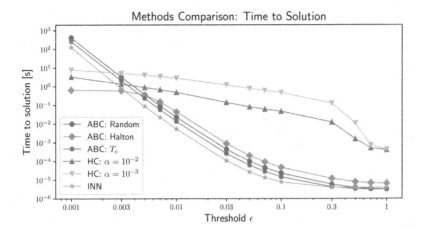

Fig. 4. Time to solution, i.e. of a single acceptance, of different approaches for obtaining $p(\mathbf{x}|\mathbf{y}^\star)$ in dependence of acceptance threshold ϵ, averaged over 1000 different electron spectra.

normal distribution, and not from a quasi-random sequence. Therefore, for the full range of ϵ, the INN always surpasses the acceptance rate of ABC: Random and ABC T_e, since they are also both based on random numbers rather than a quasi-random sequence.

4.2   Runtimes

While the acceptance rate is more interesting for theoretical analysis, in practice we are interested in the actual computational cost, e.g. in terms of the runtime. We performed the same experiment as before, but instead we measured the total runtime relative to the number of accepted samples, $t_{\text{total}}/m_{\text{acc}}$. Again, we average our results over the same 1000 electron spectra from the test set. The result is depicted in Fig. 4.

We can see that general trends are preserved, e.g. that the INN is the fastest method up until $\epsilon \geq 3 \cdot 10^{-3}$ and that ABC with informed prior is always faster than naive ABC. HC is still a fast method for very small thresholds. However, the relative runtimes difference between HC and all other methods decreased by around two order of magnitude when compared to the relative difference in acceptance rate. This can be understood as HC uses loops and needs to call $f(\cdot)$ many times, while e.g. ABC calls the forward function only once for all proposal vectors and therefore takes advantage of optimized matrix operations. Hence, to ensure efficient computation, HC should as well be embedded in parallel procedures. We can also see that using the INN does not cause any significant overhead, since the relative speedup is approximately conserved with respect to the relative increase in acceptance rate.

Thus, in order find uncorrelated samples for the inverse problem, the method should be chosen having the required accuracy in mind. An algorithm based on

Algorithm 1. INN-HC: Inverse solver optimized for low acceptance thresholds.

```
 1: procedure INVERSESOLVER(y*, m, f, inn, d, ϵ, α)
 2:     Y* ← vstack(y*, m)                    ▷ Vertically stack y*, i.e. Y* ∈ ℝ^(m×n_y)
 3:     Z ← rand(𝒩(0,1), (m, n_z))                              ▷ Z ∈ ℝ^(m×n_z)
 4:     X ← inn⁻¹([Y*, Z])
 5:     for i in 1, ..., m do
 6:         x ← X_{i,·}
 7:         if d(y*, f(x)) > ϵ then
 8:             x ← FirstChoiceHillClimbing(y*, f, d, ϵ, x, α)
 9:         X_{i,·} ← x
10:     return X

11: procedure FIRSTCHOICEHILLCLIMBING(y*, f, d, ϵ, x₀, α)
12:     x ← x₀
13:     while d(y*, f(x)) > ϵ do
14:         ξ ← rand(𝒰([−1, 1]), (n_x))         ▷ Generate vector with random direction
15:         ξ ← ξ/|ξ|                            ▷ Normalize to unit length
16:         x̃ ← x + αξ
17:         if d(y*, f(x̃)) ≤ d(y*, f(x)) then
18:             x ← x̃.
19:     return x
```

the combination of an INN and HC, which is designed to also work for very small thresholds, is provided in Algorithm 1.

5 Conclusion

In this work, we have studied INNs on synthetic electron spectra in the context of near-critical laser-plasma physics. In particular, we compared INNs with other standard statistical methods for solving the inverse process. We found that INNs perform, both in terms of acceptance rates as well as runtimes, better than all other methods up to a small threshold distance. Furthermore, we show that naive ABC based on random numbers has lower acceptance rates and larger runtimes than our INN model by a factor of approximately 10 for any threshold. INNs also surpass informed ABC, where we used a modified prior $p(a_0|T_e)$ that we motivated due to physical considerations, by a significant amount. Moreover, we demonstrate the importance of quasi-random numbers and recommend to use them as well in conjunction with INNs. On the other hand, our results suggest that iterative approaches, in our case hill-climbing, surpass INNs for small thresholds $\epsilon \leq 3 \cdot 10^{-3}$, especially in terms of the acceptance rate. Therefore, due to the relative strengths of the different algorithms, we propose a composite algorithm for obtaining the conditional posterior that combines both hill-climbing and INNs.

References

1. Ardizzone, L., Kruse, J., Rother, C., Köthe, U.: Analyzing inverse problems with invertible neural networks (2018). http://arxiv.org/abs/10.48550/ARXIV.1808.04730
2. Beaumont, M.A.: Approximate bayesian computation. Ann. Rev. Stat. Appl. **6**, 379–403 (2019). https://doi.org/10.1146/annurev-statistics-030718-105212
3. Birdsall, C.K., Langdon, A.B.: Plasma Physics via Computer Simulation. CRC Press, Boca Raton (2018)
4. Burau, H., et al.: Picongpu: a fully relativistic particle-in-cell code for a GPU cluster. IEEE Trans. Plasma Sci. **38**(10), 2831–2839 (2010). https://doi.org/10.1109/tps.2010.2064310
5. Derouillat, J., et al.: Smilei: a collaborative, open-source, multi-purpose particle-in-cell code for plasma simulation. Comput. Phys. Commun. **222**, 351–373 (2018). https://doi.org/10.1016/j.cpc.2017.09.024
6. Dinh, L., Krueger, D., Bengio, Y.: Nice: Non-linear independent components estimation. arXiv preprint arXiv:1410.8516 (2014). https://doi.org/10.48550/ARXIV.1410.8516
7. Dinh, L., Sohl-Dickstein, J., Bengio, S.: Density estimation using real NVP (2016). https://doi.org/10.48550/ARXIV.1605.08803
8. Djordjević, B.Z., et al.: Modeling laser-driven ion acceleration with deep learning. Phys. Plasmas **28**(4), 043105 (2021). https://doi.org/10.1063/5.0045449
9. Gibbon, P.: Short-Pulse Laser Interactions with Matter: an Introduction. World Scientific, Singapore (2005)
10. Gretton, A., Borgwardt, K.M., Rasch, M.J., Schölkopf, B., Smola, A.: A kernel two-sample test. J. Mach. Learn. Res. **13**(1), 723–773 (2012)
11. Hockney, R.W., Eastwood, J.W.: Computer Simulation using Particles. CRC Press, Boca Raton (2021)
12. Kingma, D.P., Ba, J.: Adam: a method for stochastic optimization (2014). https://doi.org/10.48550/ARXIV.1412.6980
13. Kingma, D.P., Dhariwal, P.: Glow: Generative flow with invertible 1×1 convolutions. In: Advances in Neural Information Processing Systems, vol. 31 (2018)
14. Kluge, T., Cowan, T., Debus, A., Schramm, U., Zeil, K., Bussmann, M.: Electron temperature scaling in laser interaction with solids. Phys. Rev. Lett. **107**(20), 205003 (2011). https://doi.org/10.1103/PhysRevLett.107.205003
15. Macchi, A.: A review of laser-plasma ion acceleration (2017). https://doi.org/10.48550/ARXIV.1712.06443
16. Mora, P.: Plasma expansion into a vacuum. Phys. Rev. Lett. **90**(18), 185002 (2003). https://doi.org/10.1103/PhysRevLett.90.185002
17. Niederreiter, H.: Random number generation and quasi-monte Carlo methods. SIAM (1992). https://doi.org/10.1137/1.9781611970081
18. Russel, S., Norvig, P., et al.: Artificial Intelligence: A Modern Approach. Pearson Education Limited, London (2013)
19. Wilks, S.C., et al.: Energetic proton generation in ultra-intense laser-solid interactions. Phys. Plasmas **8**(2), 542–549 (2001). https://doi.org/10.1063/1.1333697

4th Workshop on Applied High Performance Numerical Algorithms for PDEs

MATLAB Implementation of Hp Finite Elements on Rectangles Using Hierarchical Basis Functions

Alexej Moskovka[1] and Jan Valdman[2,3(✉)]

[1] Department of Mathematics, Faculty of Applied Sciences, University of West Bohemia, Technická 8, 30100 Plzeň, Czech Republic
[2] Department of Computer Science, Faculty of Science, University of South Bohemia, Branišovská 31, 37005 České Budějovice, Czech Republic
[3] The Czech Academy of Sciences, Institute of Information Theory and Automation, Pod vodárenskou věží 4, 18208, Prague 8, Czech Republic
jan.valdman@utia.cas.cz

Abstract. A MATLAB implementation of hierarchical shape functions on 2D rectangles is explained and available for download. Global shape functions are ordered for a given polynomial degree according to the indices of the nodes, edges, or elements to which they belong. For a uniform p-refinement, the hierarchical structure enables an effective assembly of mass and stiffness matrices. A solution to a boundary value problem is approximated for various levels of uniform h and p refinements.

Keywords: MATLAB vectorization · finite elements · mass and stiffness matrices · uniform hp-refinement · boundary value problem

1 Introduction

hp-FEM is a numerical method for solving partial differential equations based on piecewise polynomial approximations that employ elements of variable size (h) and degree of the polynomial (p). The origins of hp-FEM date back to the work of Ivo Babuška and his coauthors in the early 1980 s s (e.g. [11,12]) who discovered that the finite element method converges exponentially fast when the mesh is refined using a suitable combination of h-refinements (dividing elements into smaller ones) and p-refinements (increasing their polynomial degree). Many books (e.g. [3,4,6,9]) have been written explaining the methodology of hp-FEM accompanied by software codes [13,14] in C++. Implementing hierarchical shape functions, particularly in the case of hp adaptivity, is not straightforward, and

A. Moskovka was supported by the MSMT CR project 8J21AT001 Model Reduction and Optimal Control in Thermomechanics. J. Valdman announces the support of the Czech Science Foundation (GACR) through the GF21-06569K grant Scales and shapes in continuum thermomechanics.

© The Author(s), under exclusive license to Springer Nature Switzerland AG 2023
R. Wyrzykowski et al. (Eds.): PPAM 2022, LNCS 13827, pp. 287–299, 2023.
https://doi.org/10.1007/978-3-031-30445-3_24

special data structures are needed [5,10]. A recent MATLAB contribution [8] provides an object-oriented approach to implement hp-FEM on triangles with adaptive h-refinement.

Our focus is on a simple hp-FEM implementation on rectangles directly based on [4]. We provide eight examples that demonstrate the basics of hp-FEM assemblies, including:

- constructions of basis functions and their isoparametric transformations to general quadrilaterals (Sect. 2),
- the ordering of global shape functions using indexing matrices (Sect. 3),
- assemblies of the mass and stiffness matrices (Sect. 4),
- solution of a particular diffusion-reaction boundary value problem using uniform h and p refinements (Sect. 5).

A complementary software for this paper is available at

https://www.mathworks.com/matlabcentral/fileexchange/111420

for download and testing. The codes for the evaluation of the shape functions were provided by Dr. Sanjib Kumar Acharya (Mumbai). The assemblies of FEM matrices are partially based on vectorization techniques of [1,2]. The names of most of the mesh attributes and the domain triangulation algorithms are taken from [7].

2   Hierarchic Shape Functions

We consider the basis functions for the dimensions of space $d \in \{1,2\}$ (see [4]). For a reference element $T_{ref} = [-1,1]^d$ and $p \in \mathbb{N}$ we denote by

$$S^p(T_{ref}) \tag{1}$$

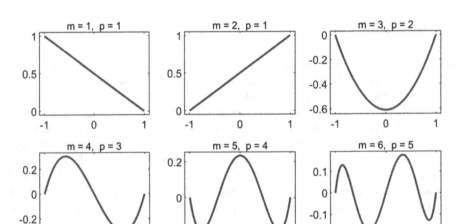

Fig. 1. The hierarchic shape basis functions $N_m(\xi)$, $m = 1, \ldots, 6$, where p is the corresponding polynomial degree.

the space of polynomials of degree p defined on T_{ref}. The basis functions that span the space are called shape functions. We define them using Legendre polynomials for $x \in [-1, 1]$:

$$P_0(x) = 1, \quad P_1(x) = x,$$

$$P_{n+1}(x) = \frac{(2n + 1) \, x \, P_n(x) - n \, P_{n-1}(x)}{n + 1}, \qquad n \geq 1. \tag{2}$$

Hierarchic shape functions on $T_{ref} = [-1, 1]$ are functions $N_m(\xi) : T_{ref} \to \mathbb{R}$, $m \in \mathbb{N}$ defined using (2) as:

$$N_1(\xi) = \frac{1 - \xi}{2}, \quad N_2(\xi) = \frac{1 + \xi}{2},$$

$$N_m(\xi) = \frac{1}{\sqrt{2(2m - 3)}} \left(P_{m-1}(\xi) - P_{m-3}(\xi) \right), \qquad m \geq 3. \tag{3}$$

All $N_m(\xi)$, $m \geq 3$ vanishes at the endpoints of T_{ref}.

Example 1. The first hierarchical shape functions are shown in Fig. 1 and the pictures can be reproduced by the script

```
example1_draw_hp_basis_1D
```

2.1   Hierarchic Shape Functions on $T_{ref} = [-1, 1]^2$

For $p \in \mathbb{N}$ we define the trunk space $S^p(T_{ref})$ spanned by polynomials $\xi^i \eta^j$, where $i, j \in \mathbb{N}_0$ satisfies $i + j \leq p$, supplemented by the polynomial $\xi \eta$ for $p = 1$ and the polynomials $\xi^p \eta$, $\xi \eta^p$ for $p \geq 2$. Its dimension is given by

$$n_{p,ref} = \dim(S^p(T_{ref})) = \begin{cases} 4p, & p \leq 3 \\ 4p + (p - 2)(p - 3)/2, & p \geq 4. \end{cases} \tag{4}$$

There are three types of 2D shape functions: nodal (Q1), edge, and bubble (sometimes called internal). The nodal shape functions that span the space $S^1(T_{ref})$ are defined as follows:

$$N_1(\xi, \eta) = \frac{1}{4}(1 - \xi)(1 - \eta), \qquad N_2(\xi, \eta) = \frac{1}{4}(1 + \xi)(1 - \eta),$$

$$N_3(\xi, \eta) = \frac{1}{4}(1 + \xi)(1 + \eta), \qquad N_4(\xi, \eta) = \frac{1}{4}(1 - \xi)(1 + \eta). \tag{5}$$

The function of the i-th nodal shape is equal to one in the i-th node of T_{ref} and vanishes in other nodes. The edge shape functions are constructed by multiplying one-dimensional shape functions $N_m(\xi)$, $m \geq 3$ from (3) by linear blending functions. We define $\phi_p(x) = N_{p+1}(x)$, $p \geq 2$, and the edge shape functions by

$$N_p^{(1)}(\xi, \eta) = \frac{1}{2}(1 - \eta) \, \phi_p(\xi), \qquad N_p^{(2)}(\xi, \eta) = \frac{1}{2}(1 + \xi) \, \phi_p(\eta),$$

$$N_p^{(3)}(\xi, \eta) = \frac{1}{2}(1 + \eta) \, \phi_p(-\xi), \qquad N_p^{(4)}(\xi, \eta) = \frac{1}{2}(1 - \xi) \, \phi_p(-\eta). \tag{6}$$

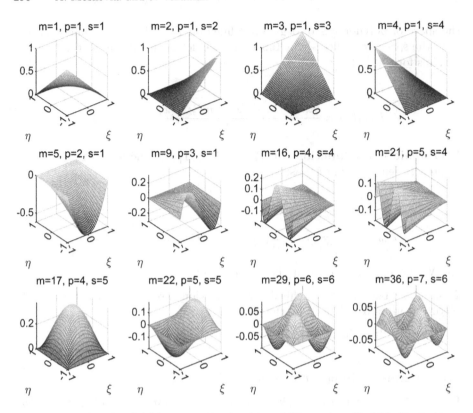

Fig. 2. Examples of nodal (the top row), edge (the middle row) and bubble (the bottom row) shape functions. Here, m denotes the index of the shape function, p its polynomial degree and s is the local index.

For $j \in \{1,2,3,4\}$, the restriction of $N_p^{(j)}$ on the j-th edge is equal to the corresponding one-dimensional edge shape function of the p-th degree, and it vanishes along the other edges. The bubble functions are defined as

$$N_p^{\beta}(\xi,\eta) = \phi_{p-(\beta+1)}(\xi)\,\phi_{\beta+1}(\eta)\,, \qquad 1 \leq \beta \leq p-3\,, \quad p \geq 4 \qquad (7)$$

and any of them attains zero values on all edges. Table 1 shows the number of shape functions in T_{ref} for $1 \leq p \leq 7$.

Local Indexing. The shape functions of the p th degree in T_{ref} are ordered by a unique index $m \in \mathbb{N}$ given by

$$m = \begin{cases} 4(p-1) + s\,, & \text{for } p \leq 4\,, \\ 4(p-1) + (p-3)(p-4)/2 + s\,, & \text{for } p \geq 5\,, \end{cases} \qquad (8)$$

where for $p = 1$: s is the index of a node $i \in \{1,2,3,4\}$,
for $p \geq 2$: s is the index of an edge $j \in \{1,2,3,4\}$,

Table 1. The numbers of shape functions.

polynomial degree p	# of nodal functions	# of edge functions	# of bubble functions	# of all functions
1	4	0	0	4
2	4	4	0	8
3	4	8	0	12
4	4	12	1	17
5	4	16	3	23
6	4	20	6	30
7	4	24	10	38

for $p \geq 4$: $s = 4 + \beta$, where β is the local index of a bubble function (7).

Example 2. Several shape functions are depicted in Fig. 2 and can be reproduced by the script

```
example2_draw_hp_basis_2D
```

The degree of the polynomial p and the local index s are evaluated by the function [s,p] = shapeindx(m).

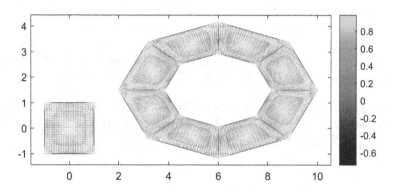

Fig. 3. The isoparametric transformation of T_{ref} indicated by the blue frame (bottom-left) to eight quadrilaterals indicated by red frames (right) and the transformation of the function $\cos\left(\frac{3\pi}{4}\xi\right)\cos\left(\frac{3\pi}{4}\eta\right)$ approximated for $p = 4$. (Color figure online)

Mapping From T_{ref} to a quadrilateral T. Transformation of a reference element T_{ref} to a quadrilateral T is performed by the isoparametric mapping $Q : T_{ref} \to T$ defined as $(x,y)(\xi,\eta) = Q(\xi,\eta)$, where

$$Q(\xi,\eta) = \left(\sum_{i=1}^{4} X_i \, N_i(\xi,\eta), \sum_{i=1}^{4} Y_i \, N_i(\xi,\eta) \right), \tag{9}$$

and (X_i, Y_i), $i \in \{1,2,3,4\}$ are the coordinates of the i-th node of T. For a given $p \in \mathbb{N}$, we denote by

$$S^p(T) \tag{10}$$

the space of functions spanned by $N_m\big(Q^{-1}(x,y)\big)$, where $N_m \in S^p(T_{ref})$.

Example 3. The transformation of T_{ref} into eight different quadrilaterals form-ing a flattened annulus is shown in Fig. 3 and can be reproduced using the script

```
example3_isoparametric_transformation
```

It also visualizes the approximation of the function $f(\xi, \eta) = \cos\left(\frac{3\pi}{4}\xi\right)\cos\left(\frac{3\pi}{4}\eta\right)$, $(\xi, \eta) \in T_{ref}$ for $p = 4$ and its transformation into quadrilaterals.

3   Global Shape Functions

A domain $\Omega \subset \mathbb{R}^2$ is approximated by a triangulation T into closed elements (quadrilaterals). We denote by $\mathcal{N}, \mathcal{E}$ and T the sets of nodes, edges, and elements, respectively, and by $|\mathcal{N}|, |\mathcal{E}|$ and $|T|$ their sizes. For a given $p \in \mathbb{N}$ we define it by

$$S^p(T) \tag{11}$$

the space of all global shape functions on T and by n_p its dimension given by

$$n_p = \begin{cases} |\mathcal{N}| + (p-1)|\mathcal{E}|, & p \le 3, \\ |\mathcal{N}| + (p-1)|\mathcal{E}| + \frac{1}{2}(p-2)(p-3)|T|, & p \ge 4. \end{cases} \tag{12}$$

We denote by $N_m^{(g)}$, $1 \le m \le n_p$ the m-th global shape function defined by its restrictions on elements $T_k \in T$, $1 \le k \le |T|$ in the following way:

$N_m^{(g)}$ is a nodal shape function corresponding to the i-th node: If T_k is adjacent to the i-th node, then $N_m^{(g)}\big|_{T_k} = \tilde{N}_{l,k}$, where $\tilde{N}_{l,k}$ is the l-th local nodal shape function on T_k which is equal to one in the i-th node. Otherwise, $N_m^{(g)} = 0$.

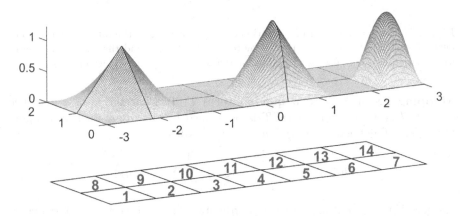

Fig. 4. Function $u \in S^p(T) \in$ of (13) and the underlying rectangular mesh with indices of elements.

$N_m^{(g)}$ is an edge shape function corresponding to the j-th edge: If T_k is adjacent to the j-th edge, then $N_m^{(g)}\big|_{T_k} = \tilde{N}_{l,k}$, where $\tilde{N}_{l,k}$ is the l-th local edge shape function on T_k whose restriction on the j-th edge is the corresponding edge shape function in 1D. Otherwise, $N_m^{(g)} = 0$.

$N_m^{(g)}$ is a bubble shape function corresponding to the k-th element: $N_m^{(g)}\big|_{T_k} = \tilde{N}_{l,k}$, where $\tilde{N}_{l,k}$ is the corresponding l-th local bubble shape function on the k-th element. Otherwise, $N_m^{(g)} = 0$.

Example 4. We assume a triangulation $\mathcal{T}$ of $\Omega = (-3,3) \times (0,2)$ with $|\mathcal{N}| = 24$, $|\mathcal{E}| = 37$, $|\mathcal{T}| = 14$, $n_p = 149$ and the function $u \in S^4(\mathcal{T})$ defined as

$$u(x,y) = N_{10}^{(g)}(x,y) - 2N_{34}^{(g)}(x,y) - 2N_{142}^{(g)}(x,y), \qquad (x,y) \in \Omega \qquad (13)$$

shown in Fig. 4. The nodal function $N_{10}^{(g)}$ corresponds to the node adjacent to T_1, T_2, T_8, T_9, the edge function $N_{34}^{(g)}$ to the edge adjacent to T_4, T_5, and the bubble function $N_{142}^{(g)}$ is defined in T_7. Figure 4 is generated by the script

```
example4_draw_hp_basis_2D_global
```

3.1   Global Indexing

The relation between the topology of $\mathcal{T}$ and the global shape function indices is represented by three essential matrices.

Table 2. The matrix $B(\mathcal{T},p)$ for $\mathcal{T}$ with $|\mathcal{N}| = 4$, $|\mathcal{E}| = 4$, $|\mathcal{T}| = 1$ and $p = 5$. Zero values are replaced by symbol $'-'$.

p	the global node index	the global edge index	the global element index	the local bubble index
1	1	–	–	–
1	2	–	–	–
1	3	–	–	–
1	4	–	–	–
2	–	1	–	–
2	–	2	–	–
2	–	3	–	–
2	–	4	–	–
3	–	1	–	–
3	–	2	–	–
3	–	3	–	–
3	–	4	–	–
4	–	1	–	–
4	–	2	–	–
4	–	3	–	–
4	–	4	–	–
4	–	–	1	1
5	–	1	–	–
5	–	2	–	–
5	–	3	–	–
5	–	4	–	–
5	–	–	1	1
5	–	–	1	2

A Matrix $B(\mathcal{T}, p)$ is of size $n_p \times 5$ and stores the key attributes of the global shape functions $N_m^{(g)} \in S^p(\mathcal{T})$, $1 \le m \le n_p$ which are uniquely determined by: the degree of $N_m^{(g)}$ (the first column of $B(\mathcal{T}, p)$), the type of $N_m^{(g)}$ (nodal, edge or bubble) specified by the global index of the respective node (the 2nd column), edge (the 3rd column), or element (the 4th column). Additionally, the type of bubble requires a local index of a bubble (the 5th column). The key advantage of this approach is that for the same $\mathcal{T}$ and $1 \le p_1 < p_2$ the first n_{p_1} rows of both matrices $B(\mathcal{T}, p_1)$ and $B(\mathcal{T}, p_2)$ are the same.

A Matrix $C(\mathcal{T}, p)$ of size $n_{p,ref} \times |\mathcal{T}|$ collects for individual elements the indices of the corresponding global functions. In particular, $C_{l,k}(\mathcal{T}, p) = m$ means that $N_m^{(g)}\big|_{T_k}$ corresponds to the l-th local shape function on the k-th element.

A Matrix $S(\mathcal{T}, p)$ of size $n_{p,ref} \times |\mathcal{T}|$ for the l-th row and the k-th column returns the sign of the l-th local function on the k-th element. For edges adjacent to two elements, the corresponding local edge functions of odd degrees have to be assigned opposite signs to ensure the continuity of the corresponding global edge functions.

Example 5. We assume a triangulation $\mathcal{T}$ with $|\mathcal{N}| = 4$, $|\mathcal{E}| = 4$, and $|\mathcal{T}| = 1$. Tab. 2 depicts for $p = 5$ the corresponding matrix $B(\mathcal{T}, p)$ with 23 (the value of n_p) rows and 5 columns that can be generated by the script

```
example5_B_matrix
```

Example 6. We assume a triangulation $\mathcal{T}$ with $|\mathcal{N}| = 6$, $|\mathcal{E}| = 7$ and $|\mathcal{T}| = 2$. Tab. 3 depicts for $p = 3$ the corresponding matrices $C(\mathcal{T}, p)$ and $S(\mathcal{T}, p)$ with 12 (the value of $n_{p,ref}$) rows and 2 (the value of $\mathcal{T}$) columns that can be generated by script

```
example6_C_S_matrices
```

Fig. 5 shows the global edge function $N_{17}^{(g)}$ of the 3rd degree. The left part exploits the right orientation with opposite signs providing continuity, and the right part exploits the wrong orientation leading to discontinuity.

Table 3. Matrices $C(\mathcal{T}, p)$ (left) and $S(\mathcal{T}, p)$ (right) of Example 6.

l	T_1	T_2		l	T_1	T_2
1	1	2		1	1	1
2	2	3		2	1	1
3	5	6		3	1	1
4	4	5		4	1	1
5	7	9		5	1	1
6	10	11		6	1	1
7	12	13		7	1	1
8	8	10		8	1	1
9	14	16		9	1	1
10	17	18		10	-1	1
11	19	20		11	1	1
12	15	17		12	1	1

4   Mass and Stiffness Matrices

4.1   The Reference Mass and Stiffness Matrices

are for a given $p \in \mathbb{N}$ matrices of size $n_{p,ref} \times n_{p,ref}$ defined by

$$M_{i,j}^{ref} = \int_{T_{ref}} N_i N_j \mathrm{dx}, \qquad K_{i,j}^{ref} = \int_{T_{ref}} \nabla N_i \cdot \nabla N_j \mathrm{dx}. \qquad (14)$$

Functions

```
mass_matrixQp_2D_reference(p)
```

```
stiffness_matrixQp_2D_reference(p)
```

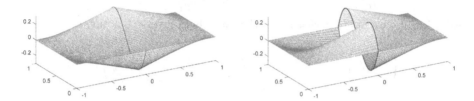

Fig. 5. The right (left) and wrong (right) orientation of $N_{17}^{(g)}$ of Example 6.

evaluate the corresponding reference mass and stiffness matrices using the Gaussian quadrature rule. For a given p, the function $[\texttt{X,W}] = \texttt{intrec\_hp(p)}$ returns the Gauss points $X \in T_{ref}$ together with the corresponding weights stored in a vector W.

4.2   The Global Mass and Stiffness Matrices

are for a specific p and $\mathcal{T}$ matrices of size $n_p \times n_p$ defined by

$$M_{i,j} = \int_{\mathcal{T}} N_i^{(g)} N_j^{(g)} \mathrm{dx}, \qquad K_{i,j} = \int_{\mathcal{T}} \nabla N_i^{(g)} \cdot \nabla N_j^{(g)} \mathrm{dx} \qquad (15)$$

and assembled by adding the contributions of local mass and stiffness matrices $M(T_k)$ and $K(T_k)$ of size $n_{p,ref} \times n_{p,ref}$ to the corresponding entries. In particular, $M_{i,j}(T_k)$ and $K_{i,j}(T_k)$ contribute to the c_i^k-th row and the c_j^k-th column of M and K, respectively, where c^k is the k-th column vector of $C(\mathcal{T},p)$.

For any $T_k \in \mathcal{T}$, $1 \leq k \leq |\mathcal{T}|$ the local mass matrix $M(T_k)$ is given by

$$M(T_k) = \frac{|T_k|}{|T_{ref}|} M^{ref} = \frac{|T_k|}{4} M^{ref}, \qquad (16)$$

however, this formula cannot be applied to the assembly of the local stiffness matrix $K(T_k)$. Instead, we apply the chain rule to evaluate

$$
\begin{aligned}
K_{i,j}(T_k) &= \int_{T_k} \nabla \tilde{N}_i(x,y) \cdot \nabla \tilde{N}_j(x,y)\mathrm{d}\mathbf{x} = \\
&= \int_{T_k} \nabla N_i(Q^{-1}(x,y)) \cdot \nabla N_j(Q^{-1}(x,y))\mathrm{d}\mathbf{x},
\end{aligned}
\tag{17}
$$

where $\tilde{N}_i$ and N_i, $1 \le i \le n_{p,ref}$ are the i-th local function on T_k and T_{ref}, respectively. Using the chain rule, one can write

$$
\nabla \tilde{N}_i(Q^{-1}(x,y)) = \left(\frac{\partial \tilde{N}_i}{\partial \xi}\frac{\partial \xi}{\partial x} + \frac{\partial \tilde{N}_i}{\partial \eta}\frac{\partial \eta}{\partial x}, \frac{\partial \tilde{N}_i}{\partial \xi}\frac{\partial \xi}{\partial y} + \frac{\partial \tilde{N}_i}{\partial \eta}\frac{\partial \eta}{\partial y} \right),
\tag{18}
$$

where

$$
\left(\frac{\partial \xi}{\partial x}, \frac{\partial \eta}{\partial x} \right) = \frac{\partial Q^{-1}}{\partial x}(x,y), \quad \left(\frac{\partial \xi}{\partial y}, \frac{\partial \eta}{\partial y} \right) = \frac{\partial Q^{-1}}{\partial y}(x,y).
$$

Additionally, we apply derivative of the formula of inverse function to evaluate

$$
\begin{pmatrix} \frac{\partial \xi}{\partial x} & \frac{\partial \xi}{\partial y} \\ \frac{\partial \eta}{\partial x} & \frac{\partial \eta}{\partial y} \end{pmatrix} = \nabla Q^{-1}(x,y) = \left(\nabla Q(\xi,\eta) \right)^{-1} = \begin{pmatrix} \frac{\partial x}{\partial \xi} & \frac{\partial x}{\partial \eta} \\ \frac{\partial y}{\partial \xi} & \frac{\partial y}{\partial \eta} \end{pmatrix}^{-1}.
\tag{19}
$$

Table 4. Mesh properties (left) of the uniform mesh refinements of Example 7 and numbers of global shape functions for different polynomial orders (right).

level	$|\mathcal{N}|$	$|\mathcal{E}|$	$|\mathcal{T}|$	level	n_1	n_2	n_3	n_4	n_5
2	$2.5 \cdot 10^1$	$4.0 \cdot 10^1$	$1.6 \cdot 10^1$	2	$2.5 \cdot 10^1$	$6.5 \cdot 10^1$	$1.1 \cdot 10^2$	$1.6 \cdot 10^2$	$2.3 \cdot 10^2$
3	$8.1 \cdot 10^1$	$1.4 \cdot 10^2$	$6.4 \cdot 10^1$	3	$8.1 \cdot 10^1$	$2.3 \cdot 10^2$	$3.7 \cdot 10^2$	$5.8 \cdot 10^2$	$8.5 \cdot 10^2$
4	$2.9 \cdot 10^2$	$5.4 \cdot 10^2$	$2.6 \cdot 10^2$	4	$2.9 \cdot 10^2$	$8.3 \cdot 10^2$	$1.4 \cdot 10^3$	$2.2 \cdot 10^3$	$3.2 \cdot 10^3$
5	$1.1 \cdot 10^3$	$2.1 \cdot 10^3$	$1.0 \cdot 10^3$	5	$1.1 \cdot 10^3$	$3.2 \cdot 10^3$	$5.3 \cdot 10^3$	$8.4 \cdot 10^3$	$1.3 \cdot 10^4$
6	$4.2 \cdot 10^3$	$8.3 \cdot 10^3$	$4.1 \cdot 10^3$	6	$4.2 \cdot 10^3$	$1.3 \cdot 10^4$	$2.1 \cdot 10^4$	$3.3 \cdot 10^4$	$5.0 \cdot 10^4$
7	$1.7 \cdot 10^4$	$3.3 \cdot 10^4$	$1.6 \cdot 10^4$	7	$1.7 \cdot 10^4$	$5.0 \cdot 10^4$	$8.3 \cdot 10^4$	$1.3 \cdot 10^5$	$2.0 \cdot 10^5$
8	$6.6 \cdot 10^4$	$1.3 \cdot 10^5$	$6.6 \cdot 10^4$	8	$6.6 \cdot 10^4$	$2.0 \cdot 10^5$	$3.3 \cdot 10^5$	$5.3 \cdot 10^5$	$7.9 \cdot 10^5$
9	$2.6 \cdot 10^5$	$5.3 \cdot 10^5$	$2.6 \cdot 10^5$	9	$2.6 \cdot 10^5$	$7.9 \cdot 10^5$	$1.3 \cdot 10^6$	$2.1 \cdot 10^6$	$3.2 \cdot 10^6$

Example 7. For $\Omega = T_{ref} = [-1,1]^2$ the script

```
example7_M_K_matrices_times
```

runs a nested loop on different p and levels of uniform refinements of Ω. The mass and stiffness matrices are assembled by the functions `mass_matrixQp_2D(mesh)` and `stiffness_matrixQp_2D(mesh)`, respectively. Tables 4 and 5 contain the properties of the mesh and the corresponding assembly times. Assembly times were obtained on a MacBook Air (M1 processor, 2020) with 16 GB memory running MATLAB R2022a.

Table 5. Assembly times of mass and stiffness matrices in Example 7 measured in seconds.

level	$p = 1$ M [s]	K [s]	$p = 2$ M [s]	K [s]	$p = 3$ M [s]	K [s]	$p = 4$ M [s]	K [s]	$p = 5$ M [s]	K [s]
2	0.00	0.01	0.00	0.00	0.00	0.00	0.00	0.01	0.01	0.01
3	0.00	0.01	0.00	0.00	0.00	0.01	0.01	0.01	0.01	0.01
4	0.00	0.01	0.00	0.00	0.01	0.02	0.01	0.02	0.01	0.03
5	0.00	0.01	0.00	0.01	0.01	0.02	0.01	0.05	0.02	0.09
6	0.00	0.02	0.01	0.04	0.02	0.08	0.03	0.16	0.07	0.33
7	0.01	0.08	0.03	0.15	0.07	0.32	0.25	0.71	0.45	1.46
8	0.04	0.31	0.15	0.66	0.48	1.44	0.98	3.14	2.00	6.20
9	0.22	1.29	0.91	2.86	1.94	6.01	5.26	12.43	11.17	27.31

5   Solving Partial Differential Equation in 2D

We solve a diffusion-reaction boundary value problem

$$-\Delta u + \nu u = f \quad \text{in } \Omega, \qquad \frac{\partial u}{\partial n} = 0 \quad \text{on } \partial\Omega \tag{20}$$

by applying the hp-FEM method to the weak formulation of (20) given by

$$\int_T \nabla u \cdot \nabla N_m^{(g)} \mathrm{dx} + \nu \int_T u \, N_m^{(g)} \mathrm{dx} = \int_T f \, N_m^{(g)} \mathrm{dx}, \quad \forall N_m^{(g)} \in S^p(T). \tag{21}$$

It leads to an algebraic system of linear equations in the form of

$$(K + \nu M)\,\tilde{u}_n = b, \tag{22}$$

where M and K are global mass and stiffness matrices, u_n is the numerical solution of (21) represented by the vector $\tilde{u}_n \in \mathbb{R}^{n_p}$ of coefficients in the corresponding hp basis and the vector $b \in \mathbb{R}^{n_p}$ is given by $b_m = \int_T f N_m^{(g)} \mathrm{dx}$. We assume the domain $\Omega = T_{ref} = [-1, 1]^2$ and the parameter $\nu = 0.1$. It is easy to show that

$$u(x, y) = (1 - x^2)^2 (1 - y^2)^2$$

represents the solution of (20) corresponding to the function

$$f(x, y) = \nu \, u(x, y) - 4\big(-2 + 5y^2 - y^4 + x^4(-1 + 3y^2) + x^2(5 - 12y^2 + 3y^4)\big)$$

for $(x, y) \in \Omega$. To study the convergence of hp approximations, we take several levels of uniform refinements of Ω defined by $|T|$ squares of same size, where $|T| = 4^{level}$, $level = 1, \ldots, 7$ and solve (22) for different polynomial orders p, $1 \le p \le p_{max} = 5$. The exact solution u is approximated in $S^{\tilde{p}}(T)$, $\tilde{p} = p_{max} + 2$ by the vector $\tilde{u}$. The corresponding error e in the energy norm is given by

$$e^2 = \int_T \big(\|\nabla u - \nabla u_n\|^2 + (u - u_n)^2\big) \mathrm{dx} \approx (\tilde{u} - \tilde{u}_n)^T (K + M)(\tilde{u} - \tilde{u}_n). \tag{23}$$

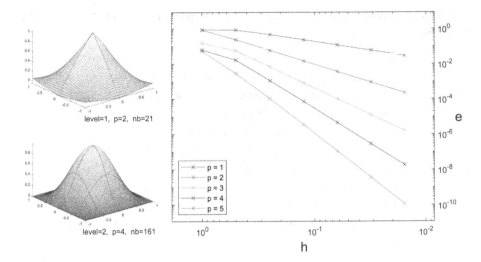

Fig. 6. Examples of solutions of (21) and convergence in the energy norm.

The script **example8_diffusion_reaction_BVP** utilizes a nested for loop on p (inside) and mesh refinement levels (outside). Two particular numerical solutions are shown in Fig. 6 (left). The corresponding errors (23) are shown in Fig. 6 (right), where the crosses on different lines correspond to the mesh refinement levels and both x and y labels are log-scaled. The calculation confirms a theoretical expectation $e \approx h^p$, where p is a chosen polynomial order and h is a chosen square size satisfying $|\mathcal{T}| = 4\,h^{-2}$.

References

1. Anjam, I., Valdman, J.: Fast MATLAB assembly of FEM matrices in 2D and 3D: Edge elements. Appl. Math. Comput. **267**, 252–263 (2015)
2. Rahman, T., Valdman, J.: Fast MATLAB assembly of FEM matrices in 2D and 3D: Nodal elements. Appl. Math. Comput. **219**, 7151–7158 (2013)
3. Szabó, B., Babuška, I.: Finite Element Analysis. Wiley-Interscience, New York (1991)
4. Szabó, B., Babuška, I.: Introduction to Finite Element Analysis, John Wiley & Sons (2011)
5. Bangerth, W., Kayser-Herold, O.: Data structures and requirements for hp finite element software. ACM Trans. Math. Softw. (TOMS) **36**(1), 1–31 (2009)
6. Šolín, P., Segeth, K., Doležel, I.: Higher-Order Finite Element Methods, Chapman & Hall/CRC (2004)
7. Moskovka, A., Valdman, J.: Fast MATLAB evaluation of nonlinear energies using FEM in 2D and 3D: nodal elements. Appl. Math. Comput. **424**, 127048 (2022)
8. Innerberger, M., Praetorius, D.: MooAFEM: an object oriented Matlab code for higher-order adaptive FEM for (nonlinear) elliptic PDEs. Appl. Math. Comput. **442**, 127731 (2023)

 9. Demkowicz, L.: Computing with hp-ADAPTIVE FINITE ELEMENTS, Volume 1, Chapman & Hall/CRC (2007)
10. Demkowicz, L., Oden, J.T., Rachowicz, W., Hardy, O.: Toward a Universal h-p Adaptive Finite Element Strategy. Part 1. Constrained Approximation and Data Structure. Comput. Methods Appl. Mech. Eng. **77**(1–2), 79–112 (1989)
11. Babuška, I., Szabó, B., Katz, I.: The p-version of the finite element method. SIAM J. Num. Anal. **18**(3), 515–545 (1981)
12. Babuška, I., Guo, B.Q.: The h-p version of the finite element method. Comput. Mech. **1**, 21–41 (1986)
13. Schöberl, J.: C++11 Implementation of Finite Elements in NGSolve. Vienna University of Technology, Institute for Analysis and Scientific Computing (2014)
14. Šolín, P., Korous, L., Kus, P.: Hermes2D, a C++ library for rapid development of adaptive hp-FEM and hp-DG solvers. J. Comput. Appl. Math. **270**, 152–165 (2014)

Adaptive Parallel Average Schwarz Preconditioner for Crouzeix-Raviart Finite Volume Method

Leszek Marcinkowski[1]([⊠])([iD]) and Talal Rahman[2]

[1] Faculty of Mathematics, Informatics, and Mechanics, University of Warsaw, Banacha 2, 02 -097 Warszawa, Poland
Leszek.Marcinkowski@mimuw.edu.pl
[2] Faculty of Engineering and Science, Western Norway University of Applied Sciences, Inndalsveien 28, 5063 Bergen, Norway
Talal.Rahman@hvl.no

Abstract. In this paper, we describe and analyze an Average Schwarz Method with spectrally enriched coarse space for a Crouzeix-Raviart finite volume element discretization of a multiscale problem. The derived preconditioner is symmetric and we apply GMRES iterative method to the preconditioned problem obtaining the convergence rate of GMRES weakly dependent on the ratio of the coarse to fine mesh h/H if the enrichments of the coarse space contain sufficiently many specially constructed eigenfunctions.

Keywords: Average Schwarz method · Domain Decomposition · Finite Volume Element Method · Crouzeix-Raviart

1 Introduction

The finite volume element method is quite popular in science and engineering, and therefore quite many works in which the method is analyzed have been published, cf. e.g. [7,8,12,13,15,23] and references therein.

The Domain Decomposition Methods (DDMs) are a very powerful and effective way of solving in parallel the linear and non-linear systems of equations arising from discretizations of PDEs.

There are not many DDMs for solving the systems arising from Finite Volume Element Discretizations, in particular a Crouzeix-Raviar Finite Volume Element (CRFVE) discretization. To our knowledge those papers [9,16–19,29] are the only published results concerning this topic. The last three papers are related to DDMs for the CRFVE discretizations. In this paper, we extend the results of [16] where there is the analysis of the classical (no enrichments) average Schwarz method for a CRFVE discretization of a multiscale problem. Those results show that the coefficients must satisfy quite restrictive assumptions to get

R. Wyrzykowski et al. (Eds.): PPAM 2022, LNCS 13827, pp. 300–312, 2023.
https://doi.org/10.1007/978-3-031-30445-3_25

a fast convergence. Here we propose a new version of the coarse space of the average Schwarz method, i.e. the coarse space is harmonically enriched. We described the details of this new version, in particular the new enriched coarse space. Then, we show that the convergence speed of the GMRES iterative method with the preconditioner obtained by this method is independent of the distribution of the contrast if the coarse space is sufficiently enriched. It can be done adaptively, namely, we can set a threshold and include into the coarse space all eigenfunctions of some specially defined local eigenproblems problems whose eigenvalues are above the threshold. The other option is to include a preset number of eigenfunctions, the number can be selected by a user. e.g. it may equal the number of inclusions.

The idea of enriching the coarse space by the specially defined eigenfunctions is not a very new one, the first results appeared in the 2010 s,s, cf. e.g. [14,27] and the references therein.

Presented here version of the Average Schwarz method is based on the abstract scheme of the Additive Schwarz Method (ASM), and is a very simple domain decomposition method. Perhaps one of the simplest. It was first proposed in [2], cf. also [1,10,20,22]. Both the construction and the analysis are based on this abstract ASM scheme, cf. e.g. [26,28].

Throughout the paper, the following notations are being used: $x \lesssim y$ and $w \gtrsim z$ denote that there exist positive constants c, C independent of the mesh parameters, the number of subdomains, and the jump of coefficients such that $x \leq cy$ and $w \geq Cz$, respectively.

The remainder of the paper is organized as follows: in the Sect. 2 a finite volume element discretization is introduced. Section 3 is devoted to a presentation of an Additive Schwarz Method (ASM), in particular, we describe a spectrally enriched coarse space. Finally, in the last Sect. 4 we describe the main theoretical results of this work.

2   Discrete Problem

First, we introduce a multiscale second-order elliptic differential problem. For a given polygonal domain Ω on the plane we want to find $u^* \in H_0^1(\Omega)$ that

$$-\nabla \cdot (A(x)\nabla u)(x) = f(x), \quad x \in \Omega,$$
$$u(s) = 0, \quad s \in \partial\Omega,$$

where $A \in (L^\infty(\Omega))^{2\times 2}$ is a symmetric matrix-valued function satisfying the uniform ellipticity as follows,

$$\exists \alpha > 0 \quad \text{such that} \quad \xi^T A(x)\xi \geq \alpha|\xi|_2^2 \quad \forall x \in \Omega \text{ and } \forall \xi \in \mathbb{R}^2,$$

where $|\xi|_2^2 = \xi_1^2 + \xi_2^2$. Further, we can assume that α equal to one which can be always obtained by scaling the original problem by α^{-1}.

The weak formulation of the differential problem is the following: find $u \in H_0^1(\Omega)$ such that

$$a(u, v) = f(v) \quad \forall v \in H_0^1(\Omega), \tag{1}$$

where

$$a(u, v) = \int_{\Omega} \nabla u^T A(x) \nabla v \, dx \quad \text{and} \quad f(v) = \int_{\Omega} f v \, dx.$$

We now introduce a triangulation, namely, let $T_h = T_h(\Omega)$ be a quasiuniform triangulation of Ω, cf. [4] or [3], hereon referred to as the primal mesh consisting of triangles $\{\tau\}$ with the size parameter $h = \max_{\tau \in T_h} \text{diam}(\tau)$.

We assume that the coefficient matrix function $A(x)$ is continuous and smooth in each triangle $\tau \in T_h$, namely,

$$\forall \tau \in T_h \quad |A|_{W^{1,\infty}(\tau)} \leq C, \tag{2}$$

where C is a positive constant.

Further, we also assume that

$$\forall \tau \in T_h \, \exists \lambda_\tau > 0 \quad \text{s.t.} \quad \xi^T A(x)\xi \geq \lambda_\tau |\xi|_2^2 \geq |\xi|_2^2 \quad \forall x \in \tau \text{ and } \forall \xi \in \mathbb{R}^2. \tag{3}$$

Due to $A \in (L^\infty(\Omega))^{2 \times 2}$, we see that

$$\forall \tau \in T_h \, \exists \Lambda_\tau > 0 \text{ such that } \quad |\nu^T A(x)\xi| \leq \Lambda_\tau |\nu|_2 |\xi|_2 \quad \forall x \in \tau \text{ and } \forall \xi, \nu \in \mathbb{R}^2.$$

We also assume that $\Lambda_\tau \lesssim \lambda_\tau$ for any $\tau \in T_h$.

Summing up the coefficients in each triangle $\tau \in T_h$ are smooth and do not vary too much, but between triangles jumps of coefficients are arbitrary.

We then have that

$$\lambda_\tau |u|_{H^1(\tau)}^2 \leq \int_\tau \nabla u^T A(x) \nabla u \, dx \leq \Lambda_\tau |u|_{H^1(\tau)}^2 \quad \forall u \in H^1(\tau). \tag{4}$$

We assume that Ω is decomposed into a set of disjoint polygonal subdomains $\{\Omega_j\}_{j=1}^N$ aligned to the triangulation, i.e. each fine triangle of T_h is contained in one of the subdomains Ω_k, i.e. $\overline{\Omega} = \bigcup_i \overline{\Omega}_i$, for any $\tau \in T_h$ there is Ω_i such that $\tau \subset \Omega_i$. We also assume that these substructures form a coarse triangulation of the domain which is shape regular in the sense of [5] and let $H = \max_j \text{diam}(\Omega_j)$ be its coarse parameter, cf. Fig. 1.

2.1   Crouzeix-Raviart Finite Volume Element Method

To introduce the discrete problem we have to define another partition of finite covolumes of Ω so-called dual mesh of Ω.

Let $\mathcal{E}_h(\tau)$ be the set of edges of $\tau \in T_h$ and let define $\mathcal{E}_h = \cup_{K \in T_h} \mathcal{E}_h(K)$, i.e. the union of all edges in the triangulation T_h. We also need to introduce a set of interior edges $\mathcal{E}_h^{in}$ of the triangulation T_h, i.e. $e \in \mathcal{E}_h^{in}$ if and only if $e \in \mathcal{E}_h$ and $e \not\subset \partial\Omega$.

We also need the sets of so-called Crouzeix-Raviart (CR) nodal points i.e. we denote the CR nodal points, i.e. the midpoints of edges $e \in \mathcal{E}_h$, belonging

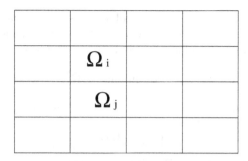

Fig. 1. A coarse decomposition of Ω into subdomains.

to $\Omega, \Omega_i, \partial\Omega$ and $\partial\Omega_i$ by $\Omega_h^{\mathrm{CR}}, \Omega_{i,h}^{\mathrm{CR}}, \partial\Omega_h^{\mathrm{CR}}$ and $\partial\Omega_{i,h}^{\mathrm{CR}}$, respectively. Correspondingly, the set of P_1 conforming nodal points, i.e., vertices of elements in $\mathcal{T}_h$ are denoted by $\Omega_h, \Omega_{i,h}, \partial\Omega_h$ and $\partial\Omega_{i,h}$, respectively.

Let for any fine edge $e \in \mathcal{E}_h^{\mathrm{in}}$ which is the common edge of two triangles $\tau_1, \tau_2 \in \mathcal{T}_h$ we define a domain V_e as the polygon with the vertices v_1, v_2 which are the ends of e (which are the common vertices of τ_1, τ_2) and two centroids: c_1, c_2 of τ_1 and τ_2, respectively, i.e. the V_e is the polygon enclosed by the straight lines connecting v_1, v_2, c_1, c_2. We see that

$$\overline{V}_e = \overline{V}_{1,e} \cup \overline{V}_{2,e}$$

where $V_{k,e}$ is the open triangle whose vertices are the ends v_1, v_2 of $e \in \mathcal{E}_h^{\mathrm{in}}$ and the centroid c_k of τ_k, see Fig. 2.

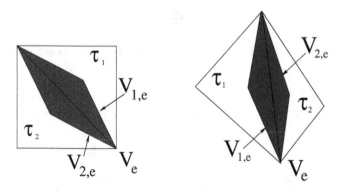

Fig. 2. Control volume of CRFVE: V_e related to the common edge e of two triangles τ_1 and τ_2.

The region V_e is called the control volume of the edge $e \in \mathcal{E}_h^{\mathrm{in}}$ and we introduce the dual mesh

$$T_h^* = \{V_e\}_{e \in \mathcal{E}_h^{\mathrm{in}}}$$

Naturally, T_h^* is not a triangulation of Ω, it is just a dual mesh to T_h. The solution space will be the Crouzeix-Raviart (CR) finite element space (cf. e.g. [3]), or nonconforming P_1 element space defined as follows: let

$$V_h = \{v \in L^2(\Omega) : v_{|\tau} \in P_1(\tau), \ v \text{ continuous at } \Omega_h^{CR}, \quad v(m) = 0 \ \ m \in \partial\Omega_h^{CR}\}$$

where $P_k(\tau)$ is the space of polynomial of degree less or equal to k. Naturally, we see that $V_h \in L^2(\Omega)$ but

$$V_h \not\subset H^1(\Omega).$$

The degrees of freedom of CR finite element function u on a triangle τ with the three edges e_k $k = 1, 2, 3$, are:

$$\{u(m_{e_k})\}_{k=1,2,3},$$

where m_{e_k} is the midpoint of the fine edge e_k, cf. Fig. 3.

Next, we define the control volume space as follows: let

$$V_h^* = \{v \in L^2(\Omega) : v_{|V_e} \in P_0(V_e) \ ; e \in \mathcal{E}_h^{in}\}$$

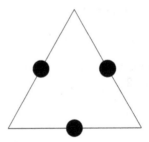

Fig. 3. The degrees of freedom (DOFs) of Crouzeix-Raviart nonconforming element

We can introduce the nodal basis of V_h as: $\{\phi_e\}_{e \in \mathcal{E}_h^{in}}$ where $\phi_e \in V_h$ is a nodal function associated with an fine edge $e \in \mathcal{E}_h^{in}$ whose midpoint is $m_e \in \Omega_h^{CR}$ such that

$$\phi_e(s) = \begin{cases} 1 & s = m_e \\ 0 & s \neq m \end{cases} \qquad \forall s \in \Omega_h^{CR}.$$

Analogously we define the basis of V_h^*: $V_h^* = \text{span}(\chi_e)_{e \in \mathcal{E}_h^{in}}$ where χ_e is the characteristic function of the control volume V_e related to the interior fine edge $e \in \mathcal{E}_h^{in}$

We can also introduce two interpolation operators: I_h and I_h^* defined for a function that has the unique values at Ω_h^{CR}:

$$I_h u = \sum_{e \in \mathcal{E}_h^{in}} u(m_e)\phi_e \quad \text{and} \quad I_h^* u = \sum_{e \in \mathcal{E}_h^{in}} u(m_e)\chi_e.$$

Here m_e is the midpoint of an edge $e \in \mathcal{E}_h^{\text{in}}$.

We are now able to define the CRVME discrete problem: find $u_h^{FV} \in V_h$ such that

$$a_h^{FV}(u_h^{FV}, v) = (f, v) \quad \forall v \in V_h^* \tag{5}$$

where $(\cdot, \cdot)$ is L^2 inner product on Ω, or equivalently

$$a_h^{FV}(u_h^{FV}, I_h^* v) = (f, I_h^* v) \quad \forall v \in V_h, \tag{6}$$

where

$$a_h^{FV}(u, v) = - \sum_{e \in \mathrm{E}_h^{\text{in}}} v(m_e) \int_{\partial V_e} \nabla u^T A(s) \mathbf{n} \, ds \qquad u \in V_h, v \in V_h^*. \tag{7}$$

where $\mathbf{n}$ is the unit outer vector to V_e.

The existence of the unique solution to the CRFVE discrete problem and the error estimates are given in [16].

Naturally, the second formulation (6) allows us to interpret the CRFVE discrete problem as a discrete variational problem posed in V_h.

We also define a corresponding CRFE discrete problem: find $u_h^{FE} \in V_h$ such that

$$a_h^{FE}(u_h^{FE}, v) = (f, v) \qquad \forall v \in V_h, \tag{8}$$

where the broken form is defined for $u, v \in V_h$ as follows:

$$a_h^{FE}(u, v) = \sum_{\tau \in T_h} \int_\tau \nabla u^T A \nabla v \, dx. \tag{9}$$

The last bilinear form induced the corresponding broken energy norm by

$$\| \cdot \|_a = \sqrt{a_h^{FE}(\cdot, \cdot)}.$$

Formally, as defined it is a seminorm but an easy standard argument shows that it is indeed a norm, cf. e.g. [3].

3   Additive Average Schwarz Method

In this section, we introduce an Additive Average Schwarz method. The method is introduced using the abstract scheme of the Additive Schwarz method (ASM), cf e.g. [26,28], i.e., we introduce the decomposition of the space V_h into a coarse space and local subspaces together with respective coarse and local bilinear forms.

3.1   Local Spaces

The local spaces are defined as simple local CR spaces with the CR zero boundary conditions on its local boundary and extended as zero at all CR nodes outside Ω_k, i.e. let

$$V_k = \{u \in V_h : u(m) = 0 \quad m \notin \Omega_k^{CR}\}. \tag{10}$$

The local forms are equal to $a_h^{FE}(u, v)$. Note that local spaces V_k $k = 1, \ldots, N$ are $a_h^{FEM}(u, v)$ orthogonal, thus we see that $\bigoplus_{k=1}^N V_k \subset V_h$ is $a_h^{FEM}(u, v)$ orthogonal decomposition, however we have that $V_h \neq \bigoplus_{k=1}^N V_k$.

3.2   Harmonically Enriched Coarse Space

We first introduce a coarse interpolation operator

$$I_0 : V_h \to V_h \tag{11}$$

defined as follows: for any $u \in V_h$ let $I_0 u \in V_h$ satisfies:

$$I_0 u(m) = \begin{cases} u(m) & m \in \bigcup_{k=1}^N \partial\Omega_{k,h}^{CR} \\ \bar{u}_k & m \in \Omega_{k,h}^{CR} \quad k = 1, \ldots, N \end{cases}. \tag{12}$$

where $\bar{u}_k = \frac{1}{M_k}\sum_{m \in \partial\Omega_{k,h}^{CR}} u(m)$ with $M_k = \#\partial\Omega_{k,h}^{CR}$, i.e. $\bar{u}_k$ is the discrete average over $\partial\Omega_{k,h}^{CR}$.

Then the classical additive average Schwarz coarse space is the range of I_0:

$$V_0^{class} = I_0 V_h. \tag{13}$$

Its dimension is equal to the number of interface nodal points. Then we have the decomposition of the discrete CR space:

$$V_h = V_0^{class} + \bigoplus_{k=1}^N V_k.$$

Further, we introduce local generalized eigenspaces. Let $V_h(\Omega_k)$ be the space of restrictions of V_k to Ω_k or equivalently we can define $V_h(\Omega_k)$ as the CR local space with the CR zero boundary condition on the local triangulation $T_h(\Omega_k)$ inherited from T_h.

We also need two local bilinear forms:

$$a_k(u, v) = \sum_{\tau \in T_h(\Omega_k)} \nabla u^T A \nabla v \, dx,$$

$$b_k(u, v) = \sum_{\tau \in T_h(\Omega_k)} \lambda_{\Omega_k} \nabla u^T \nabla v \, dx.$$

where $\lambda_{\Omega_k} = \min_{\tau \in T_h(\Omega_k)} \lambda_\tau$, cf. (3). Note that the both forms are symmetric and positive definite on $V_h(\Omega)$, since the first one is the broken local form of the FEM original one, and the second is a scaled local H^1 bilinear form.

Then, a generalized eigenvalue problem is to find all eigenpairs: $(\lambda_{i,k}, \psi_{i,k})$ such that

$$a_k(\psi_{i,k}, v) = \lambda_{i,k} b_k(\psi_{i,k}, v) \qquad \forall v \in V_h(\Omega) \tag{14}$$

and

$$b_k(\psi_{i,k}, \psi_{i,k}) = 1,$$

i.e., the eigenfunctions are normalized in the norm induced by the form $b_k(u, v)$. Note that since $a_k(u, u) \geq b_k(u, u)$ for any $u \in V_h(\Omega_k)$, we see that $\lambda_{i,k} \geq 1$.

We can order the eigenvalues in decreasing order:

$$\lambda_{1,k} \geq \lambda_{2,k} \geq \ldots \lambda_{N_k,k} \geq 1,$$

where $N_k = \dim(V_h(\Omega_k))$.

Formally, an eigenfunction $\psi_{i,k} \in V_h(\Omega_k)$, i.e. is a locally defined only but we can extended it by zero elsewhere, i.e. to all $\overline{\Omega}_h^{CR}$ with zero values. Further, we will denote this extended function by the same symbol $\psi_{i,k}$.

Then the local harmonical enrichment space is defined as:

$$V_k^{harm} = \mathrm{span}(\psi_{i,k})_{i=1}^{n_k} \tag{15}$$

where $0 \leq n_k \leq N_k$ is any number selected by an user. One possibility is to pre-select a threshold $\nu_k > 1$ and include all $\psi_{i,k}$ such that $\lambda_{i,k} \geq \nu_k$. Naturally, the number $n_k = 0$ means there is no enrichment related to Ω_k, i.e. formally $V_k^{harm} = \{0\}$ is the zero space. Potentially, in a 'bad' case the n_k may have any value less or equal to N_k to get a good condition number.

Finally, our enriched coarse space is introduced:

$$V_0 = V_0^{class} + \sum_{k=1}^{N} V_k^{harm}. \tag{16}$$

Remark 1. The form $b_k(u, v)$ can be defined in a bit different way, namely, we can take: $b_k(u, v) = \lambda_{\Omega_k} H_k^{-2} \int_{\Omega_k} uv \, dx$ and get similar results.

3.3 ASM Operator

Next as in the abstract scheme of the ASM method, cf. e.g. [26], we define so-called projections: $T_k : V_h \to V_k \ k = 0, \ldots, N$:

$$a_h^{FE}(T_k u, v) = a_h^{FV}(u, I_h^* v) \qquad \forall v \in V_k \tag{17}$$

and the global operator $T = T_0 + \sum_{k=1}^{N} T_k$. Finally, we replace our CRFVE discrete problem (5) by:

$$T u_h^{FV} = g \tag{18}$$

where u_h^* is the solution of (5) and $g = g_0 + \sum_k g_k$ with $g_k = T_k u_h^*$, i.e.

$$a_h^{FE}(g_k, v) = a_h^{FV}(u_h^*, I_h^* v) = (f, v) \qquad \forall v \in V_k$$

for $k = 0, \ldots, N$. Note, that g_k can be computed without knowing u_h^*, cf. e.g. [26,28].

The new problem can be represented as a preconditioned old problem, i.e. if we represent algebraically the old problem as $Au_h^{FV} = f$ then the new one can be represented as $B_{ASM}Au_h^{FV} = B_{ASM}f$. One can see that the original problem is non-symmetric in general, but the parallel preconditioner B_{ASM} is symmetric.

Naturally, the preconditioner is parallel as computing the residual $r = g - Tv$ in an implementation of an iterative solver, e.g. PCG, is equivalent to solving independent local problems and a coarse problem. The adaptivity of the method lies in the possibility of automatic selection of the number of the eigenfunctions included in the spaces V_k^{harm}, cf. (15).

4   Convergence

4.1   GMRES Method

Since the problem (18) is nonsymmetric, it can be solved with GMRES method, cf. e.g. [24]. We now state the convergence results of GMRES applied to the problem (18). The original convergence results of GMRES were stated in the l_2 norm, cf. [11], however, the results carry over to the general Hilbert space, in our case to V_h equipped with the energy norm $\|\cdot\|_a$, cf. [6,25]. The convergence rate estimates of the GMRES are based on two parameters: the smallest eigenvalue of the symmetric part of the operator T denoted by γ_1 and the norm of the operator T denoted by γ_2, respectively, as follows:

$$\gamma_1 = \inf_{u \neq 0} \frac{a_h^{FE}(Tu, u)}{\|u\|_a^2} \quad \text{and} \quad \gamma_2 = \sup_{u \neq 0} \frac{\|Tu\|_a}{\|u\|_a}. \tag{19}$$

Then the estimate of the convergence rate of the GMRES iteration, in the $\|\cdot\|_a$ norm can be obtained:

Theorem 1 (Eisenstat-Elman-Schultz [11]). *Provided γ_1 is strictly positive, the GMRES method for solving the linear system (18) converges for any starting value $u_0 \in V_h$ and the following estimate holds:*

$$\|g - Tu_m\|_a \leq \left(1 - \frac{\gamma_1^2}{\gamma_2^2}\right)^{m/2} \|g - Tu_0\|_a,$$

where u_m is the m-th iterate of the GMRES iteration method.

4.2   Main Results

Our main result is the following theorem:

Theorem 2. *There exists positive h_0, H_0 such that for all $h \leq h_0$ and $H \leq H_0$ we have that*

$$\|Tu\|_a \lesssim \|u\|_a \qquad \forall u \in V_h, \tag{20}$$

$$a_h^{FE}(Tu, u) \gtrsim \left(\left(1 + \max_k \lambda_{n_k+1,k}\right)^{-1} \frac{h}{H} - Ch \right) \|u\|_a^2 \qquad \forall u \in V_h, \tag{21}$$

where C is a constant independent of coefficients, the mesh parameter h or the subdomain size H, and the eigenvalues $\lambda_{n_k+1,k}$ are from (14).

Note that in particular for sufficiently small h_0 the right-hand side of (21) is positive. This theorem gives us directly the corollary which estimates the convergence rate of GMRES iteration applied to the problem (18).

Corollary 1. *The constants (19) in the convergence theory of GMRES, i.e. in Theorem 1, for our ASM operator T can be bounded as follows*

$$\gamma_1 \gtrsim \left(\left(1 + \max_k \lambda_{n_k+1,k}\right)^{-1} \frac{h}{H} - Ch \right), \qquad \gamma_2 \lesssim 1.$$

The proof of Theorem 2 is based on the scheme proposed in [18]. We have to check three assumptions:

Assumption I: which requires that the two forms are close to each other:

$$|a_h^{FV}(u, I_h^* v) - a_h^{FE}(u, v)| \lesssim h \|u\|_a \|v\|_a \qquad \forall u, v \in V_h$$

This assumption is satisfied, cf. Lemma 2.5 in [16].

Assumption II: The next assumption is called *a stable decomposition* in the abstract theory of the Additive Schwarz Method, cf. e.g. [26, 28], i.e. we want to check if for any $u \in V_h$ there exist the following decomposition: $u_k \in V_k$, $k = 0, \ldots, N$ such that

$$\sum_{k=0}^{N} a_h^{FE}(u_k, v_k) \lesssim \left(1 + \max_k \lambda_{n_k+1,k}\right) \frac{h}{H} a_h^{FE}(u, u).$$

The proof of this assumption follows the lines of the proof of a similar one for the main results of [21].

Assumption III: The final assumption to be checked is that the spectral radius of the matrix of the constants of the strengthened Cauchy-Schwarz inequalities is bounded independently of coefficients or mesh parameters, i.e. the strengthen Cauchy-Schwarz inequalities for local spaces in the ASM abstract framework hold with the minimal constants $\{\epsilon_{kl}\}_{k,l=1}^{N}$ if

$$a_h^{FE}(u_k, u_l) \leq \epsilon_{k,l} \sqrt{a_h^{FE}(u_k, u_k)} \sqrt{a_h^{FE}(u_l, u_l)} \qquad \forall u_k \in V_k, \forall u_l \in V_l.$$

Then the estimate of γ_2 is dependent on $\rho(\mathcal{E})$ the spectral radius of the symmetric matrix: $\mathcal{E} = (\epsilon_{kl})_{k,l=1}^{N}$. In our case, it is satisfied with the constant one as the local spaces V_k and V_l are $a_h^{FE}(u, v)$ orthogonal since the functions of both subspaces have disjoint supports. Thus the matrix $\mathcal{E}$ is equal to Id and its spectral radius is equal to one. This is always the case in all versions of average Schwarz methods and can be considered a small advantage of this class of DDMs.

Finally, those three assumptions and Theorem 5.2 in [18] proves the estimates in the statement of Theorem 2.

5   Implementation

Due to the lack of space, we cannot provide a full description of the implementation. We refer to [16] or [20] for some details and standard DDM textbooks like e.g. [26]. In general to apply an iterative method like GMRES, one has to compute the residual $r = g - Tv$ for a given iterate v, which is equivalent to computing $r_k = g_k - T_k v$ for $k = 0, \dots, N$ what can be done in parallel as the problems are independent. This is an intrinsic property of the Additive Schwarz Method.

References

1. Bjørstad, P.E., Dryja, M., Rahman, T.: Additive Schwarz methods for elliptic mortar finite element problems. Numer. Math. **95**(3), 427–457 (2003). https://doi.org/10.1007/s00211-002-0429-6
2. Bjørstad, P.E., Dryja, M., Vainikko, E.: Additive Schwarz methods without subdomain overlap and with new coarse spaces. In: Domain decomposition methods in sciences and engineering (Beijing, 1995), pp. 141–157. Wiley, Chichester (1997)
3. Braess, D.: Finite elements. Cambridge University Press, Cambridge, third edn. theory, fast solvers, and applications in elasticity theory, Translated from the German by Larry L. Schumaker (2007). https://doi.org/10.1017/CBO9780511618635,
4. Brenner, S.C., Scott, L.R.: The mathematical theory of finite element methods, Texts in Applied Mathematics, vol. 15. Springer, New York, third edn. (2008). https://doi.org/10.1007/978-0-387-75934-0
5. Brenner, S.C., Sung, L.Y.: Balancing domain decomposition for nonconforming plate elements. Numer. Math. **83**(1), 25–52 (1999)
6. Cai, X.C., Widlund, O.B.: Domain decomposition algorithms for indefinite elliptic problems. SIAM J. Sci. Statist. Comput. **13**(1), 243–258 (1992). https://doi.org/10.1137/0913013
7. Chatzipantelidis, P.: A finite volume method based on the Crouzeix-Raviart element for elliptic PDE's in two dimensions. Numer. Math. **82**(3), 409–432 (1999). https://doi.org/10.1007/s002110050425
8. Chatzipantelidis, P.: Finite volume methods for elliptic PDE's: a new approach. M2AN Math. Model. Numer. Anal. **36**(2), 307–324 (2002). https://doi.org/10.1051/m2an:2002014
9. Chou, S.H., Huang, J.: A domain decomposition algorithm for general covolume methods for elliptic problems. J. Numer. Math. **11**(3), 179–194 (2003). https://doi.org/10.1163/156939503322553072

10. Dryja, M., Sarkis, M.: Additive average Schwarz methods for discretization of elliptic problems with highly discontinuous coefficients. Comput. Methods Appl. Math. **10**(2), 164–176 (2010). https://doi.org/10.2478/cmam-2010-0009
11. Eisenstat, S.C., Elman, H.C., Schultz, M.H.: Variational iterative methods for non-symmetric systems of linear equations. SIAM J. Numer. Anal. **20**(2), 345–357 (1983). https://doi.org/10.1137/0720023
12. Ewing, R.E., Li, Z., Lin, T., Lin, Y.: The immersed finite volume element methods for the elliptic interface problems. Math. Comput. Simulation **50**(1–4), 63–76 (1999). https://doi.org/10.1016/S0378-4754(99)00061-0, modelling '98 (Prague)
13. Ewing, R.E., Lin, T., Lin, Y.: On the accuracy of the finite volume element method based on piecewise linear polynomials. SIAM J. Numer. Anal. **39**(6), 1865–1888 (2002). https://doi.org/10.1137/S0036142900368873
14. Galvis, J., Efendiev, Y.: Domain decomposition preconditioners for multiscale flows in high-contrast media. Multiscale Model. Simul. **8**(4), 1461–1483 (2010). https://doi.org/10.1137/090751190
15. Lin, Y., Liu, J., Yang, M.: Finite volume element methods: an overview on recent developments. Int. J. Numer. Anal. Model. Ser. B **4**(1), 14–34 (2013)
16. Loneland, A., Marcinkowski, L., Rahman, T.: Additive average Schwarz method for a Crouzeix–Raviart finite volume element discretization of elliptic problems with heterogeneous coefficients. Numer. Math. **134**(1), 91–118 (2015). https://doi.org/10.1007/s00211-015-0771-0
17. Loneland, A., Marcinkowski, L., Rahman, T.: Edge-based Schwarz methods for the Crouzeix-Raviart finite volume element discretization of elliptic problems. Electron. Trans. Numer. Anal. **44**, 443–461 (2015)
18. Marcinkowski, L., Rahman, T., Loneland, A., Valdman, J.: Additive Schwarz preconditioner for the finite volume element discretization of symmetric elliptic problems. BIT Numer. Math. **56**(3), 967–993 (2015). https://doi.org/10.1007/s10543-015-0581-x
19. Marcinkowski, L., Loneland, A., Rahman, T.: Schwarz methods for a crouzeix-raviart finite volume discretization of elliptic problems. In: Dickopf, T., Gander, M.J., Halpern, L., Krause, R., Pavarino, L.F. (eds.) Domain Decomposition Methods in Science and Engineering XXII. LNCSE, vol. 104, pp. 595–602. Springer, Cham (2016). https://doi.org/10.1007/978-3-319-18827-0_61
20. Marcinkowski, L., Rahman, T.: Additive average Schwarz with adaptive coarse spaces: scalable algorithms for multiscale problems. Electron. Trans. Numer. Anal. **49**, 28–40 (2018). https://doi.org/10.1553/etna_vol49s28
21. Marcinkowski, L., Rahman, T., Khademi, A.: Adaptive Schwarz method for Crouzeix-Raviart multiscale problems in 2d. In: Domain decomposition methods in science and engineering XXVI. Lect. Notes Comput. Sci. Eng., Springer, Cham (2022). https://doi.org/10.1007/978-3-030-95025-5_48
22. Rahman, T., Xu, X., Hoppe, R.: Additive Schwarz methods for the Crouzeix-Raviart mortar finite element for elliptic problems with discontinuous coefficients. Numer. Math. **101**(3), 551–572 (2005). https://doi.org/10.1007/s00211-005-0625-2
23. Rui, H., Bi, C.: Convergence analysis of an upwind finite volume element method with crouzeix-raviart element for non-selfadjoint and indefinite problems. Front. Math. China **3**(4), 563–579 (2008)
24. Saad, Y., Schultz, M.H.: GMRES: a generalized minimal residual algorithm for solving nonsymmetric linear systems. SIAM J. Sci. Statist. Comput. **7**(3), 856–869 (1986). https://doi.org/10.1137/0907058

25. Sarkis, M., Szyld, D.B.: Optimal left and right additive Schwarz preconditioning for minimal residual methods with Euclidean and energy norms. Comput. Methods Appl. Mech. Engrg. **196**(8), 1612–1621 (2007). https://doi.org/10.1016/j.cma.2006.03.027

26. Smith, B.F., Bjørstad, P.E., Gropp, W.D.: Domain decomposition: Parallel multilevel methods for elliptic partial differential equations. Cambridge University Press, Cambridge (1996)

27. Spillane, N., Dolean, V., Hauret, P., Nataf, F., Pechstein, C., Scheichl, R.: Abstract robust coarse spaces for systems of PDEs via generalized eigenproblems in the overlaps. Numer. Math. **126**(4), 741–770 (2013). https://doi.org/10.1007/s00211-013-0576-y

28. Toselli, A., Widlund, O.: Domain decomposition methods—algorithms and theory, Springer Series in Computational Mathematics, vol. 34. Springer-Verlag, Berlin (2005). https://doi.org/10.1007/b137868

29. Zhang, S.: On domain decomposition algorithms for covolume methods for elliptic problems. Comput. Methods Appl. Mech. Engrg. **196**(1–3), 24–32 (2006)

Parareal Method for Anisotropic Diffusion Denoising

Xiujie Shan$^{(\boxtimes)}$ and Martin B. van Gijzen

Delft Institute of Applied Mathematics, Delft University of Technology,
2628 CD Delft, The Netherlands
xiujieshan@gmail.com

Abstract. This paper studies time-domain parallelisation using Parareal to speed up the computations of anisotropic diffusion filtering. We consider both explicit and implicit Euler based method for the propagation in time for Parareal. The Preconditioned Conjugate Gradient (PCG) method is used to solve the systems that arise in the implicit based method. The estimation of the iteration numbers of PCG allows us to predict the running time of Parareal calculation, which further guides us in the experimental stage. Parallelisation of the method is implemented using Coarray Fortran. We illustrate the experimental results on 3D low-field MRI images using up to 960 cores. The computational improvement in time is achieved.

Keywords: Image denoising · Parareal · Nonlinear Diffusion equation · High performance computing

1 Introduction

The nonlinear diffusion equation has many applications, and one of the most important is image denoising. The classical paper by Perona and Malik [18] proposed image denoising by considering denoising as a diffusion process, in which the diffusion parameter is chosen such that edges are preserved. Computationally this amounts to integrating time into a nonlinear diffusion equation. This process can be quite expensive. An option to speed up the computations is to use a parallel-in-time integration method.

Parallelisation in time was first considered by Nievergelt [16], to make full use of the potential of massively parallel computers. Parareal was proposed by Lions, Maday, and Turinici in 2001 [15]. The method was a real breakthrough, and it is now one of the most widely used parallel-in-time methods, particularly for the time discretization of partial differential evolution equations. A further concise version of the method, which is also commonly used now, was given in [3]. In [2], Bal and Maday gave the convergence analysis of Parareal for the heat equation and also the application to a nonlinear partial differential equation for pricing of an American put. Maday and others have been working on this topic continuously. Others developed a Parareal version for nonlinear PDEs [2] and a stable Parareal method for first- and second-order hyperbolic systems [5].

© The Author(s), under exclusive license to Springer Nature Switzerland AG 2023
R. Wyrzykowski et al. (Eds.): PPAM 2022, LNCS 13827, pp. 313–322, 2023.
https://doi.org/10.1007/978-3-031-30445-3_26

Analysis of the Parareal algorithm has provided new insights into the relations with other algorithms, which has led to new parallel-in-time algorithms. In 2007, Gander and Vandewalle [12] analyzed the connection between the Parareal algorithm, space-time multigrid, and the multiple shooting methods. A historical review of Parareal can be found in [12] as well. Gander et al. further explored this topic in [11], and interpreted the Parareal algorithm as a multigrid method which led to the multigrid-reduction-in-time (MGRIT) algorithm. By considering Parareal a preconditioned iterative process, where the coarse time integration method acts as the preconditioner, the authors extended Parareal (two-level) to a multi-level method in 2014 [8]. Wu [24] proposed a parallel coarse grid correction diagonalization technique and analyzed the convergence rate of this method. Gander and Wu developed a diagonalization-based Parareal algorithm for dissipative and wave propagation problems. A new Parareal algorithm for ODEs with discontinuous source in time has been proposed [10]. By defining a smooth input according to the coarse discretization, the authors illustrate that the coarse propagator can capture a highly oscillatory or discontinuous source in time.

The research about domain decomposition methods for image denoising includes successive space correction methods, parallel space correction methods, etc. [4]. These methods aim to do parallel computing by decomposing the image (space domain) and they have been used to solve some convex minimization problems, and variational inequalities with the convex set constraint [7,9,25]. The Parareal algorithm to solve the anisotropic diffusion denoising belongs to a different category, in which the algorithm is designed to do the parallel calculation in the time domain. We consider both explicit time and implicit based integration methods for the coarse and fine grids. The implicit Euler based method requires solving an extensive nonlinear system at every time step. To linearise the equation, we compute the diffusion based on the solution of the previous time step. The resulting linear system is solved with preconditioned conjugate gradient (PCG) method. We refer to [22] for the details of this solver and the preconditioners. We will analyse the possible speed-up for both the explicit and implicit method by estimating the computing time per Parareal iteration, using the upper bounds on the number of CG iterations provided in [22]. The results are validated by numerical experiments using up to 960 cores of the DelftBlue supercomputer of the Delft University of Technology [6].

Our paper is organized as follows. Section 2 presents the denoising model and its numerical discretization. Section 3, discusses Parareal to integrate the equations in time. Section 4 investigates potential speedup of Parareal. Section 5 presents the numerical experiments. Section 6 makes some concluding remarks.

2   Model and Discretization

This section describes the anisotropic diffusion denoising model and its numerical discretization in space and time.

2.1 Diffusion Model

The idea of using a diffusion equation for image denoising was first considered by Koenderink in [1] by connecting the linear heat equation to the Gaussian filter. The nonlinear diffusion model we use was proposed by Peron and Malik in 1990 in [18] and is given by

$$
\begin{cases}
\dfrac{\partial u}{\partial t} = \nabla \cdot (c(\|\nabla u\|_2)\nabla u), & \text{in} \quad \Omega \times (0,T), \\[2mm]
\dfrac{\partial u}{\partial \boldsymbol{n}} = 0, & \text{on} \quad \partial\Omega \times (0,T), \\[2mm]
u(0) = \hat{u}_0, & \text{in} \quad \Omega,
\end{cases}
\tag{1}
$$

where $\Omega \subseteq \mathbb{R}^d$ for $d = 2,\ 3$. Choices for the diffusion coefficient are given by $c_1(\|\nabla u\|_2) = e^{-(\|\nabla u\|_2/K)^2}$, $c_2(\|\nabla u\|_2) = \dfrac{1}{1+\left(\frac{\|\nabla u\|_2}{K}\right)^2}$, where K is a damping parameter. The idea behind this nonlinear diffusion model is explained as follows. Since the edges of the image can be approximately estimated by $\|\nabla u\|_2$, diffusion coefficient $c(\|\nabla u\|_2)$ is also called as edge detector. $c(\|\nabla u\|_2) \to 0$ as $\|\nabla u\|_2 \to +\infty$, this means that in the neighbourhood of an edge (where $\|\nabla u\|_2$ is large), the diffusion coefficient is small, i.e., the diffusion is slow. Similarly, in a flat area, $c(\|\nabla u\|_2) \to 1$, when $\|\nabla u\|_2 \to 0$. This means that the nonlinear diffusion behaves like linear diffusion in a flat area, and noise is smoothed out quickly. Apart from image processing, this model also arises in other contexts, for example, faceted crystal growth [13] and continuum mechanics [14].

For the one dimensional space case, we consider $\Omega = [0,\ 1]$ and step size $h_x = \frac{1}{N_x}$, where N_x is the number of spatial grid points. $\frac{\partial}{\partial x}(c(|\frac{\partial u}{\partial x}|) \cdot \frac{\partial u}{\partial x})$ can be discretized as

$$
\frac{\partial}{\partial x}\left(c(|\frac{\partial u}{\partial x}|) \cdot \frac{\partial u}{\partial x}\right)_{x_i} \approx c_{i+\frac{1}{2}}\frac{(u_{i+1} - u_i)}{h_x^2} - c_{i-\frac{1}{2}}\frac{(u_i - u_{i-1})}{h_x^2},
$$

where $c_{i\pm\frac{1}{2}} = \frac{c_{i\pm1}+c_i}{2}$. $c_i := c(|u_x|_i) = c(|\frac{u_{i+1}-u_{i-1}}{2h_x}|)$ for $0 \le i \le N_x - 1$. Because of the Neumann boundary conditions, we have that $u_{-1} = u_0$ and $u_{N_x-1} = u_{N_x}$. The discretization in space is given by

$$
\frac{d\mathbf{u}}{dt} = \frac{1}{h_x^2}
\begin{pmatrix}
-c_{\frac{1}{2}} & c_{\frac{1}{2}} & & & \\
c_{\frac{1}{2}} & -(c_{\frac{1}{2}}+c_{1+\frac{1}{2}}) & c_{1+\frac{1}{2}} & & \\
& \ddots & \ddots & \ddots & \\
& & c_{N-\frac{5}{2}} & -(c_{N-\frac{5}{2}}+c_{N-\frac{3}{2}}) & c_{N-\frac{3}{2}} \\
& & & c_{N-\frac{3}{2}} & -c_{N-\frac{3}{2}}
\end{pmatrix}
\mathbf{u},
$$

where $\mathbf{u} = (u_0, u_1, \ldots, u_{N-1})^T$. The higher-dimensional case can be discretised analogously.

2.2   Linearization and Time Discretization

After spatial discretisation we obtain a system of ordinary equations

$$\frac{d\mathbf{u}}{dt} = C(\mathbf{u})\mathbf{u}.$$

To integrate this system in time we consider the explicit and implicit Euler based method. Using explicit Euler method, we have for $m = 0, 1, 2, \ldots$

$$\frac{\mathbf{u}_{m+1} - \mathbf{u}_m}{\tau} = C(\mathbf{u}_m)\mathbf{u}_m. \tag{2}$$

We rewrite it into $\mathbf{u}^{m+1} = (\lambda(I + \tau C(\mathbf{u}^m)))\mathbf{u}^m$.

The implicit Euler based method follows $\frac{\mathbf{u}_{m+1} - \mathbf{u}_m}{\tau} = C(\mathbf{u}_{m+1})\mathbf{u}_{m+1}, m = 0, \ldots, N - 1$. To linearise the right-hand side, we approximate $C(\mathbf{u}_{m+1})$ by $C(\mathbf{u}_m)$. With this modification the implicit Euler based method is given by

$$\left(\frac{1}{\tau}I - C(\mathbf{u}_m)\right)\mathbf{u}_{m+1} = \frac{1}{\tau}\mathbf{u}_m, \tag{3}$$

which is a linear system of the form

$$A\mathbf{u} = \tilde{\mathbf{f}}. \tag{4}$$

In every time iteration, we solve a linear system (4) by using the preconditioned Conjugate Gradient method (PCG) [20]. Since A is strongly diagonally dominant we use diagonal scaling (Jacobi preconditioner) as preconditioner, which means setting the preconditioned matrix M as the main diagonal elements of A.

3   Parareal Algorithm for the Anisotropic Diffusion Model

This section starts with explaining the idea of Parareal algorithm as a multiple shooting method [12] and giving the algorithm for solving model (1).

Divide the time interval $(0, T)$ into subintervals $I_n = (T_n, T_{n+1})$ of size ΔT, $n = 0, 1, \ldots P - 1$. Then sub-interval I_n is decomposed further into smaller sub-interval with size δt. Now we consider solve the problem

$$\begin{cases} \dfrac{\partial \mathbf{u}}{\partial t} = C(\mathbf{u})\mathbf{u}, & t \in (0, T), \\ u(0) = u_0. \end{cases} \tag{5}$$

The initial value problems on each coarse time intervals are given by

$$\begin{cases} \dfrac{\partial \mathbf{u}_n}{\partial t} = C(\mathbf{u}_n)\mathbf{u}_n, & t \in (T_n, T_{n+1}), \\ \mathbf{u}_n(T_n) = U_n \end{cases}$$

and the matching conditions are $U_0 = \mathbf{u}_0$ and $U_{n+1} = u_n(T_{n+1}, U_n)$.

These conditions compose a nonlinear system which we denote it by $\mathbf{F}(\mathbf{U}) = 0$, where $\mathbf{U} = (U_0, U_1, \ldots, U_P)^T$. Solving this system by Newton method leads to

$$\begin{cases} U_0^{k+1} = \mathbf{u}_0, \\ U_{n+1}^{k+1} = \mathbf{u}_n(T_{n+1}, U_n^k) + \dfrac{\partial \mathbf{u}_n}{\partial U_n}(T_{n+1}, U_n^k)(U_n^{k+1} - U_n^k), \end{cases}$$

where $k = 0, 1, \ldots$.

Approximating $\mathbf{u}_n(T_{n+1}, U_n^k)$ by the fine propagator $F(U_n^k)$ and $\frac{\partial \mathbf{u}_n}{\partial U_n}(T_{n+1}, U_n^k)(U_n^{k+1} - U_n^k)$ by the coarse propagators $G(U_n^{k+1}) - G(U_n^k)$, the recursion formula of the Parareal method is

$$\begin{cases} U_0^{k+1} = \mathbf{u}_0, \\ U_{n+1}^{k+1} = F(U_n^k) + G(U_n^{k+1}) - G(U_n^k), \end{cases}$$

For the explicit Euler scheme, we have $G(U_n) = (I + \Delta T \cdot C(U_n))U_n$ and $F(U_n) = (I + \delta t \cdot C(U_n))U_n$. For the implicit Euler based method, we have $G(U_n) = (I - \Delta T \cdot C(U_n))^{-1} U_n$ and $F(U_n) = ((I - \delta t \cdot C(U_n))^{-1})^{\frac{\Delta T}{\delta t}} U_n$.

One usual initial guess for U_{n+1}^0 is $G(U_n^0)$. As the iteration converges and $U_{n+1}^{k+1} - U_{n+1}^k \to 0$, the results from the coarse method $G(U_n^{k+1})$ and $G(U_n^k)$ will cancel out and Parareal will only reproduces the fine time solution. It has been proven in [12] that Parareal converges after a maximum of P iterations.

Algorithm 1. Parareal algorithm for solving the model

$U_0^0 \leftarrow \tilde{U}_0^0 \leftarrow \mathbf{u}_0$
for $n = 0$ to $P - 1$ **do**
    $\tilde{U}_{n+1}^0 \leftarrow G(\tilde{U}_n^0)$
    $U_{n+1}^0 \leftarrow \tilde{U}_{n+1}^0$
end for
$U_0^1 \leftarrow \mathbf{u}_0$
for $k = 0$ to $K_{max} - 1$ **do**
    for $n = 0$ to $P - 1$ **do** (parallel)
        $\hat{U}_{n+1}^k \leftarrow F(U_n^k)$
    end for
    for $n = 0$ to $P - 1$ **do**
        $\tilde{U}_{n+1}^{k+1} \leftarrow G(U_n^{k+1})$
        $U_{n+1}^{k+1} \leftarrow \hat{U}_{n+1}^k + \tilde{U}_{n+1}^{k+1} - \tilde{U}_{n+1}^k$ which equals to:
        $U_{n+1}^{k+1} \leftarrow F(U_n^k) + G(U_n^{k+1}) - G(U_n^k)$
    end for
    if $\dfrac{\|U_{n+1}^{k+1} - U_{n+1}^k\|_2}{\|\mathbf{u}_0\|_2} < \epsilon$ **then**
        BREAK
    end if
end for

---

4   Analysis of the Algorithm

The speed-up of Parareal has been estimated in [2]. The cost of the fine iteration method is proportional to $\frac{T}{\delta t}$. The computational cost of Parareal is proportional to $k(\frac{T}{\Delta T} + \frac{\Delta T}{\delta t})$. Fixing k, the cost of Parareal is optimal when $\frac{T}{\Delta T} = \frac{\Delta T}{\delta t}$. For the aim of comparison, keeping $\frac{T}{\delta t}$ fixed leads to $\Delta T = \sqrt{T \delta t}$. Therefore, the maximum gain in computational time is $S = \frac{1}{4}\sqrt{\frac{T}{\delta t}}$ for $k = 2$.

In our paper, for solving the problem with the implicit method, the iteration number of PCG can be bounded. Later we will use the bounds to estimate the algorithm's running time. Since $\max_i(|C_{i,i}|) \leq \frac{2d}{h^2}$, by using the Gershgorin's theorem, we have

$$\kappa_\tau \leq 1 + \frac{4d\tau}{h^2},$$

where τ is the time step and d is the space dimension. For the details we refer to [22]. The iteration number of PCG is given as

$$N_\tau = \ln\left(\frac{\epsilon}{2\sqrt{\kappa_\tau}}\right) / \ln\left(\frac{\sqrt{\kappa_\tau} - 1}{\sqrt{\kappa_\tau} + 1}\right). \tag{6}$$

4.1   Potential Speedup by Parareal (Ideal Case)

The total amount of calculation for the fine method with the time step δt is $\frac{T}{\delta t}$. By using the explicit Euler method as fine and coarse propagators, we have the speedup for Parareal method is:

$$S \approx \frac{\frac{T}{\delta t}}{\left((k+1)\frac{T}{\Delta T} + k\frac{\Delta T}{\delta t}\right)},$$

where $k + 1$ is from the initialization of Parareal.

For implicit Euler based method with PCG as fine and coarse propagators, we have

$$S \approx \frac{\frac{T}{\delta t}N_{\frac{T}{\delta t}}}{\left((k+1)\frac{T}{\Delta T}N_{\frac{T}{\Delta t}} + k\frac{\Delta T}{\delta t}N_{\frac{\Delta T}{\delta t}}\right)}, \tag{7}$$

where $N_{\{\cdot\}}$ stands for the PCG iterations for different time step. By fixing k, T and δ_t, we can search the maximal gain in time.

4.2   Potential Speedup by Parareal (with Communication Time)

Assuming that one communication time between fine and coarse is $T_{co} = T_{f2c} + T_{c2f}$, we have total communication time for Parareal is kT_{co}. By calculating the CPU time for one step time iteration T_f in the sequential case, we have the estimated CPU time for Parareal as $T_f\left((k+1)\frac{T}{\Delta T} + k\frac{\Delta T}{\delta t}\right)$. The total time for Parareal calculation for the explicit Euler in the super computer is then $T_{total} = T_f\left((k+1)\frac{T}{\Delta T} + k\frac{\Delta T}{\delta t}\right) + kT_{co}$. By denoting the CPU time for one PCG iteration as $T_{f_{cg}}$, we have $T_{total} = T_{f_{cg}}\left((k+1)\frac{T}{\Delta T}N_{\frac{T}{\Delta t}} + k\frac{\Delta T}{\delta t}N_{\frac{\Delta T}{\delta t}}\right) + kT_{co}$ for the implicit Euler based method.

5   Experimental Results

This section will give the run time and image results tested by the denoising model. Image data and parameter choices for the Parareal algorithm are provided as well, including the CG iteration number, tolerance ϵ for Parareal, ΔT for coarse method, and δt for fine method.

The parallel implementation for the Parareal method is done in Fortran using Coarray Fortran (CAF). CAF follows the SPMD model. Each process (called image) has its private variables. Variables which have a so-called codimension are addressable from other images. We use CAF to implement the fine propagator in parallel on each coarse interval. We run the fine steps parallel in time indicating the number of cores.

The numerical tests have been performed on the DelftBlue supercomputer, which now has 228 Intel Xeon compute nodes with 48 cores each. We test a 3D melon image ($128 \times 128 \times 128$) scanned by low-field MRI machine [17] using model (choosing diffusion coefficient to be c_1 with $K = 20$) in Table 1 and Table 2. The fine time step is $1e^{-7}$ and the total number of time steps is 960, meaning that $T = 960 \times 1e^{-7}$. The relative tolerance for Parareal and PCG to converge is $1e^{-6}$.

Table 1 shows the results for explicit method. When the number of coarse steps equals 48, we have the lowest run time, with a speed-up of about two. The estimated time is obtained from the ideas described in Sect. 4.2 without communication time. This estimated time predicts well the optimal number of coarse steps for this example. The estimated times are consistently lower than the measured run times. This can be explained by the fact that we did not consider communication time in the estimated time.

The results for implicit Euler based method are tabulated in Table 2. The CG iterations we got from the experiments match the theoretical iterations in (6). We again observe that the estimated times predict well the optimal number of cores, which is 48, and again we see a speed-up of about a factor of two for the optimal number of cores. We do observe that, with for increasing number of cores, our estimation for the run time becomes too pessimistic. For this we do not have a satisfactory explanation yet (Fig. 1).

Table 1. Parareal times obtained for explicit Euler. ("Coarse" stands for coarse step $T/\Delta T$, "Parareal" the total Parareal iterations, "Elapsed time" the running time for the algorithm, "Total iterations" the fine and coarse iterations with Parareal iterations, "Estimated time" is calculated as T_{total}.)

Coarse	Parareal	Elapsed time	Total iterations	Estimated time
1	1	286	960	286.00
12	12	480	1116	332.48
48	4	127	320	95.33
96	3	136	414	123.34
192	3	243	783	233.27
480	2	449	1444	430.19
960	1	646	1921	572.30

Table 2. Parareal time obtained for implicit Euler based method. ("CG coarse" stands for the iterations of CG for one coarse propagation, "CG fine" iterations of CG for one fine propagation, "Total iterations" the CG iterations for coarse and fine propagations with Parareal iterations, "Estimated time" is calculated as T_{total}.)

Coarse	Parareal	CG coarse	CG fine	Elapsed time	Total iterations	Estimated time
1	1	2	2	1102	1920	1102
12	8	7	2	1413	2036	983
48	5	4	2	656	1352	578
96	4	3	2	690	1520	707
192	3	3	2	874	2334	1075
480	3	2	2	1882	3852	2211
960	1	2	2	1502	3842	2205

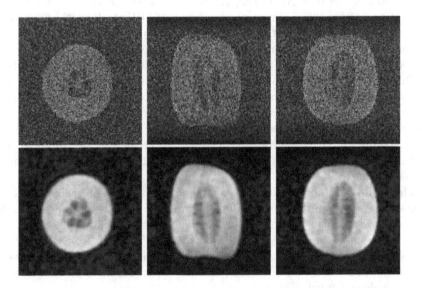

Fig. 1. Three slides from the 3D melon image, the model is with diffusion coefficient c_2 and $K = 15$. The total diffusion time is $2.4e^{-6}$.

6   Conclusions

In this paper, we have investigated the use of the Parareal method to speed up anisotropic diffusion filtering. The parallelisation in time can be done with only local modifications to the code, without the need to completely restructure the program. We have derived theoretical estimates for the run time that can be used to predict the optimal number of cores. A modest but useful speedup with a factor of two is obtained to denoise a 3D low-field MR image of a melon.

Acknowledgements. The authors thank the Leiden University Medical Center for providing the low-field MR image and the reviewers' comments to help improve the paper.

A   Appendix

So far, we have focused on the classical denoising models as proposed in [18] by Perona and Malik. The total variational model proposed in [19] is a widely used alternative. In this appendix, we give numerical results for this technique. We use Parareal with the linearised implicit Euler method. As explained in [21], it is not possible to derive a useful upper bound on the number of CG iterations for the total variation model and make an a priori prediction for the optimal number of cores for this method. Solving the total variation model with gradient descent method equals solving (1) with $c(\|\nabla u\|_2) = \frac{1}{\|\nabla u\|_2}$. Following the idea of [23], we solve it with a lagged diffusivity fixed point iteration. For the numerical experiments, we use $\frac{1}{\|\nabla u\| + \epsilon}$ instead of $\frac{1}{\|\nabla u\|}$, where $\epsilon = 1e^{-5}$. One fine time step is $1.5e^{-6}$ and the total evaluation time is $7.2e^{-4}$ (Table 3).

Table 3. Parareal times obtained for implicit Euler. ("Coarse" stands for coarse step $T/\Delta T$, "Parareal" the total Parareal iterations, "Elapsed time" the running time for the algorithm.)

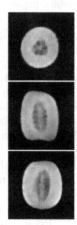

Coarse	Parareal	Elapsed time
1	1	2023.48
12	5	1580.85
48	2	1495.60
96	2	2717.97
240	1	2173.66
480	1	2263.87

References

1. The structure of images: biological cybernetics **50**, 363–370 (1984)
2. Bal, G., Maday, Y.: A "parareal" time discretization for non-linear PDE's with application to the pricing of an American put. In: Pavarino, L.F., Toselli, A. (eds.) Recent Developments in Domain Decomposition Methods, vol. 23, pp. 189–202. Springer, Berlin (2002). https://doi.org/10.1007/978-3-642-56118-4_12
3. Bal, G.: Parallelization in time of (stochastic) ordinary differential equations (2006)
4. Chang, H., Zhang, X., Xue-Cheng, T., Yang, D.: Domain decomposition methods for nonlocal total variation image restoration. J. Sci. Comput. **60**, 79–100 (2014). https://doi.org/10.1007/s10915-013-9786-9

5. Dai, X., Maday, Y.: Stable parareal in time method for first- and second-order hyperbolic systems. SIAM J. Sci. Comput. **35**(1), A52–A78 (2013)
6. Delft High Performance Computing Centre (DHPC): DelftBlue Supercomputer (Phase 1) (2022)
7. Duan, Y., Tai, X.C.: Domain decomposition methods with graph cuts algorithms for total variation minimization Adv. Comput. Math. **36**, 175–199 (2012). https://doi.org/10.1007/s10444-011-9213-4
8. Falgout, R.D., Friedhoff, S., Kolev, T.V., MacLachlan, S.P., Schroder, J.B.: Parallel time integration with multigrid. SIAM J. Sci. Comput. **36**(6), C635–C661 (2014)
9. Firsov, D., Lui, S.: Domain decomposition methods in image denoising using gaussian curvature. J. Comput. Appl. Math. **193**(2), 460–473 (2006)
10. Gander, M.J., Kulchytska-Ruchka, I., Niyonzima, I., Schöps, S.: A new parareal algorithm for problems with discontinuous sources. SIAM J. Sci. Comput. **41**(2), B375–B395 (2019)
11. Gander, M.J., Kwok, F., Zhang, H.: Multigrid interpretations of the Parareal algorithm leading to an overlapping variant and MGRIT. Compu. Vis. Sci. **19**, 59–74 (2018)
12. Gander, M.J., Vandewalle, S.: Analysis of the parareal time-parallel time-integration method. SIAM J. Sci. Comput. **29**(2), 556–578 (2007)
13. Kobayashi, R., Giga, Y.: Equations with singular diffusivity. J. Stat. Phys. **95**, 1187–1220 (1999). https://doi.org/10.1023/A:1004570921372
14. Kohn, R., Temam, R.: Dual spaces of stresses and strains, with applications to hencky plasticity. Appl. Math. Optim. **10**, 1–35 (1983). https://doi.org/10.1007/BF01448377
15. Lions, J.L., Maday, Y., Turinici, G.: Résolution d'edp par un schéma en temps «pararéel?». Comptes Rendus de l'Académie des Sciences - Series I - Mathematics **332**(7), 661–668 (2001)
16. Nievergelt, J.: Parallel methods for integrating ordinary differential equations. Commun. ACM **7**(12), 731–733 (1964)
17. O'Reilly, T., Teeuwisse, W., Webb, A.: Three-dimensional MRI in a homogenous 27.cm diameter bore Halbach array magnet. J. Magn. Reson. **307**, 106578 (2019)
18. Perona, P., Malik, J.: Scale-space and edge detection using anisotropic diffusion. IEEE Trans. Pattern Anal. Mach. Intell. **12**(7), 629–639 (1990)
19. Rudin, L.I., Osher, S., Fatemi, E.: Nonlinear total variation based noise removal algorithms. Physica D: Nonlinear Phenomena **60**(1), 259–268 (1992)
20. Saad, Y.: Iterative methods for sparse linear systems. Society for Industrial and Applied Mathematics Philadelphia, PA, USA (2003)
21. Shan, X., van Gijzen, M.: Deflated preconditioned conjugate gradients for nonlinear diffusion image enhancement. In: Vermolen, F.J., Vuik, C. (eds.) Numerical Mathematics and Advanced Applications ENUMATH 2019. LNCSE, vol. 139, pp. 459–468. Springer, Cham (2021). https://doi.org/10.1007/978-3-030-55874-1_45
22. Shan, X., van Gijzen, M.B.: Deflated preconditioned conjugate gradient methods for noise filtering of low-field MR images. J. Comput. Appl. Math. **400**, 113730 (2022)
23. Vogel, C., Oman, M.: Fast, robust total variation-based reconstruction of noisy, blurred images. IEEE Trans. Image Process. **7**(6), 813–824 (1998)
24. Wu, S.L.: Toward parallel coarse grid correction for the parareal algorithm. SIAM J. Sci. Comput. **40**(3), A1446–A1472 (2018)
25. Xu, J., Tai, X.C., Wang, L.L.: A two-level domain decomposition method for image restoration. Inverse Probl. Imaging **4**(3), 523–545 (2010)

Comparison of Block Preconditioners for the Stokes Problem with Discontinuous Viscosity and Friction

Piotr Krzyżanowski[✉]

University of Warsaw, Warsaw, Poland
p.krzyzanowski@mimuw.edu.pl

Abstract. Several block preconditioning strategies for the Stokes problem with piecewise discontinuous viscosity and friction are investigated for their efficiency and independence of the contrast in both viscosity and friction. The constituting blocks correspond to inexact solvers, based on algebraic multigrid. It follows that the block triangular preconditioner is the most robust choice.

Keywords: Stokes problem · discontinuous coefficients · block preconditioner

1 Introduction

Let us consider a stationary Stokes system with friction:

$$
\begin{aligned}
-\operatorname{div}(\nu \nabla u) + \kappa u + \nabla p &= f, \\
\operatorname{div} u &= 0,
\end{aligned}
\tag{1}
$$

in a domain $\Omega \subset R^d$, where $d = 2, 3$, supplemented with boundary conditions

$$
u = u_D \text{ on } \partial\Omega_D, \qquad \nu\frac{\partial u}{\partial n} - pn = 0 \text{ on } \partial\Omega_N,
$$

where both $\partial\Omega_D$ and $\partial\Omega_N$ have a positive $(d-1)$-dimensional measure and they together form a splitting of $\partial\Omega$ into the Dirichlet part and the Neumann part, respectively. For the notational simplicity, in this section, without loss of generality, we will restrict ourselves to the case $u_D = 0$.

We assume that Ω can be split into two disjoint subdomains, $\bar\Omega = \bar\Omega_1 \cup \bar\Omega_2$ and $\Omega_1 \cap \Omega_2 = \emptyset$ and that the intersections of both $\partial\Omega_1$ and $\partial\Omega_2$ with $\partial\Omega_D$ have a positive measure. Further, we restrict ourselves to the case when both the viscosity ν and the friction κ are discontinuous across the interface between Ω_1 and Ω_2,

$$
\nu = \begin{cases} \nu_1 & \text{in } \Omega_1, \\ \nu_2 & \text{in } \Omega_2, \end{cases} \qquad
\kappa = \begin{cases} \kappa_1 & \text{in } \Omega_1, \\ \kappa_2 & \text{in } \Omega_2, \end{cases}
$$

© The Author(s), under exclusive license to Springer Nature Switzerland AG 2023
R. Wyrzykowski et al. (Eds.): PPAM 2022, LNCS 13827, pp. 323–330, 2023.
https://doi.org/10.1007/978-3-031-30445-3_27

and both $0 < \nu_1 \leq \nu_2$, and $\kappa_1, \kappa_2 \geq 0$ as well, are constants. The unknowns are the fluid velocity $u : \bar{\Omega} \to R^d$ and the pressure $p : \Omega \to R$, while the external force f is prescribed.

Such a problem arises in many applications. For example, it appears as a part of a linearization scheme of geophysical fluid flows [11], where different viscosities correspond to different physical properties of the rock. It also results from the so called one-fluid approach to two-phase flows where one assumes that i-th phase ocuppies Ω_i [10]. Another application is to use (1) to approximate flow in Ω_1 around obstacle Ω_2 via introduction of artificial penalizing parameters inside Ω_2: either large friction κ_2 [7] or large viscosity ν_2 [9], or both.

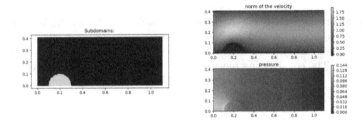

Fig. 1. Left: The geometry of the domain and its subdomains: Ω_1 marked in dark color, Ω_2 painted in yellow. Right: example solution (see Sect. 3)(Color figure online).

After finite element discretization of (1), one arrives at a large system of linear equations with a block 2×2 structure, consisting of sparse matrices (cf. Sect. 2). The condition number of this system is adversely affected not only by the mesh size h, but also by the viscosity contrast ν_2/ν_1 and the friction coefficient κ. In turn, iterative solvers for the system will converge very slowly, unless adequately preconditioned.

Preconditioners for the Stokes system with high contrast in the viscosity have recently been investigated by numerous scientists. Probably the first to analyze a preconditioning method to (4)–(5), which was based on block diagonal preconditioning as specified below, were Olshanskii and Reusken [10]. In [11], a block diagonal preconditioner was introduced, exploring the so called BFBT approach [4] customized by introducing weights. Recently, a matrix–free preconditioner was proposed and evaluated in [13], mixing Chebyschev smoothers with Zulehner's [15] approach to preconditioning saddle point problems. Seemingly, the question how these preconditioners perform in the case when $\kappa_1 = 0 \neq \kappa_2$ was not investigated so far. While all these works deal with high contrast cases, they mostly use only one type (usually block diagonal) of a block preconditioner. Hence, in what follows we compare the efficiency of various types of block preconditioners.

2 Finite Element Discretization and Matrix Formulation

Setting
$$V = \{v \in H^1(\Omega)^d : v = 0 \text{ on } \partial\Omega_D\}, \qquad W = L^2(\Omega),$$

the weak formulation of (1) is to find $(u, p) \in V \times W$ such that for any $(v, w) \in V \times W$, there holds

$$\sum_{i=1}^{2} \int_{\Omega_i} (\nu_i \nabla u \cdot \nabla v + \kappa_i u\, v)\, dx - \int_{\Omega} p\, \nabla \cdot v\, dx = \int_{\Omega} f\, v\, dx, \qquad (2)$$

$$\int_{\Omega} \nabla \cdot u\, w\, dx = 0. \qquad (3)$$

In order to discretize (2)–(3) with the finite element method, we assume that both Ω_1 and Ω_2 are polyhedrons and equip them with conforming triangulations $\mathcal{T}_{h_i}(\Omega_i)$, $i = 1, 2$, where h_i denotes the corresponding mesh size. We further assume that $\mathcal{T}_h = \mathcal{T}_{h_1}(\Omega_1) \cup \mathcal{T}_{h_2}(\Omega_2)$, $h = \max\{h_1, h_2\}$, is still a proper conforming triangulation of entire Ω. Next, we choose two finite element spaces, $V_h \subset V$ and $W_h \subset W$, satisfying the uniform inf-sup condition; one example of such a pair of spaces is the Taylor–Hood element [6]. Then we formulate the discretized problem as follows:

Problem 1. *Find* $(u_h, p_h) \in V_h \times W_h$ *such that for any* $(v_h, w_h) \in V_h \times W_h$ *there holds*

$$\sum_{i=1}^{2} \int_{\Omega_i} (\nu_i \nabla u_h \cdot \nabla v_h + \kappa_i u_h\, v_h)\, dx - \int_{\Omega} p_h\, \text{div } v_h\, dx = \int_{\Omega} f\, v_h\, dx, \qquad (4)$$

$$\int_{\Omega} w_h\, \text{div } u_h\, dx = 0. \qquad (5)$$

Taking standard nodal basis functions, we can express (4)–(5) as a system of linear equations with a 2×2 block matrix $\mathcal{M}$:

$$\mathcal{M} \begin{pmatrix} U \\ P \end{pmatrix} \equiv \begin{pmatrix} A & B^T \\ B & 0 \end{pmatrix} \begin{pmatrix} U \\ P \end{pmatrix} = \begin{pmatrix} F \\ 0 \end{pmatrix}, \qquad (6)$$

where A is an SPD matrix which corresponds to the discrete reaction–diffusion term, while matrix B is a discretized counterpart to the divergence operator.

3 Block Preconditioners

All these preconditioners are derived from two possible variants of block LU decomposition of a block matrix:

$$\begin{pmatrix} A & B^T \\ B & -C \end{pmatrix} = \begin{pmatrix} I & \\ B\,A^{-1} & I \end{pmatrix} \begin{pmatrix} A & \\ & S_A \end{pmatrix} \begin{pmatrix} I & A^{-1}B^T \\ & I \end{pmatrix}$$

$$= \begin{pmatrix} I & -B^T C^{-1} \\ & I \end{pmatrix} \begin{pmatrix} S_C & \\ & -C \end{pmatrix} \begin{pmatrix} I & \\ -C^{-1}B & I \end{pmatrix},$$

where $S_A = -C - BA^{-1}B^T$ and $S_C = A + B^T C^{-1}B$ are the corresponding
Schur complements. Motivated by the above decompositions, two main types of
block preconditioning matrices arise which can, in principle, be applied to (6)
(cf. [8] and the literature cited therein):

- dual block preconditioners:

$$
\mathcal{P}_d^{-1} = \begin{pmatrix} I & -dA_0^{-1}B^T \\ & I \end{pmatrix} \begin{pmatrix} A_0^{-1} & \\ & S_0^{-1} \end{pmatrix} \begin{pmatrix} I & \\ -cBA_0^{-1} & I \end{pmatrix} \tag{7}
$$

- primal block preconditioners

$$
\mathcal{P}_p^{-1} = \begin{pmatrix} I & \\ -cS_0^{-1}B & I \end{pmatrix} \begin{pmatrix} A_0^{-1} & \\ & S_0^{-1} \end{pmatrix} \begin{pmatrix} I & -dB^T S_0^{-1} \\ & I \end{pmatrix}. \tag{8}
$$

where A_0 and S_0 are assumed symmetric, positive (or negative) definite matrices
and c, d are prescribed real numbers (in what follows, we will limit ourselves only
to several specific choices when $c, d \in \{-1, 0, 1\}$).

It can easily be verified that applying $\mathcal{P}_d^{-1}$ to a vector requires one solve
with S_0 and at most two solves with A_0, while applying $\mathcal{P}_p^{-1}$ to a vector takes
one solve with A_0 and at most two solves with S_0.[1] In consequence, the costs of
vector multiplication by $\mathcal{P}_d^{-1}$ or $\mathcal{P}_p^{-1}$ may differ when $cd \neq 0$.

Our goal here is to assess which of three block preconditioning strategies:

- block diagonal, $c = d = 0$ (abbr. „diag" in Sect. 3),
- block triangular, $c = 1$, $d = 0$ (abbr. „triang"),
- block indefinite, $c = d = 1$ (in both dual and primal versions) (abbr. „indef"),

leads to the most efficient iterative method, while being insensitive to the mesh
size, the viscosity contrast and the friction coefficient.

The key point to satisfactory performance of these preconditioners is to
choose the founding blocks (A_0, S_0) as good preconditioners to either the pair
(A, S_A) or (S_C, C), depending whether one uses dual or primal block preconditioning, respectively [8].

Choosing S_0 For the standard Stokes system (that is, $\nu_1 = \nu_2 = 1$ and
$\kappa_2 = 0$), it is long known that S_A is spectrally equivalent (uniformly in h) to the
mass matrix, so in this specific case S_0 can be chosen as a preconditioner to the
mass matrix.

For the system (1) with discontinuous viscosity and no friction it was proved
in [10] that S_A is uniformly spectrally equivalent (with respect to both the mesh
size and the viscosity contrast) to M_ν — the mass matrix scaled by the inverse of
the viscosity, i.e. corresponding to the bilinear form $\sum_{i=1}^{2} \int_{\Omega_i} \nu_i^{-1} p\,q\,dx$. Therefore, a rather cheap preconditioner S_0 for this scaled mass matrix M_ν should be
sufficient.

Choosing A_0 Following works mentioned above, we will set A_0 as a good preconditioner for A matrix — a matrix which corresponds to a reaction–diffusion

---

[1] When $cd = 0$, both types of preconditioners require only one solve with A_0 and one
with S_0.

Table 1. Number of iterations for exact and inexact solvers with respect to the mesh resolution N. Dual block diagonal and block triangular preconditioner case. Here, $\nu_2 = 10^6, \kappa_2 = 10^9$.

block solver →	exact			inexact		
precond ↓ N →	64	128	256	64	128	256
diag	25	27	25	63	34	34
triang	18	18	19	26	27	28

problem with discontinuous coefficients. Such preconditioner can be constructed in many ways; for example, one can take a domain decomposition based preconditioner, [3], which offers a high level of coarse grain parallelism.

Another possibility, confirmed by our experiments in Sect. 4, is to use an algebraic multigrid solver which is known to be robust with respect to high variation in the diffusion coefficient, see e.g. [14, Section 14], and can also be parallelized [5].

4   Numerical Experiments

Our experimental setting is a variation on the theme of the classical 2D benchmark [12], with an obstacle serving as Ω_2 and the geometry modified by moving the center of the obstacle to the bottom of the domain, as in [9]. Zero Dirichlet boundary conditions are imposed on the top and the bottom edges of rectangular Ω, together with a parabolic inflow profile on its left edge. On the right, the "do nothing" boundary condition is prescribed; cf. Figure 1. We set $\nu_1 = 10^{-3}, \kappa_1 = 0$ as in [12], while ν_2, κ_2 play the role of parameters which penalize the flow inside the obstacle.

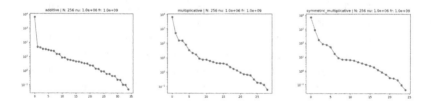

Fig. 2. Typical convergence histories for various preconditioners. Left: block diagonal; center: block triangular; right: block indefinite. Inexact block solvers, dual version. $N = 256$.

We ran the experiments in FEniCS [1] with PETSc [2] backend for linear algebra, on a 4-core Intel i5-6400 2.7 GHz machine with 16 GB of RAM. For the finite element spaces we used the classical Taylor–Hood pair. The domain was triangulated with an unstructured, shape regular mesh, refined in the vicinity of the interface between Ω_1 and Ω_2. The mesh resolution parameter $N \in \{32, 64, 128, 256\}$ was roughly inversely proportional to the mesh size (doubling N essentially quadrupled the number of unknowns). The largest system solved had approximately $8 \cdot 10^5$ degrees of freedom.

Two types of A_0 and S_0 were considered:

- „exact": $A_0 = A$, $S_0 = M_\nu$,
- „inexact": both A_0^{-1} and S_0^{-1} were defined as three iterations of the algebraic multigrid solver for A or M_ν, respectively. The algebraic multigrid solver was BoomerAMG from the hypre library [5], with default parameters.

For comparison, we also include results for the so called inexact Schur complement preconditioner. This preconditioner takes A_0^{-1} defined as two iterations of the GMRES preconditioned with BoomerAMG and S_0^{-1} defined as three iterations of the Jacobi method applied to the *inexact Schur* complement $BA_0^{-1}B^T$.

In Tables 1 and 2 we report on the total number of iterations of the GMRES(40) solver required to reduce the norm of the residual by a factor 10^5, taking zero as the initial guess. Table 3 presents the corresponding timings (in seconds). Figure 2 shows typical convergence histories for three types of preconditioners where, after a relatively short phase of fast reduction of the residual, the convergence speed becomes slower.

Table 2. Number of iterations for varying ν_2 and κ_2. $N = 256$. Inexact dual (upper part) and primal (middle part) preconditioners, followed by dual exact (lower part) preconditioner.

Precond →	diag				triang				indef				inex. schur			
$\kappa_2 \downarrow \nu_2 \rightarrow$	10^{-3}	10^0	10^3	10^6	10^{-3}	10^0	10^3	10^6	10^{-3}	10^0	10^3	10^6	10^{-3}	10^0	10^3	10^6
0	63	34	34	34	23	29	29	29	19	24	24	24	23	29	29	29
10^3	79	34	34	34	61	28	29	29	49	24	24	24	60	29	29	29
10^9	34	35	80	34	28	28	60	28	23	24	46	24	28	28	60	29
0	63	34	34	34	23	28	28	28	25	28	28	28	38	60	56	56
10^3	79	34	34	34	61	28	28	28	77	28	28	28	80	61	56	56
10^9	34	35	80	34	28	28	60	28	27	29	76	28	60	64	80	64
0	19	27	27	27	13	19	19	19	13	18	18	18	13	20	20	20
10^3	62	25	27	27	34	19	19	19	33	18	18	18	33	19	20	20
10^9	25	25	62	25	17	17	33	19	17	17	33	18	19	19	33	19

All types of block preconditioners retain their convergence rate in a very broad range of problem parameters under consideration: the discrete problem size (controlled implicitly by mesh resolution N), the viscosity contrast ν_2/ν_1. As concerns the friction parameter κ_2, their performance was essentially uniform, with two outliers observed for all N and preconditioner types, when $(\nu_2, \kappa_2) \in \{(10^{-3}, 10^3), (10^3, 10^9)\}$ — in these cases, the convergence rate, while still acceptable, was visibly reduced in comparison to other combinations of (ν_2, κ_2).

Table 3. Timings for varying ν_2 and κ_2. $N = 256$. Results for dual and primal exact, then dual and primal inexact preconditioners are presented in the subsequent parts of the table.

precond →	diag				triang				indef				inex. schur			
$\kappa_2 \downarrow \nu_2 \rightarrow$	10^{-3}	10^0	10^3	10^6	10^{-3}	10^0	10^3	10^6	10^{-3}	10^0	10^3	10^6	10^{-3}	10^0	10^3	10^6
0	95	52	52	52	37	45	45	46	59	73	73	73	70	86	85	86
10^3	116	52	52	52	92	44	45	46	145	73	73	73	174	86	86	86
10^9	49	51	117	52	42	41	89	44	67	68	137	73	78	78	173	86
0	95	52	52	52	37	44	44	44	40	45	45	44	59	91	86	85
10^3	117	52	52	52	91	44	44	44	116	45	45	45	119	92	85	86
10^9	49	50	118	52	41	41	90	44	41	43	115	45	86	91	119	96
0	33	34	34	34	32	33	32	32	34	36	36	36	34	37	36	36
10^3	43	34	34	34	36	33	32	32	43	36	36	36	42	36	36	36
10^9	34	34	42	34	32	32	35	33	36	36	42	37	36	36	41	36
0	34	34	34	35	32	33	32	33	32	33	33	33	–	–	–	–
10^3	44	34	34	34	37	33	33	33	42	33	33	33	–	–	–	–
10^9	34	34	42	34	32	32	36	33	33	33	42	33	–	–	–	–

5   Conclusions

While replacing exact solvers with inexact ones increases the number of iterations, significantly lower cost per iteration of the latter should make the inexact version more efficient if the blocks will grow large enough. It is expected to be more profound in 3D, when direct solvers struggle more. However, the relatively small-sized experiments in 2D provided here, so far show the supremacy of using direct factorization of A and M_ν. On the other hand, our inexact versions used for the comparison were indeed very crude approximations to the exact inverse.

The most efficient preconditioners turned out the triangular and the primal block indefinite ones, despite the dual block indefinite preconditioner offered the fastest convergence rate. Because of greater simplicity and potential for a better pattern of memory access and higher degree of parallelism, the former seems the best choice overall.

Acknowledgement. The author wishes to thank the reviewers whose comments and remarks helped to improve the paper.

References

1. Alnæs, M.S.: The FEniCS project version 1.5. Arch. Numer. Softw. **3**(100) (2015)
2. Balay, S., et al.: PETSc users manual. Technical Report ANL-95/11 - Revision 3.8, Argonne National Laboratory (1995)
3. Dryja, M., Sarkis, M.: Additive average Schwarz methods for discretization of elliptic problems with highly discontinuous coefficients. Comput. Methods Appl. Math. **10**(2), 164–176 (2010)

4. Elman, H.C.: Preconditioning for the steady-state navier-stokes equations with low viscosity. SIAM J. Sci. Comput. **20**(4), 1299–1316 (1999)
5. Robert D. Falgout, Jim E. Jones, and Ulrike Meier Yang. The design and implementation of hypre, a library of parallel high performance preconditioners. In Numerical solution of Partial Differential Equations on Parallel Computers, Lect. Notes Comput. Sci. Eng, pages 267–294. Springer-Verlag, 2006
6. Girault, V., Raviart, P.A.: Finite Element Method for Navier-Stokes Equations. Theory and Algorithms. Springer, Berlin (1986)
7. Kadoch, B., Kolomenskiy, D., Angot, P., Schneider, K.: A volume penalization method for incompressible flows and scalar advection-diffusion with moving obstacles. J. Comput. Phys. **231**(12), 4365–4383 (2012)
8. Krzyżanowski, P.: Block preconditioners for saddle point problems resulting from discretizations of partial differential equations. In: Axelsson, O., Karatson, J., (eds.), Efficient Preconditioned Solution Methods for Elliptic Partial Differential Equations, pp. 44–65. Bentham Publishers (2011)
9. Malikova, S.: Approximation of rigid obstacle by highly viscous fluid (2022). arxiv:2201.10299
10. Olshanskii, M.A., Reusken, A.: A Stokes interface problem: stability, finite element analysis and a robust solver. In: European Congress on Computational Methods in Applied Sciences and Engineering ECCOMAS 2004 (2004)
11. Rudi, J., Stadler, G., Ghattas, O.: Weighted BFBT preconditioner for Stokes flow problems with highly heterogeneous viscosity. SIAM J. Sci. Comput. **39**(5), S272–S297 (2017)
12. Schäfer, M., Turek, S., Durst, F., Krause, E., Rannacher, R.: Benchmark computations of laminar flow around a cylinder. In: Hirschel, E.H. (ed.) Flow Simulation with High-Performance Computers II: DFG Priority Research Programme Results 1993–1995, pp. 547–566. Vieweg+Teubner Verlag, Wiesbaden (1996). https://doi.org/10.1007/978-3-322-89849-4_39
13. Wichrowski, M.: Fluid-structure interaction problems: velocity-based formulation and monolithic computational methods. PhD thesis, Polish Academy of Sciences, Institute of Fundamental Technological Research (2021)
14. Jinchao, X., Zikatanov, L.: Algebraic multigrid methods. Acta Numerica **26**, 591–721 (2017)
15. Zulehner, W.: A class of smoothers for saddle point problems. Computing **65**(3), 227–246 (2000)

On Minimization of Nonlinear Energies Using FEM in MATLAB

Alexej Moskovka[1]([✉])[ID], Jan Valdman[2,3][ID], and Marta Vohnoutová[2][ID]

[1] Department of Mathematics, Faculty of Applied Sciences, University of West Bohemia, Technická 8, 30100 Plzeň, Czech Republic
alexmos@kma.zcu.cz
[2] Department of Computer Science, Faculty of Science, University of South Bohemia, Branišovská 31, 37005 České Budějovice, Czech Republic
[3] The Czech Academy of Sciences, Institute of Information Theory and Automation, Pod vodárenskou věží 4, 18208 Prague, Czech Republic

Abstract. Two minimization problems are added to the Moskovka and Valdman MATLAB package (2022): a Ginzburg-Landau (scalar) problem and a topology optimization (both scalar and vector) problem in linear elasticity. Both problems are described as nonlinear energy minimizations that contain the first gradient of the unknown field. Their energy functionals are discretized by finite elements, and the corresponding minima are searched using the trust-region method with a known Hessian sparsity or the Quasi-Newton method.

Keywords: minimization · nonlinear energy · finite elements · Ginzburg-Landau model · topology optimization

1 Introduction

For solving problems given by (a system of) partial differential equations, the variational approach is based on finding a minimum of the corresponding energy functional

$$J(u) = \min_{v \in V} J(v), \qquad (1)$$

where V is a space of test functions defined in a domain Ω and includes Dirichlet boundary conditions on $\partial\Omega$. Problems of this type appear in various applications of physics and are mathematically studied in the calculus of variations. The energy functionals are then described by integrals over domains in two- or three-dimensional space. The finite element method [9] can be applied as an approximation of (1) and results in a minimization problem

$$J(u_h) = \min_{v \in V_h} J(v) \qquad (2)$$

formulated in the finite-dimensional subspace V_h of V.

A. Moskovka was supported by the MSMT CR 8J21AT001 Model Reduction and Optimal Control in Thermomechanical Systems project. J. Valdman announces the support of the Czech Science Foundation (GACR) through the GF21-06569K grant Scales and shapes in continuum thermomechanics.

R. Wyrzykowski et al. (Eds.): PPAM 2022, LNCS 13827, pp. 331–342, 2023.
https://doi.org/10.1007/978-3-031-30445-3_28

A recent MATLAB implementation of [5,6] using the simplest linear nodal basis functions allows us to solve (2) efficiently. The energy formulations of the studied problems, including p-Laplace and hyperelasticity, contain the first gradient parts of searched functions discretized by the finite element method (FEM) and formulated as the sum of energy contributions from local elements. The key ingredient is the vectorization of exact or approximate energy gradients in the nodal patches (sets of elements adjacent to particular nodes). This leads to a time-efficient implementation with a higher memory cost. New attempts to apply available techniques to problems of elastoplastic deformations of layered structures and shape memory alloys are reported in [11,12].

In this contribution, we comment on the implementation of the Ginzburg-Landau model in superconductivity [1,3,4] and the topology optimization problem of the elastic medium [2,8]. The resulting MATLAB codes are provided for download and testing at the following link:

https://www.mathworks.com/matlabcentral/fileexchange/97889

Assembly times were obtained on Lenovo ThinkPad T14 Gen 1 (Intel Core i7 processor, 2021) with 16 GB memory running MATLAB R2018a.

2   Finite Element Method and Minimization

The subspace V_h is spanned by a set of n_b basis functions $\varphi_i(x) \in V_h, i = 1, \ldots, n_b$, and a trial function $v \in V_h$ is expressed by a linear combination

$$v(x) = \sum_{i=1}^{n_b} v_i\, \varphi_i(x), \qquad x \in \Omega, \tag{3}$$

where $\bar{v} = (v_1, \ldots, v_{n_b}) \in \mathbb{R}^{n_b}$ is a vector of coefficients. We consider only the case $V_h = P^1(\mathcal{T})$, where $P^1(\mathcal{T})$ is the space of piecewise linear nodal basis functions defined on a triangulation $\mathcal{T}$ of the domain Ω with a Lipschitz boundary. Note that the number of nodes corresponds to the number of all the basis functions of V_h, therefore, $n_b = |\mathcal{N}|$. Consequently, the minimizer $u_h \in V_h$ of (2) is represented by a vector of coefficients $\bar{u} = (u_1, \ldots, u_{|\mathcal{N}|}) \in \mathbb{R}^{|\mathcal{N}|}$ and some coefficients of $\bar{u}, \bar{v}$ related to the Dirichlet boundary conditions are prescribed.

An appropriate minimization method is needed to solve (2). We use the MATLAB Optimization Toolbox [10] which provides minimization techniques based on two methods. The first, the Quasi-Newton method, computes a descent direction and the corresponding optimal step length to compute a new iteration. This method does not need to know the gradient vector of $J(v)$ from (2) explicitly but instead computes the numerical gradient and the corresponding Hessian matrix using the Broyden-Fletcher-Goldfarb-Shanno (BFGS) update formula. The second, the trust-region method, is based on approximating the objective function using the quadratic model function with the appropriate trust-region radius. Contrary to the Quasi-Newton method, the trust region also requires knowledge of the discrete gradient of $J(v)$. The gradient can be explicitly derived or evaluated numerically using the central difference scheme. Additionally, the Hessian sparsity can be specified and follows directly from the FEM discretization (see Fig. 1).

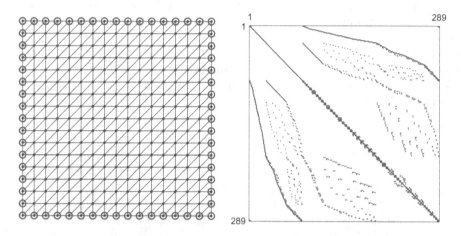

Fig. 1. Discretization of a rectangular domain (left) including Dirichlet boundary nodes (red) and the corresponding Hessian sparsity (right). (Color figure online)

If the Hessian matrix is sparse (i.e. for the Ginzburg-Landau problem), the trust-region method is much more time-efficient than the Quasi-Newton method. In contrast, if the Hessian matrix has many non-zero elements (i.e. for the topology optimization), the trust-region method can be significantly slower.

2.1   Solution Algorithm

consists for $d = 2$ of several typical steps:

- triangulation of the domain Ω into triangles and assembly of structures 'mesh' and 'patches' [6].
- defining the corresponding discrete energy functional $J(v)$ from (2) as a sum of the energy contributions of every element.
- if the trust region method is chosen, the 'patches' structure is used to define a function that represents the gradient of the discrete energy functional. This gradient can be evaluated either exactly (in the case that the partial derivatives of $J(v)$ from (2) can be derived explicitly) or numerically using the central difference scheme. The Hessian sparsity follows automatically from the FEM discretization.
- the choice of a stopping criterion of the minimization process.

3   Ginzburg-Landau Problem

Superconductors are certain metals and alloys that, when cooled below a critical (typically very low) temperature, lose their resistivity, allowing permanent currents to circulate without loss of energy. Superconductivity was discovered by Ohnes in 1911. As a phenomenological description of this phenomenon, Ginzburg and Landau introduced in 1950 the Ginzburg-Landau model, which has been proven to effectively predict the behavior of superconductors and that was subsequently justified as a limit of the Bardeen-Cooper-Schrieffer (BCS) quantum theory. It is a model of great importance in physics, and Nobel prizes have been awarded for it to Abrikosov, Ginzburg, and Landau in 2003. For more details on the physical and mathematical description of the models studied, see [3,4].

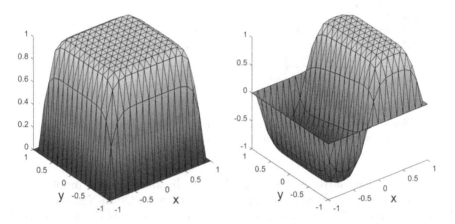

Fig. 2. Two numerical solutions of G-L problem on a rectangular domain Ω for $\varepsilon = 10^{-2}$ and zero Dirichlet boundary conditions on the boundary $\partial\Omega$. We can identify flat regions, where the solutions satisfy $u = 1$ or $u = -1$. The computational mesh consists of 512 elements and 289 nodes including 64 Dirichlet boundary nodes. The mesh is shown independently in Fig. 1.

Leaving out the dependence on the magnetic field, we consider the simpler Ginzburg-Landau minimization problem [1] for a scalar test function $v \in V$, and the minimizer $u \in V$ means the order parameter that indicates the local state of the material (normal or superconducting). The energy functional reads

$$J(v) = \int_{\Omega} \left(\frac{\varepsilon}{2} \|\nabla v\|^2 + \frac{1}{4}(v^2 - 1)^2 \right) \mathrm{d}x, \tag{4}$$

where $\Omega \subset \mathbb{R}^d$ is a given domain, ε a given small positive parameter and

$$\nabla v = \left(\frac{\partial v}{\partial x_1}, \dots, \frac{\partial v}{\partial x_d} \right)$$

denotes the vector gradient in the dimension d and $\|\cdot\|$ its euclidean norm. The space V above contains testing functions $v : \Omega \to \mathbb{R}$ having the first (generalized) derivatives and satisfying the Dirichlet boundary condition

$$v = 0 \qquad \text{on} \quad \partial \Omega. \tag{5}$$

It is possible to show that the structure of (4) allows for more minimizers that satisfy the corresponding Euler-Lagrange equation formulated as the boundary value problem for the nonlinear partial differential equation

$$\begin{aligned} \varepsilon \Delta u = u^3 - u & \quad \text{in} \quad \Omega, \\ u = 0 & \quad \text{on} \quad \partial \Omega \end{aligned} \tag{6}$$

or its weak form

$$\int_\Omega \frac{\varepsilon}{2} \nabla u \cdot \nabla v \, dx - \int_\Omega (u - u^3) v \, dx = 0 \qquad \text{for all } v \in V. \tag{7}$$

Figure 2 shows two different solutions generated by two different initial approximations, and Table 1 the performance of the trust-region method with the specified Hessian sparsity pattern for different levels of uniform refinements. The stopping criteria related to the first-order optimality, tolerance on the argument, and tolerance on the function equal to 10^{-6} are considered.

Table 1. Performance of G-L minimizations for $\varepsilon = 10^{-2}$.

level	$|\mathcal{T}|$	dofs	exact gradient			numerical gradient		
			time [s]	iters	$J(\mathbf{u})$	time [s]	iters	$J(\mathbf{u})$
2	128	49	0.39	8	0.3867	0.08	8	0.3867
3	512	225	0.06	6	0.3547	0.05	6	0.3547
4	2048	961	0.13	7	0.3480	0.12	7	0.3480
5	8192	3969	0.28	6	0.3462	0.34	6	0.3462
6	32768	16129	1.11	7	0.3458	1.26	7	0.3458
7	131072	65025	6.63	8	0.3457	7.17	8	0.3457
8	524288	261121	56.97	8	0.3456	64.98	10	0.3456

Note that the original nonvectorized implementation [1] of the Newton-Ralphson solver based on the weak form (7) requires, for example:

level 6 - 4.33s and 6 iterations,
level 7 - 54.46s and 6 iterations,
level 8 - 936.47s and 6 iterations.

Our implementation only needs a slightly higher number of iterations. The underlying MATLAB code is heavily vectorized and therefore faster. The part most computationally consuming is the function 'energy' that evaluates the corresponding energy $J(v)$ for a given vector $\mathbf{v} \in \mathbb{R}^{|\mathcal{N}|}$ together with the numerical gradient $\nabla J(v)$. The MATLAB profiler shown in Fig. 3 outputs the number of calls and the total evaluation time of every code line related to the function evaluating (4) and its gradient.

```
Time     Calls   Line

                 77    function e = energy(v,eps)
< 0.001   340    78        if nargin==1   % global energy only
4.181     170    79            v elems = v(mesh.elems2nodes);                    % values on elements
2.609     170    80            F elems = evaluate F 2D scalar(mesh,v elems);   % all gradients
2.176     170    81            densities elems = densities(v elems,F elems);
0.361     170    82            e = sum(mesh.areas.*densities elems);
< 0.001   170    83        else   % local gradient energies using the epsilon perturbation vector
0.006     170    84            e = zeros(numel(dofsMinim),size(eps,2));
11.220    170    85            v patches = v(patches.elems2nodes);
< 0.001   170    86            for comp=1:size(eps,2)
2.772     340    87                v patches eps = v patches + eps(comp)*patches.logical;
15.213    340    88                F patches = evaluate F 2D scalar(patches,v patches eps);
12.610    340    89                densities patches = densities(v patches eps,F patches);
0.995     340    90                e patches = patches.areas.*densities patches;
2.489     340    91                cumsum all e = cumsum(e patches);
2.629     340    92                e(:,comp) = [cumsum all e(indx(1)); diff(cumsum all e(indx))];
0.001     340    93            end
< 0.001   340    94        end
3.326     340    95    end
```

Fig. 3. MATLAB profiler for level 8 refinement.

The energy evaluation consists of the following steps:

- (line 79) assembly of the matrix 'v_elems' of nodal values of $\mathbf{v}$ on the elements.
- (line 80) evaluation of the cell 'F_elems' of gradients of $\mathbf{v}$ on elements stored.
- (line 81) evaluation of the vector 'densities_elems' of energy densities in the elements. This is done by the function 'densities' processing both the gradient and the reaction terms of (4). Gaussian quadrature is applied for the evaluation of the reaction term.
- (line 82) the total energy 'e' is given by the sum of the energy contributions of every element multiplied by their areas.

The energy gradient evaluation procedure is similar, but includes the for loop over two components of the input vector 'eps', which are $-\epsilon$ and $+\epsilon$. Therefore, the numbers of calls of lines 87–92 are twice as high.

- (line 85) assembly of the matrix 'v_patches' of the nodal values of $\mathbf{v}$ on patches.

- (line 87) perturbation of the nodal values by the corresponding component of 'eps' resulting in a vector 'v_patches_eps'.
- (line 88) evaluation of the cell '**F_patches**' of gradients of 'v_patches_eps' on patches.
- (lines 89–90) evaluation of the vector 'e_patches' of energy densities on patches.
- (line 91) assembly of vector '**cumsum_all_e**' containing the cumulative sums of vector 'e_patches'.
- (line 92) evaluating a vector 'e' of differences of cumulative sums using the 'indx' vector (described in detail in [6]).

This implementation facilitates an easy extension to higher-order difference schemes.

4   Topology Optimization in 2D

Structural topology optimization (TO) is a numerical method that aims, through a density function, to optimally distribute a limited amount of material within a volume, representing the initial geometry of a body that undergoes specific loads and displacement boundary conditions. Among the approaches to solving TO problems ([2]), we focus on the so-called phase field approach. We consider a domain $\Omega \in \mathbb{R}^d$ where the material is distributed using a scalar phase field variable ϕ, representing a density fraction of the material, hence $\phi \in [0,1]$ with

$\phi \equiv 0$ corresponding to the void (no material),
$\phi \equiv 1$ to the bulk material.

Adopting a linear elastic model, the state equations are of the form

$$
\begin{aligned}
\text{div}(\sigma) &= 0 \quad &\text{in} \quad &\Omega\,, \\
u &= 0 \quad &\text{on} \quad &\Gamma_D\,, \\
\sigma \cdot n &= g \quad &\text{on} \quad &\Gamma_N.
\end{aligned}
\tag{8}
$$

Here, we have the stress tensor $\sigma = \sigma(\phi)$, the displacement vector u and with zero value (in sense of traces) at the Dirichlet boundary Γ_D, the external load g vector at the Neumann boundary Γ_N with the normal unit vector n.

The stress tensor reads

$$
\sigma(\phi) = \mathbb{C}(\phi) : \varepsilon(u)
$$

with the fourth-order linear material tensor $\mathbb{C} = \mathbb{C}(\phi)$ and the symmetric strain $\varepsilon(u)$ is defined as

$$
\varepsilon(u) = (\nabla u + \nabla u^T)/2.
$$

The symbol ':' denotes the contraction of two tensors in the form that yields $\sigma_{ij} = \mathbb{C}_{ijkl}\varepsilon_{kl}$, where the Einstein summation is applied. We consider the void as a very soft material, adopting the following equation for $\mathbb{C}$:

$$
\mathbb{C}(\phi) = \mathbb{C}_{bulk}\phi^p + \mathbb{C}_{void}(1 - \phi)^p.
$$

In practical calculations, we set $p = 3$, and $\mathbb{C}_{void} = 10^{-2} \, \mathbb{C}_{bulk}$ and the matrix $\mathbb{C}_{bulk}$ is specified by two material parameters (the first Lamé parameter λ and the shear modulus μ). The weak form of the linear elastic problem (8) can be written as

$$\int_{\Omega} \sigma(\phi) : \varepsilon(v) \, dx = \int_{\Gamma_N} g \cdot v \, dx \qquad (9)$$

for any test displacement field v and $\sigma(\phi) = \mathbb{C}(\phi) : \varepsilon(v)$. The goal is to minimize the compliance of a given structure by optimally distributing a limited amount of material. For this purpose, we introduce an objective functional $J(\phi, u(\phi))$ defined as:

$$J\big(\phi, u(\phi)\big) = \int_{\Gamma_N} g \cdot u(\phi) \, dx + \kappa \int_{\Omega} \left[\frac{\gamma}{2} \|\nabla \phi\|^2 + \frac{1}{\gamma} \psi_0(\phi) \right] dx , \qquad (10)$$

where for a given ϕ the corresponding displacement $u(\phi)$ is given as the solution of (9). The first integral represents a measure of the compliance of the global system, the term $\frac{\gamma}{2}\|\phi\|^2$ penalizes nonconstant values of ϕ, while $\frac{1}{\gamma}\psi_0(\phi)$, where

$$\psi_0(\phi) = (\phi - \phi^2)^2 ,$$

represents the double-well potential function penalizing values of ϕ different from 0 and 1. The parameter γ is usually set between 10^{-4} and 10^{-2} (for a finer mesh, the lower value provides better results). Minimization of the functional (10) is imposed under the assumption of distributing a limited constant quantity of material within the domain; therefore, we introduce the constraint

$$\int_{\Omega} \phi \, dx = m|\Omega|$$

with $0 < m \leq 1$ representing a volume fraction of the target domain.

Figures 4, 5 and 6 illustrate topology optimization solutions for different domains and the corresponding Dirichlet and Neumann boundary conditions. For the sake of clarity, the computational meshes on the left side are depicted for lower levels of refinement. Red circles indicate the nodes corresponding to Γ_D and green circles indicate the nodes that belong to Γ_N.

Three models are given by the following parameters.

The first model:

- a rectangular domain $(0, 0.02) \times (0, 0.01)$,
- $\gamma = 10^{-4}$,
- the left side of the boundary is fixed,
- a constant traction force $g = 5 \cdot 10^6$ acts on the bottom side of the boundary from $x = 0.016$ to $x = 0.02$ downwards.

The second model:

- an L-shaped domain given by the union of rectangles $(0, 0.06) \times (0, 0.06)$, $(0, 0.06) \times (0.06, 0.2)$ and $(0.06, 0.2) \times (0, 0.06)$,

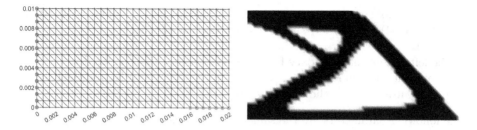

Fig. 4. The first model: triangulation of the rectangle domain (left) with 3600 elements and the solution (right).

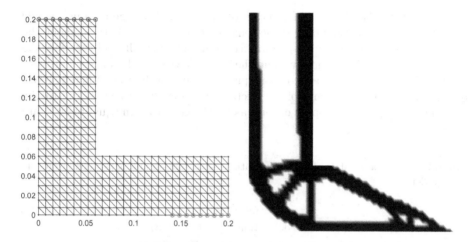

Fig. 5. The second model: triangulation of the L-shaped domain (left) with 3672 elements and the solution (right).

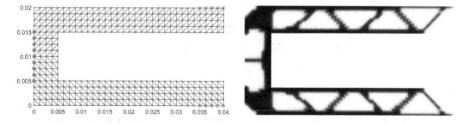

Fig. 6. The third model: triangulation of the pincer domain (left) with 3600 elements and the solution (right).

- $\gamma = 10^{-3}$,
- the top side of the boundary is fixed,
- a constant traction force $g = 10^6$ acts on the bottom side of the boundary from $x = 0.14$ to $x = 0.2$ downwards.

The third model:

- a pincer domain given by the union of rectangles $(0, 0.005) \times (0, 0.02)$, $(0.005, 0.04) \times (0, 0.005)$ and $(0.005, 0.04) \times (0.015, 0.02)$,
- $\gamma = 10^{-3}$,
- the left side of the boundary from $y = 0.005$ to $y = 0.015$ is fixed,
- a constant traction force $g = 2 \cdot 10^5$ acts on the top (upwards) and the bottom (downwards) sides of the boundary from $x = 0.035$ to $x = 0.04$.

The following parameters are the same for all models:

- $E = 12.5 \cdot 10^8$ (Young modulus), $\nu = 0.25$ (Poisson ratio),
- $\kappa = 100$, $m = 0.4$.

Contrary to the Ginzburg-Landau problem, a small change of ϕ in a single node affects the corresponding displacement $u(\phi)$ given by (9) throughout the domain. In this case, the corresponding Hessian matrix is full, and therefore the trust-region method is ineffective, and the quasi-Newton method is used instead. Table 2 shows the performance of the quasi-Newton method for different levels of uniform mesh refinements of the rectangular domain corresponding to the first model. The same stopping criteria as for the GL-problem equal to 10^{-4} are considered.

Table 2. Performance of TopOpt minimizations with domain and parameters from the first model.

			quasi-Newton		
level	$|\mathcal{T}|$	dofs	time [s]	iters	$J(\mathbf{u})$
1.0	100	120	2.11	50	28.0815
1.5	240	270	9.52	44	24.2585
2.0	400	440	25.88	52	23.5845
2.5	900	960	194.13	82	21.4105
3.0	1600	1680	1079.45	125	21.0503
3.5	3600	3720	15737.81	323	20.3108

Similarly to 3, the MATLAB profiler shown in Fig. 7 outputs the number of calls and the total evaluation time of code lines related to the function evaluating (10). The energy evaluation consists of the following steps:

- (line 48) assembly of a vector 'z_elems' containing averaged values of ϕ on the elements.
- (lines 49–50) evaluating vectors 'mu_elems' and 'bulk_elems' that store the values of shear and bulk modulus, respectively, on the elements.
- (lines 52–55) an update of the elastic stiffness matrix [7].
- (line 57) restriction of the stiffness matrix on free degrees.
- (line 58) a new displacement field in free degrees is evaluated based on (9).

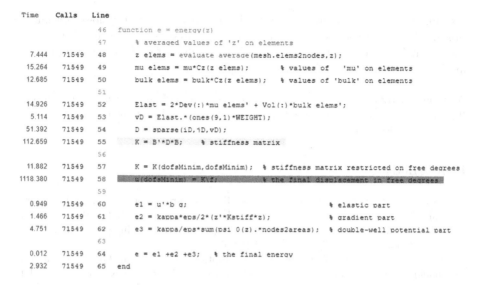

Time	Calls	Line	
		46	function e = energy(z)
		47	% averaged values of 'z' on elements
7.444	71549	48	z elems = evaluate average(mesh.elems2nodes,z);
15.264	71549	49	mu elems = mu*Cz(z elems); % values of 'mu' on elements
12.685	71549	50	bulk elems = bulk*Cz(z elems); % values of 'bulk' on elements
		51	
14.926	71549	52	Elast = 2*Dev(:)*mu elems' + Vol(:)*bulk elems';
5.114	71549	53	vD = Elast.*(ones(9,1)*WEIGHT);
51.392	71549	54	D = sparse(iD,iD,vD);
112.659	71549	55	K = B'*D*B; % stiffness matrix
		56	
11.882	71549	57	K = K(dofsMinim,dofsMinim); % stiffness matrix restricted on free degrees
1118.380	71549	58	u(dofsMinim) = K\f; % the final displacement in free degrees
		59	
0.949	71549	60	e1 = u'*b g; % elastic part
1.466	71549	61	e2 = kappa*eps/2*(z'*Kstiff*z); % gradient part
4.751	71549	62	e3 = kappa/eps*sum(psi 0(z).*nodes2areas); % double-well potential part
		63	
0.012	71549	64	e = e1 +e2 +e3; % the final energy
2.932	71549	65	end

Fig. 7. MATLAB profiler for level 3 refinement.

- (lines 60–62) evaluating the first (elastic), second (gradient) and third (double-well potential) part of (10).
- (line 64) the final energy given as a sum of its three components.

The profiler shows that the main cost of the evaluation lies in the reassembling of the elastic stiffness matrix and the solutions of the linear systems of equations in each energy evaluation.

5 Conclusions and outlooks

We introduced a Ginzburg-Landau and topology optimization problem that appears in physics and implemented them using the concept of our codes from [5] based on a minimization of energy functionals.

A comparison with the original implementation of Ginzburg-Landau [1] based on the Newton-Raphson method demonstrates the effectiveness of our vectorization concepts, leading to significantly better evaluation times, but higher memory cost. It shows that the trust region method requires only a slightly higher number of iterations. It would be interesting to apply our vectorization concepts to the assembly of the Hessian matrix in the Newton-Raphson method.

A simple implementation of topology optimization of an elastic medium using the Quasi-Newton method has proved feasible. The elasticity stiffness matrix needs to be assembled and the resulting linear system of equations solved in every energy iteration. The original assembly code of [7] is effectively split using precomputed structures that do not change during the minimization process. Practically, it still takes the majority of the evaluation time. Although this approach is highly inefficient from an optimization point of view, it should allow for a simple extension to more complicated problems, such as topology optimization of elastoplastic materials, where the elastoplasticity solver of [7] replaces the original elasticity solver. To reduce the number of evaluations, we plan to implement schemes of gradient flow type [8].

Acknowledgment. We thank Prof. Ulisse Stefanelli and Dr. Stefano Almi (University of Vienna) for inspiring discussions on topology optimization models and their numerical implementation.

References

1. Alberty, J., Carstensen, C., Funken, S.A.: Remarks around 50 lines in matlab: short finite element implementation. Numer. Algorithms **20**, 117–137 (1999)
2. Bendsoe, M.P., Sigmund, O.: Topology Optimization, Springer, Berlin (2004). https://doi.org/10.1007/978-3-662-05086-6
3. Romá, C.: Analysis of singularities in elliptic equations: the Ginzburg-Landau model of superconductivity, the Lin-Ni-Takagi problem, the Keller-Segel model of chemotaxis, and conformal geometry. Université Pierre et Marie Curie - Paris VI, Mathematical Physics (2017)
4. Bethuel, F., Brezis, H., Hélein, F.: Ginzburg-Landau vortices, Birkhäuser (2017)
5. Matonoha, C., Moskovka, A., Valdman, J.: Minimization of p-Laplacian via the finite element method in MATLAB. In: Lirkov, I., Margenov, S. (eds.) LSSC 2021. LNCS, vol. 13127, pp. 533–540. Springer, Cham (2022). https://doi.org/10.1007/978-3-030-97549-4_61
6. Moskovka, A., Valdman, J.: Fast MATLAB evaluation of nonlinear energies using FEM in 2D and 3D: nodal elements. Appl. Math. Comput. **424**, 127048 (2022)
7. Čermák, M., Sysala, S., Valdman, J.: Efficient and flexible MATLAB implementation of 2D and 3D elastoplastic problems. Appl. Math. Comput. **355**, 595–614 (2019)
8. Carraturo, M., Rocca, E., Bonetti, E., Hömberg, D., Reali, A., Auricchio, F.: Graded-material design based on phase-field and topology optimization. Comput. Mech. **2019**(64), 1589–1600 (2019)
9. Ciarlet, P.G.: The Finite Element Method for Elliptic Problems. SIAM, Philadelphia (2002)
10. MATLAB documentation on minimization with gradient and Hessian sparsity pattern. https://www.mathworks.com/help/optim/ug/minimization-with-gradient-and-hessian-sparsity-pattern.html
11. Drozdenko, D., Knapek, M., Kružík, M., Máthis, K., Švadlenka, K., Valdman, J.: Elastoplastic deformations of layered structures. Milan J. Math. **90**, 691–706 (2022)
12. Frost, M., Valdman, J.: Vectorized MATLAB implementation of the incremental minimization principle for rate-independent dissipative solids using FEM: a constitutive model of shape memory alloys. Mathematics **10**(23), 4412 (2022)

A Model for Crowd Evacuation Dynamics: 2D Numerical Simulations

Maria Gokieli[1,2]([⊠])

[1] Faculty of Mathematics and Natural Sciences - School of Exact Sciences,
Cardinal Stefan Wyszyński University, Wóycickiego 1/3, 01-938 Warsaw, Poland
[2] ICM, University of Warsaw, Tyniecka 15/17, 02-630 Warsaw, Poland
`m.gokieli@icm.edu.pl`

Abstract. In [5] we have proposed a numerical scheme for solving a macroscopic model of crowd dynamics. We apply it here to simulate a room evacuation, for velocity fields derived from the p–Poisson equation. We analyze the stability parameters and the influence of p on the dynamics.

Keywords: Finite elements method · crowd dynamics · advection–diffusion · semi–implicit scheme · CFL condition · p-Laplacian

1 Introduction

In [5] we have considered the following model for pedestrians' movement: if $\Omega \subset \mathbb{R}^2$ is the available environment, $\overrightarrow{V}(x) \in \mathbb{R}^2$ is the velocity of an individual at x, and $\rho(t, x) \in \mathbb{R}$ is the density of the pedestrians at time t and point $x \in \Omega$, the dynamics of ρ is governed by:

$$\partial_t \rho + \text{div}\left(\rho \overrightarrow{V}\right) - \kappa \, \Delta \rho = 0 \qquad \text{in } \mathbb{R}^+ \times \Omega \, . \tag{1}$$

This is a regularization ($\kappa > 0$) of the continuity equation proposed originally in this context by Hughes [7,8]

$$\partial_t \rho + \text{div}\left(\rho \overrightarrow{V}\right) = 0 \, , \qquad \text{in } \mathbb{R}^+ \times \Omega \, . \tag{2}$$

The diffusion term that we add in (1) models a natural random spread of the pedestrians, independently of the direction $\overrightarrow{V}$ they are given.

We consider here that Ω is a room that the pedestrians exit. Consequently, Ω is a bounded domain, the boundary $\partial\Omega$ of Ω is a union of disjoint parts: the walls Γ_w, the exits Γ, and the corners Γ_c. The set of corners is finite; Γ_w and Γ are regular and possess at each point an exterior normal vector $\overrightarrow{\nu}(x)$.

The model requires to be supplied with a velocity field $\overrightarrow{V}$ which defines the evacuation direction. In any nontrivial case it should of course depend on x, and most likely also on $\rho(x)$. This latter dependency appears in the original [7,8] and

R. Wyrzykowski et al. (Eds.): PPAM 2022, LNCS 13827, pp. 343–353, 2023.
https://doi.org/10.1007/978-3-031-30445-3_29

related works, see e.g. [9,13]. It makes however our problem nonlinear. It is also possible to make $\overrightarrow{V}$ depend on other, nonlocal quantities, as the mean value of ρ in some neighborhood of x. We neglect them here – as the nonlocal behaviour is present in our model (1) by the diffusion term. The basic requirement for $\overrightarrow{V}$ so as to get a model of evacuation are the following boundary conditions:

$$\overrightarrow{V} \cdot \overrightarrow{\nu} = 0 \text{ on } \Gamma_w, \tag{3}$$

$$\overrightarrow{V} \cdot \overrightarrow{\nu} > 0 \text{ on } \Gamma. \tag{4}$$

Also, we assume a homogeneous Neumann boundary condition on ρ

$$\nabla \rho \cdot \overrightarrow{\nu} = 0 \quad \text{on } \Gamma_w \cup \Gamma \tag{5}$$

and the initial condition

$$\rho(0, x) = \rho_0(x) \geq 0. \tag{6}$$

This will ensure the evacuation process (see [5, Lemma 1]).

We are interested here in presenting numerical simulations for the evacuation process, based on (1). We chose a geometry of Ω including obstacles inside the evacuated space and use the numerical scheme of [5]. We have considered there velocity fields $\overrightarrow{V}$ such that

$$\operatorname{div} \overrightarrow{V} \geq 0 \quad \text{on } \Omega. \tag{7}$$

and have shown that the L^2-norm of the exact solution decreases under the above assumption. The semi–implicit scheme of [5] was shown to be stable and preserving this monotonicity property under a CFL type condition.

We show in the present paper an explicit formula for this CFL condition when (5) is assumed and we show examples of stable and unstable evolution, depending on the choice of parameters. We also discuss concrete choices of $\overrightarrow{V}$. We investigate $\overrightarrow{V}$ which were not, as far as we know, considered in this context, and which seem to be a very natural choice for the modelled phenomenon. We show that the pointwise assumption (7) is only relevant for special $\overrightarrow{V}$, which do not depend, or depend very weakly, on ρ. For $\overrightarrow{V}$ clearly dependent on ρ, the L^2-norm of the numerical solution ρ_h is decreasing only after an initial period of time. This does not contradict the scheme stability, but shows that a new analysis of these monotonicty and stability properties is needed.

The plan of this paper is as follows. Section 2 recalls the semi–implicit numerical scheme proposed in [5]. We discuss the choice of $\overrightarrow{V}$ and its computation in Sect. 3. We show in Sect. 4 the obtained simulations and discuss the choice of the time step for particular $\overrightarrow{V}$. We show the first confirmations of the so called Braess paradox. i.e. a heuristic observation that obstacles to the movement may facilitate it, and on the contrary, lack of obstacles may slow the movement down. We illustrate this Braess paradox for evacuation, leaving a more systematic study of the role of the obstacles for the future (see Sect. 5).

2   Numerical Scheme

In all what follows, we assume the geometry of Ω as in the Introduction and (3)–(4). We assume also that $\overrightarrow{V}$ may depend of x and ρ, we note $\overrightarrow{V} = \overrightarrow{V}(\rho)$.

Definition 1. *We say that $\rho : (0,T) \times \Omega \to \mathbb{R}$ solves the model (1), (5) (in the weak sense) if, for any $t \in (0,T)$, $\rho(t) \in H^1(\Omega)$, $\rho \geq 0$ and for any $\eta \in H^1(\Omega)$, any $t \in (0,T)$*

$$\int_\Omega \partial_t \rho(t)\, \eta + \int_\Gamma \rho(t)\, \eta\, \overrightarrow{V}(\rho(t)) \cdot \overrightarrow{\nu} - \int_\Omega \rho(t)\, \overrightarrow{V}(\rho(t)) \cdot \nabla\eta + \kappa \int_\Omega \nabla\rho(t) \cdot \nabla\eta \; = \; 0.$$
(8)

We have written $\int_\Omega f(t)$ for $\int_\Omega f(t,x)\, dx$.

One can verify by classical methods that under additional assumptions on $\overrightarrow{V}$, the solution ρ exists and, with the initial condition (6), is unique. We omit here the mathematical analysis of the model; of course many mathematical properties of ρ depend on the choice of $\overrightarrow{V}$ that we do not want to impose at this point. We state however an important monotonicty property and its relation to $\overrightarrow{V}$.

Definition 2. *The functions $m : \mathbb{R}_+ \to \mathbb{R}$ defined by*

$$m(t) = M(\rho(t)) = \int_\Omega \rho(t,x)\, dx.$$
(9)

shall be called the total mass function. *The function $s : \mathbb{R}_+ \to \mathbb{R}$ defined by*

$$s(t) = S(\rho(t)) = \int_\Omega \rho(t,x)^2\, dx$$
(10)

shall be called the L^2–stability function for the equation (8) with $\rho(0) = \rho_0$.

Lemma 1. *Let $\overrightarrow{V}$ satisfy (3)–(4). Let ρ be the solution to (1) with (5) and (6). The total mass function (9) is decreasing. The L^2–stability function (10) is decreasing in the neighborhood of t_0 if and only if t_0 is such that*

$$\int_\Omega \rho^2\, \mathrm{div}\, \overrightarrow{V} + 2\kappa \int_\Omega |\nabla\rho|^2 + \int_\Gamma \rho^2 \overrightarrow{V} \cdot \overrightarrow{\nu} \geq 0.$$
(11)

This condition is in particular fulfilled for $\overrightarrow{V}$ satisfying (7).

Proof. By posing $\eta = 1$, we obtain the first statement from (3)–(4). By posing $\eta = \rho$, again from (3)-(4) and the identity

$$2\int_\Omega \rho\, \overrightarrow{V}(\rho) \cdot \nabla\rho \; = \; -\int_\Omega \rho^2\, \mathrm{div}\, \overrightarrow{V}(\rho) + \int_\Gamma \rho^2 \overrightarrow{V}(\rho) \cdot \overrightarrow{\nu}$$

we obtain:

$$\frac{1}{2}\frac{d}{dt}\int_\Omega \rho^2 \; = \; -\frac{1}{2}\int_\Omega \rho^2\, \mathrm{div}\, \overrightarrow{V}(\rho) - \kappa \int_\Omega |\nabla\rho|^2 + \int_\Gamma \rho^2 \overrightarrow{V}(\rho) \cdot \overrightarrow{\nu}.$$

$\square$

We define now the finite element spaces $V_h \subset H^1(\Omega)$, where h is, as usual, the mesh parameter, and look for the approximate solutions in V_h. Let $\Omega_h \subset \Omega$ be the triangulated, shape regular domain, with the mesh size parameter h. Let $(\cdot, \cdot)$ denote the L^2 product on Ω_h.

Definition 3 (cf. Def. 2 of [5]). *We define the sequence $\{\rho_h^n\}_{n=0}^\infty \subset V_h$ to be the* approximate FEM solution *of (8) if ρ_h^n satisfies the following semi–implicit first order scheme for any test function $\eta_h \in V_h$:*

$$\int_{\Omega_h} \left(\frac{\rho_h^{n+1} - \rho_h^n}{\Delta t} \right) \eta_h - \int_{\Omega_h} \rho_h^{n+1} \overrightarrow{V}(\rho^n) \cdot \nabla \eta_h + \kappa \int_{\Omega_h} \nabla \rho_h^{n+1} \cdot \nabla \eta_h +$$

$$+ \int_{\Gamma_h} \rho_h^n \overrightarrow{V}(\rho^n) \cdot \overrightarrow{\nu} \, \eta_h = 0. \quad (12)$$

We say that the scheme is stable *from n_0 if for any $n \geq n_0$:*

$$(\rho_h^{n+1}, \rho_h^{n+1}) \leq (\rho_h^n, \rho_h^n).$$

Remark 1. The above definition is consistent with that of the semi–implicit scheme in [5, Def. 2], if we put

$$A_0(\varphi)(\rho, \eta) = - \int_{\Omega_h} \rho \overrightarrow{V}(\varphi) \cdot \nabla \eta + \kappa \int_{\Omega_h} \nabla \rho \cdot \nabla \eta, \quad (13)$$

$$B(\varphi)\rho = -\frac{1}{2} \rho \overrightarrow{V}(\varphi) \cdot \overrightarrow{\nu}, \quad (14)$$

and, for an arbitrary $\alpha > 0$,

$$A_1(\varphi)(\rho, \eta) = \frac{1}{2\alpha} \int_\Gamma [B(\varphi)\rho - \alpha\rho] [B(\varphi)\eta - \alpha\eta], \quad (15)$$

$$A_2(\varphi)(\rho, \eta) = \frac{1}{2\alpha} \int_\Gamma [B(\varphi)\rho + \alpha\rho] [B(\varphi)\eta + \alpha\eta]. \quad (16)$$

The notion of stability is also consistent with [5]. It is strong. A future study should include a weaker notion of stability, where the L^2 norm of the numerical solution is bounded.

Theorem 1. *[5]* **(CFL condition for stability).** *Let $\alpha > 0$ be an arbitrary constant and let's define A_1 as in (14)–(15). The semi–implicit scheme (12) is stable under (11) and the abstract CFL condition*

$$\Delta t \, A_1(\rho_h)(u_h, u_h) \leq (u_h, u_h) \qquad \forall \rho_h, u_h \in V_h. \quad (17)$$

Proof. The proof is identical as in [5, Proof of Theorem 2], where the nonlinear case has already been considered. We have assumed there (7) to infer (11). □

In view of (14)–(15), we give below a more explicit form of the (CFL) condition.

Remark 2. If ρ solves the model (1), (5), the CFL condition (17) writes as

$$\frac{\Delta t \int_{\Gamma} u_h^2 \left(\overrightarrow{V}(\rho_h) \cdot \overrightarrow{\nu} - 2\alpha \right)^2}{8\alpha \int_{\Omega_h} u_h^2} \le 1. \tag{18}$$

Note that κ does not appear in (18) explicitly. Instead, it has a crucial role in (11) in the case when div $\overrightarrow{V}$, or $\int_{\Omega} \rho^2$ div $\overrightarrow{V}(\rho)$, is not positive.

This form of CFL condition allows to find an optimal α. If we assume that $|\overrightarrow{V}|$ is bounded on Ω, we obtain $2\alpha_{opt} = \max_{\Gamma} |\overrightarrow{V}|$. With these assumptions, (18) is satisfied if

$$\frac{1}{4} \Delta t \left(2 \max_{\Gamma} |\overrightarrow{V}| - \min_{\Gamma} |\overrightarrow{V}| \right) \frac{\int_{\Gamma} u_h^2}{\int_{\Omega_h} u_h^2} \le C_0 \max_{\Gamma} |\overrightarrow{V}| \frac{\Delta t}{h} \le 1. \tag{19}$$

Indeed, the last term on the lhs is of order oh $1/h$; it depends also on the mesh and on the degree of the elements. For a uniform mesh and P2 elements that we use in the sequel, $1/C_{0,u} = 6(1 + \sqrt{2}) \approx 14.5$, see e.g. [11], where the authors propose to multiply $C_{0,u}$ by 10 so as to stay clearly away from the unstable region. In most simulations, we increase this constant even more. However, $\max |\overrightarrow{V}|$ may be difficult to estimate if it is not granted by construction.

3   Velocity

The velocity field $\overrightarrow{V}$ is a crucial element of the model. Apart from satisfying (3)–(4), it should reproduce the direction that the individual at x will follow so as to reach the exit. From the modelling point of view, V should be dependent on the space variable x, and on the density $\rho(x)$. From the analytical and numerical point of view, the important properties of $\overrightarrow{V}$ are (7) and (18).

A frequent simplification, that we also admit here, is to take

$$\overrightarrow{V} = \overrightarrow{V}(\rho(x)) = v(\rho(x)) \overrightarrow{W}(x), \tag{20}$$

where $\overrightarrow{W} : \Omega \to \mathbb{R}^2$ is a vector field giving the direction to follow at x, and $v : \mathbb{R} \to \mathbb{R}$ is a non-increasing function giving the scalar value of the velocity, responsible for a slow down when the density is bigger. So as to make v meaningful, $\overrightarrow{W}$ is often normalized: $|\overrightarrow{W}(x)| = 1$.

The most natural choice for $\overrightarrow{W}$ seems to be the vector field $-\nabla \Phi(x)$, where Φ is the distance to the exit. It is well known (see e.g. [2,4,13] and related works) that Φ is given by the so-called *eikonal equation*:

$$\Phi \in W^{1,p}(\Omega) \cap C(\bar{\Omega}) : \quad |\nabla \Phi(x)| = 1 \quad \text{for } x \in \Omega, \quad \Phi(\xi) = 0 \quad \text{for } \xi \in \Gamma,$$

The eikonal equation is highly nonlinear. Many approximations of the distance function are used in applications (see [2]); a few however approximate its gradient. Among them, the most interesting one may be the solution of the p–Poisson problem. If

$$\Delta_p u = \operatorname{div}\left(|\nabla u|^{p-2}\,\nabla u\right),$$

we solve

$$\begin{cases} -\Delta_p \Psi_p(x) = 1 & \text{in } \Omega \\ \nabla \Psi_p \cdot \vec{\nu} = 0 & \text{on } \Gamma_w \\ \Psi_p = 0 & \text{on } \Gamma, \end{cases} \tag{21}$$

The result of [4] is that

$$\Psi_p \text{ converges to } \Phi \text{ strongly in } W^{1,m}(\Omega) \quad \text{as } p \to \infty, \quad \text{for all } m \geq 1.$$

This means in particular that $|\nabla \Psi_p| \to 1$ as $p \to \infty$, a property which is very important. Thus, for bigger p, by taking $\vec{W} = -\nabla \Psi_p$, and $\vec{V}$ as in (20), we have a velocity field satisfying (3)–(4), $|\vec{W}| \approx 1$ and close to the vector field resulting from the eikonal equation. The CFL condition (19) is then also easier to satisfy and to check.

For $p = 2$, (21) is the linear Poisson equation. This case is of particular interest, because if we take $\vec{V} = -\nabla \Psi_2$ in (1), the condition (7) is satisfied directly. This $\vec{V}$, even if not a perfect choice from the modelling point of view, satisfies all our assumptions, and thus helps to determine constants in the CFL condition.

4   Simulations

4.1   Settings

In the simulations, we have considered a symmetric, nearly rectangular room of dimension 1×1.5, with two identical exits. We have placed obstacles in front of the exits, as in the figures below. The code has been coded and executed with the FreeFem++ software [6]. We used $P2$ elements. The mesh is shape regular, with h of order of 0.02. The maximal step size is $\Delta t = 0.01$. The initial density ρ_0 is constant. We have used the vector field (20) in two variants: with

$$\vec{W} = -\nabla \Psi_p$$

or

$$\vec{W}(x) = \frac{\Psi_p(x)}{|\Psi_p(x)|}, \tag{22}$$

where Ψ_p solves (21) for $p \in \{2, 3, 4, 5\}$ (we have also used rational values close to those). We shall clearly note in each experiment if $\vec{W}$ is normalized or not.

The p–Poisson equation (21) has been solved numerically by two methods:

1. the Newton method, see e.g. [12, Ch. 9],

2. the fixed–point (Picard) iterations: take u_0 solving $\Delta u_0 = -1$ and

$$\text{div} \left(|\nabla u_{i-1}|^{p-2} \nabla u_{i-\frac{1}{2}} \right) = -1$$

for $i = 1, 2, \ldots$, with the boundary conditions as in (21). Additionally, we use a damping proposed in [1, (3.7), $\gamma = 0.5$], i.e. $u_i = \gamma u_{i-\frac{1}{2}} + (1 - \gamma)u_{i-1}$. The equations were solved by FEM on the same grid.

The two approaches gave essentially the same results, the Newton method being, as expected, much faster. The unexpected behaviour was the nonconvergence of both methods for p bigger than 5. This value could be even slightly lower depending on the geometry and on the method, but we were unable to get it significantly higher, and this, apparently, independently of the mesh refinement. This effect was indeed reported in [1] as for the fixed–point method.

The scalar velocity function has a piecewise linear form:

$$v(\rho) = \min \left(v_{\max}, \max \left(1 - \frac{\rho}{\rho_{\max}}, 0 \right) \right), \tag{23}$$

or a piecewise constant form:

$$v(\rho) = \frac{v_{\max}}{2} \quad \text{if } \rho \leq \rho_{\max}; \qquad v(\rho) = 0 \quad \text{otherwise}, \tag{24}$$

or a constant form

$$v(\rho) = \frac{v_{\max}}{2}. \tag{25}$$

We take $v_{\max} = 1$ and $\rho_{\max} = 8$.

4.2 Linear Model, P = 2

At first, we perform our simulations with $p = 2$. Here, $\overrightarrow{W}$ is not normalized: $\overrightarrow{W} = -\nabla \Psi_2$ and v is constant as in (25). Thus, $\overrightarrow{V}$ satisfies the condition (7), and thus, the assumptions of 1.

We use five time steps Δt between 0.001 and 0.01 and draw in Fig. 1, the functions defined in Definition 2. (Note the log scale for t). The total mass function is decreasing only for $\Delta t \leq 0.002$; the same is true for the stability function. It is clear, by Lemma 1, that these are the only cases where the scheme is stable.

4.3 p ≥ 2

When $p > 2$, or if v is not constant, the property (7) is not satisfied anymore. In Fig. 2, we show experiments with $p \in \{2, 3, 5\}$. So as to minimize 'side effects', $\overrightarrow{W}$ is still not normalized: $\overrightarrow{W} = -\nabla \Psi_p$. The scalar velocity v is piecewise constant (24). As ρ does not exceed $\rho_{\max}$, our model is still in the linear regime, but (7) is not granted for $p > 2$.

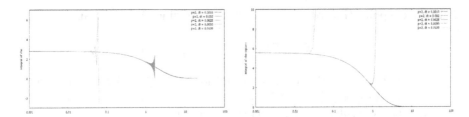

Fig. 1. Here, $\overrightarrow{V} = -0.5\nabla\Phi_2$. We compare the evolution for different time steps Δt. On the left, the total mass of pedestrians vs time. On the right, the stability function vs time. Both in log scale on the time axis. The decreasing curves correspond to $\Delta t = 0.002$ and $\Delta t = 0.001$, which fit almost perfectly. The light blue — to $\Delta t = 0.0025$, the others to bigger Δt. (Color figure online)

We take $\Delta t = 0.002$ for $p \in \{2, 3\}$ and $\Delta t = 0.01$ for bigger p, in view of the fact that $|\nabla \Psi_p|$ is considerably closer to 1 for these p. We observe on one hand, the stability of the scheme, and on the other, the effect of decreasing the total evacuation time with increasing p. In particular, for $p = 2$ the evacuation is very long. Finally, we verify that the Picard and Newton method applied to (21) give the same result. We have checked that with increasing p, the error between the two methods decreases.

4.4   Nonlinear Model, $p \geq 2$

We finally simulate the evacuation with a normed velocity field (22) and with v piecewise constant (24) and piecewise linear (23). Here, $\Delta t = 0.01$. The evolution is visualized in Fig. 3. Some violations of the non–negativity of ρ_h are observed when the model becomes nonlinear. The stability functions do not decrease in an initial period of time, after which they are all perfectly monotone, going down to zero. This means that (7) is no longer valid, and the weaker condition (11) becomes valid after this initial time. We postulate that our scheme is still stable, but within a larger definition of stability, meaning boundedness of the solution's L^2 norm. This approach should be considered in view of the properties of $\overrightarrow{V}$ itself.

We observe, as before, shortening of the evacuation time when p increases, but the influence of p is attenuated. Surpisingly enough, introducing a piecewise linear, decreasing velocity (23) does not shorten the evacuation time, and leads to bigger crowd densities. However, this comparison is still quite heuristic.

The Braess paradox clearly appears in Fig. 4: the upper part of the room, with more obstacles, evacuates more quickly and has less regions with high densities. This phenomenon can be observed for both forms of v, but a piecewise linear velocity (23) makes it clearer.

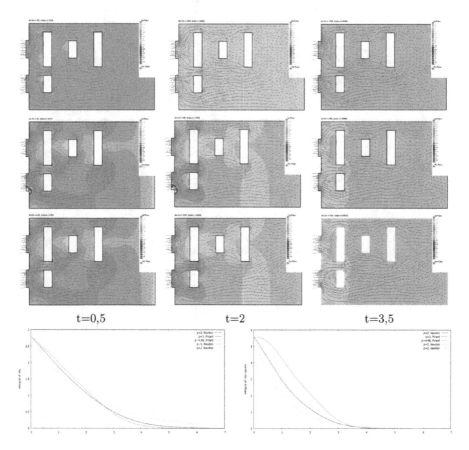

$$t=0,5 \qquad\qquad t=2 \qquad\qquad t=3,5$$

Fig. 2. The first three rows show the evolution of the crowd density with the velocity field $\overrightarrow{V} = v\nabla\Psi_p$ and p equal to, respectively, 2, 3, 5. We do not normalize the velocity field here. $\Delta t = 0.002$ when p equals 2 or 3, $\Delta t = 0.01$ for $p = 5$. In the fourth row, on the left, the evolution of the total mass of pedestrians: in yellow for $p = 2$, in blue/green for $p = 3$, in brown $p = 5$ (4.98 for the Picard method). On the right, the stability function for each case. (Color figure online)

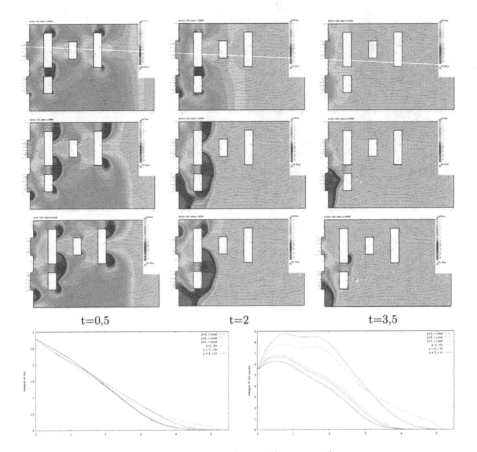

t=0,5   t=2   t=3,5

Fig. 3. Evolution with a velocity field $\overrightarrow{V} = v\overrightarrow{W}$ where $\overrightarrow{W}$ is normed according to (22). $\Delta t = 0.01$. First row, the scalar function v is piecewise constant (24) and $p = 2$. Second row, the scalar function v is piecewise linear (23) and $p = 2$. Third row, the scalar function v is piecewise linear (23) and $p = 4$. Below, on the left, the evolution of the total mass of pedestrians, with v piecewise constant and p taking the values 2, 5 (steeper functions) and v piecewise linear and p taking the values 2, 4, 5. On the right, the stability function for each case. Here, the influence of p on the dynamics is smaller than in the previous case.

5   Conclusions

We have concentrated here on the role of the velocity field $\overrightarrow{V}$ for the evacuation dynamics, in particular when the direction of $\overrightarrow{V}$ is given by the p–Poisson equation (21). We have shown that bigger p shorten the evacuation time. We have also seen the Braess paradox appearing in evacuation.

In this context, a more systematic study of the role of 1) the dependence of the velocity field on ρ 2) the parameter κ (which may also be dependent on ρ), and finally 3) the geometry, is to be performed. At this end, we need a mathematical study of a weaker condition for stability: $(\rho_h^n, \rho_h^n) \leq C$. We also hope to find a numerical method for solving the p–Poisson equation for larger p.

References

1. Bakker, J.C.: Wall-distance calculation for turbulence modelling. Bachelor Thesis, Delft University of Technology (2018)
2. Belyaev, A., Fayolle, P.-A.: On variational and PDE-based distance function approximations. Compu.r Graphics Forum **34**(8), 104–118 (2015)
3. Colombo, R.M., Gokieli, M., Rosini, M.D.: Modeling crowd dynamics through hyperbolic - elliptic equations. In: Non-Linear Partial Differential Equations, Mathematical Physics, and Stochastic Analysis – The Helge Holden Anniversary Volume, pp. 111–128. EMS Series of Congress Reports, May 2018
4. Bhattacharya, T., DiBenedetto, E., Manfredi, J.: Limits as $p \to \infty$ of $\Delta_p u_p = f$ and related extremal problems. Rend. Sem. Mat. Univ. Politec. Torino **47**, 15–68 (1989)
5. Gokieli, M., Szczepańczyk, A.: A numerical scheme for evacuation dynamics. In: Wyrzykowski, R., Deelman, E., Dongarra, J., Karczewski, K. (eds.) PPAM 2019. LNCS, vol. 12044, pp. 277–286. Springer, Cham (2020). https://doi.org/10.1007/978-3-030-43222-5_24
6. Hecht, F.: New development in FreeFem++. J. Numer. Math. **20**(3–4), 251–265 (2012)
7. Hughes, R.L.: A continuum theory for the flow of pedestrians. Transp. Res. Part B Methodol. **36**(6), 507–535 (2002)
8. Hughes, R.L.: The flow of human crowds. Annu. Rev. Fluid Mech. **35**(1), 169–182 (2003)
9. Jiang, Y., Zhou, S., Tian, F.-B.: Macroscopic pedestrian flow model with degrading spatial information. J. Comp. Sci. **10**, 36–44 (2015)
10. Kachroo, P.: Pedestrian Dynamics: Mathematical Theory and Evacuation Control. CRC Press (2009)
11. Kamga, J.-B.A., Després, B.: CFL condition and boundary conditions for DGM approximation of convection-diffusion. SIAM J. Numer. Anal. **44**(6), 2245–2269 (2006)
12. M. G. Larson and F. Bengzon. The finite element method: theory, implementation, and practice. Texts in Computational Science and Engineering 10, 2010
13. Twarogowska, M., Goatin, P., Duvigneau, R.: Macroscopic modeling and simulations of room evacuation. Appl. Math. Model. **38**(24), 5781–5795 (2014)

5th Minisymposium on HPC Applications in Physical Sciences

Parallel Identification of Unique Sequences in Nuclear Structure Calculations

Daniel Langr[1]([✉])[iD] and Tomáš Dytrych[2,3][iD]

[1] Faculty of Information Technology, Czech Technical University in Prague,
Thákurova 9, 16000 Praha, Czech Republic
`daniel.langr@fit.cvut.cz`
[2] Nuclear Physics Institute, Czech Academy of Sciences, Řež 130, 25068 Řež, Czech Republic
[3] Department of Physics and Astronomy, Louisiana State University, Baton Rouge, LA 70803, USA

Abstract. Reducing the set of sequences into the set of sequences that are unique can save a lot of memory space in computer programs. We study this problem on the symmetry-adapted no-core shell model (SA-NCSM) nuclear structure calculations, where duplicated sequences of different kinds naturally emerge in the data of the basis of the Hilbert space physically relevant to a given nucleus. For a fast solution of this problem on multicore architectures, we propose and present a multithreaded algorithm suitable for high performance computing (HPC) environments. Furthermore, we provide an experimental evaluation of this algorithm and show that, in practice, it can significantly reduce the time required to identify unique sequences in a real-world application.

Keywords: Multithreading · Nuclear structure · Parallel algorithm · Symmetry-adapted no-core shell model · Unique sequences

1 Introduction

Let us consider the programming problem of mapping indexes $0 \leq i < n - 1$ to variable-length sequences S_i, where:

$$S_i = \left(a_0^{(i)}, a_1^{(i)}, \ldots, a_{\text{len}(S_i)-1}^{(i)}\right). \tag{1}$$

For the sake of consistency with algorithm pseudocode and computer code, we stick to zero-based indexing even in the mathematical notation throughout this text. In addition, assume that $S_i = S_j$ holds for many combinations of i and j. Under this assumption, storing all the sequences $S_0, \ldots, S_{n-1}$ separately in a computer memory would take an unnecessary large space.

An alternative approach is to store only sequences that are *unique*. Let us denote these unique sequences by U_I:

$$\{U_I : 0 \leq I < N\} = \{S_i : 0 \leq i < n\} \quad \text{and} \quad U_I \neq U_J \text{ if } I \neq J. \tag{2}$$

© The Author(s), under exclusive license to Springer Nature Switzerland AG 2023
R. Wyrzykowski et al. (Eds.): PPAM 2022, LNCS 13827, pp. 357–369, 2023.
https://doi.org/10.1007/978-3-031-30445-3_30

Also, let $\text{len}(U_I)$ denote the length of U_I.

Example 1. Let $n = 5$, $S_0 = (A, C, D)$, $S_1 = (B, D)$, $S_2 = (B, D)$, $S_3 = (A)$, $S_4 = (A, C, D)$. Then, the number of unique sequences is $N = 3$ and a possible way to enumerate them is $U_0 = (A, C, D)$, $U_1 = (B, D)$, $U_2 = (A)$.

Let $X \cdot Y$ denote the operation of concatenating elements of two sequences X and Y. In Example 1, storing all $n = 5$ sequences in a computer memory would require an array of length 11:

$$elems = [S_0 \cdot S_1 \cdot S_2 \cdot S_3 \cdot S_4] = [A, C, D, B, D, B, D, A, A, C, D]. \qquad (3)$$

The mapping of indexes to sequences can then be implemented by another array:

$$first = [0, 3, 5, 7, 8, 11]. \qquad (4)$$

Here, $first[i]$ is the index of the first element of S_i in $elems$, $first[n]$ equals the length of $elems$, and the length of S_i can be derived as $\text{len}(S_i) = first[i+1] - first[i]$. Consequently,

$$S_i = \Big(elems\,[first[i]],\, elems\,[first[i]+1], \ldots, elems\,[first[i+1]-1] \Big). \qquad (5)$$

Storing the $N = 3$ unique sequences would require an array of length 6:

$$Elems = [U_0 \cdot U_1 \cdot U_2] = [A, C, D, B, D, A]. \qquad (6)$$

Similarly to $first$, we can construct the corresponding array $First$ as follows:

$$First = [0, 3, 5, 6]. \qquad (7)$$

This array is now related to unique sequences:

$$U_I = \Big(Elems\,[First[I]],\, Elems\,[First[I]+1], \ldots, Elems\,[First[I+1]-1] \Big). \qquad (8)$$

Therefore, we need to map the indexes i of S_i to the indexes I of U_I, which can be accomplished with an additional array:

$$Map = [0, 1, 1, 2, 0]. \qquad (9)$$

Now, $S_i = U_I$ where $I = Map[i]$.

In this example, it does not seem that storing unique sequences in a computer memory would be of much benefit. However, our work addresses situations where the numbers n and N are much larger and where

$$N \ll n \quad \text{and} \quad M \ll m, \quad \text{where} \quad M = \sum_{I=0}^{N-1} \text{len}(U_I) \quad \text{and} \quad m = \sum_{i=0}^{n-1} \text{len}(S_i).$$
$$(10)$$

Algorithm 1: Single-threaded unique sequences identification

Input: $S_0, S_1, \ldots, S_{n-1}$: input sequences
Output: *elems, first*: arrays encoding unique seq. $U_0, U_1, \ldots, U_{N-1}$
Output: N: number of unique sequences
Output: M: total number of elements of unique sequences
Data: *aux*: associative data structure that maps input sequences to indexes

1 $I \leftarrow 0$
2 **for** $i \leftarrow 0$ to $n - 1$ **do**
3   **if** S_i is not contained in *aux* **then**
4   insert S_i into *aux* and set $aux[S_i] \leftarrow I$
5   append current length of *Elems* to *First*
6   append elements of S_i to *Elems*
7          $I \leftarrow I + 1$
8   append $aux[S_i]$ to *Map*
9 $N \leftarrow$ length of *First*
10 $M \leftarrow$ length of *Elems*
11 append length of *Elems* to *First*

A single-threaded algorithm for the identification of unique sequences U_I in the input sequences S_i can be designed in a relatively straightforward way with the help of an auxiliary associative data structure that provides mapping $aux : S_i \rightarrow I$, where $S_i = U_I$. The pseudocode is presented as Algorithm 1.

This algorithm cannot be directly parallelized by splitting the loop iterations between multiple threads. First, this loop is inherently sequential due to appending data mainly to the *Elems* and *First* arrays with initially unknown lengths. Moreover, implementations of associative data structures provided by performance-aware programming languages (such as `std::map` or `std::unordered_map` in C++) are usually not thread-safe. Although thread-safe versions of associative data structures — such as concurrent hash tables — have been developed, they mostly come up with some restrictions and drawbacks (for instance, they commonly require keys to fit the word size of a given computer architecture to enable their processing with atomic memory operations).

We designed a generic multithreaded parallel algorithm for identification of unique sequences, which we present in Sect. 4. Furthermore, we used its efficient implementation in our *high-performance computing* (HPC) application, which is described in Sect. 2. Finally, we experimentally evaluated this implementation on real-world application problems and show the results in Sect. 6.

2   Application

Our need for parallel identification of unique sequences came from *symmetry-adapted no-core shell model* (SA-NCSM) nuclear structure calculations [1,8]. With these calculations, we try to model atomic nuclei, namely, to obtain their nuclear wave functions. The SA-NCSM first forms a *basis* for the Hilbert space relevant to a given nucleus. Since this basis is infinite-dimensional, only its finite subset of basis states/functions is taken into consideration. This subset is selected by a single even number — so-called *basis cutoff parameter Nmax* (it represents the maximum allowed number of harmonic oscillator quanta above the minimum for a given nucleus). As the next step, a Hamiltonian matrix operator is constructed such that its rows and columns are spanned by the basis functions. Finally, the resulting wave functions are obtained in the form of linear combinations of basis functions. The coefficients of these linear combinations are elements of the eigenvectors of the Hamiltonian matrix. The entire SA-NCSM workflow consists of a series of calculations with increasing *Nmax*. This process is stopped once the eigenvalues converge for all the energy states in which one is interested.

Our implementation of the SA-NCSM is the software framework called LSU3-shell [2]. It is written in the C++ programming language, and its parallelization is built upon the hybrid MPI+OpenMP programming model, which makes it applicable to practically any contemporary large-scale supercomputer [10,11]. The SA-NCSM employs a sophisticated mathematical background provided by group theory and the theory of representation, and the group of particular interest is the special unitary group SU(3) [3]. Within LSU3shell, a basis is organized into so-called *IpIn blocks*. Each IpIn block is related to a particular distribution of protons and neutrons in the harmonic oscillator shells. A combination of two IpIn blocks forms a submatrix of a Hamiltonian matrix. Internally, an IpIn block consists of multiple SU(3) proton-neutron irreducible representations (PN irreps). Each PN irrep is mapped to a block of matrix rows/columns. Their number is given by the PN irrep *dimension* and its *multiplicity factor* in the IpIn block. For more details on the construction of the basis and its organization, see [6,7].

According to the description above, a submatrix related to a particular combination of IpIn blocks consists of matrix blocks where each block is given by a combination of PN irreps. To process these blocks independently — for instance, to enable finer granularity of parallel processing — we would need to remember the first row/column index and the multiplicity factor of each PN irrep for all IpIn blocks in a basis. In practice, this would require a large amount of memory space. For illustration, the SA-NCSM basis for the 12C nucleus and $Nmax = 12$ has $n = 73,676,583$ IpIn blocks. The total number of their PN irreps is $m = 1,214,960,841$. Storing a sequence of PN irrep indexes, a sequence of first row/column indexes, and a sequence of multiplicity factors for each IpIn block would require tens of gigabytes of memory. Moreover, these numbers grow rapidly with the growing number of nucleons and increasing *Nmax*, making explicit storage of all these sequences infeasible in practice.

In the current version of LSU3shell, only sequences of PN irrep indexes are stored in memory for IpIn blocks. Recent research revealed that many of these sequences are the same for different IpIn blocks. Moreover, we found that the same holds also for the sequences of multiplicity factors. The sequences of row/column indexes are distinct for each IpIn block. However, when we consid-

Table 1. Counts of *all* and *unique* sequences and their elements for the 12C nucleus and *Nmax* = 12 SA-NCSM basis.

Sequences	Total count (n)	Total number of elements (m)	Unique count (N)	Unique number of elements (M)
PN irrep indexes	73,676,583	1,214,960,841	7,995	188,177
Row/column offsets	73,676,583	1,214,960,841	6,973	222,810
Multiplicity factors	73,676,583	1,214,960,841	3,769	141,025

ered only their offsets with respect to the first row/column index of the IpIn block, we made the same observation. The particular numbers for the 12C nucleus and *Nmax* = 12 basis are shown in Table 1. The numbers for unique sequences are several orders of magnitude lower than those for all the sequences, and storage of only unique sequences in memory requires only a few megabytes. To achieve that, we need to quickly identify these unique sequences, which is the goal of the presented algorithm.

3   Related Work

The defined problem may be considered as a specific instance of the generic problem domain referred to as *data deduplication*. Data deduplication describes methods that are mostly used to reduce the amount of data stored in a storage system or transferred over a network by eliminating redundant parts [9,13,14]. Our problem represents in-memory data deduplication for particular types of data (sequences). Problems of this type are relatively rarely addressed in the literature. We have found some relevant papers applying deduplication methods in order to compress the memory footprints of sparse matrices [4,5,12]. However, they focus on the data reduction results and acceleration of subsequent matrix operations. In contrast to our work, they do not propose efficient parallel algorithms for identification of unique/redundant data.

4   Algorithm

One way to find a parallel solution to the unique sequence identification problem may be derived directly from Algorithm 1. The first option is to use thread-local hash tables and then reduce them to a single global hash table. An alternative option is to use a concurrent hash table shared by all threads. In our auxiliary measurements, better scalability and performance were achieved using another approach, which we present here as our final proposed solution. It is based on calculating the hashes for all the input sequences and their subsequent grouping with respect to the same hashes. This then enables independent processing of a group of sequences by a single thread, since equal sequences (having the same elements) belong to a single group. Moreover, if a sufficient hash function is used, then all the sequences in the same group are likely to be equal.

Algorithm 2: Multithreaded parallel unique sequences identification; part I

Input: $S_0, S_1, \ldots, S_{n-1}$: input sequences
Input: T: number of threads
Output: *Elems, First, Map*: arrays encoding unique seq. $U_0, U_1, \ldots, U_{N-1}$
Output: N: number of unique sequences
Output: M: total number of elements of unique sequences
Data: H: array of pairs (h, i) where h is the hash for S_i
Data: *EO, FO*: integer arrays of size T

1 $Map \leftarrow$ array of size n
2 $H \leftarrow$ array of size n
3 **for all** $0 \leq i < n$ **do in parallel** $H[i] \leftarrow (\text{hash}(S_i), i)$
4 sort H in parallel using h as sorting keys
5 $begin \leftarrow$ array of size $T + 1$
6 **for all** threads **do in parallel**
7 $\quad$ $j \leftarrow$ index of current thread
8 $\quad$ $k \leftarrow \lfloor j * n/T \rfloor$
9 $\quad$ $h \leftarrow H[k].h$
10 $\quad$ **while** $k > 0$ **and** $H[k-1].h = h$ **do** $k \leftarrow k - 1$
11 $\quad$ $begin[j] \leftarrow k$
12 $begin[T] \leftarrow n$

$\quad$ // To be continued as Algorithm 3.

The pseudocode of the proposed algorithm is presented as Algorithm 2, Algorithm 3, and Algorithm 4. First, an auxiliary array H is constructed, where each element contains information about a sequence index and its hash. Then, this array is sorted considering hashes as sorting keys, which effectively places information about sequences with the same hashes next to each other. Each part of H with the same hash defines a single group of sequences. In the next step, these groups are divided into T segments, where T denotes the number of threads. Now, each thread can operate independently on its segment. Since each unique sequence corresponds to a single group, each thread can process its local groups to identify its unique sequences. The information about them is encoded in thread-local arrays $Elems_j$ and $First_j$. When thread-local unique sequences are identified, sequences within a group are compared for equality. This is necessary since two sequences with different elements may have the same hash. Information about index mapping is stored directly in the Map array, but this mapping now applies only to thread-local unique sequences. Finally, thread-local unique sequences are merged into global unique sequences, that is, into the resulting arrays $Elems$ and $First$. This requires the indexes of the elements and the indexes in Map to be incremented accordingly. The increments are computed as prefix sums (scans) on the lengths of the thread-local arrays $Elems_j$ and $First_j$.

Algorithm 3: Multithreaded parallel unique sequences identification; part II

```
13  for all threads do in parallel
14  |   j ← index of current thread
15  |   B ← begin[j]
16  |   E ← begin[j + 1]
17  |   Elems_j ← empty array
18  |   First_j ← [0]
19  |   if B = E then break
20  |   for k ← B to E − 1 do
21  |   |   i ← H[k].i
22  |   |   if k = 0 or H[k].h ≠ h then
23  |   |   |   g ← length of First_j
24  |   |   |   h ← H[k].h
25  |   |   |   append elements of S_i to Elems_j
26  |   |   |   Map[i] ← length of First_j − 1
27  |   |   |   append length of Elems_j to First_j
28  |   |   else
29  |   |   |   present ← false
30  |   |   |   for l ← g to last index of First_j do
31  |   |   |   |   b ← First_j[l − 1]
32  |   |   |   |   e ← First_j[l]
33  |   |   |   |   if S_i = (Elems_j[b], ..., Elems_j[e − 1]) then
34  |   |   |   |   |   Map[i] ← l − 1
35  |   |   |   |   |   present ← true
36  |   |   |   |   |   break
37  |   |   |   if present = false then
38  |   |   |   |   append elements of S_i to Elems_j
39  |   |   |   |   Map[i] ← length of First_j − 1
40  |   |   |   |   append length of Elems_j to First_j
41  |   remove last element of First_j
    // To be continued as Algorithm 4.
```

Almost all the steps of the algorithms are executed in parallel. There are a few single-threaded operations, which are computationally trivial (prefix sums are performed on T values only).

5   Implementation Issues

Here, we discuss some problems that are important for efficient implementation of the proposed multithreaded algorithm. Some of them are applicable to the implementation of the single-threaded algorithm as well.

First, sequences are represented in computer programs as variable-length arrays. These generally require dynamic memory allocations. If each input sequence were represented by a separate array, the number of corresponding allocations would be $O(n)$. However, if we reuse the same array for input sequences and apply exponential growth of its capacity, then the number of allocations can be reduced to $O(N + \log L)$, where L is the length of the longest input sequence.

Second, the multithreaded algorithm contains the parallel sorting step. For our implementation, we finally chose the parallel multi-way *mergesort*. Initially, we tried to use a few variants of parallel *quicksort*. However, it turned out that all of them were significantly slower than the mentioned mergesort. We attribute this behavior to the fact that quicksort is generally much more data-sensitive and does not efficiently deal with cases where there are only relatively few distinct sorting keys in the sorted data.

Third, in our application, we employed the method for hashing input sequences provided by the C++ Boost library. This method combines hashes of individual sequence elements in the following way:

$$h_0^{(i)} = \text{hash}\big(a_0^{(i)}\big),$$
$$h_{k+1}^{(i)} = \text{hashcombine}\big(h_k^{(i)}, a_k^{(i)}\big),$$
$$\text{hash}(S_i) = h_{\text{len}(S_i)}^{(i)},$$

where

$$\text{hashcombine}\big(h_k^{(i)}, a_k^{(i)}\big)$$
$$= h_k^{(i)} \oplus \Big(\text{hash}\big(a_k^{(i)}\big) + 9\text{E}3779\text{B}9_{16} + \big(h_k^{(i)} \ll 6\big) + \big(h_k^{(i)} \gg 2\big)\Big),$$

where $\oplus$, $\ll$, and $\gg$ denote the exclusive bit OR (XOR) operation, the left bit shift operation, and the right bit shift operation, respectively. The hashes of individual input sequence elements were calculated in our case by the C++ standard library `std::hash` functors.

Fourth, in the multithreaded algorithm, the input sequences S_i are accessed twice. In the first case (Line 3 of Algorithm 2), they are accessed in regular order with respect to their increasing indexes i, provided that iterations are mapped to threads such that each thread takes care of a contiguous chunk of indexes. In the second case (Line 21 of Algorithm 3), the input sequences are accessed in an irregular order given by the sorted array H. In our application presented in Sect. 2, this irregular access turned out to be several times slower than the regular one (see Sect. 7 for some details). We found that this slowdown was mainly due to the less efficient utilization of the computer memory subsystem. Namely, in the regular access case, the automatic prefetching of data into cache memories was very efficient. This automatic prefetching was mostly useless in the irregular access case. We were able to partially reduce the negative impact of irregular basis data access with explicit software prefetching.

Algorithm 4: Multithreaded parallel unique sequences identification; part III

42 $M \leftarrow$ sum of lengths of $Elems_j$ for $0 \le j < T$
43 $N \leftarrow$ sum of lengths of $First_j$ for $0 \le j < T$
44 $EO \leftarrow$ exclusive prefix sum (scan) on lengths of $Elems_j$ for $0 \le j < T$
45 $FO \leftarrow$ exclusive prefix sum (scan) on lengths of $First_j$ for $0 \le j < T$
46 $Elems \leftarrow$ array of size M
47 $First \leftarrow$ array of size $N + 1$
48 **for all** threads **do in parallel**
49 $\quad j \leftarrow$ index of current thread
50 $\quad$ copy elements of $Elems_j$ to $Elems$ from index $EO[j]$
51 $\quad$ add $EO[j]$ to all elements of $First_j$
52 $\quad$ copy elements of $First_j$ to $First$ from index $FO[j]$
53 $\quad$ **for** $k \leftarrow B$ to $E - 1$ **do**
54 $\quad\quad i \leftarrow H[k].i$
55 $\quad\quad Map[i] \leftarrow Map[i] + FO[j]$

56 $First[N] \leftarrow M$

---

6   Experiments

To evaluate the proposed algorithm, we applied it to our SA-NCSM nuclear structure calculations introduced in Sect. 2. Within experiments, we then measured runtime of the algorithm for identification of unique sequences of all three mentioned types (PN irrep indexes, PN irrep mulitplicities within IpIn blocks, and block row/column offsets) on different SA-NCSM problems.

As a testbed, we used nodes of two supercomputers with different CPU architectures. The first were the computational nodes of the Karolina supercomputer operated by IT4Innovations in Ostrava, Czech Republic. A single Karolina node consisted of two AMD EPYC 7H12 CPUs each having 64 computational cores. A single CPUs additionally consisted of 4 NUMA nodes.

The second were the computational nodes of the Frontera supercomputer operated by the Texas Advanced Computing Center (TACC), University of Texas, Austin, USA. A single Frontera node consisted of two Intel Xeon Platinum 8280 CPUs each having 28 computational cores. A single CPU was a single NUMA node as well.

The strong-scaling results obtained in the experiments conducted on these supercomputers are shown in Table 2 and Table 3. On Karolina, we used two different setups for multithreaded algorithm runs. In the first one, only a single NUMA node was used, and the number of threads was set to the number of its cores (16). In the second one, a single CPU was used, and the number of threads was set accordingly to 64. On Frontera, each NUMA node corresponded to a single CPU (socket). Therefore, we set the number of threads to the number of single CPU cores (28). The rationale behind these setups is that it is the typical way in which we map MPI processes to supercomputer nodes and split MPI processes to threads in our productive SA-NCSM calculations.

Table 2. Unique sequences identification time in seconds with single-threaded (ST) and multithreaded (MT) algorithm by using T threads on the Karolina supercomputer node. The experiments for $T = 16$ and $T = 64$ threads were mapped to a single NUMA node and to a single CPU socket, respectively.

Nucleus	$Nmax$	ST	MT ($T = 16$)	MT ($T = 64$)
10B	18	658.6	167.7	92.2
12C	14	221.6	51.5	28.9
12B	14	165.9	45.3	20.9
16O	12	129.4	34.7	17.8
18F	10	105.0	26.1	16.1
22Na	8	269.0	66.0	32.2

Table 3. Unique sequences identification time in seconds with single-threaded (ST) and multithreaded (MT) algorithm by using T threads on the Frontera supercomputer node. The experiments for $T = 28$ threads were mapped to a single NUMA node/CPU socket.

Nucleus	$Nmax$	ST	MT ($T = 28$)
10B	18	804.1	149.5
12C	14	250.2	39.1
12B	14	197.9	28.8
16O	12	154.8	24.5
18F	10	124.8	17.1
22Na	8	316.6	41.9

To evaluate the efficiency of the proposed multithreaded algorithm, we also performed experiments with the implementation of the presented single-threaded algorithm (Algorithm 1). Figure 1 shows the relative measured execution time of the multithreaded algorithm normalized to the execution time of the single-threaded algorithm on both testbed systems.

7   Discussion on Results

The results presented in Table 2 and Table 3 indicate two outcomes. First, the proposed parallel multithreaded algorithm significantly reduced the unique sequence identification time in contrast to its single-threaded variant in our SA-NCSM nuclear structure calculations, which was our main goal. Although savings of tens or hundreds of seconds might not seem to be large, we need to realize that in production SA-NCSM calculations, the number of involved supercomputer resources can be enormous.

The second outcome is that the speedup of the multithreaded algorithm compared to its single-threaded variant is far from linear (ideal). We performed some additional profiling measurements and found that the problem — specific to our application — was with the already mentioned second processing of the input sequences S_i in irregular order with respect to growing i. The measurements revealed that this irregular-order processing of the input sequences was 3 to 4 times slower than their in-order processing in the first algorithm phase. The cause of this effect stemmed mostly from the ineffective prefetching of data into caches and cache-line size-based memory access, where some data transferred from memory to CPU cache were then not used.

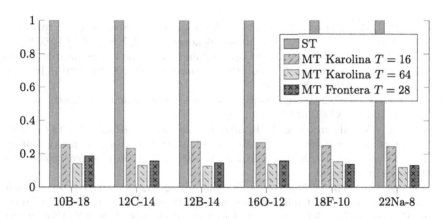

Fig. 1. Unique sequences relative identification time with the multithreaded (MT) algorithm using T threads on the Karolina and Frontera supercomputer nodes. The time is normalized by the execution time of the single-threaded algorithm (ST) on a given system.

8 Conclusions

The contribution of the presented work is the multithreaded algorithm for the problem of identification of unique sequences. This algorithm can be implemented in performance-aware programming languages such as C or C++ without the need for any special concurrent data structure (such as a concurrent hash table). Also, it does not target any particular threading mechanism; therefore, it can be implemented with different ones, such as OpenMP, C++11 threading, or the POSIX thread library. The presented experimental evaluation showed that this algorithm significantly reduced the unique seqeuneces identification step in our SA-NCSM nuclear structure calculations. However, the observed speed-ups were not linear because of irregular access to SA-NCSM basis data within our application, which caused less effective utilization of the memory and cache subsystem.

Acknowledgements. This work was supported by the Czech Science Foundation under grant number 22-14497S and by the Czech Ministry of Education, Youth and Sports under grant number CZ.02.1.01/0.0/0.0/16_019/0000765 and through the e-INFRA CZ (ID:90140).

The authors acknowledge the Texas Advanced Computing Center (TACC) at The University of Texas at Austin for providing HPC resources that have contributed to the research results reported within this paper under the allocation number PHY21002.

References

1. Barrett, B.R., Navrátil, P., Vary, J.P.: Ab initio no core shell model. Prog. Part. Nucl. Phys. **69**, 131–181 (2013). https://doi.org/10.1016/j.ppnp.2012.10.003
2. Dytrych, T., et al.: Efficacy of the SU(3) scheme for ab initio large-scale calculations beyond the lightest nuclei. Comput. Phys. Commun. **207**, 202–210 (2016). https://doi.org/10.1016/j.cpc.2016.06.006
3. Heine, V.: Group Theory in Quantum Mechanics. Pergamon Press (1960). https://doi.org/10.1016/C2013-0-01646-5
4. Karakasis, V., Gkountouvas, T., Kourtis, K., Goumas, G., Koziris, N.: An extended compression format for the optimization of sparse matrix-vector multiplication. IEEE Trans. Parallel Distrib. Syst.**24**(10), 1930–1940 (2013). https://doi.org/10.1109/TPDS.2012.290
5. Kourtis, K., Goumas, G., Koziris, N.: Optimizing sparse matrix-vector multiplication using index and value compression. In: Proceedings of the 5th Conference on Computing Frontiers, pp. 87–96. CF 2008, ACM, New York, NY, USA (2008). https://doi.org/10.1145/1366230.1366244
6. Langr, D., Dytrych, T., Oberhuber, T., Knapp, F.: Efficient parallel generation of many-nucleon basis for large-scale *Ab Initio* nuclear structure calculations. In: Wyrzykowski, R., Dongarra, J., Deelman, E., Karczewski, K. (eds.) PPAM 2017. LNCS, vol. 10778, pp. 341–350. Springer, Cham (2018). https://doi.org/10.1007/978-3-319-78054-2_32
7. Langr, D., Dytrych, T., Launey, K.D., Draayer, J.P.: Accelerating many-nucleon basis generation for high performance computing enabled ab initio nuclear structure studies. The International Journal of High Performance Computing Applications **33**(3), 522–533 (2019). https://doi.org/10.1177/1094342019838314
8. Launey, K.D., Dytrych, T., Draayer, J.P.: Symmetry-guided large-scale shell-model theory. Prog. Part. Nucl. Phys. **89**, 101–136 (2016). https://doi.org/10.1016/j.ppnp.2016.02.001
9. Meister, D.: Advanced data deduplication techniques and their application. Ph.D. thesis, Johannes Gutenberg-Univrsität (2013)
10. Message Passing Interface Forum: MPI: A Message-Passing Interface Standard Version 4.0 (June 2021). https://www.mpi-forum.org/docs/mpi-4.0/mpi40-report.pdf
11. OpenMP Architecture Review Board: OpenMP Application Programming Interface Version 5.2 (2021). https://www.openmp.org/specifications/
12. Willcock, J., Lumsdaine, A.: Accelerating sparse matrix computations via data compression. In: Proceedings of the 20th Annual International Conference on Supercomputing. pp. 307–316. ICS 2006, ACM, New York, NY, USA (2006). https://doi.org/10.1145/1183401.1183444

13. Xia, W., et al.: A comprehensive study of the past, present, and future of data dedu-plication. Proc. IEEE **104**(9), 1681–1710 (2016). https://doi.org/10.1109/JPROC.2016.2571298
14. Zhang, X., Deng, M.: An overview on data deduplication techniques. In: Balas, V.E., Jain, L.C., Zhao, X. (eds.) Information Technology and Intelligent Trans-portation Systems. AISC, vol. 455, pp. 359–369. Springer, Cham (2017). https://doi.org/10.1007/978-3-319-38771-0_35

Experimental and Computer Study of Molecular Dynamics of a New Pyridazine Derivative

Sebastian Wołoszczuk[1]([✉]), Aneta Woźniak-Braszak[1], Andrzej Olejniczak[2], and Michał Banaszak[1,3]

[1] Faculty of Physics, Adam Mickiewicz University, ul. Uniwersytetu Poznańskiego 2, 61-614 Poznań, Poland
sebastian.woloszczuk@amu.edu.pl
[2] Faculty of Chemistry, Nicolaus Copernicus University in Toruń, ul. Gagarina 7, 87-100 Toruń, Poland
[3] NanoBioMedical Centre, Adam Mickiewicz University, ul. Wszechnicy Piastowskiej 3, 61-614 Poznań, Poland

Abstract. The paper presents experimental and computer simulation studies of molecular dynamics of new pharmacological substances that are pyridazine derivatives. To obtain the information about molecular dynamics and cross-relaxation, a new pyridazine derivative was studied by the solid-state NMR spectroscopy homemade pulse spectrometer operating at the frequency of 30.2 MHz for protons and 28.411 MHz for fluorine nuclei, with complete absence of their interference. The Fourier Transform Infrared Spectroscopy (FTIR) data for triazolopyridazine derivates were analyzed and compared with the normal vibration frequency as calculated by quantum chemical methods. The standard Molecular Dynamics (MD) simulations were performed using the GROMACS package for the new pyridazine derivative. The simulation data were confronted with the experimental results.

Keywords: triazolopyridazine derivates · molecular dynamics · FTIR · computer simulations

1 Introduction

For many years, triazolopyridazine derivatives have been of great interest because of their wide use in medicine thanks to showing antimicrobial and antifungal [1,2], as well as anticancer [3,4], anxiolytic [5], hypoglycemic and hypolipidemic [6], antihistamine [7–9], analgesic and anti-inflammatory [10], antidiabetic [11] and antidepressant [12] properties. For example, fluorophenyl ring triazolopyridine is a compound with documented anxiolytic (anticoagulant) activity without undesirable sedative effect [13], difluoromethoxyphenyl substituted pyridazine is a drug known as Zardavirin showing the ability to smooth muscle relaxation with a simultaneous anti-inflammatory action [7].

© The Author(s), under exclusive license to Springer Nature Switzerland AG 2023
R. Wyrzykowski et al. (Eds.): PPAM 2022, LNCS 13827, pp. 370–381, 2023.
https://doi.org/10.1007/978-3-031-30445-3_31

The triazolopyridazines were obtained by multistep synthesis at the Department of Organic Chemistry of Poznan University of Medical Sciences [14–16]. One of the obtained triazoplopyridazine derivatives, 6-chloro-3-trifluoromethyl-1,2,4-triazolo [4,3-b] pyridazine, with the best antifungal activity was reacted with alcohol involving nucleophilic substitution to obtain C6 substituted ether derivative 6-methoxy-3-trifluoromethyl-1,2,4-triazolo[4,3-b]pyridazine. Molecular structure of $C_7H_5ON_4F_3$ (CF_3OCH_3 for short) with numbering of atoms is shown in Fig. 1. The aim of the study was to determine the structure and molecular dynamics of a new pharmacological substance using experimental and simulation methods. Solid-state NMR experiments, FTIR spectroscopy quantum chemistry calculations and standard molecular dynamics simulations were used to investigate of the structure and molecular dynamics of the new pyridazine derivative.

Fig. 1. Molecular structure of CF_3OCH_3 with numbering of atoms.

2   Results and Discussion

2.1   Cross-Relaxation NMR Experiment

The NMR cross-relaxation experiments were carried out in a wide range of temperatures [17–23]. The $1\,H-_{19}F$ cross relaxation was studied using the NMR sequence consisting of the first RF pulse of the frequency of 28.411 MHz and the amplitude equal to 1.2 Gs, which saturated the fluorine spins. The state of fluorine saturation was maintained for a time much longer than the proton spin-lattice relaxation time. After the solid-echo pulse sequence at 30.2 MHz, the echo amplitude, M_{sat}, was observed. Then, the echo amplitude, M, was determined without the fluorine saturation. On the basis of the results obtained from the cross-relaxation experiments, it was found that the same values of the signal amplitude were obtained with saturation of fluorinated spins as without this saturation. It was assumed that the cross interaction between fluorine nuclei and hydrogen spins in CF_3OCH_3 compound was weak. In order to investigate the molecular dynamics, measurements of spin-lattice T_1 relaxation times as a function of temperature were performed. The spin-lattice relaxation times were estimated using the standard saturation recovery sequence within the range from 223 K to 323 K. The uncertainties were approximately $\pm$ 10 % for all measurements.

The recovery of magnetization $M_z(t)$ was biexponential in the whole temperature range. For each temperature, the decay of magnetization was decomposed into two exponential terms characterized by different spin-lattice relaxation times $T_1(1H)$. The temperature dependence of the relaxation times $T_1(1H)$ for CF_3OCH_3 is shown in Fig. 2, together with the corresponding theoretical curves.

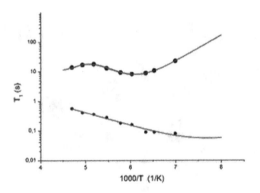

Fig. 2. Temperature dependence of the spin-lattice relaxation times $T1_1$ for 6-methoxy-3-trifluoromethyl-1,2,4-triazolo[4,3-b]pyridazine.

Figure 2 shows two courses of relaxation times as a function of temperature. A shallow minimum visible in the course of long relaxation times is equal to 6 s and appears in the vicinity of 163 K. The temperature dependence of the relaxation times, T_1, was analyzed in terms of dipole-dipole Bloembergen-Purcell-Pound (BPP) theory [24]. It was assumed that the T_1 values were determined by dipolar interactions modulated by different molecular processes and were described by Eq. 1,

$$\left(\frac{1}{T_1}\right) = \frac{2}{3}\gamma^2 \Delta M_2 \left(\frac{\tau_c}{1 + \omega_0^2\tau_c^2} + \frac{4\tau_c}{1 + 4\omega_0^2\tau_c^2}\right), \tag{1}$$

where the correlation time, τ_c, is given by Arrhenius formula $\tau_c = \tau_0 \exp(E_a/RT)$. It was suggested that the motion characterized by the relaxation time $\tau_0 = 1.0e - 14$ s and the activation energy $E_a = 23$ KJmol[1] can be the hindered rotation of the triazolopyridazyne ring. On the other hand, the short-component of the relaxation times tends to the minimum that was assigned to the hindered rotation of the methyl CH_3 group around its threefold axis C3. The activation parameters of this low temperature motion were: the relaxation time $\tau_0 = 1.2e - 12$ s and the activation energy $E_a = 8.4$ KJmol^1, which is consistent with the earlier NMR data [25–27].

2.2   FTIR Results

FTIR measurements were carried out on a Nicolet 6700 (Thermo Scientific) spectrometer equipped with a single-reflection Smart iTR attenuated total reflection (ATR) accessory with a ZnSe crystal. For each spectrum, 64 scans in the mid-infrared region ($500 - 4000$ cm^{-1}), with a resolution of 1 cm^{-1}, were accumulated.

Spectral distortion due to the nature of ATR experiment was eliminated by applying advanced ATR correction as implemented in the OMNIC 9.2 software. The molecular geometry optimization and computation of harmonic vibrational frequencies were performed in Gaussian-09 software using hybrid B3LYP functional and dispersion-corrected ω B97X-D functional, combined with Pople 6-311++G (d, p) split-valence basis set. The calculations were carried out for a single molecule in the gas phase. The assignment of the normal modes was based on the total energy distribution (TED) calculated using VEDA 4 program. Table 1 collects the calculated vibrational frequencies and proposed assignments for the lowest-energy CF_3OCH_3 conformer (Fig. 1).

Fig. 3 presents the experimental IR spectrum of CF_3OCH_3 conformer (whose structure is shown in Fig. 1) along with its spectrum calculated by B3LYP and ω B97X-D functionals.

Comparison of the experimental and calculated IR spectra (Fig. 3) shows a good agreement for the C−H bond stretching vibration in the CH_3 group, which in the experimental spectrum appears at 3030 cm^{-1}, while within the B3LYP approximation, it has a calculated frequency of 3049.9 cm^{-1}. In the range from 1624 cm^{-1} to 1517 cm^{-1}, the observed bands are attributed to the stretching vibrations of C=C and C=N bonds. The bands appearing in the range from 1493 cm^{-1} to 851 cm^{-1} correspond to the stretching and deformation vibrations of C−O, C−F, N−C, and H−C bonds. Below 829 cm^{-1}, the peaks appearing in the IR spectrum correspond to the torsion and out-of-plane stretching vibrations of H−C=C=O, C=C=C−N, C=N−N=C, N=C=N−N, F−C−F, and C=CON bonds. The calculations performed using the ω B97X-D functional, provided a better agreement between the calculated and experimental IR frequencies, especially within the C(4)-C(3)-N(8) moiety (1386 cm^{-1} band, ν C−C, ν C−N and δ C−C−N modes) and bending modes of CH_3 group (1490 − 1505 cm^{-1}). In both cases (B3LYP and ω B97X-D), however, the largest disagreement with the experimental data, is found for the vibrations of the fluorine atoms. For example, in the calculated spectra, the intensive stretching C−F mode appears at 1158 cm^{-1}, whereas in the experimental spectrum this band is much broader and upshifted to 1185 cm^{-1}. As known, fluorine atoms, especially those attached to electron withdrawing groups, can form a special type bond with halogen (the so-called fluorine bond) with acceptors as N, O, S, and pi-electrons [28]. Thus, the obtained results point out that in the solid state, the fluorine atoms are

Table 1. Calculated vibrational frequencies and proposed assignments for the low-energy conformer of CF_3OCH_3. For atom numbering see Fig. 1.

Wave- number (cm^{-1})	(M1 cm^{-1})	Assignment (TED%)[a]
27.00	62.3	τF15C12C7N10(77) + γC12N10N9C7(13)
73.67	0.7	F15C12C7N10(11) + τC17O16C2C1(18) + γC12N10N9C7(28) + γC4N10N8C3(10)
100.34	45.1	δC12C7N9(56) + γF13C7F15C12(10)
114.95	8.1	τC2N11N10C7(18) + τC17O16C2C1(29) + γC12N10N9C7(27)
154.27	140.0	τC2N11N10C7(27) + τC17O16C2C1(36)
196.22	81.5	τH18C17O16C2(36) + τH19C17O16C2(13) + τH20C17O16C2(13) + τC2N11N10C7(20)
208.33	75.6	δO16C2N11(31) + δC17O16C2(31) + γF13C7F15C12(10)
213.47	117.8	τN10C7N9N8(11) + τC17O16C2C1(11) + γF14C7F13C12(11) + γC4N10N8C3(25)
305.40	34.9	vC12C7(10) + δF13C12F15(11) + γF13C7F15C12(34)
350.61	0.8	τC1C4C3N10(14) + τN10C7N9N8(11) + γC4N10N8C3(18)
363.47	60.3	vC12C7(31) + δF15C12F14(25) + δC17O16C2(11)

Wave- number (cm^{-1})	(M1 cm^{-1})	Assignment (TED%)[a]
411.42	5.0	γN11C7C3N10(68)
420.98	10.7	δC2N11N10(26) + δC17O16C2(12)
451.11	8.1	δF13C12F15(17) + δF14C12F13(17) + τC1C4C3N10(24) + γO16C1N11C2(11)
505.38	63.4	δC2N11N10(10) + δF13C12F15(11) + δF14C12F13(12) + δF15C12F14(30)
560.33	1.9	δF13C12F15(11) + δF14C12F13(12) + τN10C7N9N8(14) + γF14C7F13C12(27)
565.44	0.8	δC4C3N8(24) + δO16C2N11(18) + δC17O16C2(21)
606.12	30.8	vC4C3(11) + δC4C3N8(11) + γF13C7F15C12(14)
621.62	10.9	δC2N11N10(12) + δC1C4C3(14) + δN11N10C3(20)
659.39	0.7	τC3N8N9C7(30) + γO16C1N11C2(39)
712.32	2.8	τC3N8N9C7(22) + τN10C7N9N8(20) + γF14C7F13C12(18) + γC12N10N9C7(11) + γO16C1N11C2(10)
738.68	84.5	vF13C12(11) + vF14C12(15) + vF15C12(15) + δF13C12F15(11) + δF14C12F13(10)
748.10	0.1	τC1C4C3N10(23) + τC3N8N9C7(13) + τN10C7N9N8(22) + γO16C1N11C2(14) + γC4N10N8C3(10)
775.49	38.0	vC4C3(19) + δC3N8N9(22) + δN8N9C7(14)
837.06	224.7	τH5C1C2O16(48) + τH6C4C3N10(21) + γC4N10N8C3(12)
864.21	91.1	vO16C2(17) + δC1C4C3(10) + δN10C7N9(14) + δO16C2N11(16)
978.98	119.7	vN10C7(15) + vO16C17(13) + δC3N8N9(17) + δC1C4C3(18) + δN8N9C7(19)
996.45	0.4	τH5C1C2O16(36) + τH6C4C3N10(53)
1021.15	180.0	vO16C17(48) + δN8N9C7(10)
1031.06	344.6	vO16C17(12) + δC3N8N9(12) + δN11N10C3(15)
1103.39	472.7	vN8N9(50)
1109.97	1062.3	vF14C12(40) + vF15C12(40) + γF14C7F13C12(11)
1140.70	11.2	vC1C4(12) + δH5C1C2(40) + δH6C4C1(27)
1160.55	515.3	vN8N9(13) + vF13C12(23) + vF14C12(17) + vF15C12(17)
1170.91	3.3	δH18C17H20(16) + δH19C17H18(16) + τH18C17O16C2(32) + τH19C17O16C2(18) + τH20C17O16C2(18)
1203.20	188.1	δH20C17H19(15) + τH19C17O16C2(22) + τH20C17O16C2(22)
1224.78	534.0	vF13C12(20) + τH19C17O16C2(11) + τH20C17O16C2(11)
1312.68	445.7	vN9C7(25) + vN11N10(25) + δN10C7N9(11)

Wave- number (cm^{-1})	(M1 cm^{-1})	Assignment (TED%)[a]
1320.67	536.6	vN8C3(19) + vO16C2(19) + δH5C1C2(18) + δH6C4C1(11)
1341.88	48.1	vN8C3(21) + δH6C4C1(22) + δC4C3N8(16)
1403.20	379.4	vO16C2(14) + δH6C4C1(10)
1445.49	1.5	vN9C7(14) + vN10C7(23) + vN11N10(18)
1472.21	39.3	vN11C2(18) + δH18C17H20(25) + δH19C17H18(25)
1483.04	33.2	δH18C17H20(38) + δH19C17H18(38) + τH18C17O16C2(16)
1496.35	38.0	δH20C17H19(70) + τH19C17O16C2(10) + τH20C17O16C2(10)
1515.61	349.1	vN11C2(10) + vN9C7(16) + vC12C7(22) + δN10C7N9(10)
1537.74	188.8	vC1C4(11) + vN11C2(33)
1581.35	220.6	vC1C4(19) + vN8C3(16) + δH5C1C2(10)
1661.20	215.7	vC1C4(35) + vN11C2(23) + vC4C3(13)
3049.85	31.8	vC17H18(17) + vC17H19(41) + vC17H20(41)
3123.96	18.3	vC17H19(50) + vC17H20(50)
3163.57	17.7	vC17H18(82)
3210.80	0.9	vC1H5(47) + vC4H6(52)
3223.80	0.2	vC1H5(52) + vC4H6(47)

v - stretching, δ - in-plane bending, τ - torsion, γ - out-of-plane modes, a - total energy distribution; contributions < 10% are not listed

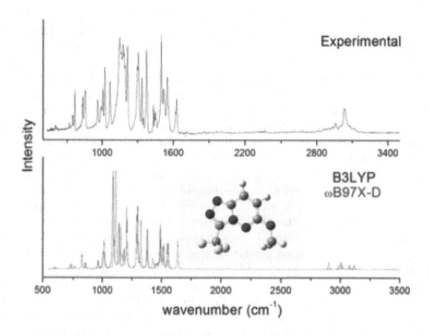

Fig. 3. Comparison of the experimental IR spectrum of the low-energy conformer with the spectrum calculated by using B3LYP and ω B97X-D functionals.

involved in intermolecular noncovalent interactions, possibly with the methoxy oxygen, basic nitrogen atoms, or the pi-electron system. Resolving the nature of this interaction requires the refinement of the crystalline structure, and will be the subject of our further study. To complement above quantum chemical calculations results, standard Molecular Dynamics simulations were also carried out for a single molecule.

2.3   Molecular Dynamics Simulation

Experimental study requires considerable amount of work in preparing the samples and then carrying out the relevant measurements. Quantum chemistry calculations presented above give the spectra of harmonic vibrational frequencies. Molecular Dynamics simulations, on the other hand, provide a relatively cheap and fairly quick rough estimation of the parameters difficult to track or inaccessible in the experimental methods as well as by the quantum chemistry calculations. Simulations were performed using the GROMACS [29] package with the OPLS–AA force field [30,31]. A single pyridazine molecule was placed in a cubic box of 3 nm in size, and standard periodic boundary conditions were applied. After the initial equilibration we performed 1×10^6 timesteps with the timestep $\Delta t = 10$ fs, that is 10 ns of simulation total time, which is long enough to capture the essential characteristic times for the methyl group. The canonical ensemble

(NVT) was applied at a constant temperature of 303 K at a v–rescaled thermostat with a time constant for coupling (= 0.1 ps). All bonds were constraine0d to the forcefield equilibrium lengths with the use of LINCS algorithm [32].

We followed the trajectory of the methyl group as shown in Fig. 4, presenting the time dependence of the dihedral angles for a few time scales, as indicated in the caption: (a) 10 ns, (b) 200 ps, and (c) 25 ps respectively. In Fig. 4(a) we can see energy minima for the dihedral angles separated by 1200°. The red line is the eye guide to show the equilibrium position at a given energy minimum. As shown, the dihedral angle is, at any given time, limited to one of the minima, and every so often there is a jump of proton from the methyl group to an adjacent minimum (or more than one minimum). The jumps between the minima are thermally driven and therefore hindered by dihedral energy barriers. Figure 4(b), which is an enlargement of a fragment of Fig. 4(a), in the region from 4200 ps to 4400 ps, reveals that the 4800° rotation, which appeared to be continuous in Fig. 4(a), actually consists of three jumps. Between these jumps the methyl group oscillates (vibrational motion around the equilibrium angle). Note that the first two jumps are separated by an angle of 1200°, while in the third case a jump by 2400° takes place. The jumps are shown in more detail in Fig. 4(c), corresponding to the time window of 25 ps, from $t = 4295$ ps to $t = 4320$ ps. This figure clearly displays the oscillations of the methyl group inside the individual energy minima. We calculated the correlation time for the methyl group (average lifetime in a given potential energy minimum) as 7e–11 s.

In Fig. 5 the time window is limited to 4 ps (between $t = 2208$ ps and $t = 2212$ ps) which allows observations of single oscillations. The oscillatory motion of the methyl group inside a given energy minimum has its characteristic time, which in this case was estimated to be 1.2e-13 s. The data presented are in agreement with the experimental results as well as the results of quantum mechanical calculations.

When it comes to the computational complexity of this type of calculations and simulations, one should look at it from two sides.

First, even though we are dealing with a single molecule with a small number of atoms, depending on what kind of movements we want to study, the simulation time as well as the frequency of trajectory snapshots should be appropriately selected. If we wanted to perform a single simulation covering all possible molecular motions with an accuracy appropriate to the fastest motions, the amount of recorded data would turn out to be unimaginably large, the vast majority of which would be completely unnecessary. Generally speaking, for a given chemical group and its movement, which has its characteristic time, the sampling interval as well as the time of the simulation itself should be appropriately selected so as to capture all the necessary data for subsequent numerical analysis. This optimizes the simulation time as well as the amount of recorded data, which, as already mentioned, even for such low-molecular compounds can be overwhelming.

In a case such as this, i.e. a single molecule in vacuo, parallelization is not needed. A single trajectory is usually tens of hours of CPU time. However,

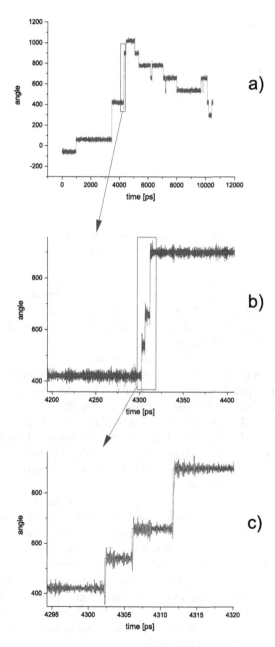

Fig. 4. Dihedral angle of the methyl group as a function of time for a few time windows: (a) 10 ns; (b) 200 ps; and (c) 25 ps. Red line is an eye guide to show the equilibrium position at a given energy minimum. (Color figure online)

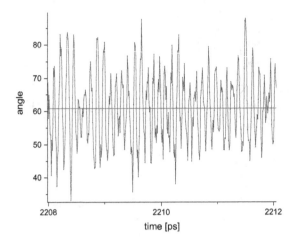

Fig. 5. Vibrational motion of the methyl group from the time dependence of a dihedral angle taken between 2208 ps and 2212 ps of the simulation.

given that simulations need to be run with slightly different parameters for each chemical group of interest and having the appropriate number of computational cores, it is possible to run quasi-parallel simulations, that is, all interesting sets should be calculated simultaneously.

It turns out, however, that very soon with increasing number of atoms/molecules, and therefore a rapid increase in the number of interactions in the system, true parallelism is a necessity. Thus, for example, in a study of a problem of adsorption and release of doxorubicin molecules at/from multi-walled carbon nanotubes [33,34] in a system containing more than 4×10^6 atoms, the parallel simulation (MPI) on the CPU only in a sweet-spot of the number of cores took about 10 weeks (60 ns of simulation), while the addition of the GPU (RTX 2060 Turbo) reduced this time five times to two weeks (here, too, a sweet-spot of the number of processor cores was used).

These examples show how large time spans can be dealt with, depending on the computational complexity of a given problem. In the case of very complex systems, the standard, if only the problem can be parallelized, is the use of paralleling libraries (e.g. MPI) and multi-core nodes. The use of GPU cards in this case often allows to reduce simulation time several times in relation to the pure CPU calculations. It should be emphasized that even in simulations of simple low-molecular compounds, where no algorithmic parallelization is possible, having access to multiple cores, it is possible to achieve a several-fold reduction in the total calculation time if we carry out quasi-parallel simulations probing different parameter sets simultaneously.

Using appropriately selected parallelization techniques, one can expect in most cases a significant shortening of the overall simulation time. Calculations and simulations were performed on a computing cluster located in the Functional

Materials Physics Division at the Faculty of Physics of the Adam Mickiewicz University on an Intel i9–10980XE processor.

3   Conclusions

The structure and molecular dynamics of a new potential drug ingredient was studied by FTIR spectroscopy, NMR technique, quantum chemistry calculations, and Molecular Dynamics simulations. Infrared spectroscopy provides information on the oscillations of individual functional groups within the structure of triazolopyridazine derivative. These measurements facilitate the confirmation of successful synthesis of the studied substance and investigate the conformation dynamics and vibrational characteristics. Quantum chemistry calculations spectra of harmonic vibrational frequencies are in very good agreement with FTIR experiment spectra.

The MD simulations performed and presented in this study gave a more detail insight into dynamical behavior of the methyl group of pyridazine derivative. The use of a number of experimental methods has provided wide information on the structure and molecular dynamics of the new pyridazine derivative.

Acknowledgement. We would like to thank Prof. Grzegorz Kamieniarz (Faculty of Physics, AMU, Poznań, POLAND) for all his valuable comments and guidance.

References

1. Glodek, M., et al.: Process robustness–a PQRI white paper. Pharm. Eng. **26**(6), 1–11 (2006)
2. Fu, J., et al.: An experimental study of the variability in the properties and quality of wet granules. Powder Technol. **140**(3), 209–216 (2004)
3. Goldszal, A., Bousquet, J.: Wet agglomeration of powders: From physics toward process optimization. Powder Technol. **117**(3), 221–231 (2001)
4. Moes, J.J., et al.: Application of process analytical technology in tablet process development using NIR spectroscopy: Blend uniformity, content uniformity and coating thickness measurements. Int. J. Pharm. **357**, 108–118 (2008)
5. Yassin, F.A.: Synthesis and antimicrobial activity of some new triazino-, triazolo-, and pyrazolopyridazine derivatives. Chem. Het. Cyclic Comp. **45**(8), 997–1003 (2009)
6. Tehrani K.H., Mashayekhi V., Azerang P., Minami S., Sardari S., Kobasarfard F.: Synthesis and antimycobacterial activity of some triazole derivatives - new route to functionalized triazolopyridazines. Iran J. Pharm. Res. **14**(Suppl.), 59–68 (2015)
7. Boukharsa, Y., Zaoui, Y., Taoufik, J., Ansar, M.: Pyridazin-3(2H)-ones: synthesis, reactivity, applications in pharmacology and agriculture. J. Chem. Pharm. Res. **6**(12), 297–310 (2014)
8. Bradbury, R.H., et al.: Discovery of AZD3514, a small-molecule androgen receptor downregulator for treatment of advanced prostate cancer. Bioorg. Med. Chem. Letters **23**(7), 1945–1948 (2013)

9. Ghidu V.P., Ilies M.A., Cullen T., Pollet R., Abou-Gharbia M.: A new and efficient synthetic route for the anxiolytic agent CL285032. Bioorg. Med. Chem. Lett. **21**(1), 259–261 (2011). Enos A., Eppler C. M.; Powell D.W.: Method for the treatment of noise phobia in companion animals, PCT Int. Appl. WO/2006/127574 (2006)

10. Boezio, A.A., et al.: Discovery and optimization of potent and selective triazolopyridazine series of c-Met inhibitors. Bioorg. Med. Chem. Letters **19**(22), 6307–6312 (2009)

11. Deeb A., El-Eraky W., El-Awdan S., Mahgoub S.: Pyridazine and its related compounds. Part 34. Hypoglycemic and hypolipidemic activity of some novel condensed pyridazine sulfonamides. Med Chem. Res. **23**, 34–41 (2014)

12. Brunnee, T., Engelstatter, R., Steinijans, V.W., Kundel, G.: Bronchodilatory effect of inhaled zardaverine, a phosphodiesterase III and IV inhibitor, in patients with asthma. Eur. Respir. J. **5**, 982–985 (1992)

13. Bansal, R., Thota, S.: Pyridazin-3(2H)-ones: the versatile pharmacophore of medicinal significance. Med. Chem. Res. **220**, 2539–2552 (2013)

14. Katrusiak, A., Melzer, E., Bałoniak, S., Bobkiewicz, T., Polcyn, P.: Triazolo- and tetrazolopyridazine derivatives and their hypotension and heart rate activity. Acta Pol. Pharm. Drug Res. **58**(3), 217–223 (2001)

15. Katrusiak, A., Ratajczak-Sitarz, M., Skierska, U., Zinczenko, W.: Nucleophilic substitution and lipophilicity - structure relations in methylazolopyridazines. Collect. Czech. Chem. Commun. **70**(9), 1372–1386 (2005)

16. Długaszewska J., Katrusiak A.: 9th Polish-German symposium on pharmaceutical sciences, Kraków 26–27.05.2017, Towards novel concepts in pharmaceutical sciences, p. 226. PQRI, Process robustness - a PQRI white paper. Pharm. Eng. **26**, 1–11 (2006)

17. Jurga, K., Fojud, Z., Woźniak-Braszak, A.: NMR strong off-resonance irradiation without sample overheating. Solid State NMR **25**, 119 (2004)

18. Baranowski M., Woźniak-Braszak A., Jurga K., High homogeneity B1 30.2 MHz nuclear magnetic resonance probe for off-resonance relaxation times measurements. J. Mag. Res. **208**, 163 (2011)

19. Czechowski, T., Baranowski, M., Jurga, K., Jurga, J., Kędzia, P.: The instrument set for generating fast adiabatic passage. Appl. Magn. Reson. **43**, 331–340 (2012). https://doi.org/10.1007/s00723-012-0372-3

20. Woźniak-Braszak, A.: Methodology for solid state NMR study of cross relaxation and molecular dynamics in heteronuclear systems. Solid State NMR **53**, 38 (2013)

21. Woźniak-Braszak A.: Study of cross-relaxation and molecular dynamics in the solid 3-(trifluoromethyl) benzoic acid by solid state NMR off-resonance. Solid State NMR **81**, 8–10 (2017). https://doi.org/10.1016/j.ssnmr.2016.12.002

22. Woźniak-Braszak, A., Jurga, K., Baranowski, M.: The Lipari-Szabo model-free analysis application in study of cross relaxation in heteronuclear systems by solid state NMR. Appl. Magn. Reson. **47**(6), 567 (2016)

23. Jurga, K., Woźniak-Braszak, A., Baranowski, M.: Methodology for solid state NMR off-resonance study of molecular dynamics in heteronuclear system. Solid State NMR **71**, 73–79 (2016)

24. Bloembergen N., Purcell E. M., Pound R. V., Relaxation effects in nuclear magnetic resonance absorption. Phys. Rev. **73**, 679–712 (1948) https://doi.org/10.1103/PhysRev.73.679

25. Dobrzyńska-Mizera M., Knitter M., Woźniak-Braszak A., Baranowski M., Sterzyński T., Di Lorenzo M.L.: Poly(l-Lactic Acid)/pine wood bio-based composites. Materials **13**, 3776 (2020). https://doi.org/10.3390/ma13173776

26. Hołderna-Natkaniec, K., Jurga, K., Natkaniec, I., Nowak, D., Szyczewski, A.: Molecular dynamics of Ethisterone studied by 1H NMR, IINS and quantum mechanical calculations. Chem. Phys. **317**, 178–187 (2005). https://doi.org/10. 1016/j.chemphys.2005.06.043
27. Woźniak-Braszak, A., Knitter, M., Markiewicz, E., Ingram, W.F., Spontak, R.J.: Effect of composition on the molecular dynamics of biodegradable isotactic polypropylene/thermoplastic starch blends. ACS Sustain. Chem. Eng. **7**, 16050–16059 (2019). https://doi.org/10.1021/acssuschemeng.9b02774
28. Eskandari, K., Lesani, M.: Does fluorine participate in halogen bonding? Chem. Euro. J. **21**(12), 4739–4746 (2015)
29. Berendsen, H.J.C., Van Der Spoel, D., Van Drunen, R.: GROMACS: a message-passing parallel molecular dynamics implementation. Comput. Phys. Commun. **91**, 43–56 (1995). https://doi.org/10.1002/chem.201405054
30. Jorgensen W.L., Maxwell D.S., Tirado-Rives J.: Development and testing of the OPLS all-atom force field on conformational energetics and properties of organic liquids. J. Am. Chem. Soc. **118**, 11225–11236 (1996). https://doi.org/10.1021/ja9621760
31. Jorgensen, W.L., Tirado-Rives J.: The OPLS [optimized potentials for liquid simulations] potential functions for proteins, energy minimizations for crystals of cyclic peptides and crambin. J. Am. Chem. Soc. **110**, 1657–1666 (1988). https://doi.org/10.1021/ja00214a001
32. Hess, B., Bekker, H., Berendsen, H., Fraaije, J.: LINCS: a linear constraint solver for molecular simulations. J. Comput. Chem. **18**, 1463–1472 (1997)
33. Chudoba, D., Łudzik, K., Jażdżewska, M., Wołoszczuk, S.: Kinetic and equilibrium studies of doxoribicin adsorption onto carbon nanotubes. Int. J. Mol. Sci. **21**, 8230 (2020)
34. Chudoba, D., Jażdżewska, M., Łudzik, K., Wołoszczuk, S., Juszyńska-Gałązka, E., Kościński, M.: Description of release process of doxorubicin from modified carbon nanotubes. Int. J. Mol. Sci. **22**, 12003 (2021)

Description of Magnetic Nanomolecules by the Extended Multi-orbital Hubbard Model: Perturbative vs Numerical Approach

Romuald Lemański[1]([✉]) [iD] and Michał Antkowiak[2] [iD]

[1] Institute of Low Temperature and Structure Research, Polish Academy of Science, ul. Okólna 2, 50422 Wrocław, Poland
r.lemanski@intibs.pl
[2] Faculty of Physics, Adam Mickiewicz University in Poznań, ul. Umultowska 85, 61614 Poznań, Poland
antekm@amu.edu.pl

Abstract. We present a microscopic description of magnetic molecules by the extended multi-orbital Hubbard model. In the limit of large Coulomb on-site interaction, we derived the spin Hamiltonian using the perturbation theory. The magnetic coupling constant between two ions we determined in two different ways: a) from the expression obtained in the perturbation calculus and b) from the analysis of distances between the lowest levels of the energy spectrum obtained by the diagonalization of the Hamiltonian of the extended multi-orbital Hubbard model. In order to speed up the very long and memory-intensive process of constructing the Hamiltonian matrix, whose size was 14400×14400, we implemented a procedure for locating the positions of non-zero elements. This significantly reduced the time of matrix creation and made it possible to perform calculations for more model parameters. The procedure we use can be applied to various nanomagnets, but the final calculations we performed for the molecular ring Cr_8. We showed that the inter-site repulsion between electrons located on neighboring ions increases the antiferromagnetic exchange coupling between magnetic moments of these ions, but this increase can be compensated for by the effect of correlated hopping of electrons.

Keywords: magnetic nanomolecules · extended multi-orbital Hubbard model · correlated hopping · Cr8 · sparse matrices · performance analysis · optimization

1   Introduction

Typical spectra of low-energy excitations of magnetic nanomolecules (MNMs) determined experimentally correspond (approximately) to the excitation spectra of the Heisenberg model [1]. For this reason, the efforts of many researchers have been directed towards determining the exchange coupling constants in a

© The Author(s), under exclusive license to Springer Nature Switzerland AG 2023
R. Wyrzykowski et al. (Eds.): PPAM 2022, LNCS 13827, pp. 382–391, 2023.
https://doi.org/10.1007/978-3-031-30445-3_32

system-appropriate version of the Heisenberg model. The calculations are usually performed with methods based on the density functional theory (DFT) [1–3]. However, in some cases these methods do not give satisfactory results [4–6]. In general, the problem with obtaining correct magnetic coupling values by these methods stems from the lack of consideration of electron dynamics and the resulting electron correlations [7].

In Ref. [8,9] it was proposed to describe MNMs using the multi-orbital Hubbard model (HM) combined with DFT calculations [8,9]. In this DFT + MB approach (MB stands for many-body), the microscopic parameters of the model are determined first, and only then the exchange constant is calculated using the second-order perturbation theory. In Ref. [8] the method was applied to study of the molecular ring Cr_8, and the magnetic coupling obtained there (after the correction, see Ref. [10]) was 1.65 meV. However, this value is slightly larger than the 1.46 meV deduced from the experiments. Later on, in Ref. [11] it was shown that the correlated hopping effect can noticeably reduce the coupling.

In fact, the effect of correlated hopping, i.e. the decrease in the amplitude of an electron jump to the orbital already occupied by an electron (with the opposite spin), as compare to the amplitude of the jump to the empty orbital, results from the mutual repulsion of the electrons. On the other hand, however, the repulsion of electrons on adjacent ions reduces the relative difference between the Coulomb energies of electrons on the same ion and on adjacent ions. And this in turn strengthens the antiferromagnetic coupling between the ions.

Here we investigate what is the effect of the repulsion between electrons, both by taking into account the correlated hopping and the direct Coulomb repulsion of electrons located on adjacent ions, on the magnetic coupling between Cr ions. Using the extended multi-orbital HM we first constructed the effective spin Hamiltonian from the perturbation theory and obtained the Heisenberg model with the exchange constant Γ. Then we diagonalized numerically the Hamiltonian (1) for the system of two Cr ions and based on the analysis of the obtained exact energy spectrum we deduced another value Γ^* for the exchange constant, which turned out to be slightly greater than Γ [11].

2   Extended Multi-orbital HM

The Hamiltonian H_{exHM} of the extended multi-orbital HM is composed of the single-ion part H_{SI} and two intersite terms H_{V}, H_{t}, representing Coulomb repulsion and electron jumps, respectively. Then

$$H_{\mathrm{exHM}} = H_{\mathrm{SI}} + H_{\mathrm{V}} + H_{\mathrm{t}} \tag{1}$$

where

$$H_{\mathrm{SI}} = U \sum_{i,m} n_{im\downarrow} n_{im\uparrow} + \tag{2}$$

$$\frac{1}{2} \sum_{i,m\neq m',\sigma} [U' n_{im\sigma} n_{im'\bar{\sigma}} + U'' n_{im\sigma} n_{im'\sigma}] +$$

$$\frac{1}{2} \sum_{i,m\neq m',\sigma} \left[J c_{im\sigma}^{\dagger} c_{im'\bar{\sigma}}^{\dagger} c_{im\bar{\sigma}} c_{im'\sigma} + J c_{im\sigma}^{\dagger} c_{im\bar{\sigma}}^{\dagger} c_{im'\bar{\sigma}} c_{im'\sigma} \right],$$

$$H_{\mathrm{V}} = V \sum_{i,j,m,n,\sigma,\sigma'} n_{im\sigma} n_{jn\sigma'} \qquad (3)$$

and

$$H_{\mathrm{t}} = \sum_{i,j,m,m',\sigma} t^{ij}_{mm'} [1 - a(n_{im} + n_{jm'} - 1 - \delta_{ij}\delta_{mm'})] c^{\dagger}_{im\sigma} c_{jm'\sigma}. \qquad (4)$$

In the above formulas i and j denote nearest-neighbor sites, m, m' label orbitals and $\sigma, \bar{\sigma}$ label spins of electrons ($\bar{\sigma} = -\sigma$), $c^{\dagger}_{im\sigma}$ ($c_{im\sigma}$) denotes the creation (annihilation) operator of an electron, $n_{im\sigma} = c^{\dagger}_{im\sigma} c_{im\sigma}$ is the occupation number and $n_{im} = n_{im\downarrow} + n_{im\uparrow}$. U, U' and U'' describe the Coulomb type on-site interactions between two electrons: U - on the same orbital and $U'(U'')$ - on different orbitals with opposite (parallel) spins, respectively. V is the Coulomb repulsion constant between two electrons on adjacent ions and J represents the on-site exchange coupling resulting from the first Hund's rule, but also the spin-flip term and the pair hopping term, which are presented in the third line of the formula for H_{SI}. The latter two interactions are essential for maintaining the correct structure of spin multiplets [9]. Here we adopt the following relations between parameters of the model: $U' = U - 2J$ and $U'' = U - 3J$. They result from the requirements of rotational symmetry [12]. The parameter $t^{ij}_{mm'}$ is the hopping amplitude ($i \neq j$) from orbital m' at site j to orbital m at site i or the energy $\varepsilon^i_m \equiv t^{ii}_{mm}$ of orbital m at site i ($i = j$ and $m = m'$).

The parameter a in (4) is a mesure of reduction of the electron hopping amplitude between two orbitals when the sum of their occupancies exceed 1. Here we assume that for all relevant pairs of orbitals it has the same value [11].

3   Performance Analysis

Calculations have been carried out using the Wolfram Mathematica software. After we have run some initial tests it appeared that the bottleneck of our program is the construction of the Hamiltonian (1) matrix. Our algorithm assumed that the matrix was the result of the outer product of vectors containing all possible states of the system. It appeared that because of the sparsity of the matrix the most of the time was spent adding and multiplying zeros. As running this part of the program took unreasonable amount of time we have found the necessity to optimize it. Knowing states combinations that give non-zero matrix elements we have written an algorithm to create the map of non-zero elements, which is simply a list of matrix indexes.

Using the map we can calculate the non-zero elements of the sparse matrix in distinctively lower time. For the largest matrices considered the time of building the matrix has been decreased 260 times and the total calculation is 140 times faster (see Table 1). Although the creation of the map takes less time than calculating the corresponding outer product it is still significant. However we have excluded it from total time as the map needs to be calculated only once for each system considered and used to construct the matrices with different sets of parameters. It can be also stored in the file for future reuse.

Table 1. Computing performance for different total spin S resulting in matrices of different matrix size and density (md). The total computing times before optimization (bo) are compared to full times (ft) of optimized algorithm, which consist of matrix building (mb) and diagonalization (ev) times. All times have been obtained running the program on 4 cores except the non-zero elements map creation time (map) obtained using 1 core.

S	size	md [%]	bo [s]	ft [s]	mb [s]	ev [s]	map [s]
0	14400	0.2	18100	127	69	58	4200
1	9450	0.3	7800	56	38	18	1820
2	2520	0.8	560	7.8	6.7	1.1	135
3	210	6.3	3.7	0.3	0.3	~ 0	0.9

The optimization tilted the balance of calculation time towards the diagonalization of the matrix. Fortunately the Mathematica supports parallelization of calculations. We performed the scalability tests running the *Eigenvalues* function on different numbers of cores ranging from 1 to 4 and calculated the speedup defined as the ratio of the run time on 1 core and n cores (see Fig. 1a). We have obtained the super-linear speedup for larger matrices which is caused by accumulation of the cache size [13]. The diagonalization time drops significantly when 2 cores are used however adding further cores causes just a small decrease. Further tests on larger system have shown no speedup when using more than 4 cores.

We have also noted that Mathematica has been using more cores while the map of non-zero elements have been built. After running that part of the code on different number of cores it appeared that it actually slows down (see Fig. 1b) with consecutive cores included into test runs. We did not investigate this further as the speed of this non-repeatable part is of less importance. However, we can see the potential of improving its parallelization as the parts of the map could be easily created separately.

More important improvement could be obtained by parallelization of matrix building algorithm as the non-zero elements of matrices can be calculated independently. Another possible optimization could be based on the fact that we are dealing with symmetric matrices, therefore we could calculate half of both the matrix and the map.

To analyze the performance we have run our code on the 4-core system with Intel Core i5-8265U CPU 1.60 GHz and 16 GB of RAM.

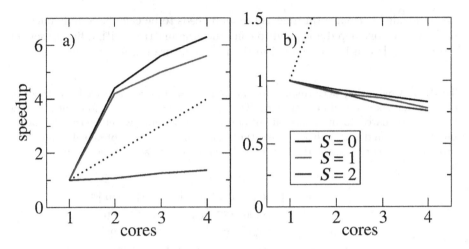

Fig. 1. Speedup of a) diagonalization and b) non-zero elements maps creation of matrices related to total spin S denoted in the legend. The ideal linear speedup is shown by dotted line.

4   Magnetic Interaction Between Two Ions

In further consideration, we will focus on the case of the Cr_8 molecular ring, in which Cr ions each have 3 electrons on the d shell. In the ground state, these 3 electrons occupy the half-filled quasi triplet, which has a significantly lower energy than the unoccupied quasi doublet formed the rest of the d shell. Due to the intra-ion exchange couplings, the diagonalization of the single-ion part H_{SI} of the Hamiltonian (1) results in formation of quartets and doublets. One of these quartets corresponding to the spin $S = 3/2$ is the ground state. Its energy E_0 is equal to

$$E_0 = \varepsilon_1 + \varepsilon_2 + \varepsilon_3 + 3U - 9J, \tag{5}$$

where $\varepsilon_m \equiv t^{ii}_{mm}$ (here we used the same notation for energies of the orbitals $m = 1, 2, 3$ as it is given in Ref. [8]).

From the perturbative calculus applied to (1) in the limit of small $t^{ii'}_{mn}$ one gets an effective Heisenberg Hamiltonian of interacting spins $S = 3/2$ with the antiferromagnetic super-exchange coupling $\Gamma^{ii'}_{SE}$. If following the discussion given in [8] we take into account also a direct ferromagnetic Coulomb exchange term $\Gamma^{ii'}_{CE}$, then the final form of the effective Hamiltonian H_{eff} is as follows.

$$H_{eff} = \frac{1}{2} \sum_{i, i'} \Gamma^{ii'} S_i \cdot S_{i'} \tag{6}$$

where $\Gamma^{ii'} = \Gamma^{ii'}_{CE} + \Gamma^{ii'}_{SE}$ and the sum is over all pairs (not ordered) of adjacent magnetic ions.

The super-exchange coupling $\Gamma_{SE}^{ii'}$ resulting from electrons kinetic can be expressed as the sum of the following two contributions

$$\Gamma_{SE}^{ii'} = \Gamma_0^{ii'} + \Delta\Gamma^{ii'}, \tag{7}$$

where the main part $\Gamma_0^{ii'}$ comes from jumps of electrons between single occupied states belonging to the quasi-triplets

$$\Gamma_0^{ii'} = \frac{2}{9}\sum_{n=1}^{3}\sum_{n'=1}^{3}\frac{|t_{nn'}^{ii'}|^2 + |t_{nn'}^{i'i}|^2}{U - V + 2J + \varepsilon_n - \varepsilon_{n'}}(1 - a)^2 \tag{8}$$

and $\Delta\Gamma^{ii'}$ results from electron jumps between single occupied states belonging to the quasi-triplet and unoccupied states belonging to the quasi-doublet

$$\Delta\Gamma^{ii'} = \frac{2}{9}\sum_{n'=1}^{3}\sum_{n=4}^{5}\frac{|t_{nn'}^{ii'}|^2 + |t_{nn'}^{i'i}|^2}{U - V + \varepsilon_n - \varepsilon_{n'}}$$
$$-\frac{2}{9}\sum_{n'=1}^{3}\sum_{n=4}^{5}\frac{|t_{nn'}^{ii'}|^2 + |t_{nn'}^{i'i}|^2}{U - V - 3J + \varepsilon_n - \varepsilon_{n'}}. \tag{9}$$

The factor $(1 - a)^2$ associated with the effect of correlated hopping occurs only in the formula for $\Gamma_0^{ii'}$ because only in this case an electron hops to the orbital which is already occupied by another electron with an opposite spin. On the other hand, $\Delta\Gamma^{ii'}$ does not depend on the parameter a, because then the electron hops to an unoccupied orbital. Since we assume that the interactions between adjacent Cr ions in Cr_8 are the same, from now we omit the upper indices i, i' in the coupling constants Γ, Γ_0 and $\Delta\Gamma$.

Let us now recall that for two spins $S = 3/2$ coupled antiferromagnetically within the Heisenberg model with the coupling constant Γ, the energy spectrum form four levels: $E = 0, \Gamma, 3\Gamma$ and 6Γ. Therefore, the measure of magnetic coupling between adjacent Cr ions is the energy difference between the lowest excited state and the ground state of the system. Using this fact, we estimated the magnetic coupling constant not only from the perturbation theory but also directly from the diagonalization of the Hamiltonian (1). Since in our case the hopping amplitudes are small with respect to U, then the lowest part of energy spectrum of the multi-orbital HM is similar to the spectrum of the Heisenberg model. Indeed, for $S_z = 0$, the four lowest energy levels then have approximately the distribution in the form of $E = 0$, Γ^*, $3\Gamma^*$, $6\Gamma^*$, but Γ^* is slightly larger than Γ. We conclude from this that the Γ^* corresponds to the magnetic exchange constant.

The diagonalization turned out to be a big challenge, because in our case the matrix has dimensions of 14400×14400. However, this task was successfully accomplished using the procedures described in the previous section, allowing us to perform calculations across a wide range of the model parameters.

If we do not take into account neither the intersite Coulomb repulsion ($V = 0$), nor the correlated hopping ($a = 0$) and put into the formulas (6–9) the

parameters taken from Ref. [8] (with the corrections given in [10]), then we get
$\Gamma \approx 1.7$ meV, whereas from the diagonalization $\Gamma^* \approx 1.71$ meV.

As already mentioned in Introduction, the parameters V and a, which are
always positive from the physical premises, affect the size of the exchange constants in the opposite way, i.e. Γ and Γ^* increase with the increase of V, but
they decrease as a increases. For Γ, the functional dependency on V and on a
is given in the formulas (8, 9). On the other hand, the dependence of Γ^* on V
and a is obtained numerically from the diagonalization of the Hamiltonian (1)
performed for the appropriately selected set of parameters V and a.

We do not have data on V and a for Cr$_8$, but it is usually agreed that V is
an order of magnitude smaller than U (here $U \approx 6$eV) and $0 < a < 0.4$ (see [11]
and the references given there), here we examined the most relevant physically
ranges: $0 < V < 0.6$eV and $0 < a < 0.1$.

The main part of our results obtained from the diagonalization of the Hamiltonian (1) (Γ^* - solid lines) and from the perturbation calculus (Γ - dotted lines)
are shown in Fig. 2 and 3. In Fig. 2 it is displayed how Γ and Γ^* change with
V for a few fixed values of a. It turns out that Γ and Γ^* grow approximately
linearly with the increase of V, but this increase is small, as it is only about 0.1
meV when V increases by 0.5 eV. On the other hand, the increase in a causes a
nearly linear decrease in Γ and Γ^*, but the decrease by 0.1 meV occurs already
at a very slight increase in a by approx. 0.023.

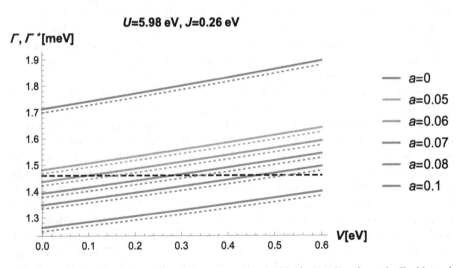

Fig. 2. Dependence of the exchange constants Γ^* (solid lines) and Γ (dotted
lines) on V for several selected values of the correlated hopping parameter $a =
0, 0.05, 0.06, 0.07, 0.08, 0.1$. The dashed line corresponds to $\Gamma = \Gamma^* = 1.46$ meV.

In Figs. 2 and 3 the dashed lines correspond to the value $\Gamma^* = 1.46$ meV,
which was obtained from the experiments. The points of intersection of this
line with solid lines correspond to such pairs of values (V, a) for which $\Gamma =$

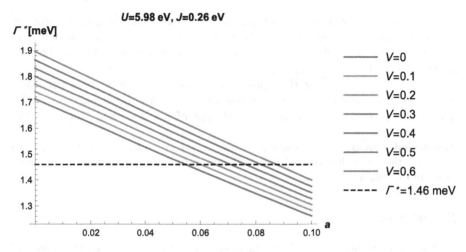

Fig. 3. Dependence of the exchange constant Γ^* on a for several selected values of $V = 0, 0.1, 0.2, 0.3, 0.4, 0.5, 0.6\,eV$. The dashed line corresponds to $\Gamma^* = 1.46$ meV.

1.46 meV. These pairs of numbers correspond to such values of V and a which mutually compensate for the increase (induced by V) and the decrease (induced by a) of the antiferromagnetic component in the exchange constant such that the resultant Γ^* value is as predicted by the experimental data. Explicit values of a meeting this condition for the set $V = 0, 0.1, 0.2, 0.3, 0.4, 0.5, 0.6$ eV (see Fig. 3) are given in Table 2.

Table 2. The correlated hopping parameter a required to keep the exchange constant Γ^* to be equal to 1.46 meV for $V = 0, 0.1, 0.2, 0.3, 0.4, 0.5, 0.6$ eV:

V [eV]	0	0.1	0.2	0.3	0.4	0.5	0.6
a	0.055	0.06	0.066	0.071	0.076	0.082	0.087

5 Summary and Conclusions

In this contribution, we examined the effect of Coulomb repulsion of electrons located on adjacent ions and of the correlated hopping of electrons on the exchange constant between magnetic moments of the ions in Cr_8. Although both of these phenomena result from the mutual repulsion of electrons, but it turned out that their influence on the value of the exchange constant is opposite. Indeed, direct Coulomb repulsion causes amplification, while the effect of correlated hopping weaken the antiferromagnetic coupling of the ions. So, if there are no other factors affecting the value of the exchange constant, then to obtain consistency with the experiment, when the electron repulsion of adjacent ions is occur, the parameter of correlated hopping should be slightly higher.

We have optimized our code replacing the time consuming outer product calculation with the creation of non-zero elements map. The computation time has dropped by two orders of magnitude, however we can still observe the possibilities of further improvements.

Anyway, after applying the optimization, we were able to perform many calculations not only by the perturbation calculus method, but also exactly by diagonalizing the Hamiltonian matrices, the size of which reached 14400×14400.

Acknowledgements. We extend our thanks to G. Kamieniarz for encouraging us to undertake the research presented here and for the fruitful discussions of some issues raised in this paper.

References

1. Furrer, A., Waldmann, O.: Magnetic cluster excitations. Rev. Mod. Phys. **85**, 367 (2013). https://doi.org/10.1103/RevModPhys.85.367
2. Kortus, J., Hellberg, C.S., Pederson, M.R.: Hamiltonian of the V_{15} spin system from first-principles density-functional calculations. Phys. Rev. Lett. **86**, 3400 (2001). https://doi.org/10.1103/PhysRevLett.86.3400
3. Milios, C.J., Winpenny, R.E.P.: Cluster-based single-molecule magnets. In: Gao, S. (ed.) Molecular Nanomagnets and Related Phenomena. SB, vol. 164, pp. 1–109. Springer, Heidelberg (2014). https://doi.org/10.1007/430_2014_149
4. Brzostowski, B., Lemański, R., Ślusarski, T., Tomecka, D., Kamieniarz, G.: Chromium-based rings within the DFT and Falicov–Kimball model approach. J. Nanopart. Res. **15**(4), 1–12 (2013). https://doi.org/10.1007/s11051-013-1528-2
5. Brzostowski, B., et al.: DFT and Falicov-Kimball model approach to Cr_9 molecular ring. Acta Phys. Pol. A **126**, 270 (2014). https://doi.org/10.12693/APhysPolA.126.270
6. Weissman, S., Antkowiak, M., Brzostowski, B., Kamieniarz, G., Kronik, L.: Accurate magnetic couplings in chromium-based molecular rings from broken-symmetry calculations within density functional theory. J. Chem. Theory Comput. **15**(9), 4885 (2019). https://doi.org/10.1021/acs.jctc.9b00459
7. Held, K., et al.: Realistic investigations of correlated electron systems with LDA + DMFT. Phys. Status Solidi B **243**, 2599 (2006). https://doi.org/10.1002/pssb.200642053
8. Chiesa, A., Carretta, S., Santini, P., Amoretti, G., Pavarini, E.: Many-body models for molecular nanomagnets. Phys. Rev. Lett. **110**, 157204 (2013). https://doi.org/10.1103/PhysRevLett.110.157204
9. Chiesa, A., Carretta, S., Santini, P., Amoretti, G., Pavarini, E.: Many-body ab initio study of antiferromagnetic Cr_7M molecular rings. Phys. Rev. B **94**, 224422 (2016). https://doi.org/10.1103/PhysRevB.94.224422
10. Chiesa, A., Carretta, S., Santini, P., Amoretti, G., Pavarini, E.: Erratum: many-body models for molecular nanomagnets. Phys. Rev. Lett. **110**, 157204 (2013). Phys. Rev. Lett. **126**, 069901(E) (2021). https://doi.org/10.1103/PhysRevLett.126.069901
11. Matysiak, J., Lemański, R.: Description of molecular nanomagnets by the multiorbital Hubbard model with correlated hopping. Phys. Rev. B **104**, 014431 (2021). https://doi.org/10.1103/PhysRevB.104.014431

12. Frésard, R., Kotliar, G.: Interplay of Mott transition and ferromagnetism in the orbitally degenerate Hubbard model. Phys. Rev. B **56**, 12909 (1997). https://doi.org/10.1103/PhysRevB.56.12909
13. Ristov, S., Prodan, R., Gusev, M., Skala, K.: Superlinear speedup in HPC systems: why and when? In: Proceedings of the Federated Conference on Computer Science and Information Systems, vol. 889 (2016). https://doi.org/10.15439/2016F498

Structural and Electronic Properties of Small-Diameter Carbon NanoTubes: A DFT Study

Bartosz Brzostowski[1]([✉]) [ID], Artur P. Durajski[2] [ID], Konrad M. Gruszka[2] [ID], and Jacek Wojtkiewicz[3] [ID]

[1] Faculty of Physics and Astronomy, University of Wrocław, pl. M. Borna 9, 50-204 Wrocław, Poland
bartosz.brzostowski@uwr.edu.pl
[2] Institute of Physics, Częstochowa University of Technology, Avenue Armii Krajowej 19, 42-200 Częstochowa, Poland
{artur.durajski,konrad.gruszka}@pcz.pl
[3] Faculty of Physics, Warsaw University, Pasteura 5, 02-093 Warszawa, Poland
wjacek@fuw.edu.pl

Abstract. One of the crucial properties of Carbon NanoTubes (CNTs) is their *conductivity*. They can be metallic, semiconducting or insulating in nature [6]. Therefore, their conducting properties are closely related to the existence and width of *CNTs energy band gap* – quantity which is (relatively) easily calculable. From a theoretical point of view, CNTs have been studied by various methods. Many results have been obtained; however, their status is quite diverse. The widespread rule claims that (n,m) CNT is metallic if $n - m = 0$ mod 3 [2,6]. This rule was based on 'gluing' of graphene sheets into tubes (or the 'zone folding' method). Moreover, the geometry of all hexagons has been assumed to be identical – the structure optimization hasn't been performed. Such an approach can be reliable for large-diameter CNTs, where curvature effects are small. However, it is at least disputable for its applicability to small-diameter CNTs. For these reasons, we undertook a systematic exploration of small-diameter CNTs to examine the significance of the 'deviation' effects (i.e. the deviation from planar regular hexagon geometry) on properties of CNTs. In particular, we wanted to check explicitly the validity of the claim that 'CNTs (n,m), where $n - m = 0$ mod 3, possess zero energy gap'.

In our paper, we present the results of calculations for $(2, m)$ and $(3, m)$ series of CNTs. These are optimized geometries, densities of states, energy gaps, and electronic band structures. The general conclusion is that the 'zone-folding' based rule predicting metallicity for those CNTs where $n - m = 0$ mod 3 is fulfilled, besides the find that hexagons forming CNTs are not planar and possess non-equal bond lengths. So this 'zone-folding' based law describes conductivity aspects of CNTs amazingly well.

Keywords: Carbon nanotubes · Band structure · Energy gap

© The Author(s), under exclusive license to Springer Nature Switzerland AG 2023
R. Wyrzykowski et al. (Eds.): PPAM 2022, LNCS 13827, pp. 392–402, 2023.
https://doi.org/10.1007/978-3-031-30445-3_33

1   Introduction

Carbon NanoTubes – one of the allotropic forms of carbon – beginning from its discovery, still are among the most intensively studied quasi-one-dimensional systems. It is due to its exceptional mechanical, electronic, and optical properties, which turns scientific interests in CNTs to this day. Due to the wide applicability of CNTs, many papers explore their diverse properties such as semiconduction/ metallicity features [7,13,20], mechanical, magnetic [6], and optical properties [17,18] to name a few.

One of the crucial properties of Carbon NanoTubes (CNTs) is their *conductivity*. Their character can be metallic, semiconducting, or insulating [6] in nature. Conducting properties are closely related to *energy gap* of CNTs – quantity (relatively) easily calculable. From a theoretical point of view, CNTs have been studied by various methods; the most popular are semiempirical and ab-initio ones. Many results have been obtained; however, their status is quite diverse. The broad 'folk knowledge' claims that (n, m) CNT is metallic if $n - m = 0$ mod 3 [2,6]. This rule was derived from simple calculations based on 'cutting and gluing' of the graphene sheets into tubes [8]. However, in such studies the geometry of all hexagons has been assumed to be identical – the structure optimization hasn't been performed. Such an approach can be reliable for large-diameter CNTs, where curvature effects are small. However, it is at least disputable for its applicability to small-diameter CNTs.

For these reasons, we undertook a systematic exploration of small-diameter CNTs to examine the significance of the curvature effects. In particular, we wanted to check explicitly the validity of the rule claiming that 'CNTs (n, m), where $n - m = 0$ mod 3, possess zero energy gap'. In our paper, we present the results of calculations for $(2, m)$ and $(3, m)$ series of CNTs. We have calculated: optimized geometries, densities of states, energy gaps, and band structures. In our study, we have also paid attention to the technical aspect of computations. One of them was a comparison between two popular packages: SIESTA and Quantum Espresso. The second one was the examination of parameters crucial for computations such as density of k–points in the grid, and the number of carbon atoms in an elementary cell.

2   Computational Methods

2.1   Quantum Software Packages

To the study electronic properties of investigated materials, we have performed first-principles calculations within the framework of the density-functional theory (DFT) [14] as implemented in the Quantum Espresso [4,5] and SIESTA [16] packages. We performed also calculations for finite CNTs using Gaussian09 package [3].

Quantum Espresso (opEn-Source Package for Research in Electronic Structure, Simulation, and Optimization) is an integrated suite of software for atomistic calculations based on electronic structure, using density functional theory, a plane-wave basis set, and pseudopotentials. Quantum Espresso is free software, released under the GNU General Public License. The compiling of Quantum Espresso packages (7.0 version) was realized by using the open-source gfortran (11.2.0 version) compiler from the GCC distribution with mpi-parallel execution provided by OpenMPI (4.1.2 version). Moreover, external libraries like BLAS and LAPACK for linear algebra and FFTW for fast Fourier transformation were used. In the case of Quantum Espresso, (GGA-PBE) approximation was used for the exchange-correlation functional together with the projector-augmented wave (PAW) method.

In the case of SIESTA, the exchange and correlation effects were accounted for by the generalized gradient approximation (GGA) with exchange-correlation potential proposed by Pedrew, Burke and Ernzerhof (PBE) [15]. SIESTA is density functional method using standard norm-conserving pseudopotentials and numerical linear combination of atomic orbitals basis set, which includes multiple-zeta and polarization orbitals. Also in the case of Gaussian09 the PBE [15] functional was used.

2.2   Computational Parameters

The optimized atomic structures were obtained by fully relaxing of both atomic positions as well as cell parameters until all forces were smaller than 10^{-6} eV/Å. All parameters critical for convergence, such as the k-points mesh and the energy cutoff were carefully tested to ensure the most accurate results. In the case of Quantum Espresso after proper convergence tests, we obtained well-converged values for the kinetic energy cutoff of the wavefunction equal to 80 Ry and the kinetic energy cutoff for charge density equal to 400 Ry. For the Siesta package, the parameters of the calculations were systematically tested also in terms of further calculations of phononic properties. Since unit cells were used for calculations, which for some nanotubes are small and contain few atoms, it was necessary to use larger values of parameters such as plane-wave cutoff (MeshCutoff) and Brillouin zone sampling (k-grid Monkhorst Pack). The unit cells were constructed so that in the z direction the axis of the nanotube was oriented, while in the x and y directions they had a size of 15 Å increased by the diameter of the nanotube. Tests have shown that the 1x1xM Monkhorst-Pack grid [11] is good enough and only the M value is significant for convergence. For the smallest unit cells, the value of this parameter was tested up to 3000. To investigate the electronic properties such as the main energy gap, a sufficiently good value of this parameter is M equal to 1200, but for the phonon properties, it may not be enough. For nanotubes with a clearly non-zero energy gap, a convergence is obtained for smaller values of the M parameter. On the other hand, nanotubes with a gap of zero or close to zero make convergence difficult. As part of the tests, MeshCutoff from 1000 to 2000 Ry was checked. For the study of electronic properties, the value of 1000 Ry is large enough, but even 2000 Ry may not be enough for phonon properties. In the case of Gaussian, all calculations have been performed with the use of 6-31G(d) basis.

2.3 Relaxation Methodology

The ideal atomic positions in cells with a fixed distance of 1.41 Å between C atoms have been generated by the TubeASP applet [12]. The optimized atomic structures were obtained using different methods for maximum atomic force smaller than 10^{-6} eV/Å. In the case of Quantum Espresso, the Broyden-Fletcher-Goldfarb-Shanno (BFGS) quasi-Newton algorithm was used, whereas for the Siesta package the optimization of the coordinates was obtained using the conjugate gradients method.

The change in the initial distance between the carbon atoms given in the nanotube generator did not affect the optimization of the structure. However, choosing a value other than 1.41 Å typically resulted in the need for more molecular dynamics steps to obtain an optimized structure.

In the use of Gaussian for finite CNTs, the option 'Optimization and Frequency' has been used, i.e. after optimization, eigenfrequencies have been calculated and their positivity has been checked.

3 Results

3.1 Calculation Procedure, Energy Gaps, Band Structure

We have calculated all the CNTs of kind $(2, m)$ and $(3, m)$, i.e.: $(2, 0)$, $(2, 1)$, $(2, 2)$; $(3, 0)$, $(3, 1)$, $(3, 2)$, $(3, 3)$. Each of CNTs, were structure-optimized and for each one, we have calculated their electronic properties in terms of the band structure and density of states.

CNTs are *periodic* systems. In Fig. 1 we present structures of elementary cells for all studied seven CNTs. As can be seen, elementary cells of armchair and zig-zag CNTs are much smaller than cells for chiral CNTs. For every optimized structure, we have calculated the band structure and density of states. Plots of these results are presented in Fig. 4 for CNTs $(2, m)$ and Fig. 5 for CNTs $(3, m)$. It is seen that the band structures are much more complicated for chiral CNTs than for armchair and zig-zag ones. It can be attributed to the sizes of elementary cells. For every CNT, structural optimization has been performed. As a rule, the geometry corresponding to the optimized and non-optimized ones are quite different. We illustrate this diversity in the Fig. 2.

It is also seen that all CNTs, for which the 'zone-folding' based rule predicts metallicity (i.e. $(2, 2)$, $(3, 0)$ and $(3, 3)$) are in fact conductive, i.e. possess a non-zero density of states at the Fermi energy. Apparently, the conductivity holds also for optimized structures, which are not regular hexagons. On the other hand, the CNTs $(2, 0)$ and $(3, 2)$ are gapped with gaps 0.65 eV and 0.29 eV, respectively – as 'zone-folding' based rule predicts. Interestingly enough, we have found *two* isomers of the CNT $(3, 1)$. They differ in structure and also energy gap: One isomer with lower energy possesses a gap 0.69 eV and the second one 0.36 eV. We have described these two structures elsewhere [1]. In any case, both structures are gapped, as the 'zone-folding' based rule predicts. And last, interestingly enough, the $(2, 1)$ CNT is gapless, although it should be gapped along the 'zone-folding' based rule.

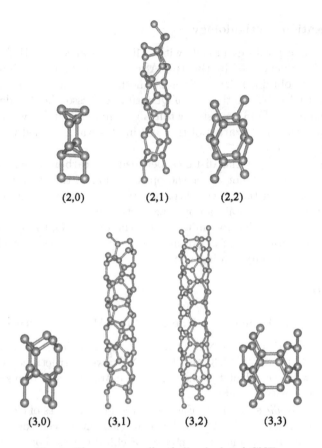

(2,0)   (2,1)   (2,2)

(3,0)   (3,1)   (3,2)   (3,3)

Fig. 1. Elementary cells of all calculated CNTs.

3.2   Comparison with Existing Results

Wherever possible, we also made comparison with literature data. We have found results for the (2, 2) CNT: [20], [9] and [10]. In all papers, authors have obtained small gaps (0.1 up to 0.2 eV, implying that (2, 2) CNT is an indirect semiconductor) - so, their results are similar to ours. The difference can be attributed to the fact that they used functionals other than ones used by us.

We have also carefully inspected results for the (3, 1) CNT in [9]. The authors found, that examined CNT possesses a gap of 0.4 eV, which is consistent with our result for one of the isomers of (3, 1) CNT.

Summarizing our calculations for infinite CNTs, our calculations show that (2,0), (3,1) and (3,2) CNTs are gapped, whereas (2,1), (2,2), (3,0) and (3,3) are gapless.

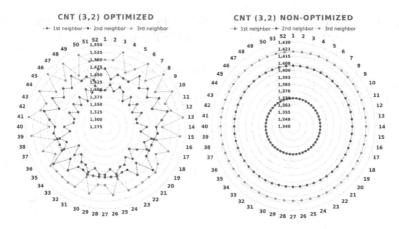

Fig. 2. Histograms of distances of atoms within elementary cell for CNT $(3,2)$ for non-optimized case (right panel) and optimized one (left panel).

3.3 Finite CNTs

For the sake of comparison, we have also calculated the *finite* CNTs, as real systems are finite ones. We treat these results as preliminary, as the sizes of CNTs calculated were limited by our computational facilities and we were able to calculate systems up to about 150 atoms.

We performed our calculations with the aid of the Gaussian 09 package [3]. The CNT was generated with the use of the same generator as infinite ones. We used the PBE functional as implemented in Gaussian 09. In such systems, we encounter a problem with how to 'end' it, in the order to avoid artifacts coming from unpaired bonds. We decided to take the simplest solution, i.e. to saturate the unpaired bonds by the hydrogen atoms. For an illustration, see Fig. 3 (Table 1).

Table 1. Results of DFT calculations for energy band gaps of finite (upper part) and infinite (lower part) CNTs. All energies are in eV. Energy gaps for infinite CNT $(3,1)$ correspond to two geometric isomers, see [1].

CNT	$(2,0)$	$(2,1)$	$(2,2)$	$(3,0)$	$(3,1)$	$(3,2)$	$(3,3)$
No. of elementary cells	12	4	12	8	3	2	13
Energy gap [eV]	0.73	0.23	0.08	0.11	0.27	0.49	0.20
Chemical formula	C_{96}	$C_{112}H_6$	$C_{128}H_8$	$C_{96}H_6$	$C_{156}H_8$	$C_{152}H_{10}$	$C_{156}H_{12}$
Gap for infinite system	0.65	0	0	0	0.69/0.36	0.29	0

We see that all finite CNTs have a non-zero energy gap. It is not unexpected, as they are finite systems. Yet, the values of the gap for finite CNTs $(2,1)$, $(2,2)$, $(3,0)$ and $(3,3)$ (corresponding to zero-gap infinite CNTs) are substantially smaller than $(2,0)$, $(3,1)$ and $(3,2)$ (corresponding to non-zero-gap infinite CNTs). Moreover, gaps of finite CNTs are greater than their infinite counterparts (with one exception of $(3,1)$ CNT). We should note here that it would be especially interesting to see how finite-size data tend to the limit of infinite objects. Preliminary study in this direction has been made in [19]. It is also worth noting, that this behavior is consistent and can be a guide if used properly, to find the finite gap CNT's using only small computational cells.

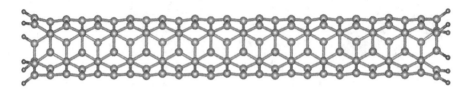

Fig. 3. Finite CNT $(3,3)$ with 13 elementary cells and hydrogen atoms (presented as blue spheres) at the ends.

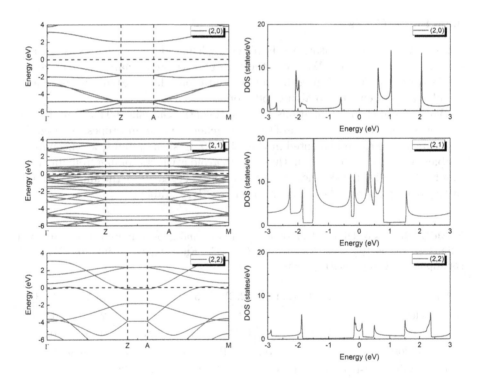

Fig. 4. Band structures (left panels) and densities of states for CNTs $(2,0)$, $(2,1)$ and $(2,2)$. Fermi energy is located at zero.

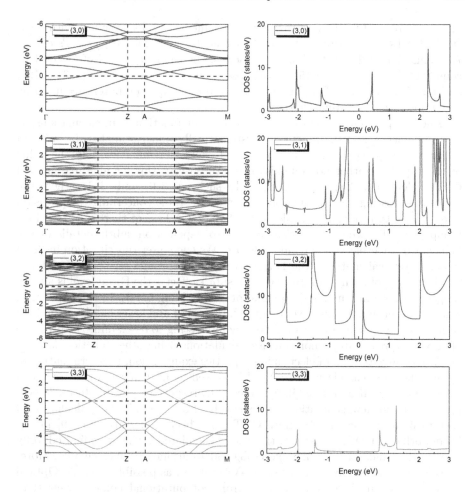

Fig. 5. Band structures (left panels) and densities of states for CNTs $(3,0)$, $(3,1)$, $(3,2)$ and $(3,3)$. Fermi energy is located at zero.

4   Summary, Conclusions, Outlook

The general conclusion is that the simple 'zone-folding' based rule predicting metallicity for those CNTs where $n - m = 0$ mod 3 is fulfilled, besides the opportunity that hexagons forming CNTs are not planar and possess non-equal bond lengths. It is a little bit surprising that this simple law describes conductivity aspects of CNTs amazingly well. Apparently, conductivity is not closely related to the regularity of hexagons, but rather to the proliferation of conjugate double bonds parallelly to the CNT axis.

Having developed the methodology and values of parameters of computation, we would like to continue our calculations for subsequent CNTs. However, such an extension of calculations is very demanding from the computational point of view. It is related to the fact that sizes of elementary cells grow fast with n for (n, m) CNTs. For instance, the largest elementary cell for $(3, m)$ CNTs counts 76 atoms (for $(3, 2)$ CNT). For $(4, m)$ series, the elementary cell of CNT $(4, 3)$ counts 148 atoms, and for $(5, m)$ the size of an elementary cell of $(5, 3)$ is 196, and for $(5, 4)$ it is 244. For this reason, the use of supercomputers seems to be inevitable in more systematic studies.

Another problem is the examination of other functionals in calculations. It is well known that PBE functional systematically underestimates the value of the energy gap. For large-gap CNTs, this effect can influence only the value of the gap, but rather not its existence. We observe this for all three gapped CNTs calculated. Another case is CNTs such as $(3, 0)$ and $(3, 3)$, where the bands are crossing and presumably this effect is stable concerning the precision of calculations, resulting in gaplessness of these CNTs. Yet there is also a third group of CNTs, where the existence of gap depends on subtle details of the behavior of their electronic band structure. We encounter this situation in $(2, 2)$ CNT. In our calculations, the Fermi level passes through an upper and lower band and we obtain no gap. But this is a subtle effect – the Fermi level is almost tangent to both minimal and maximal of nearby lying bands. In the paper [20], where another functionals have been used, the upper and lower bands are divided by a small gap. Therefore it would be very interesting to re-examine the presence of gaps by (presumably) more precise calculations using other functionals.

A natural extension of electronic properties examination, is determination of *optical* ones, i.e. calculation of UV-VIS, as well as near-infrared spectra. Such calculations are also of great importance with respect to possible technological applications in new generations of solar cells. Such a study, i.e. calculation of spectra of more than thirty finite CNTs, has been undertaken in [19] in the framework of TDDFT. However, the size of calculated CNTs were limited: only those with elementary cells not exceeding 150 atoms have been calculated. Moreover, is some cases only part of the UV-VIS range was possible to cover. Optical properties are much more demanding from computational point of view than densities of states – in particular, more memory is necessary. To achieve further progress in examination of optical properties of CNTs, it is mandatory to use more advanced computational resources, i.e. multiprocessor stations with parallel processing and large amount of memory. This aspect concerns two routes of calculations, i.e. periodic infinite systems and finite ones. We hope to be able to extend in planned future research the computations reported in [19].

In the case of calculations for infinite nanotubes, the basic problem is the necessity to use a dense set of k-points. This causes a significant increase in computation time and increases the amount of required RAM. For a software whose parallelization limits its use on one node, with a typical 7-day queue walltime it is possible to calculate basic electronic properties, however, the calculation of phonon or optical properties is troublesome or impossible. This problem can be avoided in a way by performing calculations for finite nanotubes. In this case, however, detailed studies of the scalability of the obtained results in terms of the number of unit cells included should be carried out. While for armchair or zig-zag nanotubes it is easy to do, because unit cells consist of a relatively small number of atoms, for chiral nanotubes with a large number of atoms in the unit cell it is difficult, because the calculation time increases significantly with an increase in the number of atoms in the studied structure.

Acknowledgements. BB acknowledges the access to the PSNC supercomputing resources.

APD is grateful to the Czestochowa University of Technology - MSK CzestMAN for granting access to the computing infrastructure built-in project no. POIG.02.03.00-00-028/08 "PLATON - Science Services Platform" and POIG.02.03.00-00-110/13 "Deploying high-availability, critical services in Metropolitan Area Networks (MAN-HA)".

References

1. Brzostowski, B., Durajski, A., Gruszka, K., Wojtkiewicz, J.: Geometric isomers of the (3,1) carbon nanotube: a theoretical study. Acta Phys. Pol. A **142** (2022). https://doi.org/10.12693/APhysPolA.142.21
2. Fox, M.: Optical Properties of Solids. Oxford University Press, Oxford (2010)
3. Frisch, M.J., et al.: Gaussian 09 Revision D.01, Gaussian Inc., Wallingford CT (2013)
4. Giannozzi, P., Andreussi, O., Brumme, T., et al.: Advanced capabilities for materials modelling with Quantum ESPRESSO. J. Phys. Condens. Matter **29**, 465901 (2017). https://doi.org/10.1088/1361-648x/aa8f79
5. Giannozzi, P., Baroni, S., Bonini, N., et al.: Quantum espresso: a modular and open-source software project for quantum simulations of materials. J. Phys. Condens. Matter **21**, 395502 (2009). https://doi.org/10.1088/0953-8984/21/39/395502
6. Jorio, A., Dresselhaus, G., Dresselhaus, M.S. (eds.): TAP, vol. 111. Springer, Heidelberg (2008). https://doi.org/10.1007/978-3-540-72865-8
7. Kamal, C., Chakrabarti, A.: Comparison of electronic and geometric structures of nanotubes with subnanometer diameters: a density functional theory study. Phys. Rev. B **76**, 075113 (2007). https://doi.org/10.1103/PhysRevB.76.075113
8. Kataura, H., et al.: Optical properties of single-wall carbon nanotubes. Synth. Metals **103**(1), 2555–2558 (1999). https://doi.org/10.1016/S0379-6779(98)00278-1
9. Mao, Y.L., Yan, X.H., Xiao, Y., Xiang, J., Yang, Y.R., Yu, H.L.: The viability of 0.3 nm diameter carbon nanotubes. Nanotechnology **15**(8), 1000–1003 (2004). https://doi.org/10.1088/0957-4484/15/8/024
10. Mao, Y.L., Yan, X.H., Xiao, Y., Xiang, J., Yang, Y.R., Yu, H.L.: First-principles study of the (2,2) carbon nanotube. Phys. Rev. B **71**, 033404 (2005). https://doi.org/10.1103/PhysRevB.71.033404
11. Monkhorst, H.J., Pack, J.D.: Special points for brillouin-zone integrations. Phys. Rev. B **13**, 5188–5192 (1976). https://doi.org/10.1103/PhysRevB.13.5188
12. https://nanotube.msu.edu/tubeASP/
13. Niranjan, M.K.: Theoretical investigation of electronic bandgaps of semiconducting single-walled carbon nanotubes using semi-empirical self-consistent tight binding and ab-inito density functional methods. J. Phys. Commun. 4(1), 015004 (2020). https://doi.org/10.1088/2399-6528/ab62c0
14. Parr, R., Yang, W.: Density-functional theory of atoms and molecules. Oxford University Press, Oxford (1995). https://doi.org/10.1093/oso/9780195092769.001.0001

15. Perdew, J.P., Burke, K., Ernzerhof, M.: Generalized gradient approximation made simple. Phys. Rev. Lett. **77**, 3865–3868 (1996). https://doi.org/10.1103/PhysRevLett.77.3865

16. Soler, J.M., et al.: The SIESTA method for ab initio order-N materials simulation. J. Phys.Conden. Matter **14**, 2745–2779 (2002). https://doi.org/10.1088/0953-8984/14/11/302

17. Spataru, C.D., Ismail-Beigi, S., Benedict, L.X., Louie, S.G.: Quasiparticle energies, excitonic effects and optical absorption spectra of small-diameter single-walled carbon nanotubes. Appl. Phys. A **78**(8), 1129–1136 (2004). https://doi.org/10.1007/s00339-003-2464-2

18. Wojtkiewicz, J., Brzostowski, B., Pilch, M.: Electronic and optical properties of carbon nanotubes directed to their applications in solar cells. In: Wyrzykowski, R., Deelman, E., Dongarra, J., Karczewski, K. (eds.) Parallel Processing and Applied Mathematics, pp. 341–349 (2020). https://doi.org/10.1007/978-3-030-43222-5_30

19. Wojtkiewicz, J., Pilch, M.: Theoretical study of carbon nanotubes as candidates for active layer in solar cells. Comput. Theoret. Chem. **1216**, 113846 (2022). https://doi.org/10.1016/j.comptc.2022.113846

20. Yuan, J., Huang, Y.: Structural, electronic and optical properties of smallest (2, 2) carbon nanotube: a plane-wave pseudopotential total energy calculation. J. Mol. Struct. THEOCHEM **942**(1–3), 88–92 (2010). https://doi.org/10.1016/j.theochem.2009.11.041

8th Minisymposium on High Performance Computing Interval Methods

Need for Techniques Intermediate Between Interval and Probabilistic Ones

Olga Kosheleva◉ and Vladik Kreinovich(✉)◉

University of Texas at El Paso, El Paso, TX 79968, USA
{olgak,vladik}@utep.edu

Abstract. In high performance computing, when we process a large amount of data, we do not have much information about the dependence between measurement errors corresponding to different inputs. To gauge the uncertainty of the result of data processing, the two usual approaches are: the interval approach, when we consider the worst-case scenario, and the probabilistic approach, when we assume that all these errors are independent. The problem is that usually, the interval approach leads to too pessimistic, too large uncertainty estimates, while the probabilistic approach – that assumes independence of measurement errors – sometimes underestimates the resulting uncertainty. To get realistic estimates, it is therefore desirable to have techniques intermediate between interval and probabilistic ones. In this paper, we propose such techniques based on the assumption that, in each practical situation, there is an upper bound $b \in [0, 1]$ on the absolute value of all correlations between measurement errors – the bound that needs to be experimentally determined. The assumption that measurement errors are independent corresponds to $b = 0$; for $b = 1$, we get interval estimates, and for intermediate values b, we get the desired intermediate techniques. We also provide efficient algorithms for implementing the new techniques.

Keywords: Interval uncertainty · Probabilistic uncertainty · High performance computing

1 Formulation of the Problem

Need to Take Uncertainty into Account in High-performance Computing. One of the main applications of high performance computing is estimating the values of some quantities y based on the inputs $x_1, \ldots, x_n$. For example,

---

This work was supported in part by the National Science Foundation grants 1623190 (A Model of Change for Preparing a New Generation for Professional Practice in Computer Science), and HRD-1834620 and HRD-2034030 (CAHSI Includes), and by the AT&T Fellowship in Information Technology. It was also supported by the program of the development of the Scientific-Educational Mathematical Center of Volga Federal District No. 075-02-2020-1478, and by a grant from the Hungarian National Research, Development and Innovation Office (NRDI).

R. Wyrzykowski et al. (Eds.): PPAM 2022, LNCS 13827, pp. 405–414, 2023.
https://doi.org/10.1007/978-3-031-30445-3_34

in weather prediction, we estimate tomorrow's temperature y at some location based on the results x_i of meteorological measurements in the vicinity of this location.

The problem is that even when the data processing algorithm

$$y = f(x_1, \ldots, x_n)$$

describes the exact relation between y and x_i, the value $\widetilde{y} = f(\widetilde{x}_1, \ldots, \widetilde{x}_n)$ – that we obtain by processing measurement results $\widetilde{x}_i$ – is not exact: since the measurement results $\widetilde{x}_i$ are, in general, different from the actual (unknown) values x_i of the corresponding quantities. Because of the measurement errors $\Delta x_i \stackrel{\text{def}}{=} \widetilde{x}_i - x_i$, the result $\widetilde{y}$ of data processing is, in general, different from the desired value y. It is important to provide an estimate for the resulting uncertainty $\Delta y \stackrel{\text{def}}{=} \widetilde{y} - y$; see, e.g., [7].

What Do We Usually Know and What We Usually Do not Know About the Measurement Errors Δx_i. For each measuring instrument, we know the upper bound Δ_i on the absolute value of the measurement error, i.e., a value for which $|\Delta x_i| \leq \Delta_i$. Indeed, if no such bound is guaranteed, this would mean that for any measurement result, the actual value can be anything – this would be a wild guess, not a measuring instrument.

In many practical applications, each measuring instrument is calibrated: before using this instrument, we several times compare its results with the results of a much more accurate instrument; thus, if the mean value of the measurement error was not 0, we can find this mean value (known as *bias*) and correct for it by subtracting this mean value from all the measurement results. Thus, we can safely assume that for each instrument, the mean value of the measurement error is 0.

In most applications, we can also safely assume that the measurement errors are relatively small. So we can safely ignore terms which are quadratic or higher order in terms of these errors. For example, even if the relative measurement error is 10%, its square is 1%, which can be safely ignored in comparison with 10%.

This is often all we know. Ideally, we should also know the probability distributions of all the measurement errors and all the correlations between them. In simple computations, when the number n of inputs is small, it is possible to extract this information for all n instruments and all $n^2/2$ pairs of instruments. So, for simple computations, this information is sometimes available. However, for high-performance computing, when n is large, it is not feasible to extract all this information, so this information is usually not available.

Possibility of Linearization. By definition of the measurement errors, we have $x_i = \widetilde{x}_i - \Delta x_i$, thus

$$\Delta y = f(\widetilde{x}_1, \ldots, \widetilde{x}_n) - f(\widetilde{x}_1 - \Delta x_1, \ldots, \widetilde{x}_n - \Delta x_n).$$

Since the measurement errors Δx_i are small, we can expand the expression $f(\widetilde{x}_1 - \Delta x_1, \ldots, \widetilde{x}_n - \Delta x_n)$ in Taylor series in terms of Δx_i and keep only linear terms in this expansion. As a result, we get

$$\Delta y = \sum_{i=1}^{n} c_i \cdot \Delta x_i, \tag{1}$$

where

$$c_i \stackrel{\text{def}}{=} \frac{\partial f}{\partial x_i}_{|x_1 = \tilde{x}_1, \ldots, x_n = \tilde{x}_n}. \tag{2}$$

How Δy is Estimated Now: Interval Technique. Since we have no information about the correlation between the measurement errors, a natural idea is to consider all possible correlations. In general, since $|a + b| \leq |a| + |b|$ and $|a \cdot b| = |a| \cdot |b|$, from the formula (1), we get

$$|\Delta y| \leq \sum_{i=1}^{n} |c_i| \cdot |\Delta x_i|.$$

Since $|\Delta x_i| \leq \Delta_i$, we get

$$|\Delta y| \leq \Delta_{\text{int}} \stackrel{\text{def}}{=} \sum_{i=1}^{n} |c_i| \cdot \Delta_i. \tag{3}$$

This value Δ_{int} is the exact upper bound, in the sense that it is possible to have $|\Delta y| = \Delta_{\text{int}}$ with probability 1. Indeed, this happens when:

- with probability $1/2$, we have $\Delta x_i = \Delta_i \cdot \text{sign}(c_i)$, where, as usual, $\text{sign}(x) = +1$ for $x > 0$ and $\text{sign}(x) = -1$ for $x < 0$; and
- with probability $1/2$, we have $\Delta x_i = -\Delta_i \cdot \text{sign}(c_i)$.

In this case:

- with probability $1/2$, we have $\Delta y = \Delta_{\text{int}}$, and
- with probability $1/2$, we have $\Delta y = -\Delta_{\text{int}}$.

This worst-case estimate (3) is known as the *interval estimate*, since this is the only estimate that we can guarantee based on the available information – that all measurement errors Δx_i are located within the corresponding interval $[-\Delta_i, \Delta_i]$; see, e.g., [2,4,5].

Interval Technique: Efficient Algorithms. How can we compute the value Δ_{int}? A natural idea is to explicitly use the expression (3). When the function $f(x_1, \ldots, x_n)$ is given by an *explicit expression*, we can simply differentiate it with respect to all the variables x_i and then compute c_i by using the Formula (1).

Often, the algorithm $f(x_1, \ldots, x_n)$ is only given as a proprietary *black box*: we do not know the exact algorithm, so we cannot differentiate this function. In this case, to find the values c_i, we can use numerical differentiation techniques.

For example, we can take into account that, in general, the derivative is the limit of the ratios

$$c_i = \lim_{h_i \to 0} \frac{f(\tilde{x}_1, \ldots, \tilde{x}_{i-1}, \tilde{x}_i + h_i, \tilde{x}_{i+1}, \ldots, \tilde{x}_n) - \tilde{y}}{h_i}.$$

Thus, we can estimate c_i as the value of this ratio for some small h_i.

The limitation of this natural idea is that for large n, it requires applying the algorithm $f(x_1, \ldots, x_n)$ $n + 1$ time: 1 times to compute $\tilde{y} = f(\tilde{x}_1, \ldots, \tilde{x}_n)$ and n times to compute n values $c_1, \ldots, c_n$. In practice, the algorithm $f(x_1, \ldots, x_n)$ is often time-consuming – it may require several hours on a high-performance computer, and the number of inputs n may be in the thousands. In this case, the overall time needed to apply this natural idea is unrealistically large.

In such situations, we can use a faster algorithm based on using Cauchy distribution, with probability density proportional to $1/(1 + (x/\Delta)^2)$; see, e.g., [1]. This algorithm is based on the fact that if we have n independent random variables δ_i each of which is Cauchy-distributed with parameter Δ_i, then their linear combination $\sum c_i \cdot \delta_i$ is also Cauchy-distributed, with parameter $\Delta = \sum |c_i| \cdot \Delta_i$ – which is exactly the desired expression (3). Thus, to estimate Δ_{int}, we, several times $k = 1, \ldots, K$, simulate the Cauchy-distributed values $\delta_i^{(k)}$ and compute

$$\delta^{(k)} = f(\tilde{x}_1 + \delta_1^{(k)}, \ldots, \tilde{x}_n + \delta_n^{(k)}) - \tilde{y}$$

for which, according to the formula (1), we have

$$\delta^{(k)} = \sum_{i=1}^{n} c_i \cdot \delta_i^{(k)},$$

and then use the resulting Cauchy-distributed sample $\delta^{(1)}, \ldots, \delta^{(K)}$ to estimate the desired parameter $\Delta = \Delta_{\text{int}}$.

The advantage of this Cauchy-based method is that, as with all Monte-Carlo simulation methods, the number of simulations – and thus, the number of times we apply the time-consuming algorithm $f(x_1, \ldots, x_n)$ – depends only on the desired accuracy and does not depend on the number of inputs n. In general, the accuracy of a statistical estimate based on a sample of size K is approximately equal to $1/\sqrt{K}$ (see, e.g., [8]). So, to estimate Δ_{int} with accuracy 20%, it is sufficient to apply the algorithm $f(x_1, \ldots, x_n)$ $K \approx 25$ times – which is much smaller than the thousands times needed for a direct estimation.

Comment. Since the largest value of the expression (1) is attained at the end-points of the corresponding intervals, a seemingly natural idea may be to apply the Monte-Carlo idea directly: namely, to select, for each i, one of the endpoints $\Delta x_i = \Delta_i$ or $\Delta x_i = -\Delta_i$ with equal probability 1/2, repeat this several (K) times and take the largest of the resulting values $\Delta y^{(1)}, \ldots, \Delta y^{(K)}$. Unfortunately, this simple idea leads to a drastic underestimation, even in the simplest case when $f(x_1, \ldots, x_n) = x_1 + \ldots + x_n$ and when all the values x_i are measured with the same accuracy $\Delta_i = \Delta_1$.

Indeed, in this case, formula (3) leads to $\Delta_{\mathrm{int}} = n \cdot \Delta_1$ – and, as we have mentioned, it is possible that this value is actually attained. On the other hand, when we use the above seemingly natural idea, then for large n, according to the Central Limit Theorem (see, e.g., [8]), the distribution of the sum is close to Gaussian, with mean 0 (equal to the sum of the means) and variance $V = \sigma^2$ equal to the sum of the variances $V = n \cdot \Delta_1^2$. Thus, e.g., with confidence 99.9%, we can conclude that the resulting values $\Delta y^{(k)}$ are within the 3-sigma interval, i.e., smaller that $3\sigma = 3\sqrt{n} \cdot \Delta_1$. For large n, we have $3\sqrt{n} \ll n$. So indeed, this seemingly natural idea can lead to a drastic underestimation.

Interval Technique: Limitation. The main problem with this approach is that the resulting worst-case estimates are too pessimistic. In most practical situations, the actual value Δy is much smaller than Δ_{int}.

How Can We Explain this Limitation. The above limitation can be easily explained. Indeed:

- In the arrangement that leads to $\Delta y = \Delta_{\mathrm{int}}$, all measurement errors are highly correlated, with correlation coefficients ± 1.
- In practice, it is possible that common factors affect several measurement instruments, but there are also usually other factors which affect only one measuring instrument, so the correlation is usually larger than -1 and smaller than 1.

How Δy is Estimated Now: Probabilistic Technique. Another idea is that since we have no reason to prefer negative or positive correlation, it is reasonable to assume that the correlation is 0, and, more generally, that different measurement errors are independent.

This is also what follows from the Maximum Entropy approach [3], when out of all possible joint distributions $\rho(\Delta x_1, \ldots, \Delta x_n)$ for which mean of each variable is 0 and which are located on the given intervals $[-\Delta_i, \Delta_i]$, we select the distribution with the largest value of entropy

$$S \stackrel{\mathrm{def}}{=} -\int \rho(\Delta x_1, \ldots, \Delta x_n) \cdot \ln(\rho(\Delta x_1, \ldots, \Delta x_n)) \, d\Delta x_1 \ldots d\Delta x_n.$$

Independence implies that for each $i \neq j$, the expected value $E[\Delta x_i \cdot \Delta x_j]$ of the product $\Delta x_i \cdot \Delta x_j$ is equal to the product of expected values

$$E[\Delta x_i \cdot \Delta x_j] = E[\Delta x_i] \cdot E[\Delta x_j],$$

i.e., since the mean value of each measurement error is 0, to

$$E[\Delta x_i \cdot \Delta x_j] = 0.$$

In this case, the expected value of $(\Delta y)^2$ is equal to

$$E[(\Delta y)^2] = \sum_{i=1}^{n} c_i^2 \cdot V_i,$$

where by

$$V_i \overset{\text{def}}{=} E[(\Delta x_i - E[\Delta x_i])^2] = E[(\Delta x_i)^2],$$

we denoted the variance of the i-th measurement error.

As is well known in statistics, for large n, the deviation from this expected value is small – since deviation grows with n as $\sqrt{n}$, while the expected value itself grows as n [8], so we conclude that the actual value $(\Delta y)^2$ is, with high accuracy, equal to this expected value:

$$(\Delta y)^2 \approx \sum_{i=1}^{n} c_i^2 \cdot V_i.$$

We do not know the variances V_i, but, since $|\Delta x_i| \le \Delta_i$, we have $(\Delta x_i)^2 \le \Delta_i^2$. Thus, the expected value V_i of the square $(\Delta x_i)^2$ is also bounded by the same bound Δ_i^2:

$$V_i \le \Delta_i^2.$$

This upper bound on the variance V_i is the best we can have – it is attained if:

– we have $\Delta x_i = \Delta_i$ with probability $1/2$, and
– we have $\Delta x_i = -\Delta_i$ with probability $1/2$.

Thus, we conclude that

$$(\Delta y)^2 \le \sum_{i=1}^{n} c_i^2 \cdot \Delta_i^2,$$

i.e., that

$$|\Delta y| \le \Delta_{\text{prob}} \overset{\text{def}}{=} \sqrt{\sum_{i=1}^{n} c_i^2 \cdot \Delta_i^2}. \tag{4}$$

Probabilistic Technique: Eficient Algorithms. How can we estimate the value Δ_{prob}? A natural idea is to explicitly use the expression (1): when describing interval techniques, we have already mentioned how we can estimate the values c_i.

The limitation of this natural idea is the same as for the similar interval idea: that for large n, it requires applying the algorithm $f(x_1, \ldots, x_n)$ too many times and thus, the overall time needed to apply this natural idea is sometimes unrealistically large.

To speed up computations, we can use the fact that if we have n independent random variables δ_i each of which is normally distributed with mean 0 and standard deviation Δ_i, then their linear combination $\sum c_i \cdot \delta_i$ is also normally distributed, with the standard deviation equal to the desired expression (1). Thus, to estimate Δ_{prob}, we, several times $k = 1, \ldots, K$, simulate the normally distributed values $\delta_i^{(k)}$ and compute the value

$$\delta^{(k)} = f(\tilde{x}_1 + \delta_1^{(k)}, \ldots, \tilde{x}_n + \delta_n^{(k)}) - \tilde{y}$$

for which, according to the formula (1), we have

$$\delta^{(k)} = \sum_{i=1}^{n} c_i \cdot \delta_i^{(k)},$$

and then use the resulting normally distributed sample $\delta^{(1)}, \ldots, \delta^{(K)}$ to estimate the desired standard deviation Δ_{prob}.

This method has the same advantage as the Cauchy method: that when we use this method, the number of times we apply the time-consuming algorithm $f(x_1, \ldots, x_n)$ depends only on the desired accuracy and does not depend on the number of inputs n.

Probabilistic Technique: Limitation. The main problem with this probabilistic technique is that it is too optimistic, it often drastically decreases the approximation error Δy.

We had an example of such a drastic underestimation when we explained why a seemingly natural Monte-Carlo algorithm does not lead to a reasonable estimate for interval uncertainty.

How Can We Explain this Limitation. The above limitation can be easily explained. Indeed:

– This technique assumes that all the measurement errors are independent.
– However, as we have mentioned, in reality, there may be common factors affecting several instruments, and thus, there is correlation.

Need for Intermediate Techniques. Since the interval techniques are too pessimistic and the probability techniques are too optimistic, it is desirable to have intermediate techniques that would provide more realistic estimates.

The main objective of this paper is to provide such estimates.

2   Main Idea and the Resulting Formula and Algorithm

Main Idea. As we have mentioned, the problem with the interval technique is that it assumes that the absolute value of the correlation can be 1, while in practice, it is always smaller than 1. Similarly, the problem with the probabilistic technique is that it assumes that all correlations are 0s, while in practice, they can take non-zero values.

So, a natural idea is to assume that there is some number b between 0 and 1 that provides an upper bound for absolute values $|r_{ij}|$ of all the correlations

$$r_{ij} \stackrel{\text{def}}{=} \frac{E[\Delta x_i \cdot \Delta x_j]}{\sigma_i \cdot \sigma_j},$$

where $\sigma_i \stackrel{\text{def}}{=} \sqrt{V_i}$:

$$|r_{ij}| \leq b.$$

This value can be determined empirically, by computing absolute value of the correlation for several randomly selected pairs of measuring instruments and selecting the largest of these values.

Comments

- It should be mentioned that while the experimental determination of the correlations is possible, it is not easy to do in the field. Hopefully, when several different sensors are produced by the same manufacturer, this manufacturer will be able to provide these correlation values.
- Our estimates are based on computing the largest absolute value of the observed correlations. Instead of estimating it as the largest of the observed values, we can instead make a usual reasonable assumption that correlations are normally distributed. Then, based on the observed correlation values, we can find the sample mean μ and the sample standard deviation σ and conclude, with some confidence, that the actual correlation values are within the interval $[\mu - k_0 \cdot \sigma, \mu + k_0 \cdot \sigma]$, where, as usual, $k_0 = 2$ corresponds to reliability 95%, $k_0 = 3$ to 99.9%, and $k_0 = 6$ to reliability $1 - 10^{-8}$.

Comment About Novelty. While the proposed idea sounds natural, to the best of our knowledge, this idea has not been previously followed – in spite of the fact that several methods for processing statistical data under interval uncertainty have been developed; see, e.g., [6].

From the Idea to the Resulting Formula. From the formula (1), we conclude that

$$(\Delta y)^2 = \sum_{i=1} c_i^2 \cdot (\Delta x_i)^2 + \sum_{i \neq j} c_i \cdot c_j \cdot \Delta x_i \cdot \Delta x_j,$$

hence

$$E[(\Delta y)^2] = \sum_{i=1}^{n} c_i^2 \cdot E[(\Delta x_i)^2] + \sum_{i \neq j} c_i \cdot c_j \cdot E[\Delta x_i \cdot \Delta x_j],$$

i.e.,

$$E[(\Delta y)^2] = \sum_{i=1}^{n} c_i^2 \cdot V_i + \sum_{i \neq j} c_i \cdot c_j \cdot r_{ij} \cdot \sigma_i \cdot \sigma_j.$$

We know that $(\Delta y)^2 \approx E[(\Delta y)^2]$, we know that $|r_{ij}| \leq b$, so we conclude that

$$(\Delta y)^2 \leq \sum_{i=1}^{n} c_i^2 \cdot \sigma_i^2 + \sum_{i \neq j} |c_i| \cdot |c_j| \cdot b \cdot \sigma_i \cdot \sigma_j.$$

We have mentioned that $\sigma_i \leq \Delta_i$, thus

$$(\Delta y)^2 \leq \sum_{i=1}^{n} c_i^2 \cdot \Delta_i^2 + \sum_{i \neq j} |c_i| \cdot |c_j| \cdot b \cdot \Delta_i \cdot \Delta_j. \tag{5}$$

Here,

$$\Delta_{\text{int}}^2 = \left(\sum_{i=1}^{n} |c_i| \cdot \Delta_i \right)^2 = \sum_{i=1}^{n} c_i^2 \cdot \Delta_i^2 + \sum_{i \neq j} |c_i| \cdot |c_j| \cdot \Delta_i \cdot \Delta_j,$$

thus the formula (5) takes the form

$$(\Delta y)^2 \leq b \cdot \Delta_{\text{int}}^2 + (1 - b) \cdot \left(\sum_{i=1}^{n} c_i^2 \cdot \Delta_i^2 \right),$$

i.e., the form

$$(\Delta y)^2 \leq b \cdot \Delta_{\text{int}}^2 + (1 - b) \cdot \Delta_{\text{prob}}^2.$$

So, we arrive at the following final formula.

Resulting Formula

$$|\Delta y| \leq \Delta_b \stackrel{\text{def}}{=} \sqrt{b \cdot \Delta_{\text{int}}^2 + (1 - b) \cdot \Delta_{\text{prob}}^2}. \tag{6}$$

How to Compute this Estimate. As we have mentioned earlier, there exist efficient algorithms:

- for computing Δ_{prob} – based on Monte-Carlo simulation of normally distributed measurement errors – and
- for computing Δ_{int} – based on using Cauchy distribution [1].

In both algorithms, the number of simulations depend only on the desired accuracy and does not depends on the number n of inputs.

By using these algorithms, we can efficiently compute the new estimate (6).

Future Work. How realistic is this new estimate? How close is it to the actual error Δy? To answer these questions, it is necessary to test this method on real-life examples.

Acknowledgments. The authors are greatly thankful to the anonymous referees for valuable suggestions.

References

1. Kreinovich, V., Ferson, S.: A new Cauchy-based black-box technique for uncertainty in risk analysis. Reliab. Eng. Syst. Saf. **85**(1–3), 267–279 (2004)
2. Jaulin, L., Kiefer, M., Didrit, O., Walter, E.: Applied Interval Analysis, with Examples in Parameter and State Estimation, Robust Control, and Robotics. Springer, London (2001). https://doi.org/10.1007/978-1-4471-0249-6
3. Jaynes, E.T., Bretthorst, G.L.: Probability Theory: The Logic of Science. Cambridge University Press, Cambridge (2003)

4. Mayer, G.: Interval Analysis and Automatic Result Verification. de Gruyter, Berlin (2017)
5. Moore, R.E., Kearfott, R.B., Cloud, M.J.: Introduction to Interval Analysis. SIAM, Philadelphia (2009)
6. Nguyen, H.T., Kreinovich, V., Wu, B., Xiang, G.: Computing Statistics under Interval and Fuzzy Uncertainty. Springer Verlag, Berlin (2012)
7. Rabinovich, S.G.: Measurement Errors and Uncertainty: Theory and Practice. Springer Verlag, New York (2005)
8. Sheskin, D.J.: Handbook of Parametric and Nonparametric Statistical Procedures. Chapman and Hall/CRC, Boca Raton (2011)

A Cross-Platform Benchmark for Interval Computation Libraries

Xuan Tang[1(✉)], Zachary Ferguson[1], Teseo Schneider[2], Denis Zorin[1], Shoaib Kamil[3], and Daniele Panozzo[1]

[1] New York University, New York City, USA
txstc55@gmail.com
[2] University of Victoria, Victoria, Canada
[3] Adobe Research, San Jose, USA

Abstract. Interval computation is widely used in Computer Aided Design to certify computations that use floating point operations to avoid pitfalls related to rounding error introduced by inaccurate operations. Despite its popularity and practical benefits, support for interval arithmetic is not standardized nor available in mainstream programming languages.

We propose the first benchmark for interval computations, coupled with reference solutions computed with exact arithmetic, and compare popular C and C++ libraries over different architectures, operating systems, and compilers. The benchmark allows identifying limitations in existing implementations, and provides a reliable guide on which library to use on each system for different CAD applications. We believe that our benchmark will be useful for developers of future interval libraries, as a way to test the correctness and performance of their algorithms.

Keywords: Interval Arithmetic · Transcendental Functions · Certified Computations · Collision Detection · Robust Computation · Open-Source Library · Benchmark

1 Introduction

Interval computation allows performing floating-point operations with certifiable correctness, by accounting for rounding errors. Every floating-point number is replaced by a pair of numbers, representing an interval that contains the exact result of the computation, independently from the rounding. While this approach increases the cost and memory usage of computations, it is a staple for many algorithms in computer aided design, geometric computing, image processing, computer graphics, and scientific computing. For example, they are used for Boolean computation [24], intersections between parametric patches [23], continuous collision detection [20], subdivision surfaces [28], and precision manufacturing [25]. More applications are discussed in the survey [15].

While the formal correctness of interval computation has been proven [22], ensuring that an implementation of interval arithmetic is correct is a daunting

R. Wyrzykowski et al. (Eds.): PPAM 2022, LNCS 13827, pp. 415–427, 2023.
https://doi.org/10.1007/978-3-031-30445-3_35

	BOOST	FILIB	NATIVE SWITCHED	MULTIPLICATIVE	PRED-SUCC	BIAS
CORRECTNESS (ARITHMETIC)	✓	✓	✓	✓	✓	✓
CORRECTNESS (TRANSCENDENTAL)	✗	✓	✓	✓	✓	✓
CORRECTNESS (COMPOSITE)	✗	✓	✗	✓	✓	✗
INTERVAL WIDTH (ARITHMETIC)	1	2	1	3	2	1
INTERVAL WIDTH (TRANSCENDENTAL)	1	2	2	2	2	1
SPEED	6	3	4	1	2	5
CONSISTENCY	✗	✓	✗	✓	✗	✗
PORTABILITY	✓	✓	✗	✗	✗	✗

Fig. 1. We introduce a benchmark for interval arithmetic computation and test it on four C/C++ libraries: filib, filib++ (including the native_switched, multiplicative, and pred_succ methods), Boost, and BIAS. We evaluate each library for their correctness, output interval size, speed, consistency, and portability. The table shows a summary of our benchmark where the numbers indicate a ranking from best (small) to worst (large).

task, as the proof relies on assumptions on the order of operations (which can be altered by the compiler or the reordering buffers on the CPU) and on a set of hardware assumptions on the ALUs, which are architecture-dependent. At the same time, users rely on interval computation to certify the correctness of their algorithm, assuming that the interval computation library is correct, which, as we will show in this paper, is not always true for specific combinations of compilers, operating systems, and architectures.

Because a formal proof for every hardware and software combination is impractical (requiring to adapt the proof at every new software or hardware update), we propose an experimental approach: we introduce a large benchmark of test expressions and real-world algorithms for which the exact answer is computed using exact computation. The benchmark can then be used to test existing implementations, and identify issues. We note that a library passing our benchmark problems might still contain errors, as our benchmarks do not exhaustively test all possible combinations of operations and operands.

We use our benchmark to evaluate four popular C/C++ interval libraries (filib, filib++, Boost, BIAS) for correctness, interval size, speed, and consistency. The results are summarized in Table 1. The only library that is at the same time correct, consistent, portable, and has a reasonable speed is filib, which does not rely on using special hardware instructions to control the underlying rounding mode.

We provide the complete source code and scripts to run our benchmark, and in addition we provide a CMake build system for using filib on Windows, Linux, and macOS operating systems with both x86 and ARM architectures. We believe that our benchmark will be a useful tool to continue to assess the correctness of existing interval libraries as new compilers and architectures are developed, and also to provide a standardized set of tests for developers of interval libraries.

2   Background

In the past two decades, numerous interval arithmetic libraries have been developed in various languages. While the logic behind interval arithmetic has been explored in many works [3,12], the actual implementations vary from library to library and may produce different results.

2.1   Hardware Rounding Mode Control

Many modern programming languages comply with the IEEE 754 standard for implementing floating point datatypes, which supports different rounding rules (round to nearest, towards ∞, and towards $-\infty$) [14]. These rounding modes provide good lower and upper bounds on basic arithmetic operations. Libraries like Boost [21] or CGAL [24] use this functionality to build interval operations. Their implementation focuses on setting the correct rounding mode before calling the default math library [4]. Other libraries like Profil/BIAS [16] and filib++ [18] also use or include this implementation for basic algebraic operations.

Such strategies work well for basic arithmetic operations but require a lot of care when computing transcendental functions, where many rounding changes need to happen to evaluate a single transcendental function [10]. Some of them, like CGAL, sidestep the problem by not supporting transcendental operations.

2.2   Software Implementations

It is possible to avoid relying on hardware rounding mode support by using a pure software implementation. There are two main approaches.

Multiplicative. While it is hard to obtain the exact floating point error of an expression, the relative error of single operations can be generalized [11,17] since there are only a finite number of bits representing a number [7]. Hence, one can carefully analyze the error to generate a number ϵ such that if the true result is α and the computed result is β, $(1 - \epsilon)\beta \leq \alpha \leq (1 + \epsilon)\beta$ holds and $1 - \epsilon$, $1 + \epsilon$ can be exactly represented in floating-point. Filib++, BIAS, and GAOL [8] all provide such implementations, although the choice of ϵ varies depending on how the analysis is performed.

Changing Binary Representation. Since nowadays almost all floating-point numbers implementations follow the IEEE 754 standard, one can deconstruct the binary representation of a number and directly change the result to obtain an interval [1]. Filib and filib++ adopt this approach, by directly modifying the mantissa and exponent of a double, generating a reasonably-small interval without sacrificing performance.

2.3   Other Implementations

Some libraries rely on others as part of their implementation of interval arithmetic. For example, IBEX [5] and XSC [13] both use filib as the backend for interval computation. These libraries generally do not provide better performance or smaller interval width, but they focus on providing a more user-friendly interface. Other interval libraries exist in other programming languages. For example, IntervalArithmetic.jl [2] in Julia, interval-arithmetic [19] in Javascript. Since our goal is on C/C++ libraries we do not include such libraries for our study.

3   Methodology

A good interval library should maintain four traits: (1) correctness, (2) small interval widths, (3) efficiency, and (4) consistency across different architectures and compilers. We design our benchmark to test these four traits. We recognize that in many applications, an interval itself is initialized from a single number rather than an actual range since the goal is to compute an interval that includes the true value of an expression. Hence, the initialization of an interval in our benchmark is always from a single value. In our benchmark, we compare the following four popular open source libraries that complies with IEEE 754 standard: filib, filib++, Boost, and BIAS.

Filib++ supports three modes for interval computations: `native_switched` (uses system rounding modes), `pred_succ` (directly manipulates the bit representation of a double), and `multiplicative` (multiplies two numbers to generate an interval). BIAS includes three rounding modes (ROUND DOWN, ROUND UP, and ROUND NEAR) which can be set before an interval operation. Their documentation is unclear how an interval operation is affected by these rounding modes, thus we treat them as three different interval types.

3.1   Expressions

We list the expressions that will later be referred to in this paper here:

$$\frac{a(a + bc)}{(b + cd)} - \frac{d\,(e + f/g)}{(g + h)} - \frac{i}{j} \tag{1}$$

$$\cos\left(\left(\cos\left(\cos(f) + \exp\left(\frac{d}{c}\right)\right)\right)\left(\sin\left(\sqrt{e} + a + b - \sqrt{d + c}\right)\right)\right) \tag{2}$$

$$\exp\left(\sqrt{\exp\left(\sqrt{\exp\left(\sqrt{a}\right)}\right)}\right) \tag{3}$$

$$\exp\left(\frac{\sqrt{\exp\left(\cos\left(a/d\right)\right)/\exp\left(\cos\left(\sqrt{f}\right)\right)}}{\sqrt{\cos(\cos(\cos(c)))/\sqrt{\sin(\cos(b))}}}\right) \tag{4}$$

3.2   Correctness

While libraries can optimize interval operations for every single arithmetic or transcendental function, composite expressions that combine multiple operations can potentially cause the library to produce incorrect (interval does not include the true result) or empty (lower bound is greater than upper bound) intervals. In our benchmark, we test each library on 28 different basic expressions and 104 expressions from FPBench [6], a floating point accuracy benchmark that covers a variety of application domains. The basic benchmark is composed of: four basic arithmetic operations (addition, subtraction, multiplication, and division); four transcendental functions (sqrt, exp, sin, cos); ten composite expressions that only contain basic arithmetic operations; and ten composite expressions containing both arithmetic operations and transcendental functions. These expressions are randomly generated from a fixed seed and listed on the website.

For each expression, we generate one million valid inputs for evaluation. To ensure that the representation of the input and result are precise, and no additional floating point error is introduced during validation, we convert every input and output to rational format using GMP [9]. A typical query has the form

$$\frac{n_l}{d_l} \leq \text{expression}(\frac{n_1}{d_1}, \dots) \leq \frac{n_u}{d_u}$$

for $n, d \in \mathbb{Z}$. Using this format, the queries can be evaluated later by an arbitrary precision software to get an exact answer. In our benchmark, we use Mathematica [27].

3.3   Interval Width

To report the interval width we utilize a similar procedure to when checking correctness. Instead of outputting the actual query, we compute the interval width by using a rational subtraction (i.e., we convert the upper and lower bound to rational numbers).

3.4   Speed

To test the speed of an interval library, we measure the execution time for each expression: we generate 1,000 inputs for each expression and execute the expression 10,000 times for every input. Finally, we accumulate the total execution time for each library and expression to report the performance. It is important to execute different sets of inputs since input values may affect the performance of some operations due to range reduction.

3.5   Consistency and Portability

We deployed our benchmark on four different platforms with different compilers:

- Windows (Intel Core i7 8700k, x86-64, Windows 10, MSVC 14.27.29110)

- macOS Intel (2.4 GHz 8-Core Intel Core i9, x86-64, macOS Big Sur, Darwin Kernel Version 20.1.0, Apple clang version 12.0.0)
- macOS Arm (3.2 GHz 4-Core/2 + 2 GHz 4-Core Apple M1, arm64, macOS Big Sur, Darwin Kernel Version 20.1.0, Apple clang version 12.0.0)
- Linux (AMD EPYC 7452 32-Core Processor, x86-64, Ubuntu 19.10, GCC 9.2.1).

4   Results

We discuss in detail how each interval type perform over different platform and expressions.

4.1   Correctness

As discussed before, we test each library on 28 (constructed by us) and 104 (extracted from FPBench) expressions. We check for correctness by ensuring that the interval computation produces an interval containing the exact solution, evaluated with arbitrary precision with Mathematica [27].

We begin with the 28 expressions. All of the libraries produce correct results for basic arithmetic operations. However, when it comes to transcendental functions, Boost is not correct (since it deals with transcendental functions by setting rounding modes before calling the standard math library). Specifically, it fails for exp and trigonometry functions, where the implementation is based on Taylor expansion [10]. For composite expressions that only contain basic arithmetic operations, all libraries are correct. When transcendental functions are included in a composite expression, BIAS produces incorrect intervals for Expression (2).

Filib and filib++'s three interval modes are correct for the 28 expressions, the native_switched mode for filib++ is not correct on four of the expressions from FPBench. For example, "polarToCarthesian, x", that computes

$$r \cos(\theta \cdot (3.14159265359/180.0))$$

which contains transcendental function cos. Another example is the expression "sineOrder3"

$$(0.954929658551372x_0) - (0.12900613773279798((x_0\, x_0)\, x_0))$$

which only contains basic arithmetic operations, and is designed to find floating point problem caused by the order of evaluation.

We conclude that only filib and filib++'s pred_succ and multiplicative modes produce correct intervals for all tests.

4.2   Interval Width

Due to the large number of test expressions, we show only some of the most representative expressions. Specifically, we look at one expression that contains only arithmetic operations (Expression (1)), one expression that contains only transcendental functions (Expression (3)), and one that contains both (Expression (4)).

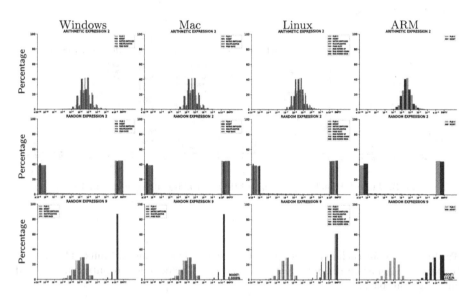

Fig. 2. Distribution of interval width. Top: Expression (1). Middle: Expression (3). Bottom: Expression (4)

Across the different platforms, the distribution of interval width does not vary much. However, within each platform, the distribution of interval width can be quite different between libraries. The top row of Fig. 2 shows that for expressions that contain only arithmetic operations, libraries that use system rounding modes (Boost, filib++ native_switched, BIAS) produce smaller interval widths compared to others. The multiplicative mode of filib++ produces the largest interval widths. However, the differences are small across libraries.

When transcendental functions are added into the expression, the interval widths can be unpredictable (Fig. 2). The difference of overall distribution of the libraries can also be quite large depending on the expression, but within filib and filib++'s three interval modes, the interval widths are quite similar. We also see that Boost produces empty intervals, an indication that Boost's results are sometimes incorrect.

4.3 Performance

We show the accumulated time in milliseconds for each expression on the Linux platform since the relative performance across platforms is similar. We also highlight the fastest method for each expression. From Table 1, we see that Boost has the worst performance on all of the 28 expressions, followed by BIAS, then filib. While filib++'s `native_switched` mode also sets rounding mode for basic arithmetic operations, it is highly optimized and is significantly faster than the other two libraries.

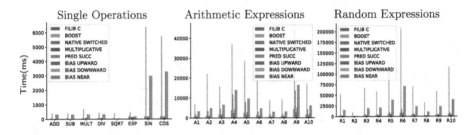

Fig. 3. Time for each expression ($1,000 \times 10,000$ runs) in ms on Linux.

Table 1. Time for each expression ($1,000 \times 10,000$ runs) in ms on Linux. The relative timings are similar on different platforms and OS. The complete results can be found on our github page.

	FILIB C	BOOST	NATIVE SWITCHED	MULTIPLICATIVE	PRED SUCC	BIAS UPWARD	BIAS DOWNWARD	BIAS NEAR
ADDITION	66.52	405.78	18.49	3.94	**3.92**	327.93	328.69	327.94
SUBTRACTION	80.08	405.35	18.37	9.20	**3.90**	327.60	327.44	327.44
MULTIPLICATION	78.40	649.62	25.81	**13.59**	90.03	339.43	338.87	338.61
DIVISION	84.43	451.78	**38.13**	68.97	81.12	344.25	343.87	344.13
SQUARE ROOT	84.85	434.21	24.19	24.26	**24.18**	61.76	60.44	60.40
EXPONENTIAL	199.08	462.47	**143.28**	143.43	143.43	196.44	196.34	200.39
SIN	202.25	7115.77	**171.54**	172.79	172.94	2088.65	2088.34	2087.43
COS	190.21	6776.14	168.64	168.65	**168.54**	2425.19	2424.21	2423.90
ARITHMETIC EXPRESSION 1	861.49	6848.71	1969.52	**589.98**	1053.79	4126.49	4097.03	4091.17
ARITHMETIC EXPRESSION 2	1292.77	23227.45	3170.62	**699.40**	1040.81	5706.45	5672.61	5661.78
ARITHMETIC EXPRESSION 3	1844.20	15082.05	4984.85	**1318.50**	1900.36	7790.34	7769.46	7757.53
ARITHMETIC EXPRESSION 4	3758.37	30943.47	11407.83	**2354.18**	4077.55	16086.02	16062.78	16054.29
ARITHMETIC EXPRESSION 5	2635.54	21860.23	7910.95	**1626.65**	2888.93	10891.99	10883.80	10871.13
RANDOM EXPRESSION 1	2449.01	55822.93	3454.41	**2112.71**	2350.52	12849.99	12853.38	12858.24
RANDOM EXPRESSION 2	1354.32	4737.32	1465.94	1441.29	1440.93	**1323.64**	1327.30	1324.32
RANDOM EXPRESSION 3	3382.98	69212.48	5741.97	**2945.31**	3689.13	17524.99	17485.55	17498.33
RANDOM EXPRESSION 4	3067.34	56868.36	4927.13	3063.33	**3593.86**	17996.21	17975.26	17973.13
RANDOM EXPRESSION 5	5870.61	121944.99	9633.84	**5146.98**	6081.06	32546.81	32577.18	32540.89

Within filib++, the performance of the three modes on basic operations is comparable. However, for more complex arithmetic expressions, `native_switched` mode is consistently the slowest, likely because it changes the rounding mode for each operations. The multiplicative mode is always the fastest, while `pred_succ` method is between the two. Since filib++ ignores interval mode when computing transcendental functions, the performance on sqrt, exp, sin, cos are similar. As a result, when computing more complicated expressions, multiplicative mode remains the fastest one among three modes and among all the interval types, followed by pred_succ mode, then native_switched mode. Although the speed of filib++ can drop below filib or even BIAS on some expressions, the relative difference is minimal.

4.4   Consistency and Portability

While Boost can be deployed on all platforms we test on, it does not produce consistent results due to its system specific rounding modes.

While filib++ does well in terms of both correctness and speed, it does not produce the same result across different platforms: we found that it produces different results on the Linux platform. As seen in Fig. 4, the pred_succ's distribution of interval width differs from Linux to Mac. Additionally, its portability is limited due to the lack of updates since 2011 and the use of autoconf to generate the makefile.[1]

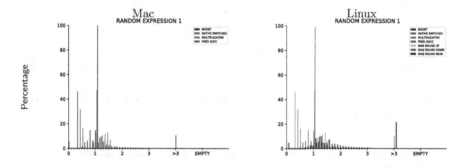

Fig. 4. Distribution of each library's interval width on expression 2, normalized.

BIAS is not maintained[2] and currently does not compile out of the box on modern windows and macOS versions. We thus only tested it on Linux.

4.5   Application on Continuous Collision Detection Queries

As a further benchmark of correctness, we integrate three interval libraries in the continuous collision detection (CCD) benchmark of [26]. The CCD benchmark features two interval based algorithms to detect collisions along a continuous linear trajectory. Both the univariate and multivariate interval-based CCD perform interval-based bisection root finding [22] and use interval arithmetic to compute

---

[1]   filib++ source: http://www2.math.uni-wuppertal.de/wrswt/software/filib.html, last updated in 2011.

[2]   BIAS source: https://www.tuhh.de/ti3/keil/profil/index_e.html, last updated in 2009,.

424 X. Tang et al.

an estimate of the codomain of a function. The correctness of the interval arithmetic ensures that no false negatives (no collision is reported when there is a collision) occur and smaller interval width helps to reduce the number of false positives (a collision is reported when there is no collision).

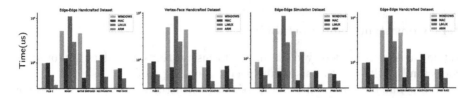

Fig. 5. Average time of each query using different interval types on different platform in univariate interval root finder test.

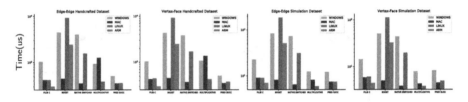

Fig. 6. Average time of each query using different interval types on different platform in multivariate interval root finder test.

Timing-wise (Fig. 5, 6), all libraries are in a similar ballpark, with the exception of Boost being slightly slower than the others in certain tests.

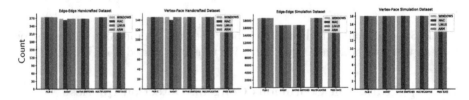

Fig. 7. Number of false positives using different interval types on different platform in univariate interval root finder test.

None of the libraries produces false negatives in this benchmark. The number of false positives varies as expected, as the intervals are different (Fig. 7, 8). It is concerning to see that Boost and filib++'s native_switched produce different numbers of false positives on different architectures. filib, filib++'s pred_succ, and filib++'s multiplicative method produce consistent results across all operating systems and architectures.

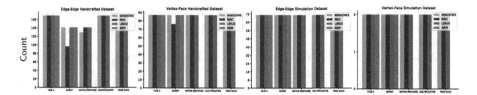

Fig. 8. Number of false positives using different interval types on different platform in multivariate interval root finder test.

5 Conclusion

In this paper, we designed a benchmark that tests interval libraries for correctness, interval width, speed, and consistency. Using our benchmark we evaluated four interval libraries: filib, filib++, Boost, and BIAS (Table 1). We also provide the complete results along with all the expressions on our github page.[3]

In our study, filib is the only library that is correct, consistent, portable, and efficient. We believe it is the best option between the libraries we tested. To make deployment on multiple platforms easier, we provide a copy of the library with a modern cmake build system on github.[4]

References

1. Abrams, S., et al.: Efficient and reliable methods for rounded-interval arithmetic. Comput.-Aid. Des. **30**(8), 657–665 (1998). https://doi.org/10.1016/S0010-4485(97)00086-9, http://www.sciencedirect.com/science/article/pii/S0010448597000869
2. Benet, L., Sanders, D.: Juliaintervals.jl package - Rigorous numerics with interval arithmetic & applications (2015). https://github.com/JuliaIntervals/IntervalArithmetic.jl
3. Benhamou, F., Older, W.J.: Applying interval arithmetic to real, integer, and Boolean constraints. J. Logic Program. **32**(1), 1–24 (1997). https://doi.org/10.1016/S0743-1066(96)00142-2, http://www.sciencedirect.com/science/article/pii/S0743106696001422
4. Brönnimann, H., Melquiond, G., Pion, S.: The design of the Boost interval arithmetic library. Theor.l Comput. Sci. **351**(1), 111–118 (2006). https://doi.org/10.1016/j.tcs.2005.09.062, http://www.sciencedirect.com/science/article/pii/S0304397505006110, real Numbers and Computers
5. Chabert, G.: IBEX (2007). http://www.ibex-lib.org/
6. Damouche, N., Martel, M., Panchekha, P., Qiu, C., Sanchez-Stern, A., Tatlock, Z.: Toward a standard benchmark format and suite for floating-point analysis. In: Bogomolov, S., Martel, M., Prabhakar, P. (eds.) NSV 2016. LNCS, vol. 10152, pp. 63–77. Springer, Cham (2017). https://doi.org/10.1007/978-3-319-54292-8_6

---

[3] https://geometryprocessing.github.io/intervals/.

[4] https://github.com/txstc55/filib.

7. Goldberg, D.: What every computer scientist should know about floating-point arithmetic. ACM Comput. Surv. **23**(1), 5–48 (1991). https://doi.org/10.1145/103162.103163
8. Goualard, F.: Gaol: NOT Just Another Interval Library (2005). https://sourceforge.net/projects/gaol/
9. Granlund, T., Team, G.D.: GNU MP 6.0 Multiple Precision Arithmetic Library. Samurai Media Limited, London, GBR (2015)
10. Harrison, J., Tak, P., Tang, P.: The Computation of Transcendental Functions on the IA-64 Architecture. Intel Technol. J. **4**, 234–251 (1999)
11. Harrison, J.: Formal verification of floating point trigonometric functions. In: Hunt, W.A., Johnson, S.D. (eds.) FMCAD 2000. LNCS, vol. 1954, pp. 254–270. Springer, Heidelberg (2000). https://doi.org/10.1007/3-540-40922-X_14
12. Hickey, T., Ju, Q., Van Emden, M.H.: Interval arithmetic: from principles to implementation. J. ACM **48**(5), 1038–1068 (2001). https://doi.org/10.1145/502102.502106
13. Hofschuster, W., Krämer, W.: C-XSC 2.0 – A C++ library for extended scientific computing. In: Alt, R., Frommer, A., Kearfott, R.B., Luther, W. (eds.) Numerical Software with Result Verification. LNCS, vol. 2991, pp. 15–35. Springer, Heidelberg (2004). https://doi.org/10.1007/978-3-540-24738-8_2
14. IEEE: IEEE standard for binary floating-point arithmetic. ANSI/IEEE Std 754–1985, pp. 1–20 (1985). https://doi.org/10.1109/IEEESTD.1985.82928
15. Kearfott, R.: Interval computations: introduction, uses, and resources. Euromath Bulletin **2** (1996)
16. Knüppel, O.: PROFIL/BIAS—A fast interval library. Computing **53**(3), 277–287 (1994). https://doi.org/10.1007/BF02307379
17. Lefevre, V., Muller, J.: Worst cases for correct rounding of the elementary functions in double precision. In: Proceedings 15th IEEE Symposium on Computer Arithmetic. ARITH-15 2001, pp. 111–118 (2001). https://doi.org/10.1109/ARITH.2001.930110
18. Lerch, M., Tischler, G., Gudenberg, J.W.V., Hofschuster, W., Krämer, W.: FILIB++, a fast interval library supporting containment computations. ACM Trans. Math. Softw. **32**(2), 299–324 (2006). https://doi.org/10.1145/1141885.1141893
19. Poppe, M.: interval-arithmetic (2015). https://github.com/mauriciopoppe/interval-arithmetic
20. Redon, S., Kheddar, A., Coquillart, S.: Fast Continuous Collision Detection between Rigid Bodies. Comput. Graphics Forum **21** (2002)
21. Schling, B.: The Boost C++ Libraries. XML Press (2011)
22. Snyder, J.: Interval Analysis For Computer Graphics. In: ACM SIGGRAPH, pp. 121–130. ACM (August 1992). https://www.microsoft.com/en-us/research/publication/interval-analysis-computer-graphics/
23. Snyder, J.M., Woodbury, A.R., Fleischer, K., Currin, B., Barr, A.H.: Interval Methods for multi-point collisions between time-dependent curved surfaces. In: Proceedings of the 20th Annual Conference on Computer Graphics and Interactive Techniques, pp. 321–334. SIGGRAPH '93, Association for Computing Machinery, New York, NY, USA (1993)
24. The CGAL Project: CGAL User and Reference Manual. CGAL Editorial Board, 5.3 edn. (2021). https://doc.cgal.org/5.3/Manual/packages.html
25. Tibken, B., Hofer, E.P., Seibold, W.: Quality control of valve push rods using interval arithmetic. IFAC Proc. **32**(2), 409–412 (1999), 14th IFAC World Congress 1999, Beijing, Chia, 5–9 July

26. Wang, B., Ferguson, Z., Schneider, T., Jiang, X., Attene, M., Panozzo, D.: A large scale benchmark and an inclusion-based algorithm for continuous collision detection. ACM Trans. Graphics **40**(5) (2021)
27. Wolfram Research Inc.: Mathematica 12.0 (2020). http://www.wolfram.com
28. Zorin, D.: A method for analysis of C1-continuity of subdivision surfaces. SIAM J. Num. Anal. **37**(5), 1677–1708 (2000). https://doi.org/10.1137/s003614299834263x

Testing Interval Arithmetic Libraries, Including Their IEEE-1788 Compliance

Nathalie Revol[1]($\boxtimes$)(ID), Luis Benet[2](ID), Luca Ferranti[3](ID), and Sergei Zhilin[4](ID)

[1] INRIA - LIP UMR 5668, ENS Lyon, University Lyon 1, Inria,
CNRS, Lyon, France
Nathalie.Revol@inria.fr
[2] Instituto de Ciencias Físicas, Universidad Nacional Autónoma de México,
Cuernavaca, Mexico
benet@icf.unam.mx
[3] University of Vaasa, Vaasa, Finland
luca.ferranti@uwasa.fi
[4] CSort LLC, Barnaul, Russia
szhilin@gmail.com

Abstract. As developers of libraries implementing interval arithmetic, we faced the same difficulties when it came to testing our libraries. What must be tested? How can we devise relevant test cases for unit testing? How can we ensure a high (and possibly 100%) test coverage? In this paper we list the different aspects that, in our opinion, must be tested, giving indications on the choice of test cases. Then we examine how several interval arithmetic libraries actually perform tests. Next, we present two existing frameworks developed specifically to gather test cases and to incorporate easily new libraries in order to test them, namely JInterval and ITF1788. Not every important aspects of our libraries fit in these frameworks and we list extra tests that we deem important, but not easy, to perform.

Keywords: Unit tests for interval arithmetic libraries · Test cases for interval arithmetic · Testing IEEE 1788–2015 compliance

1 Introduction

Many libraries implement interval arithmetic, from XSC [1] and FILIB [2] among the pioneers, to Octave/Interval [3], ValidatedNumerics.jl [4] and Moore [5] for the more recent ones. An early comparison of several libraries [6] indicated that the underlying approach of the definition of interval arithmetic was, more or less, different and specific to each library. It was thus impossible to compare the results obtained by different libraries, as so many differences impacted the computations. To enable comparisons, it was decided to standardize interval arithmetic. A collective effort, launched in 2008, led to the standardization of interval arithmetic, specified in the IEEE 1788–2015 standard [7].

© The Author(s), under exclusive license to Springer Nature Switzerland AG 2023
R. Wyrzykowski et al. (Eds.): PPAM 2022, LNCS 13827, pp. 428–440, 2023.
https://doi.org/10.1007/978-3-031-30445-3_36

The development of IEEE 1788–2015 compliant libraries, and thus the comparison of their results, was therefore made possible. However, before even considering comparisons between libraries, the developers of an interval arithmetic library need to check their developments, to ensure that their library behaves correctly, in particular with respect to IEEE 1788–2015 compliance. How do they usually proceed? Through intensive tests. Formal proof that each operation is correct is the next step, but it will not be considered in what follows.

Another use of tests is, for users, at installation time, to check that the newly installed library behaves properly on one's platform. This is not a 100% guarantee of correctness, but it increases the user's confidence.

Developers test for many aspects of their libraries, not only for IEEE 1788–2015 compliance, but also for instance the handling of exceptional or invalid inputs and so on. *Unit tests* are very common: for each operation or function, one prepares a set of inputs and checks whether the library computes the expected output, or at least an enclosure of it. Rapidly, the developers realize that, in order to get sufficient confidence in the implementation of a given operation, in order to test a high enough coverage of the code (or 100% of it), a huge number of cases must be tested. This implies that, *for each implemented operation*, a large part of the development time is devoted to devising these test cases. We are developers of different libraries, we faced the same situation and we elaborated similar tests. We decided to make our expertise easily available to everyone interested. The preliminary result of this collaboration is the content of this article.

In what follows, we propose to list, in Sect. 2, the different features that must be tested. We then compare, in Sect. 3, this list of recommended tests with the tests that are actually included in some well-known libraries (for which we have access to their test suites). Our goal is to devise test cases for each situation we have identified and to share them: in Sect. 4 we introduce two existing frameworks that, on the one hand, ease the integration of a new library to be tested, and that, on the other hand, offer a significant set of test cases, as well as a convenient mechanism to add new ones. As no setup is perfect, in Sect. 5, we then give a list of other types of tests deemed useful in our development of interval arithmetic libraries, but still missing. Our short- to midterm-goal is to enrich and share test suites, and to enhance the capabilities of the frameworks introduced in Sect. 4.

2   What Must Be Tested?

Testing floating-point arithmetic has been studied thoroughly, as testified by Nelson Beebe's web page for software [8] and more generally by the huge amount of bibliographic references and of available programs. Similarly, in this article, we gather and organize the important features that must be tested in order to assess the correctness, compliance and possibly quality of a library implementing interval arithmetic.

2.1   General Remarks About Unit Tests

Let us denote by $\mathcal{L}$ the tested library, and intervals using boldface: $\mathbf{x}$, $\mathbf{y}$. We focus here on unit tests, for a function, denoted by f. A unit test case is a pair composed of the input argument $\mathbf{x}$ and the expected output $\mathbf{y}$.

First, the output $\mathbf{y}$ must be the tightest representable interval enclosing $f(\mathbf{x})$; otherwise a very accurate library could compute $\mathbf{z}$ such that $\mathbf{z} \subsetneq \mathbf{y}$ and still $\mathbf{z} \supseteq f(\mathbf{x})$. To ensure the tightness property for $\mathbf{y}$, typically, one computes the endpoints $\underline{y}$ and $\bar{y}$ of $\mathbf{y} = [\underline{y}, \bar{y}]$ using a precision higher than the computing precision of $\mathcal{L}$. Let us illustrate this with $\mathcal{L}$ using `Binary64` floating-point numbers, on the (simple) example of the exponential function. We assume that the given floating-point implementation of exp does not provide correct rounding, but that, for any precision q, it satisfies $RD_q(\exp(x)) \leq \exp(x) \leq RU_q(\exp(x))$ for RD_q rounding downwards and RU_q rounding upwards, both in precision q. Given $\mathbf{x} = [\underline{x}, \bar{x}]$, to compute the infimum $\underline{y}$ of $\mathbf{y}$, one gets the approximations $RD_q(\exp(\underline{x}))$ and $RU_q(\exp(\underline{x}))$ of $\exp(\underline{x})$ in high precision q, and finally round them downwards in the target precision $= 53$. If $RD_{53}(RD_q(\exp(\underline{x})))$ and $RD_{53}(RU_q(\exp(\underline{x})))$ are equal, then they are the sought value $\underline{y}$ for the infimum of $\exp(\mathbf{x})$.

Once the test cases are devised, what conclusions can be drawn from the comparison between $\mathbf{y}$ and $\mathbf{z}$ the result computed by $\mathcal{L}$? Requiring equality may be too demanding. Inclusion is required, but we want to dismiss, for instance, an implementation of sin that returns $[-1, 1]$ for any argument. If the accuracy of the function is given in the specification of the library, how can it be used and checked?

A last general recommendation is to incorporate the following procedure: if $(\mathbf{x}, \mathbf{y})$ is given as a pair of input and output, pick at random (a reasonably large number of) values $x \in \mathbf{x}$ and check whether $f(x) \in \mathbf{y}$ with $f(x)$ computed by the underlying arithmetic, and whether $f([x, x]) \subseteq \mathbf{y}$. Those tests are disconnected from the knowledge of the implementation of f and may hit a zone not considered (forgotten) in the development of f, such as an overlooked quadrant for a trigonometric function.

2.2   Tests Common to All Interval Arithmetic Libraries

- **Easy test cases.** First, easy cases are tested: these test cases are both easy to devise and easy to compute. They constitute preliminary tests, at an early stage of the implementation of the function, to identify and correct the most obvious bugs. These test cases are chosen to cover, roughly speaking, the various possible magnitudes of the arguments, but without any exhaustivity. They also span positive and negative values, if the domain and range of the function so permit.
- **Special and exceptional values.** A time-consuming task, when implementing a function, is the handling of special and exceptional values. In floating-point arithmetic, 0 is a special value, because it has two representations, $+0$ and -0, that is, signed zeros. It is thus valuable to test whether one gets the

same result, independently of the sign of the representation of 0, when 0 is an endpoint of either an input argument or of the output.

1 is not a special value for floating-point arithmetic. However, it is often considered as a special value, for instance for the logarithmic functions and the arc-cosine: its image is the special value 0.

Infinities are also special values in floating-point arithmetic. If they are supported by the library, one must have test cases containing infinities as their endpoints, both for inputs and for outputs. If infinities are not supported by the library, it is even the more so important to test input arguments that yield overflow, such as the addition or the multiplication of $[c * \text{MAXREAL}, \text{MAXREAL}]$ by itself, with c either 0 or $c = 0.75$. Another example is $\exp([\underline{x}, \bar{x}])$ with $\underline{x}$ such that $\exp(\underline{x})$ is rather small and $\bar{x}$ such that $\exp(\bar{x})$ overflows, or both $\underline{x}$ and $\bar{x}$ such that their exponential overflow.

Again, when floating-point arithmetic is used, NaN is an exceptional value, that is the result of an invalid computation. How is a NaN handled when it occurs as the endpoint of an input interval? The answer should be that, even if it has no mathematical meaning, in practice NaNs propagate. Some libraries use NaN to denote the emptyset, as is the case in Intlab [9]. Care must then be taken for the union or intersection of two intervals.

- **Cornercases.** Another family of test cases is designed in order to test the difficulties encountered during the implementation, such as difficult-to-round values, or values at the boundaries of the domain of the function, or close to points whose image is an extremum. A typical example is a floating-point input close to an integer multiple of $\frac{\pi}{2}$, for trigonometric functions. The various tools for testing *floating-point* arithmetic can be a source of inspiration. Indeed, with floating-point arithmetic, as there is a sudden change in absolute error between two consecutive floating-point numbers when the binade (i.e. an interval of the form $[2^k, 2^{k+1})$ with $k \in \mathbb{Z}$) changes, it is worth exploring several binades, both for the inputs and output values. This is particularly true for mid-rad representation of the intervals, that is, the representation of intervals by their midpoint and radius. With floating-point arithmetic, another delicate zone concerns subnormal numbers (i.e., numbers with the minimum possible exponent). Test cases should contain intervals $[0, \bar{x}]$ and $[\underline{x}, \bar{x}]$ such that $\underline{x}$ and $\bar{x}$ are subnormals – for the logarithmic functions, or intervals $[\underline{x}, \bar{x}]$ such that their exponential has subnormal endpoint(s).
- **Functions specific to intervals.** Functions such as the union (convex hull of the union) or the intersection must be tested when one, or both endpoints are special or exceptional values, or when one argument is the empty set, if it is supported by the library.

  Functions such as the midpoint or radius have been thoroughly studied in [10], test cases can be taken from this reference.
- **Input and Output.** Finally, I/O is the place where the most unexpected things can happen: much creativity is needed to cover a large variety of input values given as strings.

2.3   Tests About IEEE-1788 Compliance

The IEEE 1788–2015 standard [7] was developed to enable comparisons of interval methods and their implementation. It mandates operations in Sect. 9; it provides "hooks" to integrate several flavors of interval arithmetic and it defines the so-called "set-based" flavor along with its set of recommended operations in Sect. 10; it mandates that intervals are decorated with flags that sum up the history of their computation (such as "every operation and function involved in this computation is defined and continuous on its arguments") in Sect. 8. It also specifies the handling of exceptions in Sect. 12.1.3 and the grammar for I/O in Sect. 13. Last but not least, it offers the possibility to return either the tightest possible result, or simply an accurate one, or a valid one in Sect. 12.10.1. "Compressed arithmetic" will not be mentioned, as it is not yet widely used. Testing IEEE 1788–2015 compliance means testing all of these aspects:

- **testing flavor compliance:** each test case must be accompanied with the indication of the corresponding flavor: how can it be specified? If several flavors are tested (once they are defined by a new revision of the standard), either the testing framework or the library must offer a mechanism to change the current flavor in use. This is needed to test for instance $\emptyset + [1, 2]$ or $\exp([-\infty, 0])$ in the set-based flavor and then $[3, 2] + [4, 1]$ in the (future?) Kaucher flavor.
- **required functions / recommended functions:** the standard mandates that some functions are implemented by the library, such as cosh, but only recommends other ones, such as expm1 ($\mathrm{expm1}(x) = \exp(x) - 1$) for the set-based flavor. The tests must allow for executing functions if they exist in the library but not crashing when a recommended function is not available.
- **testing decorations:** the set-based flavor defines 5 decorations. To test every possible meaningful combination of decorations for inputs and output, one must devise close to 5 test cases for unary operations and up to 25 test cases for binary operations. Care must be taken to exhaust the complete list of possibilities.
- **testing the different accuracies: tightness/accurate/valid:** we already discussed the difficulty to validate a computed result, to compare it with the expected output, when it is not the tightest possible one. The standard defines three possible levels of accuracy. Test cases must include all three possibilities for each pair of input and output, and check if the corresponding levels are available in the library. They must include the description of this level, the testing framework must be able to check whether the result is tight or valid (both are easy), or accurate (by computing the enclosing interval that is only slightly larger, as defined by the standard).
- **exceptional behavior:** exceptions have already been mentioned above. The standard defines the different exceptions that must be signalled, the test cases must include these exceptions and check whether the correct exception is signalled.
- **standard specific I/O system:** the standard defines precisely the various forms of inputs and outputs. At least one test case per form must be present

in the test case. If one wants to test every possibility, with at most 3 values for each variable field lengths, one obtains a thousand test cases.

2.4 Tests Specific to Some Libraries

Some libraries must need specific test cases, corresponding to their specificities.

- **Representations of intervals.** A library that uses, for instance, the mid-rad representation of intervals must test that operations and I/O operate correctly on this representation. There are libraries that keep track of the openness or closedness of each endpoint: test cases must be provided to check that this information is correctly computed. If each possibility is tested, this can multiply by 4 the number of test cases. Some libraries do not employ floating-point types to represent intervals, either in inf-sup or mid-rad representation. Exact rational numbers can be used instead, as in MPRIA [11] and JInterval [12]. Other libraries, such as ARB [14], also allow complex intervals, that is, they use complex arithmetic as their underlying arithmetic.
- **Precision.** A library that accomodates several floating-point formats, such as `Binary32` and `Binary64`, must test that it operates soundly with both formats and with combinations of both. Moreover, a library that uses arbitrary precision, such as MPFI [13] or ARB [14] must include tests for largely varying precisions, without claiming exhaustivity.
- **Directed roundings.** In order to guarantee the inclusion property, libraries rely on directed roundings. They must have tests which are specific to how directed rounding is achieved. If it is achieved by changing the rounding mode, ideally it should be tested that this is thread safe and that using multiple threads doesn't lead to undefined behavior. If it is achieved via software, by emulating directed rounding in round to nearest (as it is done e.g. by default in IntervalArithmetic.jl), then they very likely rely heavily on the use of Error-Free Transforms, or EFT in short. Thus, hard to round cases and corner cases for EFT (when it overflows, underflows, returns NaN) should also be tested.

2.5 On Tests Timing

An important issue related to tests is time. To illustrate this question, let us mention that MPFI currently implements about 30 test cases for each function, and running the tests (`make check`) takes 20 s of user's time on a reasonably fast PC. If all these recommended test cases were implemented, there would be at least a few hundred test cases, at most a few thousands. The testing time will be multiplied according by a factor between 10 and 100. Shall we stick to our limited number of test cases and risk to have not enough tests performed, or shall we risk to have a more complete test cases coverage and no test performed at all, because of the time it takes? This latter risk decreases when the library is stable, as tests are performed once and for all at installation time and this is not frequent.

2.6 Need for a Unified Framework for Testing Interval Arithmetic Libraries

While there are several shared features between all interval arithmetic libraries, they are all also somehow unique in design choices (how to handle direct rounding, tightness vs speed, etc.). This calls for a unified framework to test interval arithmetic libraries. This has several benefits. First, a standard framework makes it easier to compare libraries against each other. It would also offer a tool for developers, to easily verify whether their library is compliant with the standard or not. Finally, an important use case of interval arithmetic is to perform rigorous computations, that can be used as mathematical proofs. While several theorems for rigorous computations have been proved, they all rely on the assumption that the underlying implementation of interval arithmetic is correct. For this reason, a unified testing framework, developed through inputs from several interval libraries developers, would increase the reliability of *all* libraries.

Based on the above discussion, we identify the following requirements in a unified interval testing framework:

1. **Modularity:** tests should be structured in a modular way, to allow users and developers choosing what parts to test. For example, tests for decorated intervals should be separated from tests for bare intervals. Tests for recommended functions should be separated from tests for required functions.
2. **Completeness:** there should be tests for all functions required and recommended by the standard. The tests should contain both some simple normal cases and cornercases, as well as exceptional behavior (handle NaN, overflow, underflow) and hard to round cases for finite precision data types.
3. **Support for different number systems**: allow to test when the bounds of the interval are `Binary64`, `Binary32`, arbitrary precision floats etc.
4. **Test for tightness:** verify that the computed interval is the smallest valid interval.
5. **Test for validity:** achieving tight bounds can be challenging or at least computationally expensive. Libraries at early stages or libraries with a focus on efficiency may prefer to test only that the computed interval is valid, i.e. an enclosure of the expected result. A unified framework should allow the user to switch between testing tightness and validity, ideally also allowing to set a threshold on how much wider the returned interval is allowed to be.
6. **Self-validated:** it should be possible for the user to verify that the results expected by the tests are indeed correct.

3 Interval Arithmetic Libraries and Their Test Sets

During decades, several interval arithmetic libraries have been developed, each with its own design choices. Since we are interesting in testing, here we only list some of the ones for which tests are freely available.

1. **MPFI** [13]: C library for arbitrary precision interval arithmetic. Based on MPFR. Unit tests for each function: some "easy" values, exceptions, exact cases. Currently not IEEE-1788 compliant.

2. **JInterval** [12,18]: Java library providing preliminary standard IEEE P1788 compliant exact implementation of interval arithmetic operations and controllable arbitrary precision for elementary functions. Use the set of rational numbers extended by $-\infty$ and $+\infty$ as a basic number type for intervals endpoints. On top of this implementation, tightest approximations of interval arithmetic and elementary functions are supported for float types `binary16`, `binary32`, `binary64`, `binary128`, etc.

3. **libieeep1788** [20,21]: C++ implementation of the preliminary IEEE P1788 standard. Relies on MPFR. Unit tests for IEEE-1788 compliance.

4. **Octave interval package** [3,22]: GNU Octave interval arithmetic package compliant with the standard. Test sets derived from `libieeep1788`, `MPFI`, `C-XSC`, `FILIB` plus several new tests for most of the standard functions. These tests constitute the current ITF1788 testsuite. Relies on MPFR for both arithmetic operations and elementary functions.

5. **ValidatedNumerics.jl** [4,23]: Julia set of packages for interval arithmetic and applications. Currently not conformant with the standard. By default, direct rounding is handled via the software emulator RoundingEmulator.jl. However, it also supports changing rounding modes. Correctly rounded elementary functions are computed via CRlibm when possible, and using MPFR as fallback. For `Binary64` bounds, uses the ITF1788 testsuite. Also has hardcoded tests for other non-standard functionalities (complex intervals, interval boxes, other number formats)

6. **GAOL** [24]: C++ library not compliant with the standard, e.g. lacks decorated intervals. Tight bounds on arithmetic operations using round upwards mode only. Supports CRlibm and IBM Accurate Portable Mathematical Library for elementary functions computations. Uses its own unit tests.

4 Existing Frameworks

4.1 Why They Are Needed?

As a motivating example, consider Kuliamin's paper [25] about testing floating-point mathematical functions. The paper defines several criteria for devising tests, such as considering exceptional cases (overflow, underflow, NaN), inputs out of domain, special values (signed zero, subnormal numbers) etc.

However, this leads to more than 15,000 values to test for the exponential function alone. When interval arithmetic is tested, this means that each endpoint must take 15,000 values: the combinatorics (even if one restricts the tests to proper intervals, where the left endpoint is not greater than the right endpoint) are discouraging if one plans to develop individually, manually, such intensive tests for each new library.

A natural way to increase effectiveness of individual libraries developers is to unite their efforts in order to accumulate tests in a properly structured common shared database of tests equipped by appropriate tools for tests usage. That is why the frameworks briefly described in the next two subsections are worth our attention.

4.2   JInterval P1788 Test Launcher

P1788 Test Launcher [12,19] is an interval arithmetic libraries testing application based on the JInterval library. The features of JInterval entail a freedom for P1788 Test Launcher in the selection of computation modes corresponding to a tested library.

P1788 Test Launcher loads dynamic libraries (.so/.dll) with third party implementation of P1788 and checks the results obtained from a library with the tightest results computed internally using JInterval. Operations and functions from a tested library are called through the unified adaptor wrapper interface which must be preliminary implemented for the library being checked. The structure of the wrapper interface is adapted from C++ templates of the libieeep1788 library. So, technically, the implementation of the interface in most of cases boils down to overloading methods of libieeep1788 classes describing set-based flavor of interval arithmetic for Binary64 value set as a rule. Wrappers for the following interval arithmetic libraries are already included in P1788 Test Launcher: Profil/BIAS, boost/interval, C-XSC, FILIB, libieeep1788, libMoore, MPFI.

The launcher reads tests from plain text files of simple human-readable format and writes the results computed using the tested library and JInterval and their relation into a plain text report. Test set included in the Launcher consists of over 14,000 tests which partly originated from libieeep1788, FILIB, libMoore while the others are original.

4.3   ITF1788 – Interval Test Framework for IEEE 1788

The idea behind ITF1788 is to simplify the development of unit tests for an interval arithmetic library independently of the programming language it is written in, the testing framework used and library peculiarities, such as custom function names. ITF1788 is a Python engine for converting pre-calculated tests from domain specific language, called the Interval Test Language (ITL), to the code of unit tests according to the configuration describing the syntax of the language, the testing framework and the interval library.

The notation of ITL is easy to read and write and covers all notions of IEEE-1788 necessary to test an implementation. The following small example of test description from [26] gives a general understanding of ITL composition.

```
/* Testing the addition function */
testcase addition.test {
    add [ -1.0, 1.0 ] [ empty ] = [ empty ];
    add [ 1.0, 2.0 ] [ 3.0, infinity ] = [ 4.0, infinity ];
    add [ 1.0, infinity ] [ -infinity, 4.0 ] = [ entire ];
    // using hexadecimal notation
    add [ 0X1.FFFFFFFFFFFFP+0 ] [ 0X1.999999999999AP-4 ] =
        [ 0X1.0CCCCCCCCCCC4P+1, 0X1.0CCCCCCCCCCC5P+1 ];
}
```

```
/* Testing the division function */
testcase division.test {
    div [ empty ] [ empty ] = [ empty ];
    div [ -30.0, 15.0 ] [ entire ] = [ entire ];
}
```

ITF1788 inputs ITL-files and converts tests to the code of unit tests for specified language, test framework and library.

One can easily customize ITF1788 to support new programming languages, test frameworks and library specific features. The developer simply has to prepare several YAML configuration files. Additional flexibility can be obtained using implementation of Python callback functions for proper modifications of ITF1788 output.

Original ITF1788 engine and accompanying test sets for IEEE-1788 compliance testing have been developed by M. Kiesner, M. Nehmeier and J. Wolff von Gudenberg [26]. Later O. Heimlich contributed a lot to the original project and to its own fork of ITF1788 [27]. The latter now contains:

- configurations for programming languages C++, Octave, Julia, Python;
- configurations for test frameworks Boost Test Library, test frameworks for Octave, Julia and Python;
- plugins for libraries:
  - libieeep1788, C-XSC, GAOL, Ibex (in C/C++);
  - interval package, INTLAB toolbox (in GNU Octave);
  - pyIbex (in Python);
  - ValidatedNumerics (in Julia).
- almost 10,000 tests in ITL.

Most of the tests accumulated in ITF1788 are derived from unit tests of C-XSC, FILIB, MPFI, libieeep1788.

5   What Is Missing? A Roadmap for Testing

A first important requirement, which is perhaps too obvious but still worth mentioning, is that a standard framework for tests must be open. It should also be portable across architectures and languages, and be properly documented. The ITF1788 test suite has developed an interesting approach to solve these particular issues. This is achieved by introducing a domain specific language for storing the unit tests, and allowing the user to pass the syntactic information necessary of the language through the configuration of some files [26].

The unit tests of the ITF1788 suite cover numerous cases, including some cornercases, allow modularity and allow to test the tightness (equality assertion) or correctness (asserting containment). Both of these aspects are desirable and should be included with certain redundancy. For instance, to avoid that an implementation of sin trivially returns $[-1, 1]$ and passes all containment assertions, tests that involve the radius of the returned interval (to be less than two) can be introduced that break the trivial implementation.

Yet, the unit tests of the ITF1788 suite are restricted to the `binary64` floating point format. In our view, it is desirable to have the unit test coverage enlarged to include unit tests for quadruple and extended precision, including different precision values (e.g., $256, 512, 1024$). Similarly, concrete tests should be included for other IEEE754 numeric formats, such as `binary32`.

Other unit tests should choose randomly (floating-point) values $x \in \mathbf{x}$ and evaluate that the inclusion $f([x, x]) \subseteq f(\mathbf{x})$ holds true. While these tests are certainly redundant, in particular if the implementation is correct, they serve to check values not explicitly covered in previous tests, in particular worst-case accuracy. Such tests may be particularly interesting during the early stages of development, considering specially the power function and the transcendental functions, in particular for extended precision intervals.

In other communities, also a priori interested in reliable computations, "friendly competitions" are organized, to compare what each tool offers: methods, limitations, new aspects, etc. The code of the tools must be publicly available, and the benchmarks must be reproducible. See for instance https://cps-vo. org/group/ARCH/FriendlyCompetition. Organizing such a friendly competition would be a sane motivation for developers, to update and increase the depth of unit tests.

6   Conclusions

This paper focused on testing strategies for interval arithmetic libraries. During the years, different libraries have adopted different design choices and as such comparison and reproducibility has been a challenge. The IEEE 1788–2015 standardization is a big step to solve this issue, but broad adoption of the standard is a slow process. Moreover, testing is critical in software development and, due to its rigorous nature, even more central in interval arithmetic. It is thus fundamental to have an extensive unified testing framework. In this work, we sketched a possible structure for such framework. Hopefully, developers of interval libraries will join forces and share experience to develop an extensive open-source cross platform testing framework.

References

1. Hofschuster, W., Krämer, W.: C-XSC 2.0 - A C++ Library for Extended Scientific Computing. In: Alt, R., Frommer, A., Kearfott, R.B., Luther, W. (eds) NUMERICAL SOFTWARE WITH RESULT VERIFICATION, LNCS, vol. 2991, pp. 15–35. Springer, Berlin, Heidelberg (2004). https://doi.org/10.1007/978-3-540-24738-8_2
2. Lerch, M., Tischler, G., Wolff von Gudenberg, J., Hofschuster, W., Krämer, W.: FILIB++, a Fast Interval Library Supporting Containment Computations. ACM TOMS **32**(2), 299–324 (2006). http://www.xsc/de

3. Heimlich, O.: Interval arithmetic in GNU Octave. In: SWIM 2016, 9th Summer Workshop on Interval Methods. ENS de Lyon, France (2016)
4. Sanders, D.P., Benet, L., Ferranti, L., et al.: ValidatedNumerics.jl. https://github.com/JuliaIntervals/ValidatedNumerics.jl
5. Mascarenhas, W.F.: Moore: Interval arithmetic in modern C++ (2016) arXiv preprint arXiv:1611.09567
6. Revol, N.: Standardized interval arithmetic and interval arithmetic used in libraries. In: Fukuda, K., Hoeven, J.V.D., Joswig, M., Takayama, N. (eds.) ICMS 2010. LNCS, vol. 6327, pp. 337–341. Springer, Heidelberg (2010). https://doi.org/10.1007/978-3-642-15582-6_54
7. IEEE: Institute of Electrical and Electronic Engineers: 1788–2015 IEEE Standard for Interval Arithmetic. In: IEEE STD 1788–2015, 1–97 (2015)
8. Beebe, N.: IEEE 754 floating-point test software. https://www.math.utah.edu/~beebe/software/ieee/
9. Rump, S.M.: INTLAB - INTerval LABoratory. In: Developments in Reliable Computing, Tibor Csendes (eds), pp. 77–104. Kluwer Academic Publishers (1999)
10. Goualard, F.: How do you compute the midpoint of an interval? ACM TOMS **40**(2), 1–25 (2014)
11. MPRIA: GNU Multi-Precision Rational Interval Arithmetic Library https://www.gnu.org/software/mpria/manual/
12. Nadezhin, D.Y., Zhilin, S.I.: JInterval library: Principles, development, and perspectives. Reliable Comput. **19**(3), 229–247 (2013)
13. Revol, N., Rouillier, F.: Motivations for an arbitrary precision interval arithmetic and the MPFI library. Reliable Comput. **11**(4), 275–290 (2005). https://doi.org/10.1007/s11155-005-6891-y
14. Johansson, F.: Arb: a C library for ball arithmetic. ACM Commun. Comput. Algebra **47**(4), 166–169 (2013)
15. Lerch, M., Tischler, G., Wolff von Gudenberg, J., Hofschuster, W., Krämer, W.: The Interval Library FILIB++ 2.0 - Design, Features and Sample Programs. Preprint 2001/4, Universität Wuppertal (2001)
16. FILIB++ Interval Library http://www2.math.uni-wuppertal.de/wrswt/software/filib.html
17. Boost Interval Arithmetic Library v. 1.79.0 https://www.boost.org/doc/libs/1_79_0/libs/numeric/interval/doc/interval.htm
18. JInterval Library https://github.com/jinterval/jinterval/
19. P1788 Test Launcher (based on JInterval Library) https://github.com/jinterval/jinterval/tree/master/p1788-launcher-java
20. Nehmeier, M.: libieeep1788: a C++ implementation of the IEEE interval standard P1788. In: 2014 IEEE Conference on Norbert Wiener in the 21st Century (21CW), pp. 1–6. IEEE, Massachusetts, USA (2014) https://doi.org/10.1109/NORBERT.2014.6893854
21. libieeep1788 https://github.com/nehmeier/libieeep1788
22. Heimlich, O.: GNU Octave interval package https://octave.sourceforge.io/interval/index.html https://sourceforge.net/p/octave/interval/ci/default/tree/
23. Sanders, D.P., Benet, L., Ferranti, L., et al.: JuliaIntervals/IntervalArithmetic.jl: v0.20.5. Zenodo. https://doi.org/10.5281/zenodo.6337817
24. Goualard, F.: Goal: not just another interval library (2005) https://sourceforge.net/projects/goal/
25. Kuliamin, V.V.: Standardization and testing of implementations of mathematical functions in floating point numbers. Prog. Comput. Softw. **33**(3), 154–173 (2007)

26. Kiesner, M., Nehmeier, M., Wolff von Gudenberg, J.: ITF1788: An Interval Test-framework for IEEE 1788. Report number 495, Department of Computer Science, University of Würzburg (2015) https://www.researchgate.net/publication/278620157_ITF1788_An_Interval_Testframework_for_IEEE_1788
27. ITF1788 - Interval Test Framework for IEEE STD 1788–2015 https://github.com/oheim/ITF1788

A Survey of Interval Algorithms for Solving Multicriteria Analysis Problems

Bartłomiej Jacek Kubica$^{(\boxtimes)}$ (iD)

Institute of Information Technology, Warsaw University of Life Sciences – SGGW,
ul. Nowoursynowska 159, 02-776 Warsaw, Poland
bartlomiej_kubica@sggw.edu.pl

Abstract. This paper surveys the research effort of several authors to solve various multicriteria problems, using interval methods. These efforts fall naturally into two categories: approximating the whole Pareto sets and seeking a single solution point optimal with respect to the preferences of a specific decision maker. In both kinds of problems, the interval calculus turns out to be useful. For several of the outlined approaches, their assumptions and practical importance is discussed. Parallelization (potential or actual) of the methods is also investigated. In particular, the discussion on parallelization of the algorithm of Fernandez and Toth seems to be an original contribution of this paper, as well, as an analysis of applicability of various interval goal programming and TOPSIS approaches.

Keywords: multiple criteria analysis · interval computations · Pareto sets · goal programming · TOPSIS

1 Introduction

Problems of multicriteria decision making are ubiquitous in several branches of engineering and economical sciences. Several methods have been developed for treating such decision problems [4], and we can be interested in finding various kinds of solution(s).

2 Basic Notions

We are interested in solving the following problem:

$$\max_{x} q_k(x) \qquad k = 1, \ldots, N , \tag{1}$$

s.t.

$$g_j(x) \leq 0 \qquad j = 1, \ldots, m ,$$
$$x_i \in [\underline{x}_i, \overline{x}_i] \qquad i = 1, \ldots, n .$$

We assume all criteria to be maximized. In general, we have three kinds of criteria:

© The Author(s), under exclusive license to Springer Nature Switzerland AG 2023
R. Wyrzykowski et al. (Eds.): PPAM 2022, LNCS 13827, pp. 441–456, 2023.
https://doi.org/10.1007/978-3-031-30445-3_37

- maximized ones, as in the above example: we want the value to be as large as possible;
- minimized ones: we want the value to be as small as possible;
- stabilized ones: there is an optimal value, and we want the actual value to deviate from it, as little as possible.

Obviously, assuming all criteria to be maximized does not reduce the generality of our considerations – all problems can be transformed to such form. Instead of using a minimized criterion 'min q', we can set 'max$(-q)$', and instead of a stabilized criterion, we can set 'max$(-||q - q^0||)$', where q^0 is the desired value of the criterion.

The solution of Problem (1) can be defined in a few manners. By aggregating all criteria, using some scalarization function, we can reduce the problem to unicriterion optimization (cf. Subsect. 3.2). But in several cases, we are interested in so-called Pareto-optimal solutions.

Definition 1. *A feasible point x is* Pareto-optimal *(non-dominated), if there exists no other feasible point x' such that:*

$$(\forall k) \quad q_k(x') \geq q_k(x) \text{ and } (\exists i) \quad q_i(x') > q_i(x) .$$

Now, by solving Problem (1) we can mean finding two sets. First, the *Pareto-optimal set*, i.e., the set of Pareto-optimal points, i.e., feasible points that are non-dominated according to criteria. Second, the *Pareto frontier*, i.e., the set of N-tuples of criteria values for Pareto-optimal points. For convenience, in the following text, we shall call them together Pareto sets.

In the remainder, one more definition will be needed.

Definition 2. *A point y dominates a set B, iff $D(y) \cap B = \emptyset$, and similarly a set B' dominates a set B, iff $(\forall y \in B')D(y) \cap B = \emptyset$, where the cone $D(y_1, \ldots, y_N) = \{(y'_1, \ldots, y'_N) \mid (\forall k)y'_k \geq y_k \text{ and } (\exists i)y'_i > y_i\}$.*

The interpretation of the definitions is straightforward. A feasible point is Pareto-optimal if there is no other feasible point that would improve some criterion without causing a simultaneous worsening in at least one other criterion. Pareto-front is the image of Pareto-set in criterion space and D is the cone of domination in this space.

3 Classical (i.e., Non-interval Methods)

Before we shall present interval methods for solving Problem (1), let us briefly recall the classical methods.

3.1 Pareto-Sets Approximation

In many applications, it is sufficient to find a single solution point, but obtaining the whole Pareto frontier (and its corresponding Pareto set) can be very useful, as well. Not only for cognitive reasons, but also for practical ones: it is just convenient to choose an appropriate solution point, when having all non-dominated solutions presented.

The majority of the classical methods are actually not appropriate to approximate a set. They are usually better at dealing with a single solution than with a set of solutions. When there is more than one solution (especially, when the solution set is uncountable), the problem is usually considered to be *ill-posed*.

The most prominent (and pretty successful) algorithms designed to deal with this sort of problems are based on *population methods*, in particular on genetic and evolutionary algorithms. Specific algorithms that have been designed are: SPEA (Strength Pareto Evolutionary Algorithm), SPEA2, NSGA (Nondominated Sorting Genetic Algorithm), NSGA-II, etc.; see, e.g., [5,42] and the references therein.

3.2   Decision Making

Nevertheless, for several applications, the decision maker is interested in finding just a single point – the one that is either 'optimal', or at least 'sufficient', corresponding to their preferences. But how to measure the 'optimality' in the case of several, possibly non-homogeneous, criteria?

There are a few approaches to obtain it. Most of them involve some form of *scalarization function*: $q(x) = f(q_1(x), \ldots, q_N(x))$, where q_i's are the criteria. But what should the formula for q be like?

Linear scalarization function. The simplest scalarization function is, obviously, a linear one: $q(x) = w_1 q_1(x) + \ldots + w_N q_N(x) = \sum_{i=1}^{N} w_i \cdot q_i(x)$, where w_i is the weight of the i-th criterion, for $i = 1, \ldots, N$.

While this approach might seem simple, elegant and straightforward, there is a serious issue with it: there are nondominated points that will never maximize $q(x)$, regardless of the choice of w_i's. Other words: some solutions that may be desired by rational decision-makers can never be chosen using a linear scalarization function. To be more precise: this approach tends to favor extreme solutions. Let us explain it on a specific example.

Example 1. Let us consider a problem with two maximized criteria presented on Fig. 1.

There are three possibilities:

1. The weight of criterion 1 is higher than this of criterion 2. In this case, the point to maximize the scalarization function is $(y_1 = 8, y_2 = 0)$.
2. The weight of criterion 1 is lower than this of criterion 2. In this case, the point to maximize the scalarization function is $(y_1 = 0, y_2 = 8)$.
3. The weights of both criteria are equal. In this case, both points $(y_1 = 8, y_2 = 0)$ and $(y_1 = 0, y_2 = 8)$ maximize the scalarization function.

In any case, none of the other solutions: $(1, 6)$, $(3, 3)$, or $(6, 1)$ can be as good as the two extreme solutions, although all five points are Pareto-optimal!

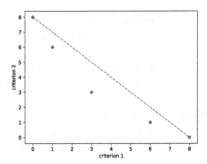

Fig. 1. The paradox of linear scalarization function.

This problem has been first described by Pekka Korhonen, but according to [40], it has not been published in a paper, but 'only in diverse discussions'. This *Korhonnen's paradox* causes a very limited usefulness of linear scalarization functions, unless some auxiliary tools are used, e.g., to convexify the solution set. Obliviousness about this issue can lead to taking wrong decisions. The book of Wierzbicki and Nakamori [40] gives an interesting example in Subsect. 12.6.1.

A possible fix is using nonlinear scalarization functions; e.g., polynomial ones. But such an approach would be hard both to parameterize and to justify. Also, such scalarization functions may be unstable with respect to their arguments and parameters.

Another approach was needed.

Goal programming. An alternative to using linear (or non-linear) scalarization functions has been proposed by the theory of so-called *satisficing decision*, credited to Herbert Simon. The word 'satisficing' is a neologism, combining the words 'satisfying' and 'sufficient'. This approach states that a decision maker does *not* want to take an *optimal* decision, but a *sufficiently good* decision. Hence, instead of trying to maximize or minimize the criteria, we choose some 'aspiration levels' for them, and we try to find the solution that is either at least as good (according to all criteria), or as close as possible to satisfying the 'aspirations'.

The discussion of the origin and importance of the concept of 'satisficing decision making' (for which Simon received the Nobel Prize in Economics, in 1978) is far beyond the scope of this survey. Let us focus on the algorithms that can be used to find such decisions.

Ironically, the search for *satisficing* decision points can be performed using optimization. This is done by so-called *goal programming*, credited to Charles and Cooper (again, many references could be done here; cf. [40]). The essence of *goal programming* is to choose a single goal: a point in the decision space, that the decision maker considers 'satisficing'. Having this point, we choose the solution by minimizing the distance from the 'goal' point.

Please note, this is equivalent to using the scalarization function:

$$q(x) = -||q(x) - q^{goal}|| \, , \tag{2}$$

where $q^{goal} = (q_1^{goal}, \ldots, q_N^{goal})$ is obviously the aspiration point, and the minus sign before the expression is used, as we decided to perform maximization.

We can use various distance measures (e.g., norms L1, L2, L∞, etc.). For instance, for the L1 norm, (2) takes the form:

$$q(x) = -\sum_{i=1}^{N} |q_i(x) - q_i^{goal}| , \tag{3}$$

It is worth noting that when $q(\cdot)$ is linear and the L1 norm is used, the problem remains linear; we shall get back to this topic in Paragraph 'Multiobjective linear programming'. The method might seem ambiguous, because various norms can be chosen, but the choice of distance measure has usually a minor importance for the result. A more serious issue with goal programming is that it can choose a dominated point as the most desired solution. In fact, the decision maker can choose an arbitrary goal, and if they do it obliviously of the actual geometry of the Pareto frontier, they can choose a point that is 'not good enough'. And the function (2) will be maximized in this very point, having smaller values for points that dominate it. A good survey of goal programming methods can be found in [17].

Utopia and nadir points. While choosing a goal allows selection of any nondominated point, setting weights to criteria may be more intuitive, or more comfortable to some decision makers. It is pretty simple to combine both approaches. For instance, (3) would be replaced by: $q(x) = -\sum_{i=1}^{N} w_i \cdot |q_i(x) - q_i^{goal}|$. Such a scalarization function is still not prone to the Korhonnen's paradox.

As we are choosing various weights for various criteria, the choice of the 'goal' becomes less significant. It is convenient to use the *ideal solution* (also called the *utopia* point) in this place. This is the point in the criteria space, almost always having no counterpart in the decision space, where all criteria have optimal values, i.e., values that they achieve when optimizing the given single criterion, ignoring the others.

For the example on Fig. 1, the 'ideal solution' would be the point $(8, 8)$, where both criteria have maximal values.

A great popularity has been achieved by the so-called TOPSIS method (Technique for Order of Preference by Similarity to Ideal Solutions), using both positive and negative ideal solutions.

The *negative ideal solution*, also called the *anti-ideal solution*, is obviously the opposite of the utopia point: the point with worst possible values of all criteria. Such a point can also be called the *nadir* point; on Fig. 1. the point $(0, 0)$ can be considered to be the nadir.

Why the phrase 'can be considered' was used in the previous sentence? Actually, the definition(s) of nadir and negative ideal solution are less obvious than in the case of the utopia point. Some authors (e.g., [17]) distinguish these two notions: nadir is considered only among the values from the Pareto frontier, while the negative ideal – from the whole achievable set. However, we shall not distinguish these notions in this paper.

Nevertheless, it is worth noting that precisely estimating the nadir point, especially for nonlinear problems, may be much more difficult, than estimating the utopia point.

TOPSIS. Let us describe the algorithm of the aforementioned TOPSIS method, first described in [12].

Usually, it is assumed that we have a finite number of alternatives. Let them be stored in the matrix $Y = [Y_{ij}]$, where $i = 1, \ldots, m$ is the number of alternative, and $j = 1, \ldots, N$ is the number of criterion (following the interval notation from [20], matrix elements are denoted as capital letters).

The first step of the TOPSIS method is the normalization of all criteria values:

$$R_{ij} = \frac{Y_{ij}}{\sqrt{\sum_{k=1}^{m} Y_{kj}^2}} . \tag{4}$$

Using the weights, it is transformed to the weighted normalized decision matrix: $V_{ij} = R_{ij} \cdot w_j$, for $i = 1, \ldots, m$, and $j = 1, \ldots, N$. Then we choose the 'ideal solutions'. Assuming all criteria are maximized, the positive ideal solution is: $V_j^+ = \max_i V_{ij}$, and the negative ideal solution (or anti-ideal solution) is: $V_j^- = \min_i V_{ij}$. Obviously, we could also separate the criteria into subsets of maximized and minimized ones (and such a formulation is used, e.g., in [14,38]); we omit this for simplicity, as because stabilized criteria would be hard to fit in such a schema. Now, having both 'ideal' solutions, we can compute the separation measure from it, for each of the alternatives:

$$d_i^+ = ||V_{i:} - V^+|| \, , d_i^- = ||V_{i:} - V^-|| \, .$$

All papers known to the author use the L2 norm in the above equations, but other norms would be feasible, as well.

Having the separation measures from both ideal solutions, we can aggregate them into the *relative closeness to the ideal solution* measure (in [8] called the 'separation index'): $c_i = \frac{d_i^-}{d_i^+ + d_i^-}$, for each solution. Obviously, $c_i \in [0, 1]$, and we choose the alternative i with c_i as close to 1, as possible (d_i^- as large as possible; d_i^+ as small as possible).

Multiple criteria linear programming. Solving multiobjective linear programming (MOLP) problems is of particular importance, and much effort has been made in this area; see, e.g., the textbooks [29,41]. In particular, a multiobjective version of the simplex method has been developed, and also other methods (Benson's algorithm [2]). Section 2.4 of [32] describes, how nadir points can be estimated for linear problems (which is, in general, not possible in the nonlinear case).

4   Interval Algorithms

Interval calculus is a branch of numerical analysis and mathematics that operates on intervals rather than numbers. It has been described in numerous textbooks, including, in particular, [10,15,19,28,33,39], or a most recent one [21]. Arithmetic (and other) operations on intervals are designed, so that the following condition was fulfilled:

$$\odot \in \{+, -, \cdot, /\}, \ a \in \mathbf{a}, \ b \in \mathbf{b} \ \text{ implies } \ a \odot b \in \mathbf{a} \odot \mathbf{b} \ . \tag{5}$$

In other words, the result of an operation on numbers will be contained in the result of an analogous operation on intervals, containing these numbers. The size of this paper does not allow to present the details, but this seems unnecessary due to the aforementioned wide literature. Interval methods appear to be a proper tool for various approaches to multicriteria optimization.

4.1 Pareto-Sets Approximation

As we have already stated, computing the Pareto sets (or even approximating them precisely enough) is a hard task (although computable, as proven by Toth and Kreinovich in [7]), especially for nonlinear problems; moreover classical algorithms turned out to be not well-suited for this purpose.

Hence, interval methods are a useful tool to obtain such an approximation. They can be used in at least three manners:

– reducing the problem to repeated unicriterion global optimization;
– branch-and-bound type (B&BT) procedure performed in the decision space;
– branch-and-bound type procedure performed in the criteria space and resulting boxes inverted to the decision space.

Let us present them briefly.

Reducing to global optimization. Fernandez and Toth [6] present a sophisticated algorithm for a bicriteria problem. An inspiration for their approach was the ε-constraint method, presented by Miettinen [32].

Suppose we are solving the following problem:

$$\max_{x}\{f_1(x), f_2(x)\} \ ,$$
$$\text{s.t.}$$
$$x \in X \ .$$

In [6], minimization is considered, but we change it to maximization to remain consistent with other examples.

In this approach, one of the criteria is treated as the objective and the other as a constraint. A sequence of constrained optimization problems is then solved.

Precisely, in each step we are seeking the set of δ-optimal points of the following problems:

$$\max_{x} f_1(x) \ , \tag{6}$$
$$\text{s.t.}$$
$$f_2(x) \geq f_2^{(i)} \ ,$$
$$f_1(x) \leq f_1(\check{x}^{(i)}) + \delta \cdot |f_1(\check{x}^{(i)})| \ ,$$
$$x \in X \ ,$$

where δ is a parameter of the method (δ = 0.01 was used in the numerical experiments of [6]).

In the above problem, $\check{x}^{(i)}$ is the optimal solution of (6) for the previous value of i, and $f_2^{(i)}$ – the lower bound on $f_2(x)$ over the set of δ-optimal points).

Obviously, the search starts with $f_2^{(0)} = -\infty$, and the first optimization problem boils down to:

$$\max_{x \in X} f_1(x) \ . \tag{7}$$

Thanks to reducing the problem to global optimization, tools analogous to typical global optimization problems can be used. As much information as possible is extracted from the solution of each problem of type (6); in particular, boxes that cannot contain solutions of further optimization problems get discarded, not to be considered in subsequent algorithm's stages. Obviously, the process stops when all boxes get discarded. All details can be found in [6].

The branch-and-bound type search in decision space of the problem. This approach, most similar to algorithms currently used in global optimization or equations solving, was presented in the paper of Ruetsch [36]. While processing the boxes he uses two kinds of tests to discard them:

– comparing the bounds on criteria values in boxes, to delete dominated ones,
– a 'differential approach' – some procedure using the information about gradients, probably equivalent (or almost equivalent) to the 'multicriteria variant of the monotonicity test', introduced by Kubica and Woźniak [23].

Unfortunately, paper [36] lacks important information, useful to implement the algorithm. It does not describe, how are the boxes stored and chosen for comparisons? In particular, is linear search necessary? Also, it gives no details on the 'differential procedure'.

The branch-and-bound type search in criteria space of the problem. This approach was first presented by Barichard and Hao [1] and then in a series of papers of Kubica and Woźniak [23–27].

Barichard and Hao proposed an algorithm storing pairs of boxes – the box in the decision space and in the criteria space. They perform bisection in the criteria space and use constraint propagation to narrow the corresponding box in decision space. Also, some algorithm, called "substitution procedure" is used to find a feasible point in each box. Having feasibility of some points verified, boxes dominated by them can be discarded.

Paper [1] lacks several important details about the substitution and the constraint propagation procedures, which makes it difficult to implement it. Also, presented results lack information about computation time or number of iterations (criteria evaluations).

Kubica and Woźniak [22,25] proposed an algorithm similar in general assumptions, but different in significant details. Among others, boxes obtained from B&BT procedure are inverted to the decision space. This means that with each box **y** in the criteria space a set of boxes {**x**} in the decision space is associated, not a single box. This set is represented by three lists of boxes:

- boxes verified to lie in the interior of reverse image of **y**,
- boundary boxes of the reverse image of **y**,
- boxes yet to be checked.

To invert the boxes, a version of the SIVIA procedure [16] is used. In contrast to classical SIVIA, the procedure in Kubica and Woźniak's algorithm stops when the first interior box is found – even, if there are still unchecked boxes. This allows a relatively early approximation of the Pareto front, and consequently a possibility to discard dominated boxes in the criteria space.

After obtaining the desired accuracy (given by the parameter ε_y) of the Pareto front approximation, we enter the "second phase" in which all boxes from the decision space, yet unchecked (because SIVIA was stopped), are investigated until a desired accuracy ε_x is obtained. This second phase does not allow discarding boxes from the criteria space or affect the approximation of the Pareto front.

4.2 Tools

Tools that can be applied in all three algorithms to compute Pareto sets are (at least to some extent) distinct in all cases. In particular, a multicriterion analog of the monotonicity test has been introduced in [23]. As Goldsztejn et al. pointed in [9], the formulation in [23] is not completely correct; an improved version is presented in their paper. Details of using the interval Newton operator have been discussed in [22]. Hence, the 2nd-order Pareto-optimality conditions (analogous to Fritz John conditions) have been proposed in [26] and specialized heuristics for bisection [27]. Martin et al. [31] consider advanced use of constraint propagation techniques. Also the PhD thesis of Martin [30] describes several other tools.

Parallelization. An important topic is the potential for parallel implementation of the described algorithms. Indeed, as pointed by the author in the book [21], interval branch-and-bound-type algorithms are natural candidates for parallel implementation. Let us quote directly what was written in this book: 'Both phases of a B&BT algorithm parallelize well, as different boxes can be processed independently. Yet, they are (in general) *not* 'embarrassingly parallel' – for both basic kinds of parallel implementation (shared or distributed memory) some problems have to be addressed'.

As for the algorithms for Pareto sets approximation, the first known multithreaded implementation seems to have been presented by the author in [24]. Further development of our algorithms has been presented in the subsequent papers: [25–27].

A distributed memory implementation for a cluster or cloud environment does not seem to ever have been considered, although such an implementation would be more laborious to implement than a multithreaded one. All details can be found in a thorough discussion of parallelizing interval branch-and-bound-type algorithms in Chap. 7 of [21].

Finally, it is worth mentioning that authors other than Kubica and Woźniak do not seem to use parallelization in their implementations.

The algorithm of Fernandez and Toth. The author would like to pay a particular attention to the algorithm presented by Fernandez and Toth [6]. Seemingly this algorithm is harder to parallelize than typical branch-and-bound-type algorithms: it performs several steps, each including a branch-and-bound procedure, but the steps are sequential.

How to parallelize such a procedure?

Firstly, each step can be parallelized, using the aforementioned techniques of parallelizing branch-and-bound type methods. This is however not the only possibility.

Please note that in each step i of this algorithm, we consider only boxes generated by the previous step, and the new value of $f_2^{(i)}$ can only be better (higher, in the case of maximization), than the previous one. Hence, we can implement this algorithm as a *pipeline*, where two or more steps will get executed concurrently, with boxes passed between them. Such an implementation is another interesting area of possible further research.

4.3   Decision Making

When we are interested in locating a single solution, most desired by a specific decision maker, interval methods can be very useful, as well.

MOLP with interval coefficients. As in the case of non-interval algorithms, linear problems are of particular interest; also specific theoretical results have been obtained for multicriteria linear problems.

There are several kinds of interval MOLP problems, as the uncertainty can be encountered in various places:

– coefficients in the objective function can be interval-valued:
  $q(x) = \sum_{i=1}^{n} \mathbf{c}_i \cdot x_i,$
– parameters of the constraints can be interval-valued: $\mathbf{A} \cdot x \gtreqless \mathbf{b}.$

The paper of Oliveira and Antunes [34] gives a nice survey of various approaches.

The first kind of uncertainty turns out to be particularly important. In his influential paper from 1980, Bitran [3] observed that we can distinguish 'necessary' and 'possible' non-dominated points. *Necessarily non-dominated* points are Pareto-optimal for all values of the coefficients $c \in \mathbf{c}$, while *possibly non-dominated* ones – for at least one of the values $c \in \mathbf{c}$.

Bitran emphasizes the importance of *necessarily efficient solutions*, and he proposes a 'branch-and-bound implicit enumeration algorithm' to enclose all such points.

Hladik introduces several improvements to the Bitran's approach, in particular proposing an enhanced sufficient condition for the point to being necessarily efficient, and analysing the complexity of the resulting problem [11].

All the above approaches consider optimization of all criteria. What about the *satisficing* approach? It is adopted by the version of goal programming, with an interval goal. Let us consider this approach in a separate paragraph.

Goal programming with an interval-valued reference 'point'. Interval goal programming turns out to be a quite popular research topic; see, for instance, the following papers: [13,35,37] and the references therein.

What is worth noting is that virtually all of these papers consider the linear case. The author is aware of very little, or even none at all, effort related to investigating nonlinear goal programming with interval-valued goals, and such investigations might be quite interesting.

As for linear problems, a few methods have been developed. In the non-interval case, we have been minimizing a norm (or maximizing its opposite number), as in Eq. (2). How to 'intervalize' this formula?

Inuiguchi and Kume [13] propose solving four problems that arise from two decisions:

- the subtraction between $q(x)$ and q^{goal} can be done either using classical interval subtraction ($[\underline{a}, \overline{a}] - [\underline{b}, \overline{b}] = [\underline{a} - \overline{b}, \overline{a} - \underline{b}]$) or using the Kaucher's [18] inner subtraction ($[\underline{a}, \overline{a}] \ominus [\underline{b}, \overline{b}] = [\underline{a} - \underline{b}, \overline{a} - \overline{b}]$); they call these operations the 'possible' and 'necessary' subtractions, respectively,
- we can minimize the lower or upper endpoint of the resulting interval-valued expression.

It is worth noting that other approaches are possible, as well: for instance, we could minimize some other metrics or quasi-metrics between the intervals $q(x)$ and q^{goal} (cf. Sect. 2.7 of [21], for a discussion of various metrics on the space of intervals). A compatible approach, but in a different context, was used in [27]. The author is not aware of any papers using this approach for goal programming.

Finally, it should be discussed, why one would use interval-valued goals? Most of the aforementioned papers do not address this question, and it seems pretty significant: can we not simply use the upper bound (for maximized criteria), or lower bound (for minimized ones), and transform interval-valued goals to precise ones?

Indeed, we can. Yet, it may be very convenient to specify goal values for stabilized criteria, in the form of a range. Hence, in the author's opinion, for problems with a large number of stabilized criteria, the interval-valued goal programming can be a very natural and intuitive approach.

TOPSIS method with interval-valued criteria. The TOPSIS method has found several versions with interval-valued criteria. We shall consider three of them: [8,14,38], but even the references of these papers provide links to many other ones.

Why so many variations of the interval TOPSIS approach have been developed? Because there are at least a few significant features that can be implemented in various ways.

Firstly, the normalization procedure. How to normalize a set of interval values? The paper [8] ignores the problem completely, while both [14,38] use the formula:

$$\mathbf{R}_{ij} = \frac{\mathbf{Y}_{ij}}{\sqrt{\sum_{k=1}^{m} (\underline{Y}_{kj}^2 + \overline{Y}_{kj}^2)}} . \tag{8}$$

Such a normalization is pretty controversial. Please note that in the case of all $\mathbf{Y}_{ij}$ values being degenerate, (8) does not reduce to the non-interval case of (4). What is more, values of the 'normalized' intervals can never reach 1; the maximal possible value is close to $\frac{\sqrt{2}}{2}$.

Another important question, when adapting TOPSIS to the interval case, is how should the ideal solutions be represented. Should they be precise points? Intervals? More general sets of values? Or maybe yet something else (e.g., [8] implements them as so-called fuzzy bags).

In the version of Jahanshahloo et al. [14], they are precisely known points: the optimal values of all intervals. Sevastjanov et al. criticize this approach in [38]. According to them, the approach of Jahanshahloo et al. 'seems to be justified only in the case when there are no any intersections of these intervals' (criteria).

As an example, they consider the situation, when $\mathbf{Y}_{11} = [5,7]$, and $\mathbf{Y}_{21} = [0,10]$. We can ignore normalization, as it just divides both of these intervals by the same quantity. Also, assume equal weights for all criteria, and $\mathbf{V} = \mathbf{Y}$.

So, according to the methodology of Jahanshahloo et al., the positive ideal solution would be $V_1^+ = 10$, and the negative ideal solution $V_1^- = 0$. Sevastjanov et al. claim that this is 'wrong', and the components of ideal solutions should be the proper components of the matrix $\mathbf{V}$, as it is in the non-interval case. Hence, in their opinion, we should have $\mathbf{V}_1^+ = \mathbf{V}_{11} = [5,7]$, and $\mathbf{V}_1^- = \mathbf{V}_{21} = [0,10]$, because mid $\mathbf{V}_{11} >$ mid $\mathbf{V}_{21}$.

In the author's opinion, both approaches seem rather arbitrary. When we consider all possible multicriteria problems arising from choosing $V_{11} \in \mathbf{V}_{11}$ and $V_{21} \in \mathbf{V}_{21}$, we would see that V_1^+ can be far from the value 10 (e.g., for $V_{11} = V_{21} = 5$, but it does not have to belong to the range $[5,7]$ (e.g., for $V_{11} = 5$ and $V_{21} = 10$. As for V_1^-, please note that it can never take any values exceeding 7, so the interval $[0,10]$ is definitely overestimated.

A reasonable approach seems to take the ideal solutions as intervals of all possible values; in the case of maximized criteria, this results in:

$$\mathbf{V}_i^+ = [\max_j \underline{V}_{ij}, \max_j \overline{V}_{ij}] , \mathbf{V}_i^- = [\min_j \underline{V}_{ij}, \min_j \overline{V}_{ij}] .$$

In the considered example, it would result in $\mathbf{V}_1^+ = [5,10]$, $\mathbf{V}_1^- = [0,7]$, which seems reasonable.

Yet another question is how the choice of these 'ideal solutions' will affect the final selection of an actual solution from the Pareto frontier. This might be hard to analyze in the general case. It seems, the approach of Jahanshahloo [14] tends to favor narrower intervals, while using interval-valued ideal solutions does not result in such a bias. On the other hand, it is difficult to judge whether such a bias would be an unwanted phenomenon.

This brings us to the next important point that has to be decided in the 'intervalization' of the TOPSIS method: how to measure the distance between solutions, i.e., between intervals or interval vectors. Various metrics can be used here, in particular [14] uses the Euclid distance (i.e., the one generated by the L2 norm), while [8, 38] use the Manhattan distance (L1 norm). In the author's opinion, using the L1 norm is superior to the Euclid distance: it is computationally less intensive, and equally good in describing the separation.

Finally, let us discuss the question why one would want to use interval solutions in the TOPSIS method. We have already raised a similar question for goal programming, but now the answer will be different. TOPSIS-like methods are not well suited for stabilized criteria (unless, of course, we transform them to some other ones – minimized or maximized), so using such criteria is a poor excuse for the interval TOPSIS approach. Nevertheless, approximating the negative ideal solution (aka nadir, aka anti-ideal) is often difficult, as we had already stated. Hence, interval methods may be very convenient to bound it.

Also, although TOPSIS methods are usually used for a finite number of alternatives, thanks to the virtues of the interval approach, we can extend them to the continuous case.

5 Conclusions

We have reviewed several versions of algorithms for solving multicriteria analysis problems. We have shown how interval algorithms can contribute to both approximating Pareto sets and decision making in the case of multiple conflicting criteria.

The performed survey has shown at least a few significant points where additional research would be very advisable. These include, in particular, interval goal programming for the nonlinear case.

It is also very desired to provide novel implementations of the described algorithms for approximating the Pareto sets (cf. Subsect. 4.1). Such implementations should use proficient techniques of modern programming languages and, in particular, advanced parallelization, and use comparable interval techniques for box processing. Such unified and up-to-date implementations would allow to perform efficiency tests of the three presented approaches.

References

1. Barichard, V., Hao, J.K.: Population and interval constraint propagation algorithm. Lect. Notes Comput. Sci. **2632**, 88–101 (2003)
2. Benson, H.P.: An outer approximation algorithm for generating all efficient extreme points in the outcome set of a multiple objective linear programming problem. J. Global Optim. **13**(1), 1–24 (1998)

3. Bitran, G.R.: Linear multiple objective problems with interval coefficients. Manage. Sci. **26**(7), 694–706 (1980)
4. Ceberio, M., Modave, F.: Interval-based multicriteria decision making. In: Bouchon-Meunier, B., Coletti, G., Yager, R.R. (eds.) Modern Information Processing, pp. 281–294. Elsevier Science, Amsterdam
5. Deb, K., Agrawal, S., Pratap, A., Meyarivan, T.: A fast elitist non-dominated sorting genetic algorithm for multi-objective optimization: NSGA-II. In: Schoenauer, M., et al. (eds.) PPSN 2000. LNCS, vol. 1917, pp. 849–858. Springer, Heidelberg (2000). https://doi.org/10.1007/3-540-45356-3_83
6. Fernandez, J., Toth, B.: Obtaining an outer approximation of the efficient set of nonlinear biobjective problems. J. Global Optim. **38**, 315–331 (2007)
7. G-Tóth, B., Kreinovich, V.: Verified methods for computing pareto sets: general algorithmic analysis. Int. J. Appl. Math. Comput. Sci. **19**(3), 369–380 (2009)
8. Giove, S.: Interval TOPSIS for multicriteria decision making. In: Proceedings of the 13th Italian Workshop on Neural Nets, Lecture Notes in Computer Science 2486, pp. 56–63 (2002)
9. Goldsztejn, A., Domes, F., Chevalier, B.: First order rejection tests for multiple-objective optimization. J. Global Optim. **58**(4), 653–672 (2014)
10. Hansen, E., Walster, W.: Global Optimization Using Interval Analysis. Marcel Dekker, New York (2004)
11. Hladík, M.: Complexity of necessary efficiency in interval linear programming and multiobjective linear programming. Optim. Lett. **6**(5), 893–899 (2012)
12. Hwang, C.L., Yoon, K.: Multiple attribute decision making: methods and applications. Springer-Verlag (1981)
13. Inuiguchi, M., Kume, Y.: Goal programming problems with interval coefficients and target intervals. Euro. J. Oper. Res. **52**(3), 345–360 (1991)
14. Jahanshahloo, G.R., Lotfi, F.H., Izadikhah, M.: An algorithmic method to extend TOPSIS for decision-making problems with interval data. Appl. Math. Comput. **175**(2), 1375–1384 (2006)
15. Jaulin, L., Kieffer, M., Didrit, O., Walter, É.: Applied Interval Analysis. Springer, London (2001). https://doi.org/10.1007/978-1-4471-0249-6
16. Jaulin, L., Walter, É.: Set inversion Via interval analysis for nonlinear bounded-error estimation. Automatica **29**(4), 1053–1064 (1993)
17. Jonez, D., Tamiz, M.: Practical Goal Programming, International Series in Operations Research & Management Science, vol. 141. Springer, New York (2010). https://doi.org/10.1007/978-1-4419-5771-9
18. Kaucher, E.: Interval analysis in the extended interval space $\mathbb{IR}$. In: Fundamentals of Numerical Computation (Computer-Oriented Numerical Analysis), pp. 33–49. Springer, Vienna (1980). https://doi.org/10.1007/978-3-7091-8577-3_3
19. Kearfott, R.B.: Rigorous Global Search: Continuous Problems. Kluwer, Dordrecht (1996)
20. Kearfott, R.B., Nakao, M.T., Neumaier, A., Rump, S.M., Shary, S.P., van Hentenryck, P.: Standardized notation in interval analysis. Vychislennyie Tiehnologii (Computational Technologies) **15**(1), 7–13 (2010)
21. Kubica, B.J.: Interval Methods for Solving Nonlinear Constraint Satisfaction, Optimization and Similar Problems. SCI, vol. 805. Springer, Cham (2019). https://doi.org/10.1007/978-3-030-13795-3
22. Kubica, B.J., Woźniak, A.: Interval componentwise Newton operator in computing the Pareto-front of constrained multicriterial problems. In: Proceedings of KKA 2008 Conference. EXIT (2008)

23. Kubica, B.J., Woźniak, A.: Interval methods for computing the Pareto-front of a multicriterial problem. In: Lecture Notes in Computer Science 4967, pp. 1382–1391 (2009). PPAM 2007 Proceedings
24. Kubica, B.J., Woźniak, A.: A multi-threaded interval algorithm for the Pareto-front computation in a multi-core environment. In: Lecture Notes in Computer Science 6126/6127 (2010). Accepted for publication. PARA 2008 Proceedings
25. Kubica, B.J., Woźniak, A.: Optimization of the multi-threaded interval algorithm for the Pareto-set computation. J. Telecommun. Inf. Technol. 1, 70–75 (2010)
26. Kubica, B.J., Woźniak, A.: Using the second-order information in pareto-set computations of a multi-criteria problem. In: Jónasson, K. (ed.) PARA 2010. LNCS, vol. 7134, pp. 137–147. Springer, Heidelberg (2012). https://doi.org/10.1007/978-3-642-28145-7_14
27. Kubica, B.J., Woźniak, A.: Tuning the interval algorithm for seeking pareto sets of multi-criteria problems. In: Manninen, P., Öster, P. (eds.) PARA 2012. LNCS, vol. 7782, pp. 504–517. Springer, Heidelberg (2013). https://doi.org/10.1007/978-3-642-36803-5_38
28. Kulisch, U.: Computer Arithmetic and Validity - Theory Implementation and Applications. De Gruyter, Berlin, New York (2008)
29. Luc, D.T.: Multiobjective Linear Programming. Springer, Cham (2016). https://doi.org/10.1007/978-3-319-21091-9
30. Martin, B.: Rigorous algorithms for nonlinear biobjective optimization. Ph.D. thesis, Université de Nantes (2014)
31. Martin, B., Goldsztejn, A., Granvilliers, L., Jermann, C.: Constraint propagation using dominance in interval branch & bound for nonlinear biobjective optimization. Euro. J. Oper. Res. 260(3), 934–948 (2017)
32. Miettinen, K.: Nonlinear Multiobjective Optimization, International Series in Operations Research & Management Science, vol. 12. Kluwer Academic Publishers, Dordrecht (1999)
33. Moore, R.E., Kearfott, R.B., Cloud, M.J.: Introduction to Interval Analysis. SIAM, Philadelphia (2009)
34. Oliveira, C., Antunes, C.H.: Multiple objective linear programming models with interval coefficients - an illustrated overview. Euro. J. Oper. Res. 181(3), 1434–1463 (2007)
35. Rivaz, S., Yaghoobi, M.A., Hladík, M.: Using modified maximum regret for finding a necessarily efficient solution in an interval MOLP problem. Fuzzy Optim. Decis. Making 15(3), 237–253 (2016)
36. Ruetsch, G.R.: An interval algorithm for multi-objective optimization. Struct. Multi. Optim. 30(1), 27–37 (2005)
37. Sen, S., Pal, B.B.: Interval goal programming approach to multiobjective fuzzy goal programming problem with interval weights. In: Procedia Technology, Proceedings of International Conference on Computational Intelligence: Modeling Techniques and Applications (CIMTA) 2013, vol. 10, pp. 587–595 (2013)
38. Sevastjanov, P., Tikhonenko, A.: Direct interval extension of TOPSIS method. In: Wyrzykowski, R., Dongarra, J., Karczewski, K., Waśniewski, J. (eds.) PPAM 2011. LNCS, vol. 7204, pp. 504–512. Springer, Heidelberg (2012). https://doi.org/10.1007/978-3-642-31500-8_52
39. Shary, S.P.: Finite-dimensional Interval Analysis. Institute of Computational Technologies, SB RAS, Novosibirsk (2013)
40. Wierzbicki, A.P., Nakamori, Y.: Creative Environments: issues of creativity support for the knowledge civilization age, vol. 59. Springer (2007). https://doi.org/10.1007/978-3-540-71562-7

41. Zeleny, M.: Linear multiobjective programming, Lecture Notes in Economics and Mathematical Systems, vol. 95. Springer Science & Business Media (2012). https://doi.org/10.1007/978-3-642-80808-1
42. Zitzler, E., Laumanns, M., Thiele, L.: SPEA2: Improving the strength Pareto evolutionary algorithm. TIK-report 103 (2001)

7th Workshop on Complex Collective Systems

Social Fragmentation Transitions in Large-Scale Parameter Sweep Simulations of Adaptive Social Networks

Hiroki Sayama[1,2]([✉]) [iD]

[1] Center for Collective Dynamics of Complex Systems, Binghamton University, State University of New York, Binghamton, NY 13902-6000, USA
[2] Waseda Innovation Lab, Waseda University, Shinjuku, Tokyo 169-8050, Japan
sayama@binghamton.edu

Abstract. Social fragmentation transition is a transition of social states between many disconnected communities with distinct opinions and a well-connected single network with homogeneous opinions. This is a timely research topic with high relevance to various current societal issues. We had previously studied this problem using numerical simulations of adaptive social network models and found that two individual behavioral traits, homophily and attention to novelty, had the most statistically significant impact on the outcomes of social network evolution. However, our previous study was limited in terms of the range of parameter values examined, and possible interactions between multiple behavioral traits were largely ignored. In this study, we conducted a substantially larger-scale parameter sweep numerical experiment of the same model with expanded parameter ranges by an order of magnitude in each parameter dimension, resulting in a total of 116,640 simulation runs. To capture nontrivial interactions among behavioral parameters, we modeled and visualized the dependence of outcome measures on the model parameters using artificial neural networks. Results show that, while the competition between homophily and attention to novelty is still the primary determinant of social fragmentation, another transition plane emerges when individuals have strong social conformity behavior, which was not previously known. This implies that social fragmentation transition can also occur in the homophily-social conformity trade-off, the two behavioral traits that have very similar microscopic individual-level effects but produce very different macroscopic collective-level outcomes, illustrating the nontrivial macroscopic dynamics of complex collective systems.

Keywords: adaptive social networks · social fragmentation · large-scale numerical simulations · homophily · attention to novelty · social conformity

---

This work was supported in part by JSPS KAKENHI Grant Number 19K21571.

1   Introduction

The study of temporal evolution of social structure is one of the significant application domains of complex collective systems research. In particular, social fragmentation transition, i.e., transition of social states between many disconnected communities with distinct opinions and a well-connected single network with homogeneous opinions, is a timely research topic with high relevance to various current societal issues [1–8]. We had previously studied this problem using numerical simulations of adaptive social network models [9] and found that two individual behavioral traits, homophily (i.e., tendency to strengthen connections to similar individuals and weaken those to dissimilar ones) [10–12] and attention to novelty (i.e., tendency to strengthen connections to individuals whose opinions stand out compared to others), had the most statistically significant impact on the outcomes of social network evolution [9]. Specifically, when homophily was strong, the social network evolved into fragmented states of many disconnected clusters with diverse opinions, but when attention to novelty was strong, the social network evolved to well-connected yet informationally homogeneous states. However, the previous study was rather limited in terms of the range of parameter values examined, and possible interactions between multiple behavioral traits were largely ignored, especially about the other behavioral trait, social conformity (i.e., how strongly individuals assimilate themselves to social neighbors).

In this study, we examined a broader spectrum of social network dynamics through a larger-scale parameter sweep experiment of the same model with expanded parameter ranges by an order of magnitude in each parameter dimension, resulting in a total of 116,640 simulation runs. To capture nontrivial interactions among behavioral parameters, we modeled and visualized the dependence of outcome measures on the model parameters using artificial neural networks. Results show that, while the competition between homophily and attention to novelty is still the primary determinant of social fragmentation when social conformity behavior of individuals is weak, another transition plane emerges at an intermediate homophily level when individuals have strong social conformity behavior, which was not previously known.

In what follows, we describe the model of adaptive social networks and the settings and results of the large-scale parameter sweep numerical experiments. We further discuss implications of the results for social evolution and potential future research directions.

2   Model

Our original model [9] describes distributed opinion dynamics on an adaptive social network made of n nodes. Adaptive networks [13, 14] are a class of dynamical network models in which node states and edge connectivities co-evolve in adaptation to each other. In our model, node i has its own opinion state $x_i \in \mathbb{R}$.

Nodes are connected through weighted directed edges that represent the information flow from source to target nodes. The edge weight is denoted as $w_{ij} \in \mathbb{R}_{\geq 0}$, where i is the target node and j is the source node.

The adaptive network dynamics, i.e., the co-evolution of node states and edge weights, are governed by the following differential equations:

$$\frac{dx_i}{dt} = c\left(\langle x \rangle_i - x_i\right) + \epsilon \tag{1}$$

$$\frac{dw_{ij}}{dt} = hF_h(x_i, x_j) + aF_a(\langle x \rangle_i, x_j) \tag{2}$$

$$\langle x \rangle_i = \frac{\sum_j w_{ij} x_j}{\sum_j w_{ij}} \tag{3}$$

Here, $\langle x \rangle_i$ (Eq. (3)) represents the weighted local average of neighbors' opinions (i.e., social norm) perceived by node i. Parameter c and noise term ϵ in Eq. (1) represent the strength of social conformity and stochastic fluctuation of node states, respectively. Parameters h and a in Eq. (2) represent the strength of homophily and attention to novelty, respectively. F_h and F_a in Eq. (2) are functions that describe the increase/decrease of edge weights because of homophily and attention to novelty, respectively. F_h and F_a can be any functions that monotonically decrease (for F_h) or increase (for F_a) as the distance between the two arguments increase. In this study, we used the following simple functions for F_h and F_a:

$$F_h(x_i, x_j) = \theta_h - |x_i - x_j| \tag{4}$$

$$F_a(\langle x \rangle_i, x_j) = |\langle x \rangle_i - x_j| - \theta_a \tag{5}$$

Here θ_h and $-\theta_a$ are the default values of F_h and F_a, respectively, when the two given arguments are equal. These functions describe that the edge from node j to node i tends to become strengthened when j's state is similar to i's (i.e., homophily) and distant from the local average (i.e., attention to novelty), or weakened otherwise. We restricted w_{ij} to be always nonnegative, and any negative values resulted from numerical simulation of Eq. (2) would be rounded up to zero.

Simulating this adaptive social network model from a random initial condition produces a sequence of social network configurations in which node states (opinions) spread through social ties and edge weights (connection strengths) also change due to node states (an example is shown in Fig. 1). We implemented the numerical simulator of the model in Python 3.7 with NetworkX [15] and PyCX [16][1].

This model is known to exhibit social fragmentation transition, i.e., transition between fragmented and homogenized social network states, as the individuals' behavioral parameters are varied (Fig. 2) [1–4]. Our previous study [9] showed that, when homophily (h) is stronger or attention to novelty (a) is weaker, the

---

[1] The simulator code is available from the author upon request.

Fig. 1. A snapshot of the proposed adaptive social network model visualized in the middle of a simulation. Colors of nodes represent their states (opinions) using Matplotlib's "spectral" color map, while the shade of edges represent their weights (connection strengths).

social network is more inclined to become fragmented into many disconnected small clusters with various opinion states (Fig. 2, left), and in the opposite settings social homogenization is more likely to occur (Fig. 2, right). Meanwhile, the potential effect of social conformity (c) was unclear in the previous analysis, which is the main focus of the present study.

3   Experiments

3.1   Settings

We conducted numerical simulations of the above adaptive social network model to systematically investigate the effects of individual behavioral parameters (c, h, a, θ_h, and θ_a) on the course of social network evolution. The parameter values used are as follows:

- Network size: $n \in \{30, 100, 300\}^2$
- Behavioral parameters: c, h, a, θ_h, $\theta_a \in \{0.003, 0.01, 0.03, 0.1, 0.3, 1.0\}$

The above range of values for behavioral parameters was an order-of-magnitude larger in each dimension than what was examined before [9]. Each parameter value combination was simulated 5 times with independently generated random initial conditions. This resulted in a total of $3 \times 6^5 \times 5 = 116,640$ simulation runs,

---

^{2} Simulations with a larger network size ($n = 1,000$) were also conducted in our earlier work [9] and we confirmed that their results did not differ much from those with $n = 300$.

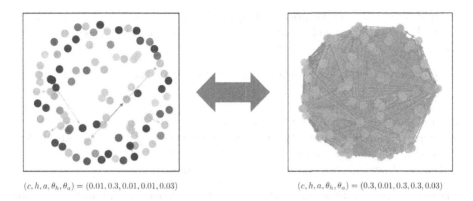

$(c, h, a, \theta_h, \theta_a) = (0.01, 0.3, 0.01, 0.01, 0.03)$ $(c, h, a, \theta_h, \theta_a) = (0.3, 0.01, 0.3, 0.3, 0.03)$

Fig. 2. Examples of final states of the adaptive social network simulation with $n = 100$ that demonstrate social fragmentation transition. Left: Fragmented state with large h and small a. Right: Homogenized state with small h and large a. Specific parameter settings are shown beneath each panel. Visualizations were done in the same way as in Fig. 1.

taking a substantial amount of computational time and resource. Simulations were thus conducted in parallel on four designated PCs for over a few months.

In each simulation, the initial configuration of the network was randomly generated so that every pair of nodes were connected by two directed edges (in both directions) with a randomly generated weight sampled from a standard uniform distribution $(w_{ij} \in [0, 1])$ in each direction[3] and each node had a random node state sampled from the normal distribution $\mathcal{N}(0, 1)$. Equations (1) and (2) were numerically simulated using a simple Euler forward method with time step size $\Delta t = 0.1$ for $t \in [0, 100]$. The stochastic behavior of node states represented by ϵ in Eq. (1) was simulated by adding a random number sampled from $\mathcal{N}(0, 0.1^2)$ to x_i at each discrete time step Δt.

3.2   Outcome Measures

At the end of each simulation run $(t = 100)$, we converted the final network configuration into an undirected network by replacing the two directed edges between each pair of nodes with a single undirected edge whose weight was the average of the original two edges' weights. Then the Louvain modularity maximization method [17] was applied to the undirected network to detect community structure in the final network configuration. Within each detected community,

---

[3] We did not use more realistic social network structures like those with long-tailed degree distributions or modular community structures. This is because, in order to understand social self-organization, those structures should arise as an *outcome* of dynamical interactions among agents rather than used as the initial condition given *a priori*.

we calculated the average node state (called "average community state" hereafter). Using the results of these steps, we calculated the following five network metrics as final outcome measures:

1. Average edge weight (= arithmetic average of all the edge weights in the network)
2. Number of communities
3. Modularity of the community structure
4. Range of average community states (= difference between largest and smallest average community states)
5. Standard deviation of average community states

These outcome measures were averaged over five independent simulation runs for each combinations of parameter values. The first three outcome measures capture the structural properties of the social network, while the last two capture the opinion diversity in the social network. When the social network is fragmented, the average edge weight takes a small value, while all the other measurements takes large values. The opposite pattern is realized when the social network is homogenized. This allows us to easily detect which state the adaptive social network evolved into in quantitative ways.

4   Results

In order to capture and visualize the effects of the five behavioral parameters on the five outcome measures (including possible nonlinear interactions among those behavioral parameters), we modeled the parameter-outcome mapping using artificial neural networks with Wolfram Research Mathematica 12's artificial neural network predictor [18]. Natural logarithms of the five behavioral parameter values were used as five-dimensional input vectors, and the five outcome measures obtained from simulation results under those parameter settings were used as five-dimensional output vectors. The combinations of these input and output vectors were gathered for the whole simulation runs for each network size ($n \in \{30, 100, 300\}$) and used as the data set to train an artificial neural network model for specific n. The performance goal of training was set to maximizing the accuracy of outcome prediction [18].

Illustrative results with $n = 300$ are shown as heat maps of each outcome measure in Fig. 3 (for final network structure) and Fig. 4 (for final node states). The competition between homophily (h) and attention to novelty (a) is still observed as the primary determinant of social fragmentation in a low-conformity (c) regime (top rows of all panels in Figs. 3 and 4), seen as the diagonal transition plane in the plots. However, another vertical transition plane emerges at an intermediate homophily level in a high-conformity regime (bottom rows of all panels in Figs. 3 and 4), which was not previously known. Similar patterns were observed for other outcome measures and network sizes. This new result shows that, when individuals' social conformity (c) is sufficiently strong, homogenization of the social network can occur even without attention to novelty. This

(a) Number of communities

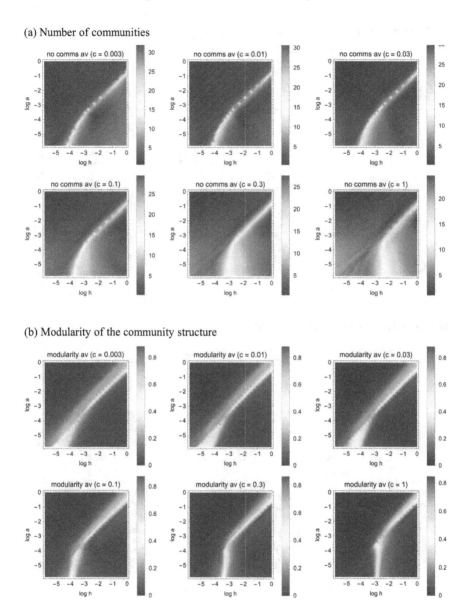

(b) Modularity of the community structure

Fig. 3. Phase diagrams of adaptive social network evolution in terms of network structure outcome measures. Each plot shows outcome dependence on homophily (h, horizontal axis), attention to novelty (a, vertical axis) and conformity (c, varied from top-left to bottom-right) modeled using artificial neural networks. (a) How the number of communities depends on h, a and c. (b) How the modularity of the community structure depends on h, a and c. Red and blue regions correspond to fragmented and homogenized network states, respectively. $n = 300$, $\theta_h = 0.1$, and $\theta_a = 0.1$. Similar patterns were observed for other outcome measures and network sizes. (Color figure online)

(a) Range of average community states

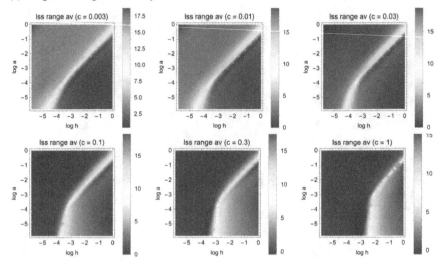

(b) Standard deviation of average community states

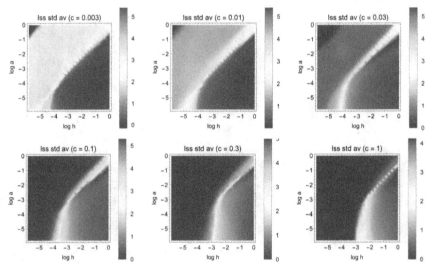

Fig. 4. Phase diagrams of adaptive social network evolution in terms of node state outcome measures. Each plot shows outcome dependence on homophily (h, horizontal axis), attention to novelty (a, vertical axis) and conformity (c, varied from top-left to bottom-right) modeled using artificial neural networks. (a) How the range of average community states depends on h, a and c. (b) How the standard deviation of average community states depends on h, a and c. Red and blue regions correspond to fragmented and homogenized network states, respectively. $n = 300$, $\theta_h = 0.1$, and $\theta_a = 0.1$. Similar patterns were observed for other outcome measures and network sizes. (Color figure online)

implies that social conformity and attention to novelty, while very different in their intentions and actions at microscopic individual levels, have similar effects of promoting connections among individuals in an adaptive social network.

The result shown above also reveals a previously unrecognized competition between social conformity (c) and homophily (h) when attention to novelty is weak (i.e., low-a regions; near the bottom edge of each heat map in Figs. 3 and 4). Namely, when c is low social fragmentation dominates, but when c is high social homogenization becomes possible for smaller values of h. This is quite intriguing because these two behaviors (social conformity and homophily) have very similar effects at an individual level (i.e., they both make ego and alter similar to each other). In fact, their differences are often very vague and undetectable in empirical social network studies [19]. Meanwhile, these two behaviors are mechanistically distinct, because social conformity is about node dynamics while homophily is about edge dynamics. This finding, that their competitive balance may lead to very different societal outcomes down the road, offers a lot of implications for how we should consider our social interactions and behaviors in this highly interconnected world.

5   Conclusions

In this study, we conducted large-scale parameter sweep simulations of our adaptive social network model to investigate the transition points between fragmentation and homogenization of social networks in a multidimensional behavioral parameter space. Artificial neural network-based modeling and visualization of the parameter-outcome mapping revealed a new transition plane for strong social conformity (c) and weak attention to novelty (a) regimes, which was previously unrecognized. The overall multidimensional phase space structure shows a nonlinear interaction among the three key behavioral mechanisms (social conformity, homophily, and attention to novelty). Within the range of parameter values tested so far, it appears that social homogenization (blue regions in Figs. 3 and 4) occupied a greater volume in the log-scale parameter space than social fragmentation did.

This study presents a concrete example of complex collective systems research to study *Artificial Society*, i.e., study of hypothetical models of *society-as-it-could-be*. Such theoretical/mathematical/computational exploration of social systems can play valuable roles complementary to more empirical social science research, in the same spirit of Artificial Life research [20] that complements traditional biology. Computational examination of hypothetical scenarios, such as changing individual behaviors in our model, allows for exploration of various possible forms of our society and may lead to a discovery of novel possible social states which would not be realized just by analyzing empirical data obtained from real society [5]. Such exploratory endeavor is becoming increasingly important and relevant in today's highly automated, interconnected society, as our daily interactions are moving away from traditional, "natural" forms and becoming more and more mediated by artificially designed, "engineered" communication platforms. This has become even more manifested because of the recent COVID-19 pandemic (think about Zoom, YouTube, Slack, and other social media/collaboration platforms). We hope that studies like ours presented here may help re-evaluate and re-design the algorithms and interfaces of online human communications and interactions for the betterment of our social network evolution.

This study is still limited in several aspects. First, we did not explore variations of the amplitude of stochastic fluctuations (ϵ) or functional shapes of homophily and attention to novelty (F_h and F_a). Second, transition planes were identified only by numerical simulations while analytical estimate of transition conditions is not accomplished yet. Third, we assumed that the behavioral parameter values would apply uniformly to all individuals in society with zero behavioral diversity. Fourth, the size of the simulated networks was relatively small (only up to 300 nodes). Future research directions are naturally to address each and all of these limitations in the current model. In particular, introducing individual behavioral diversity within a collective complex system is known to produce unexpected, nontrivial macroscopic outcomes [5, 21]. Such behavioral heterogeneity should be represented in future models to gain more nuanced, more realistic collective outcomes. High Performance Computing frameworks for agent-based models [22] also may be used to increase the simulated network size and to expand parameter sweep ranges further. Finally, quantitative comparison and validation of model behaviors with actual social network evolution data will ultimately be needed. However, obtaining such empirical data of social network evolution has been extremely difficult, and this will remain one of the major challenges in adaptive social network modeling research.

References

1. Holme, P., Newman, M.E.: Nonequilibrium phase transition in the coevolution of networks and opinions. Phys. Rev. E **74**(5), 056108 (2006). https://doi.org/10.1103/PhysRevE.74.056108
2. Zanette, D.H., Gil, S.: Opinion spreading and agent segregation on evolving networks. Physica D **224**(1–2), 156–165 (2006). https://doi.org/10.1016/j.physd.2006.09.010
3. Kozma, B., Barrat, A.: Consensus formation on adaptive networks. Phys. Rev. E **77**(1), 016102 (2008). https://doi.org/10.1103/PhysRevE.77.016102
4. Böhme, G.A., Gross, T.: Analytical calculation of fragmentation transitions in adaptive networks. Phys. Rev. E **83**(3), 035101 (2011). https://doi.org/10.1103/PhysRevE.83.035101
5. Sayama, H., Yamanoi, J.: Beyond social fragmentation: coexistence of cultural diversity and structural connectivity is possible with social constituent diversity. In: Masuda, N., Goh, K.-I., Jia, T., Yamanoi, J., Sayama, H. (eds.) NetSci-X 2020. SPC, pp. 171–181. Springer, Cham (2020). https://doi.org/10.1007/978-3-030-38965-9_12
6. Blex, C., Yasseri, T.: Positive algorithmic bias cannot stop fragmentation in homophilic networks. J. Math. Sociol. **46**(1), 80–97 (2020). https://doi.org/10.1080/0022250X.2020.1818078

7. Levin, S.A., Milner, H.V., Perrings, C.: The dynamics of political polarization. Proc. National Acad. Sci. **118**(50), e21169 (2021). https://doi.org/10.1073/pnas.2116950118

8. Sasahara, K., Chen, W., Peng, H., Ciampaglia, G.L., Flammini, A., Menczer, F.: Social influence and unfollowing accelerate the emergence of echo chambers. J. Comput. Soc. Sci. **4**(1), 381–402 (2021). https://doi.org/10.1007/s42001-020-00084-7

9. Sayama, H.: Extreme ideas emerging from social conformity and homophily: an adaptive social network model. In: ALIFE 2020: the 2020 Conference on Artificial Life (pp. 113–120). MIT Press (2020). https://doi.org/10.1162/isal_a_00349

10. McPherson, M., Smith-Lovin, L., Cook, J.M.: Birds of a feather: homophily in social networks. Ann. Rev. Sociol. **27**(1), 415–444 (2001). https://www.jstor.org/stable/2678628

11. Kossinets, G., Watts, D.J.: Origins of homophily in an evolving social network. Am. J. Sociol. **115**(2), 405–450 (2009). https://doi.org/10.1086/599247

12. Bakshy, E., Messing, S., Adamic, L.A.: Exposure to ideologically diverse news and opinion on Facebook. Science **348**(6239), 1130–1132 (2015). https://doi.org/10.1126/science.aaa1160

13. Gross, T., Sayama, H.: Adaptive Networks. Springer (2009). https://doi.org/10.1007/978-3-642-01284-6

14. Sayama, H., et al.: Modeling complex systems with adaptive networks. Comput. Math. Appl. **65**(10), 1645–1664 (2013). https://doi.org/10.1016/j.camwa.2012.12.005

15. Hagberg, A.A., Schult, D.A., Swart, P.J.: Exploring network structure, dynamics, and function using NetworkX. In: Proceedings of 7th Python in Science Conference (SciPy 2008; Pasadena, CA USA), pp. 11–15 (2008). https://www.osti.gov/biblio/960616

16. Sayama, H.: PyCX: a Python-based simulation code repository for complex systems education. Complex Adaptive Syst. Model. **1**(1), 1–10 (2013). https://doi.org/10.1186/2194-3206-1-2

17. Blondel, V.D., Guillaume, J.L., Lambiotte, R., Lefebvre, E.: Fast unfolding of communities in large networks. J. Stat. Mech: Theory Exp. **2008**(10), P10008 (2008). https://doi.org/10.1088/1742-5468/2008/10/P10008

18. Wolfram Language & System Documentation Center Predict. https://reference.wolfram.com/language/ref/Predict.html

19. Shalizi, C.R., Thomas, A.C.: Homophily and contagion are generically confounded in observational social network studies. Sociol. Methods Res. **40**(2), 211–239 (2011). https://doi.org/10.1177/0049124111404820

20. Langton, C.G.: Preface. Artificial Life II (pp. xiii-xviii). Addison-Wesley (1992)

21. Sayama, H.: Swarm chemistry. Artif. Life **15**(1), 105–114 (2009). https://doi.org/10.1162/artl.2009.15.1.15107

22. Paciorek, M., Turek, W.: Agent-based modeling of social phenomena for high performance distributed simulations. In: Paszynski, M., Kranzlmüller, D., Krzhizhanovskaya, V.V., Dongarra, J.J., Sloot, P.M.A. (eds.) ICCS 2021. LNCS, vol. 12743, pp. 412–425. Springer, Cham (2021). https://doi.org/10.1007/978-3-030-77964-1_32

Parking Search in Urban Street Networks: Taming Down the Complexity of the Search-Time Problem via a Coarse-Graining Approach

Léo Bulckaen[1,2], Nilankur Dutta[1], and Alexandre Nicolas[1(✉)]

[1] Institut Lumière Matière, CNRS and Université Claude Bernard Lyon 1,
69622 Villeurbanne, France
{leo.bulckaen,alexandre.nicolas}@polytechnique.edu
[2] Ecole polytechnique, 91128 Palaiseau, France

Abstract. The parking issue is central in transport policies and drivers' concerns, but the determinants of the parking search time remain relatively poorly understood. The question is often handled in a fairly *ad hoc* way, or by resorting to crude approximations. Very recently, we proposed a more general agent-based approach, which notably takes due account of the role of the street network and the unequal attractiveness of parking spaces, and showed that it can be solved analytically by leveraging the machinery of Statistical Physics and Graph Theory, in the steady-state mean-field regime. Although the analytical formula is computationally more efficient than direct agent-based simulations, it involves cumbersome matrices, with linear size proportional to the number of parking spaces. Here, we extend the theoretical approach and demonstrate that it can be further simplified, by coarse-graining the parking spot occupancy at the street level. This results in even more efficient analytical formulae for the parking search time, which could be used efficiently by transport engineers.

Keywords: on-street parking · parking search time · street network · graph theory

1 Introduction

Parking is a complex problem of great practical as well as theoretical interest. On the theoretical side, its complexity arises from the interaction between multiple entities (cars) which have different destinations and parking preferences, as well as several possible states (driving, searching for parking, or parked), and whose motion is constrained by the network of streets: this complexity would obviously vanish into thin air if one were to consider a predictable single driver trying to park in an empty city. The problem thus presents a singular interplay between facets including collective effects, complex networks, psychological factors, impact of transport policies.

© The Author(s), under exclusive license to Springer Nature Switzerland AG 2023
R. Wyrzykowski et al. (Eds.): PPAM 2022, LNCS 13827, pp. 470–480, 2023.
https://doi.org/10.1007/978-3-031-30445-3_39

On the practical side, the quandary of parking search is all too well known to individual drivers as well as transport authorities in virtually all large metropolitan areas [16]. Motorists may spend several dozens of hours every year searching for parking, according to INRIX survey data [6], whereas the former increasingly regard parking as a lever to enforce their transport policy. It has been assessed that cars cruising for parking may represent a significant share of the total traffic in many large cities (e.g., 15% in central Stuttgart, 28% to 45% in New York) [12,16] and aggravate congestion and pollution in city centres.

A deeper understanding of the process of parking search is thus crucial, so as to be able to predict the impact of hypothetical measures. Very recently, we put forward a general framework which goes beyond conventional numerical and theoretical approaches to parking search and which notably suitably accounts for the role of the street network and the unequal attractiveness of parking spaces [8]. One major asset of this framework is that, despite its generality, it permits analytic progress. Indeed, the problem can be solved not only by means of a computationally efficient agent-based algorithm that we developed, but also by leveraging the powerful machinery of Statistical Physics and Graph Theory to obtain analytical formulae relating the search time and the occupancy of parking spots. While we showed [8,9] that this approach can be applied to complex, large-scale networks such as that of the city of Lyon, France, the analytical formulae were fairly impractical because they involved cumbersome (even though sparse) matrices representing the graph of parking spots in the city. In this contribution, we purport to show that the complexity of the problem can be tamed down even more by considering a coarse-grained graph, whose smallest elements are street portions instead of individual parking spots.

2 Modelling Framework

2.1 Short Review of Existing Agent-Based Approaches

To start with, we very succinctly review some previous models developed to predict parking search times. The most basic model is probably the *binomial approximation* [2], which expresses the search time as $T_s \simeq \frac{T_0}{1-\phi}$, where T_0 is the time to drive from one spot to the next one. Unfortunately, this expression seems to strongly underestimate search times, if it is used in conjunction with the reported occupancy ϕ in city districts; it can hardly be reconciled with the empirical observation of surging search times long before ϕ reaches 100% [1,3,11,18].

To get insight into this mismatch, Arnott et al. [1] considered a simple model in which cars moved along a circle with 100 spots along its contour and parked in the first available spot; they found that spatial and temporal correlations in the occupation of spots, among other factors, underlay the failure of the binomial approximation. Belonging to the same kind of approaches revolving around simplified networks, aimed at gaining general insight into the problem of parking search, Krapivsky and Redner described the optimal parking strategy on a lane of parking spaces through the lens of statistical physics [13], while

Dowling and colleagues analysed parking search in a regular network using the theory of network of finite-capacity queues [7].

Aiming for a more detailed description, Levy et al. [15] put forward the PARKAGENT model, more suitable for practical use, in which cars drive towards their destination on a spatially described network of streets and decide to park or not when driving by a vacant spot by estimating their odds to find another vacant spot closer to their target, on the basis of the occupancy of spots that they have seen so far. Should they reach their destination without having parked before, they will start circling and accept the first vacant spot and, after a fixed time threshold, they will drive to an off-street parking lot. Vo et al. [17] designed a simple, easy-to-use model in NETLOGO to predict the car movements in a parking lot. The model is based on a decision tree, which considers factors such as the existence of a vacant spot near the ticket machine or the entrance and the gender of the driver.

Game-theoretic approaches have also been employed to address this problem, by supposing that a Nash equilibrium is reached by drivers intent on finding the best spot within a given, agent-specific search time, provided the reaching times for every parking space are known [5].

2.2   Presentation of the Model

The model that we recently introduced [8] can be regarded as a general framework encompassing many of these agent-based models, insofar as drivers also move on a spatially described network of streets, with parking spots located along the streets, but their turn-choices and parking decisions can be prescribed arbitrarily.

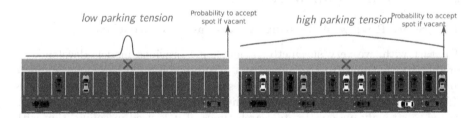

Fig. 1. Illustration of the effect of the parking tension on the probability to accept to park at a vacant spot. On the left, parking tension is low, corresponding to $\beta \to \infty$, and drivers will only accept to park at their favourite spots.

More precisely, several categories $\alpha = 1, 2, \ldots$ of drivers can be defined depending on their destination, trip purpose, etc., and, at an intersection, drivers of each category have different probabilities to turn into the possible outgoing street links; these are given by the corresponding entry of a (category-dependent) turn-choice matrix $\underline{T}^{(\alpha)}$. Thus, each category of drivers may be routed to a different destination.

Besides, drivers of distinct categories will naturally differ in their decision to park or not when driving by a vacant spot: they will choose to park there (if it is vacant) with probability $p_i^{(\alpha)}$, which in practice depends on a variety of explanatory variables, first of which how far it is from the destination, how much it costs, but also what are the odds of finding a 'better' spot, e.g., closer to the target [4,14]. To avoid prescribing specific rules for these parking choices, which are likely to depend on the local context, we chose to subsume all these factors into two generic variables, which can be tuned arbitrarily: (i) an attractiveness $A_i^{(\alpha)}$ reflecting how attractive a spot i is perceived to be *intrinsically*, (ii) the driver's perception of how easy it currently is to park, $\beta^{(\alpha)} \in [0, \infty)$.

$$p_i^{(\alpha)}(t) = f(A_i^{(\alpha)}, \beta^{(\alpha)}(t)). \tag{1}$$

For simplicity, at present, the parameter $\beta^{(\alpha)}(t)$ measuring parking tension will always be a function of the *global* occupancy $\phi(t)$, i.e., $\beta^{(\alpha)}(t) = f[\phi(t)] \equiv \beta$, even though more realistic dependencies could readily be contemplated.

As illustrated in Fig. 1, when the occupancy is very low, parking seems extremely easy, which implies that $\beta \to \infty$, and the driver will refuse to park anywhere but in their preferred spot, of attractiveness $A_{\max}$. To the opposite, when the occupancy is very high, β will tend to zero and the driver will accept virtually any admissible spot (of perceived attractiveness $A_i^{(\alpha)} > -\infty$), viz. $p_i^{(\alpha)} = 1$. Since $p_i^{(\alpha)} \in [0, 1]$, these extreme cases are conducive to expressing p_i with a Boltzmann-like functional form, viz.,

$$p_i^{(\alpha)} = e^{\beta \cdot (A_i^{(\alpha)} - A_{\max})}. \tag{2}$$

Finally, parked cars leave their space at a rate $D^{(\alpha)}$, which is the reciprocal of the average parking duration. These departing cars are removed from the simulation, because the interaction between cruising cars and the rest of the traffic is discarded here: cars move at fixed speeds in each street.

Thus formulated, our model offers a generalisation of existing agent-based approaches. For instance, if they prescribe to park in the first vacant spot within a radius of the destination [10], this can be encoded in the model as $\beta^{(\alpha)} \simeq 0$ and A_i equal to $-\infty$ outside the admissible radius and 0 inside.

2.3 Mean-Field Expression for the Search Time

A major asset of the foregoing generic framework is that it can be addressed not only by means of numerical simulations, but also more theoretically. Let us recall the major theoretical results that we obtained in this regard in [8], while referring the reader to that manuscript for the details of the derivation.

First, every street position associated with a parking spot as well as every intersection were handled as nodes of a 'graph of spots' (this means that the street position where the car starts to park and the parking spot are amalgamated). This graph contains N_{nodes} nodes. The numbers of cars of category α, i.e., α-cars, passing by each node per time unit is represented by a vector $\underline{I}^{(\alpha)}(t)$

of size N_{nodes}, where $I_i^{(\alpha)}(t)$ is the rate of cars passing by node i at time t, averaged over random realisations. The drivers' turn choices at the nodes define a transition matrix $\underline{\underline{T}}^{(\alpha)}$ such that $T_{ij}^{(\alpha)} \in [0,1]$ is the probability that an α-car chooses to move from node i to node j along an edge of the graph in one arbitrary time step, *if it does not park in the meantime*. In this graph theoretical approach, α-cars initially injected at nodes j (hence, $I_j^{(\alpha)}(t=0) > 0$) will be located at positions represented by $\underline{I}^{(\alpha)}(t=1) = \underline{I}^{(\alpha)}(0) \cdot \underline{\underline{T}}^{(\alpha)}$ at the next time step and at

$$\underline{I}^{(\alpha)}(K) = \underline{I}^{(\alpha)}(0) \cdot \left(\underline{\underline{T}}^{(\alpha)}\right)^K \tag{3}$$

after K steps, *if they do not park in the mean-time*. However, it is crucial to remark that cars may actually have parked in the meantime, with a probability $\tilde{p}_i^{(\alpha)}$ given (for each spot i) by $\tilde{p}_i^{(\alpha)} = p_i^{(\alpha)} \hat{n}_i$, where $\hat{n}_i = 1 - n_i$ is zero (one) if the spot is vacant (occupied). Taking this possibility into account, the transition matrix $\underline{\underline{T}}^{(\alpha)}$ should be substituted by $M_{ij}^{(\alpha)} = (1 - p_i^{(\alpha)} \hat{n}_i) \cdot T_{ij}^{(\alpha)}$ and the spatial distribution of cars at $t = K$ is actually

$$\underline{I}^{(\alpha)}(K) = \underline{I}^{(\alpha)}(0) \cdot \left(\underline{\underline{M}}^{(\alpha)}\right)^K. \tag{4}$$

Provided that the occupancy field (n_i) is known, the probability that an α-car reaches spot j and parks there reads

$$P_j^{(\alpha)} = \underbrace{H_i^{(\alpha)}(0)\left[\left(\underline{\underline{\mathbb{I}}} - \underline{\underline{M}}^{(\alpha)}\right)^{-1}\right]_{ij}}_{R_j^{(\alpha)}} \tilde{p}_j^{(\alpha)}, \tag{5}$$

where Einstein's summation convention (on repeated indices, excluding fixed index j here) is implied, $\underline{\underline{\mathbb{I}}}$ is the identity matrix, and $H_j^{(\alpha)}(0) = I_j^{(\alpha)}(0)/I^{(\alpha)} \in [0,1]$ is a renormalised rate, with $I^{(\alpha)}$ the total injection rate of α-cars. $R_j^{(\alpha)}$ denotes the probability to reach spot j without accepting any parking spot before.

Along the same lines, the average 'driving, searching, and parking' time $\mathrm{T}_s^{(\alpha,j)}$ of an α-car finally parking at spot j (in arbitrary time steps) can be derived; it is the average number of steps K needed to park at spot j, weighted by the probability $H_j(K) \cdot \tilde{p}_j^{(\alpha)}$ to reach j after K steps and park there. Accordingly, summing over all spots j, and skipping the algebra detailed in [8],

$$\mathrm{T}_s^{(\alpha)} = H_i^{(\alpha)}(0) \cdot \left[\underline{\underline{M}}^{(\alpha)} \cdot \left(\underline{\underline{\mathbb{I}}} - \underline{\underline{M}}^{(\alpha)}\right)^{-2}\right]_{ij} \cdot \tilde{p}_j^{(\alpha)}. \tag{6}$$

In reality, however, drivers will not keep cruising forever if they cannot find any vacant spot and will quit searching for on-street parking after a given time, represented here by a maximum number of steps K_{max}. Taking into account this upper bound, the foregoing expressions turn into

$$\bar{P}_j^{(\alpha)} = P_j^{(\alpha)} - H_i^{(\alpha)}(0)\left[\left(\underline{\underline{\mathbb{I}}} - \underline{\underline{M}}^{(\alpha)}\right)^{-1} \cdot \underline{\underline{M}}^{(\alpha)\,K_{\mathrm{max}}+1}\right]_{ij} \tilde{p}_j^{(\alpha)} \tag{7}$$

$$\bar{T}_s^{(\alpha)} = T_s^{(\alpha)} - H_i^{(\alpha)}(0) \cdot \left[(\underline{\underline{\mathbb{I}}} - \underline{\underline{M}}^{(\alpha)})^{-2} \cdot \underline{\underline{M}}^{(\alpha)\,K_{\max}+1} \right]_{ij} \tilde{p}_j^{(\alpha)}. \tag{8}$$

Unfortunately, computing $\underline{\underline{M}}^{(\alpha)\,K_{\max}+1}$ may be numerically very costly, as this is no longer a sparse matrix.

Before explaining how this complexity can be overcome, let us note that, in the above formulae, the search time was expressed in arbitrary units, each unit corresponding to a hop between two nodes of the 'graph of spots'. Real time units can be recovered by making use of an auxiliary 'generating' function $\underline{\underline{N}}(z)$ defined by $N_{ij}(z) = z^{\tau_{ij}} M_{ij}^{(\alpha)}$, where z is a real variable and τ_{ij} is the travel time between neighbouring nodes i and j [8], viz.

$$T_s^{(\alpha)} = H_i^{(\alpha)}(0) \cdot \left[(\underline{\underline{\mathbb{I}}} - \underline{\underline{M}}^{(\alpha)})^{-1} \cdot N'(z=1) \cdot (\underline{\underline{\mathbb{I}}} - \underline{\underline{M}}^{(\alpha)})^{-1} \right]_{ij} \tilde{p}_j^{(\alpha)}, \tag{9}$$

where the derivative of $\underline{\underline{N}}(z)$ satisfies $N'_{ij}(z=1) = \tau_{ij} M_{ij}^{(\alpha)}$

The foregoing formulae were derived for a *given* configuration of the occupancy $\underline{n}$. To get the actual *mean* search time requires averaging over an ensemble of equivalent realisations of $\underline{n}$. This step is tricky in general, but can be approximated by plainly substituting $\langle n_j \rangle \in [0,1]$ for $n_j = 0$ or 1 in the definition of the M_{ij} matrix (mean-field approximation).

2.4 Stationary State Occupancy

Up to now, it has been assumed that the occupancy of each spot (or its time average) is known. This section explains how this occupancy field can be derived theoretically in the stationary regime. It is worth mentioning that the reasoning of [8] is here extended to the important case of inhomogeneous departure rates $D^{(\alpha)}$.

This is achieved by writing a conservation equation, which balances incoming α-cars and departing ones, viz.,

$$\phi^{(\alpha)} = \frac{1}{N} \cdot \frac{I^{(\alpha)}}{D^{(\alpha)}}, \tag{10}$$

if all incoming drivers eventually manage to park.

In addition to this global balance, the rate at which α-cars park *at any given spot* j must be balanced by the departure rate $D^{(\alpha)}$ of parked α-cars, viz.,

$$I^{(\alpha)} P_j^{(\alpha)} = D^{(\alpha)} \langle n_j^{(\alpha)} \rangle. \tag{11}$$

It follows, using Eq. 5 and dropping the angular brackets, that $n_i^{(\alpha)} = \frac{I^{(\alpha)}}{D^{(\alpha)}} R_i^{(\alpha)} p_i^{(\alpha)} \hat{n}_i$ so that, summing over all categories α, one finally arrives at

$$\hat{n}_i = \frac{1}{1 + \sum_\alpha I^{(\alpha)} R_i^{(\alpha)} p_i^{(\alpha)} / D_i^{(\alpha)}}, \tag{12}$$

where $R_j^{(\alpha)}$, defined in Eq. 5, implicitly depends on the $\langle n_i \rangle$'s. This completes the derivation of the stationary occupation field (n_i), insofar as Eq. 12 is an implicit equation which self-consistently defines (n_i) and can be solved by means of a fixed-point iterative method.

2.5   Validation in a Large-Scale Test Case

In Ref. [8], we validated the theoretical approach on the large-scale street network of the city of Lyon and showed that the foregoing formulae giving the stationary occupation field (Eq. 12) as well as the travel time by car category (Eq. 9) are in excellent agreement with the steady-state results of numerical simulations of the agent-based model, for unbound search times. Unfortunately, the computational complexity of calculating $\underline{\underline{M}}^{(\alpha)^{K_{\max}+1}}$ in Eq. 7-8 hampered our endeavour to extend the comparison to the more realistic case in which cars quit searching after a given time.

3   Coarse-Graining Occupation Fields at the Street Level

To sum up, despite the success of the theoretical approach, there remains a difficulty associated with it: it involves multiplications and inversions of matrices such as $\underline{\underline{M}}^{(\alpha)}$, with a linear size of order the number of spots in the network. This reflects the fact that parking decisions are made with respect to each parking space individually. The $\underline{\underline{M}}^{(\alpha)}$ matrices are particularly sparse and can therefore be handled with dedicated algorithms, but exponentiating these matrices is particularly inconvenient.

3.1   Coarse-Graining Method

Here, we aim to simplify the problem by coarse-graining the occupation fields at the level of the streets, in order to be able to reason in terms of the 'graph of streets', rather than the 'graph of spots'. The gist of this simplification consists in

(i) deriving an average occupancy $\phi_{\text{street}} = \frac{1}{N_s} \sum_{i=1}^{N_s} n_i$ per street link, where N_s is the number of spots in the street, knowing the rate of incoming cars I_{street} and the characteristics of spots, and then

(ii) using these ϕ_{street} to define a coarse-grained counterpart to the $\underline{\underline{M}}^{(\alpha)}$ matrices of Eq. 9.

More concretely, for point (i), we take advantage of the fact that street links are linear, which enables us to derive the occupancies n_i in a sequential way, starting with the first spot, $i = 1$, etc. Let $I_{\text{street}}^{(\alpha)}$ be the injection rate of α-cars at the entrance of the street link. Then, applying Eq. 11 to the first spot,

$$\hat{n}_1 = \frac{1}{1 + \sum_\alpha I_{\text{street}}^{(\alpha)} p_i^{(\alpha)} / D^{(\alpha)}}, \tag{13}$$

which enables us to derive $R_2^{(\alpha)} = (1 - \hat{n}_1 p_1^{(\alpha)})$, and so on, until all n_i have been calculated. (This operation takes a time proportional to the number of spots N_s.) Finally, the mean occupancy ϕ_{street} is obtained, and, along with it, the probability that an α-car injected in the street exits from it without parking,

$$R_\infty^{(\alpha)}([I_{\text{street}}^{(\alpha)}]) = \prod_{i=1}^{N_s}(1 - \hat{n}_i p_i^{(\alpha)}). \tag{14}$$

To achieve point (ii), one simply has to notice that Eq. 9 still holds for the 'graph of streets', provided that $\underline{\underline{M}}^{(\alpha)}$ is suitably adjusted. More precisely, in the coarse grained version, this matrix should turn into

$$\underline{\underline{M}}^{(\alpha)}{}_{\mathcal{IJ}} \leftarrow [R_\infty^{(\alpha)}([I_{\text{street}}^{(\alpha)}])]_{\mathcal{I}}\, T_{\mathcal{IJ}}^{(\alpha)}, \tag{15}$$

where nodes $\mathcal{I}$ and $\mathcal{J}$ are now intersections marking the beginning of a street-link, and no longer spots.

The previous derivation within each street comes down to assuming that the spot occupancies within each street equilibrate (i.e., reach their stationary state) between every iteration of the fixed-point method for the whole network. While this may not be true from a dynamical perspective, it is reasonable to expect that it tends to the same fixed-point as the non-coarse-grained method.

3.2 Validation

At this stage, the coarse-grained method should be validated and its computational efficiency ought to be compared with that of the *bona fide* method. Regarding the latter point, coarse-graining has reduced the linear size of the involved matrices $\underline{\underline{M}}^{(\alpha)}$ (in Eq. 15) by a factor of order N_s (the number of spots per street), at the expense only of performing a number of order N (the number of spots in the network) of operations at each iteration of the fixed point method. Accordingly, this strongly reduces the computational expense of all calculations involving these matrices, which are ubiquitous in the formulae we derived, and the reduction is all the stronger as street links contain many spots.

Turning to the validation, we considered the part of Lyon which lies to the West of the river Saône, which represents about one third of the total street network. Eight car categories $\alpha = 0 \ldots 7$ are defined, each corresponding to a distinct destination within this zone, in line with what was done in [8]; the turn-choice matrices $\underline{\underline{T}}^{(\alpha)}$ guide cars from their injection point to their destination along a route that is allowed to fluctuate around the shortest path, to some extent. For these simulations, the parameter β controlling parking tension is set to 0.01 and 24 cars are injected per minute, while the mean parking duration is set to 20 min. Most importantly, an upper bound was imposed on the cruising time: drivers quit searching for on-street parking after 25 min (we also tried 15 min). Previously, this capped condition could not be handled using our analytical formulae, because of the difficulty to exponentiate the per-spot matrix $\underline{\underline{M}}^{(\alpha)}$; this is now possible. Thus, an intractable equation has thus become within

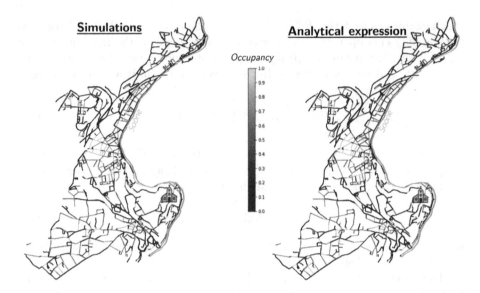

Fig. 2. Map of the stationary occupancy of street links in the Western part of Lyon (west of the river Saône): Comparison of the results obtained by numerical simulations of the agent-based model (left) and of the analytical predictions with the coarse-grained method described in this section (right).

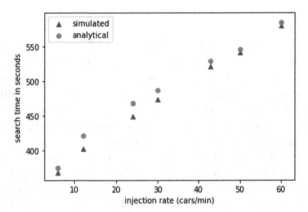

Fig. 3. Comparison of the travel (driving and searching) times obtained with direct numerical simulations and with the coarse-grained analytical method introduced here. The maximal time before drivers quit searching was set to 15 min here.

our reach. (On the other hand, the convergence of our fixed-point method to determine the stationary occupancy may be tricky, which has prevented us from theoretically handling the whole street network of Lyon so far.) Fig. 2 proves that the parking occupancy field obtained with our revised (coarse-grained) analytical expressions are in very good agreement with the result of direct numerical simulations; the slight differences (less than a few percent) mostly occur in high-density parking zones. Furthermore, the travel times given by the analytical expressions also nicely reproduce the numerical outcome, as shown in Fig. 3 for various global car injection rates, for one category of drivers. The agreement is not quite as good as that found with the original method, for non-capped search times, prior to coarse-graining; this is not very surprising, insofar as considering the network at the level of street links instead of parking spaces introduces some inaccuracy in the assessment of the final driving time, in the last street-link.

4 Conclusions

In summary, we have built on a very recently proposed framework that generalises existing agent-based models for parking search and puts greater emphasis on factors such as the topology of the street network and the unequal attractiveness of parking spaces. It was previously shown that, despite its generality, this model can be solved analytically in the mean-field stationary regime. A matricial formula relating the total driving time (including the search time) to the occupancy of parking spaces was thus derived. Here, the formula was extended to allow different categories of drivers to have different parked times (i.e., departure rates), which is naturally of practical relevance.

Furthermore, the foregoing formula was fairly cumbersome, involving very large matrices. In this contribution, we have demonstrated that the analytic expression can be further simplified by aggregating parking spots by street link, so that one now handles a 'graph of streets' instead of a 'graph of spots' (the former containing much fewer nodes, of course). This simplification drastically reduces the dimension of the matrices involved in the foregoing formula and makes them even more tractable, which could be used efficiently by transport engineers. It paves the way for a treatment of practical issues which would otherwise be computationally costly to simulate, in particular optimisation problems in the context of redesigns of the transport network.

For sure, our model currently presents some limitations, notably the lack of interactions between the cruising traffic and the underlying one, as well as the absence of feedback between the experienced search times and the parking demand. There is no reason why these limitations could not be overcome in the near future; for instance, the second limit can be overcome by integrating our model for parking search as a module in a multimodal choice model.

References

1. Arnott, R., Williams, P.: Cruising for parking around a circle. Transp. Res. Part B: Methodol. **104**, 357–375 (2017)
2. Axhausen, K.W., Polak, J.W., Boltze, M., Puzicha, J.: Effectiveness of the parking guidance information system in frankfurt am main. Traffic Eng. Control **35**(5), 304–309 (1994)
3. Belloche, S.: On-street parking search time modelling and validation with survey-based data. Transp. Res. Procedia **6**, 313–324 (2015)

4. Bonsall, P., Palmer, I.: Modelling drivers' car parking behaviour using data from a travel choice simulator. Transp. Res. Part C: Emerg. Technol. **12**(5), 321–347 (2004)
5. Calise, G., Murano, A., Stranieri, S.: The parking problem: a game-theoretic solution. arXiv preprint arXiv:2204.01395 (2022)
6. Cookson, G., Pishue, B.: The impact of parking pain in the US, UK and Germany. Tech. rep, INRIX (2017)
7. Dowling, C.P., Ratliff, L.J., Zhang, B.: Modeling curbside parking as a network of finite capacity queues. IEEE Trans. Intell. Transp. Syst. **21**(3), 1011–1022 (2019)
8. Dutta, N., Charlottin, T., Nicolas, A.: Parking search in the physical world: calculating the search time by leveraging physical and graph theoretical methods. Transp. Sci (2023). https://doi.org/10.1287/trsc.2023.1206
9. Dutta, N., Nicolas, A.: Searching for parking in a busy downtown district: an agent-based computational and analytical model. In: 2021 International Symposium on Computer Science and Intelligent Controls (ISCSIC), pp. 348–354. IEEE (2021)
10. Fulman, N., Benenson, I.: Approximation method for estimating search times for on-street parking. Transportation Science (2021)
11. Gu, Z., Najmi, A., Saberi, M., Liu, W., Rashidi, T.H.: Macroscopic parking dynamics modeling and optimal real-time pricing considering cruising-for-parking. Transp. Res. Part C: Emerg. Technol. **118**, 102714 (2020)
12. Hampshire, R.C., Shoup, D.: What share of traffic is cruising for parking? J. Transp. Econ. Policy (JTEP) **52**(3), 184–201 (2018)
13. Krapivsky, P., Redner, S.: Where should you park your car? the rule. J. Stat. Mech: Theory Exp. **2020**(7), 073404 (2020)
14. Levy, N., Martens, K., Benenson, I.: Exploring cruising using agent-based and analytical models of parking. Transportmetrica A: Transp. Sci. **9**(9), 773–797 (2013)
15. Levy, N., Render, M., Benenson, I.: Spatially explicit modeling of parking search as a tool for urban parking facilities and policy assessment. Transp. Policy **39**, 9–20 (2015)
16. Shoup, D.: Parking and the City. Routledge (2018)
17. Vo, T.T.A., van der Waerden, P., Wets, G.: Micro-simulation of car drivers' movements at parking lots. Procedia Eng. **142**, 100–107 (2016)
18. Weinberger, R.R., Millard-Ball, A., Hampshire, R.C.: Parking search caused congestion: where's all the fuss? Transp. Res. Part C: Emerg. Technol. **120**, 102781 (2020)

A Multi-agent Cellular Automata Model of Lane Changing Behaviour Considering the Aggressiveness and the Autonomy

Krzysztof Małecki[(✉)] [iD], Piotr Wróbel, and Patryk Górka

West Pomeranian University of Technology, Żołnierska 52 Str., Szczecin, Poland
kmalecki@wi.zut.edu.pl, {wp44555,gp46518}@zut.edu.pl

Abstract. Various macroscopic and microscopic road traffic models allow traffic flow analysis. However, it should be emphasised that standard traffic flow models do not include drivers' behaviour. Thus, we propose a multi-agent microscopic model for analysing the traffic flow considering the various type of agents. Agents represent both autonomous cars and various drivers' behaviour (standard and aggressive drivers). Additionally, the presented model is based on accurate data, because it considers the actual dimensions of the vehicles. To accurately reflect the acquired dimensions of the cars, a small cell cellular automaton was used, where a set of cells represents one car. The obtained numerical results allowed us to bring both trivial and non-trivial conclusions.

Keywords: Agent-Based Modeling (ABM) · Cellular Automata (CA) · Traffic Flow · Data-Driven Model

1 Introduction

There are many different models of car traffic and its effectiveness [1–4]. Regarding microscopic approach one can point out classical models, including on the one hand, continuous ones like Intelligent Driver Model - a time-continuous car-following model [5]. On the other hand there are discrete models like classical ones: Nagel-Schreckenberg model [6] and Chopard- Luthi-Queloz traffic model [7], where CA paradigm was applied. Although these models are relatively simple they allow for analysis of different relationships [8–13], etc. One can also identify a trend where drivers/cars are represented as agents. They have different abilities and define various styles of driving [14,15].

A specific group of road traffic models are models aimed at lane changing. In [9], the authors introduced the rules of changing lanes, setting three factors: safety (safe distance both at the front and rear of the vehicle), legal restrictions (German system - overtaking only in the left lane, American system - possible overtaking in the left and right lane), optimal passage (vehicles change lanes when the car in front of is moving slower and there is more free space in the destination lane, which will allow the vehicle to move faster). Additionally, the

R. Wyrzykowski et al. (Eds.): PPAM 2022, LNCS 13827, pp. 481–491, 2023.
https://doi.org/10.1007/978-3-031-30445-3_40

so-called view range was introduced, determining how many CA cells are in the adjacent lane and forward that the car sees. This parameter is crucial because drivers will often overtake frequently with a large field of view, which causes frequent changes in lane density.

In [16] the authors based on hexagonal CA cells to more accurately map the lateral movement. There is a virtual lane between the left and right lanes, and a lane-changing consists of two stages: first, the vehicle enters the virtual road lane, and then from this lane, it exits into the destination lane. In addition, the parameters (vehicle speed, vehicle position, and vehicle angle) during overtaking were investigated in an experiment on a two-kilometer road [17]. The sensors collected data from the tested vehicles every 0.2 s. Research has shown that 77% of cars overtake between 40 km/h and 60 km/h. Additionally, a model was implemented in which CA cells were 0.5 m wide and 2 m long each. Each of the vehicles occupied 15 CA cells, and the cell in the centre represented the vehicle's position. The authors investigated the effect of vehicle compaction and speed on the frequency of overtaking. They did not consider the different driving styles of road drivers.

In this article, the authors proposed a multi-agent, multi-cell CA model to study the impact of drivers' behaviour on the road on the lane changing behaviour. The novelty of this work is to develop a CA model that allows vehicles to move sideways while varying driving styles. This was achieved by mapping each road lane as a grid of small cells and defining cars as agents with their behaviours. With the help of computer simulation, it was investigated whether the aggressive driving style (the road being cut by other vehicles during the overtaking manoeuvre) impacted road traffic capacity.

2   Proposed Model

A one-way two-lane road has been mapped. Vehicles move in two directions - forward and sideways. To get high accuracy simulation, the road was divided into many small cells. The grid of the CA consists of two lanes of road divided into cells of 0.5 m long and 0.5 m wide. It was assumed (according to polish regulations [18]) that a single road lane is 3 m wide, which is 6 CA cells (Fig. 1a). Figure 1b presents a vehicle representation as a set of CA cells with selected corners.

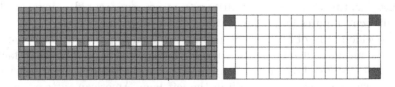

Fig. 1. (a) An empty two-lane road of 13 CA cells wide. (b) A vehicle representation as a set of CA cells with selected corners.

A few type of vehicles are considered (Table 1). The dimensions of the real vehicles are divided into few types, differing in length and width. The developed model uses small CA cells to allow the vehicles to move sideways.

Table 1. Types of vehicles (based on real sizes [15]).

Type of vehicle	Av. size (length; width) [mm]	Size (length; width) [CA cells]
A	3522; 1567	7; 3
B	4015; 1721	8; 3
C	4430; 1728	9; 3
D	4895; 1862	10; 4
E	5262; 2003	11; 4

In each iteration, the vehicle retrieves information about the distances of cars in its immediate vicinity. This allows him to make decisions based on his environment in a situation that changes dynamically with each iteration. In the simulation, there are several types of agents with different characteristics that differentiate the decision making.

The boundary condition for the developed model is periodic, i.e. the cars move along a closed track. This makes it easier to control the density of the road. The state space contains two states; the CA cell may be occupied by part of the vehicle or empty. Additionally, each vehicle was presented as an agent with strictly defined properties: standard drivers and aggressive drivers (Subsect. 2.2).

2.1 CA Transition Function

The transition function consists of following steps:

1. Establishing a safe distance – small cells allow to simulate of a broad spectrum of speeds. According to the road traffic law, the safe space in non-built-up areas is half the speed value in meters. However, it is not specified in built-up areas, and it is recommended that the time of reaching the vehicle in front during braking should not be less than two seconds. This means that when the car in front suddenly brakes, the car behind it should have such a speed that the distance between them takes no less than 2 s. Hence, the relationship that determines the safe space has been established:

$$g_i(t) = v_i(t) * 2 * gm,$$

where: $v_i(t)$ – the speed of the car in i-th CA cell in the time t, $g_i(t)$ – the safe space, gm – a factor for modifying the distance between the vehicles.
2. Acceleration – cars will increase their speed by a constant amount if their speed is lower than V_{max} and the change in acceleration does not violate the safe distance from the vehicle in front.

$$V_i(t) < V_{max} \wedge g_i(t) <= d_i(t) - (V_i(t) + v_a) \rightarrow V_i(t+1) = V_i(t) + v_a,$$

where: $V_i(t)$ – the speed of the car in i-th CA cell in the time t, V_{max} – maximum speed, $g_i(t)$ – the safe space, $d_i(t)$ – the distance to the vehicle in front, v_a – acceleration value.

3. Sudden braking – a step performed when, as a result of aggressive driving, during a lane-changing, priority was forced, and the distance to the vehicle in front is less than the safe space:

$$d_i(t) < g(t) \rightarrow V_i(t+1) = d_i(t) - 1,$$

where: $V_i(t+1)$ – the speed of the car in i-th CA cell in the time $t+1$, $g(t)$ – the safe space, $d_i(t)$ – the distance to the vehicle in front.

4. Braking – takes place when the speed of the vehicle must be adapted to that of the car in front, keeping a safe distance:

$$g_i(t) < d_i(t) + V_i(t) \rightarrow V_i(t+1) = d_i(t) - 1,$$

where: $V_i(t)$ – the speed of the car in i-th CA cell in the time $t+1$, $g_i(t)$ – the safe space, $d_i(t)$ – the distance to the vehicle in front.

5. Lane-changing – according to Fig. 2, i-th car is marked as a vehicle with the intention to change lanes; vehicles running in the same lane are marked as $i-1$ and $i+1$ respectively, for the vehicle following the vehicle i and for the vehicle preceding the vehicle i . Similarly, a car in the target lane behind the i-th car is denoted as $j-1$ and $j+1$ is on the adjacent line in front of the i-th car.

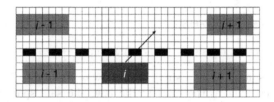

Fig. 2. The description of individual vehicles.

First, the i vehicle must check that no car in the adjacent lane runs parallel to the i-th vehicle. Changing lane requires checking that the distance to the vehicle $j-1$ is appropriate:

$$g_i(t) < d_{j-1}(t),$$

where: $g_i(t)$ – the safe distance in time t, $d_{j-1}(t)$ – the space to the car $j-1$.

The next step is to check that the distance to the vehicle $j+1$ does not violate the safe space:

$$g_i(t) < d_{j+1}(t),$$

where: $g_i(t)$ – the safe distance, $d_{j+1}(t)$ – distance to the car $j+1$.
Then, the vehicle changes the lane and can thus overtake the vehicle in front. The lane-changing takes two iterations. When any conditions are not met, the vehicle rechecks the lane-changing conditions in the next step $(t+1)$. However, if vehicle $i + 1$ has increased its speed in $t + 1$ step $(V_t(i) < V_{t+1}(i+1))$, then car i may abandon the lane change maneuver. With equal probability, vehicle i, after overtaking vehicle $i + 1$, may remain in its current lane or return to its original lane.

6. Random events – according to [9]:

$$V_i > 0 \land P(t) < p \rightarrow V_i(t+1) = V_i(t) - 1,$$

where: $V_i(t)$ – the speed of the car in i-th CA cell in the time t, $d_i(t)$ – the distance to the vehicle in front, in time t, p – the probability with which a random event occurs.

2.2 Classification of Agents Representing Drivers and Vehicles

Three types of agents have been defined, corresponding to standard or aggressive drivers, and autonomous vehicles:

– standard drivers – they follow the transition function described above,
– autonomous vehicles – follow the transition function, but their parameter $gm = 0.5$, which results in the reduction of the safe distance by a factor of two; thanks to that these vehicles keep a smaller distance from other cars, also when overtaking. It is assumed that the control mechanisms of such vehicles are accurate and there are no random events,
– aggressive drivers – their safe distance is constant and has the value of $gm = 2$, during braking, their speed diminishes twice, which is expressed by the formula:

$$gm < d_i(t) + V_i(t) \rightarrow V_i(t+1) = (d_i(t) - 1)/2,$$

where: $V_i(t)$ – the speed of the car in i-th CA cell in the time $t+1$, gm – the safe distance, $d_i(t)$ – the distance to the vehicle in front in time t.
In addition, priority may be forced during the lane-changing process. In a situation when an aggressive driver wants to overtake while there is another vehicle in the adjacent lane parallel to the analysed car i, aggressive lane-changing is understood as approaching this vehicle and forcing it to brake, and give way, as shown in the Fig. 3. The arrows indicate the direction of the vehicle's movement in the next iteration and the values above them are the number of CA cells that the car will travel in the next iteration.

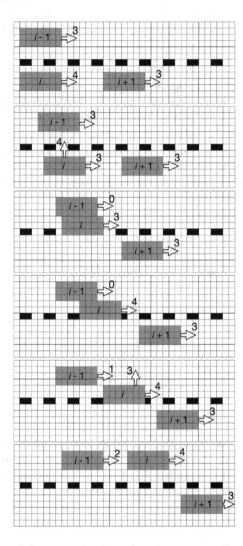

Fig. 3. Visualisation of the aggressive lane-changing process. To overtake the $i+1$ car in front of it, the i vehicle forces the priority when changing lanes and forces the $i-1$ vehicle to yield.

3   Numerical Results

Numerical tests were conducted for a fixed length of road 0.6 km. The system was upgraded every 1 s. All charts show the results of the arithmetic mean of 100 simulations. The probability of the occurrence of random events was 30%. The reference point for the performed tests was the control group consisting entirely of standard drivers.

3.1   The Autonomy

The first study shows the impact of autonomous vehicles on traffic flow. The
acceleration value was $v_a = 15$ CA cells per one iteration. In each of the analysed cases (Fig. 4b-d), i.e. for 20%, 40% and 60% of autonomous vehicles in the
entire stream of vehicles, the traffic flow improved, compared to the control sample (Fig. 4a). The maximum value of the road traffic capacity in the fundamental diagram (Fig. 5) changes its position as the number of autonomous vehicles
increases, moving to the right in relation to the axis representing the density
of vehicles on the road. The road traffic stability (spreading of single simulation samples) is on a similar level for the analysed road. The differences become
apparent when the road density exceeds 70%, especially when autonomous vehicles account for 60% of the total vehicle stream.

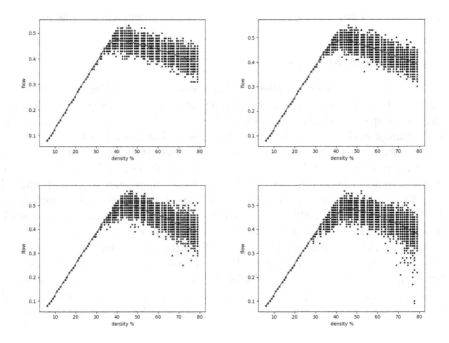

Fig. 4. (a) The control sample for the road with two lanes, (b) 20% of autonomous
cars, (c) 40% of autonomous cars, (d) 60% of autonomous cars.

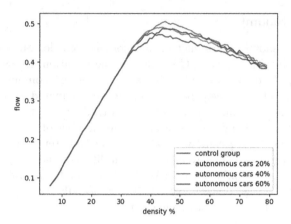

Fig. 5. Comparison of traffic flow for the control sample and autonomous vehicles.

3.2   The Aggressiveness

The second study shows the effect of aggressive drivers on the traffic flow. By analysing Figs. 6 and 7, one can observe the difference between the control group and the samples in which aggressive drivers accounted for 20% and 40% of the total number of drivers. There was an increase in flow from 35% to 60% relative to the control group. On the other hand, the decrease in the flow value is visible in the range from 60% to 80%. This is because aggressiveness reduced the distance between vehicles, hence greater throughput. When aggressive drivers accounted for 60% of all drivers, the traffic flow decreased from the control sample in the range from 30% to 80% of the density (Fig. 7). It follows that too much aggressiveness has a negative impact on the traffic flow.

At the same time, it is necessary to point out the non-trivial aspect of the simulation research conducted. Along with the increase in the number of aggressive drivers in the entire stream of vehicles, the instability of road traffic increases significantly (Fig. 6). It is especially visible in the charts presenting 40% and 60% share of aggressive drivers in the entire stream of vehicles (Fig. 6 c, d).

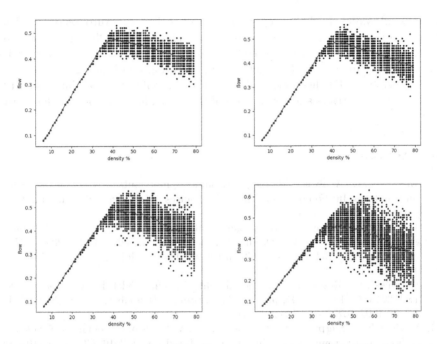

Fig. 6. (a) The control sample, (b) 20% of aggressive drivers, (c) 40% of aggressive drivers, (d) 60% of aggressive drivers.

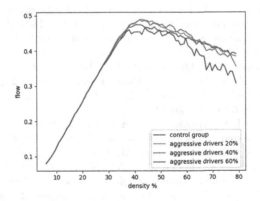

Fig. 7. Comparison of traffic flow for the control group and aggressive drivers.

4   Conclusions

The most important conclusions from work carried out can be formulated as follows: (1) The use of small cells of cellular automaton enables efficient modelling of lateral shifts in lane-changing simulation. (2) The agent-based approach enables observation of traffic flow concerning the characteristics of drivers or types of vehicles. (3) The use of a model that takes into account the actual dimensions of vehicles allows for a reliable representation of reality. (4) Autonomous vehicles have a positive effect on road traffic, resulting in higher traffic flow. (5) Aggressive drivers significantly disturb road traffic stability, understood as increasing traffic dynamics, i.e. increasing the number of acceleration and braking performed by other road users. Further work will be focused on obtaining real data related to the behavior of drivers and verification of the model in conditions similar to real ones.

References

1. Macioszek, E.: Analysis of driver behaviour at roundabouts in Tokyo and the Tokyo surroundings. In: Volume 1083 AISC of Advances in Intelligent Systems and Computing (2020)
2. Macioszek, E.: Models of critical gaps and follow-up headways for turbo roundabouts. In: Macioszek, E., Akçelik, R., Sierpiński, G. (eds.) TSTP 2018. LNNS, vol. 52, pp. 124–134. Springer, Cham (2019). https://doi.org/10.1007/978-3-319-98618-0_11
3. Sierpiński, G.: Revision of the modal split of traffic model. In: Mikulski, J. (ed.) TST 2013. CCIS, vol. 395, pp. 338–345. Springer, Heidelberg (2013). https://doi.org/10.1007/978-3-642-41647-7_41
4. Macioszek, E., Sierpiński, G., Czapkowski, L.: Methods of modeling the bicycle traffic flows on the roundabouts. In: Mikulski, J. (ed.) TST 2010. CCIS, vol. 104, pp. 115–124. Springer, Heidelberg (2010). https://doi.org/10.1007/978-3-642-16472-9_12
5. Treiber, M., Hennecke, A., Helbing, D.: Congested traffic states in empirical observations and microscopic simulations. Phys. Rev. E **62**, 1805–1824 (2000)
6. Nagel, K., Schreckenberg, M.: A cellular automaton model for freeway traffic. J. Phys. I France **2**, 2221 (1992)
7. Chopard, B., Luthi, P.O., Queloz, P.A.: Cellular automata model of car traffic in a two-dimensional street network. J. Phys. A Math. General **29**, 2325–2336 (1996)
8. Schadschneider, A., Schreckenberg, M.: Traffic flow models with 'slow-to-start' rules. Ann. Phys. **509**, 541–551 (1997)
9. Nagel, K., Wolf, D.E., Wagner, P., Simon, P.: Two-lane traffic rules for cellular automata: a systematic approach. Phys. Rev. E **58**, 1425 (1998)
10. Rickert, M., Nagel, K., Schreckenberg, M., Latour, A.: Two lane traffic simulations using cellular automata. Phys. A **231**, 534–550 (1996)
11. Liu, M., Shi, J.: A cellular automata traffic flow model combined with a BP neural network based microscopic lane changing decision model. J. Intell. Transp. Syst. **23**, 309–318 (2019)
12. Małecki, K.: The use of heterogeneous cellular automata to study the capacity of the roundabout. In: Rutkowski, L., Korytkowski, M., Scherer, R., Tadeusiewicz, R., Zadeh, L.A., Zurada, J.M. (eds.) ICAISC 2017. LNCS (LNAI), vol. 10246, pp. 308–317. Springer, Cham (2017). https://doi.org/10.1007/978-3-319-59060-8_28
13. Małecki, K., Gabryś, M.: The computer simulation of cellular automata traffic model with the consideration of vehicle-to-infrastructure communication technology. SIMULATION **96**, 911–923 (2020)

14. Chmielewska, M., Kotlarz, M., Wąs, J.: Computer simulation of traffic flow based on cellular automata and multi-agent system. In: Wyrzykowski, R., Deelman, E., Dongarra, J., Karczewski, K., Kitowski, J., Wiatr, K. (eds.) PPAM 2015. LNCS, vol. 9574, pp. 517–527. Springer, Cham (2016). https://doi.org/10.1007/978-3-319-32152-3_48
15. Małecki, K., Kamiński, M., Wąs, J.: A multi-cell cellular automata model of traffic flow with emergency vehicles: effect of a corridor of life and drivers' behaviour. J. Comput. Sci. **61**, 101628 (2022)
16. Shang, X.C., Lin, X.G., Xie, D.F., Jia, B., Jiang, R.: Two-lane traffic flow model based on regular hexagonal cells with realistic lane changing behavior (2020)
17. Ma, Y., Lv, Z., Zhang, P., Chan, C.Y.: Impact of lane changing on adjacent vehicles considering multi-vehicle interaction in mixed traffic flow: a velocity estimating model (2020)
18. Dz, U.: Announcement of the minister of infrastructure and construction of the Republic of Poland of 23 december 2015 on The Technical Conditions to be met by Public Roads, vol. 124, pp. 9–10 (2015)

Comparison of the Use of UWB and BLE as Positioning Methods in Data-Driven Modeling of Pedestrian Dynamics

Dariusz Pałka[1] , Robert Lubaś[1] , Giuseppe Vizzari[2] ,
and Jarosław Wąs[1,2](✉)

[1] Faculty of Electrical Engineering, Automatics, IT and Biomedical Engineering,
AGH University of Science and Technology, Mickiewicza 30,
30-059 Krakow, Poland
`jaroslaw.was@agh.edu.pl`
[2] Dipartimento di Informatica, Sistemistica e Comunicazione, Università degli Studi
di Milano-Bicocca, Viale Sarca 336, Building U14, 20126 Milan, Italy

Abstract. We conducted experiments on measuring the positioning of
people using standard (custom) *BLE* and *UWB* positioning systems
in an indoor test environment. Then, we analyzed and compared the
results in terms of using the data obtained from the sensors for data-
driven crowd simulations using Cellular Automata grids. Our research
confirmed the usability of both technologies as positioning methods in
data-driven modeling of pedestrian dynamics. Positioning using standard
UWB configuration revealed to be much more accurate than the standard
BLE configuration. In our experiments, based on standard configuration
of both devices, the accuracy of the UWB results equated to standard
deviation did not exceed $0.1\,\mathrm{m}$ - which is an order of magnitude (10
times) less than in the case of BLE.

Keywords: Positioning of people · Modeling of pedestrian dynamics ·
Positioning using BLE · Positioning using UWB

1 Introduction

Modeling of pedestrians' dynamics based on data from position sensors has
recently been perceived as a very promising research methodology. However,
it should be emphasized that the accuracy of positioning is still a limitation.

Currently, crowd modeling is possible using a variety of methods. Navigation
and goal setting of pedestrians are quite a challenge [13]. The solution here is
to use agent systems [11], that can be based on exact grids [2,12]. In particular,
one can point out: continuous methods, discrete methods and hybrid methods.
Continuous methods, such as the social force method, known as Helbing - Mol-
nar - Vicsek model [4], assume a simulation with the use of continuous space and
time, although they use discretization, e.g. when assessing the range of forces

R. Wyrzykowski et al. (Eds.): PPAM 2022, LNCS 13827, pp. 492–501, 2023.
https://doi.org/10.1007/978-3-031-30445-3_41

(the so-called truncation radius). In turn, discrete methods are based on Cellular Automata (CA) framework, which is composed of a grid and transition function [7,12]. CA lattice can be constant or adaptively change over time or space [1]. The grid size is closely correlated with the human size, and in the case of 2D and 2.5D simulations - with the projection of a human silhouette onto a plane. A standard lattice size for pedestrian dynamics is 40 cm [8], 25cm [12], 50 cm [5], and, if necessary, an adaptive size of a grid can be also applied [1]. Any modeling approach, and especially data-driven ones, requires data about real-world pedestrian dynamics, for several potential reasons, ranging from simulation initialization to validation of achieved results.

In our work, we decided to analyze two emerging measurement technologies regarding data-driven crowd modeling, namely Ultra - Wideband (UWB) and Bluetooth Low Energy (BLE), which were applied in data-driven schemes of crowd simulation, in particular, methods based on discrete grids. The aim of our experiment was to evaluate and compare the precision of the two technologies within the same indoor experimental setting.

2 Application of UWB and BLE in the Positioning of Pedestrians

The ultra-wide band UWB waveform is based on an impulse radio signalling scheme using band-limited pulses. There are three independent bands of operation: the sub-gigahertz band, low band and high band. According to the standard IEEE 802.15.4-2011, UWB uses a combination of burst position modulation (BPM) and binary phase-shift keying (BSPK) and transmits a very short (nanosecond order) time domain single pulse or a burst of pulses. Regarding UWB the DWM1001 development board with DWM1001 module produced by Decawave was selected for the experiment.

Bluetooth Low Energy (BLE) is a 2.4 GHz ISM wireless technology developed by the Bluetooth Special Interest Group (SIG) for short-range communication. BLE uses Gaussian Frequency Shift Keying (GFSK) and Adaptive Frequency Hopping. It has 40 channels with a separation of 2 MHz. It achieves the throughput of the physical layer at the level of 1 Mbit/s and the transmission power from -20 dBm to +10 dBm, in order to ensure low power consumption.

We use standard configurations of both devices: UWB and BLE. For both UWB and BLE, the system configuration is similar - the system consists of two types of devices:

- Beacons (anchors): located in specific, known position in space (generally, the position is fixed);
- Tags (receivers): carried by pedestrians, whose position we want to determine.

Every specified time interval, the distance between the tag and individual beacon is measured, then using trilateration (or multilateration), the position of the receiver in 3D space is computed.

Considered Decawave's set is rather low-cost solution (under 30 Euro per tag). Tag dimension is less than 8 cm and weighing a few grams. The system uses supply voltage: 2.8 V to 3.6 V. Tags must be placed every few meters, then the solution can handle a larger area of space.

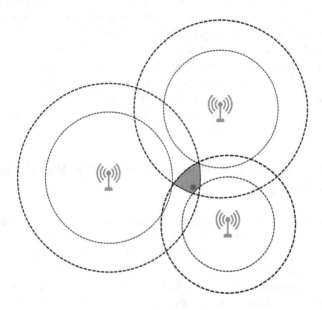

Fig. 1. Trilateration. Annuli with dashed outlines possible position taking into account distance reading error, green area, common area of annuli - possible tag position, red dot - example real position of the tag. (Color figure online)

3   Experiments

The purpose of the experiments was to estimate the minimum error of position determination using BLE and UWB. In both cases, standard devices (transmitters and receivers) were used without any modifications (both hardware and software) to improve positioning accuracy.

3.1   Experiment BLE

The first experiment measured recorded signal strength at different distances of BLE devices from each other. The configuration of the experiment was as follows:

- One of the BLE devices was programmed as a BLE Peripheral (acted as a beacon/anchor). This device was in the advertising state and sent out advertisement packets at short intervals (less than 500 ms).

- The second BLE device was programmed as a BLE Observer (receiver/tag role), it recorded the received signal strength value represented as RSSI (Received Signal Strength Indication).
- Measurements were taken for different distances of the devices from each other (ranging from 10 cm to 500 cm), with no obstacles between the devices. For each distance, 500 RSSI readings were recorded.

As can be seen in Fig. 3, the graph of the receiver's recorded signal strength (RSSI) is banded - the observed readings are grouped around 2 or 3 different values.

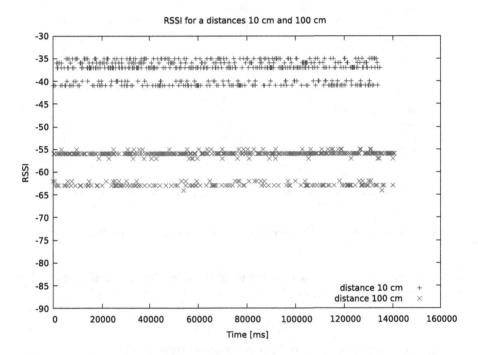

Fig. 2. Read RSSI values for the distance between BLE devices of 10 and 100 cm.

The exact distributions of RSSI values for 15 distances are shown in Fig. 3. For each distance, 500 measurements were recorded.

Dependence of measured RSSI on distance (along with the standard deviation) is shown in Fig. 4. A linear function was fitted to the measured data using

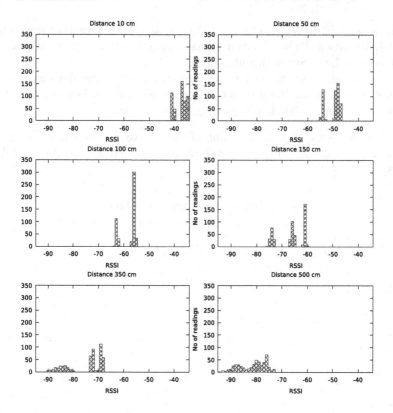

Fig. 3. Histograms of RSSI values for various distances between BLE devices.

a linear regression method with error weights (shown in the same figure). The function has the linear form:

$$f(x) = a_0 + a_1 \cdot x \tag{1}$$

with the coefficients (determined using linear regression):

- $a_0 = -11.6131$
- $a_1 = -23.9092$

Disregarding the last row in the Table 1 (since the corresponding readings have a high fluctuation), the accuracy (max error) of the distance reading between beacon and tag in the 10cm to 450cm range is approximately 1.1 m (113 cm).

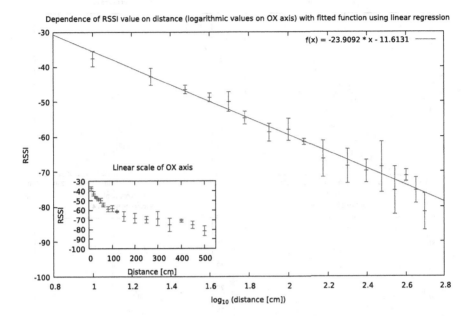

Fig. 4. Dependence of RSSI on distance for BLE devices.

Table 1. The difference between the distance resulting from the fitted linear function f(x) and the mean readout of the measurements

Distance [cm]	Mean RSSI value read	Value of the fitted function f(x)	Distance error [cm]
10	−37.6	−35.5	2
20	−42.7	−42.7	0
30	−46.5	−46.9	1
40	−48.6	−49.9	5
50	−49.9	−52.2	10
60	−54.6	−54.1	3
80	−58.7	−57.2	13
100	−57.9	−59.4	13
120	−61.4	−61.3	1
150	−66.4	−63.6	45
200	−68.4	−66.6	38
250	−69.9	−68.9	23
300	−68.6	−70.8	57
350	−75.3	−72.4	**113**
400	−71.1	−73.8	92
450	−75.3	−75.0	13
~~500~~	~~−81.5~~	~~−76.1~~	~~334~~

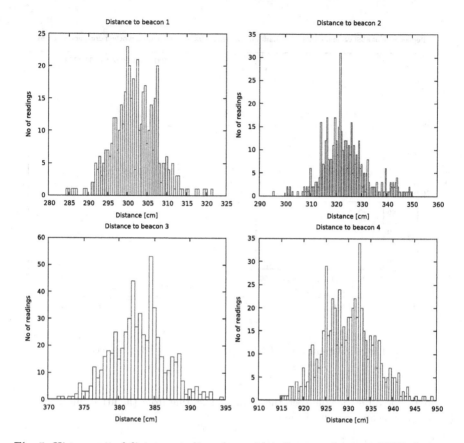

Fig. 5. Histograms of distance readings for various distances between UWB devices.

3.2   Experiment UWB

In the experiment on positioning using UWB, Qorvo DWM1001 development boards were used both as beacons (anchors) and tag. To measure the distance, DWM1001 uses two-way ranging (TWR) which is based on determining the "time of flight" (TOF) of signals between devices, rather than on a signal strength reading (as in the case of BLE).

DWM1001 firmware provides data on both the position between the tag and individual beacons and the quality of a specific position (quality factor).

The experiment aimed at determining positioning accuracy consisted of measuring the distance of a UWB device acting as a tag from four devices acting as anchors (beacons). All devices were stationary (their positions did not change), so based on the fluctuation of distance readings, the positioning error can be determined. The standard deviation for the distribution of distance readings was taken as a measure of accuracy (error).

Graphs showing the distribution of the measured values of distance from each anchor are shown in Fig. 5.

Table 2. Distance reading values to individual UWB beacons

Beacon number	Mean of the distance [cm]	Standard deviation of the distance [cm]
1	301.8	5.6
2	323.4	8.9
3	382.8	3.8
4	930.0	5.8

The mean values and standard deviations calculated from the distributions are shown in Table 2.

For UWB, the accuracy (equated to standard deviation) did not exceed 0.1 m (8.9 cm) - which is an order of magnitude (10 times) less than in the BLE case.

As in the case of BLE, measurements were made under good conditions, with all beacons in line of sight with the tag.

4   Data-Driven Simulation of Crowd Dynamics Using UWB and BLE

Modeling of pedestrians' dynamics based on data from position sensors has recently been perceived as a very promising research methodology [6,10]. How-

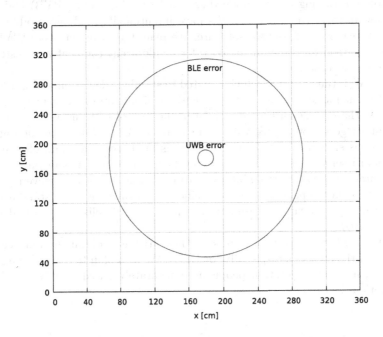

Fig. 6. Comparison of positioning accuracy using UWB and BLE - reference to a 40 cm × 40 cm grid

ever, it should be emphasized that the accuracy of positioning is still a limitation
[3]. In our work, we decided to analyze two emerging technologies, namely Ultra-
Wideband (UWB) and Bluetooth Low Energy (BLE), in terms of their use in
data-driven schemes of crowd simulation, in particular, for methods based on discrete lattice. The lattice can be constant or adaptively change over time and/or
space [1].

When using positioning and placing agents (representation of a pedestrian)
on the grid, we can observe different error values. Using a UWB Tag to determine
the position of a pedestrian increases the accuracy of the position measurement
and thus allows using denser grids for Cellular Automata.

Denser grids allow the mapping of objects and pedestrians with greater accuracy, which is important especially in situations with high density of pedestrians.
In Fig. 4 we can observe that with the standard UWB configuration, the positioning accuracy on the 40 cm × 40 cm cellular automaton grid (customarily used for
crowd modeling) is sufficient for precise pedestrian positioning. Unfortunately,
the standard configuration for BLE sensors gives a much lower positioning accuracy, which is insufficient in the precise microscopic simulation of pedestrians
based on Cellular Automata.

5   Conclusions

The main aim of our experiment was to experimentally compare the accuracy
of people positioning using standard sets of Ultrawide band (UWB) and Bluetooth low energy (BLE) sensors. We have intentionally made no modifications
or optimizations to the sensor software. We placed a set of detectors UWB and
BLE in identical locations in the corridor - indoor environment and tested the
positioning accuracy.

For UWB, the accuracy, which equated to standard deviation, did not exceed
0.1 m (in our measurements it was 8.9 cm) - which is an order of magnitude 10
times less than in the BLE case. Whilst in the case of BLE, measurements were
made under good conditions, with all beacons in line of sight with the tag.

This has significant implications in terms of the usability and effectiveness
of standard sensor arrays for positioning people in space. It can be seen that
the accuracy of UWB positioning in relation to a grid of 40 cm or even 25 cm is
sufficient to place a pedestrian in a specific cell. In the case of the standard BLE
sensor settings, we can only roughly define the set of cells where a pedestrian
can be placed.

In the next steps, we plan to modify the software to obtain greater accuracy
for each of the methods (especially for BLE). We also plan to expand the sensor
fusion [9] method to position peoplemore accurately based on integrated data
from various sensors.

References

1. Bazior, G., Pałka, D., Wąs, J.: Using Cellular Automata to Model High Density Pedestrian Dynamics. In: Krzhizhanovskaya, V.V., Závodszky, G., Lees, M.H., Dongarra, J.J., Sloot, P.M.A., Brissos, S., Teixeira, J. (eds.) ICCS 2020. LNCS, vol. 12137, pp. 486–498. Springer, Cham (2020). https://doi.org/10.1007/978-3-030-50371-0_36
2. Burstedde, C., Klauck, K., Schadschneider, A., Zittartz, J.: Simulation of pedestrian dynamics using a two-dimensional cellular automaton. Physica A: Statistical Mechanics and its Applications **295**(3 - 4), 507 – 525 (2001). https://doi.org/10.1016/S0378-4371(01)00141-8, https://doi.org/10.1016/S0378-4371(01)00141-8
3. Colmer, M.: UWB vs BLE whitepaper. GS Technology (09 2019)
4. Helbing, D., Molnár, P.: Social force model for pedestrian dynamics. Phys. Rev. E **51**, 4282–4286 (May 1995). https://doi.org/10.1103/PhysRevE.51.4282, https://link.aps.org/doi/10.1103/PhysRevE.51.4282
5. Huo, F., Song, W., Lv, W., Liew, K.M.: Analyzing pedestrian merging flow on a floor–stair interface using an extended lattice gas model. SIMULATION **90**(5), 501–510 (2014). https://doi.org/10.1177/0037549714526294, https://doi.org/10.1177/0037549714526294
6. Lee, C., Um, G., Park, S., Lee, K.: Moving object performance analysis system using multi-camera video and position sensors. In: Lee, W., Chen, L., Moon, Y., Bourgeois, J., Bennis, M., Li, Y., Ha, Y., Kwon, H., Cuzzocrea, A. (eds.) 2020 IEEE International Conference on Big Data and Smart Computing, BigComp 2020, Busan, Korea (South), February 19-22, 2020. pp. 441–445. IEEE (2020). https://doi.org/10.1109/BigComp48618.2020.00-31, https://doi.org/10.1109/BigComp48618.2020.00-31
7. Renc, P., Pęcak, T., De Rango, A., Spataro, W., Mendicino, G., Wąs, J.: Towards efficient GPGPU cellular automata model implementation using persistent active cells. Journal of Computational Science **59**, 101538 (2022). https://doi.org/10.1016/j.jocs.2021.101538, https://www.sciencedirect.com/science/article/pii/S1877750321001964
8. Sarmady, S., Haron, F., Talib, A.: Simulating crowd movements using fine grid cellular automata. In: International Conference on Computer Modeling and Simulation. pp. 428–433 (01 2010). https://doi.org/10.1109/UKSIM.2010.85
9. Szlachetka, M., Borkowski, D., Wąs, J.: The downselection of measurements used for free space determination in ADAS. Journal of Computational Science **63**, 101762 (2022). https://doi.org/10.1016/j.jocs.2022.101762, https://www.sciencedirect.com/science/article/pii/S1877750322001454
10. Tian, Q., Wang, K.I.K., Salcic, Z.: An ins and uwb fusion-based gyroscope drift correction approach for indoor pedestrian tracking. Sensors **20**(16), 4476 (Aug 2020). https://doi.org/10.3390/s20164476, http://dx.doi.org/10.3390/s20164476
11. Vizzari, G., Crociani, L., Bandini, S.: An agent-based model for plausible wayfinding in pedestrian simulation. vol. 87 (2020). https://doi.org/10.1016/j.engappai.2019.103241, https://doi.org/10.1016/j.engappai.2019.103241
12. Wąs, J., Lubaś, R.: Towards realistic and effective agent-based models of crowd dynamics. Neurocomputing **146**, 199–209 (2014). https://doi.org/10.1016/j.neucom.2014.04.057, https://doi.org/10.1016/j.neucom.2014.04.057
13. Zeng, Y., Ye, R., Song, W., Luo, S., Meng, F., Vizzari, G.: Entropy analysis of the laminar movement in bidirectional pedestrian flow. Physica A: Statistical Mechanics and its Applications **566**, 125655 (2021). https://doi.org/10.1016/j.physa.2020.125655, https://www.sciencedirect.com/science/article/pii/S0378437120309535

An Insight into the State-of-the-Art Vehicular Fog Computing with an Opportunistic Flavour

Krzysztof Ostrowski$^{(\boxtimes)}$ ⓘ and Krzysztof Małecki ⓘ

West Pomeranian University of Technology, Szczecin, Poland
krzysztof.ostrowski@zut.edu.pl, kmalecki@wi.zut.edu.pl

Abstract. Vehicular fog computing constitutes an environment for execution of demanding computation and storage tasks. There formed a hierarchical decentralised and distributed architecture supports the resource-constrained devices in completion of assignments too complex for them, and too latency-sensitive to be delegated to a cloud. This paper evaluates the recent advances in the research on vehicular fog computing focused on the exploitation of resources of the moving vehicles that operate in the opportunistic device-to-device dynamic networking environments. The proposed evaluation criteria consider structural, behavioural, and functional safety aspects of such systems. A set of research directions concludes this article.

Keywords: vehicular fog computing (VFC) · opportunistic computing · mobility-aware

1 Introduction

Fog computing is an emerging paradigm of massively distributed computing that aims to provide the benefits of cloud computing to the constrained devices in the Internet of Things (IoT) [3]. Although direct cooperation between IoT devices and the far-end cloud data centres is technically possible, it turns out to be practically infeasible due to high latencies and extensive communication resource consumption [1,40]. A wide variety of solutions that bring the cloud services "closer" to the service requester were proposed throughout the years. However, fog computing is considered as a more general form of them [41]. Fog computing addresses multiple concerns in a standardised reference architecture by providing a concept for a highly virtualised platform that distributes computation, storage, and networking tasks over the heterogeneous service providers (called fog nodes) placed between the IoT and the cloud [19]. The act of task distribution is customarily called an offloading, and includes phases like offloading targets (offloadees) discovery and selection, task placement and execution, result delivery, and workload migration.

A model of the fog computing concept, the vehicular fog computing (VFC [16]) enables vehicles to act as both the service requesters and service

© The Author(s), under exclusive license to Springer Nature Switzerland AG 2023
R. Wyrzykowski et al. (Eds.): PPAM 2022, LNCS 13827, pp. 502–513, 2023.
https://doi.org/10.1007/978-3-031-30445-3_42

providers. Vehicles include legacy and resource-rich smart road vehicles and, in a broader perspective, also ships [10], drones [21,26], and satellites [44]. Figure 1 illustrates the system context for VFC. Vehicular fog computing deals with dynamic networking environments where both the mobility and capabilities of the vehicle nodes vary over time. Those characteristics pose multiple issues that include i.a., scalability, availability of nodes, and the resulting service continuity. Researchers constrained the dynamicity of VFC by leveraging vehicular ad-hoc networks (VANETs) as a networking foundation. These simplifications enhance mobile ad-hoc networks (MANETs [6]) with a set of immobile infrastructure nodes located in the vicinity of the vehicles (e.g. roadside units (RSUs), cellular base stations with edge servers, etc.). However, with the introduction of a direct vehicle-to-vehicle (V2V [43]) communication, the previously ameliorated problem of a high dynamicity comes back with a vengeance.

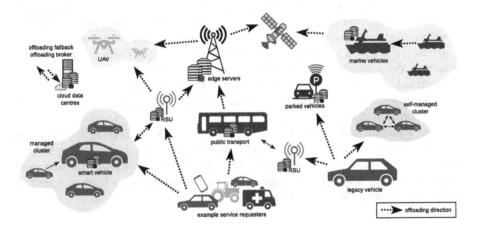

Fig. 1. Vehicular fog computing.

Leveraging the peer-to-peer communication channels in the vehicular fog computing with V2V requires new and incorporating of the existing paradigms that operate in the environments based on the "relaxed" MANETs. Relaxed denotes here that nodes in such a network are not statically supplied with prior knowledge about the network topology. In this regard, opportunistic networking [30] is a good candidate for a background study. Opportunistic networking deals with relaxed MANETs where it runs sophisticated routing strategies to cope with intermittent connectivity caused by the mobility of network nodes. Routing decisions are local and take advantage of knowledge inferred from contextual information unless simple data dissemination (flooding) is applied. The computing paradigm founded atop that networking environment, the opportunistic computing [8,9], explores human social network structures to build context-awareness and effectively utilises mobile users' devices in opportunistic routing, clustering, and computing. Vehicular fog computing is likely to take advantage of the accomplishments in the opportunistic networking and computing at its fine-grained peer-to-peer scale: on the level of V2V interactions, both within a cluster and between the clusters.

This paper verifies the state-of-the-art research in vehicular fog computing, where the mobility of vehicular fog nodes plays a pivotal role in establishing the underlying networking facilities in the process of task offloading. Aside from the similar review works that deal with mobile service requesters, this paper focuses on the moving vehicular nodes that serve as offloading targets in an opportunistic environment. According to the authors' knowledge, no survey publication is entirely dedicated to the listed aspects. For example, [29] points out the virtualisation as a leading enabler for vehicular fogs, but roughly discusses dynamic setups with moving vehicles. Similarly, [17] makes the fog node mobility characteristic as optional, then briefly presents VFC as an application of fog computing. Papers in [18,31] classify smart vehicles as the data generation layer only, and place fog nodes in the immobile network. Authors in [24] discuss vehicles that offload to infrastructure fog nodes, and cooperatively to the parked vehicles. However, collaborative offloading between vehicles is not sufficiently covered. Work in [14] surveys algorithms for the selection of the offloading target nodes, then provides a rough insight into the behaviour modelling under uncertainty of the network and system information. None of the works clearly associate VFC with opportunistic computing, nor try to evaluate the existing works using the association thus derived.

The remainder of this article is organised as follows. Section 2 categorises existing works in the area of vehicular fog computing focused on leveraging opportunistic behaviours in dynamic networks. Section 3 discusses the surveyed articles, and provides a set of open issues and an outlook for further research, while Sect. 4 concludes this article.

2   Evaluation of Approaches

This section briefly introduces the evaluation criteria (C1–C4), then presents the existing works that address there covered concerns. Table 1 summarises the coverage of the criteria in the surveyed research papers.

2.1   C1: Connectivity

Reliable communication in the opportunistic communication environments requires the dynamic application of message routing strategies that reactively or proactively cope with intermittent connectivity and delays. While most of the works deal with one-hop network neighbourhoods, the authors of [20,23,33] deal with multi-hop networking contexts. Due to the mobility of the network nodes, there are many additional hurdles to overcome with sophisticated node discovery and network monitoring algorithms. [23] elaborates on the reduction of redundant sensor data reception in dynamic networks of low connectivity, then proposes an algorithm to forward the chunks of sensor data through an on-demand sequence of relay nodes established in a decentralised manner. [20,37] enhance connectivity with a set of mobile gateways recruited from vehicles with stable connectivity characteristics to proxy the cloud services for other nodes. [32] explores the heterogeneity of the communication media to predict connection opportunities and its quality indicators. [33] devises an on-request cluster lifetime extension, where an infrastructure node either shares its own resources, or coordinates intra-cluster collaboration to increase the serviceability.

2.2 C2: Cooperativeness

Both the collaboration, understood as workload sharing to achieve a common goal jointly, and cooperation, thought as a relaxed of the form of work as job delegation, play pivotal roles in the maintenance of the heterogeneous and distributed vehicular computing networks. Cooperation in VFC is associated with a last-resort fallback offloading to a cloud, or cloud-originated task delegation. Collaboration is observable in both flat (clustered, peer-to-peer) and hierarchical architectures. Several works propose delegation of the workload from infrastructure to mobile nodes to support collaborative connectivity monitoring tasks [32], or RSU-managed cooperative offloading in case of insufficient resources or excess service handovers [22,25]. On the other hand, [38] discusses the delegation of the offloading algorithm itself from mobile to infrastructure nodes. [33] considers supervising upper layers that maintain clusters' lifetime and handle upstream escalation requests. Moreover, [5] enables vehicles to either offload to an existing or form a new resource pool cluster, as well as collaboratively aggregate the offloading results of an application distributed to the cluster. [39] discusses inter-cluster collaborative task offloading, while [4,15] cover also intra-cluster collaboration with autonomic task distribution, and parallel execution, respectively. Additionally, [36] uses nodal collaboration to share context-aware local decisions, while [23] exploits it for multi-hop data forwarding. In [11] vehicles collaborate to elect backup nodes, and to announce their willingness to leave the cluster. Furthermore, [45] enables the infrastructure and mobile nodes to establish a VFC platform of voluntary vehicular nodes cooperatively. [12] proposes a cooperative sensing solution within a platoon of vehicles, while [34] envisions a collaborative sensing platform with data mules involved in the opportunistic routing of incentives. [42] models federated learning platform with, assisted by a base station, cooperative replacement of the RSU-cached data upon movement of a vehicular cluster.

C2a: Context-Aware Clustering. Vehicular fog nodes are typically organised into subnetworks called clusters [2]. Clusters are managed either centrally or locally by the members. Clusters communicate with other clusters through an elected broker (cluster head member). Appropriate clustering and further dynamic reconstructions of clusters impact VFC systems' effectiveness, availability, and overall solution scalability. Both the metrics and triggers required to establish and maintain the clusters are derived from the current system and network contextual information. [39] arranges vehicles into clusters based on the road lane occupied and their turning directions at the next crossing. [5,28] use relative mobility level between two vehicles and mobility patterns as clustering metrics. Works [15,36] propose centrally-managed vehicular resource pools of communities of the recruited and incentivised vehicles. [11] nominates cluster heads to build a temporary cluster that reflects the offloaded application structure. [27,34] determine clusters through inspection of the temporal information derived from the historical locations of buses. [33] constructs clusters by fusing the locally calculated QoS value with information received from the two-hop neighbourhood. [4] proposes a fuzzy logic-based heuristic to elect cluster heads in a decentralised fashion, using information exchanged between one-hop neighbours. [20] establishes two-hop clusters based on mobility, connectivity, and centrality measures with the application of fuzzy logic and ant colony optimisation.

C2b: Distributed Decisions. In VFC systems decisions are taken either centrally by the infrastructure nodes, locally by the individual fog nodes and the clusters, or a multi-step hybrid approach run within the fog hierarchy is engaged. [36] applies nodal collaboration to share locally taken decisions, later fused with globally available information, to form and manage vehicular resource pools. [23] distributes iterative route planning decisions to establish a carrier for delivery of sensor data to fog nodes. [32] gathers the locally-calculated connection estimates to rank and classify the candidate offloadees. [45] proposes a two-step scheme based on contract theory and machine learning (multi-armed bandit, MAB) that actively involves both the offloader and offloadees in the pricing-based matching and task allocation under information asymmetry and uncertainty. [22] formulates a multi-stage incentive-aware Stackelberg game between the nodes in the hierarchical VFC.

C2c: Federated Learning. Uncertainties in VFC are typically handled with machine learning that solves the modelled Markov decision processes. However, such solutions incur high computation demands, especially in highly dynamic environments. Federated learning distributes the learning process, so that the models are locally trained in parallel with multiple datasets. [42] selects subsets of fog nodes to collaboratively learn the adversarial autoencoder (AAE) shared global learning model used in mobility-aware proactive caching with content popularity prediction. A general survey in the federated learning for vehicular environments is provided in [13].

2.3 C3: Redundancy

Redundancy is a conventional approach to assure fault tolerance using replicated tasks and computing nodes. [35] estimates the number of task replicas with a two-step distributed algorithm where the offloaders sequentially refine the RSU-originated approximation with a combinatorial MAB (CMAB) learning model. [11] proposes redundant fog nodes that compute at reduced rates, and are expected to speed up their computations to reach the states of the fog nodes that are about to leave the cluster.

2.4 C4: Migration

Migration of workload is essential to provide uninterrupted services in mobility-oriented systems. Fog nodes in VFC communicate with their neighbourhoods to collaboratively offload the workload or rely on the infrastructure in the results handover and task migration. [28] discusses online migration of containerised tasks between clustered fog nodes triggered by a latency condition.

Table 1. Coverage of the evaluation criteria concerning the analysed literature.

Year	2022		2021										2020						2019		
Ref.	[22]	[27]	[23]	[42]	[39]	[36]	[37]	[5]	[15]	[25]	[35]	[38]	[4]	[11]	[12]	[32]	[33]	[34]	[28]	[20]	[45]
C1		×					×									×	×			×	
C2	×	×	×	×	×	×		×	×	×		×	×	×	×	×	×	×			×
C2a		×		×	×			×	×				×	×		×	×	×	×		
C2b		×					×										×				×
C2c			×																		
C3											×			×							
C4																			×		

3 Discussion

This paper presented the recent advances in the vehicular fog computing with the mobile fog nodes that exploit opportunistic networking. Research works were evaluated with four criteria that focused on structural (C1), behavioural (C2), and functional safety (C3, C4) aspects. The selected papers exploit the dynamic computing environment as either an extension of the static infrastructure or a self-managing autonomic system. While the former is predominant, the latter slowly gains attention as with device-to-device LTE sidelink communication becomes available with C-V2X. Peer-to-peer interactions between the cluster members interwoven with indirect communication within the hierarchical architecture enable authors to embrace the structural complexity of the VFC environments. However, the dynamicity of the VFC clusters poses multiple open issues that can be jointly considered as dynamic community detection problems. Authors employ context-aware metrics and event monitoring to form and maintain the communities. While it is very beneficial to use historical data to organise the communities initially, further reconstructions are likely to be led locally by interpreting the neighbours' contexts enhanced with third-party information (e.g. social graph [7]). The instability of the clusters mainly stems from the mobility of fog nodes that results in high churn rates, but also from their over-whelming heterogeneity, autonomous local decisions and intermittent connec-tivity that introduce uncertainties. Constraining the execution environments of solutions to those of controllable mobility (e.g. highways, predictable bus trajec-tories, slowly-moving vehicles, etc.) is prevailing in the examined works. Unfor-tunately, such limitations effectively narrow down the area of deployment. Note that solutions with unmanned aerial vehicles (UAVs) are indisputably quasi-static [21] as they follow the planned paths to hover at predefined areas. In that sense, resource pools offered by UAVs correspond to the terrestrial ones formed by parked vehicles. Only a few authors explicitly perceive high network density and mobility as friends [23,45]. Nevertheless, the basic fault-tolerance techniques like redundancy and workload migration between the mobile nodes attracted few researchers. One can risk the statement that the burden of error handling has been implicitly shifted to the underlying networking layer. That might be true for low-level message routing and forwarding, which are extensively covered in the opportunistic networks, but does not hold for the application layer in which vehicular fog computing operates first and foremost. As fog computing relies on highly virtualised environments of varying computation and communication resources, and the number of resource-rich smart vehicles constantly increases, VFC is expected to relieve the infrastructure of decision tasks by splitting and distributing the problems to vehicular fog nodes. This trend is visible in hybrid management, where rough estimations are offloaded to clusters for local refine-ments, and in federated learning.

3.1   Research Directions

The following paragraphs briefly present the noticed research opportunities in VFC that emphasise the role of mobile nodes in providing a highly scalable fog computing environment. Furthermore, Fig. 2 provides an overview in the research areas of the tomorrow's VFC. Three aggregate domains that include VFC management, simulated solutions' benchmarking, and offloadee selection are considered. These areas directly benefit from the achievements brought by the works that contribute to the presented research directions.

Optimisation Problems, System, and Mobility Modelling. Surveyed research works formulate optimisation problems as either binary or mixed integer-linear. As such formulations are not efficiently solvable with a growing number of variables and constraints, their authors lean towards heuristic-based solutions to take advantage of multiple search agents. Problems with uncertain-ties are conventionally solved with machine learning. Interestingly, even with the non-exact solutions, the computation overhead is significant and will presumably exceed the complex resource and time limits of the vast majority of fog nodes spatiotemporally available in dynamic VFC environments. Future works should apply localised adaptive and hybrid approaches, where the decentralised and distributed computing for offloading management is exploited. Moreover, as the

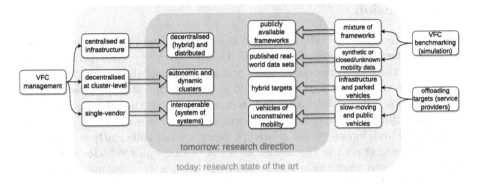

Fig. 2. Current state-of-the-art and research areas.

proposed VFC systems are theoretically evaluated, the choice of either synthetic or simulator-generated (e.g. out of real-world data sets) mobility patterns of fog nodes significantly affect the overall system performance and behaviour. That, in turn, makes solutions generally incomparable. To cope with that, both the simulation frameworks and data sets should be published, too.

Collaborative, Cooperative, and Replicated. Even in centrally-managed solutions, where an RSU or a base station maintains the global network state, VFC should take advantage of at least nodal collaboration and in-hierarchy cooperation. While collaboration is typically associated with local context sharing and distributed operation, cooperation serves as a last-resort fallback offloading (e.g. to cloud data centres), provides a path for problem escalation, and helps to unload the congested network nodes in both the horizontal and vertical directions within the hierarchy. These are considerable challenges to simultaneously enable the security-oriented interoperability between VFC service providers, dynamically reflect the offloaded application structure in the dynamic network of fog nodes, and maintain the service continuity through both the multi-factor induced migration and adaptive redundancy.

Multi-aspect Context-Awareness. Contextual operation is essential for dynamic environments. Lack of context-awareness component leads to stale information and inadequate behaviours resulting from no longer valid system states. In VFC, contextual information comes from multiple sources and dynamically changes with time. The intensity of changes is not constant. Future works in VFC should focus on identification, exploitation, and consolidation of the time-varying contextual information to predict the network and system states efficiently and to improve the robustness, and simplify the VFC systems using localised decisions and distributed responsibilities.

4   Conclusion

This work discusses the vehicular fog computing enabled for opportunistic networking, where the mobile vehicular nodes are also the service providers. An insight into the related research papers was provided, and the contents evaluated according to the derived four criteria: connectivity, cooperativeness, redundancy, and migration. By careful inspection, it has been noted that the vast majority of studies address the structural aspects of opportunistic-aware VFC, while the behavioural and, foremost, the reliability issues are not sufficiently covered. The authors foresee growth in the market of resource-rich smart vehicles in the near future, thus encourage the researchers to pay particular attention to the need to ensure the fault-tolerant and secure infrastructure-less and hybrid vehicular computing. As this paper is the very first survey in those topics, it is expected that it can serve as a starting point to explore the uncharted territories of VFC.

References

1. Al-Fuqaha, A., Guizani, M., Mohammadi, M., Aledhari, M., Ayyash, M.: Internet of things: a survey on enabling technologies, protocols, and applications. IEEE Commun. Surv. Tutorials **17**(4), 2347–2376 (2015). https://doi.org/10.1109/COMST.2015.2444095
2. Baker, D., Ephremides, A., Flynn, J.: The design and simulation of a mobile radio network with distributed control. IEEE J. Sel. Areas Commun. **2**(1), 226–237 (1984). https://doi.org/10.1109/JSAC.1984.1146043
3. Bonomi, F., Milito, R., Zhu, J., Addepalli, S.: Fog computing and its role in the internet of things. In: Proceedings of the First Edition of the MCC Workshop on Mobile Cloud Computing, pp. 13–16. MCC 2012, Association for Computing Machinery, New York, August 2012. https://doi.org/10.1145/2342509.2342513
4. Buda, S., Guleng, S., Wu, C., Zhang, J., Yau, K.A., Ji, Y.: Collaborative vehicular edge computing towards greener ITS. IEEE Access **8**, 63935–63944 (2020). https://doi.org/10.1109/ACCESS.2020.2985731
5. Cha, N., Wu, C., Yoshinaga, T., Ji, Y., Yau, K.L.A.: Virtual edge: exploring computation offloading in collaborative vehicular edge computing. IEEE Access **9**, 37739–37751 (2021). https://doi.org/10.1109/ACCESS.2021.3063246
6. Chlamtac, I., Conti, M., Liu, J.J.N.: Mobile ad hoc networking: imperatives and challenges. Ad Hoc Netw. **1**(1), 13–64 (2003). https://doi.org/10.1016/S1570-8705(03)00013-1
7. Ciobanu, R.I., Negru, C., Pop, F., Dobre, C., Mavromoustakis, C.X., Mastorakis, G.: Drop computing: ad-hoc dynamic collaborative computing. Future Gener. Comput. Syst. **92**, 889–899 (2019). https://doi.org/10.1016/j.future.2017.11.044
8. Conti, M., Giordano, S., May, M., Passarella, A.: From opportunistic networks to opportunistic computing. IEEE Commun. Mag. **48**(9), 126–139 (2010). https://doi.org/10.1109/MCOM.2010.5560597
9. Conti, M., Passarella, A.: The internet of people: a human and data-centric paradigm for the next generation internet. Comput. Commun. **131**, 51–65 (2018). https://doi.org/10.1016/j.comcom.2018.07.034
10. Cui, K., Lin, B., Sun, W., Sun, W.: Learning-based task offloading for marine fog-cloud computing networks of USV cluster. Electronics **8**(11), 1287 (2019). https://doi.org/10.3390/electronics8111287

11. Dong, L., Ni, Q., Wu, W., Huang, C., Znati, T., Du, D.Z.: A proactive reliable mechanism-based vehicular fog computing network. IEEE Internet Things J. **7**(12), 11895–11907 (2020). https://doi.org/10.1109/JIOT.2020.3007608

12. Du, H., Leng, S., Wu, F., Chen, X., Mao, S.: A new vehicular fog computing architecture for cooperative sensing of autonomous driving. IEEE Access **8**, 10997–11006 (2020). https://doi.org/10.1109/ACCESS.2020.2964029

13. Du, Z., Wu, C., Yoshinaga, T., Yau, K.L.A., Ji, Y., Li, J.: Federated learning for vehicular internet of things: recent advances and open issues. IEEE Open J. Comput. Soc. **1**, 45–61 (2020). https://doi.org/10.1109/OJCS.2020.2992630

14. Hamdi, A.M.A., Hussain, F.K., Hussain, O.K.: Task offloading in vehicular fog computing: state-of-the-art and open issues. Future Gener. Comput. Syst. **133**, 201–212 (2022). https://doi.org/10.1016/j.future.2022.03.019

15. Hameed, A.R., ul Islam, S., Ahmad, I., Munir, K.: Energy- and performance-aware load-balancing in vehicular fog computing. Sustain. Comput. Inf. Syst. **30**, 100454 (2021). https://doi.org/10.1016/j.suscom.2020.100454

16. Hou, X., Li, Y., Chen, M., Wu, D., Jin, D., Chen, S.: Vehicular fog computing: a viewpoint of vehicles as the infrastructures. IEEE Trans. Veh. Technol. **65**(6), 3860–3873 (2016). https://doi.org/10.1109/TVT.2016.2532863

17. Hu, P., Dhelim, S., Ning, H., Qiu, T.: Survey on fog computing: architecture, key technologies, applications and open issues. J. Netw. Comput. Appl. **98**, 27–42 (2017). https://doi.org/10.1016/j.jnca.2017.09.002

18. Huang, C., Lu, R., Choo, K.R.: Vehicular fog computing: architecture, use case, and security and forensic challenges. IEEE Commun. Mag. **55**(11), 105–111 (2017). https://doi.org/10.1109/MCOM.2017.1700322

19. IEEE: IEEE Std 1934-2018. IEEE standard for adoption of OpenFog reference architecture for fog computing. https://doi.org/10.1109/IEEESTD.2018.8423800, https://ieeexplore.ieee.org/document/8423800/

20. Jabri, I., Mekki, T., Rachedi, A., Ben Jemaa, M.: Vehicular fog gateways selection on the internet of vehicles: a fuzzy logic with ant colony optimization based approach. Ad Hoc Netw. **91**, 101879 (2019). https://doi.org/10.1016/j.adhoc.2019.101879

21. Jia, Z., Wu, Q., Dong, C., Yuen, C., Han, Z.: hierarchical aerial computing for internet of things via cooperation of HAPs and UAVs. IEEE Internet Things J. 1 (2022). https://doi.org/10.1109/JIOT.2022.3151639

22. Li, Y., Yang, B., Wu, H., Han, Q., Chen, C., Guan, X.: Joint offloading decision and resource allocation for vehicular fog-edge computing networks: a contract-stackelberg approach. IEEE Internet Things J. 1 (2022). https://doi.org/10.1109/JIOT.2022.3150955

23. Liang, J., Zhang, J., Leung, V.C., Wu, X.: Distributed information exchange with low latency for decision making in vehicular fog computing. IEEE Internet Things J. 1 (2021). https://doi.org/10.1109/JIOT.2021.3075516

24. Liu, L., Chen, C., Pei, Q., Maharjan, S., Zhang, Y.: Vehicular edge computing and networking: a survey. Mob. Netw. Appl. **26**(3), 1145–1168 (2020). https://doi.org/10.1007/s11036-020-01624-1

25. Lv, B., Yang, C., Chen, X., Yao, Z., Yang, J.: Task offloading and serving handover of vehicular edge computing networks based on trajectory prediction. IEEE Access **9**, 130793–130804 (2021). https://doi.org/10.1109/ACCESS.2021.3112077

26. Madan, N., Malik, A.W., Rahman, A.U., Ravana, S.D.: On-demand resource provisioning for vehicular networks using flying fog. Veh. Commun. **25**, 100252 (2020). https://doi.org/10.1016/j.vehcom.2020.100252

27. Mao, W., et al.: Data-driven capacity planning for vehicular fog computing. IEEE Internet Things J. 1 (2022). https://doi.org/10.1109/JIOT.2022.3143872

28. Mseddi, A., Jaafar, W., Elbiaze, H., Ajib, W.: Intelligent resource allocation in dynamic fog computing environments. In: 2019 IEEE 8th International Conference on Cloud Networking (CloudNet), pp. 1–7, November 2019. https://doi.org/10.1109/CloudNet47604.2019.9064110

29. Olariu, S.: A survey of vehicular cloud research: trends, applications and challenges. IEEE Trans. Intell. Transp. Syst. **21**(6), 2648–2663 (2020). https://doi.org/10.1109/TITS.2019.2959743

30. Pelusi, L., Passarella, A., Conti, M.: Opportunistic networking: data forwarding in disconnected mobile ad hoc networks. IEEE Commun. Mag. **44**(11), 134–141 (2006). https://doi.org/10.1109/MCOM.2006.248176

31. Raza, S., Wang, S., Ahmed, M., Anwar, M.R.: A Survey on vehicular edge computing: architecture, applications, technical issues, and future directions. Wirel. Commun. Mob. Comput. **2019**, e3159762 (2019). https://doi.org/10.1155/2019/3159762

32. Saad, A., Grande, R.E.D.: MDP-based vehicular network connectivity model for VCC management. In: 2020 IEEE/ACM 24th International Symposium on Distributed Simulation and Real Time Applications (DS-RT), pp. 1–8, September 2020. https://doi.org/10.1109/DS-RT50469.2020.9213698

33. Sami, H., Mourad, A., El-Hajj, W.: Vehicular-OBUs-as-on-demand-fogs: resource and context aware deployment of containerized micro-services. IEEE/ACM Trans. Networking **28**(2), 778–790 (2020). https://doi.org/10.1109/TNET.2020.2973800

34. Sun, G., Sun, S., Yu, H., Guizani, M.: Toward incentivizing fog-based privacy-preserving mobile crowdsensing in the internet of vehicles. IEEE Internet Things J. **7**(5), 4128–4142 (2020). https://doi.org/10.1109/JIOT.2019.2951410

35. Sun, Y., Zhou, S., Niu, Z.: Distributed task replication for vehicular edge computing: performance analysis and learning-based algorithm. IEEE Trans. Wirel. Commun. **20**(2), 1138–1151 (2021). https://doi.org/10.1109/TWC.2020.3030889

36. Tang, C., Xia, S., Li, Q., Chen, W., Fang, W.: Resource pooling in vehicular fog computing. J. Cloud Comput. **10**(1), 1–14 (2021). https://doi.org/10.1186/s13677-021-00233-x

37. Wang, P., Yu, R., Gao, N., Lin, C., Liu, Y.: Task-driven data offloading for fog-enabled urban IoT services. IEEE Internet Things J. **8**(9), 7562–7574 (2021). https://doi.org/10.1109/JIOT.2020.3039467

38. Wang, Z., Zhao, D., Ni, M., Li, L., Li, C.: Collaborative mobile computation offloading to vehicle-based cloudlets. IEEE Trans. Veh. Technol. **70**(1), 768–781 (2021). https://doi.org/10.1109/TVT.2020.3043296

39. Wu, Y., Wu, J., Chen, L., Zhou, G., Yan, J.: Fog computing model and efficient algorithms for directional vehicle mobility in vehicular network. IEEE Trans. Intell. Transp. Syst. **22**(5), 2599–2614 (2021). https://doi.org/10.1109/TITS.2020.2971343

40. Yannuzzi, M., Milito, R., Serral-Gracià, R., Montero, D., Nemirovsky, M.: Key ingredients in an IoT recipe: fog computing, cloud computing, and more fog computing. In: 2014 IEEE 19th International Workshop on Computer Aided Modeling and Design of Communication Links and Networks (CAMAD), pp. 325–329, December 2014. https://doi.org/10.1109/CAMAD.2014.7033259

41. Yousefpour, A., et al.: All one needs to know about fog computing and related edge computing paradigms: a complete survey. J. Syst. Archit. **98**, 289–330 (2019). https://doi.org/10.1016/j.sysarc.2019.02.009

42. Yu, Z., Hu, J., Min, G., Zhao, Z., Miao, W., Hossain, M.S.: Mobility-aware proactive edge caching for connected vehicles using federated learning. IEEE Trans. Intell. Transp. Syst. **22**(8), 5341–5351 (2021). https://doi.org/10.1109/TITS.2020.3017474
43. Zeadally, S., Guerrero, J., Contreras, J.: A tutorial survey on vehicle-to-vehicle communications. Telecomm. Syst. **73**(3), 469–489 (2019). https://doi.org/10.1007/s11235-019-00639-8
44. Zhang, Z., Zhang, W., Tseng, F.: Satellite mobile edge computing: improving QoS of high-speed satellite-terrestrial networks using edge computing techniques. IEEE Network **33**(1), 70–76 (2019). https://doi.org/10.1109/MNET.2018.1800172
45. Zhou, Z., Liao, H., Zhao, X., Ai, B., Guizani, M.: Reliable task offloading for vehicular fog computing under information asymmetry and information uncertainty. IEEE Trans. Veh. Technol. **68**(9), 8322–8335 (2019). https://doi.org/10.1109/TVT.2019.2926732

Author Index

A

Aaraj, Najwa I-399
Ababaei, Ahmad I-359
Abduljabbar, Mustafa I-249
Abeykoon, Vibhatha I-291
Afonso, Sergio I-371
Afzal, Ayesha I-155
Aliaga, José I. I-16
Aljaberi, Saeed I-399
Almeida, Francisco I-371
Alonso-Jordá, Pedro II-236
Andersson, Måns I. I-333, I-383
Andresen, Daniel II-260
Antkowiak, Michał II-382
Anzt, Hartwig I-113

B

Bader, David A. I-71
Balis, Bartosz I-197
Banaszak, Michał II-370
Beams, Natalie I-113
Bečka, Martin I-464
Benet, Luis II-428
Bielecki, Wlodzimierz II-51
Blanco, Vicente I-371
Bosque, Jose Luis I-237
Bottalico, Davide II-101
Brzostowski, Bartosz II-392
Bulckaen, Léo II-470
Bulkhak, Artem II-248
Bungartz, Hans-Joachim I-139
Bystrov, Oleg I-171

C

Cabrera, Alberto I-371
Carracciuolo, Luisa II-101
Carretero, Jesus II-77
Cascajo, Alberto II-77
Castrillon, Jeronimo I-249
Chandra, M Girish II-153
Chung, Minh Thanh I-263

Cuocolo, Reanto II-115
Cuomo, Salvatore II-115
Czajkowski, Marcin I-126
Czarnul, Paweł I-429

D

Das Sarma, Aditya II-153
De Lucia, Gianluca II-127
Dimov, Ivan I-55
Dmitruk, Beata II-63
Du, Zhihui I-71
Dubey, Anshu I-279
Durajski, Artur P. II-392
Dutka, Łukasz I-305
Dutta, Nilankur II-470
Dytrych, Tomáš II-357

E

Eitzinger, Jan I-321
Exposito, David II-77

F

Fato, Francesco II-115
Ferguson, Zachary II-415
Ferranti, Luca II-428
Fohry, Claudia II-14
Fomperosa, Jaime I-237
Fox, Geoffrey I-291
Fredriksson, Albin I-383
Fürlinger, Karl I-263

G

Ganzha, Maria I-55
García-Risueño, Pablo I-3
Garzón, Ester M. II-165
Gepner, Paweł II-223
Giampaolo, Fabio II-115
Gielerak, Roman II-187
Gokieli, Maria II-343
Górka, Patryk II-481

Grabowski, Michal I-197
Graillat, Stef I-16
Gruszka, Konrad M. II-392
Grzeszczak, Jakub I-414

H
Hager, Georg I-155
Halver, Rene II-3
Hambitzer, Anna I-399
Hardenbicker, Kai II-14
Hoekstra, Alfons I-183
Hoffmann, Nico II-273
Hoshi, Takeo I-453
Hsu, William II-260
Hutchison, Scott II-260

I
Iakymchuk, Roman I-16
Ibañez, Mario I-237
Imamura, Toshiyuki I-40
Iserte, Sergio II-223

J
John, Joseph I-225
Junghans, Christoph II-3
Jurczuk, Krzysztof I-126

K
Kačeniauskas, Arnas I-171
Kaliszewski, Ignacy II-139
Kamburugamuve, Supun I-291
Kamil, Shoaib II-415
Kanewala, Thejaka Amila I-291
Karbowiak, Łukasz I-441
Kitowski, Jacek I-305
Kjelgaard Mikkelsen, Carl Christian I-3
Klosterman, Tom I-279
Kluge, Thomas II-273
Kobayashi, Masato I-453
Kolotinskii, Daniil I-346
Kosheleva, Olga II-405
Köstler, Harald I-321
Kotara, Piotr II-209
Kranzlmüller, Dieter I-263
Kreinovich, Vladik II-405
Kretowski, Marek I-126
Kryza, Bartosz I-305
Krzywaniak, Adam II-223
Krzyżanowski, Piotr II-323

Kubanek, Mariusz I-441
Kubica, Bartłomiej Jacek II-441
Kudo, Shuhei I-453
Kumar, A Anil II-153
Kurowski, Krzysztof II-177

L
Laccetti, Giuliano II-89
Langr, Daniel II-357
Lapegna, Marco II-127
Lemański, Romuald II-382
Lenadora, Damitha I-291
Lewandowski, Michał I-30
Liu, Felix I-383
López-Villellas, Lorién I-3
Lubaś, Robert II-492

M
Maithree, Hasara I-291
Majumder, Utso II-153
Małecki, Krzysztof II-481, II-502
Marcinkowski, Leszek II-300
Markidis, Stefano I-155, I-333, I-383
Marowka, Ami II-27, II-39
Martín Garzón, Gracia Ester II-139
Martínez, Héctor II-236
Martins, Wellington Santos I-83
Mele, Valeria II-89
Michel, Antoine I-359
Michelino, Davide II-101
Miethlinger, Thomas II-273
Mikitiuk, Artur I-414
Milthorpe, Josh I-225
Miroforidis, Janusz II-139
Montella, Raffaele II-77
Moreno, Juan José II-139
Moskovka, Alexej II-287, II-331
Mukunoki, Daichi I-40
Murugan, Natarajan Arul I-333

N
Neckel, Tobias I-139
Neilsen, Mitchell II-260
Nichita, Pavel I-371
Nicolas, Alexandre II-470

O
Ogita, Takeshi I-40
Okša, Gabriel I-464

Olejniczak, Andrzej II-370
Ortega, Gloria II-165
Orts, Francisco II-165
Orzechowski, Michał I-305
Ostrowski, Krzysztof II-502
Ozaki, Katsuhisa I-40

P

Pacevič, Ruslan I-171
Pałka, Dariusz II-492
Palkowski, Marek II-51
Panozzo, Daniele II-415
Paprzycki, Marcin I-55
Parsons, Benjamin II-260
Pavlov, Daniil I-346
Perera, Niranda I-291
Pericàs, Miquel I-249
Piccialli, Francesco II-115
Pimentel, Andy D. I-183
Pires, Julio Cesar Batista I-83
Podobas, Artur I-333
Pramanik, Sayantan II-153
Puertas, Antonio M. II-165

Q

Quintana-Ortí, Enrique S. II-236

R

Rahman, Talal II-300
Ramírez, Cristian II-236
Ravedutti Lucio Machado, Rafael I-321
Reitz, Lukas II-14
Reiz, Severin I-139
Revol, Nathalie II-428
Rojek, Krzysztof II-223
Romano, Diego II-127
Rosa, Bogdan I-359
Rościszewski, Paweł II-223
Rycerz, Katarzyna II-199, II-209

S

Sabella, Gianluca II-101
Sasak-Okoń, Anna I-95
Satpute, Nitin I-399
Sawerwain, Marek II-187
Sayama, Hiroki II-459
Schneider, Teseo II-415

Shaikhislamov, Denis I-209
Shan, Kaiying I-291
Shan, Xiujie II-313
Sikorski, Andrzej I-30
Słota, Renata G. I-305
Slysz, Mateusz II-177
Soomro, Pirah Noor I-249
Spadarella, Gaia II-115
Spisso, Bernardino II-101
Stafford, Esteban I-237
Stegailov, Vladimir I-346
Stpiczyński, Przemysław II-63
Strazdins, Peter I-225
Sutmann, Godehard II-3

T

Tang, Xuan II-415
Todorov, Venelin I-55
Toporkov, Victor II-248
Trojanowski, Krzysztof I-414
Tsai, Yu-Hsiang Mike I-113
Tudruj, Marek I-95

U

Ugga, Lorenzo II-115
Uyar, Ahmet I-291

V

Vaidya, Vishnu II-153
Valdman, Jan II-287, II-331
van Dijk, Jelle I-183
van Gijzen, Martin B. II-313
Varbanescu, Ana-Lucia I-183
Vizzari, Giuseppe II-492
Voevodin, Vadim I-209
Vohnoutová, Marta II-331

W

Wąs, Jarosław II-492
Węglarz, Jan II-177
Weidendorfer, Josef I-263
Wellein, Gerhard I-155, I-321
Widanage, Chathura I-291
Wieczerzak, Dawid I-429
Wojtkiewicz, Jacek II-392
Wołoszczuk, Sebastian II-370
Woźniak-Braszak, Aneta II-370

Wróbel, Piotr   II-481
Wrosz, Izajasz   I-30
Wrzeszcz, Michał   I-305

Y

Yamamoto, Yusaku   I-453
Yemelyanov, Dmitry   II-248

Z

Zavodszky, Gabor   I-183
Zawadzki, Tomasz   II-209
Zawalska, Justyna   II-199
Zhang, Sen   I-71
Zhilin, Sergei   II-428
Zorin, Denis   II-415

Printed in the United States
by Baker & Taylor Publisher Services